PERSONAL COMPUTER APPLICATIONS

A Strategy for the Information Society

Bryan Pfaffenberger
University of Virginia

Little, Brown and Company
Boston Toronto

[redacted]

Library of Congress Cataloging-in-Publication Data

Pfaffenberger, Bryan, 1949–
Personal computer applications.

Includes index.
1. Microcomputers. I. Title.
QA76.5.P3987 1987 004.16 86-33799
ISBN 0-316-70402-4

Library of Congress Catalog Card No. 86-33799

ISBN 0-316-70402-4

9 8 7 6 5 4 3 2 1

DON

Published simultaneously in Canada
by Little, Brown & Company (Canada) Limited

Printed in the United States of America

Photo Credits

Page 2: Xerox Corporation. Pages 23, 35 (top and bottom), 36, 38 (top): IBM Archives. Page 38: National Physical Laboratory. Page 40 (top): IBM Archives. Page 40 (bottom): Alan Richards, The Institute of Advanced Study. Page 43: The Sperry Corporation. Pages 46, 47: IBM Archives. Pages 88, 93: Apple Computer, Inc. Page 110: Tom Tracy. Page 159: Aldus Corporation. Page 179: Grolier Publishing, Inc. Page 196: Tom Tracy. Page 248: Lotus Development Corporation. Page 314: Hewlett Packard, Inc. Pages 323, 324: Apple Computer, Inc. Page 332: Miles Computing. Page 348: AT & T Bell Laboratories. Page 355: Apple Computer, Inc. Page 379: Lotus Development Corporation. Page 383: Borland International. Page 384: Microsoft, Inc. Page 387: Calcomp. Page 388: Xerox Corporation. Page 440: Chrysler Corporation. Page 451: Apple Computer, Inc.

For my parents

Preface

TO THE INSTRUCTOR: WHY USE THIS BOOK?

Civilization is entering a new era — the information era. More knowledge has been created in the past twenty years than in the entire previous 5,000 years of civilization. It's a time of tremendous opportunities and equally tremendous challenges.

THE CHALLENGE: INFORMATION WORKER PRODUCTIVITY

One challenge lies in finding ways to cope with the increasing deluge of information in every career and profession. At present, information-processing burdens are coming close to paralyzing science, scholarship, government, business, and industry. In business, for example, large corporations find that they must spend up to 40 or 50 percent of their operating budgets on paperwork alone. Scientists must spend between one-fourth and one-half of their time just to keep up with an avalanche of journal articles, conference papers, books, and research reports. The need for information-processing productivity has never been greater. Yet the people who do this paperwork, white-collar information workers, show one of the lowest rates of productivity growth anywhere in our economy. These workers — clerks, professionals, technical specialists, middle managers, and executives — now predominate in the American work force. If the United States is to retain its position among world economic leaders, ways must be found to improve information worker productivity.

THE SOLUTION: PERSONAL COMPUTER APPLICATIONS

Increasingly, the answer is being found in personal computers and application software. "The personal computer," says Amy D. Wohl, president of an office automation consulting firm, "has been accepted as *the* workstation" in the office. A major reason is the availability of productivity-enhancing application software. Word processing, data base management, and spreadsheet programs have become the new tools for day-to-day information work in offices everywhere. These tools put information processing power where it is most needed: on the desks of information workers.

The chief objective of this book is to teach application software productivity techniques for today's college students, the information workers of the future. The vast majority of today's college students will work with information, and they'll do so somewhere in the office's occupational structure. A 1984 survey undertaken by the Carnegie Foundation showed that 84.5 percent of college undergraduates expected to take jobs somewhere in the world of white-collar workers. Almost every college student can benefit, therefore, by learning productivity-enhancing computer skills for information work.

Higher productivity, however, does not follow automatically from personal computer use. Most personal computer users exploit only a small fraction of their computers' power and potential. Personal computing is more challenging, and more deserving of disciplined study, than the industry made it out to be in the hype-laden boom years of the early 1980s. This book points the way toward advanced, productive, and personally satisfying work with personal computers.

THE CONCEPTS APPROACH

To help students toward mastery of personal computer applications, this book focuses on computer and software *concepts* rather than on the particulars of keyboard commands. Its aim is not to teach students how to use an IBM PC or an Apple Macintosh and three programs. On the contrary, this book strips away the superficial differences among personal computers and application programs. It emphasizes, instead, the fundamentals of productive personal computing for information work. This understanding makes learning any computer or program easy, and it points the way toward the productive use of personal computer technology.

Here's an example of the concepts focus and its value for future information workers. Most word processing programs include commands for block moves. The block move commands can be learned easily enough. What is more important to learn, however, is why word processing software tends to produce poorly organized manuscripts, what strategies writers can use to overcome this problem, and how block moves can be worked into proven manuscript revision techniques. To learn a word processing program command is to learn a skill. To learn the relationship between word processing and tightly organized writing, in contrast, is to acquire what Richard Van Horn, president of the University of Houston, calls *exportable* knowledge: knowledge that can be readily applied or exported to new programs, new computers, and new contexts.

It is no longer in doubt that personal computers and application software will be used for information work. But what *is* still in doubt is whether these tools will be used well and productively. Exportable knowledge about personal computing, not just a set of skills, is required. And to point the way toward this kind of knowledge, and toward the fulfillment of personal computing's promise, is the underlying aim of every page of this book.

USEFUL WITH ANY COMBINATION OF HARDWARE AND SOFTWARE

The concepts focus chosen for this book makes it useful with any combination of application programs. The book is neither machine- nor software-specific. You can choose to use precisely the programs you think best suited to your students and your institution's resources.

TEACHING PROGRAMS . . . AND TEACHING *HOW TO LEARN* PROGRAMS

Many computer literacy textbooks teach students particular programs, such as WordStar or Lotus 1-2-3. This book does something different. It teaches students how to learn any application program. Here's how the approach works. For each chapter that explores the use of application software, there's a tear-out *Quick Reference Guide* that looks like this one (from Chapter 4):

MANAGING THE PROGRAM AND DOCUMENTS

If you want to:	Do this:
Load the program	______________________
Load an existing document	______________________
Merge two documents	______________________
Save a document to disk	______________________
Quit the program	______________________

As students read the chapter, they consult the program's documentation and experiment with the program. If you wish, you may assign supplementary texts on specific programs [such as Stephen C. Ross, *Understanding and Using Lotus 1-2-3* (St. Paul, MN: West Publishing Co., 1968)]; students may then use the *Quick Reference Guides* to inform their approach to the supplements. However you decide to integrate the *Quick Reference Guides* into your instructional strategy, students will discover for themselves how to do the functions discussed in the chapter, and they write down the procedure in the "Do this" column.

The advantages of this approach for learning purposes cannot be overemphasized. Psychological studies have shown conclusively that students learn best when they read with questions in mind. As they read the chapters on application software in this book, the quick reference guides will help them confront the software they're using, explore its documentation and the supplementary texts (if any), experiment with the programs, and discover how to accomplish everything from the simplest to the most advanced program functions. As your students use this technique, they will learn something far more important and far more valuable than learning a program. They will *learn how to learn* a program. This is exportable knowledge. And in our rapidly evolving and changing information society, exportable knowledge may be the only kind that will still prove of value 20 years down the road.

BALANCED COVERAGE

The focus on personal computers does not rule out coverage of the wider world of larger computers or of computer programming. Indeed, the personal computer focus encourages coverage of all three. Here's why.

Larger computers will not disappear now that the PC is here; on the contrary, they will become even more useful because PCs provide new gateways to their resources. For this reason, this book covers networking topics such as electronic mail and online data base research.

An introduction to programming can benefit even those who plan to use only application software. For example, understanding the idea of IF/THEN and DO/WHILE structures helps one grasp the logic of Lotus 1-2-3 macros. Part 5 of this book introduces computer programming. If desired, this text can be supplemented with a book on Pascal or BASIC programming.

LEARNING AIDS

Personal Computer Applications has been designed with the student in mind. Among the learning aids included are:

Quick Reference Guides help students learn word processing, data base management, and spreadsheet programs;

Case Studies show how computer technology has affected the lives of people and organizations;

Boxed Inserts highlight and expand on the information presented in the chapters;

Chapter Summaries provide an executive abstract of each chapter's contents, and may be read both before and after the chapter is read;

Lists of Key Terms are presented, in alphabetical order, at the end of each chapter; the terms are keyed to entries in a carefully written glossary at the end of the book;

Chapter Review Questions and Exercises provide students with an intellectually engaging guide to studying the contents of each chapter; and

Extensive Reading Lists map out the best of the literature for every subject covered in this book.

SUPPLEMENTS FOR *PERSONAL COMPUTER APPLICATIONS*

To aid you in weaving *Personal Computer Applications* into the fabric of your course, an instructor's manual is available. This manual includes:

Sample Syllabus Suggestions for organizing your course around *Personal Computer Applications*;

Filled-in Quick Reference Guides for a variety of popular application packages;

Software Suggestions Reviews of the strengths and weaknesses of many alternative word processing, data base management, and spreadsheet programs for instructional uses;

Chapter-by-Chapter Teaching Strategies including specific suggestions for computer laboratory exercises;

Test Item Bank containing nearly 1,000 questions, which may be directly reproduced from the manual.

You may use *Personal Computer Applications* with any combination of personal computer software, supplementary textbooks on specific programs, and ancillary texts.

ACKNOWLEDGMENTS

No one who writes a textbook like this one can claim that it was a single-handed effort, and this point is particularly true for *Personal Computer Applications*. My wife, Suzanne, and two children (Julia and Michael) have been patient and supportive throughout. Avery Catlin played a major role helping me shape the focus of this book in informal discussions. Luther Gore read the manuscript critically before its final revision and made many helpful criticisms — as well as providing no small support and encouragement.

I should like to thank the many equipment manufacturers, publishers, and photo agencies who have contributed photographs, text excerpts, and other materials for this book. Their contributions are acknowledged individually where they appear.

Special appreciation is due to Tom Casson and all the other Little, Brown publishing professionals whose creative ideas and encouragement have left their mark throughout this book. I would also like to thank Victoria Keirnan, production editor, Helen Webber, copyeditor, Melinda Grosser, designer, Monica Suder, photo researcher, and Anne Starr, editorial assistant, for their contributions. Very special thanks are due to Denise Clinton, who furnished me with the ideal climate for creativity: room enough to soar with exciting ideas and new approaches, and criticism honest enough to help me understand the best ways to achieve my goals.

It has been my privilege to work with a distinguished team of reviewers, whose constructive suggestions, penetrating critiques, and dedication to the teaching of computing have been an inspiration throughout: William Pritchard, University of South Florida; Lauren Arango, Ohio Wesleyan University; Rose Laird, Northern Virginia Community College; David Olson, Western Oregon State College; Andrea Wachter, Point Park College; R. Wayne Headrick, Texas A & M University; Mardi Horton, American River College; David Callaghan, Bentley College; Carla Thompson, Tulsa Junior College; Phyllis Dunlevy, Conley

Johnson, A.C.; Gerald Meyer, La Guardia Community College; Earl Jackson, North Texas State University; Ben Guild, Wright State University; Donald Cooley, Utah State University; David G. Kay, University of California — Los Angeles; Murray Black, George Washington University; Barbara Rich, Marymount Manhattan College; Elizabeth W. Hodges, North Carolina State University; Thomas L. Van Valey, Western Michigan University; Sheila L. Cory, Chapel Hill Carrboro City Schools; David E. Anderson, Allegheny College; and Patrick Schwab, Chemeketa Community College.

Bryan Pfaffenberger
Charlottesville, Virginia

Contents

Prologue 1

PART ONE ▪ *The New Tools for Personal Productivity* 2

1 *Working Smarter: Computer Applications for the Information Age* 5

A Nation of Office Workers 6
The office and information work 7
The office's occupational structure 10
The office bottleneck 11
Computer Applications for Information Workers 11
Personal computers 13
Application software 13
Application software for information work 14
The Productivity Promise 16
Summary 18
Key Terms 18
Review Questions and Exercises 19
For Further Reading 20

2 *The World of Computing: Personal Computers in Perspective* 21

Basics: The Idea of the Computer 22
Input 22
Storage 28
Processing 29
Output 30
The computer's functional organization 30
A Question of Scale 32
The conquest of time 32
Origins: The Foundations of Modern Computing 34
Roadblocks 34
Trailblazers 37
A Computer Genealogy 41
The first generation (1946–1958) 41
The second generation (1958–1964) 45
The third generation (1964–1971) 46
The fourth generation (1971–Present) 50
Computer Horizons: Toward the Fifth Generation? 58
The short term: Slow, steady evolution 60
The long term: Revolution? 60
The information society 62
Summary 64
Key Terms 65
Review Questions and Exercises 66
For Further Reading 67

3 *The Personal Computer: Fourth-Generation Technology for Ordinary People* 70

Personal Computer Hardware: A Guided Tour 72
The microprocessor: The key to a personal computer's personality 73
Internal memory: The key to processing convenience 76
Auxiliary storage 78
Input devices: Getting information into the computer 84
Output devices: Viewing the results of processing operations 89
System Software: Getting It All Together 94
The file manager: Operating the disk drives 95
The command processor: Communicating with the user 96
System utilities: Tools for day-to-day work 100
Application Software: The Key to Productivity 105

Summary 105
Key Terms 106
Review Questions and Exercises 107
For Further Reading 108

PART TWO ▪ *Word Processing: Strategies for Writing* 110

4 *Using Word Processing Software: Tools for Writing* 113

Writing with Word Processing Software: An Overview 114
Exploring a Word Processing Program 117
Understanding the document display screen 118
Giving commands 119
Writing and revising the text 121
Formatting the text: Two approaches 127
Formatting the text: Default settings 131
Formatting the text: Character, paragraph, and document formats 132
Printing the text 135
The Limitations of Word Processing 135
Summary 137
Key Terms 138
Review Questions and Exercises 139
For Further Reading 139

5 *Advanced Word Processing: Beyond Electronic Typewriting* 141

Advanced Writing Techniques 142
Glossaries 142
Boilerplate 143
Automating command entry 146
Multiple windows 147
Footnotes 149
Advanced Editing Techniques 151
Revising from printed copy 151
The search command 153
The search-and-replace command 154

Advanced Printing Techniques 154
Producing attractive text 155
Generating form letters 156
Desktop publishing 157
Additional Advanced Features 160
Summary 161
Key Terms 162
Review Questions and Exercises 163
For Further Reading 164

6 *Word Processing Horizons: Accessory Software You Can Use* 166

Accessory Programs for Writing 167
Outlining programs 167
Memory-resident outlining programs 174
Outlining features in word processing programs 175
The memory-resident thesaurus 175
Horizons of computer writing aids 178
Accessory Programs for Editing 179
Spelling checkers 179
Style analysis software 181
The Computer's Limitations as a Critical Editor 189
Summary 190
Key Terms 192
Review Questions and Exercises 192
For Further Reading 193

PART THREE ▪ *Data Base Management: Strategies for Managing Information* 196

7 *Using File Management Software: Tools for Managing Information* 198

Managing a Data Base with File Management Software: An Overview 199
Data base management by hand 199
Advantages of computerized file management 202

Exploring a File Management Program 204
Creating a form 204
Entering data 206
Finding records 208
Modifying records 211
Sorting records 211
Selecting records 214
Printing records 218
Potential Pitfalls of File Management Software 219
Summary 221
Key Terms 222
Review Questions and Exercises 223
For Further Reading 223

8 *The Relational Connection: Introducing Data Base Management Systems* 225

Managing Data with a DBMS: An Introduction 226
Why users grow out of file management programs 227
A note on data base design 232
Exploring a Relational DBMS 232
Creating a data base 232
Adding records 234
Retrieving information 234
Updating information 237
Deleting information 237
Aggregate functions 237
Other relational DBMS features 238
Using Two or More Data Bases 239
Why multiple data bases are useful 239
Using the join command 240
The advantages of eliminating data redundancy 241
The Relational Model 242
DBMS Horizons 242
Natural language interfaces 243
Improving the user interface 243
Multiple-user DBMS packages 244
Summary 244
Key Terms 245
Review Questions and Exercises 245
For Further Reading 246

PART FOUR ▪ *Electronic Spreadsheets: Strategies for Number-Crunching* 248

9 *Electronic Spreadsheets: Tools for Manipulating Numbers* 251

Loading the Program 252
Using a Blank Spreadsheet 252
The command menu 255
Changing the Spreadsheet's Appearance 260
The default formats 260
Global formatting 261
Range formatting 262
Entering Labels 262
Entering Constants 264
Using Formulas 265
Entering formulas 265
Operators 266
Copying formulas 271
Absolute and relative cell references 272
Keys 274
Built-in functions 275
Range naming 277
Controlling recalculation 277
Editing the Spreadsheet 280
Saving to Disk 280
Printing 281
Quitting 282
The Limitations of Spreadsheet Software 283
Summary 284
Key Terms 285
Review Questions and Exercises 286
For Further Reading 286

10 *Advanced Spreadsheet Skills: Making the Most of the Visible Calculator* 287

Principles of Good Spreadsheet Design 288
Documenting your work 288
Using keys 289

Using calculation areas 290
Using appropriate cell formats 291
Splitting up complex formulas 291
Using cell protection 294
Checking your work 295
Creating a template 295
Using small spreadsheets 295
Modeling and Forecasting 299
Modeling 299
Forecasting 300
Using Advanced Spreadsheet Features 305
Advanced built-in functions 305
Using titles 306
Macros 307
Lookup tables 309
Summary 310
Key Terms 311
Review Questions and Exercises 311
For Further Reading 312

PART FIVE ▪ *Application Horizons* 314

11 ***Personal Computer Graphics: Making Your Point with Pictures*** 316

Hardware for Graphics 317
Video circuits for graphics applications 318
Resolution 322
Graphics input and output devices 323
Graphics Software and Applications 327
Analytic graphics packages 327
Presentation graphics: Presenting the data 331
Paint programs 334
Computer-aided design (CAD) 334
Graphics Horizons 335
Summary 336
Key Terms 337

Review Questions and Exercises 338
For Further Reading 338

12 *Personal Computer Communications: Strategies for Computer Networking* 340

Telecommunications: An Introduction 341
Hardware for telecommunications 342
Value-added networks 345
Software for communications 347
Telecommunications Applications 349
Electronic mail 350
Bulletin boards 353
Computer conferencing 354
Telecommuting 356
Online bibliographic data base research 357
Direct-Wire Communications 361
Local area networks 364
Micro-to-mainframe connections 366
Summary 366
Key Terms 369
Review Questions and Exercises 369
For Further Reading 370

13 *Integrated Software: Putting It All Together* 373

Integrated Software: The Promise 374
Context switching 374
Data transfer 375
Consistency of user interface 378
Integrated Software: The Reality 378
Complexity 378
Inadequate software functions 378
An Alternative to Integrated Software: Windowing Environments 380
Desktop organizers 380
Windowing environments 383
Horizons of Software Integration 385
Summary 388
Key Terms 389

Review Questions and Exercises 390
For Further Reading 390

14 *Special-Purpose Software: Tailored to Get a Specific Job Done* 391

Business 392
Accounting 392
Encrypting data 394
Investment planning 396
Project management 397
Education 399
Computer-assisted instruction (CAI) 399
Computer-managed instruction (CMI) 402
Science 402
Bibliographic management 402
Statistical packages 403
Technical word processing software 404
Utilities 404
Creating a RAM disk 404
Enhancing the keyboard 405
Printing while performing other tasks 405
Recovering deleted files 406
Special-Purpose Program Horizons 406
Summary 407
Key Terms 408
Review Questions and Exercises 409
For Further Reading 409

15 *Application Programming: From Problem to Solution* 411

Speaking Computerese: An Introduction 412
Machine language 413
Assembly language 414
High-level languages 415
Structured Programming 423
Traditional programming 424
The structured approach 426
Programming Application Software 432
Programming Horizons 433

Automatic programming 433
Very high level languages 434
Summary 434
Key Terms 437
Review Questions and Exercises 437
For Further Reading 438

PART SIX ▪ *The Impact of Computing* 440

16 *The Benefits and Risks of Personal Computing* 442

Benefits 443
New tools for small business 443
Improved public access to knowledge 443
Helping the handicapped 444
New channels for communication 445
New employment opportunities 446
Risks 446
Displaced blue-collar workers 446
Low quality of employment in service occupations 448
Computers and women 449
New risks for businesses 452
The Future 453
Summary 453
Key Terms 455
Review Questions and Exercises 455
For Further Reading 455

Appendix A Guidelines for Selecting Personal Computer Hardware and Software 457

Appendix B Resources for Personal Computing 462

Notes 464

Glossary 469

Index 497

Quick Reference Guides A–1

Operating system basics A–1
Word processing basics A–5
Advanced word processing A–13
File management basics A–17
DBMS basics A–25
Electronic spreadsheet basics A–33

PERSONAL COMPUTER APPLICATIONS

Prologue: The First Crisis in Information Management

Clay tokens served the record-keeping needs of the world's first accountants, the farmers and artisans of ancient Mesopotamia. Kept on strings or sealed in clay pots, the tokens helped villagers keep track of everything from seed stocks to bolts of textiles. Appearing around 8500 B.C., the tokens did their job adequately for 5,000 years.

By 3400 B.C., however, Mesopotamians were caught up in an unprecedented revolution: the transition to urban life. With the rise of cities came a major expansion in commerce. The waterways of the Fertile Crescent, the Tigris and Euphrates rivers, teemed with merchants' boats, and overland traders forged economic links with faraway lands and peoples. With the explosion of commerce, however, the potential for thievery and accounting mistakes multiplied dangerously. The tokens that had served so well, and for so long, could do the job no longer. And so the ancient Mesopotamians invented writing.

The world's first writers did little more than mimic the old, familiar clay tokens by incising their shapes on tablets. But the advantages of writing soon became clear, and writing developed quickly. Scribes learned to record large inventories, lengthy bills of lading, complex contracts, and intricate accounts. These documents were far more complex — and accurate — than anything that could have been done with the old tokens. Unfettered by the tokens' limitations, the pace of commerce accelerated even more rapidly. By 2900 B.C., Mesopotamians were the wealthiest people in the world, and their civilization — humanity's first — was in full swing.[1]

The first information management crisis happened a long time ago, but it has lessons for us today. In times of increasing social and economic complexity, people have to learn new, more efficient techniques for managing information. To do so is the pathway to wealth, success, and progress.

PART ONE

*"**Homo sapiens,** who stood at the dawn of the first civilization at the end of the last glacial age, is now standing at the threshold of the second, the information civilization."*

Yoneji Masuda

The New Tools for Personal Productivity

No ancestor of ours, Mesopotamians included, has ever witnessed an information management crisis like the one going on right now. Consider a few facts:

Each half hour produces enough new knowledge to fill an entire twenty-four volume set of the *Encyclopaedia Britannica*. By the time today's college freshmen reach age 50, 97 percent of all known information will have been discovered in their lifetime.

Since 1965, an estimated 100 million scientific, technical, and scholarly journal articles have been indexed in computer-readable data bases. A data base of chemicals now contains over 10,500,000 substances.

Businesses must cope with an estimated 45,000 new pages of government regulations per year. Responding to the regulations, the oil company Exxon had to submit a report to the Department of Energy that ran just shy of 500,000 pages. Documentation for just one major contract forced RCA's Missile and Surface Radar facility to crank out more than 100,000 pages of technical manuals per year.

Marks and Spencer, a huge British retailing firm, found ten years ago that its employees had to process more than 30 million pages of paperwork per year. American corporations generate enough paperwork each day to circle the globe forty times. In 1984 alone, 14 million new file cabinets were manufactured so that an estimated 200 billion pieces of paper would have some place to go.

In the face of an information explosion of this magnitude, the road to survival isn't to work harder, it's to work smarter. Happily, another explosion — this one of technology — has put just the tool we need right on our desks: the personal computer.

Part One, "The New Tools for Personal Productivity," introduces this new technology for information work. Chapter 1, "Working Smarter: Computer Literacy for the Information Age," stresses the need for information worker productivity and introduces personal computer technology. Chapter 2, "The World of Computing: Personal Computers in Perspective," introduces the idea of computing and locates the personal computer in five generations of technological progress. Chapter 3, "The Personal Computer: Fourth-Generation Technology for Ordinary People," introduces personal computer hardware and system software, laying the foundation for productive work with application software.

1 *Working Smarter:* Computer Applications for the Information Age

"With only a cheap personal computer and a communications link, you have what people have only been talking about: the office of the future."
Gus Morck *Atlantic Richfield Company*

A dairy farm may not seem like the best place to see the future. Yet well over one-third of the nation's dairy cattle are bred, fed, and milked with computer assistance — and with major benefits in efficiency and productivity. The average "computerized" cow, fed and milked at optimum times, produces 30 percent more milk than its predecessors. Using computers, the dairy industry now produces just as much milk as it did fifteen years ago — but with far fewer cows.[1]

Dairy farmers didn't achieve this major productivity increase by working harder. They did it by working smarter — with computers. Working smarter means working more productively with information: acquiring it, manipulating it, and communicating it more rapidly and effectively than ever before. That's what computers are for. And now that the personal computer has arrived, you can put the same computing power to work for you.

A NATION OF OFFICE WORKERS

Most readers of this book are almost as unlikely to wind up on dairy farms as they are counting tokens in Mesopotamia. American farming has become so productive that it requires only 3 percent of the United States work force to feed the entire United States population and a good portion of the rest of the world besides. You're most likely to wind up, not on a farm, and not even in a factory, but rather in the new capital of American work: the office. **White-collar workers** — professional and technical workers, managers and administrators, sales workers, and clerical workers — now make up more than 50 percent of the United States work force, and almost all of them work in offices (Figure 1–1).

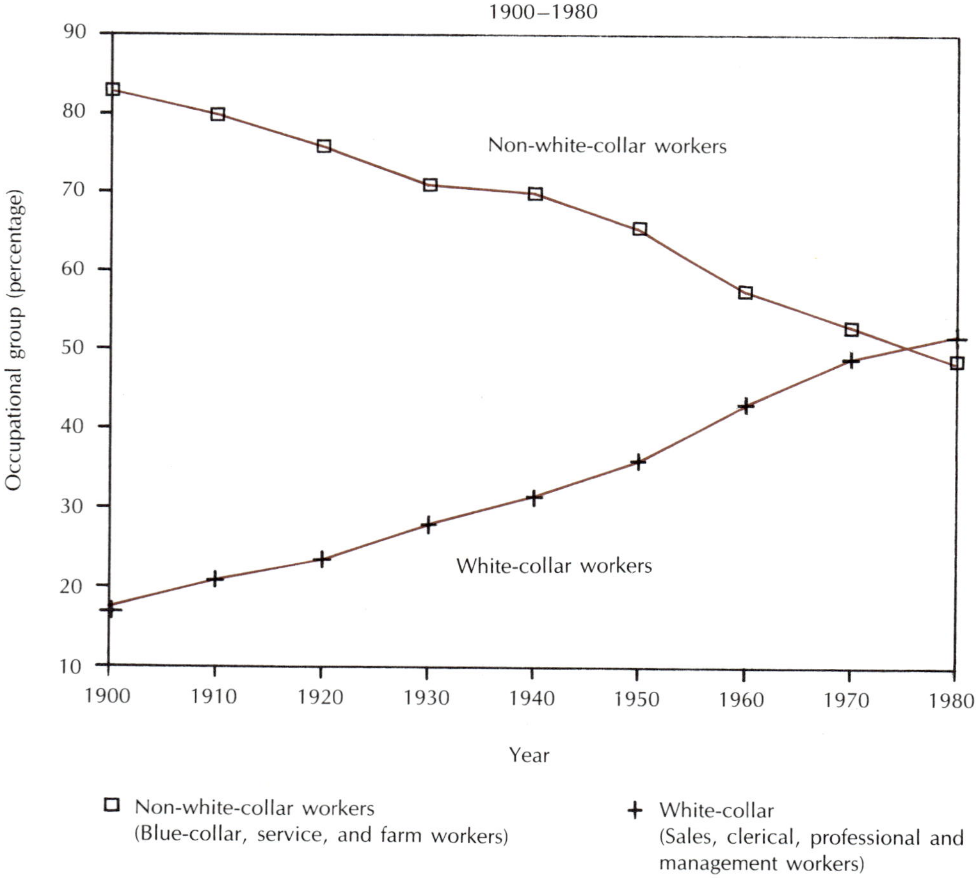

FIGURE 1–1 The Changing U.S. Work Force
Source: From Vincent E. Giuliano, "The Mechanization of Office Work," *Scientific American* (September 1982), p. 154.

The percentage of white-collar workers is still rising. And here's what it means: no matter what subject you study in college or what your career goals are — whether you choose to pursue medicine, the law, business administration, journalism, teaching, or any other career that requires a college education — the productivity tools best suited to your needs are the ones that will help you with office work. To understand these needs, let's look more closely at just what office work involves.

THE OFFICE AND INFORMATION WORK

What is an office? All of us have stereotypes aplenty about offices — the tyrannical boss, the boring work, the harassed secretary, the petty politics. Yet the stereotypes obscure a fundamental point: the office is the primary place where information work goes on. To be more precise, an **office** is a place where people carry out six fundamental activities with information (Figure 1–2):

1. *Creating information.* To create information is to take raw, unorganized **data** — facts about the world — and put them together in a way that's useful and meaningful to people. A cardboard box full of customer receipts is an example of unorganized data. It's not of much use until someone processes the data — for example, putting all the customer names and addresses in alphabetical order. Processing data produces **information.** Information is organized, useful data.
2. *Storing and retrieving information.* A major — and tedious — part of office work involves storing and retrieving massive amounts of information. Manual methods are slow and costly. According to one estimate, it takes $9,600 in labor and other costs just to fill two drawers of a four-drawer filing cabinet.
3. *Analyzing information.* To analyze something means to understand it better by looking at its component parts. In businesses, for example, managers analyze information by doing forecasts. In a forecast, you begin with the information you have, such as sales figures for the past three years, and you try to determine what sales will be in the coming year. Forecasts are essential: you have to know in advance, for instance, how many employees you'll need to cope with a growing business.
4. *Summarizing information.* Offices deal with so much information that it wouldn't be of much use without organizing and summarizing it. People who make decisions don't have time to go through all the customer records, for instance, to find out the average income of regular customers; they need someone to produce a summary of the information. Many business people spend much of their time summarizing information for top management.

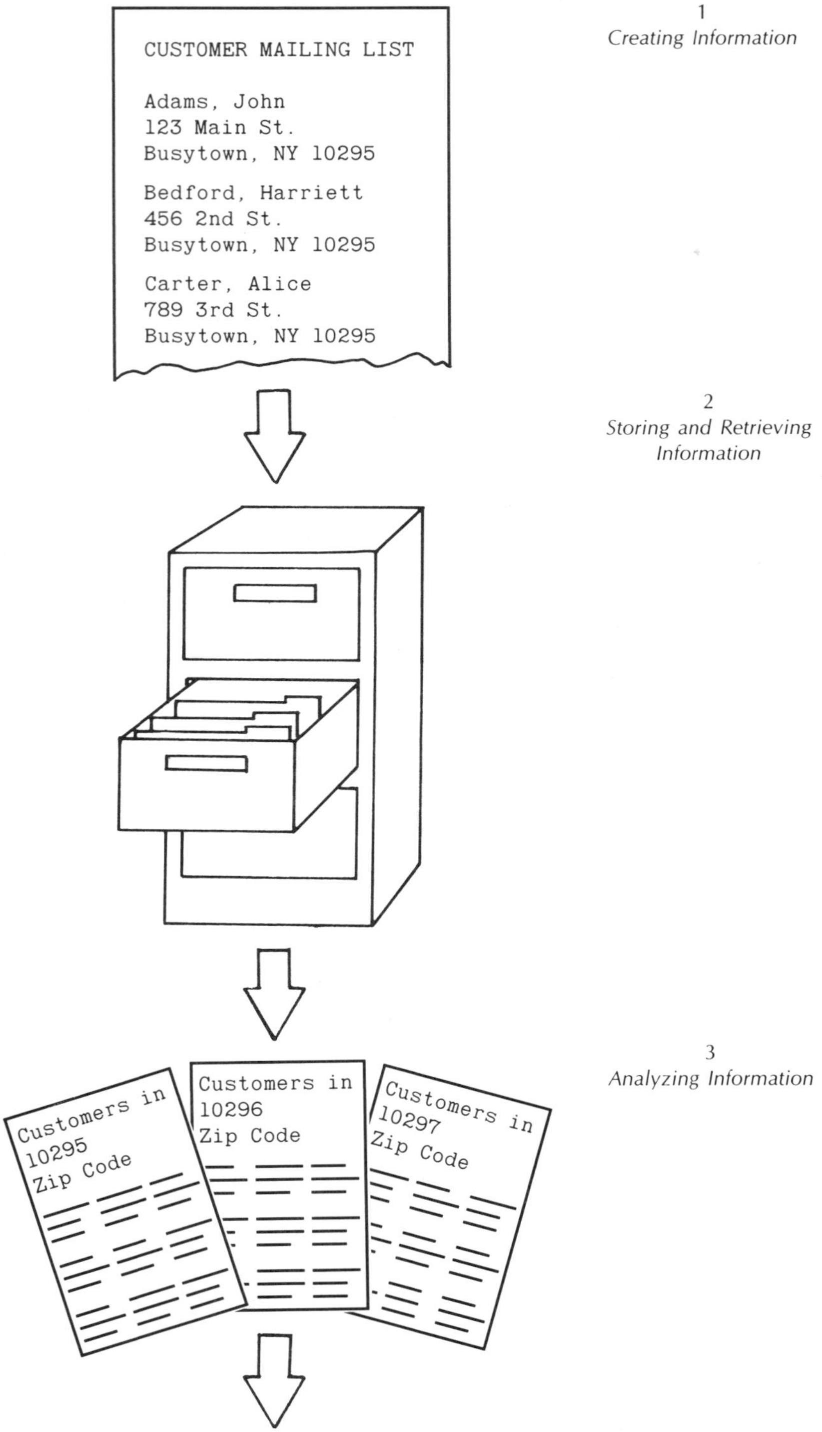

FIGURE 1–2 Information Work in the Office: Six Steps

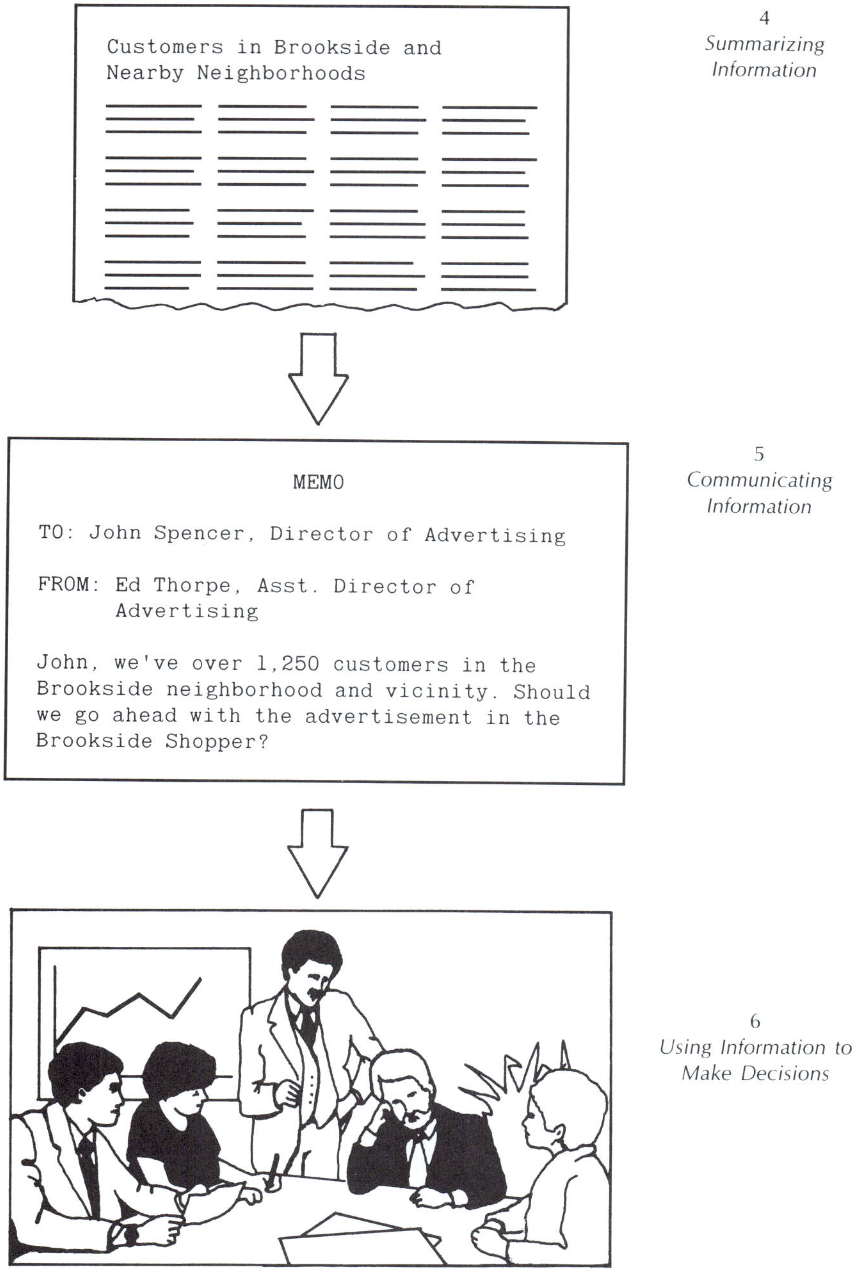

FIGURE 1–2 Information Work in the Office: Six Steps *(continued)*

5. *Communicating information*. Most communication that went on in eighteenth- and nineteenth-century businesses was by word of mouth, but businesses have grown. They're so big, in fact, that most of the people who must communicate seldom see each other; they have to communicate, for the most part, in writing. Creating documents — periodic reports, analytical reports, letters, and memos — occupies an increasingly large percentage of information worker time.
6. *Using information to make decisions*. Once information has been created or acquired, summarized, analyzed, and communicated to top management, it's used to make decisions — decisions, for example, about whether to proceed with the marketing of a product or to hire a new staff of salespeople.

Most of today's workers with college degrees are involved in these activities. Just which ones you'll concentrate on, however, depends on where you wind up in the office's occupational structure.

THE OFFICE'S OCCUPATIONAL STRUCTURE

Information workers are a varied lot and include virtually everyone who works in an office, from the highest executive down to clerks and secretaries. They work with information in different ways.[2]

Chief Executive Officers (CEOs) deal with broad issues and long-range problems; they must decide where the organization is headed and determine its fundamental objectives. They receive summaries of the organization's performance from middle-level managers and keep abreast of social and economic trends affecting the organization's environment.

Middle-level managers collect and summarize information about the organization and give it to the CEO; they also translate the organization's objectives into practical guidelines for all to follow.

Professionals and specialists exercise such skills as accounting, training, financial analysis, legal advising, marketing, public relations, and running computers.

Sales workers carry out sales transactions with the firm's clients.

Clerical and secretarial personnel do the hand processing of information (typing from dictation, sorting mail, etc.).

This occupational structure is increasingly pervasive in our society. It's found everywhere: in nonprofit organizations, highly competitive corporations, engineering firms, universities, scientific research institutes, the offices of retail and manufacturing firms, and government bureaucracies. Most readers of this book will pursue careers at the professional, specialist, sales, or middle-managerial levels. And it is in precisely these jobs that the workload of information-related activities is the highest.

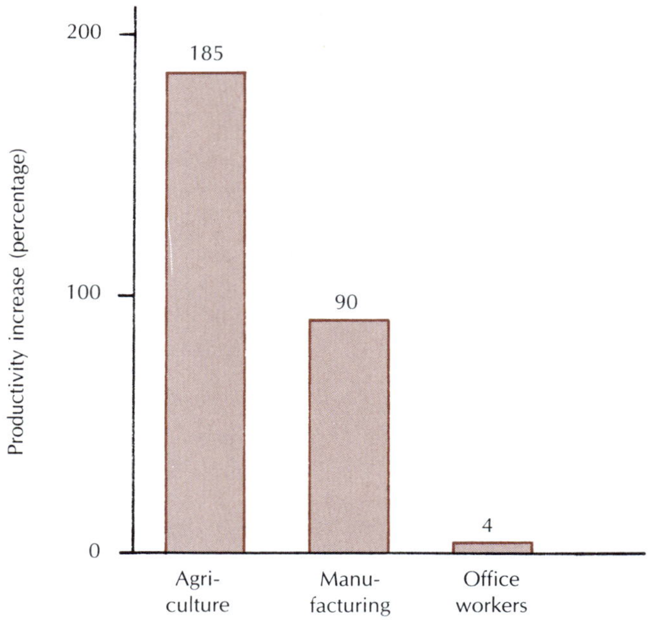

FIGURE 1–3
Productivity Increases of U.S. Workers, 1960–1970
Source: U.S. Department of Commerce figures, cited in Donald Sanders, *Computers Today* (New York: McGraw-Hill, 1983), p. 297.

THE OFFICE BOTTLENECK

The growing predominance of white-collar workers and of information work in our economy has brought with it an increasingly serious problem: slow productivity growth. The growth of white-collar productivity has been dismal at best, and it has made the office a bottleneck for economic and technical progress. Still working with tools that date back to the horse-and-buggy era, white-collar workers improved their productivity only 4 percent in the 1960s, a mediocre performance (Figure 1–3). To put that figure into perspective, during the same period industrial worker productivity rose 90 percent and farm worker productivity rose 185 percent. Not surprisingly, the cost of office work has swelled monstrously; it now makes up 40 to 50 percent of all costs in many companies. Small wonder that there's a growing cry for **office automation** — the computerization of office work — and for a new generation of computer-literate office workers.

COMPUTER APPLICATIONS FOR INFORMATION WORKERS

The computer literacy that information workers need focuses on personal computers and application software. These, to be sure, are only part of a wider world of computing (see box, "Computers at Work and Play"). Computers are

Computers at Work and Play

Computers outnumber people in the United States right now, and over one million more are being built each day. Most of these computers are mass-produced on tiny chips of silicon and find their way into everything from toasters to personal computers. Large or small, computers are changing American life.

Business. Computer-based point-of-sale terminals automatically total a day's transactions, adjust inventory records, and order new stock. Information utilities such as Dow Jones News Service give business investors with personal computers direct access to stock quotes and investment information. There's even a new generation of Coca-Cola machines that talk to customers — saying "Thank you" after dispensing a Coke.

Science and Engineering. Using computer-aided design (CAD) techniques for designing the new 767 jet aircraft, Boeing engineers cut design time and increased aerodynamic efficiency. The computer's ability to simulate or mimic complex phenomena on the display screen is leading to major advances in virtually every scientific field. The computer makes possible what-if modeling techniques, in which scientists change key variables to see what happens. In this way complex experiments can be performed without expensive equipment and laboratories.

Medicine. Implanted computerized devices are making possible a new generation of prostheses, or replacements for damaged or missing body parts. Examples include heart pacemakers that smooth out erratic heartbeats. In multiphasic health testing, a computer analyzes patient questionnaires and determines likely patterns of disease. Expert systems, or "intelligent" programs that simulate an expert's knowledge, help diagnose diseases.

Sports. Computerized analyses help Olympic athletes develop effective training programs. Baseball coaches use them to decide whether to put in left- or right-handed pinch hitters, and football teams use them to decide on draft picks. Personal computers helped climbers pick the best route up Everest, considering factors such as temperature, winds, and snowfall.

Education. With the help of IBM's "Writing to Read" program, computers in the classroom are helping first graders learn to read faster than they do by conventional methods. By simulating scientific experiments, computers permit more advanced students to gain laboratory experience without expensive equipment.

The Arts. The Broadway hit *A Chorus Line* received a Tony award for its computerized lighting system, which is now used to control the lights for operas and ballets at Lincoln Center for the Performing Arts. Computerized music synthesizers can be heard in just about every pop record (and in increasing numbers of classical compositions).

The diffusion of computer technology throughout our society is not without its costs. Industrial robots are displacing blue-collar factory workers. Grocery-store clerks are complaining of carpal tunnel syndrome, a painful ailment brought on by dragging groceries over computerized barcode readers. A new generation of "smart" weapons has changed the ground rules of conventional warfare. Like it or not, however, computers are here to stay. All of us — collectively as well as individually — will have to adapt to this major new force that is shaping the world around us.

indeed touching virtually every part of our lives. Yet you, as an ambitious student with career goals at the professional, sales, or managerial levels, will find it helpful to concentrate on the slice of the computing pie that's most relevant to your needs: the personal computer as a tool for information-related work.

PERSONAL COMPUTERS

Personal computers are easy to use, inexpensive, and small — small enough, in fact, to fit on office desks. They're designed for use by ordinary people with little previous background in computers or computer programming. What's more, they're designed to meet the computing needs of individuals. That's why they're called personal computers.

And that's just what distinguishes them from other kinds of computers (see Chapter 2). Larger computers are designed to meet the computing needs of entire organizations (or departments within them). Personal computers, as the chief scientist of IBM puts it, are — at least potentially — "responsive personal servants to ordinary people,"[3] people who don't want to become computer programmers because they have other jobs to do, such as seeing patients, helping clients win suits, and managing businesses. As you'll see, application software turns that productivity potential into a reality for information workers of all kinds.

APPLICATION SOFTWARE

The computer itself — the **hardware,** or the physical parts you can see and touch — is as useless as a stereo system without any records, cassettes, or compact disks. To make it useful, **software** is needed. The term software refers to all the programs that run on a computer, giving it the instructions it needs in order to do something useful. Absolutely necessary is **system software,** the programs that help the computer's components to work together and provide programmers the tools they need to create new programs. Chapter 3 looks at system software in more detail. Also necessary for widespread computer use is **application software,** or ready-to-run programs created to do specific tasks such as word processing or accounting.

Most people do not have the time to become proficient programmers. They need application software to make effective use of computers. This point was proven dramatically in a 1978 *Wall Street Journal* experiment. The paper presented a staff reporter, Mitchell Lynch, with an early personal computer and asked him to take it home for six months. Lynch reported:

> I thought it would straighten out the family budget; it didn't. The ads said it would help educate the kids; it didn't. Certainly it would do my tax returns; it

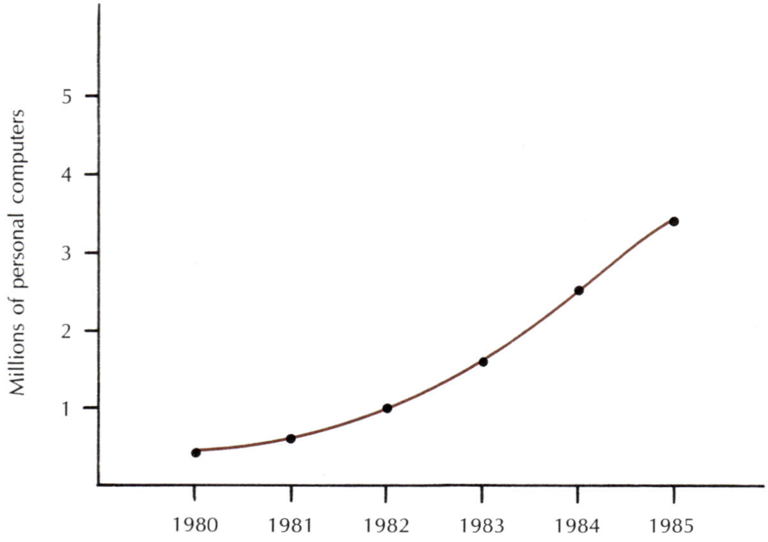

FIGURE 1–4 Growth of Personal Computer Sales, 1980–1985
Source: Wall Street Journal (September 16, 1985), p. 36.

> can't. At least it would teach me to prepare those fancy programs for computers; it didn't. Indeed, if I hadn't been assigned to work with my computer, it would be gathering dust in my closet.

What went wrong? The problem: lack of quality software. For people who don't have the time to learn programming, and that includes most white-collar workers, application software is the key to personal computer productivity. It's no wonder personal computer sales rose more than 800 percent from 1980 to 1985 (Figure 1–4), a period in which application software became readily available.

APPLICATION SOFTWARE FOR INFORMATION WORK

The three most popular application programs are *word processing, data base management,* and *spreadsheet programs* (Figure 1–5).

Word processing programs turn a computer into a supple, responsive tool for creating, revising, and printing written work. By dramatically lowering the tedium, cost, and inconvenience of revising, word processing software is a major productivity booster for anyone who communicates information in writing. There's no more erasing, cutting and pasting, or laborious retyping; a writer can revise and reorganize until the document is just right.

Data base management programs provide computerized tools for working with information normally stored in file cabinets, such as mailing lists, customer account data, patient records, or lists of franchised dealers. Like word processing programs, they put speed, convenience, and flexibility in the place of wasted time, drudgery, and rigidity. Considering that, according to one estimate, it costs $9,600 to fill just two drawers of a four-drawer cabinet using hand methods, you'll know right away why data base management programs are so popular. They dramatically ease the tasks of creating, storing, retrieving, and summarizing information.

FIGURE 1–5 Application Software for Information Work

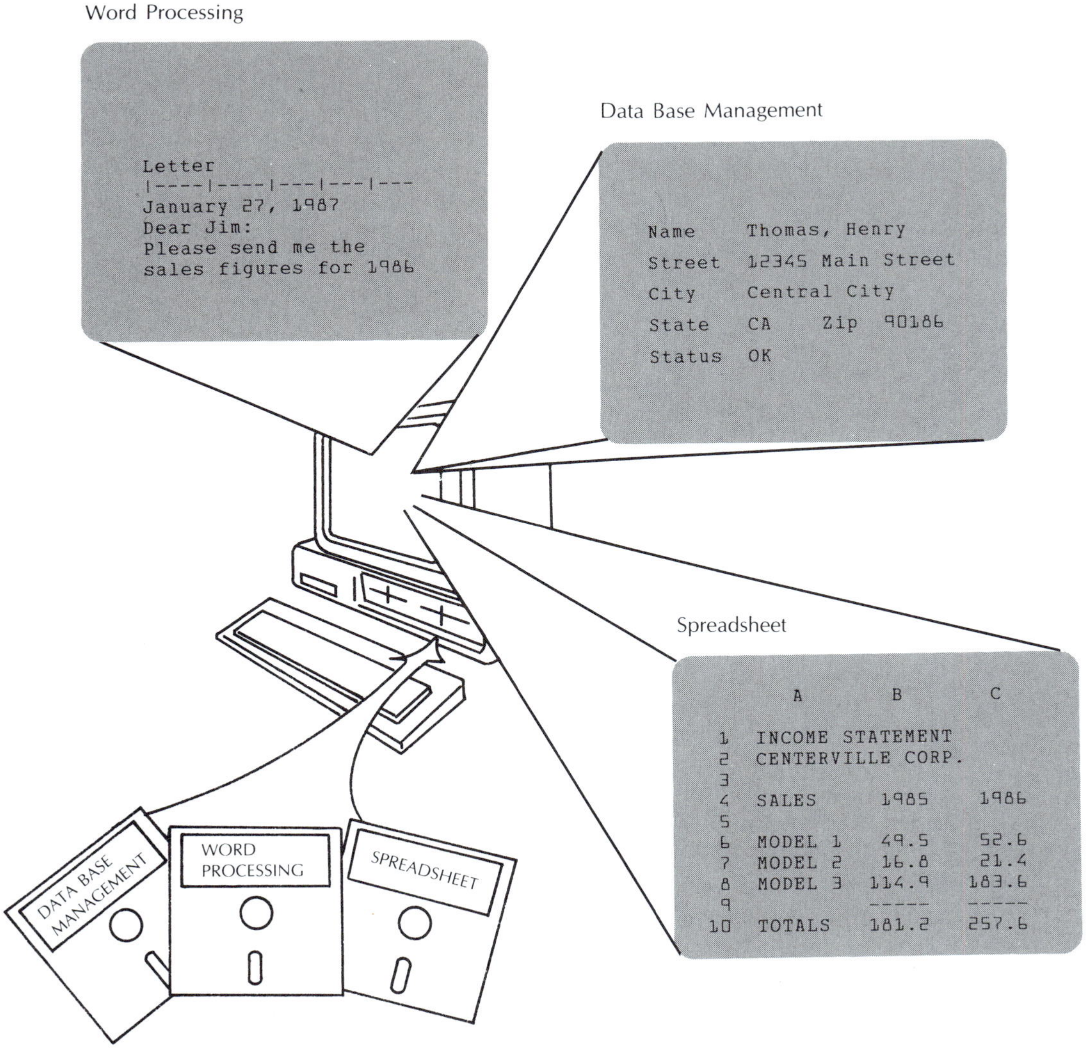

Spreadsheet programs do for numerical work what word processing programs do for writing and data base management programs do for filing. Such a program simulates an accountant's worksheet, with its many numerical entries, but with one major difference: because the numbers are linked by hidden formulas, changing one leads to a speedy, automatic recalculation of totals and averages. Spreadsheets have many applications, but one particularly useful one is for *what-if operations,* in which a key variable is changed to see what its effect is on the total picture. Spreadsheet programs are extremely useful tools for analyzing information and using information to make decisions.

The prevalence of these three kinds of application programs in the software marketplace is far from surprising. After all, the three activities they automate — writing, managing information, and reasoning with numbers — are jobs information workers perform daily. Anyone who works in an office, from the clerk up to the CEO, can use these programs to increase productivity. As you have probably concluded by now, a personal computer isn't just for people who compute, that is, work with numbers. It is far more than a machine for calculations. It's a one-person information system designed to help you create, store and retrieve, analyze, summarize, and communicate information, as well as to help you make wise and fruitful decisions.

THE PRODUCTIVITY PROMISE

The personal computer's true significance is that it puts computing power right where it's most needed: on the desks of white-collar workers. There's plenty of evidence that personal computers with application software can lead to big productivity gains. The Bank of Miami, for example, reported a 30 percent productivity gain after installing them in its offices.[4] The credit management offices of Associated Grocers of New England found that they increased credit managers' productivity by 60 to 70 percent.[5] Personal computers supplied with word processing software can lead to productivity gains of up to 400 percent over typewriters.[6]

Productivity gains of this sort, however, are far from automatic, as businesses everywhere are learning to their dismay. People who learn how to use personal computers unsystematically often tap only a tiny fraction of their computers' true power. According to Intel Corporation president Andrew Grove, information workers are exploiting only 5 percent of their computer's capabilities. Part of the reason for this low level of performance is the industry's own hype, which insists that personal computers are easy to use. That's true, but only in comparison to their predecessors. To exploit the personal computer and application software fully, something more than a casual encounter is needed. You need an encounter with personal computing that goes beyond the superficial, and shows you how to get the most out of this exciting new technology.

Case Study: Managers Reveal Their Computer Experiences

Robert Hightower, business unit manager of Systems Products United/Wavetek Inc., San Diego, California: Hightower uses his IBM Personal Computer and Lotus 1–2–3, a spreadsheet program, to produce analytical reports. Hightower figures that each report now takes about one-half hour instead of the two or three hours required previously. "More important than the time involved," Hightower says, "is the immediacy and better quality of the results. I also analyze customer survey data and the cross correlations I get were impossible before the PC."

Sherman Frankston, president Corpcom New Jersey Inc., Teaneck, New Jersey: "For me the PC is another employee, one who saves my company and my clients a great deal of money." Frankston uses his Radio Shack computer primarily for writing reports and brochures for corporate clients, transmitting the copy directly to the typesetter. Savings of 15 percent or more are gained by eliminating duplicate keyboarding. He concludes: "A PC . . . can turn a harried executive into a much more efficient presenter of ideas."

Excerpted from *Administrative Management,* Copyright 1984, by Dalton Communications, Inc., New York.

This encounter is needed, moreover, *before* you take your place in the world of white-collar work. Today's companies are groaning under the cost of training and supporting workers who try to apply personal computer technology to their jobs. For 500 workers, the training and support bill can go as high as $4 million.[7] That's why companies are looking for people who already know how to use these productivity tools. You'll be wise to learn as much as you can about them right now.

Even though training costs are high at present, United States companies are still investing heavily in equipment to automate information work. A study by Honeywell Corporation suggests that it is worth spending up to 60 percent of an information worker's annual salary on computers if that equipment brings a productivity gain of just 10 percent. With this kind of return in mind, United States firms are now putting more money per worker into computerized office equipment than into factory equipment. In late 1984, almost half the white collar workers in twenty-three leading firms and universities used personal computers for information work, and that figure is expected to rise significantly by 1990.[8] By 1990, every white-collar worker in the federal bureaucracy is expected to have a personal computer on his or her desk.

The information society, office automation, and the personal computer are here to stay. The only remaining question is whether you'll be ready for them. And that's precisely why this book was written. Its computer application strategy for the information society begins in Chapter 2, which places the personal computer in its historical context.

SUMMARY

No matter what career you choose to follow, you're likely to wind up working in an office. An office is a place where people do six kinds of information work: creating information, storing and retrieving information, analyzing information, summarizing information, communicating information, and using information to make decisions. Office workers are of five basic types: chief executive officers, middle managers, professionals, salespeople, and clerical workers. Most readers of this book will take their first jobs in the professional, technical, sales, or middle-management ranks.

White-collar workers' productivity grew only slowly during the 1960s, and a major effort is now under way to automate offices. To staff the computer-equipped offices of the future, a new generation of computer-literate, white-collar workers will be needed. If you're headed for a job at the professional, specialist, or middle-management level, your best bet is a computer literacy focus that emphasizes personal computers and application software.

Personal computers are designed for use by individuals who lack programming or technical expertise. By itself, a personal computer is next to useless for white-collar workers, who lack the time to do much programming. It becomes useful only when a wide variety of application programs are available. The three most popular are word processing, data base management, and spreadsheet programs. You need more than a superficial involvement with these programs to use them productively. You'll be wise to make personal computers and these three application programs the focus of your computer literacy effort.

KEY TERMS

application software
data
data base management program
hardware
information
office
office automation
software
spreadsheet program
system software
white-collar workers
word processing program

Note: The glossary at the back of the book contains definitions of all key terms.

REVIEW QUESTIONS AND EXERCISES

1. Define the term *white-collar worker*. Think of an organization that you have come to know well, such as an elementary school, a retail business, a university, or a corporation. What proportion of workers fall into the white-collar category? Think of your own career goals. Will you find yourself somewhere in the white-collar work force?
2. What is an office?
3. Find examples from something you're familiar with, such as a hobby or sports, which illustrate the terms *data* and *information*. How do you create information out of data?
4. Draw on your own experience to provide an example of an information storage and retrieval job that you did with hand methods.
5. From coursework you've already done, provide an example of information analysis.
6. Think of the job that business managers have to do. Why are information summaries so important to them?
7. Drawing on your own experience, think of an instance in which you used information to make a decision. How did you acquire or create the information?
8. Name and define the six basic forms of information-related work commonly done in offices.
9. Why has white-collar productivity grown so slowly?
10. Why is a focus on personal computing particularly appropriate for future white-collar workers?
11. Provide some examples of ways in which computers of all kinds (including large computing systems) are touching virtually every aspect of our lives.
12. Define the personal computer. Why is a focus on personal computing especially helpful for people with career objectives outside of computer science and programming?
13. Contrast the terms *hardware* and *software*. In what sense could these terms be meaningfully used with reference to a high-fidelity audio system? What would be the hardware? The software?
14. Contrast the terms *system software* and *application software*. How useful would you find a personal computer that had adequate system software but virtually no application software? Why?
15. Define the terms *word processing software, data base management software,* and *spreadsheet software*. Now explain how each of these application programs can be applied to the six basic forms of information work.
16. Why should you apply yourself to learning personal computer skills now, while you're still in school?

FOR FURTHER READING

INFORMATION OVERLOAD: THE CHALLENGE OF LIFE AND WORK IN THE INFORMATION AGE

Drucker, Peter F. *The Age of Discontinuity: Guidelines to Our Changing Society* (New York: Harper and Row, 1969).
Hawken, Paul. *The Next Economy* (New York: Holt, Rinehart, and Winston, 1983).
Naisbitt, John. *Megatrends: Ten New Directions Transforming Our Lives* (New York: Warner Books, 1984).
Schiller, Herbert I. *Who Knows: Information in the Age of the Fortune 500* (Norwood, N.J.: Ablex, 1981).
Toffler, Alvin. *Future Shock* (New York: Bantam Books, 1970).
———. *The Third Wave* (New York: William Morrow, 1980).
Zahr, Leonard. "The Paper Palace," *Wall Street Journal* (Sept. 16, 1986).

INTRODUCTION TO PERSONAL COMPUTERS AND APPLICATION SOFTWARE

Horenstein, Henry, and Eliot Tarlin. *Computerwise: An Introduction to Understanding, Buying, and Using a Personal Computer* (New York: Vintage Books, 1983).
Miller, Harry. "Up and Running: PC World's Official Beginner's Guide," *PC World* (May 1985).
Toong, Hoo-Min D., and Amar Gupta, "Personal Computers," *Scientific American* (December 1982).

2 The World of Computing: *Personal Computers in Perspective*

"First look backward in order to look forward."
Thomas J. Watson, Sr. (1874–1956) Founder of IBM

Imagine the computer's history as a single day. We're at 5:00 P.M. sharp. The earliest computer, a hand-powered abacus, appeared at 9:00 A.M. It wasn't until 4:45 P.M., however, that a significant improvement was made, the mechanical calculator. The first electronic computer was invented just two minutes ago, at 4:58 P.M., and the first personal computer hit the market just 20 seconds ago.

The computer's rapid development is matched by its equally rapid diffusion throughout society. Just thirty years ago, there were only a few dozen computers in existence. Now there are well over 16 million personal computers and 1.3 million large computers in the United States alone. Falling prices made this population explosion possible. In the past thirty years, computing costs fell at an average of 25 to 40 percent per year, while computational speed increased by a factor of 200. If Boeing had made the same progress in the same period, today's 767 jetliner would cost $500 and circle the earth in 20 minutes.[1]

To live today is to rush headlong on a rapidly accelerating train of technological progress. In a situation like this one, the intelligent thing to do isn't to sit comfortably admiring the scenery, it's to find out as much as you can about what this technology is all about, where it came from, and where it's headed. These are the aims of this chapter.

BASICS: THE IDEA OF THE COMPUTER

We like to think that the computer is new. The electronic computer is indeed recent, dating back only to World War II. But the idea of computing is very old. According to the late computer scientist Christopher Evans, the computer idea

> stretches back in time to the first occasion when . . . [a person] picked up a few small stones, or scratched marks in the earth as a kind of memory aid. What he [or she] was doing was using a physical unit or set of units to represent numbers or quantities, and the essence of computers is just this: a number or a quantity can be represented by a *physical thing,* whether it is a pebble, a bead on a wire, a mark on a bit of paper, a mechanical gear wheel, an electrical relay, a vacuum tube, or a submicroscopic area of magnetized material. Once numbers can be expressed in this way, it becomes possible to manipulate them or change their state and cause them to represent different numbers or quantities. This, in turn, means that it becomes possible to construct a machine to perform these manipulations.[2]

The **abacus** illustrates the idea of the computer in almost every detail. The term *abacus* refers to an ancient calculating device in which movable beads represent quantities and facilitate calculations. Most familiar to us is the oriental abacus (Figure 2–1), which was widely used until the 1970s arrival of the battery-powered calculator. The box, "Using the Abacus," illustrates subtraction technique with a simplified abacus. Read it now. As you'll see, the abacus — ancient as it is — fulfills the four basic functions of any computer: input, storage, processing, and output.

INPUT

Computers work with data that have been physically represented. **Input** is the process of getting that data into the computer for processing purposes. Whether you push beads to the top of the frame to represent the number 8,746 or push

FIGURE 2–1 Chinese Abacus

a modern computer's keys to represent a social security number, the underlying idea is still the same.

The input process involves **coding** the data. To *code* something is to represent it with a physical object or mark. To input the number 8 with an abacus, for instance, you use beads to represent that quantity. Figure 2–9 (page 26) shows other ways the number 8 can be represented.

Digital Computers. Most computers (including the abacus and modern personal computers) code information using **digits.** The word *digit* actually means "finger." As you know from grade-school experience, fingers are useful counting aids because each one is discrete — that is, clearly separate and differentiated from all the others. Coding data with discrete digits makes for computing accuracy. You can tell at a glance whether someone is holding up three or four fingers. The fourth finger is either there or it isn't. At a glance, you can discriminate between three and four with a high degree of accuracy.

A **digital computer** counts physical digits. An abacus is a digital computer that uses beads. **Electronic digital computers,** such as the personal computer, represent data using **bistable devices.** Bistable devices are electronic circuits that can be switched between just two states: on or off (Figure 2–10, page 27). Modern electronic computers are made up of simple switching devices in huge numbers.

Using the Abacus

The simplified abacus shown in Figure 2–2 has four wires with ten beads each, representing thousands, hundreds, tens, and ones. To represent and store the number 8,746, you'd move the beads to the top of the frame as shown. Now let's subtract 2,822.

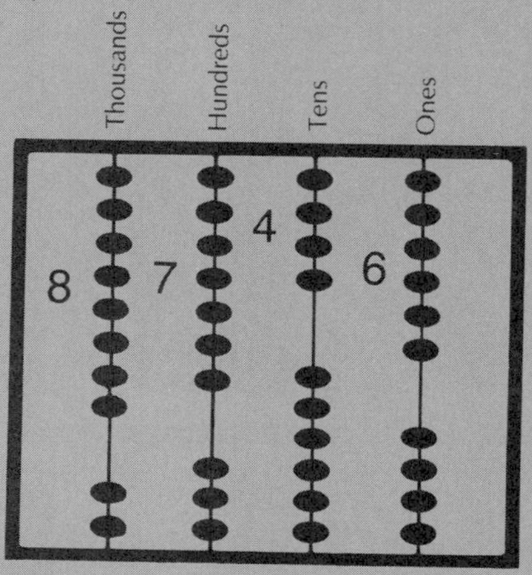

FIGURE 2–2 Using the Abacus: Step 1

With an abacus, as opposed to paper-and-pencil calculation, it's best to start on the left instead of the right. So let's take away 2,000 by moving down two beads on the left (Figure 2–3).

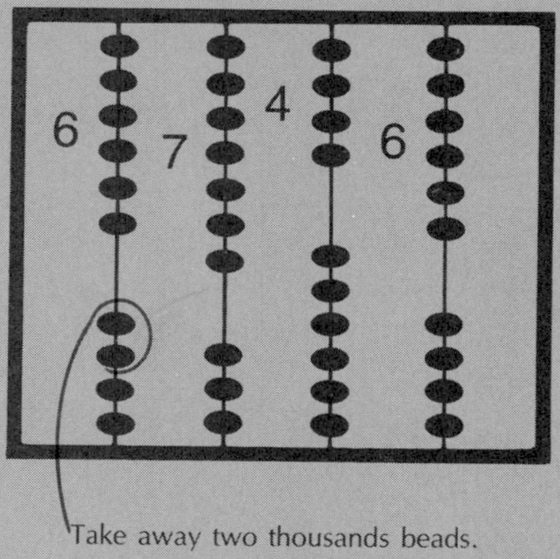

FIGURE 2–3 Using the Abacus: Step 2

So far, so good. But a problem emerges here. We need to take away 800 on the hundreds wire, but only seven beads, totaling 700, are available. Here's the procedure. First, take away as many of the hundreds beads as you can, seven in all (Figure 2–4).

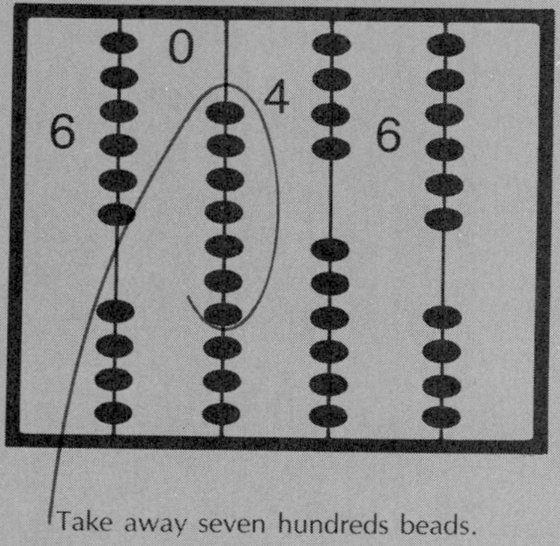

FIGURE 2–4 Using the Abacus: Step 3

Now borrow a bead from the thousands column by moving one bead down (Figure 2–5).

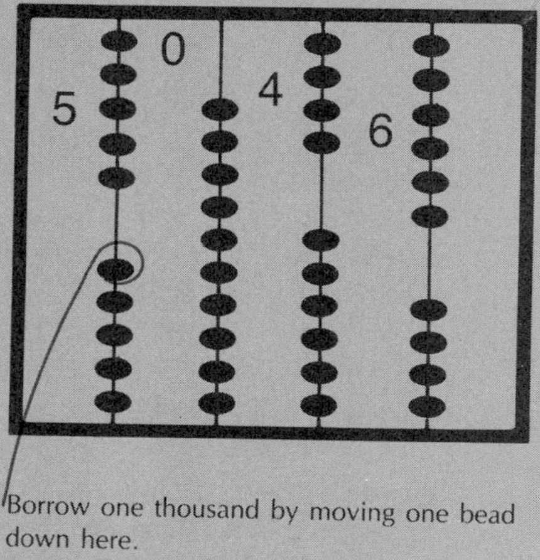

FIGURE 2–5 Using the Abacus: Step 4

Put the 1,000 you've borrowed into the hundreds column by moving all ten beads up (Figure 2–6).

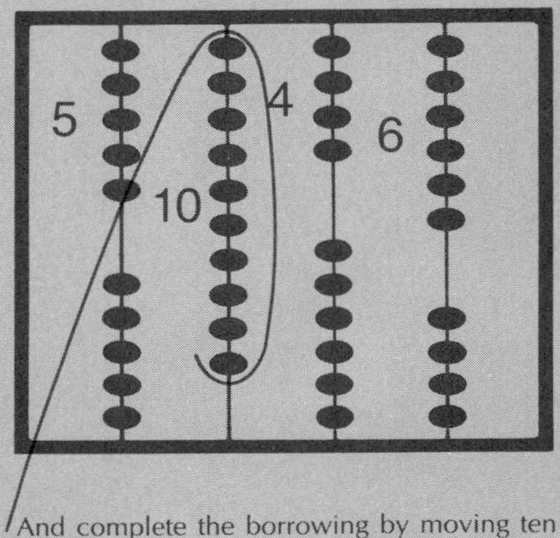

And complete the borrowing by moving ten hundreds beads up here.

FIGURE 2–6 Using the Abacus: Step 5

Take away one bead from the hundreds column. Remember, you took seven away before you borrowed 1,000, so taking one more away totals eight hundreds beads taken away (Figure 2–7).

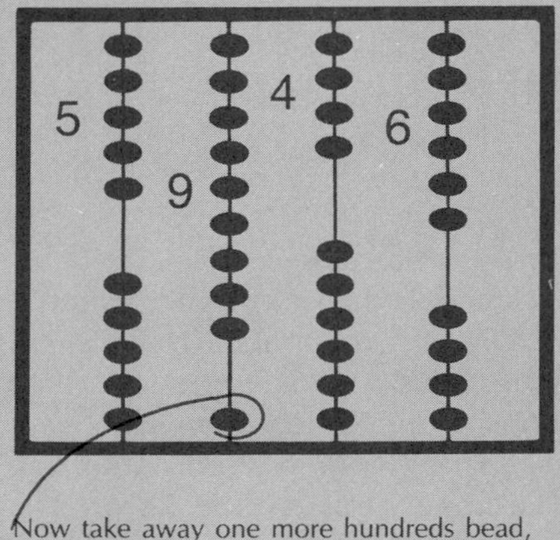

Now take away one more hundreds bead, making eight in all that you've subtracted.

FIGURE 2–7 Using the Abacus: Step 6

Now take away two tens and two ones, and you have the answer: 5,924 (Figure 2–8).

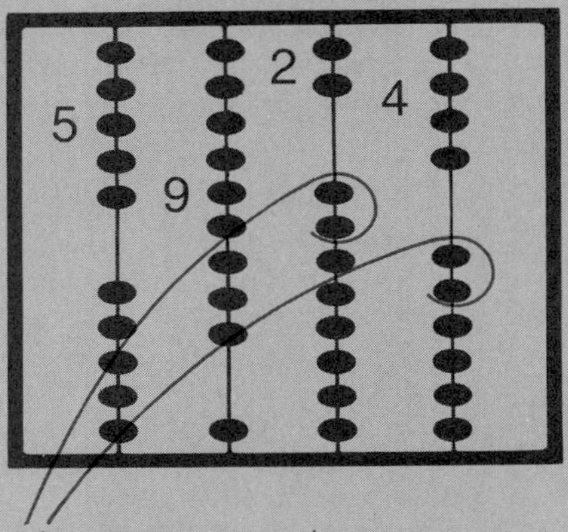

Take away two tens and two ones.

FIGURE 2–8 Using the Abacus: Step 7

In the hands of a skilled user, this and other abacus techniques can be very powerful. In 1947, Kiyoshi Matsuzake of the Japanese Ministry of Communications, an abacus clerk, was pitted against Pvt. Tom Wood, a skilled American operator of an electromechanical calculator. Matsuzake was beaten only in the multiplication contest, winning four out of five matches.*

* Michael R. Williams, *A History of Computing Technology* (Englewood Cliffs, N.J.: Prentice-Hall, 1985), p. 57.

Source: Adapted from J. M. Pullan, *The History of the Abacus* (London: Hutchinson, 1970), p. 108.

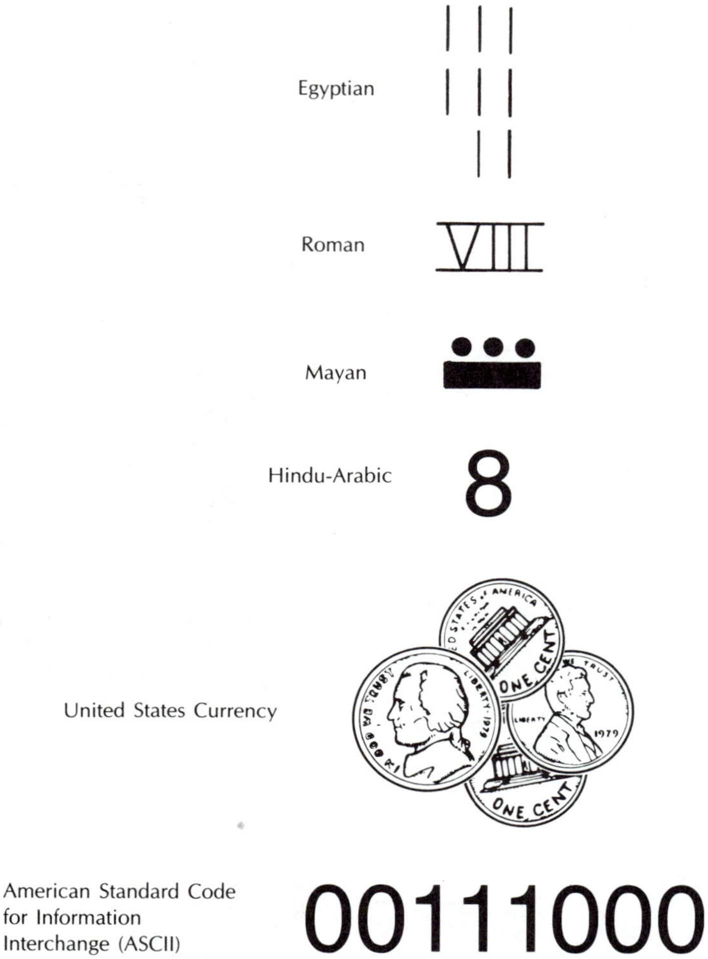

FIGURE 2–9 Some Alternative Ways to Code the Quantity 8

Analog Computers. Some computers, ancient and modern, use analog techniques to represent data. An **analog computer** draws a comparison or analogy between the representation and the thing being represented. A thermometer is a perfect example: the hotter it is, the longer the mercury gets. Analog computers can be very useful. But they have a major limitation: inaccuracy. It's easy to tell the difference between 101 and 102 degrees. But can you tell the difference between 101.2 and 101.3? Not with much accuracy. That's why most computers — ancient and modern — are digital (see the box, "The Binary Advantage"). Analog computers are often used to measure, but they're much less useful for counting (Figure 2–11).

FIGURE 2–10 Bistable Device

FIGURE 2–11 Digital Versus Analog Computers

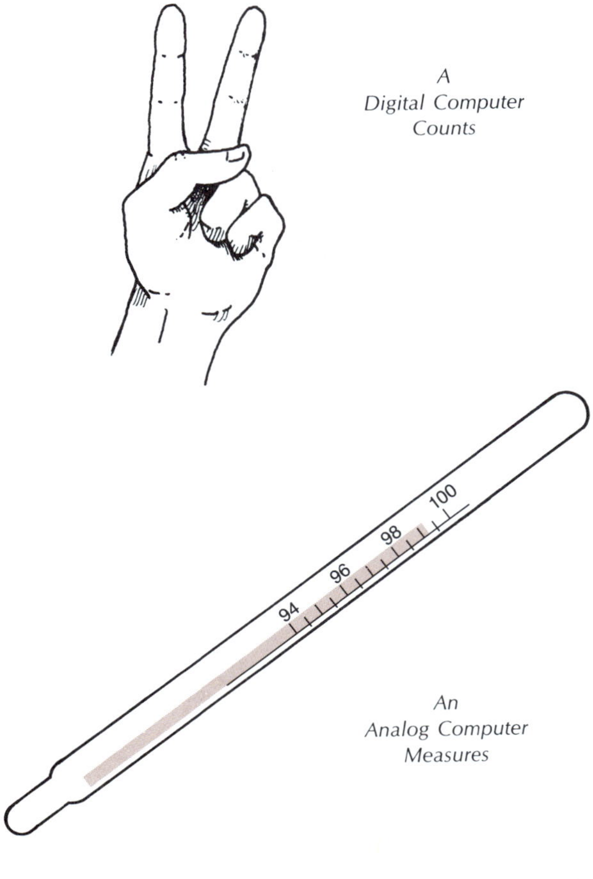

The Binary Advantage

Every number system has its own **radix,** or base. The decimal numbers we use every day have the base 10. A major exception is our timekeeping system (seconds, minutes, and hours), which uses the base 60—a holdover, amazingly enough, from Babylonian times.

Modern digital electronic computers use **binary numbers** (base 2). Binary numbers seem very peculiar the first time you see them, but they're actually very similar to the decimal numbers with which we're more familiar — they're positional, in the sense that a digit's value depends on its position in the number. But here's the big difference. In decimal numbers, you can count all the way from 0 to 9 before you carry a 1 over to the next column. In binary numbers, you can only go from 0 to 1 before you have to carry a 1 over to the next column:

Binary		*Decimal*
0	=	0
1	=	1
10	=	2
11	=	3
100	=	4
101	=	5
110	=	6
111	=	7
1000	=	8
1001	=	9

As you can see, it takes many 0s and 1s to represent numbers using binary notation, and that makes binary numbers hard for people to read. Yet they're very well suited to computers. Modern computers, as you've just seen, use bistable devices — circuits with two states, on or off — to represent data. A single bistable device can represent a single **binary digit** of data (for short, **bit**). A circuit with no current in it represents 0. A circuit *with* current represents 1. Besides this obvious convenience, binary arithmetic is far simpler than decimal arithmetic. So it's easier to build computers when binary numbers are used.

If computers could represent only two numbers (0 and 1) at a time, of course, they wouldn't be of much use. So modern computers use circuits wired in parallel (running alongside each other). In personal computers, for instance, data are represented using eight parallel circuits, each with two states (on or off). Since $2^8 = 256$, there are 256 possible combinations of these eight circuits. That leaves ample room for representing the numbers 0 through 9, uppercase letters, lowercase letters, punctuation marks, and special symbols.

STORAGE

Computers **store** the represented data so that these can be processed conveniently. The part of the computer that stores data is called the **internal memory** (or just **memory** for short). An abacus doesn't have much memory, but it's there: the memory consists of the beads pushed up to the top of the frame. The memory stores the initial value, intermediary values during processing, and the answer after processing is finished.

PROCESSING

The point of representing data in a memory is to **process** it following a series of instructions, or a **program.** In the abacus example, the processing involves subtracting one number from another. A program is a step-by-step list of instructions that enables a computer to solve a problem. You've probably heard this term *program* before, but let's look more closely at its most important characteristic: a program embodies an **algorithm.**

An algorithm, put simply, is a strategy for solving a problem when you do not know the answer right off the bat. The long division technique you learned in school is an algorithm. You don't use it when you divide 4 by 2, or 100 by 10; you already know the answer. But the algorithm comes in handy when you're dividing 32,791.396 by 1.33874. You don't know the answer to this problem, at least not in the way you know how to divide 4 by 2. Following the long division algorithm step by step, however, you obtain an accurate answer. An algorithm, in short, gives you the ability to do something, even if you don't know what you're doing.

The abacus example above illustrates this point. Pretend for a moment that you never learned how to do arithmetic with a paper and pencil and, what is more, that you understand little or nothing about math. Even so, you can still find the answer with the abacus. You simply follow a series of steps ("Begin with the leftmost wire," "If there aren't enough beads on a wire, borrow one from the next one left," etc.) and, if you follow them to their conclusion, they produce the answer. You don't have to know much about arithmetic to get accurate answers; you just follow the rules. Throughout most of its history the abacus was used by people who had no pencil-and-paper computation skills; indeed, most of them probably couldn't read and write. The abacus and its algorithms spread knowledge of arithmetic throughout societies in which arithmetic skills had been rare.

The algorithm's ability to spread knowledge of how to do things goes a long way toward explaining why computers are so valuable. Today, you can buy programs for figuring taxes, forecasting profits, analyzing writing style, and innumerable other tasks that you might not know how to do yourself. You can equip yourself with these programs, giving yourself knowledge of how to do things that you might not otherwise possess.

Since humans are prone to error, it makes good sense to build an automatic machine to carry out the algorithm's instructions. With an abacus, a human being is necessarily part of the computer: the operator has to know the "program," and carry out its instructions without error. Yet the human operator isn't necessary in principle. Since the algorithm works even if the person using it understands nothing about the problem, a machine can do it just as well. This point was doubtless recognized long before the technology for building an automatic computer existed.

OUTPUT

Every computer has one or several devices that show the end result, or **output,** of the processing operation. When you've finished carrying out a program, the abacus shows the solution using the beads pushed up to the top of the frame.

THE COMPUTER'S FUNCTIONAL ORGANIZATION

As you've just seen, an abacus performs the four basic functions of any digital computer (input, storage, processing, output). Yet it can do so only with human help. A modern computer processes information automatically, without human intervention. Automatic processing has been possible, at least theoretically, ever since algorithms were first used to solve problems with physically represented data. Lack of technological knowledge and other barriers, however, prevented the construction of an automatic digital computer until the mid-twentieth century.

Today's automatic computers are electronic, and you'd need an advanced understanding of electronic circuitry to grasp the details of how they work. Yet anyone can get a general idea of what goes on inside a computer by focusing on the computer's **functional organization:** the way it's organized to get processing done automatically. All digital computers contain just two types of components: the *central processing unit* (CPU) and *peripherals* (Figure 2–12).

Central Processing Unit (CPU). The **central processing unit** (abbreviated CPU) interprets the program's instructions to solve the problem. In modern digital computers, the CPU consists of three parts:

The Control Unit. The **control unit** supervises the computer's operation. *Supervise* makes the control unit sound intelligent, but it isn't. As you saw from the abacus example, you don't need to know anything about arithmetic to subtract with an abacus. All you need is the ability to carry out, or **execute,** a series of highly specific instructions (such as "Move two beads down," "Borrow ten beads from the next wire to the left," etc.). An abacus requires a human brain for a control unit, but a machine could do the job as well — better, in fact, since machines aren't susceptible to fatigue, boredom, and daydreaming.

The Arithmetic-Logic Unit (ALU). The **arithmetic-logic unit,** or ALU, does the computing; in modern computers, it performs both *arithmetic operations* (adding, subtracting, multiplying, and dividing) as well as *logical operations* (such as comparing two numbers to see which one is larger). An abacus requires a human hand for an arithmetic-logic unit, but again the job can be done better by a machine.

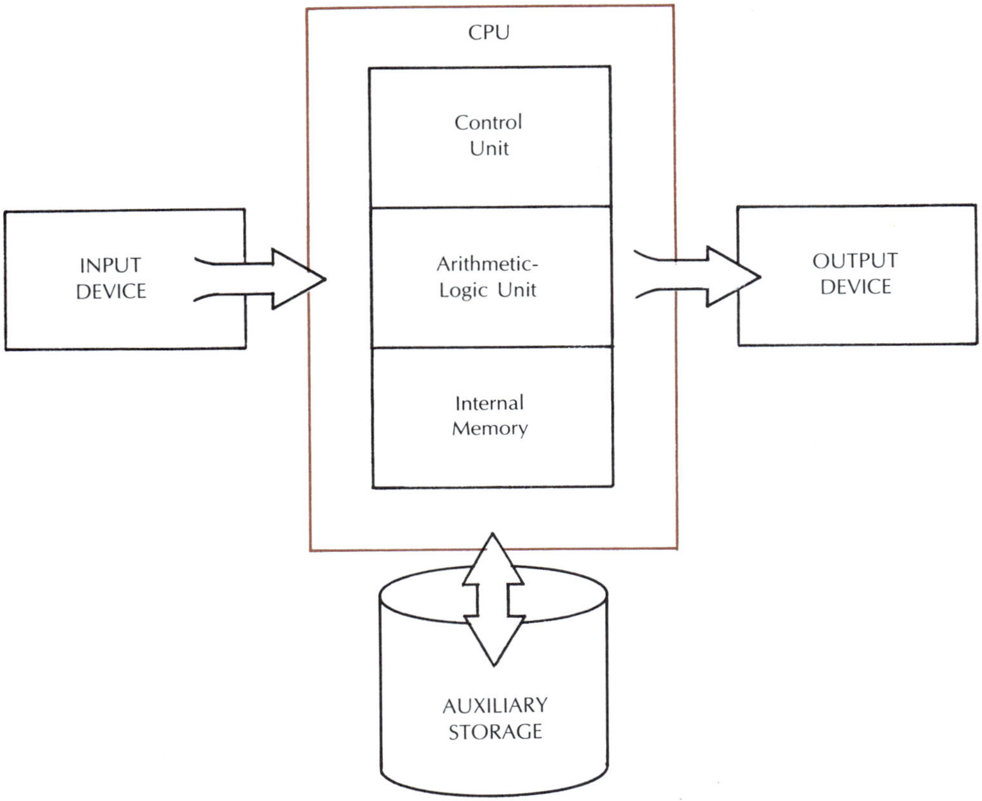

FIGURE 2–12 A Modern Computer's Functional Organization

The Internal Memory. The internal memory stores the data so that it's directly accessible to the rest of the CPU. As you saw in the abacus example, the control unit (brain) and arithmetic-logic unit (hand) must have direct access to the memory. Direct access is necessary because the memory must store intermediary values while processing as well as the final output value.

Peripherals. Every other component of modern computers is considered to be peripheral to, or outside, the computer proper, that is, the CPU. The noun **peripheral** refers to any such component.

Auxiliary Storage. One common peripheral is **auxiliary storage,** a component — such as a disk drive or tape recorder — designed for the long-term storage of large amounts of information. In contrast to the internal memory, which is designed to keep programs and data accessible for rapid processing, the auxiliary storage is used to file and retrieve programs and data that aren't needed at the moment. The auxiliary storage functions as an extension of the internal memory, and for this reason it is sometimes called extended memory.

Input and Output Devices. Other common peripherals include input and output devices, which are necessary for modern computers because they use binary numbers (1s and 0s only). Binary numbers are good choices for machine processing, but humans find them difficult to read. So **input devices** are needed to code information in machine-readable form, and **output devices** are needed to decode information so that people can read the computer's results. Common input devices are keyboards and graphics tablets (which allow the entry of pictorial images). Common output devices are cathode-ray tube (CRT) display screens and printers.

The functional organization just described is as evident in a personal computer as it is in an expensive, central computing system (Figure 2–13).

A QUESTION OF SCALE

The abacus example has provided everything you need to know to grasp how any modern digital computer functions. That includes, amazingly enough, everything from a $150 home computer to a $150 million research computer. The underlying principles are the same. Yet, as you'll see, that's like comparing ancient Chinese festival rockets with today's ultra-sophisticated spacecraft. There's a difference in scale — to put it mildly.

THE CONQUEST OF TIME

The idea of the computer is not new. What *is* new is the technology that can do the following:

Store the abstracts of 100 million journal articles in a single memory system. If stretched end-to-end, these abstracts would stretch halfway around the planet.

Use programs with more than 300,000 lines of instructions, enough to fill every page of more than a dozen average-sized textbooks.

Carry out these instructions at speeds exceeding 100 million instructions per second. In the time it takes the fastest computers to carry out an instruction, a spaceship traveling at 100,000 miles an hour would travel less than the width of a human hair.

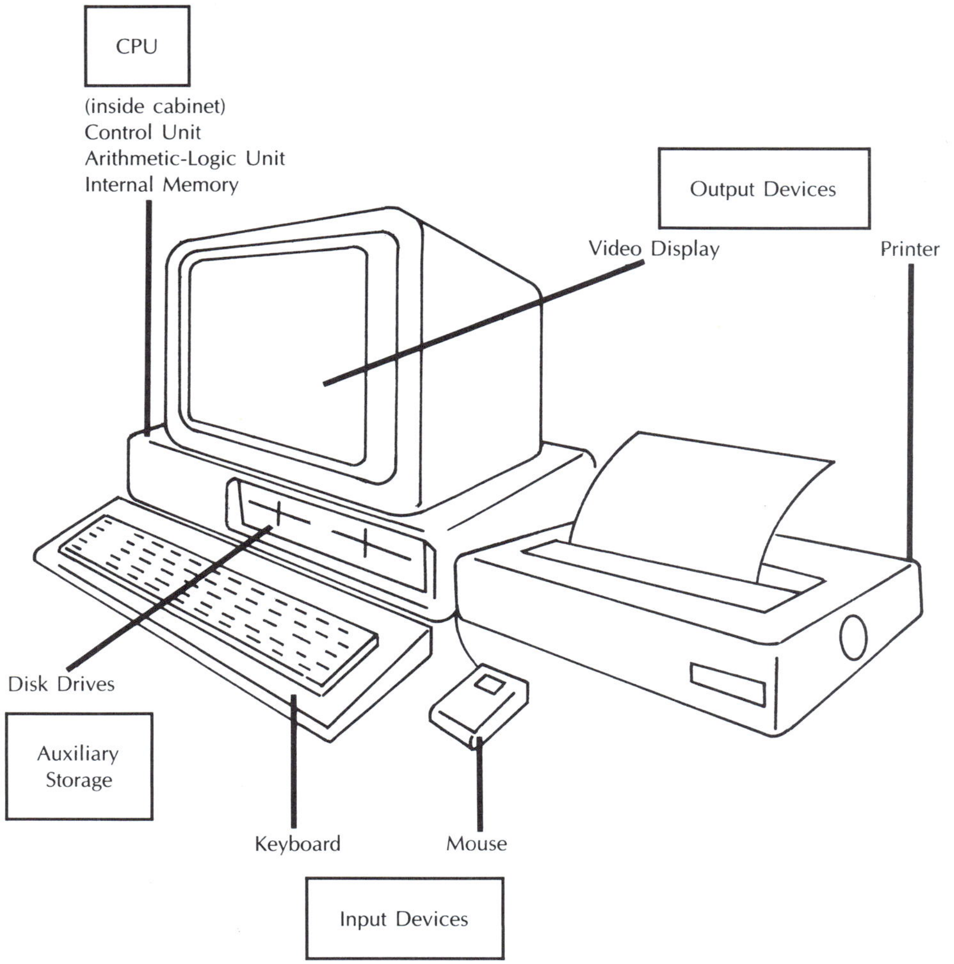

FIGURE 2–13 Functional Organization of a Personal Computer

Make mistakes only once out of every 100 billion operations. Even the most talented human mathematicians can carry out, at most, only a few instructions per second, and they'll make at least one mistake in every 5,000 calculations.

Mind-boggling memory capacities, program complexity, inconceivable speed, and phenomenal accuracy. That's the name of the game. Here's a way to put it into perspective.

Let's suppose you're going to pit yourself against an inexpensive desktop computer that stores 65,538 characters of data. Were every one of these characters written on a three-by-five-inch index card, you'd need an industrial warehouse to lay them all out; put end-to-end, they would stretch for six miles. Now — quick! — you need to locate Card 32,587, erase the number 1 on it, change it to 0, and do precisely the opposite on Card 63,211. At best, it would take you two or three minutes to do it.[3] A computer, even an inexpensive one, can do it in about one hundred-thousandth of a second. And it doesn't get tired, get bored, or make mistakes.

Our modern methods of transportation are conquering space. Our modern computers, in a very real way, are conquering time. By compressing several centuries' worth of hand calculations into a fleeting instant, computers are making it possible for people to extend their reach far beyond anything our ancestors ever dreamed of.

To grasp fully what the conquest of time means, consider this: it took seventeen technicians at Los Alamos Laboratories a full year to work out the equations required to create the first atomic bomb in 1945. By 1972, an undergraduate college student working alone at a college computer console could do them in an afternoon; today, a supercomputer can do them in a fraction of a minute. (A supercomputer is an ultrasophisticated research computer capable of performing more than 100 million arithmetic operations per second.)

No one really knows just yet what this remarkable new ability, the ability to conquer time, will mean for the future. The implications, as the atom bomb example implies, are disturbing as well as exciting. We'll return to this theme in Chapter 16, "The Benefits and Risks of Personal Computing."

ORIGINS: THE FOUNDATIONS OF MODERN COMPUTING

If the idea of computing is so old, why did today's electronic computing devices take so long to appear? A number of roadblocks — technological, socioeconomic, and intellectual — kept the electronic computer at bay until very recently.

ROADBLOCKS

Technological barriers, obviously, made the electronic computer unknown until well into the twentieth century. Clockwork calculators based on brass gears had been created by the German professor William Schickard (1592–1635) (Figure 2–14), the French philosopher Blaise Pascal (1623–1662) (Figure 2–15), and another German, the philosopher Gottfried Leibniz (1646–1716) (Figure 2–16). Leibniz's calculator could perform the four arithmetic functions (addition, subtraction, multiplication, and division).

In the nineteenth century, a British inventor named Charles Babbage (1791–

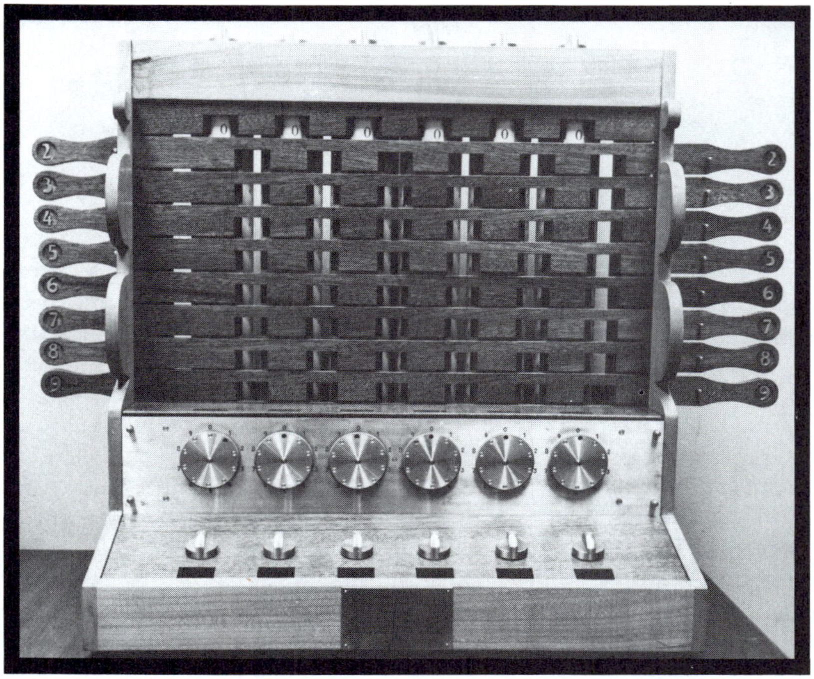

FIGURE 2–14
Schickard's Calculator

FIGURE 2–15 Pascal's Calculator

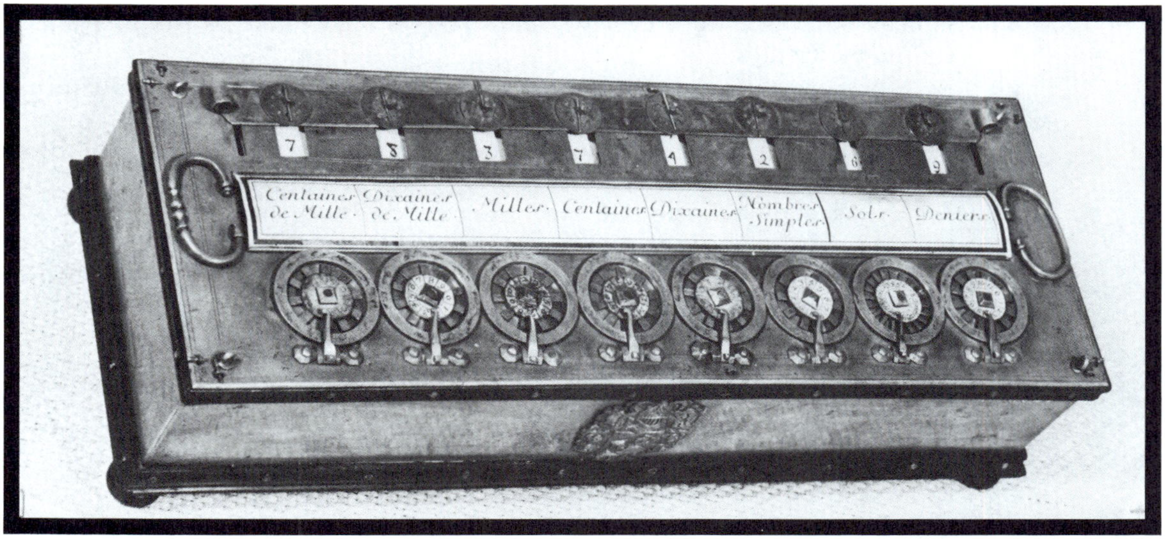

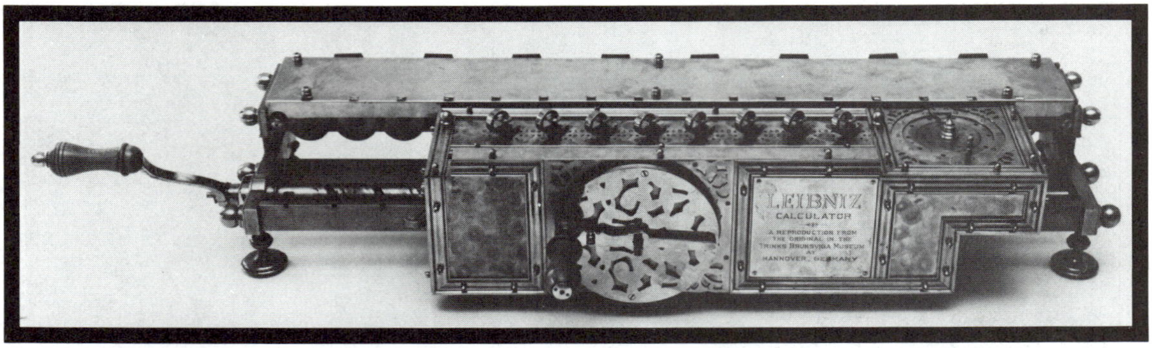

FIGURE 2–16 Leibniz's Calculator

1871) built a special-purpose calculator called the Difference Engine. It was designed to compute polynomial expressions (such as $x^2 + x + 41$), and it could do so to an accuracy of six decimal places. Later, Babbage conceived of a machine called the Analytical Engine. Far more than a calculator, the Analytical Engine — which Babbage never succeeded in building — would have been a true computer. It was to have been programmable, and it could have solved virtually any arithmetic problem. What is more, the machine would have been functionally organized; it would have had a "store," or internal memory, a "mill" (arithmetic-logic unit), and input-output devices. In developing these ideas, Babbage worked with a mathematical prodigy named Ada, the Countess of Lovelace and the daughter of Lord Byron. Ada contributed significantly to Babbage's ideas as they evolved, and deserves recognition as the first female computer scientist.

The Analytical Engine was to have been powered by steam, and if it had worked, it would have performed approximately sixty additions per minute. Despite a lifetime of effort, however, Babbage was never able to hone down the gears to the required tolerances, and the project failed. Babbage died a deeply disappointed man. He lived one hundred years ahead of his time — or more accurately, ahead of the electronic technology that could have helped him realize his dream of a computing device. In his latter years he often wished he could somehow return to this world many years later to see whether someone else had perfected the computer. How he would have enjoyed the present!

Socioeconomic barriers, too, kept computing devices in the background until the twentieth century. Pascal invented his clockwork calculator in 1642 after poring over his father's business accounts. He hoped the machine, which greatly eased arithmetic, would revolutionize accounting practices. He formed a company to market the calculator, but no one wanted it. At the time, accounting was done by drudges who worked long hours for low pay. Business owners saw that the calculator wouldn't replace the accountants; the drudges would still be necessary. All it would do would be to make life easier for them. That was close to the last thing business owners had on their minds.

Computers didn't become marketable until buying them started to make sense to businesses and governments. The market didn't arise until the twentieth century, with its explosion of social and economic complexity.

Intellectual barriers were perhaps the most formidable of all. Modern computers would never have been created if inventors had kept on trying to build them to do a limited range of jobs, such as calculating ballistics tables or sorting out the results of a national census. What makes today's computers so useful and so successful, apart from their speed and accuracy, is their ability to do a wide range of jobs. They're **general-purpose computers.** The same machine can be programmed to calculate the trajectory of spacecraft, analyze patterns of word usage in Shakespearean dramas, and play chess at world master levels. It took a series of trailblazers to point the way to modern computing.

TRAILBLAZERS

The earliest trailblazers were none other than George Babbage and Ada Byron, who together hit upon the idea of a general-purpose computer for the first time. Unfortunately, Babbage's writings were ignored until the late 1930s, and the task of developing the general-purpose computer was left to others. Chief among them were the American inventor Herman Hollerith, the British logician Alan Turing, and the American engineers John Mauchly and J. Presper Eckert.

Hollerith's Punched-Card Tabulating Machine. The U.S. Constitution calls for a census every 10 years, but the results of the 1880 census took so long to compute that they weren't announced until 1887. The way things were going, the 1890 census results wouldn't be announced until after the next census in 1900! To solve the problem, an inventor named Herman Hollerith (1860–1929) created an electrically powered tabulating machine (Figure 2–17). Picking up a cue from weaving techniques, Hollerith's device used punched cards to represent the data for fast processing. Using Hollerith's machine, the 1890 census results were announced after only six weeks of tabulation. Hollerith went on to form a corporation, which eventually came to be called International Business Machines, Inc. Until the electronic computer came on the scene, IBM produced a series of electromechanical calculators that used punched cards for data input.

Turing and the Turing Machine. Hollerith's tabulating machine was the first computer to use electricity, but it was still a special-purpose computer. The pathway to the modern, general-purpose computer became clear only after a young Cambridge University mathematics fellow, Alan Turing (Figure 2–18),

FIGURE 2–17 Hollerith's Tabulator and Sorter

FIGURE 2–18 Alan Turing

published one of the most famous papers in the history of mathematics, a 1936 paper titled "On Computable Numbers." Turing's work, little known to the public, has been compared with Darwin's and Einstein's in its elegant simplicity and scientific significance. His paper proved that any mathematical problem that is capable of solution can be solved using an algorithm — and that meant that a machine could do it. All over the world, mathematicians who read Turing's paper realized that a general-purpose, digital computer was inevitable. All that was needed now were a few technically savvy engineers to bring the general-purpose computer to fruition. To make that computer useful, programmers would be needed to devise the necessary algorithms.

Colossus. Turing himself was involved in the making of the Colossus, a supersecret British computer designed to break enemy communication codes during World War II. Kept under close wraps by MI6, the British version of the CIA, the Colossus appears to have become operational in 1943. So successful was this computer in doing its job that some say it directly contributed to the Allied victory in World War II. Turing's role in creating Colossus, however, was kept secret until 1975, and to this day much information about Colossus is still classified. It may have been the first fully operational electronic computer.

ENIAC. On the other side of the Atlantic, two American engineers named John Mauchly and J. Presper Eckert received a $400,000 grant — big money at the time — to build an electronic computer for the United States. The computer, called ENIAC, was not completed until 1946 (Figure 2–19). ENIAC firmly established the stereotype of the "electronic brain" in the public mind. A monster that contained 19,000 vacuum tubes, 70,000 resistors, and 500,000 hand-soldered connections, the computer used 100 kilowatts of electricity at a gulp, weighed 30 tons, and took up much of an 800-square-foot room. Performing up to 5,000 operations per second, ENIAC went to work on the calculations necessary to achieve the hydrogen bomb. Its use in this and other military projects helped give the United States a decisive military superiority after World War II.

The Stored Program Concept. ENIAC had many limitations, among them its unreliability: the machine could work for only a few minutes, at most, before a vacuum tube would burn out, bringing the whole system down. But an even worse problem emerged whenever the computer was reprogrammed. ENIAC's programs, the instructions it followed to process data, were wired directly into the machine. To change the program, it was necessary to rewire the machine — a tedious process at best.

Pondering ENIAC's limitations, the Princeton mathematician John von Neumann (1903–1957), Figure 2–20, hit on the **stored program concept,** or the idea of storing the program in the computer's memory right alongside the data the computer is supposed to process. Storing the program in memory meant

FIGURE 2–19 Setting Up a Problem on ENIAC

FIGURE 2–20 John von Neumann

that changing the program would be as easy as changing the data; you would just feed it in on punched cards or tape.

The stored program concept led to major progress in the design of computer programs. Since the entire program is present in memory, the computer can jump around in it as necessary (instead of executing the program instructions in a rigid sequence [Figure 2–21]). This capability allows programmers to write programs that can make decisions (**selection**) and repeat functions until a condition is fulfilled (**looping**). These features dramatically improve computer software performance.

A COMPUTER GENEALOGY

A human generation takes 25 years to run its course, but commercial computers — now only 35 years old — have already been through four of them, and some say a fifth is on the way. Each new generation of computers begins when some technological breakthrough makes its predecessors obsolete.

THE FIRST GENERATION (1946–1958)

Eckert and Mauchly, fresh from ENIAC's success, went to work in 1946 on a new computer, called UNIVAC, that would use von Neumann's stored program concept. UNIVAC (Figure 2–22) was completed in 1951 and first used by the Census Bureau, where it served until 1963. By contemporary standards, this **first-generation computer** was very difficult to use:

> Although it stored programs in memory, the programs themselves had to be entered in **machine language,** using the 1s and 0s of binary numbers. Programming in machine language is tedious because every instruction has to be spelled out in detail. To get the computer to average two numbers, for example, as many as a dozen instructions are needed.
>
> UNIVAC required its users to use **batch processing** techniques (Figure 2–23). Data and programs were fed into the machine on punched cards, processed in a batch, and the results printed out by an electromechanical typewriter. If anything went wrong with the program's execution, you didn't find out until the printout finished — and it might contain 200 pages of hopelessly garbled output.
>
> The vacuum tubes failed continually. At best, the computer would run for only a few minutes before failing ("crashing," in computer parlance).

Not surprisingly, UNIVAC found few customers outside of scientific, government, and military circles. Slow and clumsy as it was, however, UNIVAC got the

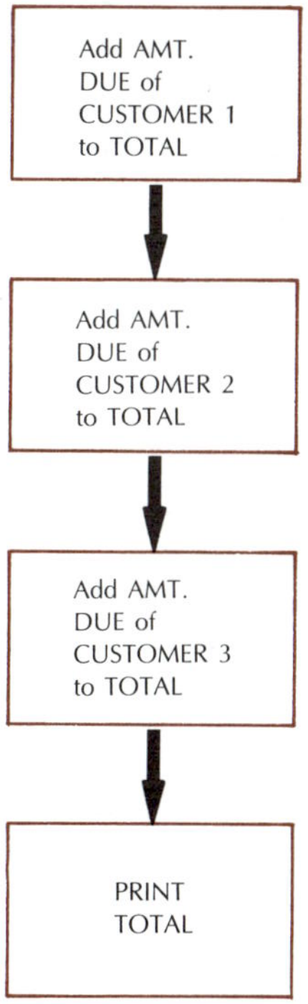

SIMPLE SEQUENCE One program statement after another is executed in a row.

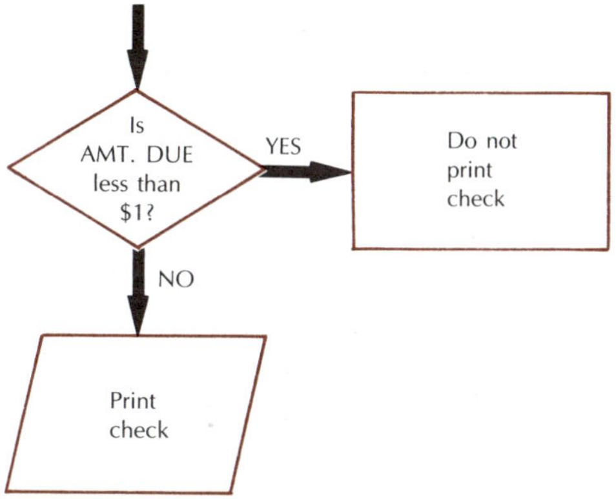

SELECTION A selection structure requires a test and, depending on the results, one of two paths is taken. Selection structures are also called IF-THEN-ELSE structures (*IF* AMT. DUE is less than $1, *THEN* do not print check; ELSE print check).

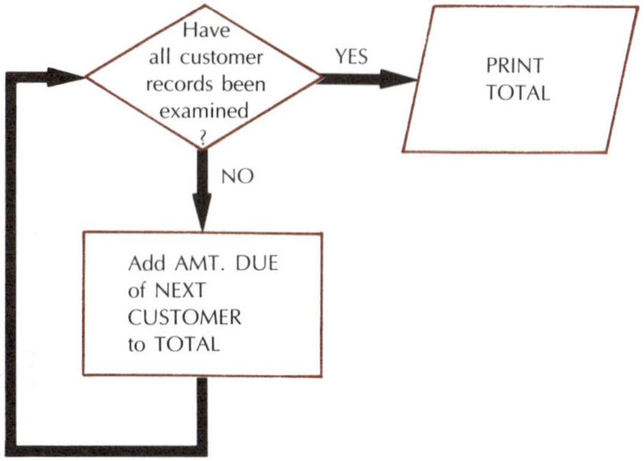

LOOP A loop structure keeps on performing the same function over and over until a condition is met. Loop structures are also called DO-UNTIL structures (DO add amt. due of next customer UNTIL all customer records have been examined).

FIGURE 2–21 Program Logic: Sequence, Selection, and Loops

FIGURE 2–22 UNIVAC

computer age started — and in more ways than one. When a UNIVAC system was installed in the Census Bureau in 1951, the new computer dislodged an IBM tabulating machine. IBM, a late entrant in the computer sweepstakes, had concentrated on punched-card tabulating machines. These tabulating machines (and IBM itself) were direct descendants of Hollerith's invention that revolutionized the census in the late nineteenth century. When UNIVAC pushed the tabulating machine out of the Census Bureau, IBM's conservative management became convinced that computers were, indeed, the wave of the future. So IBM made a major commitment to computing with the development of its 650 computer in 1953.

IBM's early forecasts showed that, at best, a market existed for about fifty or sixty of the new IBM 650 computers. Yet, in the end, IBM was forced to build more than a thousand of them! By 1956, IBM passed all other computer makers in sales, and was well on its way to becoming one of the world's largest and most successful corporations.

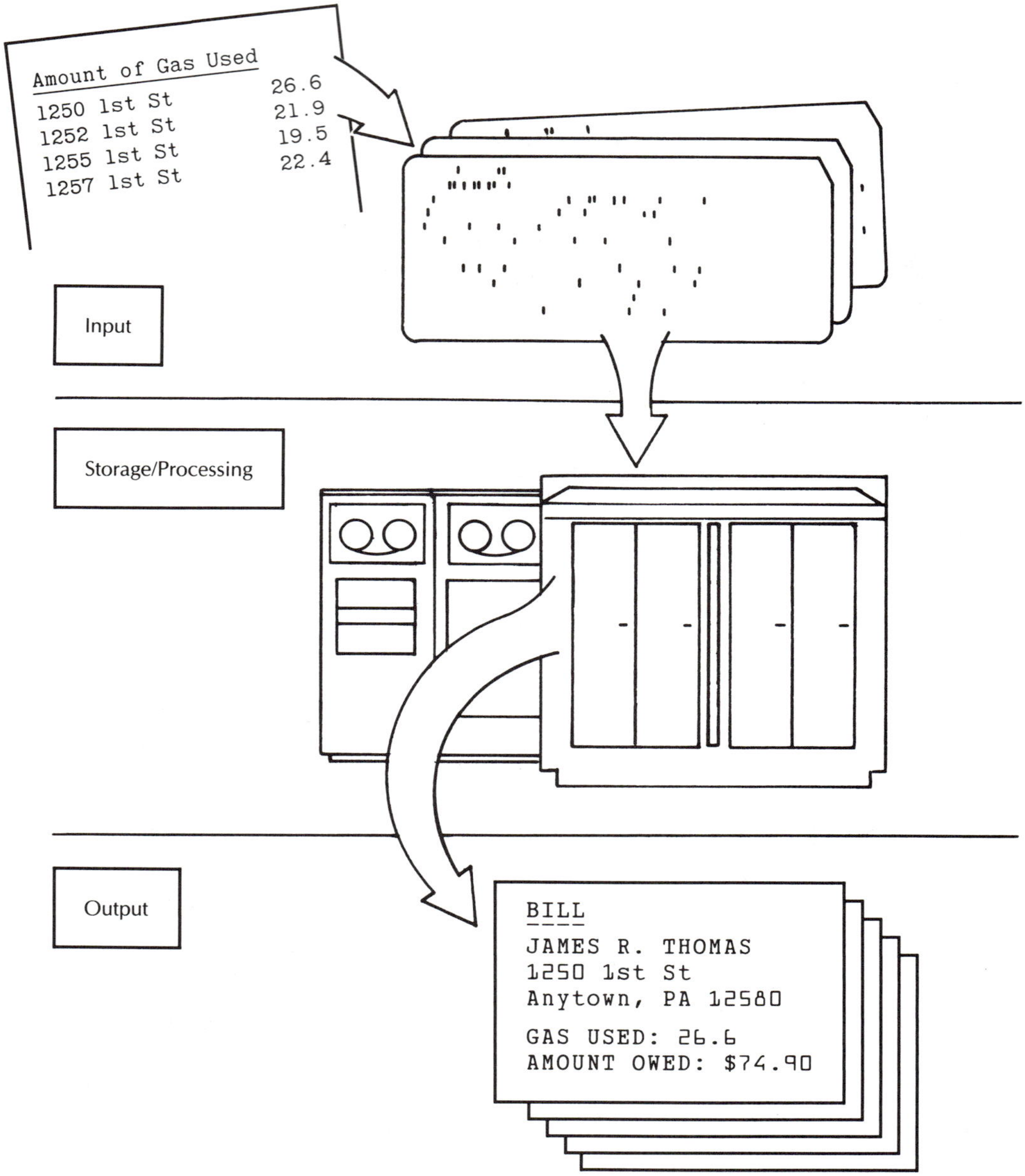

FIGURE 2–23 Batch Processing with Punched Card Input

Case Study: Computer Makes Monkey Out of Operators

It's election night, 1952. Dwight Eisenhower and Adlai Stevenson are running neck and neck in the polls; experts say it's too close to call. But CBS has set up a UNIVAC in its New York studios to predict the election results. At 9 P.M., with only 7 percent of the vote in, UNIVAC predicts an Eisenhower landslide, giving 438 electoral votes to Eisenhower and only 93 to Stevenson.

UNIVAC's programmers and CBS executives didn't believe the results when they saw them, and so the programmers "tweaked" the program (that is, adjusted it) so that it would show results more in line with the forecasts. But by morning, it became obvious that UNIVAC had been right all along. Eisenhower received 442 electoral votes to Stevenson's 89, very close to UNIVAC's original projections. A very embarrassed spokesman told the whole story to the television audience. "The trouble with machines," remarked CBS commentator Edward R. Murrow, "is people."

THE SECOND GENERATION (1958–1964)

In 1948, scientists at American Telephone and Telegraph's Bell Laboratories invented the **transistor,** an electronic component that duplicates the vacuum tube's job — but is faster, cooler, and more reliable. Using far less electricity than vacuum tubes and taking only a tiny fraction of the tubes' space, transistors led to major improvements in commercial computers. In 1958, **second-generation** computers appeared that replaced the troublesome tubes with transistorized components.

Second-generation computers were improved in other ways too:

Automatic **operating systems,** or system software for controlling computer functions and running jobs through the computer, took over the day-to-day operating routines, such as storing and retrieving programs and data on auxiliary storage devices.

High-level programming languages appeared. These languages included *COBOL* (Common Business-Oriented Language) for business programming and *FORTRAN* (Formula Translator) for scientific programming and engineering. High-level programming languages use instructions that resemble familiar English words, the Arabic numbers we use every day, and ordinary mathematical expressions (rather than cryptic instructions in binary code). After writing a program in one of these languages, the programmer uses a **compiler** to translate the program into machine language. These languages make the task of programming the computer much easier.

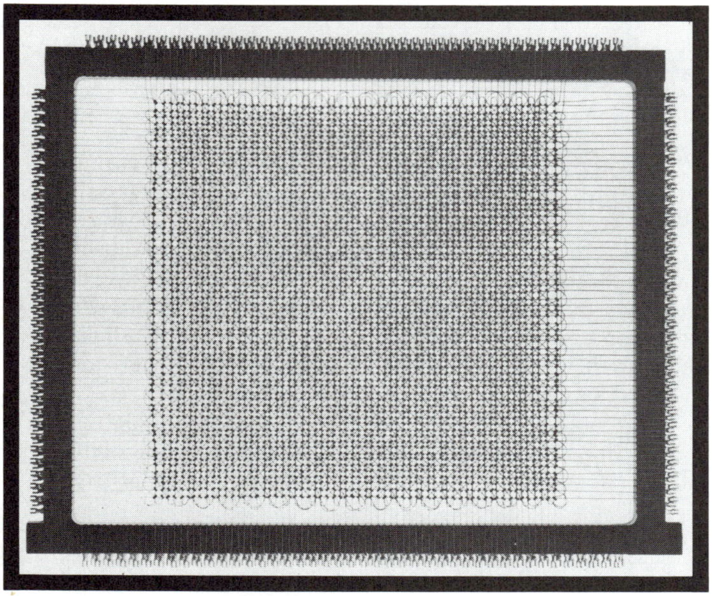

FIGURE 2–24
Magnetic Core Memory

Improvements were made, too, in the use of recording tape devices for auxiliary memory systems, which provide long-term storage for programs and data, and in the use of roomier **magnetic core memories.** Magnetic core memories, which provided internal memories for many second- (and third-) generation computers, store data by imparting a magnetic charge to a tiny section of wire (Figure 2–24). Thanks to these improvements, computer sales improved. By the close of the second generation, more than 30,000 computers were in use in the United States.

Second-generation computers took on the massive record-keeping jobs faced by rapidly growing businesses and bureaucracies. In 1961, for instance, thirty large companies began making their annual tax reports to the federal government using computer-generated tapes rather than hand-typed reports. Huge corporations began using computers to cope with equally huge payrolls. The **mainframe computer,** a large machine designed to meet the computing needs of an entire organization, was well established.

THE THIRD GENERATION (1964–1971)

An **integrated circuit** is a complex electronic component that is printed on a small, waferlike chip of silicon. The result is a tiny electronic component that replaces a much larger, hand-soldered circuit board containing many separate components. The integrated circuit integrates in one piece many electronic components that formerly had to be assembled by hand (and at great cost). And because integrated circuits are manufactured by machines that never tire or show up to work with a hangover, their overall reliability is much greater than that of hand-soldered circuits. Integrated circuits, moreover, can be mass-produced at low unit costs. Their 1959 invention set the stage for the diffusion of reliable, inexpensive computers throughout our society.

IBM was the first to capitalize on the new technology. After making a research and development investment estimated at a spectacular $5 billion, IBM released its 1964 line of computers based on integrated circuits. Called the System/360 (Figure 2–25), the 1964 line included several models to fit the computing budgets of a wide variety of organizations. With System/360, IBM achieved dominance of the computer marketplace. By 1967, IBM held 75 percent of a $6 billion market. Its dominance endures today.

The **third generation** saw the widespread use of many other innovations, most of which had their origins in second-generation research:

> *Timesharing.* New computer operating systems appeared that allowed more than one user — indeed, hundreds of them — to work with the computer simultaneously (Figure 2–26). Each user works with a **terminal,** which consists of a keyboard and video display (containing a **cathode ray tube** [**CRT**], or a television screen) connected to the central computer. Terminals are used for data input and output operations. In a **timesharing** system, everyone has the impression of having exclusive control over the computer.

FIGURE 2–25 IBM System/360

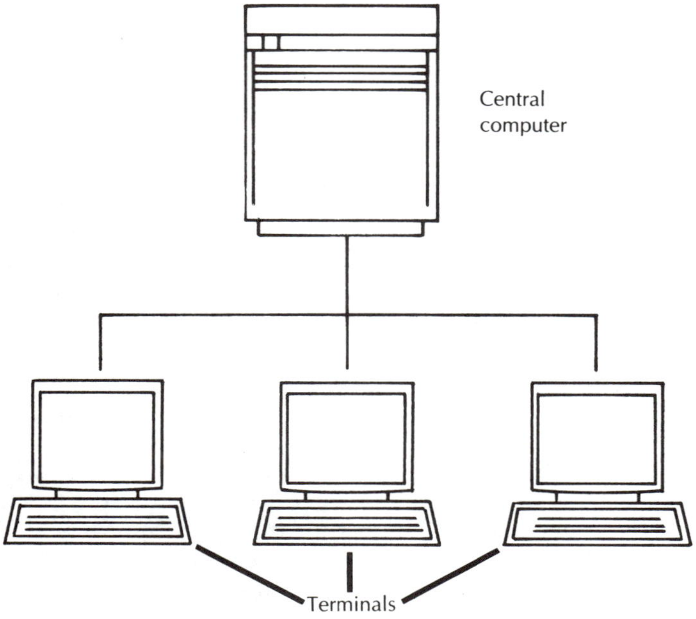

FIGURE 2–26
Timesharing System with Terminals

Interactive Processing. The development of terminals allowed users to see the results of processing operations right away instead of waiting for a printer to spit back the results (Figure 2–27). New programs allowed users to interact with the computer, permitting them to correct problems in the middle of processing operations if something went wrong. With **interactive processing,** the computer actually engages in a dialogue or interacts with the user, displaying **error messages** (messages displayed on the screen informing the user that something has gone wrong), **prompts** (messages that tell the user that the computer is ready to receive instructions), **menus** (lists of processing options from which users may choose), and **confirmation messages** (messages asking the user to confirm whether a potentially risky operation should indeed be carried out).

Data Communications. **Data communications** consisting of long-distance linkages among computers, via the telephone system or direct links, became widely used (Figure 2–28).

Improved Peripheral Devices. **Magnetic disks** replaced tapes as the major medium for long-term, auxiliary storage. Disks operate so quickly that, with new programming techniques, the auxiliary memory could be made to work as if it were an extension of the computer's internal memory. The result was the creation of computer systems with virtually unlimited memory capacities.

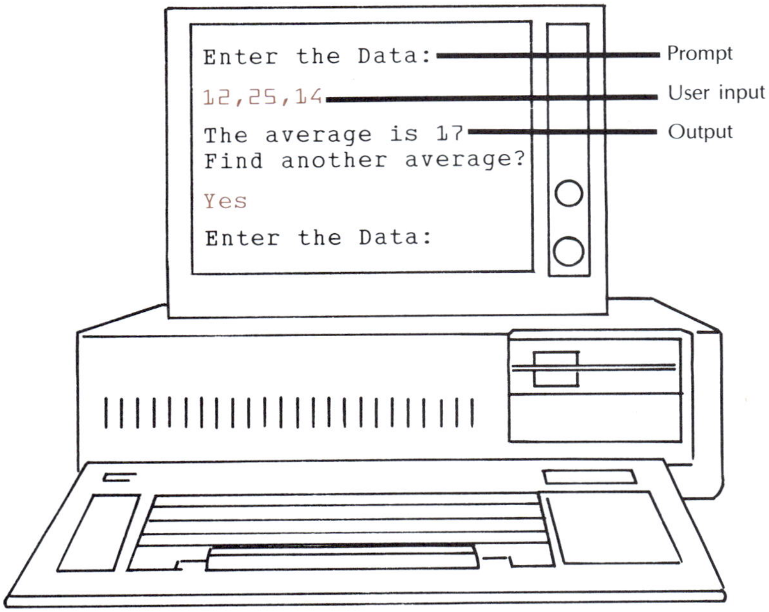

FIGURE 2–27
Interactive Processing

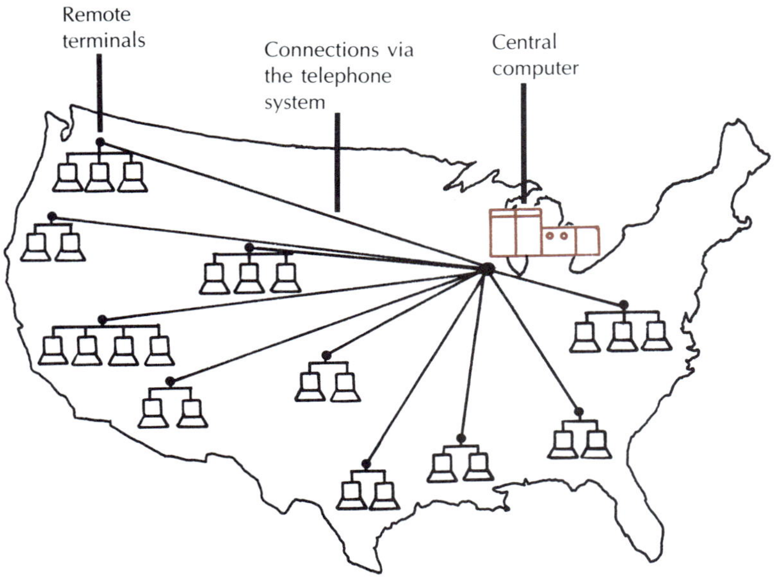

FIGURE 2–28 Data Communications

Application Software. A final third-generation development was the rise of application software as a significant factor in computer purchases. Buyers increasingly came to demand that computers come equipped with ready-to-run application programs. If the manufacturer didn't supply the software, they'd turn to third-party vendors (that is, companies other than the ones that make computers).

Taken together, timesharing, interactive processing, terminals, faster auxiliary memory devices, and application software made computers much more useful than they ever had been before. Hundreds, even thousands, of people could use them simultaneously, interacting with the computer as if each user had total control over it.

Third-generation computers firmly established the role of computer technology in large organizations. Compared to second-generation computers, third-generation machines were fast, reliable, and convenient to use. By 1965 more than 30,000 computers were in use, 5,400 of them in the federal government alone. In 1966, 1,100 universities had installed computer systems, and some of them began to offer bachelor's, master's, and doctoral degrees in computer science. In 1967, the Association for Computing Machinery had 20,000 members. By 1970, the number of installed mainframe computers had doubled, reaching 60,000 and a total value of $22 billion.[4] Computers were big business, and big businesses and other large organizations bought computers to meet their data processing needs.

THE FOURTH GENERATION (1971–PRESENT)

Integrated circuit technology advanced so rapidly that, by 1969, it was possible to put 20,000 transistors or more on a single chip of silicon. This technology, called **large-scale integration** (LSI), led to another major improvement in computers — and, many believe, to a new **fourth generation** of computers. LSI techniques make it possible to put as many as 100,000 computer components together on a single chip and to mass-produce them. The advantages are numerous. LSI-based computers are smaller and cheaper than their predecessors. What is more, they're faster: because the components can be positioned closer together, the time it takes electricity to travel through the computer is reduced.

By the late 1970s, **very large scale integration** (VLSI) — 100,000 components or more on a single chip — was achieved. By the early 1980s, as many as one million components were placed on a single chip (Figure 2–29). Each component is so small that it must be measured in microns, or millionths of a meter (Figure 2–30). Efforts are now being made to build chips with components less than one micron in width, which may lead to ultra large scale integration (ULSI) — chips with a billion or more components. However, integrated circuit technology

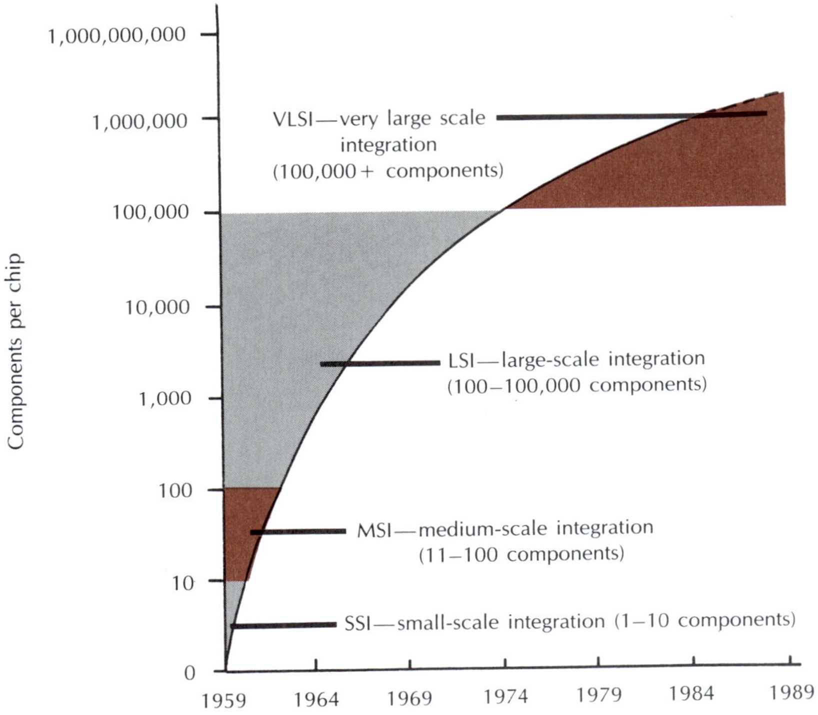

FIGURE 2–29 Advances in Integrated Circuit Complexity

FIGURE 2–30 Size of Component in VLSI Circuit

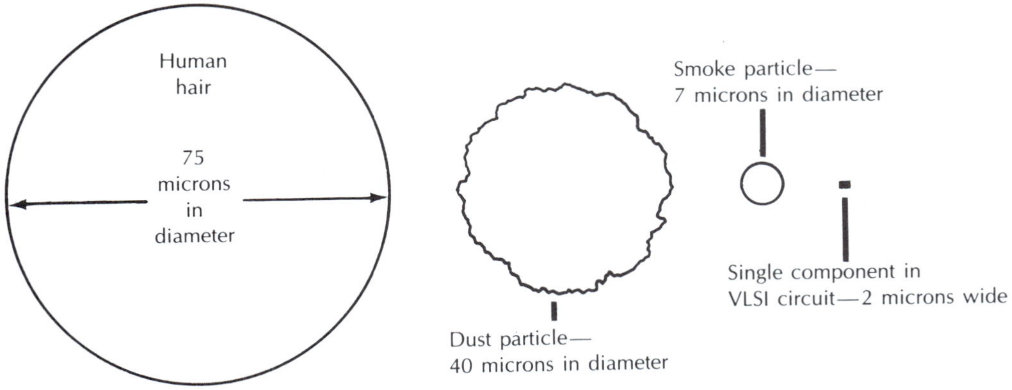

is pushing up against the ultimate barrier, the inherent granularity of matter itself. Further advances are feasible, but they will require enormous capital investments.

LSI and VLSI technology ushered in the computer age as we know it today — an age in which computers are everywhere. From 60,000 in 1970, the population of mainframes grew to over 1.3 million in 1984 — and they were joined by an estimated 16.4 million personal computers!

Memory Chips. One of the most important outcomes of LSI and VLSI technology is **semiconductor memory.** Semiconductor memories use special-purpose chips, called **memory chips,** to serve in a computer's internal memory system. Today's memory chips can store more than one million units of information each, all in a space that makes a dime look big. Because VLSI circuits can be mass-produced at low unit costs, they are bringing computing costs down at an estimated rate of 25 to 40 percent per year, a rate that's still continuing (Figure 2–31).

Minicomputers. LSI and VLSI technologies did more than just improve mainframe computers. They also improved the **minicomputer,** a junior version of a mainframe computer originally created in the 1960s. Like mainframes, minicomputers are multiple-user, timesharing machines. But they're meant to be used by, at the

FIGURE 2–31 The Downward Curve of Internal Memory Costs

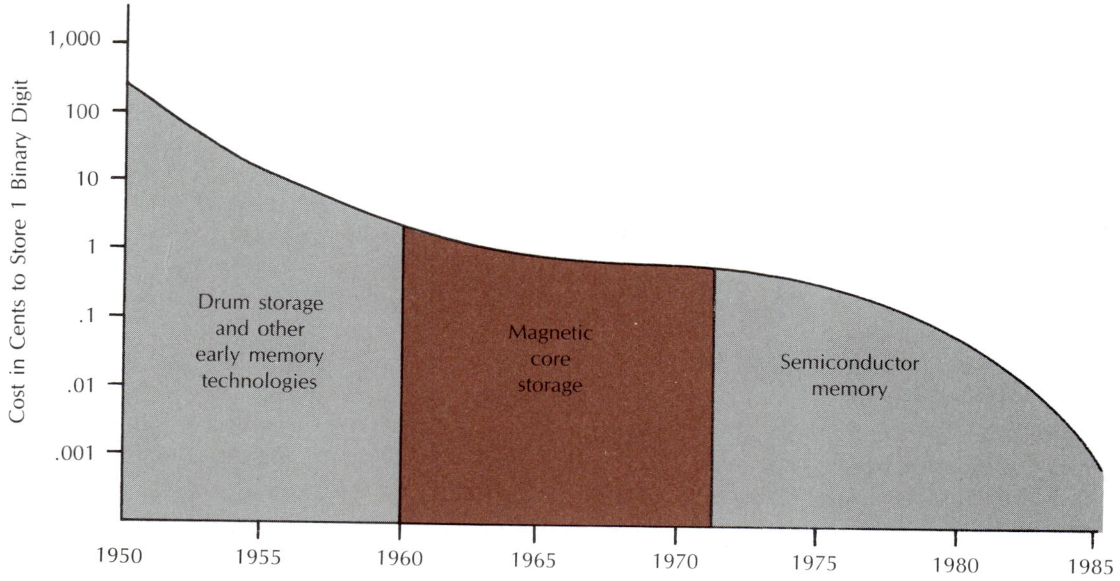

most, a few dozen people (instead of hundreds of them). VLSI techniques reduced minicomputer prices so much that small businesses (and even departments of organizations) could use them.

Distributed Computing. Improvements in data communications led to **distributed computing,** in which minicomputers linked with mainframes distribute computing resources throughout an organization. By the 1980s, mainframes and minicomputers, and huge data communication networks that linked them, had entrenched themselves firmly in every aspect of American government, commerce, and science.

Peripherals. LSI and VLSI technologies did the same thing for computer peripherals that they did for computers: they made peripherals cheaper, faster, and more reliable. New high-capacity disk drives made virtually unlimited auxiliary storage, or **mass storage,** possible. Mass storage systems are capable of storing virtually all the information used by even a large organization, such as all the current flight schedules, crew assignments, and reservations for an airline's day-to-day operations. Superfast printers, razor sharp video displays, and a host of other technical improvements also followed the introduction of VLSI technology.

Programming. Technical progress in the fabrication of fourth-generation hardware has been matched by equally impressive gains in software. Although high-level languages such as FORTRAN and COBOL continue to be widely used, new **very high-level programming languages** are now available. A very high-level programming language frees the programmer from concern about the procedure the computer must follow to carry out the program's instructions. Instead, the programmer can focus on the nature of the problem to be solved, working solely in the problem's terms (rather than those imposed by the computer). An example of a very high-level programming language is a report program generator (RPG) language, which provides extremely convenient and easy-to-use capabilities for producing printouts of information from large data bases used by businesses. Experiments have repeatedly shown that programmers working with very high-level languages can work up to ten times more productively than they can with languages such as COBOL.

Microprocessors. A major outgrowth of LSI and VLSI technologies is the **microprocessor,** a 1969 invention of Ted Hoff, an engineer at Intel Corporation. A microprocessor is a computer's central processing unit placed on a single, tiny chip of silicon. To be more precise, microprocessors do not include internal memory; they contain only the control and arithmetic-logic units. Even so, the microprocessor is a genuine technological marvel. Containing as many as 100,000 components within an area half the size of your smallest fingernail, just one microprocessor can replace the circuitry that formerly required the space of four or five filing cabinets. Creating just one microprocessor is in itself an astonishing feat, tantamount to mapping every street and freeway in Los Angeles on the head of a pin. Even more astonishing, however, is that these chips, like books, can be mass-produced. Using a process similar to modern lithographic printing, microprocessor makers print millions of exact copies from a master design. And the result is ultracheap prices. You can buy a microprocessor in any electronics supply house for just a few dollars.

The microprocessor's low cost has made it possible to embed computer intelligence in a wide variety of new, "smart" products, ranging from toasters to bombs. Automobiles, consumer appliances, industrial robots, and many more increasingly smart products use microprocessors, harnessing their computational power to special-purpose jobs such as controlling the heat in an oven. It has also made possible a new generation of smaller, general-purpose computers called microcomputers.

Microcomputers. A **microcomputer** is a general-purpose computing system constructed around a microprocessor chip. The first microcomputers appeared in 1974, five years after the invention of the microprocessor. Everyone would agree nowadays that the microcomputer is one of the most important technologies of the twentieth century, so it may seem surprising that it took five years for inventors to create it from the available parts. The fact is, however, that in the early 1970s the big computer companies failed to see the microcomputer's future. One by one, they expressed indifference to project proposals brought to them by enthusiastic employees. One computer company executive, dismissing a microcomputer project, remarked that he couldn't understand why any individual would want a personal computer!

For many years, the big computer companies left the microcomputer marketplace to a colorful collection of entrepreneurs and electronics hobbyists. First among them was Jonathan Titus, who in 1974 published a book that showed how to build a "personal minicomputer" around Intel Corporation's newest microprocessor, the 8008. To build the computer, you needed circuit boards from Titus ($47.50) and parts from an electronics supply house ($250), including the 8008 chip itself ($120). Then you had to spend days soldering all the components in place. Even so, more than 10,000 people ordered the plans.

In 1975, a calculator company named MITS offered the first microcomputer kit (complete with parts), the Altair. Based on a new Intel chip, the 8080, the Altair was a smashing success. As people soon discovered, however, the Altair couldn't do much besides twinkle lights in a distinctive pattern. That situation was soon remedied by Bill Gates (a Harvard freshman) and Paul Allen (a programmer who lived in Boston). Gates and Allen produced an Altair version of the BASIC programming language. BASIC (short for Beginner's All-purpose Symbolic Instruction Code) was invented in 1964 by two professors at Dartmouth College. Intended for teaching, the language is easy to learn. With BASIC now available for the Altair, sales accelerated even further. Gates and Allen went on to found Microsoft Corporation, one of the most respected companies in the microcomputer software business.

The Altair's success inspired other entrepreneurs, including Stephen G. Wozniak (a self-taught engineer) and Stephen Jobs (an ex-college student). Wozniak and a friend, William Fernandez, put together a prototype microcomputer built around MOS Technology's new 6502 chip. Wozniak also wrote a BASIC interpreter for the microcomputer. He tried to interest his employer, Hewlett-Packard, in the project. But the company didn't believe the machine — the Apple I — would find a market. Jobs believed in Wozniak's microcomputer, however, and talked Wozniak into founding a company (Apple Computer) to market it. After receiving some key financial support from a local electronics store owner, Jobs and Wozniak managed to sell about 500 of the microcomputer kits.

These early kits — such as the Altair, the Apple I, and others — were inexpensive, but they were far from easy to use. They appealed chiefly to hobbyists and amateur programmers.

The **personal computer,** a microcomputer designed for nonexperts and nonprogrammers, required two innovations in the microcomputer market: first, a ready-to-run microcomputer that required no assembly, and second, application software so that nonprogrammers could use it. The first requirement was met by the 1977 release of the Apple II and Tandy Corporation's TRS-80. Unlike the Apple I, the Apple II and TRS-80 were completely assembled, ready-to-run microcomputers. The second innovation occurred with the release soon afterward of word processing, spreadsheet, and other application programs for microcomputers. The spreadsheet program VisiCalc played a key role in the Apple II's success. VisiCalc, which is essentially a very high-level language for numerical reasoning, provided managers and information workers with a completely new tool for business mathematics. VisiCalc helped convince people everywhere that microcomputers were far more than interesting toys for electronics freaks.

Riding the Apple II wave, Apple Computer became the country's fastest-growing company. Sales rose from $775,000 in 1977 to $335 million in 1980. When Apple stock went public in 1980, Jobs — who had invested only a few thousand dollars in Apple — found himself worth $165 million.

Apple's success did not go unnoticed by the big computer makers, who — belatedly — recognized the huge size of the microcomputer market. IBM tossed its hat into the ring with the 1981 release of the IBM Personal Computer (popularly known as the IBM PC — or just PC). Based on the new Intel 8088 chip, a technically advanced successor of the 8080, the PC would not run application programs written for earlier computers. For this reason, PC sales were slow at first; only 35,000 were sold the first year. By 1983, however, programmers and software companies by the hundreds were writing programs for the IBM PC environment, and sales took off: 800,000 PCs were sold that year.

By 1985, IBM had achieved the same kind of dominance in the personal computer market that it had already attained in the mainframe market. More than three-quarters of the firms planning PC purchases had decided on IBM Personal Computers; only 8 percent were planning to buy Apples. A major reason for the IBM PC's enormous success lies in those three magic letters (I–B–M). Corporate buyers know they're taking a comparatively small risk when they buy IBM products; the company won't disappear overnight (as have many smaller computer companies), and IBM has a reputation for standing behind its products. Yet equally significant was IBM's choice of an open architecture for the PC.

An **open architecture** design invites third-party suppliers to provide additional circuit boards, software, and peripherals. Plug-in slots and connectors are provided so that the user can easily attach these accessories to the computer. In the PC's case, IBM actively encouraged third-party suppliers by publishing the PC's technical specifications and providing plug-in slots for circuit boards made by non-IBM suppliers. The result? Hundreds of companies market an amazing variety of accessory boards, application programs, and peripherals for the IBM PC. Users can customize the PC for a wide variety of applications, including medical laboratory analysis, foreign-language computing, retail accounting, and hundreds more. The more versatile the PC becomes, the better it sells, and the more IBM benefits.

IBM's open architecture policy has had its price, however. Almost every element of the PC's design can be copied by other computer makers without risk of patent or copyright infringements. The result is a brisk market in **PC-compatible** computers, often called (derisively) "clones." Many (but not all) PC-compatibles can use software and peripherals designed for the IBM PC, and most are significantly cheaper than IBM models. The better PC-compatibles have taken a sizable chunk out of IBM's sales. Even so, the net effect of all this competition has been to establish the IBM PC's technical specifications as a de facto standard for personal computing. Tandy Corporation acknowledged this standard tacitly when, in 1984, it gave up its attempts to create its own set of standards with its TRS-80 computers. Since then, all new Tandy computers have conformed to the IBM specifications. Apple, which refused to produce an IBM-compatible computer, watched its share of the market decline dangerously.

In 1984, Apple attempted to reverse its declining fortunes by marketing a new computer, the Macintosh, based on a sophisticated Motorola microprocessor called the 68000. Apple described the new computer as a major step forward in personal computing. The Macintosh makes good use of research findings about human-computer interaction; it offers a graphics-based user interface. The term **user interface** refers to the part of a program that handles the interaction between the user and the computer. Unfortunately, Apple underestimated the users' memory needs; the first model (the Macintosh 128) was obsolete, at least in memory capacity, on its release. Doubly unfortunate was the **closed architecture** design Apple chose for its new computer. A closed design frustrates users' attempts to expand the computer and discourages other companies from manufacturing peripherals for it. Users, for example, could not easily upgrade their Macs' memory capacity. Worse, programmers found the Macintosh to be a formidable machine; software companies released Macintosh programs six months to one year later than they had planned. With its inadequate memory, closed architecture, and paucity of application software, the Macintosh got off to a slow start. And by the time an improved version of the Macintosh came along, IBM had released its Personal Computer AT (short for "Advanced Technology") and taken the Mac out of the high-tech limelight. According to industry reports, Apple has since reconsidered its Macintosh strategy and plans to market an open-architecture version of the computer.

The 1985 release of the IBM Personal Computer AT confirmed that the boundary between microcomputers and minicomputers, already fuzzy, is fast becoming meaningless. The AT is powered by the Intel 80286 microprocessor, which is 3.5 times as fast as the IBM PC's 8088; it's capable of executing as many as 500,000 program instructions per second. Capable of storing more than 16 million characters in its internal memory, the AT comes equipped with an auxiliary storage of more than 20 million characters. It surpasses the performance of mid-1970s minicomputers (and some mainframes as well). What is more, minicomputer makers are creating microprocessors that contain all or most of a minicomputer's computational power. Digital Equipment Corporation (DEC), for example, has now released its MicroVax line of desktop computers, which provide users with much of the computing power found in its highly regarded line of VAX minicomputers. Is the MicroVax a minicomputer or a microcomputer? The terms are losing their meaning.

In the years to come, it will make more sense to talk about single-user systems and multiple-user systems than it will to talk about microcomputers and minicomputers.

> *Single-user systems* are designed for one person's use. A personal computer is a **single-user system;** it's designed to provide a person who lacks extensive computer training or programming skill with a desktop information system. Also included in this category are **professional workstations,** or special-purpose computers designed to meet the needs of professionals in disciplines such as electrical engineering, aerospace technology, and laboratory science.
>
> *Multiple-user systems* are designed to provide for the computing needs of a work team, a department within an organization, or an entire organization. Most of today's **multiple-user systems** are timesharing mainframes or mini-

computers. Tomorrow's systems will include some based on high-powered microcomputers. IBM's PC AT, for instance, can handle three remote terminals.

Supercomputers. Yet another outgrowth of VLSI technology is the **supercomputer,** an ultrasophisticated computer optimized for the solution of complex mathematical problems. Supercomputers are rated by their speed in **megaflops,** or millions of computational operations per second. Supercomputers such as the Cray X-MP perform at speeds of 50 to 80 megaflops. For comparison, personal computers operate at roughly .01 to .04 megaflops, professional workstations at .02 to .05 megaflops, minicomputers at .2 to .5 megaflops, and mainframes at 1 to 10 megaflops.

Supercomputers are now working at the frontier of our conquest of time, and the result is an explosion of scientific progress. Because supercomputers can perform so many calculations so rapidly, they can simulate highly complex natural processes, such as the weather, and speed them up so we can understand the underlying dynamics. A decade's weather can be compressed into a few minutes. Key variables can be changed to see how they determine the final outcome, and with such experiments often comes a stunning new level of understanding. Without the supercomputer, we might have been prevented from advancing our knowledge much further. Nature is incredibly complex. Cancer, for example, appears to be a collection of thousands of diseases, each related to a staggeringly complex set of variables that includes millions of bits of genetic information, hundreds of chemical substances, and a host of other factors. Supercomputers give us the tools necessary to simulate complex systems and explore their behavior.

COMPUTER HORIZONS: TOWARD THE FIFTH GENERATION?

Where's the computer headed? Here's a tip from someone who ought to know, Robert N. Noyce, who is vice-chairman of Intel Corporation, the firm that invented the microprocessor. "The usual futurist projections," says Noyce, "are too optimistic in the short term and too pessimistic in the long term."[5]

Noyce's comment is right on the mark. With the achievement of very large-scale integration, it seemed that computers would continue to develop very rapidly. Actually, what we're seeing now is a slow but steady evolution as VLSI circuitry works its way through every component of computer systems, making them smaller, cheaper, faster, and more reliable. Yet there are signs on the horizon of a major new generation of computer technology.

TABLE 2–1 Four Generations of Computer Technology

	First generation 1951–1959	Second generation 1959–1964	Third generation (1964–1971)	Fourth generation (1971–present)
Technology	vacuum tubes	transistors	integrated circuits	large-scale and very large scale integration
Failure rate	every few minutes	every few days	days to weeks	weeks to years
Speed (instructions per second)	up to 10,000	up to 1,000,000	up to 10,000,000	up to 100,000,000
Average cost (per instruction)	$10.00	$1.00	$0.10	$0.001
Internal memory (characters)	1,000 to 8,000	4,000 to 64,000	32,000 to 1 million	64,000 to 32 million
Characteristic auxiliary storage device	cards	tape	disk	mass storage
Operating characteristics	single user; manual job scheduling; batch processing	single user; automatic job scheduling; batch processing	multiple user; timesharing; data communications	multiple user; timesharing; distributed systems
Software	machine language	high-level languages	application packages	very high-level languages, "user-friendly" application programs
Used by	scientific researchers; military; government; big corporations	scientific researchers; military; government; big corporations	scientific researchers; military; government; big and medium-sized corporations; universities	scientific researchers; military; government; big and medium-sized corporations; universities; schools and colleges; small businesses; individual white-collar workers; students; writers; graphic artists; and hobbyists

THE SHORT TERM: SLOW, STEADY EVOLUTION

Computer technology will probably evolve slowly (but steadily) over the next generation. The reason is that customers care more for a computer's usefulness than they do for its technological sophistication. To be useful in most settings, a computer must come equipped with at least some application software. Application software, however, must be designed to work with a particular computer system. For this reason, very little software is available for brand-new computer systems. It takes time for a large software pool to grow up around a computer. People tend to prefer computers for which large software pools exist. And that means they prefer older, established computers over snazzy new ones, no matter how much more technologically sophisticated the new ones are. The need for application software, in other words, slows the pace of technological development.

By making computer components so much cheaper, however, VLSI technology is doing something that borders on revolution. Microprocessors are putting computing power within anyone's reach. Memory chips are making it possible for even modest computing systems to work with huge amounts of internal memory. VLSI-equipped auxiliary storage devices, printers, video display circuits, and other peripherals are improving the usefulness of all kinds of computing systems.

THE LONG TERM: REVOLUTION?

The slow, steady progress of the computer in the mid-1980s should not blind us to the possibility of major innovations. If present efforts bear fruit, tomorrow will see a very different kind of machine indeed: the fifth-generation computer. **Fifth-generation computers** will not be exclusively devoted, as today's computers are, to the production of information out of data through such techniques as sorting, comparing, or other routine tasks. On the contrary, they'll produce knowledge.

Knowledge is not the same as information. **Knowledge** is information that has been subjected to reasoning and judgment. Information, for example, is a set of statistical conclusions resulting from a marketing survey carried out in a variety of neighborhoods; knowledge, in contrast, is the judgment that a new branch of a bank will most likely succeed in neighborhood A — and *not* in neighborhood B. To the extent that reasoning and judgment are processes associated with human intelligence, fifth-generation computers will possess intelligence — specifically, **artificial intelligence** (AI).

By any standard, achieving fifth-generation computers will be challenging — if it's possible at all. Many formidable barriers exist. It's easy, for example, to represent data, such as a number, the correct spelling of a word, or a Social Security number. But how do you represent knowledge? You can't simply type an encyclopedia into the computer, ask "What shall we do to save our economy?"

Horizon Technologies

Today's new or experimental technologies could change the face of computing if they bear fruit. Here's a brief overview of what the future may hold.

Parallel Processing

In a standard computer, a single CPU executes the program instructions, one by one. Although computers based on this architecture are capable of phenomenal processing speeds, further improvements are possible — and, believe it or not, necessary. Simulations of natural phenomena, for instance, require massive numbers of computations that keep even the fastest supercomputers busy for days. One way to speed up calculations is to process work by dividing it up among many CPUs — thousands of them — and using **parallel processing.** This approach is analogous to mass-production in factories, in which thousands of workers each concentrate on one small task. The result? A computer that may be able to process one billion or more program instructions each second.

Biochips

Parallel processing is already a reality, but this next horizon technology is still on the drawing boards. It's based on the discovery that certain organic molecules can store information in very much the way semiconductor memory chips do. These genetically engineered molecules, it is believed, can be grown in the laboratory. If this technology is ever achieved, its implications border on the unthinkable. Consider this: human chromosomes store information at the molecular level, and so they provide a good idea of the information storage densities molecular storage can achieve. Just one human chromosome (according to one recent estimate) stores the equivalent of well over 500 million six-character words, which would fill 4,000 library volumes. A **biochip** mass the size of a basketball could, in theory, store all the information currently available to humanity.

Voice Recognition

Computer-based **voice-recognition** systems have already been created that recognize about one hundred spoken words. A voice-recognition system available for personal computers, for example, allows the user to give commands (such as "Recalculate!") to the computer vocally rather than typing them at the keyboard. As our understanding of voice-recognition techniques grows, computers will become more adept at understanding spoken commands. In the future, the microphone may replace the keyboard as the chief means for human-computer interaction and data input.

Robots

Industrial **robots** — machines that possess humanlike skills or dexterity — are already at work welding auto parts, working inside nuclear reactors, and amusing hobbyists. Today's robots, however, are really little more than special-purpose computers programmed to manipulate electrically powered machinery. But progress in computer vision, pattern recognition, and artificial intelligence could lead to a new generation of silicon-based, intelligent beings. If intelligent robots come about, carbon-based intelligent beings (humans) will have to adjust — and the adjustment, as science fiction writers have been telling us for many years, may not be easy.

and press "Go." For one thing, when we read an encyclopedia, we use an already enormous storehouse of linguistic knowledge, knowledge that allows us to decode and use the encyclopedia. Moreover, we bring to bear an enormous amount of experience — experience that allows us, among other things, to judge whether the encyclopedia is a good one. Unfortunately, linguists and philosophers still do not understand how all this linguistic knowledge works. On top of this problem, fifth-generation computers will require processing speeds and memory capacities far greater than those now available. Achieving the fifth generation may require an investment akin to the one that landed a man on the moon.

Japanese experience has borne out the difficulty of achieving fifth-generation technology. In 1981, Japan's Ministry of International Trade and Industry (MITI) announced a bold plan to spend tens of millions of dollars to achieve the fifth generation by the mid-1990s. United States computer scientists warned that, if the Japanese beat the United States to the fifth generation, the United States could lose its worldwide predominance in computer technology. At this writing, however, Japanese progress has been disappointing, leading MITI to cut back on the project's funding. And in the meantime, United States scientists have maintained world leadership in the supercomputer area. It is by no means clear that the United States has lost the AI sweepstakes — or, indeed, whether the contest can be won at all.

A genuine revolution in technology, if it ever occurs, may not happen until well after the turn of the century. But bear in mind Noyce's comments about overestimating the short term and underestimating the long term. At the beginning of the electronic computer era, a computer engineer remarked that no more than one or two dozen electronic computers would serve the computing needs of the entire United States! Chip-based descendants of exactly the same technology provide processing power today for millions of carburetors, toasters, and wristwatches — a development that, in 1950, no one in their right mind would have predicted.

THE INFORMATION SOCIETY

Whether or not revolutionary computer technologies are achieved, it is already apparent that the computer is assisting the creation of what some sociologists believe is a new social order, the **information society.** The information society's predecessor, the industrial society, dealt primarily with the production and distribution of goods and the provision of services. Although the production of goods and the provision of services will continue to play important roles in the information society, its chief function will be producing and distributing information and knowledge. And just as the fundamental technology of the industrial society was the steam engine, that of the information society will be the computer. Table 2–2 summarizes some of the emerging features of the

TABLE 2–2 The Industrial Society vs. the Information Society

	Industrial society	Information society
Technology		
Basis	steam engine	computer
Function	amplify physical labor	amplify mental labor
Effect	increases production and distribution of goods and services	increases production and distribution of knowledge and information
Economy and society		
Driving force of economy	technological innovation	creation of new knowledge
Employment	blue-collar workers predominate	white-collar workers predominate
Characteristic workplace	factory	office
Labor problems	Cyclic unemployment; labor-management conflict	Permanent unemployment of unskilled and semi-skilled labor
Capital resource	industrial equipment, raw materials	information and knowledge; educated workers
World economy	Western nations produce goods; Third World nations produce raw materials	Third World nations produce goods; Western nations produce information and knowledge
Communication	postal service	electronic media
Residence patterns	Centralized, near factories and arteries of transportation	Decentralized, linked by electronic media
Political system	Parliamentary democracy	Domination by special interest groups
Social Problems	War caused by conflict over resources	Shock caused by rapid pace of change; terrorism; invasion of privacy

information society, as sociologists such as Daniel Bell and Yoneji Masuda have described it.

The industrial society, to be sure, will not disappear overnight in the United States and other industrialized nations. The production and distribution of goods will continue to play a major role in our economy. Yet it is already clear, as management expert Peter Drucker pointed out a decade ago, that information and knowledge are crucial strategic resources even for firms devoted to manufacturing. What will determine an organization's success in the future, experts agree, is its ability to cope with the overabundance of information our society is producing and its commitment to using information technology in strategically advantageous ways. Exactly the same points apply to individuals, and that's why learning how to use a computer is one of the wisest things you can do.

SUMMARY

The basic idea of the computer — representing information physically and solving problems by manipulating physical objects — has been around for thousands of years. All computers perform four basic functions: input, storage, processing, and output. In the input stage, information is physically represented by digits, such as beads, gears, or current in electrical circuits. The information is stored so that it's directly accessible for processing. In the processing phase, the central processing unit (CPU) follows the instructions of a program to manipulate the represented information. A program is a computer-readable version of an algorithm, or an approach to solving a problem that uses a series of simple procedures. You can solve a problem using an algorithm even if you understand little or nothing about the problem you're working with; that's why machines can do it just as well. At the end of the processing phase, the results are displayed as output.

These four basic functions are evident in the abacus, but today's computers are a breed apart. Capable of storing millions of pages of information and executing programs longer than a college dictionary, they operate with all but inconceivable speed and accuracy. Modern computers have conquered time by making it possible to do several centuries' worth of calculations in minutes or seconds.

Achieving the modern computer took centuries because of technological, socioeconomic, and intellectual roadblocks. Beads and brass gears just wouldn't do the trick; electronic switching devices were needed. The computer, moreover, needed a market, and this market didn't exist until the nineteenth and twentieth centuries saw an explosion of population and commerce. Finally, engineers had to think their way toward a general-purpose computer, the prospects for which were not made clear until Alan Turing made a major mathematical breakthrough in 1936.

The pathway to the modern computer was cleared by Hollerith, who invented an electronic tabulating machine; Turing, who helped apply his discovery to what may have been the first electronic computer; Eckert and Mauchly, who invented the ENIAC; and von Neumann, who developed the stored program concept. By 1951, the electronic computer was a reality.

Modern computers have evolved rapidly through four generations of technology, each representing such a major advance that it made computers of previous generations obsolete. First-generation machines (1946–1958), based on vacuum tubes, were slow, unreliable, difficult to program, and difficult to use. Second-generation computers (1958–1964), based on transistors, were faster and more reliable. High-level programming languages made them much easier to program. Third-generation computers (1964–1971), based on integrated circuits, were even faster and more reliable than second-generation machines, and they were dramatically cheaper too. Improvements in system software and peripherals (such as timesharing and interactive processing) made it possible for thousands of people to use a single machine, each having the impression of full and exclusive control of its resources. Users began to demand that computers come equipped with a range of application software. Fourth-generation computers, based on very large scale integration (VLSI) technology, saw further dramatic price drops, rising minicomputer popularity, and the origin of the microcomputer. Further evolution of computer technology may result in a fifth generation of intelligent computers, but for now the demand for useful application software keeps even technologically outmoded computers on the market.

KEY TERMS

abacus
algorithm
analog computer
arithmetic-logic unit (ALU)
artificial intelligence (AI)
auxiliary storage
batch processing
binary digit
binary number
biochip
bistable device
bit
cathode ray tube (CRT)
central processing unit (CPU)
closed architecture
coding
compiler
confirmation message
control unit
data communications
digit
digital computer
distributed computing
electronic digital computer
error message
execute
fifth-generation computer
first-generation computer
fourth-generation computer
functional organization

general-purpose computer
high-level programming language
information society
input
input devices
integrated circuit
interactive processing
internal memory
knowledge
large-scale integration (LSI)
looping
machine language
magnetic core memory
magnetic disk
mainframe computer
mass storage
megaflop
memory
memory chips
menu
microcomputer
microprocessor
minicomputer
multiple-user system
open architecture
operating system
output
output devices
parallel processing
PC-compatible
peripherals
personal computer
processing
professional workstation
program
prompt
radix
robot
second-generation computer
selection
semiconductor memory
single-user system
storage
stored program concept
supercomputer
terminal
third-generation computer
timesharing
transistor
user interface
very high-level programming language
very large scale integration (VLSI)
voice recognition

REVIEW QUESTIONS AND EXERCISES

1. Develop a criticism of this statement: "The history of the computer is of no interest to me. It won't do me any good to get the perspective history is supposed to give you."
2. In what sense is the idea of the computer a very old one?
3. State why an abacus is correctly described as a digital computer.
4. What kind of analog computer are you likely to encounter in the produce or meat section of a supermarket? What is its function?
5. Think of an example of an algorithm you use every day and describe in detail the steps you must follow to apply it correctly.
6. Why is it accurate to say that we are now engaged in the conquest of time as well as space?

7. If the basic idea of computing is so old, why did it take so long for automatic computers to appear?
8. What were the limitations of first-generation computers?
9. What factors led to the commercial success of second-generation computers?
10. What are the advantages of integrated circuits over their predecessors?
11. What innovations in computer design and programming occurred during the third generation of computer technology? Why did these innovations help to establish the mainframe computer as a widely used tool in large organizations?
12. What is meant by the terms large-scale and very large scale integration? In what ways did these two technologies usher in the world of computing as we know it today?
13. In what ways were programming techniques improved as computers passed through their four generations of development?
14. What is the difference between a mainframe computer and a minicomputer? Between a minicomputer and a microcomputer? Between a microcomputer and a personal computer?
15. What role did commercial application software play in the personal computer's success in the marketplace?
16. What are the advantages — and disadvantages — of an open architecture design? Which would you prefer that your own computer used, open or closed architecture? Why?
17. Why are the terms single-user system and multiple-user system more accurate nowadays than the older terms minicomputer and microcomputer?
18. Why are supercomputers contributing to the advance of human knowledge?
19. Suppose you were working on the team that developed the ENIAC. You remark, "Someday there will be millions of computers, and people will use them in their homes." How do you think your coworkers would have received your statement?
20. Most commercially successful computers remain on the market long after they have been surpassed by technologically more sophisticated machines. Why?
21. What would an artificially intelligent computer be able to do — and why do some people believe that achieving artificial intelligence borders on the impossible?

FOR FURTHER READING

THE HISTORY OF COMPUTING TECHNOLOGY

Augarten, Stan. *Bit by Bit: An Illustrated History of Computers* (Boston: Ticknor and Fields, 1984).

———. *State of the Art: A Photographic History of the Integrated Circuit* (Boston: Ticknor and Fields, 1983).

Evans, Christopher. *The Micro Millennium* (New York: Viking Press, 1979).
Forester, Tom (ed.). *The Microelectronics Revolution: The Complete Guide to the New Technology and Its Impact on Society* (Cambridge, Mass.: MIT Press, 1984).
Goldstine, Herman H. *The Computer from Pascal to von Neumann* (Princeton, N.J.: Princeton University Press, 1980).
Hansen, Dirk. *The New Alchemists* (Boston: Little, Brown, 1983).
Hodges, Andrew. *Alan Turing: The Enigma* (New York: Simon and Schuster, 1983).
Hyman, Anthony. *Charles Babbage: Pioneer of the Computer* (Princeton, N.J.: Princeton University Press, 1983).
Osborne, Adam. *Running Wild: The Next Industrial Revolution* (Berkeley, Calif.: Osborne/McGraw-Hill, 1979.
Pullan, J. N. *The History of the Abacus* (New York: Praeger, 1969).
Randall, Brian (ed.). *The Origins of Digital Computers* (New York: Springer-Verlag, 1982).
Shurkin, Joel. *Engines of the Mind: A History of the Computer* (New York: W. W. Norton, 1984).
Sobel, Robert. *IBM: Colossus in Transition* (New York: Times Books, 1981).
Wulforst, Harry. *Breakthrough to the Computer Age* (New York: Charles Scribner's Sons, 1982).

HORIZON TECHNOLOGIES

Aleksander, Igor, and Piers Burnett. *Reinventing Man: The Robot Becomes Reality* (Harmondsworth, Eng.: Penguin, 1984).
Levine, Ronald D. "Supercomputers," *Scientific American* (January 1982).
Levinson, Stephen E., and Mark Y. Liberman. "Speech Recognition by Computer," *Scientific American* (April 1981).
Pollack, Andrew. "Computers from Bacteria," *New York Times* (February 18, 1982).
Yanchinski, Stephanie. "And Now — the Biochip," *New Scientist* (January 14 and 28, 1982).

ARTIFICIAL INTELLIGENCE

Barr, A., P. R. Cohen, and E. A. Feigenbaum. *The Handbook of Artificial Intelligence*, 3 vols. (Los Altos, Calif.: Kaufmann, 1981).
Boden, Margaret A. *Artificial Intelligence and Natural Man* (Brighton, Eng.: Harvester, 1977).
Feigenbaum, Edward A., and Pamela McCorduck. *The Fifth Generation: Artificial Intelligence and Japan's Computer Challenge to the World*, Rev. and updated ed. (New York: Signet/New American Library, 1984).
Marsh, Peter. "The Race for the Thinking Machine," *New Scientist* (July 8, 1982).
McCorduck, Pamela. *Machines Who Think: A Personal Inquiry into the History and Prospects of Artificial Intelligence* (San Francisco: W. H. Freeman, 1979).
Minksy, Marvin. "Why People Think Computers Can't," *Technology Review* (November-December 1982).
Shurkin, Joel N. "Expert Systems: The Practical Face of Artificial Intelligence," *Technology Review* (November-December 1982).
Waltz, David O. "Artificial Intelligence," *Scientific American* (October 1982).
Weizenbaum, Joseph. *Computer Power and Human Reason: From Judgment to Calculation* (San Francisco: W. H. Freeman, 1976).

THE INFORMATION SOCIETY

Bell, Daniel. *The Coming of Post-Industrial Society* (New York: Basic Books, 1973).

Ginzberg, Eli. "The Mechanization of Work," *Scientific American,* 247 (September 1982), pp. 66–75.

Giuliano, Vincent. "The Mechanization of Office Work," *Scientific American,* 247 (September 1982), pp. 148–165.

Jones, Barry. *Sleepers, Wake! Technology and the Future of Work* (New York: Oxford University Press, 1982).

Nora, Simon, and Alain Minc. *The Computerization of Society: A Report to the President of France* (Cambridge, Mass.: MIT Press, 1980).

Toffler, Alvin. *The Third Wave* (New York: Bantam Books, 1980).

3 The Personal Computer: *Fourth-Generation Technology for Ordinary People*

"Any intelligent fool can make things bigger. . . . It takes a touch of genius — and a lot of courage — to move in the opposite direction."

E. F. Schumacher

Pluck a hair and have a look at the thick end. It's roughly 100 microns in diameter (one micron equals one millionth of a meter). And now imagine a technology sophisticated enough to draw a grid of 400 squares within that 100-micron-wide circle. Imagine, too, a technology that can wire each of these squares independently so that all 400 function as transistors, or electronic switches.

Sound futuristic? It's not — in fact, it's old hat, at least in the computer world: the technology to pack more than a million transistors onto a quarter-inch-square chip of silicon was achieved in 1984.[1] Fourth-generation technology has gone so far, in fact, that IBM scientists have now managed to put the CPU of one of their large mainframe computers on a single silicon chip. The same technology has dramatically reduced the size and cost of every computer component, including disk drives, video display systems, and printers. Thanks

to fourth-generation technology, you can assemble, right on your desktop, a personal computer system that rivals the power of a third-generation mainframe.

What this means to you in brief is power — the power to extend your reach, in precisely the same way that larger computers have extended the reach of big companies and scientific researchers. With a little practical knowledge, you can put this power to work for you. Conveying this knowledge is this chapter's goal.

You can use this chapter to help you learn a personal computer's operating system. Begin by finding the sheets entitled "Quick Reference Guide: Operating System Basics," which are positioned at the end of this book. Tear them out, and staple them or put them in a folder. Keep these sheets handy as you read the section of this chapter entitled "System Software: Getting It All Together." When this chapter describes a basic operating system function, such as copying a disk, consult your operating system manual, handouts your instructor has given you, or the supplementary text you are using. Find out how to carry out the function with *your* operating system, and make a note of the procedure on the "Quick Reference Guide." When you've finished filling out the "Quick Reference Guide," keep it with you whenever you use the computer. You'll find it helpful in day-to-day operating sessions.

Think of a personal computer system as if it were a round ball with several layers (Figure 3–1). At the core is the hardware, the physical parts of the computer system. The next layer contains system software, or programs that enable the computer system to function. The outer layer, the one you see and work with, is made up of application software, programs that turn the computer system into a tool for accomplishing specific tasks. As a user of a personal computer system, you'll find that you need to know relatively little about how your computer actually works. System and application software, as Figure 3–1 suggests, insulate you from the strange doings inside your computer's maze of electronic pathways. Most of the time you're working with a personal computer, the only part of the "ball" that you see is the outermost layer, the application software. When you instruct your word processing program, for instance, to store a document on a floppy disk, you don't have to worry about just how and where the computer puts the document; system software handles the details for you.

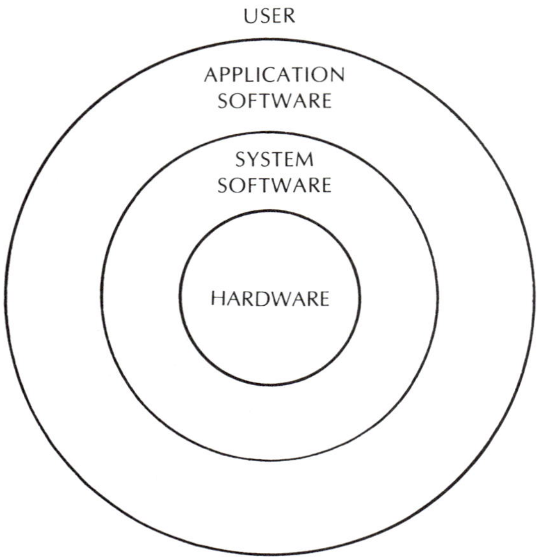

FIGURE 3–1 Three Layers of a Personal Computer System

Even so, it still makes good sense to get a more than casual grasp of how personal computer systems work — the kind of grasp that helps you understand what people mean when they say things like, "Oh, that's an 8-bit computer," or "128K of RAM just isn't enough." Such knowledge can pay off handsomely when you choose a system to meet your needs or those of an organization for which you're working. So we'll start this chapter with an overview of personal computer hardware; there follows an introduction to personal computer operating systems.

PERSONAL COMPUTER HARDWARE: A GUIDED TOUR

Like all computers, personal computers have two functional units: the central processing unit (CPU) and peripherals (see Chapter 2). The CPU follows a program's instructions and, as it does, controls the rest of the computer. A personal computer's CPU consists of its microprocessor and internal memory. Peripherals include input devices, output devices, and the auxiliary storage system.

THE MICROPROCESSOR: THE KEY TO A PERSONAL COMPUTER'S PERSONALITY

Dozens of personal computers compete for consumer favor in today's marketplace. Each claims to offer some unique bundle of features that makes it superior to all others. Yet all personal computers are based on microprocessors, and only a few brands and models of microprocessors are available. You can tell a great deal about any personal computer's personality by finding out which chip powers it.

Microprocessor chips vary in their processing capabilities, such as their processing speed and the amount of internal memory they can use. Three microprocessor design elements determine this power: (1) the number of bits that can be processed in one operation; (2) the number of bits that can be transferred to the internal memory in one operation; and (3) the maximum size of the internal memory. All three factors are determined by a microprocessor's design.

Number of Bits Processed in One Operation. The earliest microprocessor, the 1969 chip made by Intel Corporation, processes only 4 bits of data at once. A bit is a single unit of information expressed in the binary digits 0 or 1 (*bi*nary digi*t* = bit). To be useful, a microprocessor must process at least 8 bits of data at once. Performance improves when microprocessors handle 16 bits of data at once, and it improves still further when they handle 32 bits at once (Figure 3–2). To understand why, picture yourself emptying five gallons of water into a sink with a small spoon (4 bits at once), a large spoon (8 bits), a teacup (16 bits), and a coffee mug (32 bits).

Number of Bits Transferred to the Internal Memory in One Operation. Some microprocessor chips can send 8 bits of data to the internal memory in one operation, while others can send 16. Microprocessors with 16 bit data transfer capabilities are faster. To understand why, think of how much faster traffic can move on a four-lane freeway than a two-lane road.

FIGURE 3–2 8, 16, and 32 Bit Microprocessors

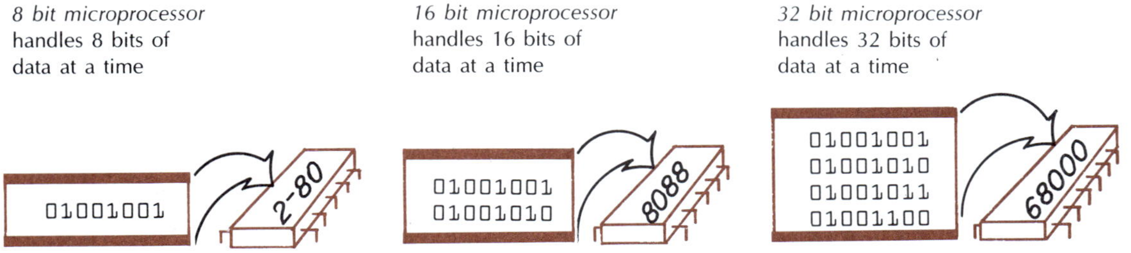

Internal Memory Limits. Every location in the computer's internal memory has its own unique **memory address,** a binary number of 16, 20, or 24 digits. The number of digits in the memory address determines the maximum of internal memory the microprocessor can use. If, for example, a microprocessor uses a 16-bit memory address, then the maximum of storage locations is 2^{16} = 65,536 (Figure 3–3). That sounds like a lot, but each storage location is only 8 bits (that is, one **byte**) in size. One byte of storage can hold only one **character** (a letter, number from 0 through 9, or a punctuation symbol). If it takes 1,500 characters to make a page of double-spaced, typed text, a memory of 65,536 bytes can hold only about 44 pages of programs and data. That's enough for some personal computer applications, but more complex programs (and lengthier data) require more memory. The microprocessor used in the IBM Personal Computer employs a 20-digit address, and it can use an internal memory of more than one million characters. Newer microprocessors use 24-digit memory addresses for a maximum memory size of more than 16 million locations — far more than many mainframe computers.

A Guide to Microprocessors. Here's a brief overview of the chips that power most microcomputers and personal computers:

Intel 8080 (1974). The 8 bit 8080, a direct descendant of the world's first microprocessor (the 1969 Intel 4004), powered the first commercially available microcomputer, the Altair. The chip transfers data 8 bits at a time and allows a maximum internal memory of 65,536 characters. Altairs were sold to thousands of computer hobbyists as kits during the mid-1970s. Because the Altair came with no software, however, this microcomputer (and its many imitators) could attract only those hobbyists with electronics or programming expertise.

Zilog Z80 (1976). A technically more sophisticated version of the Intel 8080, this 8 bit chip captured a major share of the microcomputer market during the late 1970s and early 1980s. The chip transfers data 8 bits at a time and

0110 0100 0011 0111	*16 bit memory address* allows 2^{16} = 65,536 unique memory locations
0010 0110 0100 0011 0111	*20 bit memory address* allows 2^{20} = 1,048,576 unique memory locations
0100 0010 0110 0100 0011 0111	*24 bit memory address* allows 2^{24} = 16,777,216 unique memory locations

FIGURE 3–3 Memory Addresses and Internal Memory Size

allows a maximum internal memory of 65,536 characters. It powered a variety of successful computers, such as the Radio Shack (a division of Tandy Corporation) TRS-80 and the portable Osborne 1 and Kaypro II. At this writing, the market for Z80 computers is shrinking; people prefer 16 and 32 bit computers.

6502 (MOS Technology, 1977). The 8 bit 6502 chip powers more personal computers than any other. It's the brain of Apple Computer's highly successful Apple II as well as of the most popular home computer ever made, the Commodore 64. Both machines are well suited to the educational and home markets. The chip transfers data 8 bits at a time and allows a maximum internal memory of 65,536 characters.

8088 (Intel Corporation, 1980). The 16 bit 8088 chip revolutionized the personal computer industry by making faster, more powerful personal computers possible. Able to use more than 1 million characters of internal memory, the 8088 powers the IBM Personal Computer and its imitators, or PC-compatibles. These machines now dominate the business market for personal computers. In 1985, 90 percent of businesses that planned first-time personal computer purchases anticipated buying IBM Personal Computers.[2] The 8088 transfers data 8 bits at a time. An improved version of this chip, the Intel 80286, transfers 16 bits of data at a time and can use a memory of more than 16 million characters. An even more advanced version, the 80386, transfers 32 bits of data at a time and can use more memory than most mainframes.

68000 (Motorola Corporation, 1981). The 32 bit 68000 chip puts the information-processing power of a mainframe or minicomputer on a desktop. The chip transfers 16 bits of data at a time and can use more than 16 million characters of internal memory. Apple Computer chose the 68000 chip for its 1984 Macintosh.

Computers that use 16 or 32 bit chips such as the 8088, 80286, 80386, and 68000 are technically superior to 8 bit chips — and not because they're faster. The speed differences among microprocessors are not very noticeable when running application software. Most important of all is these chips' ability to use large internal memories. The bigger the internal memory, the better: with a large memory, you can put big, complex programs to work on equally big amounts of data.

The Incompatibility Bugbear. Every microprocessor has its own unique **instruction set,** or list of several dozen tasks that it's designed to carry out. Each instruction, moreover, has its own unique code, expressed in binary numbers. Programs contain lists of instructions that use these codes. Following them, the microprocessor receives the precise instructions it needs to do processing tasks.

A major problem, however, is that one microprocessor will not recognize another's codes. No standards exist. For this reason, a program written for the Apple IIe will not run on the IBM Personal Computer. Application software written for one microprocessor, in short, is **incompatible** with a computer using a different microprocessor. To run on the IBM PC, the Apple IIe program would have to be completely rewritten to conform to the IBM PC's microprocessor. Some companies release versions of programs for two or three different machines, but the more common practice is to release application programs for only one brand of computer.

Even if two computers use the same microprocessor, they may still be incompatible (that is, unable to run each other's software). Compatibility problems can be caused by other reasons. Software must be written around the dictates not only of the microprocessor, but also the computer's operating system and disk drives. The Apple II and Commodore 64 use the same microprocessor, for instance, but they cannot run each other's software because of operating system and disk drive incompatibilities.

INTERNAL MEMORY: THE KEY TO PROCESSING CONVENIENCE

A microprocessor isn't a complete central processing unit (CPU); a complete CPU includes an internal memory. The internal memory keeps the data accessible for processing purposes. Computer memories are like the post office boxes you've probably seen in the larger post offices: there are thousands of boxes, and each has its own number (or address). Each memory location stores 8 bits of data (that is, one byte). Again, the maximum number of such boxes is determined by the microprocessor's design. Some designs permit only 65,536 boxes; others allow more than 1 million. Still others allow a maximum of 16 million.

Measuring Memory. Because computers are designed with binary numbers in mind, their memory capacities are measured in powers of 2. Common memory sizes are 65,536 (that is, 2^{16}) bytes, 262,144 (2^{18}) bytes, and 1,048,576 (2^{20}) bytes. Because these numbers are large and unwieldy, a special measurement system, using the symbols *K* and *M*, has been created to talk about them more conveniently. K, short for **kilobyte,** stands for roughly 1,000 bytes (actually, $2^{10} = 1{,}024$). M, short for **megabyte,** stands for roughly 1 million bytes (actually, $2^{20} = 1{,}048{,}576$). Advances in computer technology require the term **gigabyte,** or roughly one billion characters (actually, 1,024 megabytes).

This memory measurement system is used to describe both internal memory and auxiliary storage. You will often hear, for instance, of a personal computer that has a 640K internal memory and a 20 megabyte disk drive. This computer has room for approximately 640,000 bytes or characters in its internal memory, and its auxiliary storage system can hold roughly 20 million more.

Memory Chips. Before VLSI technology came along, it could cost as much as $25,000 just for a relatively small internal memory (about 32,000 characters of storage). A major by-product of VLSI research and development, semiconductor memory (see Chapter 2), has changed all that. Today's personal computers make use of mass-produced, inexpensive memory chips that cost as little as $5 for more than 64K of storage.

As memory costs have declined, the average size of personal computers' internal memories has grown steadily. In the early days, few of them had more than 48K of memory. Soon, however, a 64K standard emerged. With the introduction of the new 16 bit microprocessors in 1981, 128K memories became common, and by 1984 256K memories were not unusual. Experts predict that by 1990 most personal computers will have at least 1 megabyte of internal memory, a figure common in the world of mainframe computing.

RAM vs. ROM. Every personal computer has two types of internal memory, RAM (short for random-access memory) and ROM (short for read-only memory) (Figure 3–4).

FIGURE 3–4 ROM Versus RAM

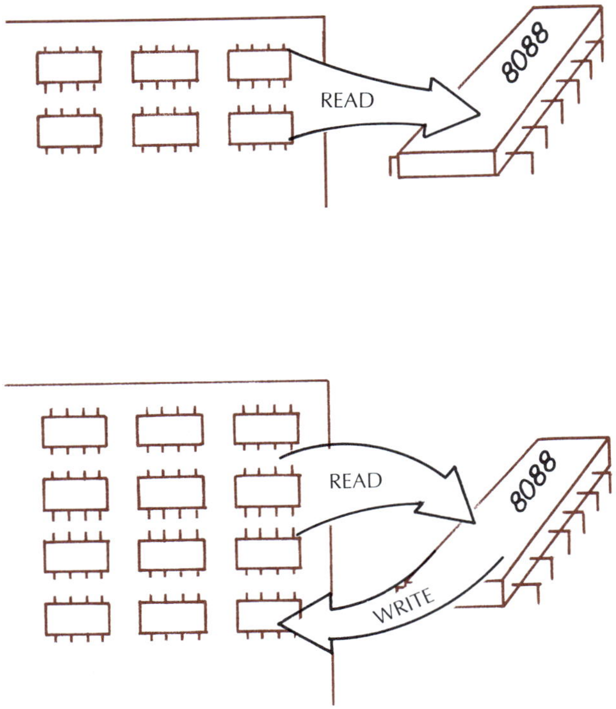

ROM transfers information to the computer on power-up; the information in ROM chips is permanent and cannot be altered by the user. The computer may read the information only.

RAM provides personal computers with internal memory. It provides a temporary storage place for programs and data. The computer can both read information from RAM and write information to it.

RAM. **Random-access memory** stores the programs and data while the computer is working. The term **random access** (also called **direct access**) refers to the memory's design; the central processing unit can gain immediate access to any part of the memory without having to go through a sequence of memory locations to get to it. That is why data are transferred between the internal memory and the microprocessor at very high speeds (10 million characters per second or more). This part of the internal memory is a **read/write memory;** the computer can both take information from it (**read**) and put information in it (**write**). RAM is **volatile,** meaning that it loses the information stored in it when the current is switched off.

ROM. **Read-only memory** is **nonvolatile;** it can contain programs and keep them even when the current is switched off. For this reason, computer manufacturers use ROM to hold programs used when you turn the computer on. Some of these programs test the computer to make sure all components are functioning properly. Others place a message on the screen telling you what to do to start an operating session.

The concept of volatility is sure to come to life for you someday when the electrical current fails. Current interruptions do happen occasionally in most areas — in some places as often as once or twice a week. Sooner or later, you will lose work when a loss of current suddenly erases everything in RAM. Cautious users safeguard their work by copying it frequently to auxiliary storage, which is nonvolatile. They also avoid working during a thunderstorm, when current interruptions are very likely.

AUXILIARY STORAGE

Auxiliary storage devices store programs and data while they are not in use. Although they're peripheral to the computer in a strict sense, no computer — personal or otherwise — is of much use without an auxiliary storage system. Because today's chip-based internal memories are volatile, some method for storing programs and data is needed while the current is switched off. In today's computers (personal and otherwise), auxiliary storage devices continue to play this role, and new ones as well:

Because semiconductor memory is volatile, auxiliary storage now serves the vital function of making backup copies of your work while you're working with the computer. As a personal computer user, you will quickly become accustomed to saving your work to disk from time to time during a working session as well as when you're finished.

Because today's auxiliary storage devices handle information at such high speeds, programmers now use them as if they were an extension of the computer's internal memory. A very large program, for example, can be set up so that only the essential parts of it are present in internal memory. Less frequently used portions of the program can be kept in auxiliary storage, to be funneled into the memory as needed. As a user, you needn't worry about these operations; they're completely automatic. So far as you know, the effect is that you're working with a much larger internal memory than your computer actually has.

Evaluating Auxiliary Storage Performance. Because auxiliary storage devices serve as extensions of a personal computer's internal memory, they must perform at high speed. Two measurements, access time and data transfer rate, provide ready indexes of an auxiliary storage system's performance.

Access time refers to the time it takes for the auxiliary storage device to locate the desired program or data and begin feeding information into the internal memory.

Data transfer rate refers to the number of bits per second transferred after the desired information has been located.

Types of Auxiliary Storage. The most commonly used auxiliary storage systems in personal computers are cassette tapes, floppy disk systems, and hard disk systems. A new, nonmagnetic technology that may prove popular is optical disk storage.

Cassette Tapes. Cassette tapes and cassette tape recorders provided the earliest personal computers with an extremely inexpensive, but slow and inconvenient, method of auxiliary storage. They are seldom used today. The problem with cassette recorders is that they store and retrieve information sequentially, a point you'll recognize immediately if you've ever wound back and forth through an audio cassette tape trying to find a song you like. This storage technique is called **sequential access** (Figure 3–5). All the information is stored in a sequence; there's no way you can get directly to what you want without winding through the sequence. Cassette recorder access times are usually more than 1 minute; data transfer rates are low, averaging around 500 bits per second. Although tape storage is slow and cumbersome, it illustrates the basic functions of an auxiliary memory device: storing and retrieving programs and data. The tape recorder's magnetic head can both *write* (that is, record) and *read* (play back) information.

Floppy Disks. The most common auxiliary storage medium for personal computers, **floppy disks** are thin, flexible disks of plastic coated with a magnetically sensitive material and wrapped in a cardboard envelope (Figure 3–6). They come in several sizes; the most popular are $5\frac{1}{4}$ inch and $3\frac{1}{2}$ inch. These disks are used in **disk drives,** which spin them at speeds of up to 300 r.p.m. Like a cassette recorder, the disk drive has a magnetic recording/playback head (called a **read/write head**), but there's an important

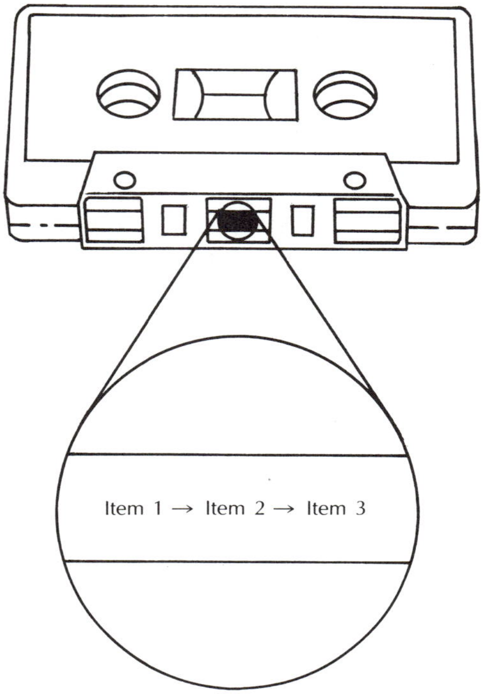

FIGURE 3–5 Tape Cassette: Sequential Access to Stored Data

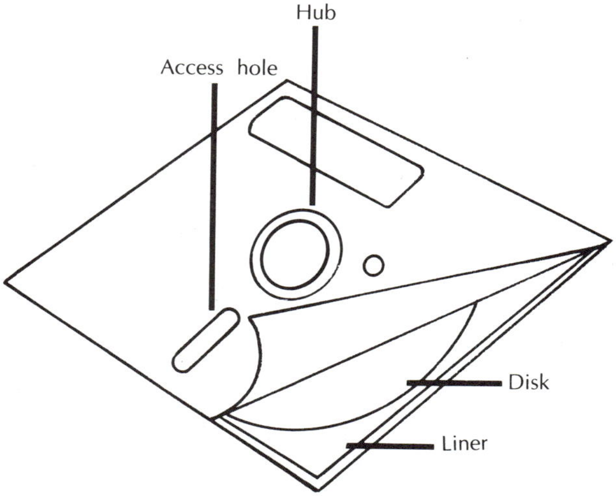

FIGURE 3–6 Floppy Disk

difference: the head can move back and forth across the surface of the rapidly spinning disk (Figure 3–7). The result is random or direct access: the drive can get to the information it's looking for without winding through a sequence of items. (To understand why, consider how much faster you can find the song you want using a record player than you can using a tape cassette recorder. With a record player, you simply move the needle across the grooves until you find the track you want.) Access times are half

FIGURE 3–7 Floppy Disk Drive: Random Access to Data Tracks

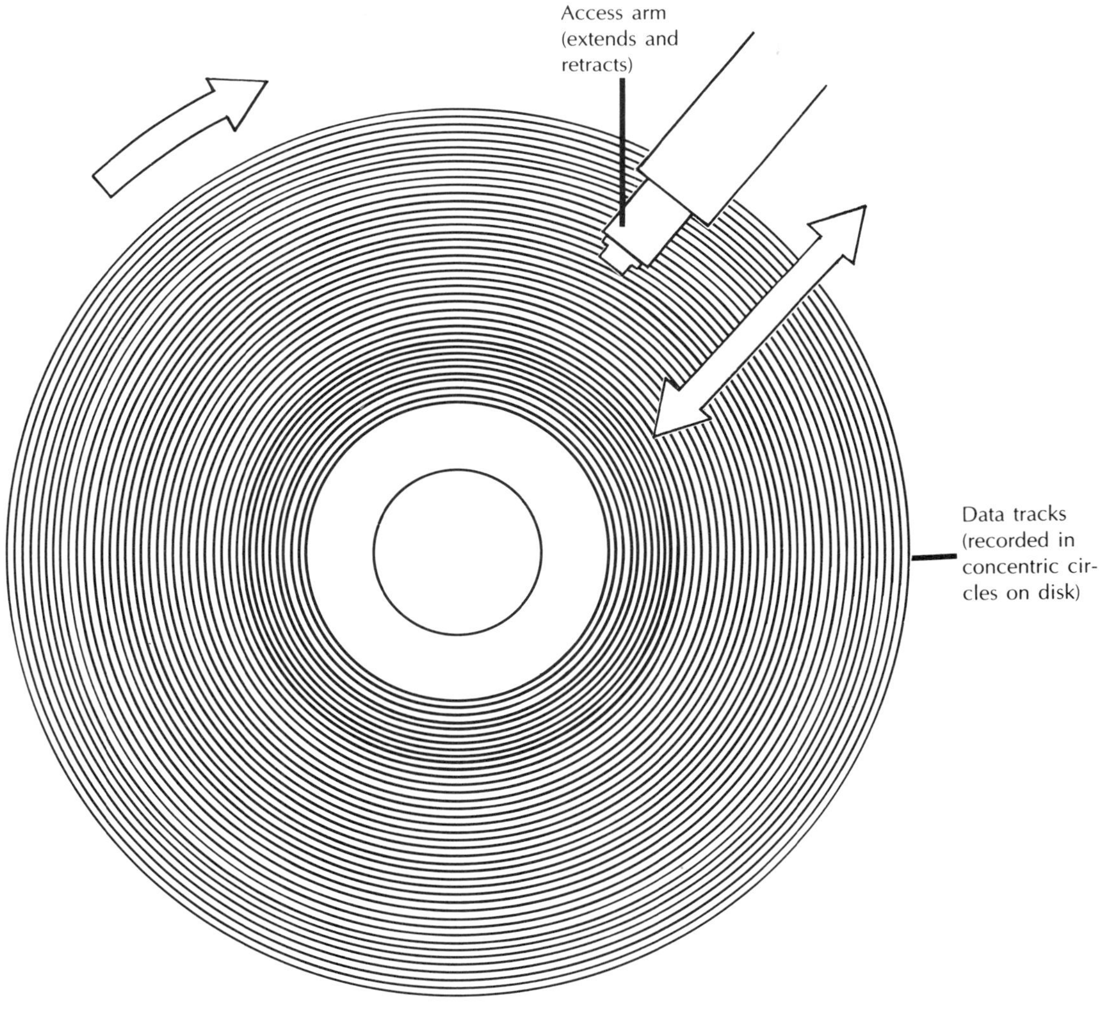

a second or less, and data transfer rates are approximately 250,000 characters per second. Floppy disks can hold as much as 1 megabyte of information per disk. Storage capacities depend on several factors, including whether the disk is single-sided or double-sided, the density with which the magnetic material can store information (measured in bits per square inch), and the number of information storage tracks on the disk's surface (Figure 3–8). Systems equipped with two flexible disk drives are convenient to use, since information can be copied easily from one drive to another.

Hard Disks. **Hard disks** (also called fixed disks or Winchester drives) are optimized versions of floppy disk technology. Spinning in a dust-proof environment at speeds of up to 3,000 r.p.m., hard disks employ rigid platters of aluminum coated with a magnetically sensitive material. The protection against dust is necessary because the read/write head "floats" a tiny fraction of an inch over the disk's surface — so close, in fact, that a dust particle or human hair on the disk would collide with the head. Most hard disk drives use two or more nonremovable platters to achieve high storage capacities (Figure 3–9). Like flexible disks, hard disks also use random- or direct-access storage techniques. But hard disks outperform flexible ones by a wide margin. Hard disk access times and data transfer rates are up to ten times faster than floppy disk drives, thanks to the disk's high r.p.m. and the head's proximity to the platter. They can transfer 5 million characters or more per second to internal memory. Hard disks, moreover, can store

FIGURE 3–8 Typical Floppy Disk Storage Capacities

	Recording Density		
	Single Density (2,768 bits per square inch)	*Double Density* (5,876 bits per square inch)	*Quad Density* (11,752 bits per square inch)
Single-sided, 40 tracks per disk	80K	180K	—
Double-sided, 80 tracks per disk	160K	360K	720K
Double-sided, double-tracked 160 tracks per disk	—	—	1.4M

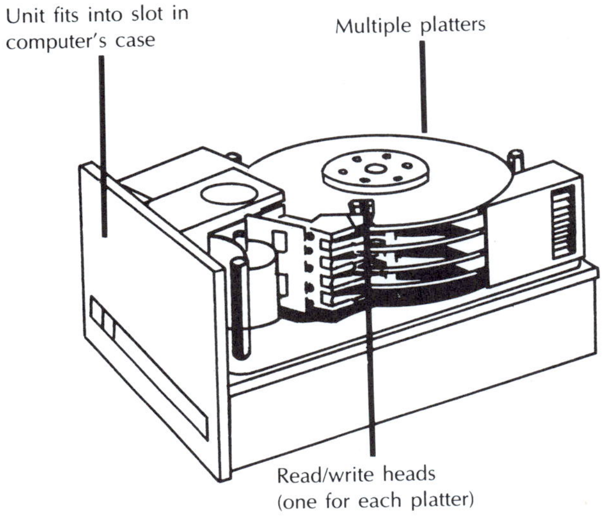

FIGURE 3–9 Hard Disk Drive

10 megabytes of information or more. The result is fast, convenient operation. Systems with hard disks usually have a flexible disk drive too. The floppy disk drive makes it easy to load new application programs into the system and back up work done with the computer.

Optical Disks. **Optical disks** store information in the form of tiny pockmarks on a reflective plastic surface. Read by a tightly focused laser beam, optical disks can store several gigabytes of information in a few square inches of space. A single optical disk can easily store the contents of an entire, twenty-four volume *Encyclopaedia Britannica*. A major drawback of commercially viable optical disk technology at this writing is that it is a **read-only storage medium;** in other words, a personal computer user can take information from optical disks, but the same user can't write new information to the disks. This auxiliary storage medium will nevertheless find increasing use as a way to distribute massive amounts of information, such as a disk-based academic encyclopedia, at low cost. Several manufacturers have released optical disk drives that read specially encoded compact disks, which are the same size as audio **compact discs** (CDs). This technology, which some expect to have enormous market potential, is known by the term **CD-ROM** (a read-only memory that uses compact disks).

The rapid decline in auxiliary storage costs has greatly increased the usability and power of personal computer systems. Ten and 20 megabyte fixed disk drives, for example, are now available for less than $500, and growing numbers of personal computers are equipped with them.

Magnetic Media No-Nos

Charles Johnson is a bit downcast today — as well he should be. He's just been posted to a branch office in the Mohave Desert, with orders to earn his commissions selling borax to hermits. The reason? He didn't make a copy of a data base of 10,000 customers kept on his PC's hard disk. And the disk drive crashed, taking all the data with it.

Auxiliary storage systems are the chief offenders in the annals of computer-assisted disaster. After all, it's difficult to erase a page of writing — you have to work at it. But it takes only a fraction of a second to wipe out all the information on a flexible or fixed disk, and with it could go hours, days, weeks, and even months of work.

You can easily protect yourself from such disasters by following three simple rules. The first rule to remember when using any magnetic storage medium is this: fear the magnetic field. Magnetic fields are, of course, produced by magnets, and this point encourages a healthy disdain for those cute little thingamajigs people like to stick to their refrigerators. But motors create magnetic fields too. Keep flexible disks at least one foot away from *anything* that might create a magnetic field, whether it's a ringing telephone or a personal cassette player. The second rule: avoid the pollutants of everyday life, such as dust, dirt, cigarette ashes, cola, and finger oil. You know that you shouldn't drink and drive; extend this rule to not drinking *anything* near a computer. Don't touch the surface of a disk; a fingerprint may hold meaning for Sherlock Holmes, but it won't for your disk drive. The third rule: *back up your work.* With flexible disk drive systems, you'll want to work with at least two drives; that way, it's easy to make a backup copy of a disk you're working with. Fixed disks present a major problem here. Since a smallish hard disk (10 megabytes) holds as much information as thirty-four flexible disks, it's a tedious job to back up everything on it. But it's essential to do so. Increasing numbers of fixed disk users are purchasing **streaming tape drives,** which back up the entire contents of a fixed disk on a single tape cartridge and do so at high speed.

INPUT DEVICES: GETTING INFORMATION INTO THE COMPUTER

Getting data into an abacus isn't much of a problem, since the abacus's arithmetic-logic unit (the hand) and its control unit (the brain) use human counting conventions. But computers work best with binary numbers, which use just two symbols: 0 and 1. Binary numbers are lengthy and people find them hard to read. For this reason, input and output devices are needed. Input devices take information that humans work with and code that information into binary numbers. Output devices do precisely the opposite; they decode binary numbers back into a form humans can read.

The ASCII Character Set. Several **coding systems** have been devised that automate the translation between decimal and binary notation. The coding system used with most personal computers is called the **ASCII** code (short for American Standard Code for Information Interchange), a coding system that is widely used for representing data with personal computers. The ASCII code represents the numbers 0 through 9, for example, using an eight-place binary number.

	Digits
1	0011 0000
2	0011 0001
3	0011 0010

Since there are $2^8 = 256$ possible combinations of these eight binary digits, there's room in the ASCII code for many more symbols than just the ten numbers 0 through 9. So the ASCII character set includes uppercase and lowercase letters, punctuation symbols, and computer control codes as well.

	Letters
A	0100 0001
B	0100 0010
C	0100 0011

Each of the eight-digit ASCII codes is called a character. A character can be a letter, a number, or a punctuation mark.

Personal Computer Input Devices. A wide variety of input devices are available for personal computers (Figure 3–10), but by far the most frequently used is the keyboard. A computer keyboard looks very much like a typewriter's, save for a few extra keys and some that have a function unique to computers (Figure 3–11).

Among the extra keys are the following:

Cursor Control Keys. These keys (also called arrow keys) control the movement of the **cursor** on the screen. The cursor, usually a blinking rectangle, vertical line, or underline character, shows where characters will appear on the screen when typed at the keyboard. The **cursor control keys** help you position the cursor on the screen. To indicate their function, these keys have arrows printed on them that show where they'll move the cursor (up, down, left, or right). Cursor movements are **nondestructive,** that is, the cursor does not rub out the characters it passes over.

Command Keys. These keys, such as **escape key (ESC), control key (CTRL),** and **alternate key (ALT),** redefine the keyboard so that you may enter commands using two or more keys. To understand how these keys work, think of what happens when you depress and hold down the SHIFT key on a typewriter. Doing so changes letters from lower case to upper case. The escape, control, and alternate keys work in much the same way; pressing them and then pressing another letter on the keyboard sends the computer

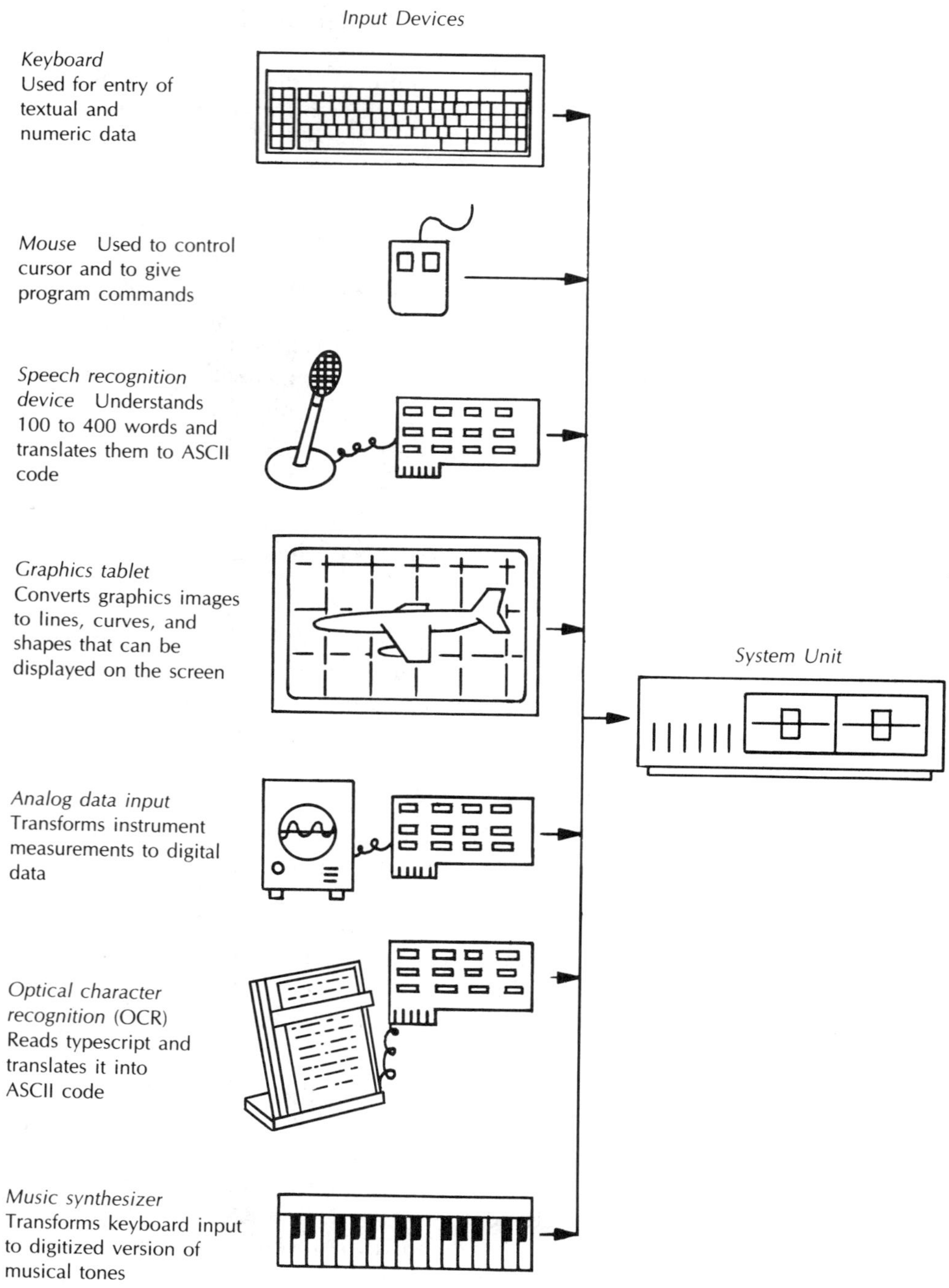

FIGURE 3–10 Input Devices

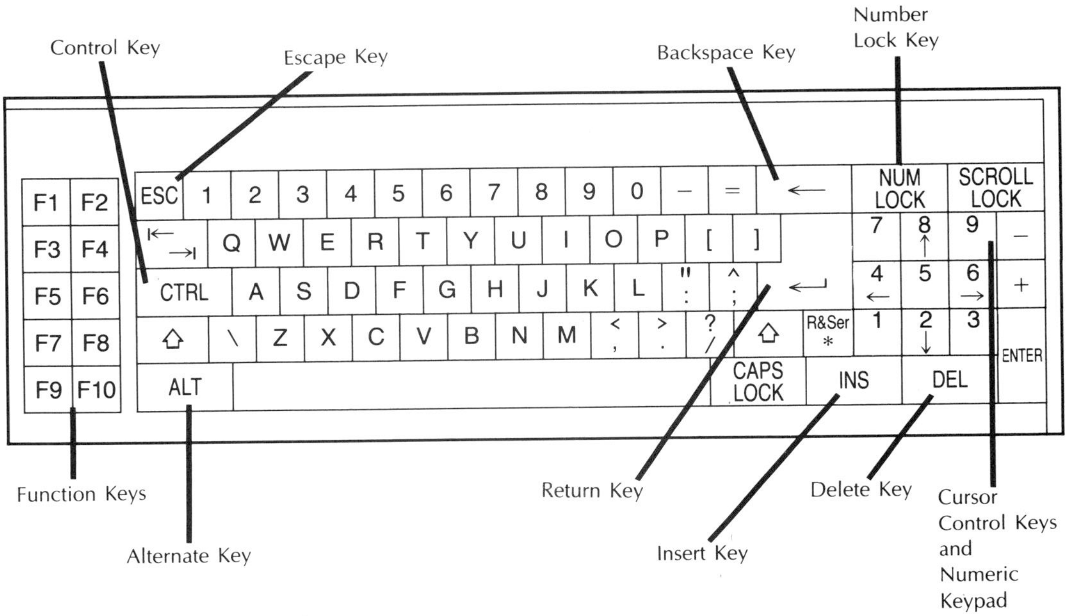

FIGURE 3–11 IBM Personal Computer Keyboard

a different signal than the one that would be sent if you hadn't used the command key. Almost all operating systems and application programs have their own distinct set of keyboard commands using **command keys** (such as CONTROL-C, ESCAPE-X, or ALTERNATE-Z). A major part of learning how to use this software is memorizing each program's list of these commands. Notice that, with most computers, it is necessary to hold down the control or alternate keys while pressing the command's second key (for instance, in the word processing program WordStar, you delete a line by holding down the control key and pressing Y). You need not hold down the escape key, however. Just press it, release it, and press the second key.

Delete Key. The **delete key,** with most computers, erases the character on which the cursor is positioned. Programs can use it for other functions, too.

Function Keys. Some computers have **function keys** (usually called F1, F2, F3, and so on), which can be used by application programs for program control purposes. If you press the F8 key while using the word processing program Microsoft Word, for instance, you will find that the word to the right of the cursor has been highlighted in reverse video. Now that it has been highlighted or selected, you can delete it with one keystroke.

Numeric Keypad. The **numeric keypad** uses a standard format for the high-speed, one-handed entry of numerical data. Many computers make the numeric keys serve as cursor control keys as well; a number lock (abbreviated numlck) key toggles or switches the numeric keypad back and forth between its two modes (controlling the cursor and entering numbers).

Some keys familiar to typists function differently on the computer keyboard:

Backspace Key. On a typewriter, pressing the backspace key is like using the left arrow key on a computer; it moves the typewriter's "cursor" left (without destroying the text it passes over). On a computer, the **backspace key** is usually **destructive;** that is, it rubs out characters as it moves left. The backspace key, in other words, is more like the automatic correction key found on some typewriter keyboards. It is very handy for correcting errors as they occur.

Return Key. Also called the enter key, the return key does not, of course, "return the carriage," for there's no carriage on a computer or its printer. The computer's return key is used in two ways. When used with the computer's operating system, pressing the return key sends a typed command to the computer's central processing unit (CPU). When used with a word processing program or some other program that allows text entry, pressing return starts a new paragraph. In Chapter 4 we discuss the return key's uses in word processing.

Another input device widely used for personal computers is the **mouse** (Figure 3–12), a hand-held computer control device that is designed to roll about on the desktop. As it rolls, its movements are reflected in the movement

FIGURE 3–12 Mouse

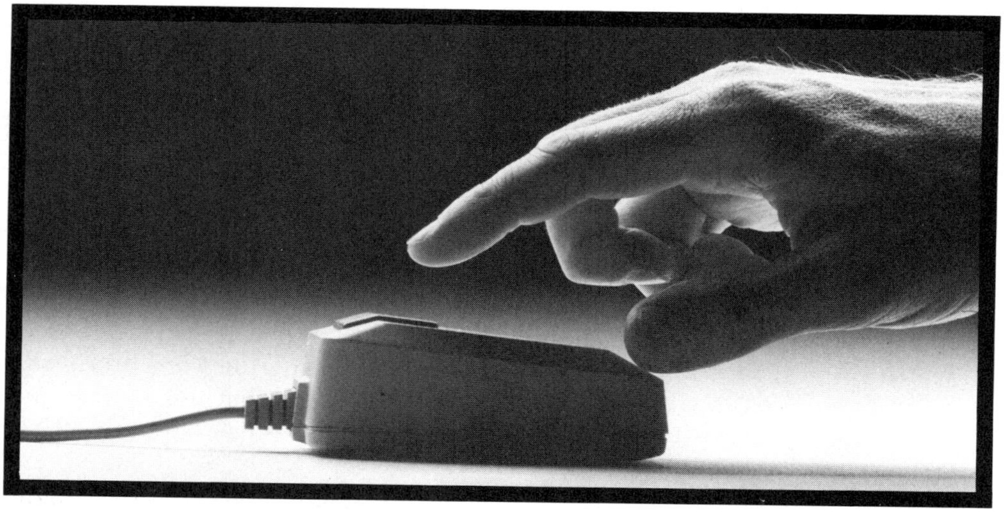

of a small arrow, or pointer, on the screen. Mice come equipped with one, two, or three buttons, which are used for command purposes.

The mouse is conveniently used for computer operations that involve selecting an item from a menu of options displayed on the screen, pointing at something on the screen, or highlighting an area of the screen in reverse video. To select an item from a menu, for example, you simply use the mouse to point at the item you want and click the button. One reason the mouse is so easy to use lies in the very high degree of hand-eye coordination humans possess. A substantial portion of our brain, in fact, is devoted to hand-eye coordination, and this portion differs from the one that controls conscious thought and spoken language. All this means that you can use the mouse to enter commands without having to think about what you're doing. For this reason, it is very easy to enter commands (and perform other computer operations) using a mouse.

OUTPUT DEVICES: VIEWING THE RESULTS OF PROCESSING OPERATIONS

All personal computers are designed to work with video display units, printers, and other output devices (Figure 3–13).

Video Display Units. Computer video display units, also called **monitors,** use the same cathode ray tube (CRT) technology that goes into the making of home television sets. In both, a cathode or electron gun shoots electrons at a screen coated with phosphor, causing individual dots (**pixels,** or *pi*cture *el*ements) to glow or not to glow (Figure 3–14). But home TVs don't work very well as computer monitors; they don't have adequate **resolution** — the ability to display information clearly and crisply on the screen. Resolution is measured by the number of horizontal and vertical lines that can be shown on the screen.

Monochrome Monitors. **Monochrome monitors** display computer output in one color only, usually green or amber against a jet-black background. A more recent trend is to use black text on a white background, simulating the reflective properties of brightly lit white papers on a desktop.

Color Monitors. Color monitors use three electron streams, corresponding to red, green, and blue. These colors can be combined to make a palette with sixteen or more colors, creating impressive-looking graphics. Yet all save the most expensive color monitors are significantly lower in resolution than monochrome ones. The best color monitors are **RGB monitors,** which have separate picture generators for each of the three basic colors (red, green, and blue).

Printers. The three most popular types of printers for personal computing are dot-matrix printers, letter-quality printers, and laser printers.

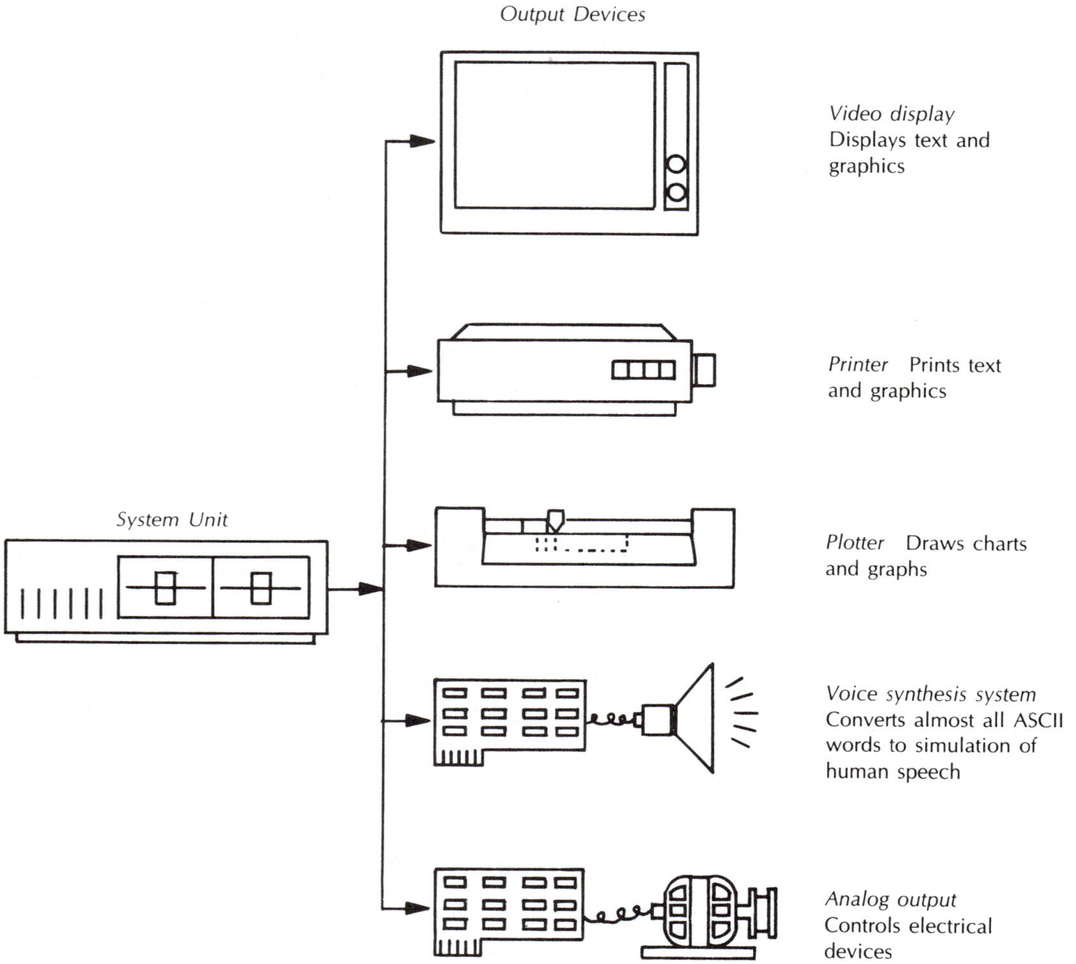

FIGURE 3–13 Output Devices

Dot-Matrix Printers. The least expensive computer printers, **dot-matrix printers,** form an image by extruding a pattern or matrix of tiny wires which strikes a ribbon, forming a character made up of tiny dots (Figure 3–15). The result is a matrix of dots printed on the page (Figure 3–16). Although dot-matrix printers work very rapidly (some print as many as 200 characters per second), the print quality is low. Some of them compensate for low quality by making repeated passes over the same material, filling in the space between the dots. This technique produces what printer companies call **near-letter-quality** results. Major advantages of dot-matrix printers are their ability to print graphic images as well as text and their low cost.

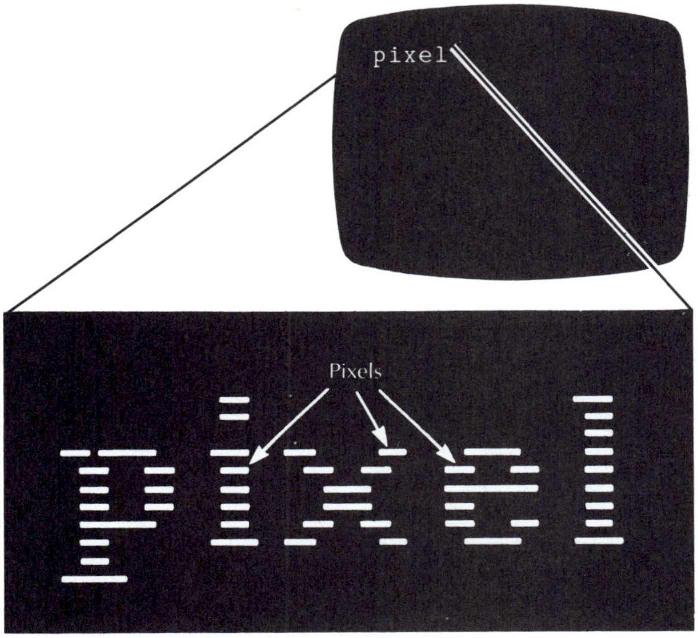

FIGURE 3–14 Pixels

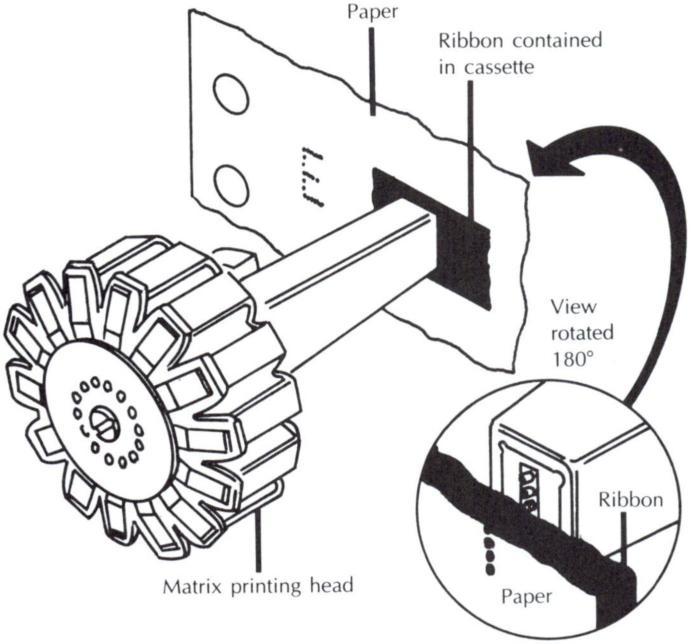

FIGURE 3–15 Dot-Matrix Printer Print Head

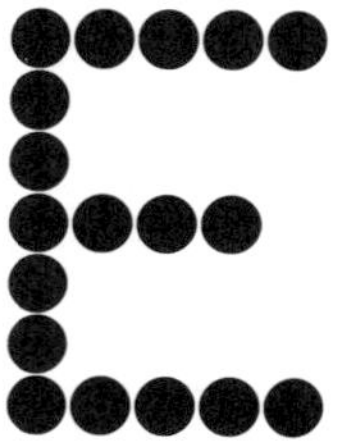

FIGURE 3–16 Dot-Matrix Printout (Magnified)

Letter-Quality Printers. **Letter-quality printers** simulate the typescript produced by a fine office typewriter. Like a typewriter, they work by striking an embossed, fully formed image of a character against a ribbon (Figure 3–17). Although quality is high, speeds are significantly lower than those of dot-matrix printers. A major disadvantage of letter-quality printers is their inability to print graphic images. Costs are low for slow printers; the faster ones cost two to three times the price of a dot-matrix printer.

Laser Printers. The newest type of personal computer printer is the **laser printer** (Figure 3–18), which is based on the technology used in office copying machines. A high-speed laser etches an image of the text to a rotating drum; the image is fused to the paper by a heat process. The result is a high-quality image that untrained eyes may not distinguish from the work of a professional printer. Laser printers work at high speeds (up to eight pages per minute), and they can print graphic images as well as text. Offsetting their advantages, however, is their high cost (which may exceed that of a personal computer).

Figure 3–19 shows samples of print produced by all three kinds of printers.

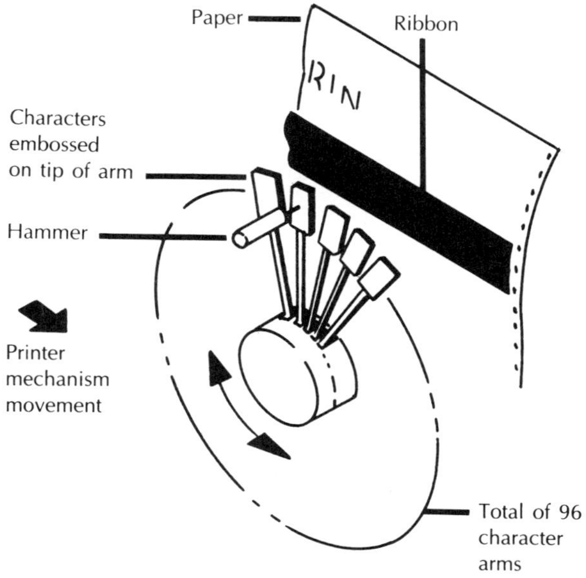

FIGURE 3–17 Letter-Quality Printer

FIGURE 3–18 Apple LaserWriter™ Printer (shown with Apple Macintosh)

FIGURE 3–19 Samples of Dot-Matrix, Letter-Quality, and Laser Printer Printouts

Dot-matrix printer (draft mode)

Dot-matrix printers can print 200 characters per second or more, but the quality of the typescript is poor.

Dot-matrix printer (near letter-quality mode)

When used in a near-letter quality mode, dot-matrix printers produce more acceptable results. However, dot-matrix printers can generate only about 25 to 50 characters per second in this mode.

Letter-quality printer

Letter-quality printers produce results indistinguishable from those of a fine, office-quality typewriter.

Laser printer

Laser printers can generate printouts that rival the quality of professionally-set type.

Laser printers can also generate printouts in a variety of type fonts and sizes. This font is called Palatino.

SYSTEM SOFTWARE: GETTING IT ALL TOGETHER

Buyers of "user-friendly" computer systems are more than dismayed when they find three or four 500 page manuals packed in with the hardware. In all likelihood, most of these pages are devoted to the system software — the many programs that control the computer system or help programmers develop new software. As a computer user (as opposed to a programmer), take heart: most of this material is irrelevant to your needs. You need know only a little about system software to use it effectively. The bulk of system software consists of tools for program development, and it won't be of concern for you unless you decide to get into programming in a big way.

Of major relevance to you, however, is the operating system, an indispensable program that manages the operation of the computer from moment to moment. Indeed, without it, the computer can't even operate. Normally, the very first thing you do when you turn on a personal computer is to insert the disk (called the **system disk**) that contains the computer's operating system. This act, called **booting the system,** loads the operating system into the computer's memory. You can't use the computer until you've booted it. To understand why, think of a taxi without a driver. By itself, the taxi is just a collection of parts that cannot work together to get you where you want to go; the driver is needed to work the controls. The operating system is like the taxi driver; it knows how to coordinate the parts of the computer so that you can use it for productive work. As this analogy suggests, operating systems are designed to work closely with system hardware. For this reason, a particular operating system usually works with just one type of microprocessor chip. CP/M-80, for example, an operating system made by Digital Research, Inc., is designed to work with chips conforming to the Intel 8080 standard.

Every personal computer operating system includes five program components, which fulfill five basic functions:

Supervisor. The **supervisor** supervises the flow of information inside the computer.

Input/Output Manager. The **input/output manager** manages the flow of information to and from input and output devices.

File Manager. The **file manager** stores and retrieves information on auxiliary storage devices such as disk drives.

Command Processor. The **command processor** handles user commands and presents error and other messages on the screen.

System Utilities. The **system utilities** provides utilities for day-to-day system maintenance.

The first two operating system functions, the supervisor and input/output manager, are automatic — as they must be, for the events they control happen far too fast for human intervention. The pages to follow survey the latter three functions, explaining what you need to know to use the operating system effectively.

THE FILE MANAGER: OPERATING THE DISK DRIVES

Obvious to the user are the auxiliary memory functions of the operating system, and for a simple reason: the file manager lets you control auxiliary memory devices (such as disk drives) through direct commands. You will use these commands to perform operations such as formatting blank disks, copying files for archival purposes, and deleting unwanted files. So prominent are these functions, in fact, that personal computer operating systems are usually called **disk operating systems** (DOS), even though they fulfill all five of the functions just listed.

Although the user controls disk drives using the operating system, it's not necessary to grasp the details of storage and retrieval processes. The details, actually, are rather disconcerting when you're working with valuable data. It's not at all uncommon for a disk drive to store data here and there all over the disk, wherever there's some extra room! So far as the user is concerned, however, a system's disk drives store data in unified **files,** each of which has its own name.

Device Independence. The file manager does more than merely mask the disconcerting details of information storage. It also masks the differences among auxiliary storage devices. A 10 megabyte fixed disk and a 360 kilobyte floppy drive, for instance, are very different machines. When both are connected to a single personal computer, however, the file manager lets the user treat both as if they were exactly the same (save that one stores many more files than the other one). This feature, called **device independence,** lets you do things such as substitute faster disk drives for slower ones without making changes to application programs. So far as you and your application programs are concerned, new devices — no matter how differently they operate from an electrical engineering standpoint — are just new, roomy places to put files.

Program Files and Data Files. As you work with operating systems, you'll find that all of them distinguish between two types of files:

> *Program Files.* The **program files** contain computer programs, such as a word processing program or spreadsheet program.
>
> *Data Files.* **Data files** contain work created with a program, such as a text document or a financial worksheet.

Program Disks and Data Disks. You will quickly learn, too, that it's easy to fill up floppy disks. Not all programs cope well with full disks, so you should take care to work with disks on which there's still plenty of room. For convenience and safe operation, it's wise to distinguish between **program disks** (disks that contain only one application program) and **data disks** (disks that contain data files). Do not store data files on program disks. When a data disk gets about three-quarters full, put it away and start using a new, blank one to store new files. That way you won't risk a program's crashing on you because you've run out of disk space.

Formatting Disks. The file manager helps you prepare new disks for use with your computer. This preparation process, called **formatting,** is necessary before you can use new, blank disks to store and retrieve information. The formatting process is necessary because new, blank disks do not contain the necessary magnetic patterns for storing information. These patterns must be laid down by the disk drive's read/write head before the disk can be used.

THE COMMAND PROCESSOR: COMMUNICATING WITH THE USER

A computer equipped for interactive processing engages you in a dialogue. You give the computer **commands;** it carries them out — and as it does, it tells you that it has done so successfully or gives you an error message telling you that something has gone wrong. The part of the operating system that handles this dialogue, the command processor, is responsible for the operating system's user interface: its method of mediating between the user and the system's hardware.

Prompts. Prompts are messages that request action from the user. You will quickly learn to recognize the **system prompt,** which tells you that the operating system has been successfully loaded into the computer's memory and is waiting for your command. By convention, the system prompt is often a "greater-than" sign (>).

Default Drive. Your computer system can be connected (or **logged on**) to only one auxiliary memory device at any one time. The current device is called the **default drive.** The operating system will automatically assume, in default of receiving other instructions, that you want to store and retrieve information from the default drive. Most systems let you know, one way or another, which drive is the current default drive. The IBM Personal Computer's operating system (PC-DOS), for instance, marries the default drive indicator and the system prompt. The message A>, for instance, tells you that the default drive is A and that the operating system is ready to receive a command (indicated by the symbol >).

File Names. Command-line operating systems typically use two-part names for files.

Primary File Name. The first part of the file name, the **primary file name,** consists of from one to eight letters, numbers, or punctuation symbols. (Not all the keys on the keyboard, however, can be used for primary file names. Some characters are illegal in file name creation and their use will generate an error message.) Examples of valid file names with PC-DOS, the IBM Personal Computer's operating system, are CHAPTER1, 5-31-87, and FILE#39. Primary file names are used to identify the material stored in the file.

Extension. The **extension,** a file name suffix of up to three letters, characters, or punctuation symbols, is optional. Extensions are often used to indicate what kind of material the file contains. Here are some customs of extension use: DOC (a word processing document), TXT (text in ASCII format), WRK (spreadsheet), COM (compiled program).

The primary file name and extension must be separated by a period, as in

```
CHAPTER1.DOC
```

Giving Commands: Command-Line Operating Systems. Most personal computer operating systems require you to type a line of commands at the keyboard (that's why they're called **command-line operating systems**). You'll have to memorize several of these commands so that you'll be able to use them without looking them up. What's more, you'll have to learn how to use a rather persnickety set of rules about typing the commands correctly.

Many commands have two parts:

Keyword. **Keyword** is a single verb such as PRINT, TYPE, or DELETE; and

Parameter or *Argument.* **Parameter** or **argument** is an object for the verb, such as a file name, that tells the operating system how to perform the function and what to do it to.

The command DELETE ESSAY1.TXT, for example, tells the operating system to erase the file ESSAY1.TXT.

File Specification. Often it is necessary, when using command-line operating systems, to provide the computer with precise information about where a file is located. If the file is on the disk contained in the default drive, there's no problem; the computer will assume that it's there and act accordingly. But if the file is contained in a disk other than the default drive, you must include a **file specification,** or an "address" telling the computer where the file is located, when you type in the file's name.

Command-line operating systems usually handle file specifications using a prefix on the file name. The prefix includes the letter corresponding to the drive on which the file is located (for instance, B for Drive B) and a colon (:), which tells the computer that the letter just typed is a file specification. Combined with a file name, a valid file specification looks like this:

```
B:CHAPTER1.TXT
```

A typed command can go wrong in several ways. You have to use exactly the right number of spaces or other symbols, called **delimiters,** or else the operating system will misunderstand the command. In many circumstances, you must be very specific about where the file you want altered is located. If you forget to tell the computer which disk drive to use, for instance, the operation may fail — or have unanticipated consequences. On the positive side, you have to learn only a few of these commands, and once you get the hang of it you'll make mistakes only occasionally. And as you'll see, the command processor presents confirmation messages to keep you from doing anything really catastrophic.

Confirmation Messages. A good operating system asks you for confirmation when you give a potentially dangerous command, such as the one that erases a whole disk:

```
ARE YOU SURE? Y/N
```

Error Messages. If something does go wrong, the command processor displays an error message, such as:

```
INSUFFICIENT DISK SPACE
```

Ideally, the command processor should present error messages in a language resembling English. After all, personal computers are designed to put an information system's power in the hands of people who aren't trained in computer science or data processing. Unfortunately, operating system error messages are often unnecessarily cryptic, obscure, or unhelpful.

Giving Commands: Object-Oriented Systems. The preceding discussion has made no attempt to disguise an unfortunate fact about personal computing: command-line operating systems present first-time computer users with a hurdle. They can't start using their computers fruitfully, moreover, until they get over it. To put it another way, command-line operating systems aren't very user-friendly; they make demands on the user that could have been avoided.

Research at Xerox's Palo Alto Research Center (PARC), a sophisticated computer think tank, suggests that operating systems should be visual (instead of textual, the way command-line systems are). Research on human cognition — that is, how we acquire knowledge and understand things — shows that people grasp the meaning of graphic images far faster than they grasp the meaning of text. The old adage "A picture is worth a thousand words" is absolutely correct. For this reason, PARC researchers advocate what they call an **object-oriented operating system.** Object-oriented operating systems first appeared with the Xerox Star information system, and Apple brought the idea to the personal computing world with its Macintosh computer. Such a system represents computer programs, files, and operations using familiar, everyday objects on the screen. A data file, for instance, is symbolized by a file folder and a word processing program by a hand writing on a piece of paper. At a glance, you can tell right away what's available on the system (Figure 3–20).

In comparison to object-oriented operating systems, command-line operating

FIGURE 3–20 Object-Oriented Operating System (Apple Macintosh)

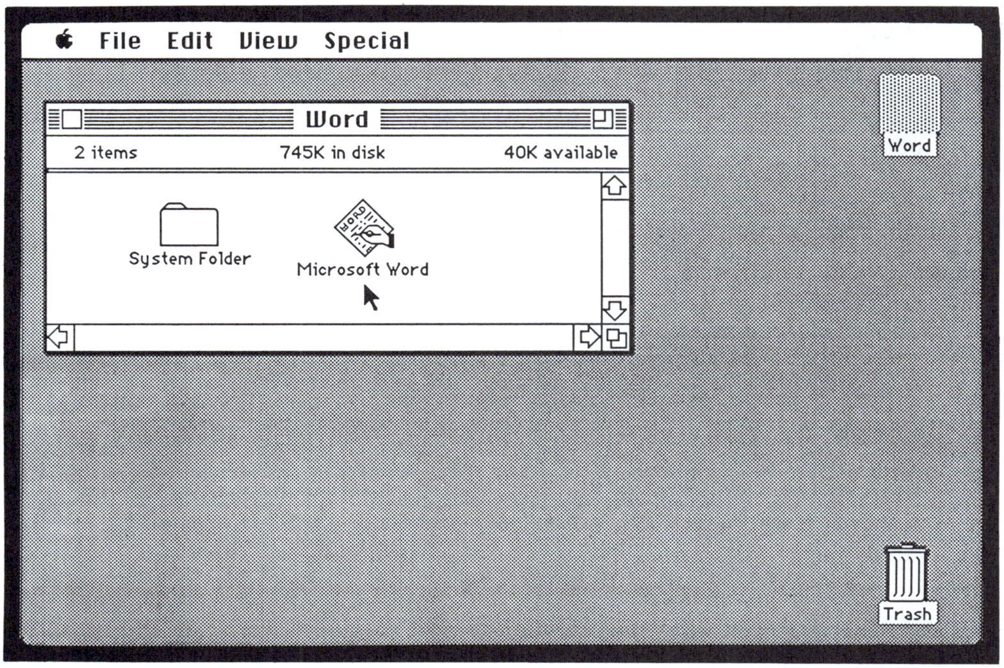

systems seem to have been made deliberately difficult. (Just pondering the terms *delimiters* and *parameters* is enough to convince anyone that these systems were hardly intended for general, public use!) Even so, it should be remembered that you need learn only a few commands and a few rules of command-line syntax to use a command-line system very effectively.

It should be remembered, too, that although a visual operating system makes personal computers easier to use, that in itself doesn't make a computer useful. To be useful for ordinary people, a personal computer needs to be equipped with a variety of application programs. The personal computer that meets your needs isn't necessarily the one that's easiest to use; it's the one for which the right application software is available.

SYSTEM UTILITIES: TOOLS FOR DAY-TO-DAY WORK

Personal computer operating systems are most frequently used for the following tasks:

Formatting new disks;

Copying and deleting disk files;

Finding out what's on disks; and

Running application programs.

System Utilities. System utilities help you do these tasks. They are of two kinds, resident and transient.

Resident Utilities. **Resident utilities** are part of the operating system itself. That means they're loaded automatically when you boot the system. You can use these utilities any time you see the system prompt. Most operating systems include at least the following resident utilities:

Switch Drives. Since only one disk drive can be online at once, a command is needed to disconnect one drive and move to the other. The **switch drive command** serves this purpose (Figure 3–21).

Directory. What's on a disk? The **directory command** tells you. After you give the command, the operating system presents a **disk directory** on the screen (Figure 3–22). All the disk's files are shown, together with the space they take up (in bytes or kilobytes) and the free space remaining.

Copy. The **copy command** copies a file from one disk to another (Figure 3–23). Using it, and using it often, is essential for personal computer productivity. All work done with the computer should be regularly and routinely copied to backup disks.

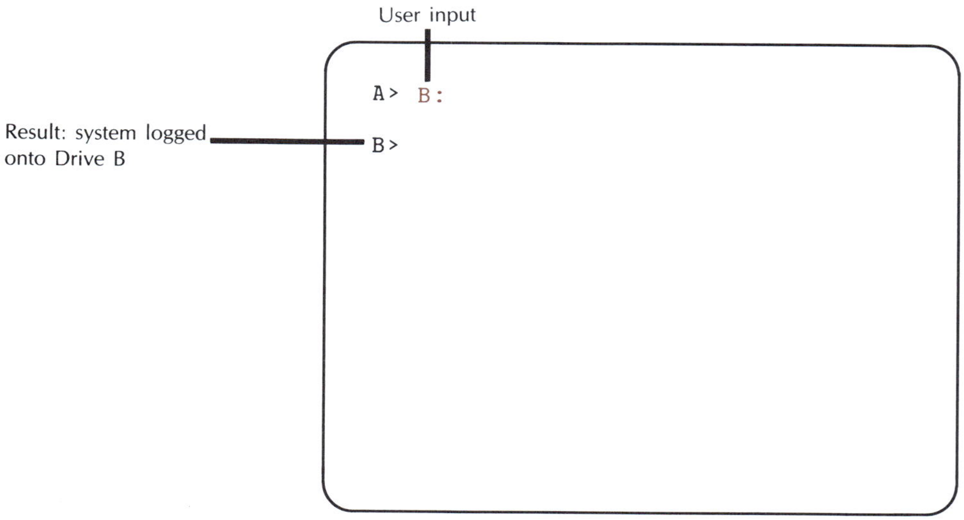

FIGURE 3–21 Switch Drives Command (PC-DOS)

FIGURE 3–22 DIR Command (PC-DOS)

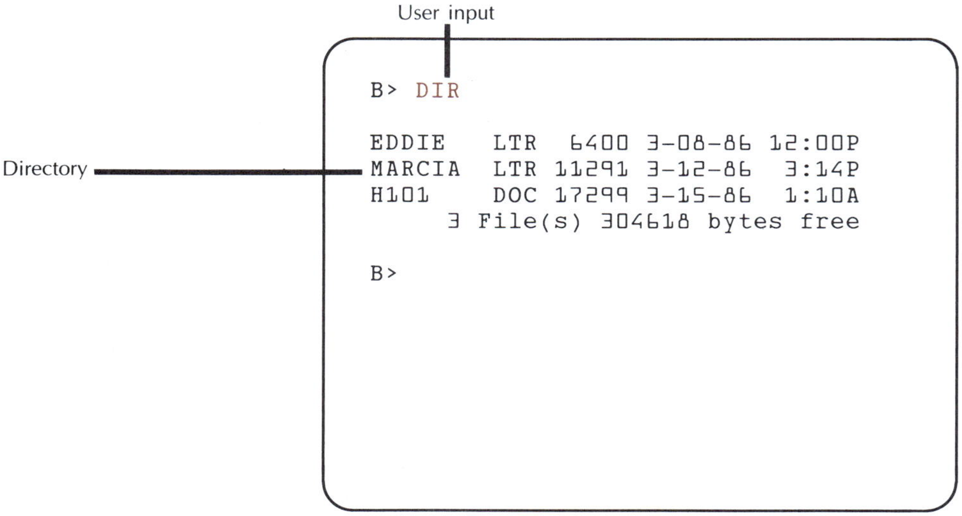

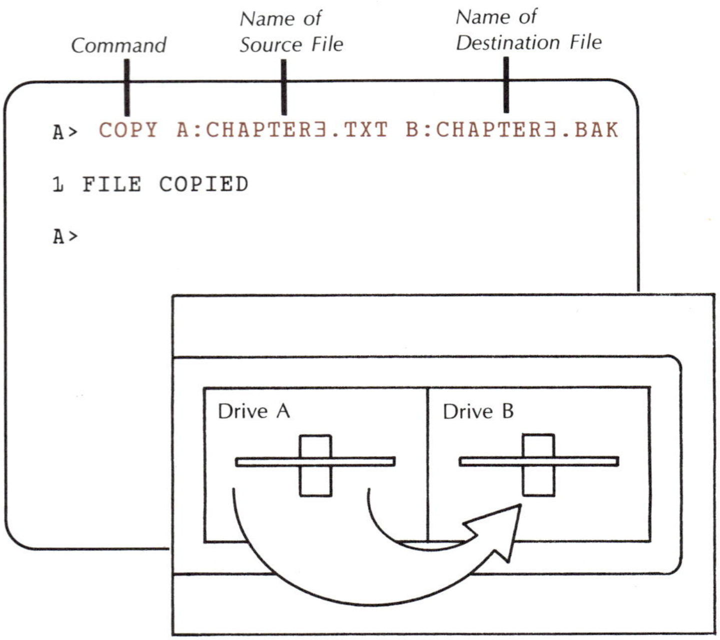

FIGURE 3–23 Copy Command (PC-DOS)

Erase. The **erase command** deletes unwanted files from a disk.

Load Program. The **load program command** transfers a ready-to-run program from a disk to the internal memory (Figure 3–24). When the program has been loaded, it takes over the computer. Actually, the disk operating system is still present in the memory, and the program makes use of it. When you terminate the program, control of the computer is returned to the operating system, and the system prompt reappears.

Reset System. Sometimes it is desirable to clear the computer's memory and start over from scratch. Sometimes programs fail or crash, locking up the keyboard, and you cannot continue to work. In such situations, the **reset command** permits you to clear the memory and start over. A reset is often called a **warm boot,** since it duplicates the effect of starting the system from scratch (booting it) except that the system is already switched on. (A **cold boot,** in contrast, occurs automatically when you turn the computer on.)

Transient Utilities. **Transient utilities** are not part of the operating system program. On the contrary, they're programs, just like application programs, that must be present on a disk in one of the drives before they can be used. (They are called transient because they move around with the disk they're on.) Transient utilities include the following programs:

Disk Format. With most personal computers, you must format new disks before you can use them in the computer. The **disk format program** does this job. Note that few standards exist for this formatting operation. One computer formats disks so that they will hold only 130K of information; another puts 1200K of information on a disk of the same size. This lack of formatting standards is a further reason that software made for one computer will probably not run on another.

Disk Copy. The resident copy command copies one file at a time. Some disk operating systems include **disk copy programs** that copy a whole disk at a time. Using a disk backup program regularly can help prevent data losses.

Unerase. Not usually included with operating systems, but available as an optional accessory program, is an **unerase program.** If used immediately after erasing a file, this program can restore the lost information.

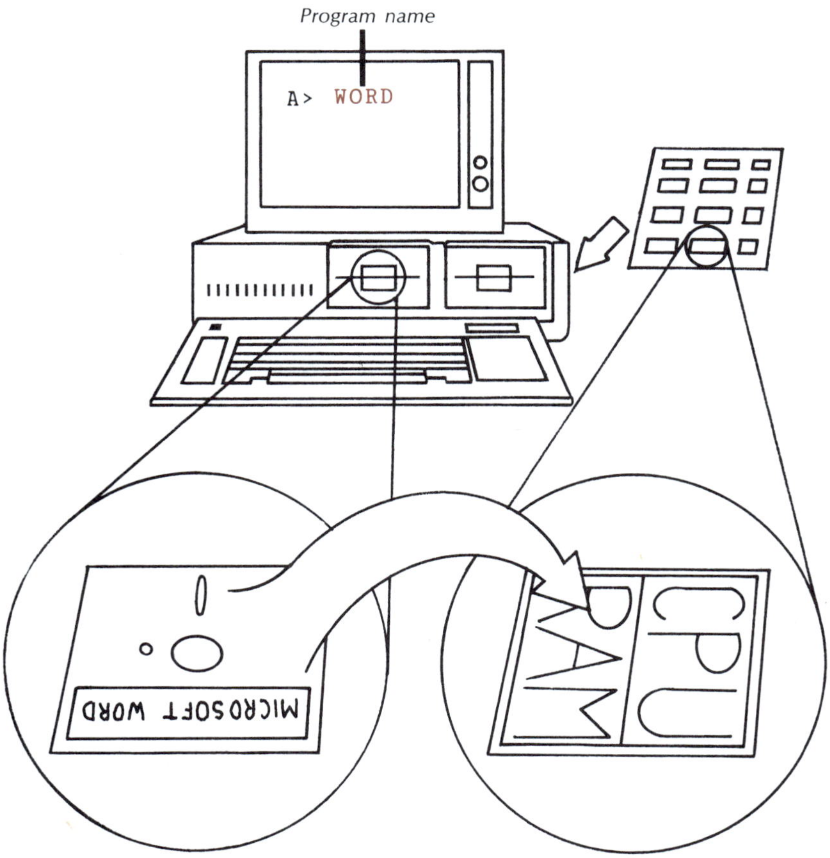

FIGURE 3–24 Loading a Program from Disk to Memory (PC-DOS)

A Survey of Personal Computer Operating Systems

Personal computer operating systems are of two kinds, **proprietary** and **nonproprietary.** Proprietary operating systems are produced by a manufacturer for its own brand of computers (and no one else's). Nonproprietary systems are those intended for two or more brands of computers. Proprietary systems, although far from dead, are on the wane in personal computing, and for reasons that have to do with simple economics.

To understand why, you need to know that an application program must be developed with a particular operating system in mind, because the application program must take over the operating system and use its functions. Now let's suppose there are two computers on the market, Computer A and Computer B, each with its own proprietary operating system (System A and System B). You're a third-party software supplier, and you're interested in marketing your program. When you look into the situation, however, you find that you have to create two versions, one for Computer A (and System A) and another for Computer B (and System B). That's expensive, so you might decide to chuck the whole idea. Now suppose that both computers A and B use a nonproprietary operating system, System Z. You can create just one version of the program, and it will run on both computers — a much more attractive proposition.

Computers with proprietary operating systems, in short, aren't likely to attract a large pool of software unless software suppliers are convinced that huge numbers of the computers will be sold. In a few cases, such as the Apple Macintosh (which has a proprietary system), the numbers look good to software suppliers. But most personal computers use nonproprietary operating systems.

Here's an overview of the chief nonproprietary operating systems in the personal computer world.

CP/M-80. CP/M (short for Control Program for Microcomputers) is the 1973 creation of Gary Kildall, who at the time was an employee of Intel Corporation. In 1975, Kildall left Intel to found Digital Research, Inc. CP/M-80, an operating system designed for Intel 8080-standard microprocessors (including the Zilog Z-80), quickly became a standard in the world of 8 bit computing, which flourished from 1975 until 1984. CP/M is a command-line operating system.

MS-DOS. In 1981, IBM approached Kildall for an operating system to be used with its new Personal Computer. Kildall, however, wasn't in his office, and the IBM executives, piqued, went to Bill Gates's Microsoft Corporation instead. Microsoft quickly came up with MS-DOS, an operating system for the Intel 8088 chip that powers the IBM Personal Computer. When sold by IBM, MS-DOS is called PC-DOS. MS-DOS is a command-line operating system that resembles CP/M-80 very closely.

UNIX. Developed in 1971 by two scientists at AT&T's Bell Laboratories, UNIX is a sophisticated operating system that supports time-sharing. What is more, UNIX can run several programs at the same time (it is, in other words, a **multitasking operating system**). Some experts believe UNIX to represent the wave of the future in personal computing. Others believe the operating system to be completely unsuitable for personal computers; current versions are notorious for their user-unfriendliness. A more balanced view focuses on UNIX's merits as a multiple-user operating system. Where several users will share time on a central microcomputer, UNIX makes sense. As an operating system for single-user systems, it doesn't.

APPLICATION SOFTWARE: THE KEY TO PRODUCTIVITY

Personal computer hardware and operating systems provide the gateway to application software, the key to personal productivity. What makes the personal computer so useful as a personal productivity tool is the existence of high-quality application programs. In Part Two, we'll meet and explore the first of the application packages featured in this book: word processing software.

SUMMARY

A personal computer system consists of hardware, system software, and application software. You do not need an electronic technician's knowledge of hardware or a programmer's knowledge of system software to use a personal computer effectively. However, you will need some practical expertise to find your way through the personal computer world.

You can understand a great deal about any personal computer's power and usefulness by knowing which microprocessor it uses, how much internal memory can be installed, and what kind of auxiliary memory devices it uses. Personal computers with 16 bit and 32 bit microprocessors process information rapidly. Large memories (256K or more) allow for more complex programs, and these programs may be easier to use because more room is available for user-friendly features. Systems equipped with two flexible disk drives or one flexible and one fixed disk drive are convenient to use. Although disk drives make for convenient operation, they must be used carefully to avoid data losses.

Input and output devices round out a personal computer system. Keyboards are the most common input devices. Output devices include monochrome and color video displays and three kinds of printers (dot-matrix, letter-quality, and laser).

System software manages the whole computer system and performs many functions. Happily, you as a computer user need worry only about the functions and commands pertaining to the computer's disk drives. Personal computer operating systems are often called disk operating systems (DOS), indicating the visible role of these disk-related operations. The operating systems store information on disks in the form of named files, which are units of related information, and they provide tools for using files, disks, and disk drives. Among these tools are commands for switching drives, viewing a disk directory, copying files, erasing files, loading programs, and resetting the system.

Operating systems are of two kinds, command-line and object-oriented. Command-line operating systems require the user to type a command at the keyboard. Theyseem very difficult to use at first, but after a little experience using the computer they become easy. Object-oriented operating systems make the learning process much easier. What makes a computer system useful for ordinary people, however, isn't so much how easy the operating system is to use; it's how much application software is available for the computer.

KEY TERMS

access time
alternate (ALT) key
argument
ASCII
backspace key
booting the system
byte
CD-ROM
character
coding system
cold boot
command
command keys
command-line operating system
command processor
compact disc (CD)
control (CTRL) key
copy command
cursor
cursor control keys
data disk
data file
data transfer rate
default drive
delete key
delimiter
destructive
device independence
direct access
directory command
disk copy program
disk directory
disk drive
disk format program
disk operating system (DOS)
dot-matrix printer
erase command
escape (ESC) key
extension
file
file manager
file specification
floppy disk
formatting
function keys
gigabyte
hard disk
incompatible
input/output manager
instruction set
keyword
kilobyte
laser printer
letter-quality printer
load program command
log on
megabyte
memory address
monitor
monochrome monitor
mouse
multitasking operating system
near-letter-quality
nondestructive
nonproprietary operating system
nonvolatile
numeric keypad
object-oriented operating system

optical disk
parameter
pixel
primary file name
program disk
program file
proprietary operating system
random access
random-access memory (RAM)
read
read-only memory (ROM)
read-only storage medium
read/write head
read/write memory
reset command
resident utilities
resolution
RGB monitor
sequential access
streaming tape drives
supervisor
switch drive command
system disk
system prompt
system utilities
transient utilities
unerase program
volatile
warm boot
wild card
write

REVIEW QUESTIONS AND EXERCISES

1. Why is it fruitful to think of a computer system as a round ball with several layers? Hint: What does the analogy mean to you, the user?
2. What is the key to any microcomputer's electronic "personality"?
3. Name three microprocessor design elements that determine a microprocessor's processing capabilities, such as its processing speed and the amount of internal memory it can use.
4. Why does a 16 bit microprocessor process information more rapidly than an 8 bit microprocessor?
5. Why, for all practical purposes, are the terms *byte* and *character* synonymous in the personal computer world?
6. Make up a chart contrasting the processing capabilities of the Zilog Z-80, MOS Technology 6502, Intel 8088, Intel 80286, and Motorola 68000 chips. Which would you prefer for your own computer system? Why? Hint: Which is more important, speed or the ability to use a large internal memory?
7. Why is it unlikely that a computer using a MOS Technology 6502 microprocessor can run a program created for the IBM Personal Computer, which uses the Intel 8088 chip?
8. What's the difference between RAM and ROM?
9. You're sitting at your computer, and you've written 10 pages of a 15-page term paper — without saving it to disk. You hear thunder in the distance. What do you do? Why?

10. Why are disk drives preferable to cassette tapes as an auxiliary storage medium? (Hint: Contrast *sequential* and *random* access.)
11. What are the advantages of hard disks compared to floppy disks?
12. What information products would you expect to see released on CD-ROM disks?
13. What are the three rules for safeguarding your work when using magnetic auxiliary storage media?
14. Make a chart identifying the special keys on your computer's keyboard (the ones which do not appear on a typewriter's keyboard or which have functions that differ from those of their typewriter equivalents).
15. What are the advantages (and disadvantages) of each of the three major types of personal computer printers? Which would you prefer for your own work? Why?
16. A friend of yours buys a computer and is dismayed when, while unpacking the box, she finds a 600-page manual for the operating system. What do you say to her that reassures her?
17. Why must an operating system be designed around a particular microprocessor?
18. Why is it that personal computer operating systems are often called *disk operating systems* (DOS) — even though they do much more?
19. What are the differences between a command-line operating system and an object-oriented operating system?
20. Why is it that even though an object-oriented operating system may make a personal computer easier to use, it does not necessarily make it useful?
21. What is the difference between transient and resident system utilities? Which of the resident utilities mentioned in the text are available with the operating system you're using? Which transient utilities are available?

FOR FURTHER READING

UNDERSTANDING PERSONAL COMPUTER HARDWARE

Braun, Ernest, and Stuart MacDonald. *Revolution in Miniature: The History and Impact of Semiconductor Electronics* (New York: Cambridge University Press, 1982).

Bylinsky, Gene. "Intel's Biggest Shrinking Job Yet," *Fortune* (May 3, 1982).

Frenzel, Louis E. *The Howard W. Sams Crash Course in Microcomputers* (Indianapolis: Howard W. Sams, 1980).

Kay, Alan C. "Microelectronics and the Personal Computer," *Scientific American* (September 1977).

Lu, Cary. "Microcomputers: the Second Wave," *High Technology* (September-October 1983).

Mayo, John S. "The Power of Microelectronics," *Technology Review* (January 1981).

Niles, Jack M. *Exploring the World of the Personal Computer* (Englewood Cliffs, N.J.: Prentice-Hall, 1982).

Noyce, Robert N. "Microelectronics," *Scientific American* (September 1977).
Rogers, Everett M., and Judith K. Larsen. *Silicon Valley Fever* (New York: Basic Books, 1984).
Toong, Hoo-Min D. "Microprocessors," *Scientific American* (September 1977).
White, Robert M. "Disk-Storage Technology," *Scientific American* (August 1980).

PERSONAL COMPUTER OPERATING SYSTEMS

Denning, Peter J., and Robert L. Brown. "Operating Systems," *Scientific American* (September 1984).
McGilton, Henry, and Rachel Morgan. *Introducing the UNIX System* (New York: McGraw-Hill, 1983).
Murtha, Stephen, and Mitchell Waite. *CP/M Primer* (Indianapolis: Howard W. Sams, 1980).
Ruff, Laura B., and Mary K. Weitzer. *Understanding and Using MS-DOS/PC-DOS* (St. Paul, Minn.: West Publishing, 1986).
Thomas, Rebecca, and Jean Yates. *A User Guide to the UNIX System* (Berkeley: Osborne/McGraw-Hill, 1982).

PART TWO

"The word processor is God's gift, or at least science's gift, to the tinkerers and the refiners and the neatness freaks. For me it was obviously the perfect new toy. I began playing on page 1 — editing, cutting, and revising — and have been on a rewriting high ever since. The burden of the years has been lifted."

William Zinsser

Word Processing: *Strategies for Writing*

Like the writing guru William Zinsser, writers everywhere are excited about word processing: about half of all American authors now use the technology. And what excites them is the malleability of electronic text. Instead of staining paper with ink, you enter text directly into a computer's memory, where it can be revised and redone until it's just the way you want it. The result? Major gains in productivity.

What's more, word processing can even improve writing quality, and in several ways. By making it easy to revise, word processing software encourages writers to continue revising and improving their work until they're satisfied with it. (Precomputer writing technologies punish revision. You'll appreciate this point immediately if you've ever retyped an eight-page paper!) Moreover, a host of word processing accessory programs, including style analysis and readability programs, provide electronic editorial assistance.

Perhaps you don't need any more convincing that word processing is a good thing. But is it for you? If you're like most college students, you're not planning on becoming a poet, novelist, or scholar, and you might think you don't need to worry about writing well and productively. Well, here's some news:

> Professional and technical workers in organizations spend nearly three times as many hours writing reports as they do performing analysis or

research. The average engineer, for example, writes approximately 800 pages each year, about the same as a doctoral candidate in the humanities.

Middle managers and executives spend up to one-fourth of their working day preparing documents (memos, letters, and reports). That's two solid hours of writing every day.

Top executives spend from 75 to 95 percent of their time communicating. Not surprisingly, executives consider writing to be the most important subject a student can study in college.

No matter what occupation or career you pursue, you're going to write. The question is, will you do so productively — and well?

Part 2 of this book presents a word processing strategy for the information society — a strategy that helps you realize word processing's promise of increased productivity and quality. Chapter 4, "Using Word Processing Software: Tools for Writing," introduces word processing technology. Chapter 5, "Advanced Word Processing: Beyond Electronic Typewriting," shows you how to maximize your word processing productivity while avoiding common pitfalls and lost work. Chapter 6, "Word Processing Horizons: Accessory Software You Can Use," introduces accessory programs that can help you achieve writing excellence.

4 *Using Word Processing Software:* Tools for Writing

"Most who use word processing programs agree that they never again want to be without one."

Judith Axler Turner Chronicle of Higher Education

All word processing programs do the same thing: they help writers create, edit, and print written work. To be sure, some word processing programs are simple, and others are complicated. Yet they all have a common core of basic functions, each designed to help you as you write, edit, and print. This chapter provides an overview of this common core.

You can use this chapter to help you learn a word processing program. Begin by finding the sheets entitled *Quick Reference Guide: Word Processing Basics*, which are positioned at the end of this book. Tear them out, and staple them or put them in a folder. Keep these sheets and your word processing program's manual (or your supplementary word processing textbook, if you're using one) handy as you read the chapter. When this chapter describes a basic function, such as loading an existing document or centering text, find out from your manual or supplementary text how to accomplish this function

with your program. Then make a note in the *Quick Reference Guide*. When you've finished filling out the *Quick Reference Guide*, keep it next to your computer. You'll find it helpful in day-to-day writing situations.

WRITING WITH WORD PROCESSING SOFTWARE: AN OVERVIEW

A typical session with a word processing program boils down to these steps (Figure 4–1):

Loading the Program. To begin a writing session with most personal computers, you turn on the computer, insert the disk containing the disk operating system (DOS), and wait until you receive the system prompt. Then you insert the disk containing your word processing program. With command-line operating systems, **loading the program** into the computer's internal memory is a simple process. You type the program's name (or an abbreviation of it) and press the RETURN key. To load WordStar, for example, you type WS and press RETURN. If you receive an error message, check to make sure that you have inserted the correct disk and spelled the program's name or abbreviation correctly.

Creating a New Document. After the program is successfully loaded, you're shown the **document display screen.** It contains a fresh, blank space for creating a new **document.** In word processing parlance, a document is a unit of written work created with a word processing program. The document may contain a poem, a letter, a short story, a technical journal article, or a novel. Notice that this usage is much broader than the everyday meaning of the word *document;* in ordinary usage, a document is a written work that is used to substantiate a claim of some sort, as in history or law.

Loading an Existing Document. If you wish, you may load a document you created and saved to disk in an earlier word processing session.

Writing. As you enter text, you don't have to worry about the right and bottom margins of the page. (If you've ever used a typewriter, you'll know right away why writers love this aspect of word processing!) Word processing programs handle **line breaks** and **page breaks** automatically. Line breaks are the places where a new line must be started to keep the text from going over the right margin; page breaks are the places where a new page must be started to keep the text from going beyond the bottom margin. As you

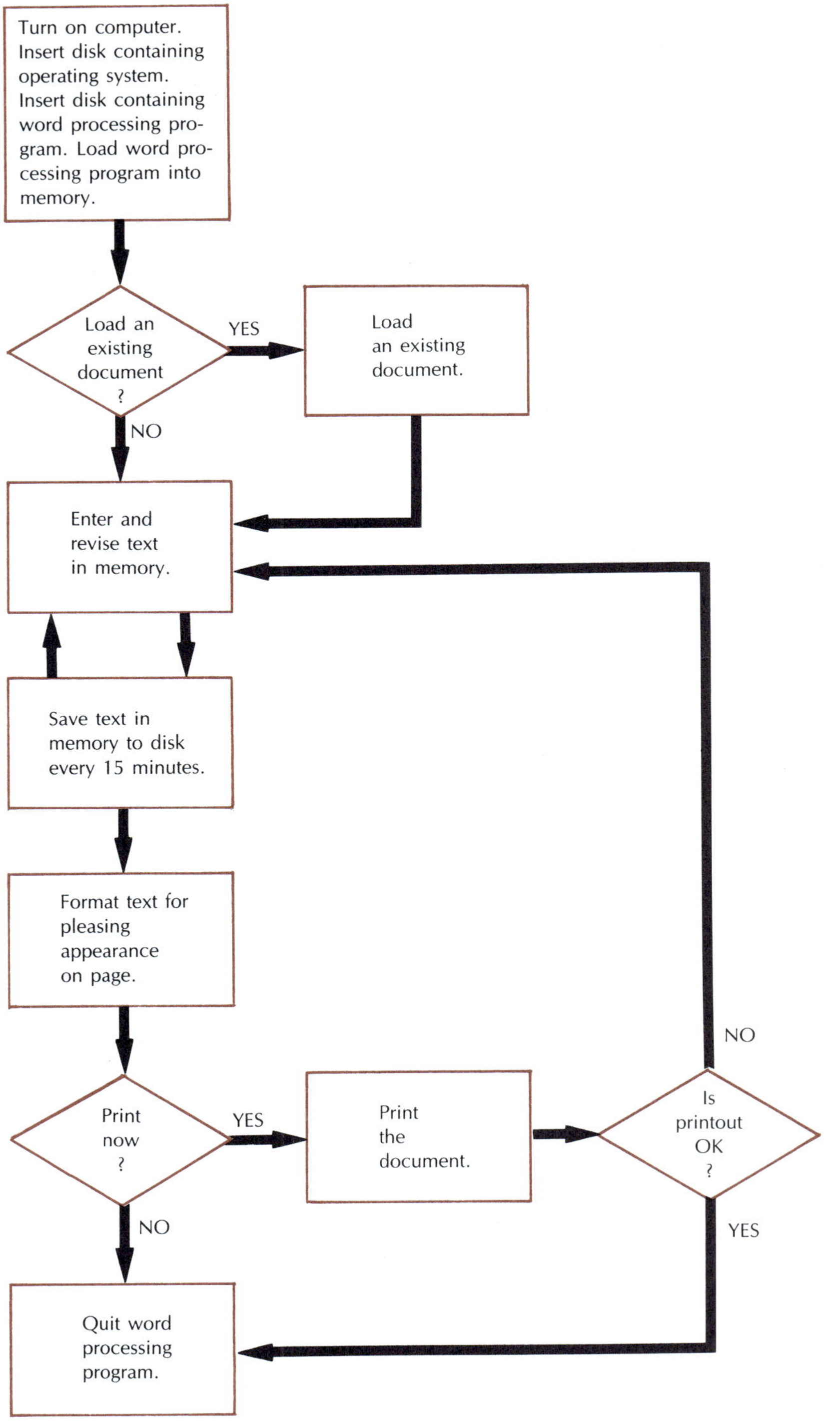

FIGURE 4–1 Typical Word Processing Session

If Zinsser Can Do It, So Can You

William Zinsser, editor of the Book-of-the-Month Club and experienced word processor, has this to say about his adventure with The Machine:

Maybe I'm not the last person in the world who would be expected to write with a word processor, but I'm one of the last. I belong to a generation of writers and editors who think of paper and pencil as holy objects. I taught myself to type at the age of ten and ever since have been banging out words onto paper, and then crossing them out and penciling other words in, and then retyping what I had revised. The feel of paper is important to me. I have always thought that a writer should have physical contact with the materials of his craft — that he should be able to spread out his notes and his early drafts and to work on them with his sacred pencil.

So how does it happen that I find myself tapping out these words on a computer keyboard and watching them appear on a terminal screen? The screen is black and the words are green — hardly my usual colors — and I have no paper anywhere. I have separated myself from paper. I'm wholly in the hands of a machine. I don't even like machines. I am not mechanical. I don't understand how mechanical objects work, and I can't fix things with my hands. I never was the typical American boy who had to have the latest gadget. Gadgets fluster me. I can't open a childproof medicine bottle. I never know which button to push — or is it pull? — at the laundromat. . . . Am I the only American car driver . . . who can't figure out how to heat or cool the car? The lever that operates this mechanism is in a slot that offers these choices: COOL, NORM-MAX, AVG, HI-LO, VENT, and HEAT. How can one selection give me both HI and LO? How does HI differ from HEAT, or from MAX? What is VENT doing in this spectrum of temperatures? Who is NORM?

For such a mechanical boob to decide to write on a word processor would seem to be a sure invitation to despair. The word processor is, after all, a computer, and most people are scared of computers. Most people are also scared of the act of writing; even the professional writer faces his daily task with a nervousness that never quite goes away. I didn't know what would happen when the fear of computers got combined with the fear of writing. But I did know that the word processor was here to stay. And I knew that if I could master it, anybody could.

From *Writing with a Word Processor* (New York: Harper and Row, 1983), pp. vii–viii.

type beyond the right margin, the program automatically moves or "wraps" overflow words down to the next line. You don't need to press the RETURN key, therefore, until you want to start a new paragraph. In the same way, you needn't worry about page breaks. As you type at the keyboard, you get the impression that you're writing on a long scroll of paper. When you enter more than a few lines of text, the "paper" on which you're writing moves or **scrolls** up, giving you fresh, new "paper" at the bottom of the screen. The program will take care of the page breaks automatically when it prints the document. If you wish, you can choose where the page breaks will occur by using a **forced page break command.** This command overrides automatic pagination and "forces" a page break where you wish it.

Editing. "Expect to revise," writing experts counsel, and word processing makes it easy. Since all the text you're creating is contained in the computer's memory (rather than in ink stains on paper), it's easy to make changes until you're satisfied. Word processing programs give you many tools for making these changes, including tools for inserting text, deleting text, copying text to a new location, and moving blocks of text around in the document. Learn to use all these tools and use them frequently. The quality of the work you do with a word processing program depends on how frequently — and how well — you revise.

Formatting. To **format** is to modify computer-based text so that it will print correctly and pleasingly on paper. Word processing programs handle formatting commands in two very different ways, as you'll see.

Saving to Disk. The work you produce when you type at the keyboard is stored temporarily in the computer's internal memory, which is volatile. That means everything you've done will be lost if you do not deliberately save it to disk. Professional writers make it a habit to save their work every 15 minutes; if the power fails, they lose no more than 15 minutes of work. You'll be wise to emulate them.

Printing. Once the text has been formatted, the computer sends it to the printer. Printing is rapid and automatic. You may, however, find errors in the printout that were not obvious on the screen. If so, correct them and print again.

Quitting. The session ends with a command that returns control of the computer to the disk operating system.

Now that you've an idea of the overall process, let's explore the particulars.

EXPLORING A WORD PROCESSING PROGRAM

To write effectively with a word processing program, you'll need to master its basic functions. The pages to follow help you toward this mastery by introducing you to the document display screen, program control commands, text revision techniques, text formatting, and printing.

UNDERSTANDING THE DOCUMENT DISPLAY SCREEN

The document display screen appears after you load a word processing program. Programs vary in what they show on the screen, but the following elements are common (Figure 4–2):

Document Window. The **document window** is the space within which text can be entered. Actually, it only shows part of that space, which is much longer (and, with some programs, wider) than the 24 line by 80 character display most programs give you. That's the reason this space is called a window; it gives you a window frame through which you see part of the document.

Status Line. The **status line** gives you information about what the program is doing. The information displayed on status lines varies, but common elements include the file name of the document you are writing and coordinates that describe the position of the cursor on the screen.

Cursor. The cursor, a blinking line or square, shows you where the characters you type will appear. You can move the cursor's position with the cursor

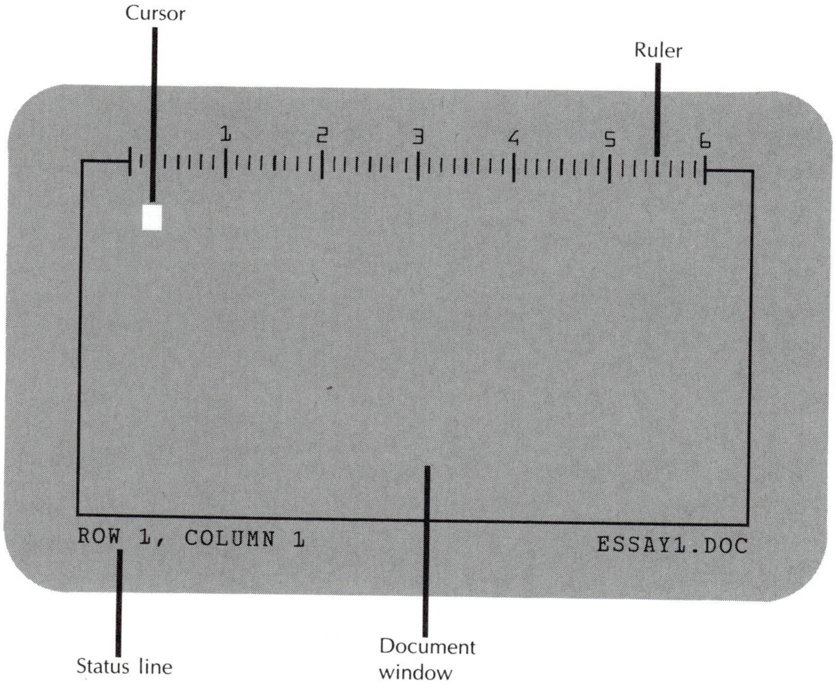

FIGURE 4–2 Document Display Screen

control keys (sometimes called arrow keys) or with a mouse, if your computer is equipped with one.

Ruler. Most programs display a **ruler** calibrated in inches. The ruler, which runs along the top or bottom margins of the document window, displays the current left and right margin settings as well as any tab stops you may have set.

These are the basic document display features. Just what other features you'll see on your program's document display screen depends on how you give it commands.

GIVING COMMANDS

Commands tell the program what to do. A big part of your proficiency with any program, therefore, depends on how well you've learned to use the commands. Programmers use three different approaches to provide commands (Figure 4–3):

The Keyboard Command Approach. **Keyboard commands** are entered by holding down one of the keyboard's command keys, such as the CONTROL or ALT keys, and pressing one or two other keys. In WordStar, for example, holding down the CONTROL key and pressing Y deletes a line of text.

The Command Menu and Pop-Up Submenu Approach. A command menu is a list (hence "menu") of command options. The list is displayed right on the screen, and the **default option** — the option that will be chosen unless you choose another one — is shown by the **pointer.** The pointer, which identifies the selected command option, highlights the option in **reverse video** (such as black letters against a green background). You may move the pointer (and, in so doing, select a different command option) using the cursor control keys. When you have highlighted the command you want, pressing RETURN causes a hidden subordinate menu (a **submenu**) to pop up. Using this **pop-up command menu,** you can then give the program detailed instructions for what you want done.

The Pull-Down Menu Approach. **Pull-down menus** work just like pop-up menus, except the command names are listed across the top of the screen. Highlighting one and pressing RETURN (or clicking the mouse button, if your computer is so equipped) causes the hidden submenu to appear.

Each command approach has its advantages and disadvantages. Good typists like the keyboard command approach because they can enter the commands without looking at the keyboard. Even so, using keyboard commands requires memorizing one or two dozen frequently used keyboard commands. The pop-up or pull-down command menu approach frees you from memorizing the

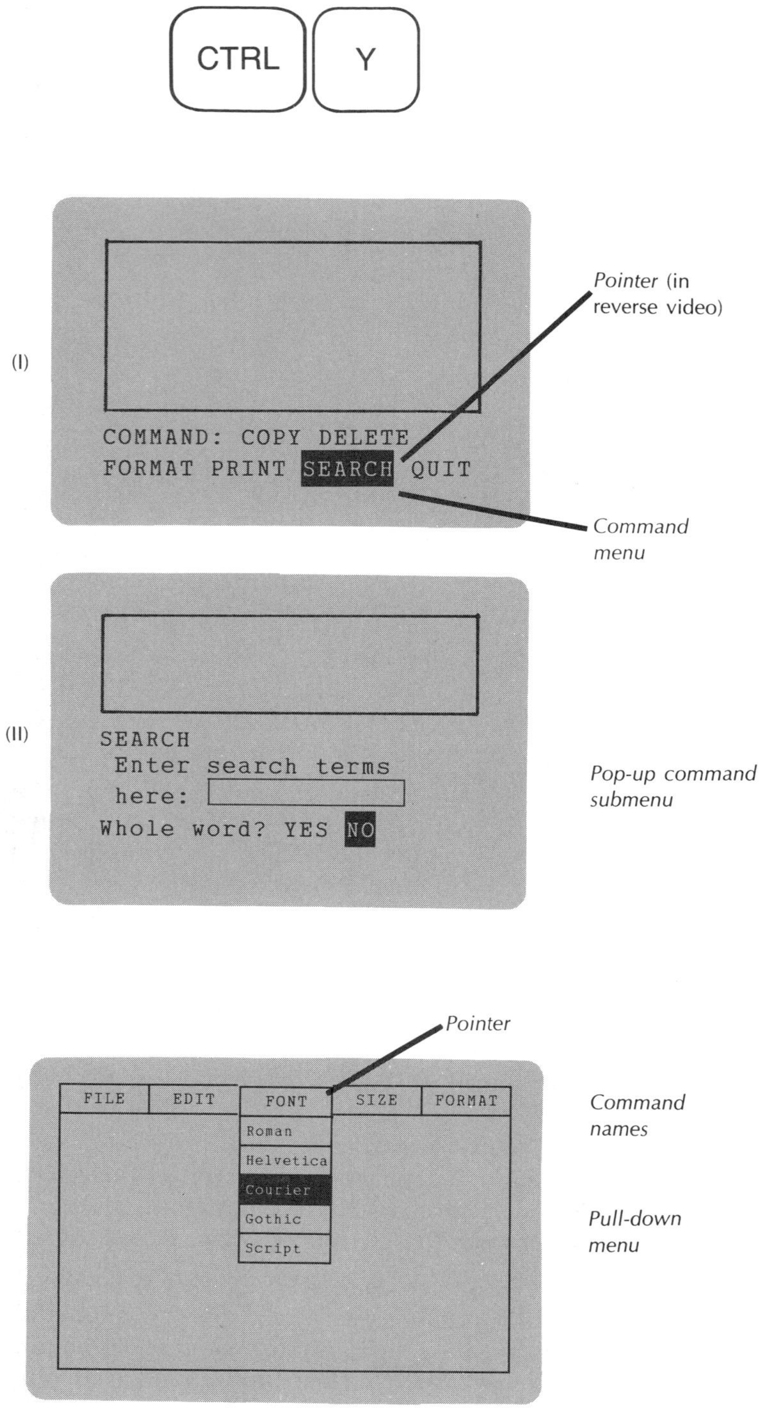

FIGURE 4–3 Three Approaches to Giving Commands

Keyboard command approach To enter a command, hold down the CONTROL key and strike another key on the keyboard.

Pop-up command menu To enter a command, use the arrow keys to highlight the command you want. Pressing the RETURN key brings into view a submenu of command options.

Pull-down command menu To enter a command, highlight the command name at the top of the screen. Pressing RETURN (or clicking the mouse button) causes the pull-down menu to appear.

commands, but it takes more time and keystrokes. Many programs combine the two approaches. Microsoft Word, for example, lets you give many program control commands in two ways. You may, if you wish, choose a command from the menu at the bottom of the screen. If you prefer, you can give the same command from the keyboard.

WRITING AND REVISING THE TEXT

The following word processing features and functions are basic to day-to-day writing and editing proficiency. Make sure you understand all of them.

Word Wrapping. As you enter text, you need not press the RETURN key at the end of every line. The program automatically detects words that go over the right margin and, with **word wrapping,** wraps them down to the next line (Figure 4–4).

Cursor Control. The cursor control or arrow keys let you position the cursor anywhere on the screen without disturbing or erasing the text. Normally,

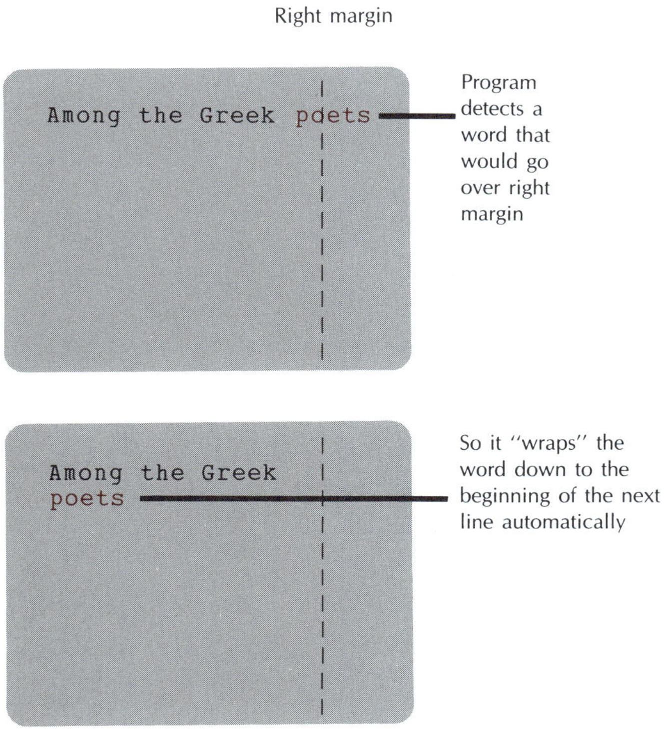

FIGURE 4–4 Word Wrapping in Action

pressing one of the arrow keys moves the cursor only one character left or right (or one line up or down). Sometimes you'll want to go farther. Most programs make these bigger jumps easier by providing additional cursor control commands (Figure 4–5). When you've learned them, you can jump to the first or last character on the screen or the beginning or end of a line in just one or two keystrokes.

Scrolling. To scroll the document is to give a command that moves the document up or down past the document window (Figure 4–6). To scroll up is to move toward the beginning of the document; to scroll down is to move toward its end. Most programs give you several scrolling commands. You may scroll one line or one window at a time. You may also move quickly to the beginning or the end of the document.

Inserting Text. Often you'll need to insert additional text in the midst of passages you've already written. To do so, simply move the cursor to the **insertion point,** the place you'd like the new text to occur, and start typing. In older programs, however, it's necessary to use a **reformatting command**

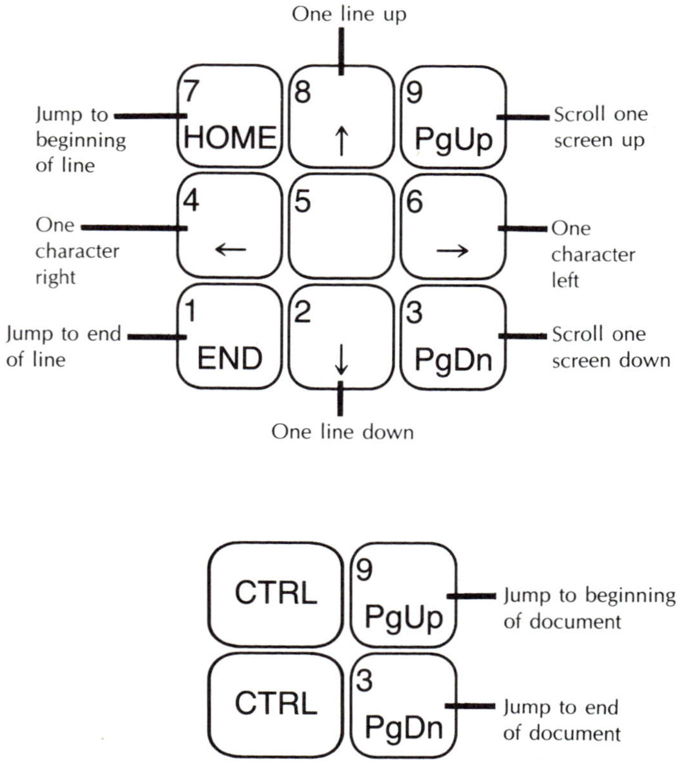

FIGURE 4–5 Cursor Control Commands Used by a Popular Word Processing Program (Microsoft Word, IBM PC Version)

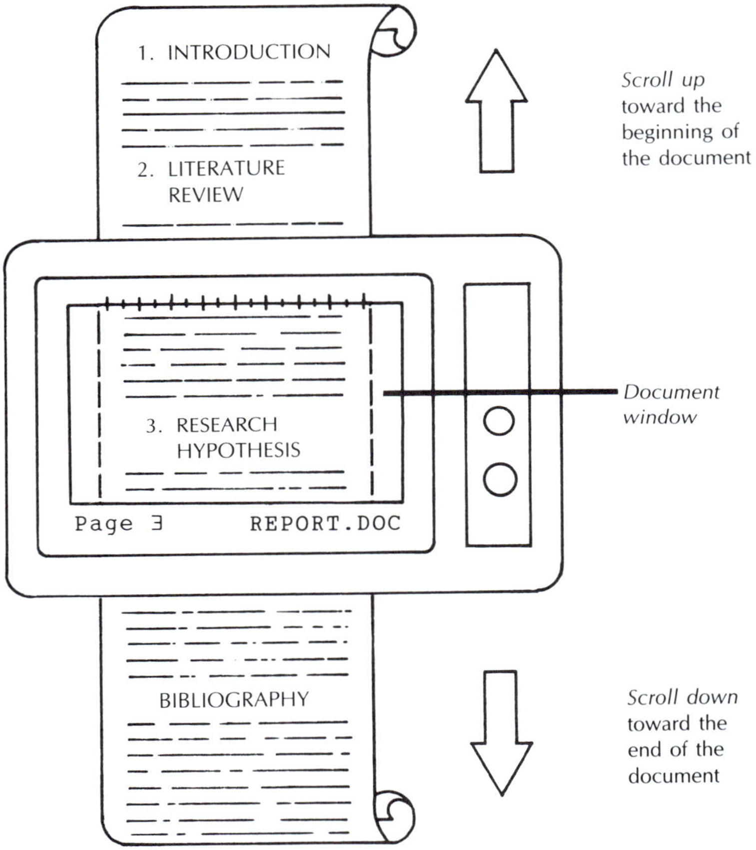

FIGURE 4–6 Scrolling Commands

to restore the right margin after insertions (Figure 4–7). Newer programs automatically reformat the right margin after insertions. This feature is called **automatic reformatting.**

Overtype and Insert Modes. Most word processing programs have two text-entry modes, an overtype mode and an insert mode. In the **overtype mode,** characters you type at the keyboard will erase characters shown on the screen. In the **insert mode,** the characters you type push existing text to the right — and down, if they would be pushed beyond the right margin. Use the overtype mode if you want to replace the old text. Use the insert mode if you just want to stick something new in the middle of it.

Deleting Text. As you write, you'll find yourself making some corrections as mistakes (such as spelling errors) occur. Most programs provide a destructive backspace key, which erases the characters it passes over. The destructive

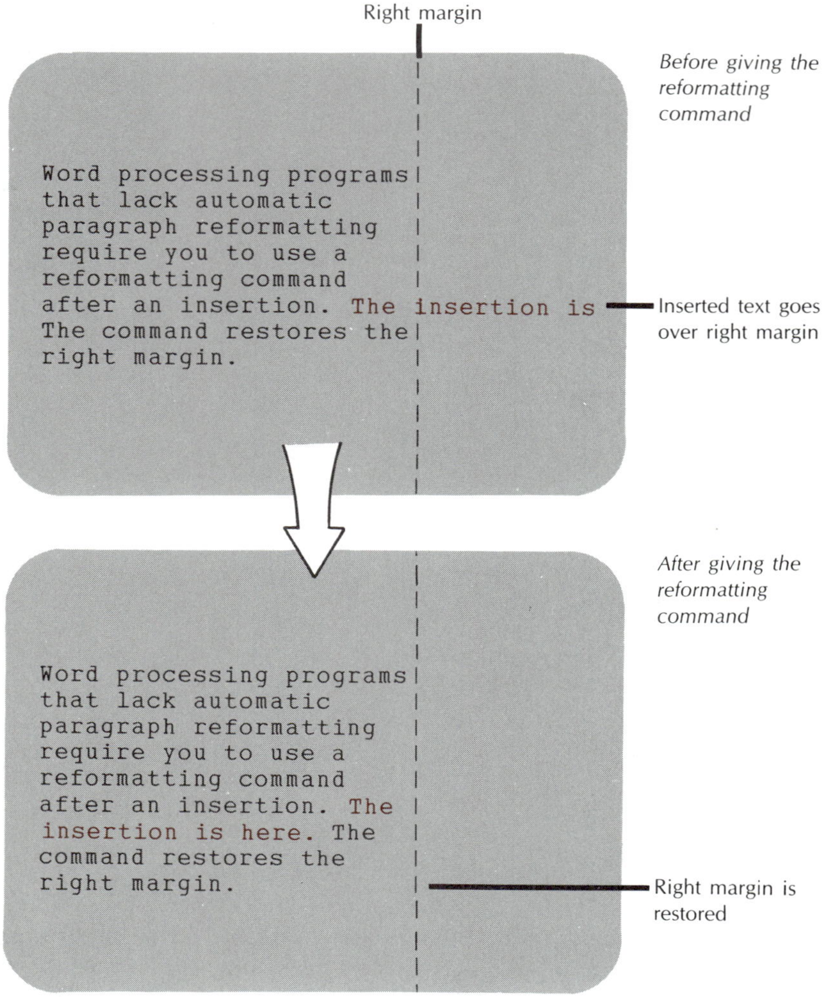

FIGURE 4–7 Manual Reformatting

backspace key erases characters to the *left* of the cursor. Also provided by most programs is a delete key, which erases the character on which the cursor is positioned. Additional text deletion commands take care of larger units of text, such as words, lines, sentences, and even paragraphs. Learn to use them; you'll find they'll vastly speed editing operations.

Defining Blocks of Text. Real revision — as opposed to the superficial kind that just makes a few insertions or deletions — almost always involves major surgery (changing the order of paragraphs or larger blocks of text). And one of the best things about word processing is how easy this surgery becomes. Word processing programs let you define a **block** of text. A block is a unit of text that you have demarcated for editing purposes, such as moving it elsewhere. With some programs, you define the block by giving a **begin block command** at the beginning of the block and an **end block command** at the end. With others, you **select** the text by highlighting it in reverse video (Figure 4–8). This technique is well suited to the mouse, which makes it easy to point to the beginning and end of the block.

Copy or Move Block. After you've defined a block, you can easily copy it or move it to a desired location. Simply move the cursor to the place you'd like the block of text to appear. Then use the **copy block command** or **move block command** (Figure 4–9). (The copy block command leaves the original block in place and makes a copy of it. The move block command

FIGURE 4–8 Two Approaches to Defining Blocks

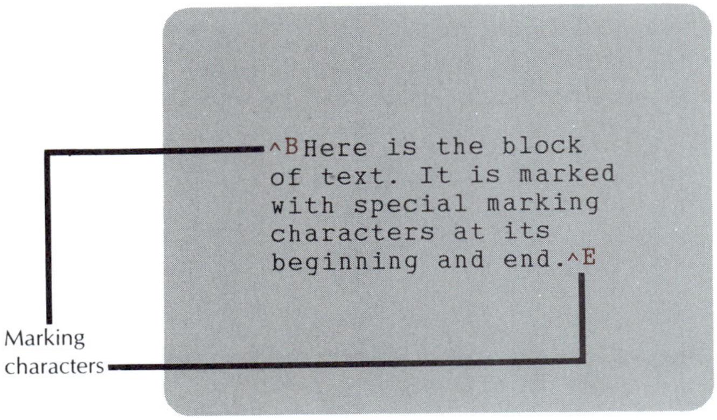

Begin block and end block commands leave marking characters in text

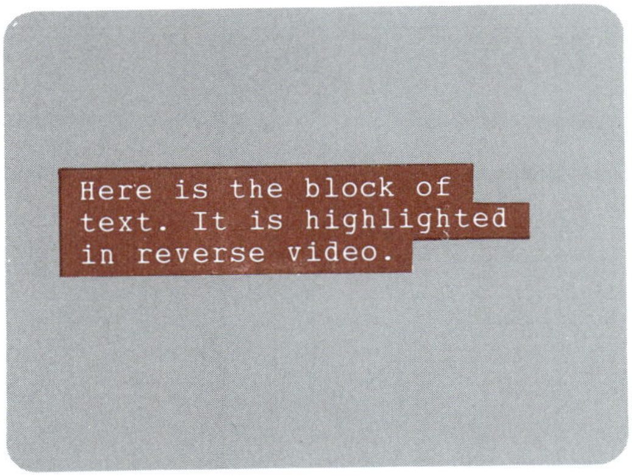

Text highlighting technique displays block in reverse video

sets a **block move** in motion: the command erases the block in its original location and moves it to the new one.)

Delete Block. Equally useful in text revision is the **delete block command,** which erases the blocked text and closes up the resulting gap automatically. The better programs temporarily store large deletions (words, sentences, paragraphs, and blocks) in a **delete buffer,** where you may recover them if you find you have made a mistake. Usually, however, the delete buffer holds only one deletion at a time. If you've made two deletions, you can get back the second one — but not the first.

Undo. Very useful for editing purposes is an **undo** command, which restores the document to the state it was in just before the last editing command was given. Suppose, for example, you've just moved a paragraph, and you decide you've made a mistake — it was better off where it was before. The undo command lets you backtrack one step, restoring the document to its state prior to the block move.

Remember that the chief benefit of word processing is the ease with which you can revise text. These revision tools, however, have no value unless you make use of them. If you treat a word processing program as if it were little more than an electronic typewriter, making only minor changes along the way,

FIGURE 4–9 Block Move

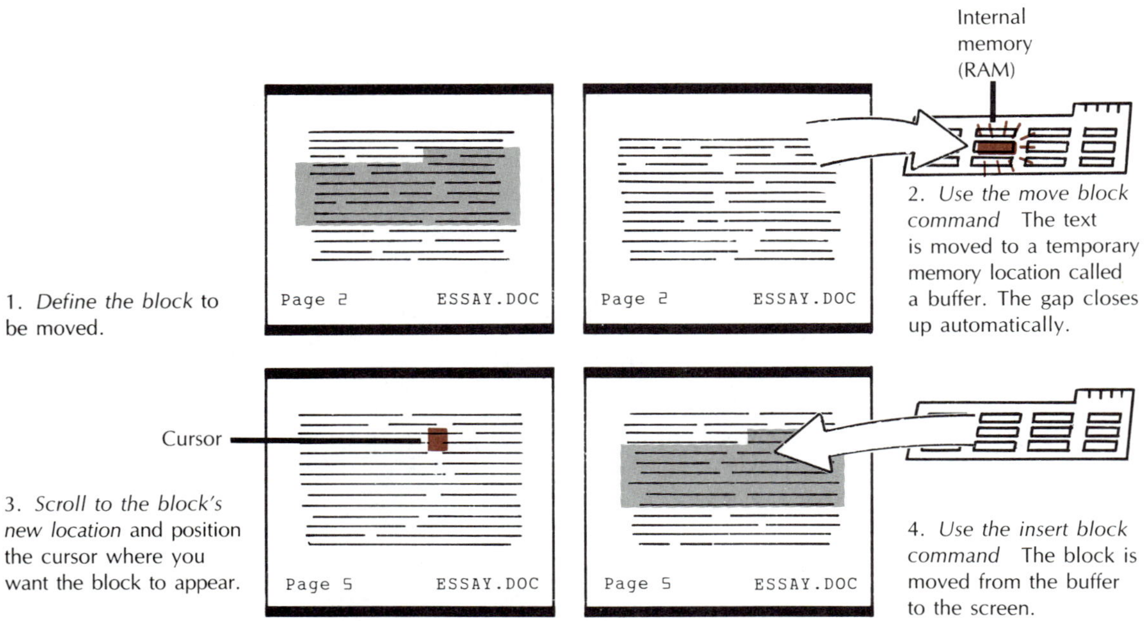

Case Study: Humanities Professors Discover Word Processing

Leroy Searle is Associate Chairman of the English Department at the University of Washington. In 1982, he bought a personal computer. "I did it," Searle recalls, "partly because computers made me incredibly nervous. Here's something on the order of the invention of print, and I didn't know anything about it. Fourteen-year-olds knew more about it."* But the computer's main attraction for Searle was word processing.

Searle and several of his colleagues in the humanities installed their computers in their campus offices, and Searle swore he'd never write with a typewriter again if he didn't have to. That kind of conviction speaks volumes to scholars who have long suffered from white-out fumes, cut-and-paste sessions, and laborious retyping. Within a year, word processing had spread like wildfire throughout the humanities and social sciences departments at the University.

Colleges throughout North America are witnessing their own versions of Washington's computer boom as humanities professors look to electronics. In 1984, for instance, half of the United States' annual yield of 30,000 Ph.D. dissertations were being prepared on computers, as was half the huge volume of scientific, scholarly, and technical works. And it's no surprise: most writers love word processing. Since writing is a major job responsibility of professors in the humanities, it's only logical that they would lead the way in the campus computer boom.

* Schuyler Ingle, "Who Needs a Mainframe?," *Pro/Files* (November/December 1983), p. 38.

it's not likely to contribute much to the quality of your writing. Word processing doesn't improve writing quality. Revision does. What word processing does is make revision easy.

FORMATTING THE TEXT: TWO APPROACHES

Formatting refers to the process by which the text is modified so that it conforms, when printed, to established aesthetic and professional standards (Figure 4–10). Word processing programs differ in the way they handle text formatting (Figure 4–11).

Offscreen Formatting. Some word processing programs do not show you what your text will look like when printed. To format your text with these programs,

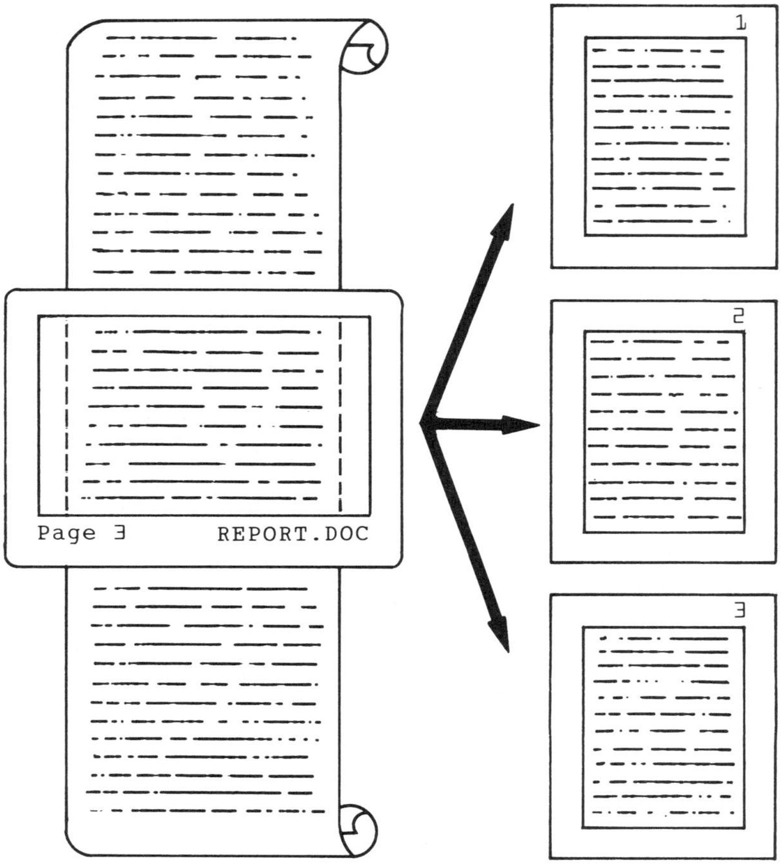

FIGURE 4–10 The Formatting Process

you have to use **embedded commands,** or commands that you place in the midst of the text, along with delimiters (usually parentheses or brackets) that mark the text to be affected. With one program, for example, an embedded command looks like this:

```
@CENTER(Chapter 1)
```

Putting this command in the text doesn't change the appearance of the text on the screen; it doesn't center "Chapter 1." The commands are read by a separate **formatting program,** which goes over the text file and constructs a **print output file. Offscreen formatting** occurs offscreen as you wait. The print output file is then sent to the printer.

Onscreen Formatting. Other programs show you the results of formatting commands right on the screen. You need not embed commands in the text.

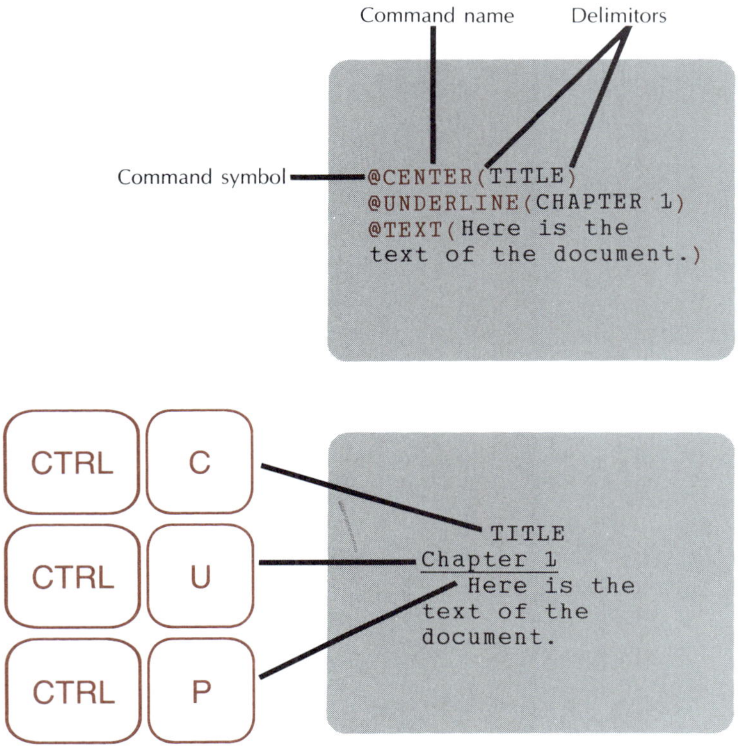

Offscreen formatting
Embedded commands are placed in text; effects of formatting are not visible on screen, which does not show how the text will print

Onscreen formatting
Formatting commands (entered with the keyboard or command menus) affect appearance of text on screen, which shows how the text will print

FIGURE 4–11 Offscreen Versus Onscreen Formatting

On the contrary, you select the text you want to format by highlighting it in reverse video. Then you choose a formatting command (either by selecting it from a command menu or using a keyboard command). If you were to select the words "Chapter 1" and choose the CENTER command, for instance, you'd see the text centered right on the screen. Because these programs show you what you will see when the document is printed, they're often called "what you see is what you get" programs (abbreviated **WYSIWYG**).

Almost all writers who use word processing software prefer WYSIWYG programs, for reasons that become obvious once you've tried an offscreen formatter. Because offscreen formatting programs do not show you how the text will appear when printed, you can't really tell how your document will look until you've saved it to disk, left the word processing program, loaded the formatting program, created the output file, and printed the document. If you find a mistake (and you surely will, the first time around), you have to repeat the whole process. Offscreen formatters waste so much time that they tend to negate the benefits of word processing (compare Figures 4–12 and 4–13).[1] Note

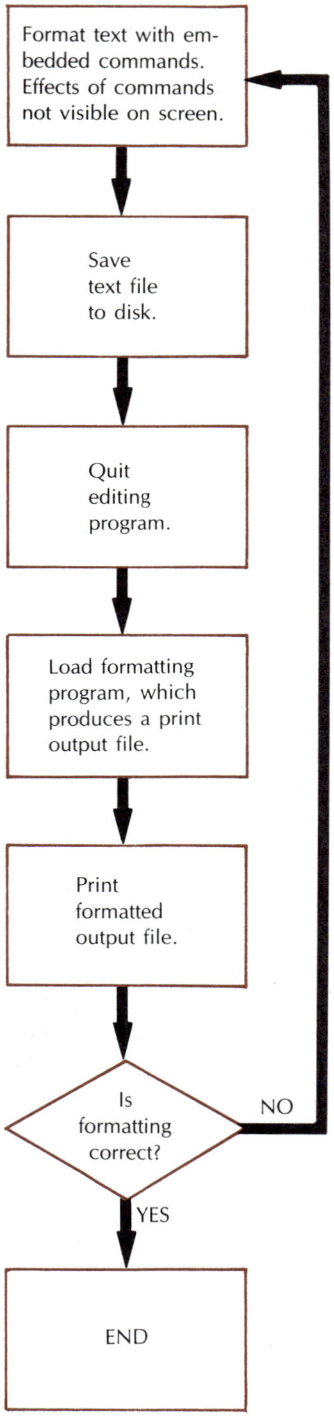

FIGURE 4–12 Formatting Text with an Offscreen Formatter

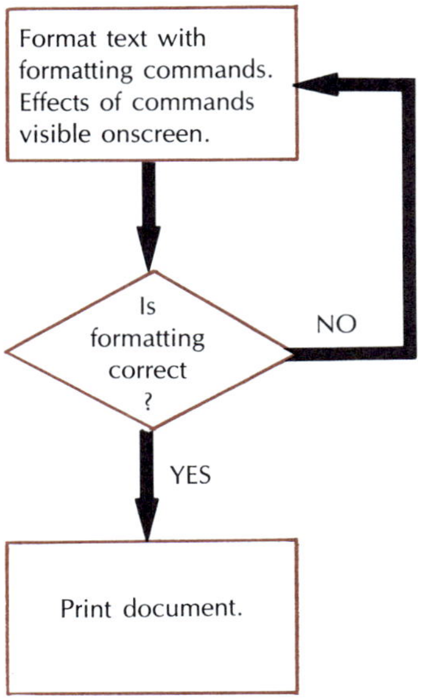

FIGURE 4–13
Formatting Text with an Onscreen Formatter

that many programs that are often described as onscreen formatters, such as WordStar and PC-Write, still require you to use some embedded commands for certain formatting purposes.

FORMATTING THE TEXT: DEFAULT SETTINGS

Every word processing program comes equipped with **default formatting settings,** the settings the program will use to format the text unless you specifically instruct it otherwise. With some programs, the default formatting settings produce results that aren't acceptable under any conditions (for instance, no margins or page breaks). Others will give you standard margins and insert page breaks where necessary. Microsoft Word, for example, inserts page breaks and inserts standard margins on the top, bottom, and sides of the page.

Part of learning a word processing program is learning its default programming settings. Consult your manual or supplementary text to find out what these settings are for your program, and note them on the *Quick Reference Guide: Word Processing Basics*, taken from the end of this book.

FORMATTING THE TEXT: CHARACTER, PARAGRAPH, AND DOCUMENT FORMATS

In almost every writing session, you'll find it necessary to depart from the default formatting settings. You'll find yourself using commands that affect three different components of your document: character, paragraph, and document formats.

Character Formats. **Character formats** are those that pertain to the appearance of individual characters (Figure 4–14). They include boldface type, italics, underlining, superscripts (one-half space above the line), and subscripts (one-half space below the line). Some newer programs also give you direct control over the diverse capabilities of today's printers, which can often print several different **fonts** and **type sizes.** A font is a set of letters, numbers, and punctuation symbols that are all designed to conform to a distinctive style, such as Times Roman or Helvetica. Type sizes are measured in printer's points and refer to the height of the characters. Common sizes for business and professional writing are 10 and 12 points.

Use character formatting sparingly. Italics, boldface, and underlining, for example, can be used for emphasis, but remember the tale of the boy who cried "Wolf!": if used too often, they lose their force. It's a good idea, too, to be conservative in your use of fonts and type sizes.

Paragraph Formats. **Paragraph formats** are those which affect the way a paragraph of text is arranged on the page (Figure 4–15). They include:

> *Left Flush Alignment.* **Left flush alignment** prints paragraphs with the left margin aligned and the right margin ragged.

boldface

italic

underline

a^2

$m_1 \quad m_2 \quad m_3$

Sans serif 8

Sans serif 10

Sans serif 20

FIGURE 4–14
Character Formats

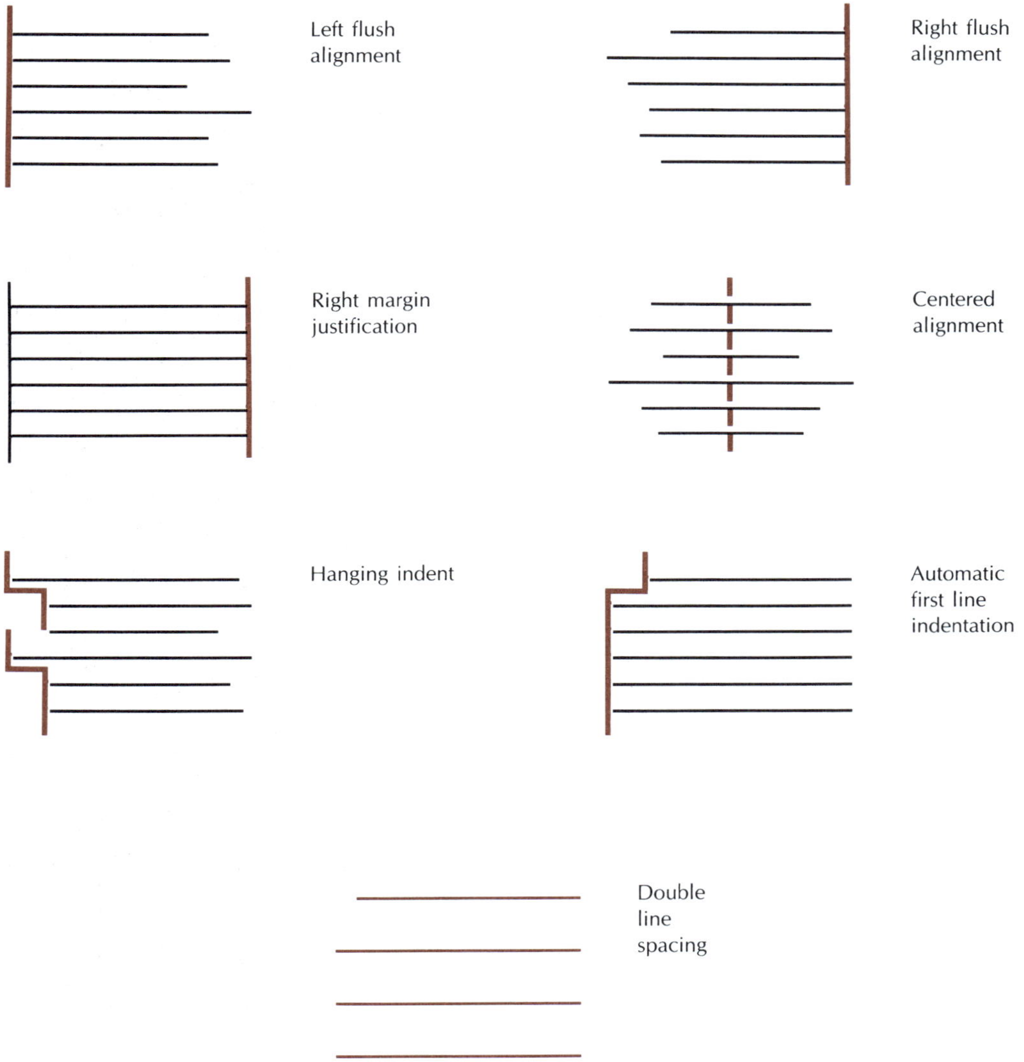

FIGURE 4–15 Paragraph Formats

Right Flush Alignment. **Right flush alignment** prints paragraphs with the right margin aligned and the left margin ragged.

Right Margin Justification. **Right margin justification** prints paragraphs with both margins aligned.

Centered Alignment. Each line is centered on the page.

Hanging Indention. **Hanging indention** prints the first line flush to the left margin, subsequent or **turnover lines** indented.

Automatic First Line Indention. The first line automatically indented.

Double Line Spacing. Each line is double-spaced. Some programs make other options available, such as 1.5 line or triple line spacing.

Document Formats. **Document formats** (Figure 4–16) control the page design. These are the chief page design elements:

Margins. Left and right margin settings control the line length. On an 8½ by 11 inch page, for example, margins of 1.25 inches on the left and right give a standard, 6 inch line length. Within the top and bottom margins is found the body of the text.

Running Heads. The space within the top and bottom margins can be used for headings that run through the document (that is, appear on every page). This book, for instance, uses **running heads** — short versions of the book's

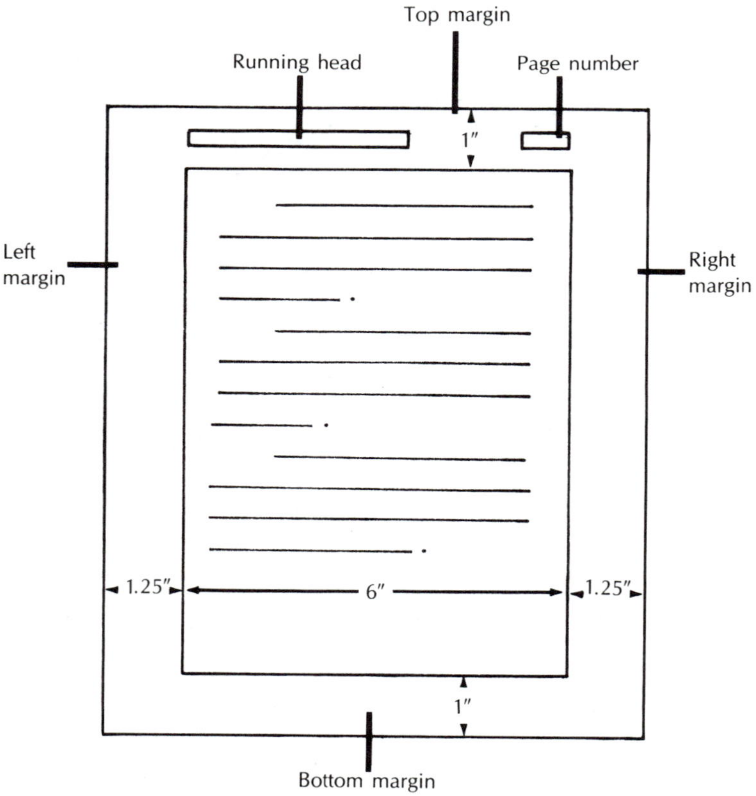

FIGURE 4–16
Document Formats

and its chapters' titles — to remind you what you're reading. For papers you write in college, it's a good idea to use your name as a running head. That way your professor can identify all the pages of your paper even if the staple falls out.

Automatic Pagination. Most word processing programs will automatically print a correct page number on each page of your document. Often, however, you must deliberately turn the pagination function on before it will put in page numbers.

PRINTING THE TEXT

Once your document has been formatted, printing is a straightforward, almost automatic process.

Selecting Printing Options. You can inform the program what kind of paper you're using, and it will adjust the printing process automatically. If you're using continuous or **tractor feed paper,** for example, the program will not pause for page breaks. If you're using single or **cut sheets,** however, it will pause to let you insert a new page. (Printers equipped with a **cut sheet feeder** do this job automatically.)

Preparing the Printer and Starting Printing. Before you give the command that starts printing the document, be sure the printer is turned on and that it's online or selected (that is, directly connected to the computer and ready to receive the computer's signals). Then use the command that initiates the printing process.

Stop Printing Command. When the printer starts printing, inspect the first page. You may find a gross error of some sort (for example, single spacing when double spacing is required). In such cases, when there's no sense in printing the whole document until the error is fixed, the stop printing command is very useful.

Printing Selected Pages or Printing Multiple Copies. Most programs let you print selected portions of your document. If you wish, you can print more than one copy.

THE LIMITATIONS OF WORD PROCESSING

Word processing, obviously, is a wonderful boon for writers. Yet the technology is not free from problems.

Underutilization of Software. Most users of word processing software learn only a fraction of the programs' commands and functions. The fraction

Four Strategies for Word Processing Excellence

Word processing doesn't automatically lead to higher productivity and better writing quality. Experienced writers use four strategies that help them get the most from word processing software. You can do the same.

1. Master your word processing program so that its full benefits are available in every writing session. Particularly important are the commands for text deletion and block moves. Their use should become second nature to you. Remember that quality goes up only when you revise, revise, and revise.
2. As you revise, however, remember that word processing makes it almost too easy to add text. Be sure the text you're adding actually improves your document. Avoid getting off on tangents; remember your aims and objectives. If you find your document growing longer, go through it and see whether you can delete some unnecessary words, sentences, or even paragraphs.
3. Save your work to disk frequently — at least as often as every 15 minutes. Most programs allow you to save a document and continue to work. You can avoid computer-assisted disaster by taking this rule to heart.
4. Develop strategies to overcome the limited view of the text. Write with an outline handy and remind yourself of your document's structure frequently. Print your work frequently and use the printed copy as a guide for revision. It's much easier to get a sense of your document's overall organization from a printed copy than it is from the screen.

they learn enables them to tackle day-to-day writing tasks, but not as well (or as productively) as they could were they to master the programs fully.

Bloated Manuscripts. Word processing makes it easy to add text — too easy, in the view of some critics. Research shows that students write longer papers with word processing programs, but the papers aren't necessarily better. When "he choked" is changed to "he felt a choking sensation," the revision changes a good, active verb to a weak, wordy cliché.

Potential for Lost Work. All work done with a word processing program is initially stored in the volatile internal memory, where it's vulnerable to loss. And sooner or later, writers who use this software will lose some of their work irretrievably.

Limited View of Text. A more serious problem is the limited view of the text provided by the twenty-four-line document window (about one-third of a page). Coupled with the slow speed of screen-by-screen scrolling, the one-third of a page view militates against a sense of your document's overall structure and organization. Research has shown that the twenty-four-line window concentrates revision efforts on the relatively trivial matters of sentence structure and word choice; it frustrates the really important domains of revision, the ones involving a document's overall structure, organization, and coherence.[2]

These limitations do not rule out the use of word processing for serious writing, but they do inspire caution. A serious writer, one who hopes for higher writing productivity and better writing quality, will take steps to circumvent these limitations. The box "Four Strategies for Word Processing Excellence" offers some suggestions; Chapters 5 and 6 contain more.

SUMMARY

All word processing programs are intended to do the same thing: to help you write, edit, and print documents. They share a core of common functions. To master any such program, you'll need to learn how it handles these functions. A typical writing session involves loading the program, creating a new document (or loading an existing one), writing or editing, formatting, saving to disk, printing, and quitting. Every word processing program presents you with a document display screen, which usually includes a document window, a status line, a cursor, and a ruler.

To control the program, you'll use commands. Some programs require you to memorize keyboard commands. Others provide pop-up or pull-down menus. Basic commands and functions include cursor control commands, scrolling commands, facilities for text insertion, the choice between an overtype and an insert mode, commands for text deletion, procedures for marking blocks of text, and commands for moving, copying, or deleting the marked block.

Word processing programs handle text formatting in two different ways. Offscreen formatting programs require you to use embedded commands. After saving the file to disk and quitting the writing/editing part of the program, a separate text formatting program reads the embedded commands and constructs a print output file. Then the print output file is sent to the printer. Onscreen formatting programs show you the effect of formatting commands right on the screen. Onscreen formatters, often called "what you see is what you get" (WYSIWYG), are preferable. If you make a mistake entering a formatting command, you see the error right away. With offscreen formatters, you may not discover formatting mistakes until you print the file.

Every program comes with default formatting settings, but you'll almost certainly want to change at least some of them every time you write. Among the formatting commands you should master are: character formats (boldface, italics, underlining, superscripts, and subscripts); paragraph formats (left flush paragraphs, right flush paragraphs, justified paragraphs, centered paragraphs, hanging indent paragraphs, automatic first line indent, and double line spacing); and document formats (margins, running heads, and automatic pagination).

Once you have formatted your document, printing is fast and straightforward. You may set the program so that it prints continuously (useful for tractor feed paper) or pauses at each page break (useful for cut sheets).

Word processing, obviously, is a genuine boon for writers, but it's not without its limitations. To get the full benefit of this technology, you'll need to master most or all of a program's commands and functions, devise ways to overcome the limited view of the text, resist the temptation to add unnecessary text, and safeguard against lost work.

KEY TERMS

automatic reformatting
begin block command
block
block move
character format
copy block command
cut sheet
cut sheet feeder
default formatting settings
default option
delete block command
delete buffer
document
document display screen
document format
document window
embedded command
end block command
fonts
forced page break command
format
formatting
formatting program
hanging indention
insert mode
insertion point
keyboard command
left flush alignment
line break
loading a program
move block command
offscreen formatting
overtype mode
page break
paragraph format
pointer
pop-up command menu
print output file
pull-down command menu
reformatting command
reverse video
right flush
right flush alignment
right margin justification
ruler
running head
scrolling
select
status line
submenu
tractor feed paper
turnover line
type sizes
undo
word wrapping
WYSIWYG

REVIEW QUESTIONS AND EXERCISES

1. Compare and contrast the overall process of writing with a word processing program (see Figure 4–1) with that imposed by other technologies, such as typewriters or pen and paper. Why does word processing increase writers' productivity so dramatically?
2. What is displayed on the document display screen of the word processing program you're using? Make a chart similar to Figure 4–2 that identifies all the features normally displayed.
3. Which approach to providing commands does your word processing program employ (keyboard commands, command menu/pop-up submenu, or pull-down menus)? Note: some word processing programs combine two or more of these approaches.
4. Which approach to text formatting does your word processing program employ, offscreen or onscreen programming? Note: some programs combine the two approaches.
5. If you do not change the default formatting settings, how will your word processing program format a three-page document?
6. Choose an academic subject in which you are likely to major or pursue a career, such as business, engineering, music, literature, or education. Identify a style manual for that subject. (A style manual sets a document formatting standard for a subject, and these standards vary from subject to subject. In psychology, for example, the style manual published by the American Psychological Association [APA] is widely used. In the humanities, however, the standard is set by the Modern Language Association's [MLA] style manual.) List the required document formats, including page margins, the position of page numbers and running heads, the number of spaces after titles and headings, and the number of spaces to indent the first line of a paragraph. Can your word processing program format a document according to the standard?
7. What are the four strategies for word processing excellence? Why are they so important?

FOR FURTHER READING

Arca, Julie A. *Practical WordStar Uses* (Berkeley: Sybex Computer Books, 1984).

Becker, Joseph D. "Multilingual Word Processing," *Scientific American* (July 1984).

Brightman, Richard W., and Jeffrey M. Dimsdale. "Will Word Processing Take the Creative Out of Creative Writing?" *Using Computers in the Information Age* (New York: Delmar Publishers, 1986).

Daiute, Colette. *Writing and Computers* (Reading, Mass.: Addison-Wesley, 1986).

Fleugelman, Andrew, and Jeremy Joan Hewes. *Writing in the Computer Age: Word Processing*

Skills and Software for Every Writer (Garden City, N.Y.: Anchor Press/Doubleday, 1983).
Hession, William, and Malcolm Rubel. *Performance Guide to Word Processing Software* (New York: McGraw-Hill, 1985).
Hinckley, Dan. *Writing with a Computer: Using Your Word Processor for a New Freedom and Creativity in Writing* (New York: Simon and Schuster, 1985).
Kater, David A., and Richard L. Kater. *The Printed Word: The Microsoft Guide to Advanced Word Processing on the Apple Macintosh* (Bellevue, Wash.: Microsoft Press, 1985).
Leserman, David H. *MacFonts* (New York: McGraw-Hill, 1985).
McGovern, Edmond. *Wordprocessing: A Writer's Guide* (Exeter: Globefield Press, 1985).
McKenzie, Alan T., ed. *A Grin on the Interface: Word Processing for the Academic Humanist* (New York: Modern Language Association of America, 1984).
McWilliams, Peter. *The Word Processing Book* (New York: Ballantine, 1983).
Naiman, Arthur. *Introduction to WordStar* (Berkeley: Sybex Computer Books, 1983).
Pfaffenberger, Bryan. *Business Communication in the Personal Computer Age* (Homewood, Ill.: Richard D. Irwin, 1987).
———. *Dynamics of Microsoft Word (IBM PC Edition)* (Homewood, Ill.: Dow Jones-Irwin, 1986).
———. *Dynamics of Microsoft Word (Macintosh Edition)* (Homewood, Ill.: Dow Jones-Irwin, 1986).
———. *The Scholar's Personal Computing Handbook: A Practical Guide* (Boston: Little, Brown, 1986).
Repohl, Roger F. *Word Processing: A Formatting Approach* (Englewood Cliffs, N.J.: Prentice-Hall, 1986).
Ross, Stephen C. *Understanding and Using WordStar* (St. Paul, Minn.: West, 1986).
Schwartz, Helen J. *Interactive Writing: Composing with a Word Processor* (New York: Holt, Rinehart and Winston, 1985).
Supplee, Kurt. "The PC Tapping at the Chamber Door," *PC Magazine* (May 29, 1984).
Weitzer, Mary K., and Laura B. Ruff. *Understanding and Using MultiMate* (St. Paul, Minn.: West, 1986).
———. *Understanding and Using pfs:WRITE* (St. Paul, Minn.: West, 1986).
Zinsser, William. *Writing with a Word Processor* (New York: Harper and Row, 1983).

5 *Advanced Word Processing:* Beyond Electronic Typewriting

"For nearly any sustained writing endeavor, treating a word processing package like a correcting typewriter can be a serious mistake. A handful of basic commands may be capable of getting the job done, but you may find yourself trying to fell a redwood with a hatchet. The textual buzzsaw lurking beneath most full-featured word processors is the best tool for the big jobs."

Christopher O'Malley *Personal Computing*

Chapter 4 covered the basic core of word processing program functions, but there's more to most word processing packages — much more. To be sure, if all you ever write with a word processing program is an occasional letter or memo, you can live without these advanced features. But your aspirations lie in the professional, managerial, and executive rungs of the office ladder. You'll write proposals and reports. You may even write technical manuals or book-length analyses. And when you do, you'll find that the "textual buzzsaw" lurking beneath your word processor's surface will prove handy indeed.

You can use this chapter to help you learn your word processing program's advanced features. Begin by finding the sheets entitled *Quick Reference Guide: Advanced Word Processing*, which are positioned at the end of this book. Tear them out, and staple them or put them in a folder. Keep these sheets, your word processing program's manual, and your supplementary text (if any)

handy as you read the chapter. When this chapter describes an advanced function, such as displaying two files on the screen at the same time, find out from your manual or supplementary text how to accomplish this function with your program. Then make a note in the *Quick Reference Guide*.

ADVANCED WRITING TECHNIQUES

Stephen Greenfield writes screenplays for a living, and it's a tough job. Movie and television studios are notorious for their complex formatting demands. One studio, for instance, wants a three-inch margin on the right, while another one wants a four-inch margin on the left. (The space is needed for the director's notes.) Greenfield needed a program that could quickly reformat his plays. He needed a powerhouse program for processing text. He found it in Microsoft Word, a full-featured program with a superb text formatting feature called style sheets. Style sheets store dozens or even hundreds of formatting keystrokes, allowing the user to format a document in seconds.

Advanced features such as style sheets can turn writing drudgery into a high-productivity steeplechase, and you get the blue ribbon at the end. The more you understand them, the more likely it is that you'll work productively with your word processing package. Covered here are several advanced writing features used by savvy writers, including glossaries, boilerplating, macros, programmable keyboard commands, style sheets, multiple windows, and footnotes. Each of these features is a "textual buzzsaw" that can cut through hours or even days of tedious work.

GLOSSARIES

Glossaries, or a memory-based text storage facility provided by some word processing programs, store frequently used passages of text and let you enter them with just a few keystrokes (Figure 5–1). Suppose you're writing a biology paper on *Sium ciutaefolium,* a name that's tedious to type. But you'll have to use it thirty-eight times in the paper. To make life easier for yourself, you can create a glossary entry (called *sc*) for the name *Sium ciutaefolium.* To enter it rapidly, you'd use the glossary command, type *sc,* press RETURN, and lo! *Sium ciutaefolium* appears.

The glossary features of most word processing programs let you store as many as several dozen glossary entries at a time, each with its own name. Stored

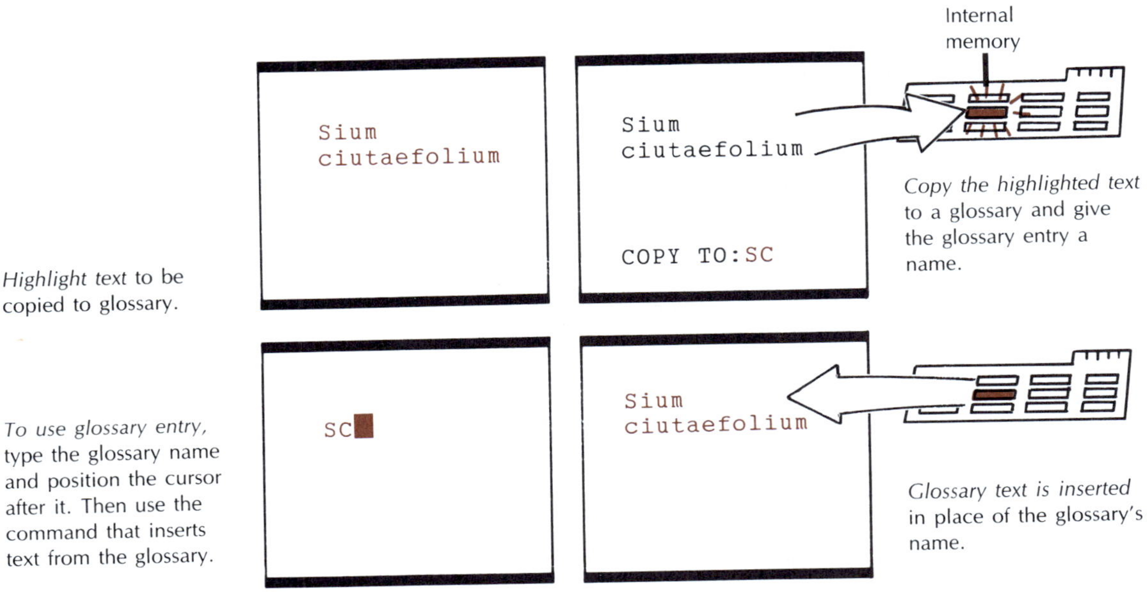

FIGURE 5–1 Creating and Using a Glossary

on disk, the entries are available with a few keystrokes any time they are needed. The owner of a small business could use multiple glossary entries, for instance, to handle routine inquiry letters. If she receives a letter asking about warranty, she can insert a standard passage filed under the glossary name *wrnty*. And if she receives one asking about professional discounts, she can insert the text filed under the glossary name *profdis*.

BOILERPLATE

Standard passages of text that are used over and over, as in the example just presented, are called **boilerplate.** They possess a well-deserved notoriety. Consider, for example, this boilerplate passage, which might be used by a company that manufactures a defective product:

> You're the *only* customer we've *ever* heard from who had problems with the Snazzy Tomato Chopper! Frankly, we're puzzled, but to show we care, a new one's on its way to you right now!

But this is only a crass (and dishonest) application of a legitimate productivity tool. There's nothing intrinsically wrong with using the same text over and over again, especially if it's the best text for a situation. In legal writing, for example,

Case Study: Boilerplating

Of all the strategies for increasing productivity with a personal computer, perhaps the most impressive — and most easily learned — is the art of boilerplating. Boilerplating, defined in simple terms, is the blending of prewritten material with new text. The prewritten text can be inserted into a document in seconds, mixing the new text so seamlessly that no one's the wiser. Boilerplating makes tedious retyping seem as old-fashioned as the quill pen. Just a few keystrokes are all that's needed to insert anything from a sentence to ten pages of prewritten text into a document.

Harvey Jones operates a used computer shop, and he has learned to put boilerplating to work. He's had to. Otherwise, he would have been swamped with the inquiry letters that stream in as a result of his modest but very successful advertising campaign. Predictably enough, people ask the same questions over and over: "What's the warranty?" "What have you done to refurbish the machines?" "Can I get service from you?" So Harvey has developed about a dozen boilerplate responses, which he stores as glossaries in Microsoft Word.

One such glossary, for example, is called WRNTY (short for "warranty"). Others are THANKS ("Thanks for your letter of . . ."), REBUILD ("All of our used computers are extensively tested, and all components that fail to meet specifications are replaced with original parts."), SERVICE ("We guarantee service overnight!"), and WHY ("Why don't you stop by and have a look?"). To answer a particular letter, Harvey might type, for instance, THANKS, REBUILD, SERVICE, and WHY, using the command that inserts the glossary text each time. In a few keystrokes (and a little customization to make sure the letter has a personal touch), Harvey's correspondence is done for the day.

boilerplate ensures that standard passages whose exact wording is crucial get entered the right way, time after time. As an attorney, you wouldn't want to give a client a will in which you left out some vital clause by mistake.

You can put a word processing program's glossary feature to work to store boilerplate. If the program you're using doesn't have glossaries, you can achieve the same result simply by storing the boilerplate passages in separate, named disk files (see Case Study 5–1). Most programs include a **file merge command** that lets you insert a file into a document you're writing. So all you need to do is use this command, tell the computer to insert ONLYCUST.TXT, and presto! the file appears ("You're the *only* customer we've *ever* heard from . . . ," etc.) (Figure 5–2).

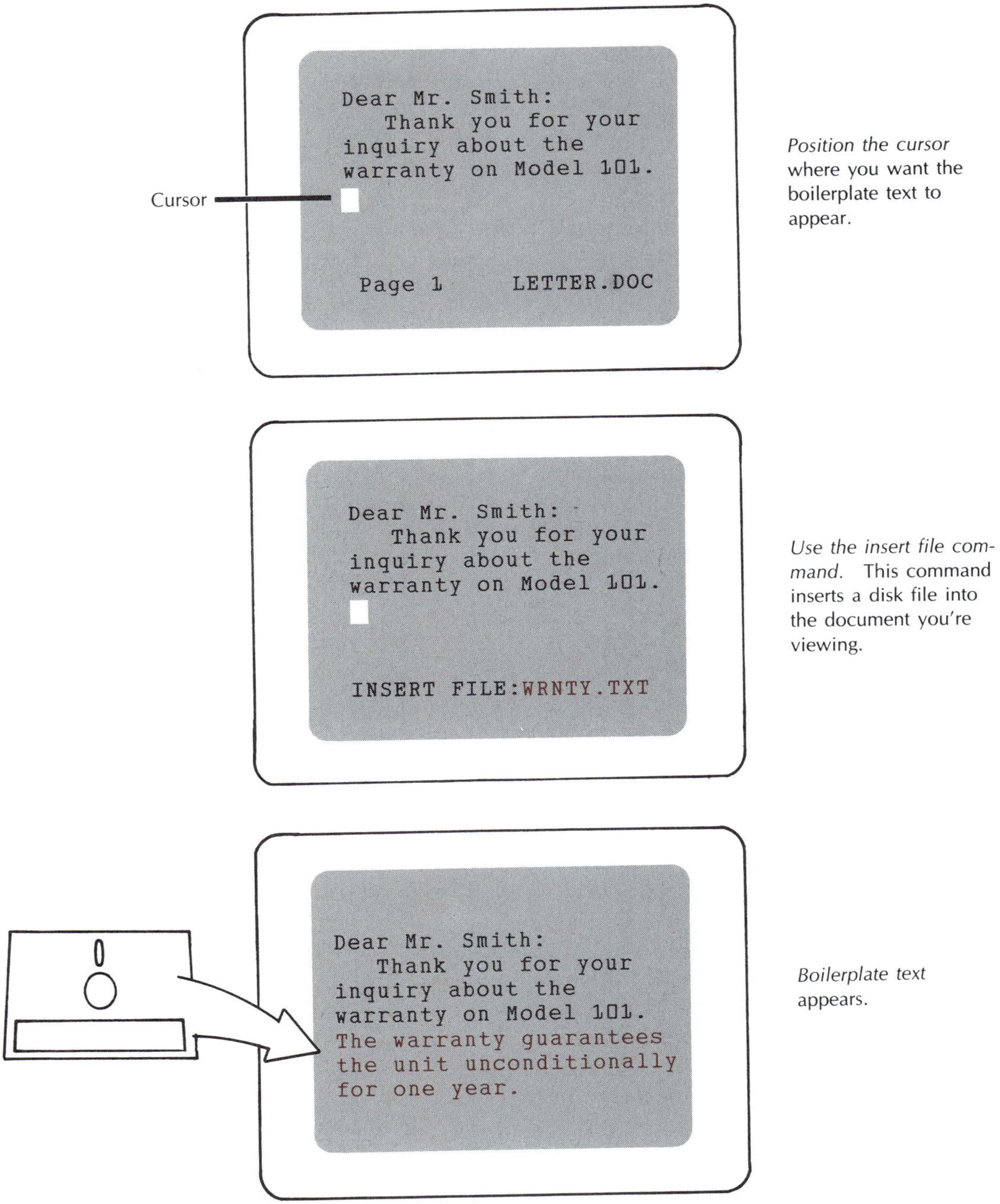

FIGURE 5–2 Boilerplating with Standard Text Passages Stored on Disk Files

AUTOMATING COMMAND ENTRY

If you write often, formatting the same kind of document over and over again becomes a tedious chore. Suppose, for example, you're unhappy with your word processing program's default formatting settings (and you probably will be). PC-WRITE, for example, starts you off with no left or right margins. Every time you start a new document, then, you'll have to set the margins manually before you start writing.

Three word processing features circumvent this problem: macros, programmable keyboard commands, and style sheets. All three do much the same job, but they use different strategies to do so:

Macros. These are similar to glossaries (stored passages of text that can be inserted by typing a few characters). Instead of text, however, the **macro** stores a series of commands that can be set in motion by using just one command. You can include in the macro virtually every command the program recognizes, including commands for positioning the cursor, scrolling the document, formatting the text, searching and replacing, and inserting boilerplate from glossaries. Using macros, you can set complex text-processing operations in motion. A macro designed to format and print text automatically, for example, would include commands to double-space the entire text, insert page numbers in the document, save the document to disk, and send the document to the printer. To use the macro, you would use the command that sets the macro in motion, and the program would read the commands in the macro file as if you were entering them from the keyboard. The commands are entered in exactly the sequence you wrote them in. It's very much like having a robot to enter all those commands for you. Macro features are included in some word processing programs. They can be added to others by using **key-enhancement programs** such as SuperKey® (Borland International).

Style Sheets. As used by professional typists, a **style sheet** is a checklist of page design specifications, such as margin settings, lines per page, header or footer position, page number position, line length, and other characteristics. The typist interviews the author and fills in the style characteristics, which guide the typist during the manuscript's production. A computer-based style sheet works the same way. A program that includes one gives you a special style sheet command which, when used, brings up a style sheet menu, or a list of options to which you can respond (such as "Text Justified or Ragged-Right?"). As you make the responses, the program saves them to a special format file, which is given a distinct name (for instance, MLA STYLE) and stored on disk. It can be attached to any document you wish to write. When you do, the formats you've selected are all entered simultaneously and affect the whole document.

These features are, unfortunately, available with only a few of today's word processing programs. As users come to grasp how useful they are, however, more and more programs will include them in the future.

MULTIPLE WINDOWS

The video display screen can be thought of as a **window** or picture frame positioned over part of a long scroll of text. Some programs allow more than one window to appear on the screen at once (a feature called **windowing** or **multiple windows**), and what is more, they let you look at two (or more) parts of the same document or two (or more) different documents (Figure 5–3).

Multiple Windows on a Single File. It's a little disconcerting to work with two windows on one file. If you think of your document as a scroll, you'd think both parts would scroll if you gave a scrolling command in one part. But they don't. If you use a scrolling command in one window, the other part of the manuscript stays put. And that's precisely why multiple windows are so useful. Try these techniques:

Displaying a Signpost Paragraph. A signpost paragraph is an introductory passage that tells your reader where you're going and what's going to be covered (for instance, "this section defines the current direction in theory, describes the evidence that cannot be explained, and suggests a direction for theoretical development"). Displaying the signpost paragraph in the top window while you're writing in the bottom helps remind you of the structure you're using.

"Anchoring" While Scrolling. Suppose, in a lengthy manuscript, you're writing on page 32 and decide you need to look briefly at something on page 6. Without multiple windows, you'll have to scroll all the way to page 6 and then scroll all the way back to page 32, a tedious prospect at best. But here's an easier technique. Split the screen so that two windows appear. Then scroll the *top* window to page 6 and read the text you want to check. Then *close* the top window. Since the bottom window never moved, you're still on page 32.

Split-Screen Editing. Multiple windows provide a fertile context for moving text around in a document. You can display a passage of text in the top window, for example, and a place in which you think it might work better in the bottom window. Using block move commands, you can cut the text out of the top window and insert it in the bottom one, and see the change in *both* places. If the change doesn't work, you can use the undo command to restore the text to its original appearance.

Two windows on one document

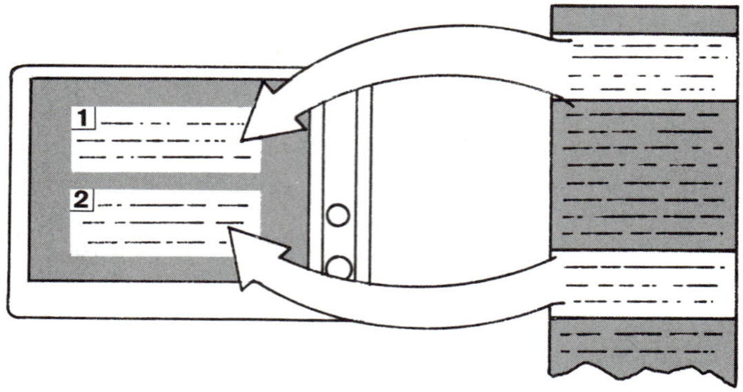

Two documents displayed simultaneously

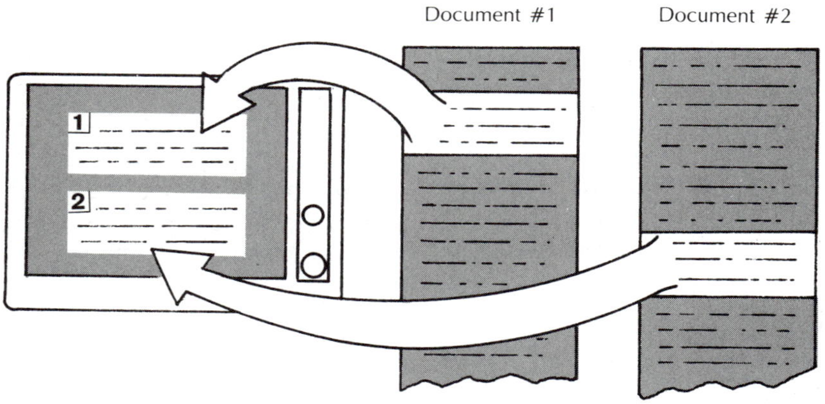

FIGURE 5–3 Multiple Windows

Typing a Table. While typing a lengthy table, try opening a narrow top window for the headings column. Enter the data in the bottom window. The bottom window will scroll but the top one won't, so the headings are always in view.

Multiple Windows on Two or More Documents. Most word processing programs with multiple window capabilities let you view two or more documents at once. Try these multiple document techniques:

Moving Text between Documents. Having both documents on the screen vastly simplifies and speeds copying or moving text from one document to the other.

Working with an Outline. Here's an excellent way to overcome the organizational problems word processing poses. Write up an outline for your essay or report, and display it in the top window. Then open a window below it and write your document. As you write, you'll see your document's structure clearly displayed, right before your eyes. If you make changes as you write, you can update the outline as easily as you can revise your document.

Working with Research Notes. Research notes written and saved with a word processor can be displayed in the top window while you're writing in the bottom one.

Figure 5–4 illustrates multiple window writing techniques.

FOOTNOTES

Writers of reports on everything from Macedonian sculpture to M-1 tanks use footnotes, and word processing programs — some of them, anyway — can help. The catch here is that not all programs include footnote utilities, and of the ones that do, some of them don't work well. The best footnote utilities include the following features (Figure 5–5):

Automatic Footnote Numbering. The program should number the footnotes automatically and adjust the numbers if you insert or delete footnotes.

Footnote Formatting Control. The program should allow you to format the footnotes any way you wish. For business reports, footnotes must be single spaced; for articles submitted to publishers, however, they must be double spaced.

Superscripts for Footnote Reference Marks. To conform to style guidelines, the program should make the **footnote reference mark** a superscript number.

"Float" Lengthy Footnotes to Next Page. If a footnote is too long to fit at the bottom of one page, the program should carry the excess text over to the next page.

Footnotes and Endnotes. You should be able to choose between footnotes positioned at the bottom of the page or **endnotes** positioned at the end of the document.

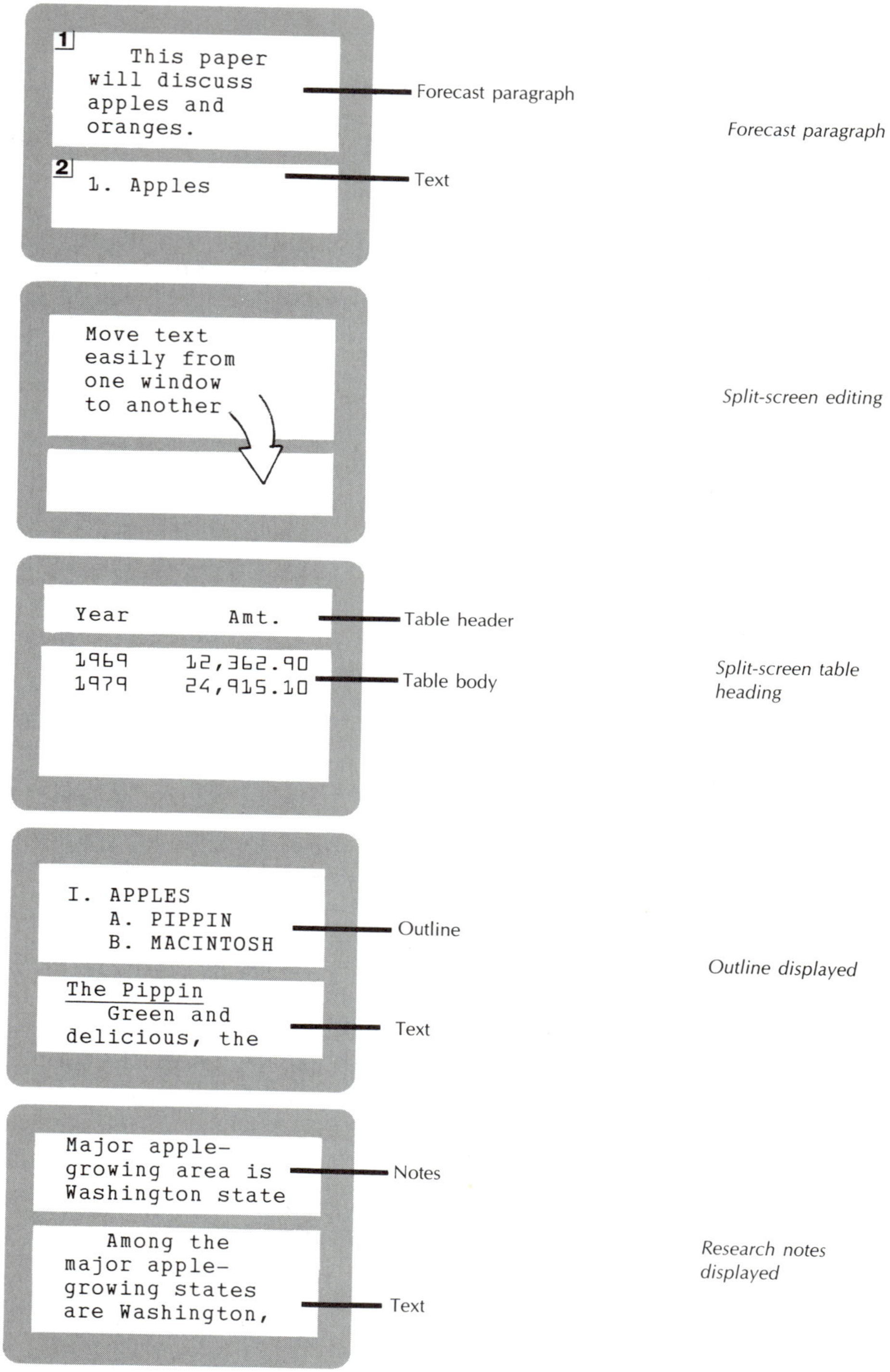

FIGURE 5–4 Multiple Window Writing Techniques

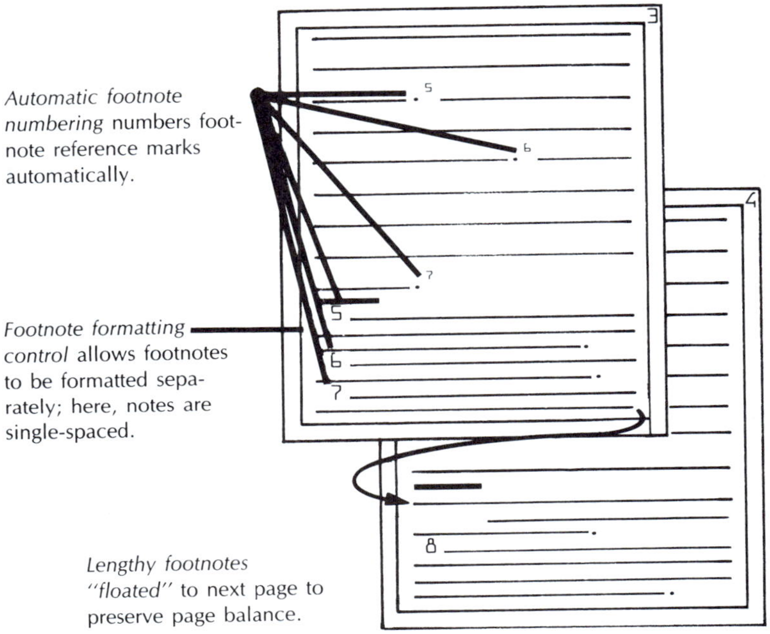

FIGURE 5–5
Footnoting Features

ADVANCED EDITING TECHNIQUES

Advanced word processing commands can help with editing, too. We'll examine two of them here: the search and search-and-replace commands. First, however, a word on the merits of editing from printed copy.

REVISING FROM PRINTED COPY

Wonderful as the computer may be, the printed page still has its merits:

Finding Errors. Detecting errors on printed copy is easier by far than finding them on the screen. Subject/verb disagreements, dangling modifiers, and other horrors seem to scream out from the printed page, even though they hide modestly and quietly among their green or amber counterparts on the video display.

Accessibility. For all the benefits of electronic writing, the paper manuscript can't be beat for accessibility. You can thumb through pages and find a passage far more quickly, in fact, than the computer can scroll you to its location in the disk file.

Ironically, it's the old-fashioned printed page — not the computer's video display — that gives the user random access to text. Scrolling on the screen saddles you with a particularly vexing variety of sequential access (Figure 5–6). (See Chapter 3 or the glossary for an explanation of the terms "sequential access" and "random access.")

For both these reasons, it makes good sense to revise your document with a printed copy at hand. This isn't to say that you need to make the actual revisions on the printed copy, although some writers will prefer to do just that. Rather, use the printed copy as a guide to the disk file's contents. You'll find that your sense of your document's overall organization, a sense that is of vital importance to writing quality, will improve measurably.

FIGURE 5–6 Advantage of Revising from Printed Copy

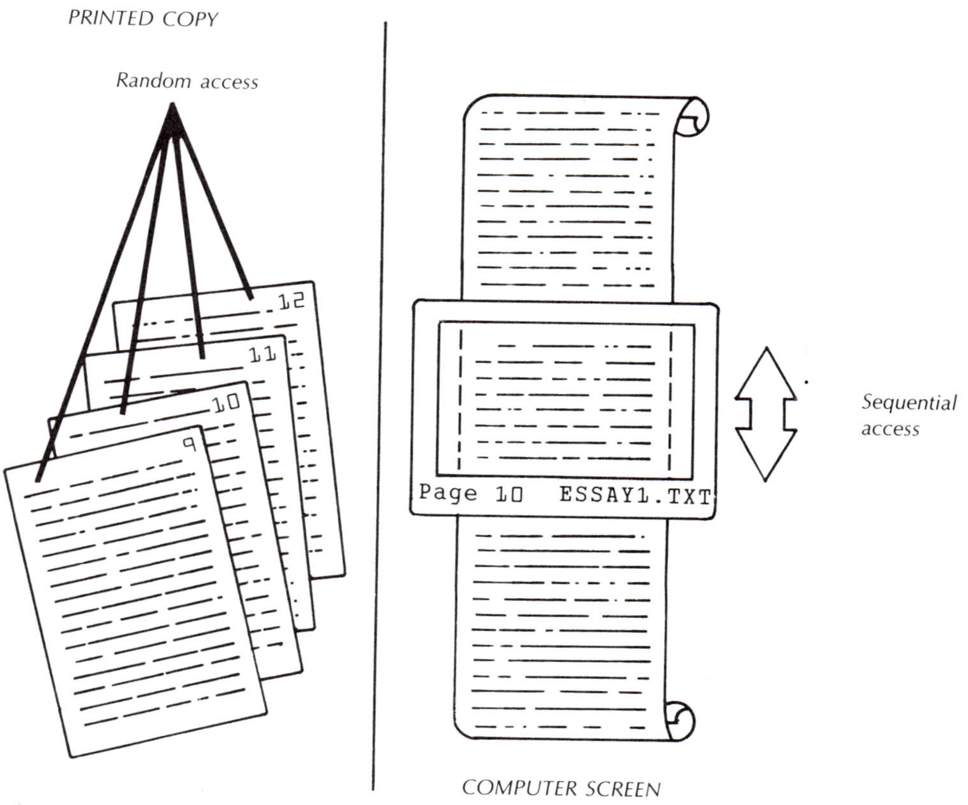

THE SEARCH COMMAND

Once you've marked up your printed copy and want to make corrections to your disk file, you can use the **search function** to locate a passage in your document quickly. To use the search function, you give the appropriate command. The program will ask you for a **search string,** or a series of characters (up to about 256 maximum) that you want to search for. The search string can include one or more words and the spaces between them. After you tell the program to go ahead and search, it looks through the file and tries to find an *exact* match (Figure 5–7).

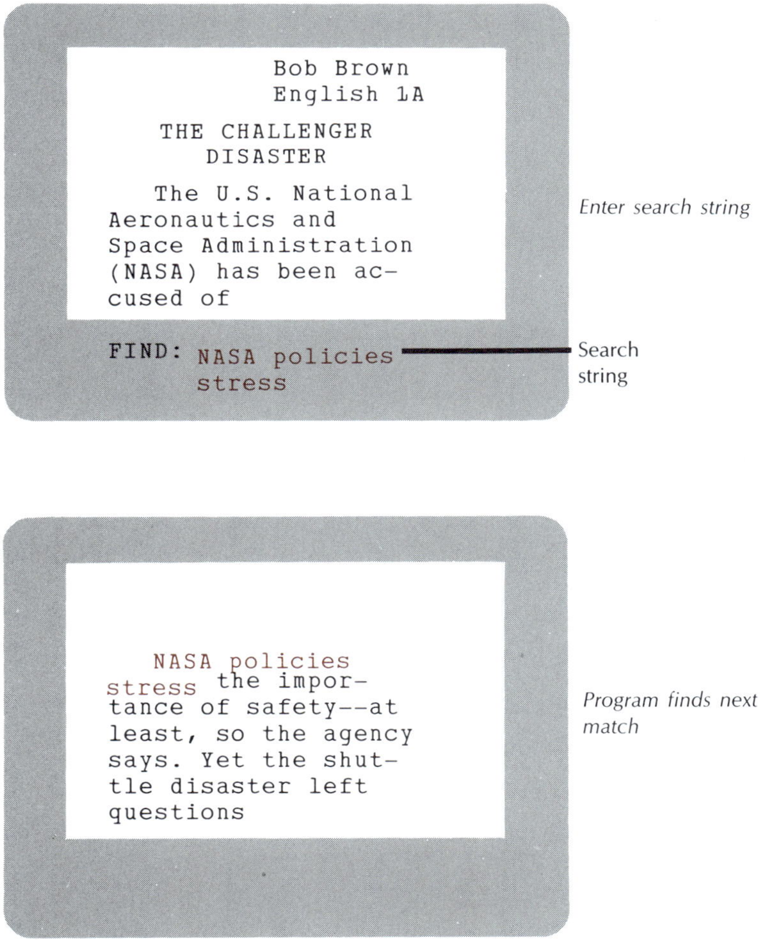

FIGURE 5–7 Search Command

It takes some forethought to use the search function effectively. Suppose, for example, you're writing a paper on the space shuttle tragedy of 1986. You want to work on a paragraph that begins "NASA policies stress the importance of safety. . . ." It doesn't make good sense to search for "NASA" since this word is likely to occur throughout the manuscript. Searching for "NASA policies stress" would almost surely take you to exactly the passage you're interested in fixing, skipping all other mentions of NASA. Be careful with your spelling when you enter the search string. If you enter, for instance, "NASA poli*tics* stress" you'd be told — after a long wait — that the program could not locate the search string in the manuscript.

Some word processing programs include search options that can help you target your search more accurately. For instance, some programs let you choose a **case-sensitive search,** one that would find "Strong" but not "strong," and a **whole-word search,** one that finds "book" but not the same four letters in "bookbinding." Often included is an option to search up (toward the beginning of the manuscript) as well as down (toward the end).

THE SEARCH-AND-REPLACE COMMAND

The **search-and-replace command** can substitute one word or phrase for another throughout a manuscript, but use it with caution. It's tempting to use the option (if available) of having all the replacements done automatically, without okaying each one, but this choice will almost certainly produce errors. Consider this example. Suppose you find you have overused the vague modifier *very.* To remove it throughout your manuscript, you use the search-and-replace command and tell it to replace *very* with nothing. The program goes through the manuscript, taking out *very* wherever it finds it and closing up the spaces left behind. The trouble is, it takes the *very* out of *antislavery, bravery, delivery, discovery, every, knavery,* and *thievery,* leaving the manuscript a mess. To avoid this problem, use the search-and-replace command with the okaying or **confirmation option** left on. This option lets you tell the program whether or not you want the change made. Another way to avoid this problem is to use the whole-word search option that some programs offer in their search-and-replace command menus. This option replaces the search word only when it's preceded and followed by blank spaces. Even so, it's still a good idea to use the confirmation option.

ADVANCED PRINTING TECHNIQUES

Advanced techniques can help you get more out of your printer, too. Introduced here are techniques for producing attractive text, generating form letters, and producing publication quality documents.

PRODUCING ATTRACTIVE TEXT

Three techniques for producing attractive-looking text are microspacing, automatic hyphenation, and proportional spacing.

Microspacing. Text printed with justified right margins often looks terrible because big gaps are inserted between words. The gaps are necessary to even out the right margin. Microspacing solves this problem. Word processing programs capable of microspacing insert tiny spaces (as small as one-twentieth of an inch) between letters and spaces to even out justified lines. Instead of a few big gaps between words, **microspacing** inserts many small gaps between letters and spaces.

Automatic Hyphenation. Another way to solve the problem of unsightly gaps between words is to hyphenate, producing more balanced character counts on each line. The problem here is the tedium of hyphenating by hand. Some programs include an **automatic hyphenation** function that goes through the text word by word. It compares the words in your document with a list of words stored on disk. When it finds words it knows how to hyphenate, it does so automatically (Figure 5–8).

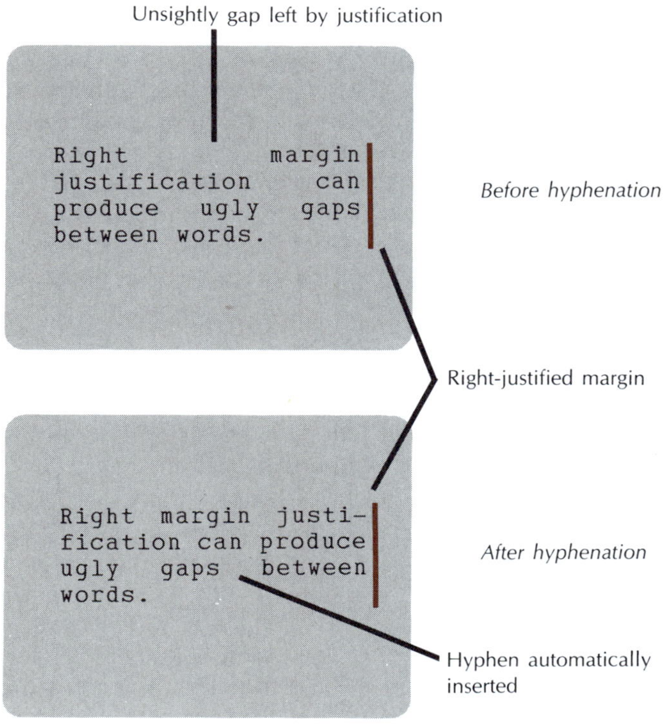

FIGURE 5–8
Automatic Hyphenation

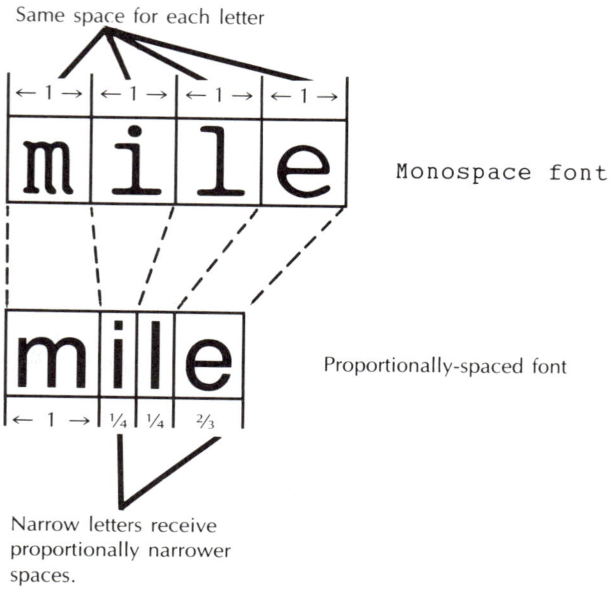

FIGURE 5–9
Proportional Spacing

Proportional Spacing. The type normally produced by personal computer printers is **monospace type.** Each character, no matter how wide or narrow, gets exactly the same amount of space. That's the one major reason computer printouts do not look like set type. Professional typesetters use **proportional spacing,** in which each letter is given a width proportional to its size; an *m* gets more space than an *i.* Some programs and printers can handle proportional spacing. They produce printouts that look as though they were professionally printed (Figure 5–9).

GENERATING FORM LETTERS

You've surely received dozens of **form letters,** a standard letter mailed to many people (often with some measure of personalization): "Dear Ms. Smith" or "Dear Mr. Jones." They begin, "You may have already won SIX BILLION DOLLARS! Just buy these $49.95 earrings and you've a chance to WIN IT BIG!" Usually, the name is inadvertently printed slightly out of register so that the ploy is obvious. For years, form letter capabilities have been the exclusive playthings of big corporations. But now (for better or worse), form letter capabilities have been handed down to the masses. Increasing numbers of personal computer word processing programs have form letter functions, and they can be made to produce excellent results. These functions are often called mail merging or print merging. At their best, form letters can send to many people a message that genuinely conveys a personal touch. That can pay off in many professions and businesses, small and large. An attorney, for example, can send out a personalized form letter to all her clients informing them that she's moved to new, more spacious quarters. A college professor can use form letters to keep colleagues informed about scholarly meetings.

Creating a form letter begins with a **main document** (sometimes called a **matrix letter**). The main document contains the text that will be printed on every letter. It also contains **data fields,** each of which has a name. The data fields tell the program what kind of information to put in the letter. The data field <<NAME>>, for example, will contain a client's name when the letter is printed. To enter the data field, it's usually necessary to use a special symbol or give a command. Doing so tells the program that the text to follow is the name of a data field.

To generate the form letters, the program goes into a list (called a **data file**) that contains all the needed information. You can create the data file with your word processing program. Each unit of information in the data file is called a **data record.** For a mailing list data base, a data record would include first name, last name, street address, city, state, and zip code. The program prints one letter for each data record, inserting the appropriate information (Figure 5–10). It usually takes some doing to get form letters to print properly. If any of the information in the data file is out of order, for instance, you'll get letters printed with information in the wrong place ("Dear Ms. 90230"). All the information in every data record has to be in exactly the right order, or the program gets confused. One by one, the program prints the letters. It begins with data record 1, putting the information from it into the correct fields in the master document. The first letter, then, is addressed to Alice Able, the second to Lester Borax, and so on.

DESKTOP PUBLISHING

With the arrival of high-quality laser printers, it's possible for personal computer users to produce documents that look like those prepared by professional typesetters. And all over the country, people are saving thousands by putting this capability, called **desktop publishing,** to good use. The term desktop publishing stems from the fact that, thanks to the personal computer, all the necessary tools will fit on a desktop (Figure 5–11). People are using their tools to prepare documents in-house, that is, without sending them out to professional typesetters.

Just about every business or professional person, sooner or later, needs a professionally printed document of some sort, even if it's just a personal letterhead. Often the needs are greater. Businesses, for instance, need such documents as brochures, price lists, and instruction sheets. Paying a professional typesetter

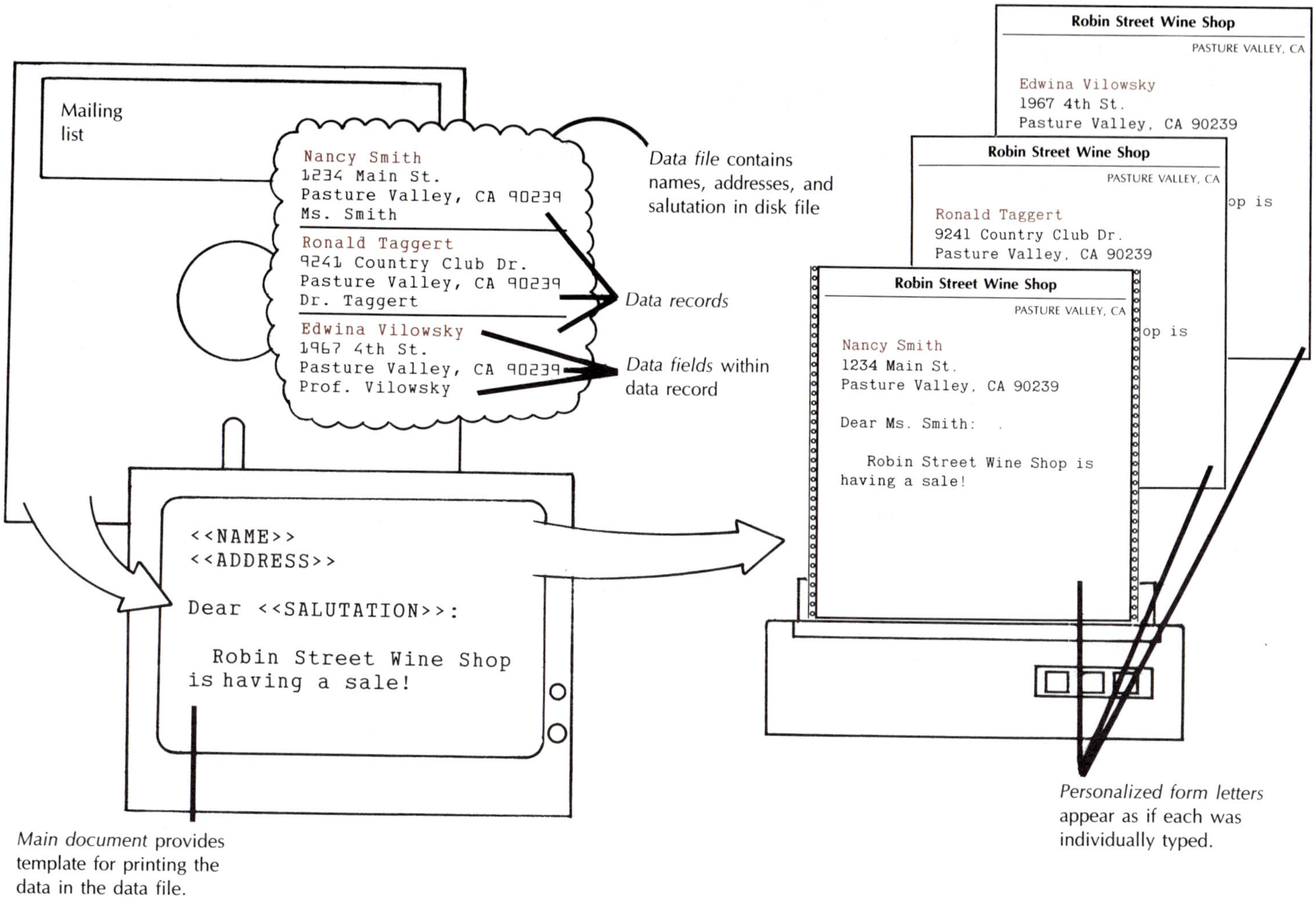

FIGURE 5–10 Mail Merging

FIGURE 5–11 Desktop Publishing with the Apple Macintosh

to design these documents is expensive. Doing it yourself on a personal computer and laser printer can lead to big savings. Of course, it's not economical to *print* thousands of copies; you'll still need the printshop. But it's much cheaper to have them run off a document you've already designed and prepared; most document production costs occur in the layout and typesetting stages.

Ordinary word processing programs such as WordStar or Microsoft Word can be used for desktop publishing, of course, but these programs provide very limited tools for controlling the appearance of text on the page. Some word processing programs, such as Word and WordPerfect, produce printouts in multiple columns running side-by-side down the page, but it's rare to find one that can incorporate graphic images, such as drawings or borders. For this reason, desktop publishers often use three programs to create documents in-house:

A Word Processing Program. The document's text is created with a word processing program and stored on disk;

A Graphics Program. Pictures and other graphic images are created with the graphics packages discussed in Chapter 11 (such as presentation graphics and paint programs); and

A Page Layout Program. Finally, the text and graphics are combined using a **page layout program,** a program that provides tools for creating and printing well-designed pages.

Desktop publishing has become one of the fastest-growing application areas in personal computing, and it has attracted many new products (and even new magazines, such as *Desktop Publishing*). A major drawback to desktop publishing, however, is that most personal computer users just don't have the graphics sensibility needed for some design jobs. It's one thing, for instance, to create a price list. It's quite another to prepare a company's annual report. In general, you should stay away from critical document designs — ones which thousands of people will see and which will reflect on the company's image — unless you've some graphics design training.

ADDITIONAL ADVANCED FEATURES

Writers in some fields need special word processing features that only a few programs provide. These fields include mathematics, statistics, foreign languages, engineering, public relations, and computer science. If you plan to pursue a career in one of these fields, you may wish to consider a program that offers some of these advanced features (see Table 5–1).

Arithmetic Functions. Performs addition, subtraction, multiplication, and division on columns or rows of figures. Useful for financial reports.

Automatic Equation Numbering. Numbers mathematical equations automatically. Useful for mathematical writing.

Equation Mode. Allows easy entry of mathematical equations.

Foreign Language/Technical Characters. Displays and prints foreign language or technical characters.

Graphics. Permits merging of graphics (charts, graphs, etc.) and text.

Horizontal Scrolling. Allows use of paper wider than 8½ inches.

TABLE 5–1 Word Processing Program Features

	Glossaries	Macros	Style sheets	Multiple windows	Automatic footnote numbering	Footnote format control
MICROSOFT WORD	yes	yes	yes	yes (6)	yes	yes
PC-WRITE	yes	yes	yes	yes (2)	yes	yes
PFS-WRITE	no	no	no	no	no	no
WORDPERFECT	no	yes	no	yes	yes	yes
WORDSTAR 3.3	no	no	no	no	no	no

* Version 3.0 and later.
† Superscript available for character formatting, but no automatic footnote function.

Index Generation. Automatically creates an index, including correct page number references, from items flagged in the text.

Multiple Columns. Prints text in two or more columns on the page. Useful for newsletters produced by public relations departments.

Table of Contents Generation. Automatically creates a table of contents for a document.

SUMMARY

Advanced features for writing, editing, and printing can help you work more productively and write better with word processing software. Advanced writing features include glossaries, boilerplating, macros, programmable keyboard commands, style sheets, multiple windows, and footnotes.

Glossaries store frequently used passages of text and let you enter them with just a few keystrokes. They can be used to insert boilerplate passages, or passages of text that deal with recurring situations. You can also store boilerplate passages in their own text files. Most word processors have a file-merging command that lets you insert a file in a document you are writing. Using this command, you can insert boilerplate files anywhere you wish.

More timesaving techniques are possible with programs that include macro, programmable keyboard command, or style sheet features. Macros are files containing a series of commands, which will be executed one by one (as if you had a robot typing at your keyboard for you). Other programs offer programmable keyboard command features, which let you enter several commands with just one keystroke. Still others offer style sheets, which let you list the formatting characteristics you want (such as margin width) and attach them in just one keystroke to any document.

Footnote superscript	Float footnotes	Search	Search-and-replace	Microspacing	Automatic hyphenation	Proportional spacing	Mail merging
yes	yes*	yes	yes	yes	yes	yes	yes
yes	no	yes	yes	yes	no	yes	yes
yes†	no	yes	yes	no	no	no	yes
yes	yes	yes	yes	yes	yes	yes	yes
yes†	no	yes	yes	yes	yes	no	optional

Programs with multiple window capabilities let you display two or more parts of the same document at the same time. Most of these programs also let you look at two or more different documents at the same time. Multiple windows make possible several useful writing techniques. You can display signpost paragraphs, outlines, and table headers in one window while you're writing in another. You can easily move text from one window to another, facilitating editing.

Few programs offer footnote utilities that work well. The best ones number the footnotes automatically, permit you to format the footnotes any way you wish, superscribe the footnote reference mark, and float lengthy footnotes to the next page.

Advanced features such as search and search-and-replace commands can help with editing. You will get the best results if you revise from printed copy. When you find a mistake, load your document. The search command can take you immediately to the passage you want to fix. Sometimes it's desirable to make a change in wording throughout a document; if so, the search-and-replace command is useful. Be sure to use it, however, with the confirmation option turned on.

Advanced printing techniques can help you produce more attractively printed documents. Microspacing and automatic hyphenation improve the appearance of right-justified text. Proportional spacing makes your work look as though it were professionally printed.

Many programs will generate form letters. First, you create a master document, which contains the text you want to appear in every letter. Then you add data fields, which tell the program what kind of information to place in the letters. Next, you make a data file, which contains the information you want inserted. Finally, you give the command that starts printing the letters. Form letter functions work best when joined with a file management or data base management program.

High-quality laser printers and desktop publishing software now make it possible for individuals and businesses to prepare many documents in-house, instead of sending them out to layout artists or typesetters. Personal computer users who lack graphics or design training, however, should not attempt to create documents that help to form a company's image.

KEY TERMS

automatic hyphenation
boilerplate
case-sensitive search
confirmation option
data field
data file
data record
desktop publishing

endnotes
file merge command
footnote reference mark
form letter
glossary
key enhancement program
macro
main document
matrix letter
microspacing
monospace type
multiple windows
page layout program
proportional spacing
search function
search string
search-and-replace command
style sheet
whole-word search
window
windowing

REVIEW QUESTIONS AND EXERCISES

1. Suppose you're the owner of a small business of some sort — say, a business that uses desktop publishing equipment to prepare brochures, newsletters, and price lists for other local businesses. Develop three or four boilerplate passages that would help you deal with routine inquiry letters (letters asking, for instance, about the kind of services you provide, the terms of payment, the typesetting options available). Now write a one-page letter in reply to a typical inquiry. Use two or three of these boilerplate passages, but add opening, closing, and other statements that give it a personal touch.
2. Find out whether your word processing program has a glossary feature. If it does, try storing the boilerplate you created in No. 1 in glossaries and reinserting the glossaries in a document. If it doesn't, find out how to insert one file into another using the file merge command. Store your boilerplate in separate disk files and practice inserting them in your document.
3. With the word processing program you're using, how many commands and keystrokes does it take to center a heading, boldface it, and leave three blank lines before and after it? Does your word processing program let you write macros? If it does, try writing a macro that accomplishes this formatting task with one command.
4. Find out whether your word processing program is capable of windowing. If it is, try splitting the screen horizontally, with equal-sized windows at the top and bottom of the screen. Write some text in both windows, and practice moving text from one window to the next.
5. Find out whether your word processing program does footnotes. If it does, determine whether it positions the notes at the bottom of the page or the end of the document. If you have a choice, how do you choose between them? How does your program print the footnote reference mark? Can

you superscribe it (i.e., position it one-half line higher than the text preceding it)? Does your program "float" lengthy footnotes to the next page? Can you double-space the text but single-space the footnotes?

6. Why is it usually better to revise from printed copy rather than on the screen?
7. Your word processing program almost certainly has search and search-and-replace features. Load a document that you've already created, and use it for searching experiments. Try the search feature first. Experiment with the default search mode, the one the program will use if you simply give the search command and type in a search string. If your program can do case-sensitive and whole-word searches, experiment with these. Now try the search-and-replace feature. What is the program's default approach to searching and replacing (that is, the approach it will use unless in default of other instructions from you)? Does it stop at each substitution and ask for confirmation? If not, how do you tell the program that you want to confirm each substitution?
8. If your word processing program has a mail merge feature, try it out. Identify four or five friends to whom you'd like to send news about what you've been up to at college. Make up a data file containing, for each data record, name, address, city, state, zip, salutation. Be sure to follow your program's rules for writing the data records as carefully as possible. Now create the main document, which is the text of the letter you want to send them. Finally, use the print merge command to start printing the form letter. If something goes wrong (it's likely), try to figure out where you made a mistake. Hint: The items in each data record must be separated by precise delimiters — usually commas or a tab keystroke.
9. Consider your postgraduate word processing needs in your chosen career or profession. Will you need any of the special features listed in the section entitled "Additional Advanced Features" (e.g., arithmetic, equation numbering, equation mode, foreign language and technical characters, graphics, horizontal scrolling, index generation, multiple columns, or table of contents generation)? Does the word processing program you're currently using have these features? If not, identify a program that does. (Hint: *PC: The Independent Guide to IBM-Standard Personal Computing* publishes periodic reviews of word processing software, and these reviews list all the features available with dozens of currently available programs.)

FOR FURTHER READING

ADVANCED WRITING AND EDITING TECHNIQUES

Bean, John C. "Computerized Word-Processing as an Aid to Revision," *College Composition and Communication* (May 1983).

Crider, Janet. "Working with WordPerfect's Column Capabilities," *IBM PC Update* (March 1986).

Cummings, Steve. "Word Processors Provide Scientific Symbols," *PC Week* (September 10, 1985).

Ditlea, Steve. "How Wordsmiths Write Smarter: You Can Profit from the Tips of These Creative Pros Who Make Their Living Using Computers to Craft Words," *Personal Computing* (March 1986).

Holz, L. "Merge, and Merge Again: The Fine Art of Boilerplating," *Business Software* (April 1985).

MacKay, Pierre A. "Typesetting Problem Scripts: Computer Typesetting Provides a Solution for Arabic and Similar Scripts," *Byte* (February 1986).

Noble, David F., and Virginia Noble. *Improve Your Writing with Word Processing* (Indianapolis: Que, 1984).

Stratton, Dorothy. *Magic Writing: A Writer's Guide to Word Processing* (New York: New American Library, 1985).

DESKTOP PUBLISHING

Benson, Roger R. "Boosting Productivity Through Timely, Tailored Documents," *Graphic Arts Monthly* (March 1985).

Carney, Tom. "Personal Publishing on Microcomputers," *Research in Word Processing Newsletter* (April 1986).

Davis, Frederic E., John Barry, and Michael Wiesenberg. *Desktop Publishing* (Homewood, Ill.: Dow Jones-Irwin, 1986).

Markoff, J., P. Robinson, and D. Osgood. "Desktop Publishing with the Macintosh," *Byte* (May 1985).

Seymour, Jim. "Desktop Publishing: The One-Stop Type Shop," *Today's Office* (August 1985).

Stultz, Russell A. *Writing and Publishing on Your Microcomputer: How to Create and Produce Professional-Quality Documentation* (Plano, Texas: Wordware Publishing, 1984).

Ulick, Terry. "An Introduction to Making Pages: Pagination Explained," *Personal Publishing* (February 1986).

Varian, Hal R. "PCTEX and MicroTEX: Professional Typesetting on MS-DOS Machines," *Byte* (April 1985).

Vose, G. Michael, and Gregg Williams. "Computer Science Considerations: Donald Knuth Speaks on His Involvement with Digital Typography," *Byte* (February 1986).

6 Word Processing Horizons: Accessory Software You Can Use

"If you don't write for a living, but regularly produce business letters, memos, or even speeches on occasion, a word processor enhanced by the right supporting software can make you a far more effective communicator."

Peter Bates *Personal Computing*

No computer can automatically turn a poor writer into a good one, but a variety of word processing accessory programs can help a good writer do a better job. In the interests of higher writing productivity and quality, you'll be wise to make these programs part of your day-to-day writing routine. Accessory programs are available for both writing and editing text.

ACCESSORY PROGRAMS FOR WRITING

Accessory programs useful during the creative part of the writing process include outlining programs and memory resident thesauruses. In the future, optical disk technology may put the equivalent of a university's reference library on your desktop.

OUTLINING PROGRAMS

Researchers and teachers who specialize in composition now agree that composition is a complex process, one that includes far more than the act of setting hand to paper (or keyboard). The great importance of prewriting, the stage of the writing process that precedes writing, is now widely recognized. Planning is a particularly important part of the prewriting process, especially when you're writing with word processing software. Since the video display screen shows you only one-third of a page at a time, it's difficult to achieve a sense of your document's overall structure. Paying attention to your document's organization, particularly through planning in the prewriting stage, may contribute significantly to writing quality.

You were probably taught one such device in high school: the outline. Most good writers do at least some outlining on paper before plunging into composition. Yet outlining on paper, although of some value, seems to defeat its own purpose. Outlining should involve a process of discovery, in which preparing the outline makes you more aware of what you're trying to say. And it should suggest fruitful ways to change the outline. Yet the difficulty and mess involved in altering a paper outline inhibits the reorganizing and restructuring that ideally ought to characterize the process. A word processing program provides a way around this problem, but introduces another. You can write an outline and revise it readily with a word processor, but once the outline gets long enough the new problem arises. You can only see one-third of a page at a time, so the outline's overall structure is hidden from your view.

Outlining programs (also called idea processing programs) were designed to overcome the limitations of word processing software for outlining purposes. Like a word processing program, an outlining program gives you tools for writing and revising an outline. Unlike a word processing program, however, it does something more: it lets you collapse or hide subordinate headings in the outline so that you can see the outline's overall structure in just one screen. If you want to see the subordinate headings, a keystroke expands the hidden headings, bringing them back into view. The box "An Idea Processor in Action" illustrates the outlining program's value.

(*text continues on p. 174*)

An Idea Processor in Action

Lisa Williams, a first-year graduate student in the humanities, is writing a paper on the famous trio sonatas of the composer Georg Philipp Telemann (1681–1767). She's done her reading and research, and now it's time to write. Instead of starting with her word processing program, however, she begins by loading ThinkTank, an idea processor. When ThinkTank's initial display screen appears, Lisa types the subject of her paper (Figure 6–1). Since this heading is the outline's subject, all other headings will be subordinate to it. To put it another way, this heading is a *first-level heading;* subordinate to it will be a *second-level heading*. Lisa adds the first of several second-level headings now (Figure 6–2).

Notice that the minus sign in front of the first-level heading has changed to a plus sign. The plus sign indicates that there's a subheading under the heading — a point that's obvious now, since the subheading is visible. But since there's a way to make subheadings disappear from view, the plus sign becomes necessary to tell you there's something under the heading.

Lisa now uses an excellent idea-generating technique called *brainstorming*. In brainstorming, the object is simply to write down everything about

FIGURE 6–1 First Heading: Subject of the Paper

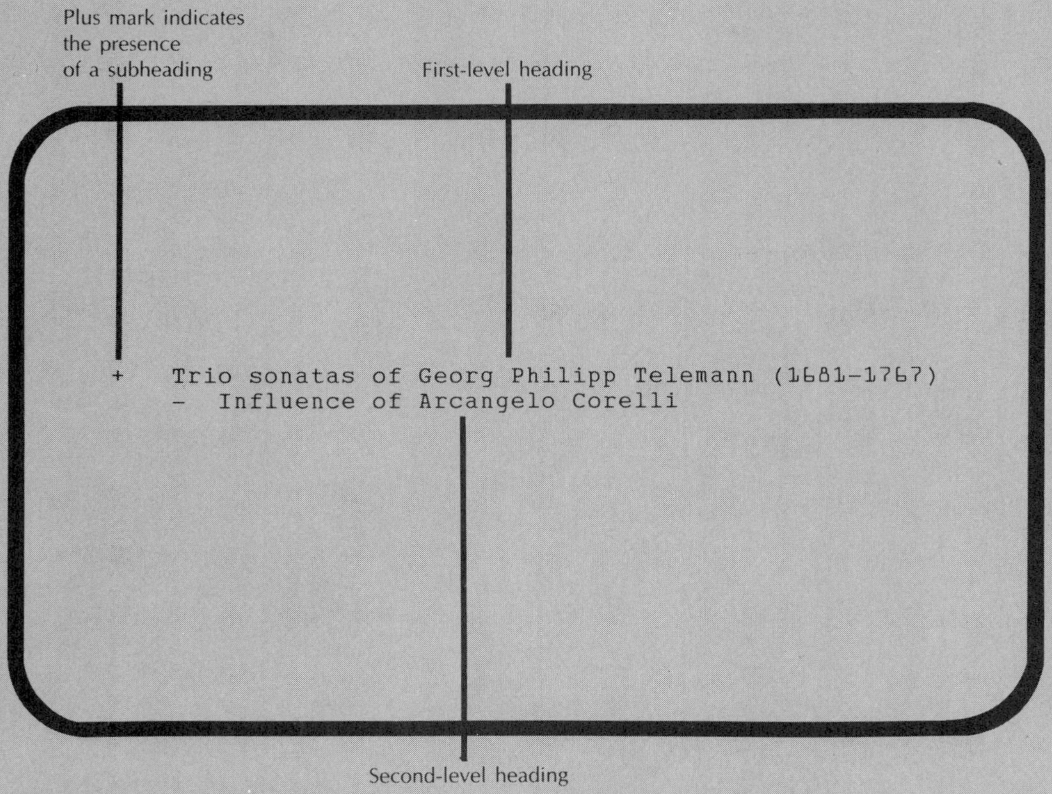

FIGURE 6–2 Second-Level Heading

the subject you can think of, in no particular order. And that's just what she does (Figure 6–3). Now that she has listed all the topics she wants to discuss, Lisa fleshes out the outline (Figure 6–4) by adding some third-level headings. Note the plus sign next to the second-level heading "Instrumentation: popular instruments predominate." Her outline is getting big enough to fill up her display screen, so she decides to collapse the third-level headings (Figure 6–5). The plus sign tells her that some third-level headings are hidden.

Now Lisa looks at her outline with an eye to restructuring it. She looks at the headings "flexibility of instrumentation possible" and "great technical

(box continues on next page)

An Idea Processor in Action (continued)

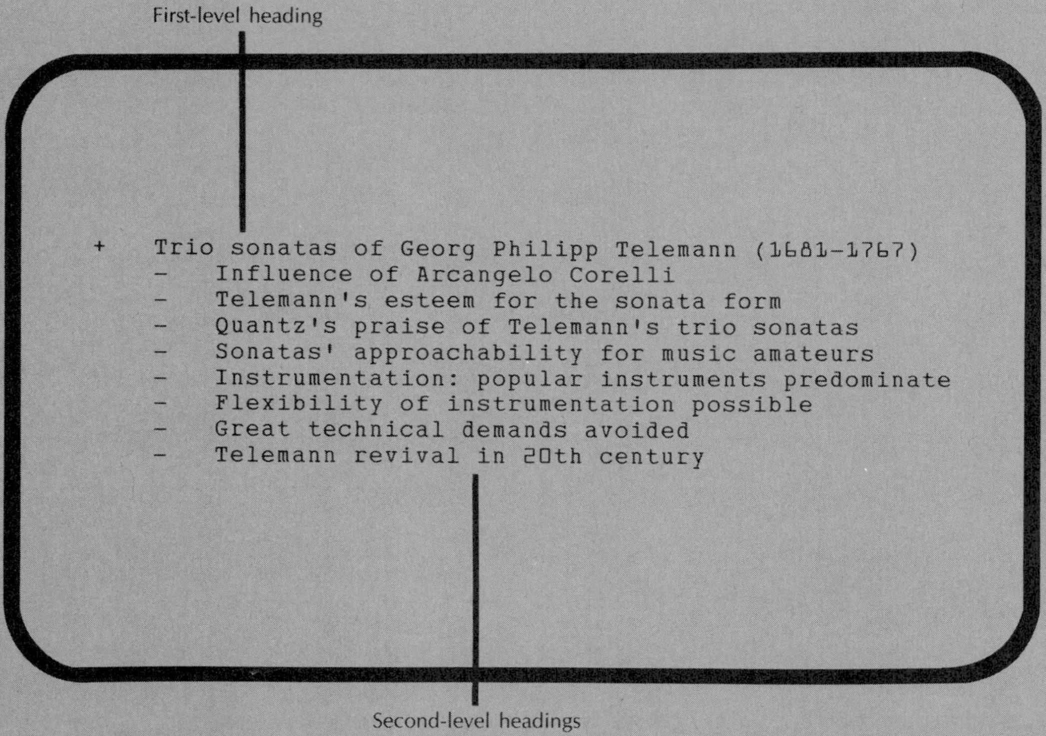

FIGURE 6–3 Brainstorming

demands avoided." Clearly, both of these headings really belong under the heading titled "sonata's approachability for musical amateurs." She uses ThinkTank's commands for restructuring the outline, producing the results shown in Figure 6–6.

Next, Lisa collapses the third-level headings again and rearranges the second-level ones (Figure 6–7). She has an appropriate plan for her paper, beginning with praise for Telemann's skills as a composer, followed by an examination of his strong

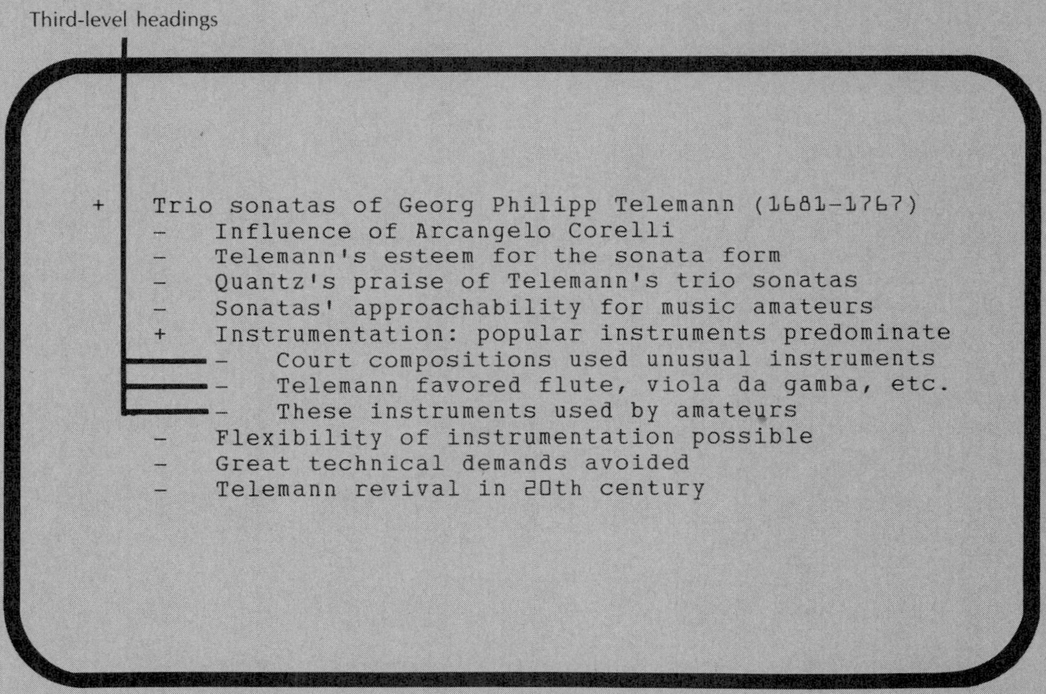

FIGURE 6–4 Adding Third-Level Headings

interest in the sonata form, and of the influence on him of the Italian master Corelli. Then the paper will discuss how Telemann brought his considerable gifts and skill to ordinary people, the amateur musicians of his day. The paper concludes with an examination of twentieth-century interest in Telemann.

Lisa rounds out her outline now by adding third-level headings. In the end, she has produced a fine guide for writing her paper.

(box continues on next page)

An Idea Processor in Action (continued)

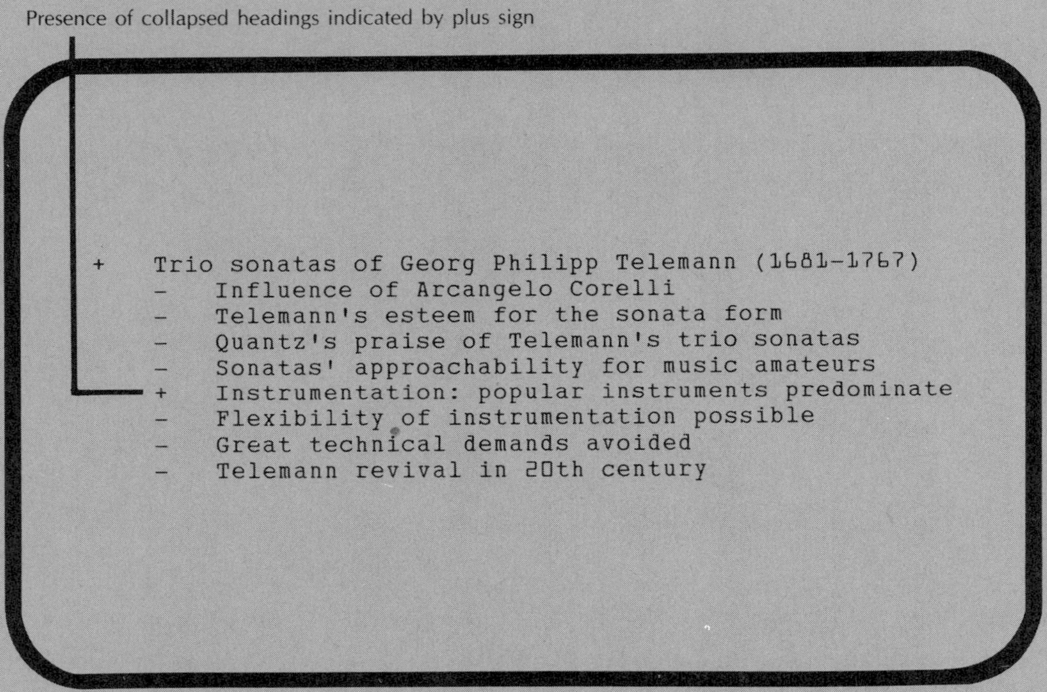

FIGURE 6–5 Collapsing the Third-Level Headings

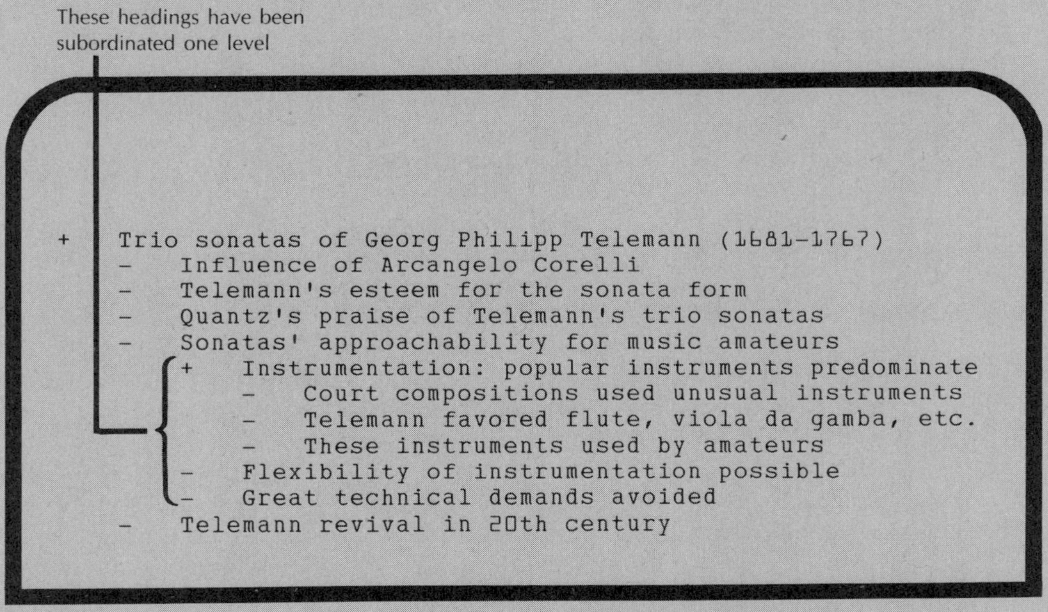

FIGURE 6–6 Restructuring the Outline

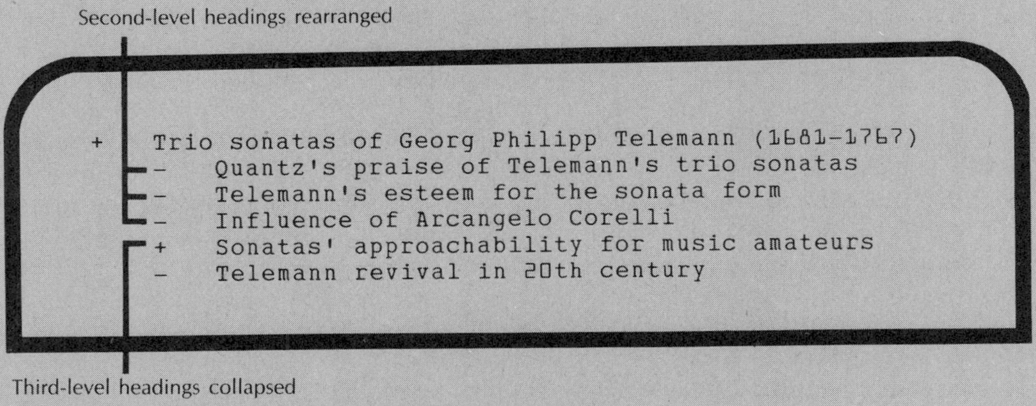

FIGURE 6–7 Rearranging the Second-Level Headings

MEMORY-RESIDENT OUTLINING PROGRAMS

Outlining programs are fun to use and, doubtless, do for outlining what word processing does for writing: they reduce the tedium and paperwork that would be involved in old-fashioned, pencil-and-paper revision. The result, moreover, is very worthwhile, especially when you're writing something that's more than a few pages long. In such cases, the outline amounts to a road map to your document's organization. Given that word processing makes it difficult to see your document's overall structure, the outline becomes especially important when you're writing with a computer.

Unfortunately, there's one important drawback to outlining programs such as ThinkTank. For reasons that will be explained in a moment, they erect barriers to revision of the outline as the writing plan changes during the document's composition. And changes in the plan will occur. As research on the composition process has demonstrated, professional writers cycle back and forth among planning, writing, and revision activities as they create a document. Writing, in short, is a discovery process, one in which the writer's sense of the document's overall structure is virtually certain to change. If the outline is to serve as an accurate road map of that structure, it must be updated as changes occur. And this is precisely where first-generation outlining programs such as ThinkTank fall down.

All outlining programs, to be sure, facilitate an outline's revision; most include text insertion, deletion, and moving commands that rival those of the best word processing software. Yet, because today's personal computers can execute only one program at a time, these tools are available only after going through a process so tedious that few writers will update their computer-generated outlines. Consider: to make an update, you'll have to save your document to disk, exit the word processing program, load the outlining program, update the outline, save the updated outline, print the updated outline, exit the outlining program, load the word processing program, scroll to the place you left off, and resume working.

Most of today's personal computers can't run two programs at once, but some clever programming has made it far easier to switch from one program to another (and back again). Many personal computers have 512K or more of RAM installed, but most popular word processing programs (such as WordStar or Microsoft Word) were designed back in the days when few computers were equipped with more than 128K or 256K. Much of a 512K or 640K computer's memory is, therefore, unused. There's room in this unused memory for a supplementary program, such as a spelling checker, an appointment calendar, or an outlining program. At a keystroke, the supplementary program — called a **memory-resident program** in computer jargon — can leap onto the screen, suspending a word processing program's execution and allowing the user to make immediate use of whatever tools the supplementary program provides.

Memory-resident outlining programs, such as Living Videotext's Ready! and SoftWorks Development's PC-OUTLINE, reduce the tedium of updating outlines considerably. Suppose you're writing a business report and, in the middle of the introduction, you realize that you need a separate chapter to talk about the research methodology. At a keystroke, the outline leaps into view on the screen. You make the changes and save them. Another keystroke returns you to the word processing program, positioning the cursor at precisely the same spot you were at when you left the program to update the outline.

OUTLINING FEATURES IN WORD PROCESSING PROGRAMS

Taking the idea of memory-resident outlining software one step further, word processing software (such as Microsoft Word, version 3.0 and later) is now available that includes outlining functions along with the standard word processing ones. Increasing numbers of writers believe that the combination is so effective that most word processing programs will incorporate this feature in the future.

What makes this combination so effective is that, when you write with one of these programs, the document and the outline are linked by the computer. When you're using the program in its outlining mode, you write a standard outline with outline headings (flush to the left margin) and indented subheadings. When you shift to the document mode, however, the headings and subheadings become titles and subheadings in a document. Now let's suppose you change the document's organization using a block move. You move a subheading and all the text under it to a new location in the document. As you do the block move, the program automatically updates the outline, restructuring the subheadings so that the outline reflects what you've done. You can also make changes on the outline. If you move a subheading in the outline mode, for example, the document will be changed: the program will automatically move the subheading — together with all the text under it — to reflect the change you've made. At any time, in short, the outline accurately reflects your document's structure, and you can see that evolving structure at a keystroke.

THE MEMORY-RESIDENT THESAURUS

At the dawn of the nineteenth century, Peter Roget, a British physician and physiologist, completed a "classed catalog of words" that he found "of much use to me in literary composition."[1] First published in 1852, the *Thesaurus* has

The Online Thesaurus at Work

Tom Chang is taking a course in creative writing, and he's decided to write a short story about a high-caste Hindu in India and the Hindu's social attitudes. He writes, "The Brahman picked his way through the crowd of pilgrims, carefully avoiding the contact that would have polluted him," and he's not sure about *crowd*. *Crowd* suggests a close gathering, particularly one in which individuality and moral purpose become submerged (hence "crowd mentality"). It works poorly with *pilgrims*, who may well have submerged their individuality, but for a high religious purpose. Highlighting *crowd* and using the thesaurus search command produces the results shown in Figure 6–8. Notice that the screen has divided into two parts; the text is shown at the bottom, with the search term highlighted, and the synonyms appear at the top.

The SPACEBAR or BACKSPACE keys can be used to highlight one of the synonyms. Pressing the ESCAPE key inserts the highlighted word in the text (Figure 6–9). *Mob* clearly isn't the right choice; it connotes a crowd bent on destruction. *Host* works better, with its connotation of a multitude sharing a single purpose (Figure 6–10).

Don't expect a memory-resident thesaurus to show you synonyms for obscure or little-used words. Most currently available electronic thesauri are designed to work with floppy disk systems, so there's rarely room for more than 50,000 synonyms of 5,000 or so words. A new memory-resident thesaurus, the Webster's NewWorld® On-Line Thesaurus, is designed for use with higher-capacity hard disks; it offers 120,000 synonyms for 20,000 words.

FIGURE 6–8 Online Thesaurus in Action

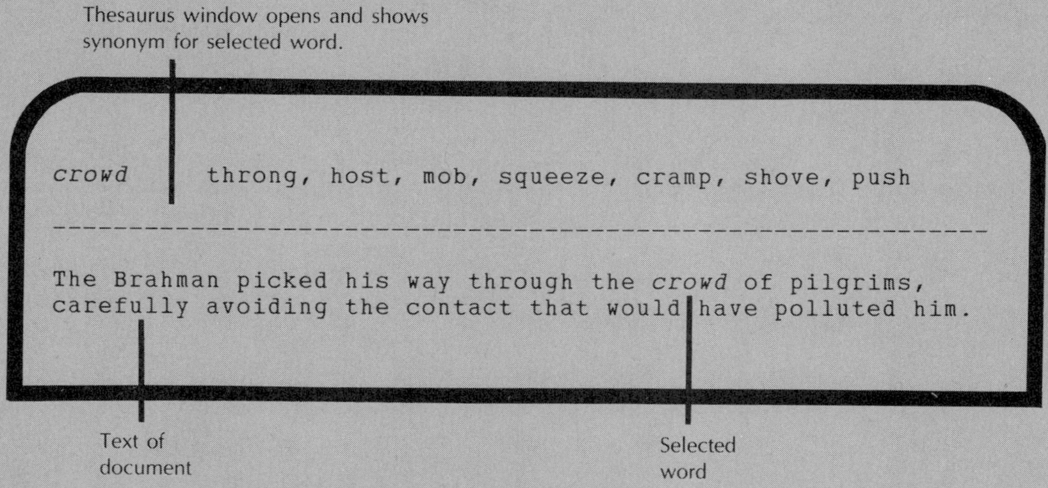

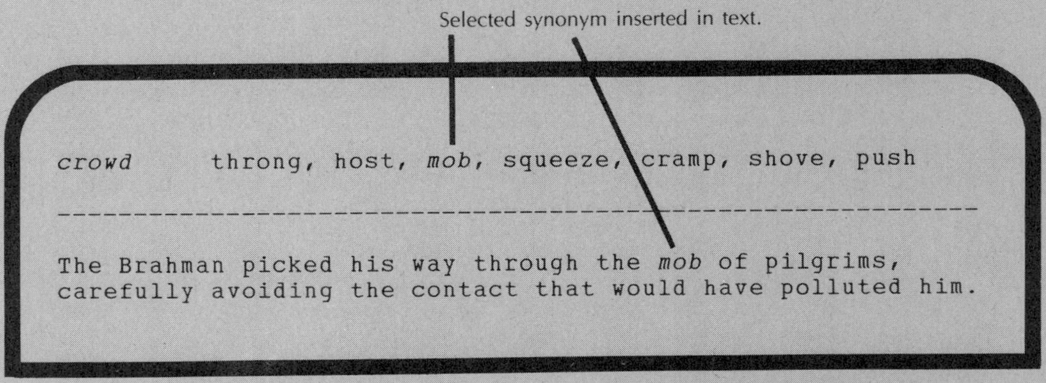

FIGURE 6–9 Selected Word Inserted in Text

FIGURE 6–10 Another Selected Word Inserted in Text

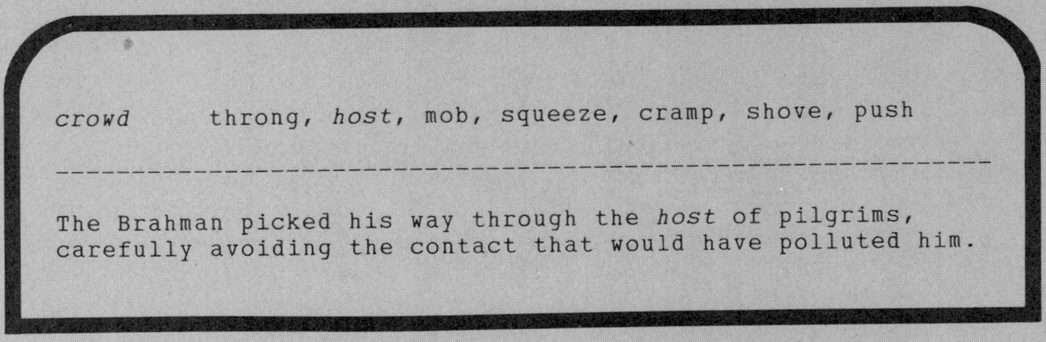

guided several generations of writers to more vivid words. But they need thumb through the book no longer: the computer can do it automatically. Roget would have been pleased: he tinkered for years trying to perfect a mechanical calculator.

What makes the computer-based thesaurus appealing to writers is that it is memory resident. A keystroke suspends operation of your word processing program and brings the **memory-resident thesaurus** program to life. As you can see in the box "The Online Thesaurus at Work," the effect is useful indeed; you needn't leave your word processing program to use it.

More than a few computer-using writers believe online thesauri to be fanciful frills, arguing that one can keep a thesaurus next to the computer. Yet there's a good case for using the computerized thesaurus. Cycling the various options into and out of your sentence can be accomplished quickly and easily; all that's required is a few keystrokes. You can see the effect of word substitutions and experiment with them. That's sure to refine your sensitivity to the language.

HORIZONS OF COMPUTER WRITING AIDS

Imagine sitting at your computer, writing a paper about the history of twentieth-century technology, and discovering that you're not quite sure how to define *transistor.* No problem. You strike a key, and a memory-resident encyclopedia pops up. You tell it to look up the word you just typed, *transistor,* and off it goes, searching through a disk-based encyclopedia in your computer's optical disk drive. In a fraction of a second, the *Academic American Encyclopedia*'s article on transistors appears on your screen. Sound futuristic? It's not (Figure 6–11). All the technology is already available, including optical disk drives, encyclopedias distributed on high-density optical disks, and the memory-resident software needed for online access. As the price of optical drives and compact disks continues to decline, computer-readable information reservoirs of this kind will become increasingly common features of personal computer systems.

Using currently available consumer technology (compact disks and disk drives), the contents of approximately 500 to 1,000 floppy disks (roughly 275,000 pages of double-spaced, typewritten text!) can be stored on a single compact disk. The implications of this technology for public information access are staggering. A museum could put a complete catalogue of its collection on optical disks, so that entering "Matisse" and "Dancers" would bring up a highly detailed, colorful reproduction on your computer screen. For brushing up on the news, disks containing two or three months of several major national newspapers could be mailed regularly to subscribers. Whether these and other optical disk applications will be commercially viable remains to be seen, but trends point in that direction.

FIGURE 6–11
CD-ROM
Disk and Disk Drive

ACCESSORY PROGRAMS FOR EDITING

Accessory programs for text revision and proofreading include spelling checkers and software for style analysis. Limited in their capabilities, these programs cannot take the place of thoughtful, hand revision efforts. A writer who understands their limitations, however, can and should use them.

SPELLING CHECKERS

Spelling checkers, programs that detect spelling mistakes and typographical errors in files created by word processing programs, are all but indispensable for all computer writing applications, but they vary considerably in quality. At one extreme are programs that simply mark the errors they find, requiring you to go through the text with a word processing program and repair them. At the other extreme are programs that identify very close to 100 percent of the errors, display them in their context, look up the correct spelling and insert it in the text file (so you don't have to do it yourself). Make sure you're working with the best spelling checker you can get.

How Spelling Checkers Work. Spelling checkers generally follow these steps to proofread a document:

Reading the Document. The checker reads the document and compiles an alphabetized list of the *unique words* it contains (that is, the list of words compiled after eliminating all duplicates).

Comparing the Unique Words to the Dictionary. Next, the checker compares the list of unique words to the words contained in its main dictionary. When one of the unique words cannot be matched with the items in the dictionary, it is put into a list of questionable words.

Displaying the Questionable Words. Finally, the spelling checker shows you the list of questionable words. High-quality programs show you the questionable word in its context (the line or paragraph in which it occurs) and permit you to type a correction, which goes into the document in place of the error (Figure 6–12).

Now that you know how spelling checkers work, you'll realize the value of a large dictionary (at least 50,000 words, and preferably 80,000 or 100,000). A program with a small dictionary (say, 20,000 words) will display as questionable many words that are actually spelled correctly. You'll have to go through the list of them, one by one. That's a waste of time.

Limitations of Spelling Checkers. Spelling checkers are likely to list as questionable many words which are correctly spelled, and there are some kinds of spelling errors which they cannot detect at all.

FIGURE 6–12 Spelling Mistake Displayed in Context

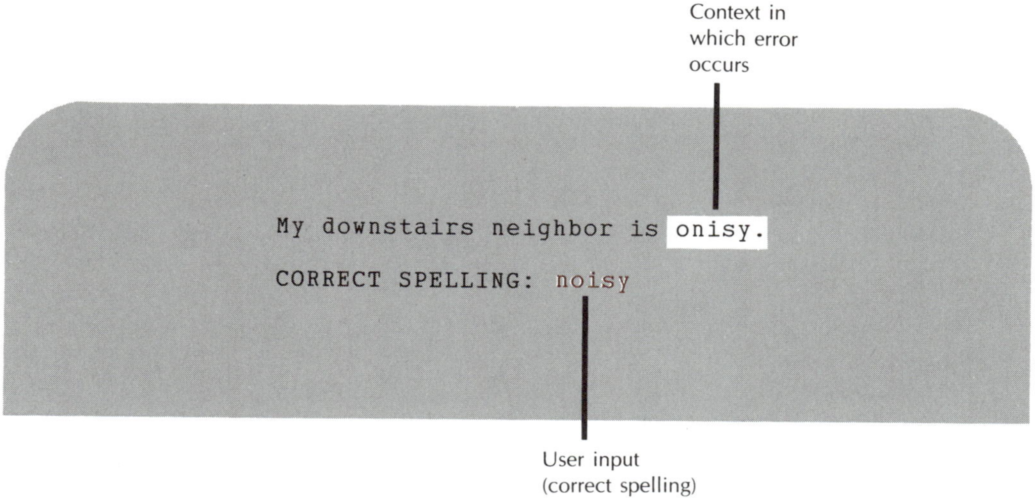

Correctly Spelled Words in the Questionable Word List. Programs with small dictionaries (for instance, 20,000 words) will report an unacceptably long list of questionable words after checking a manuscript. For that reason, such programs cannot be recommended for professional work. Even a large dictionary (for instance, 75,000 words) does not guarantee that correctly spelled words will pass inspection. One of the best spelling checkers available will list the following types of words as questionable: (1) plural forms of many words which are present in the dictionary only in their singular form (*dissertations, drawbacks, encoders*); (2) names and unfamiliar geographical terms (*Williamson, Timbuktu, Tirukittesvaram*) (note, however, that *Cucamonga* is in the program's main dictionary); (3) technical terms peculiar to a field (*pathogenesis, paraplate, stochastic*); and (4) infrequently used words with the prefixes or suffixes un-, non-, pre-, -able, -tion, -arity, etc. (*untechnical, nontutorial, preindustrial, synchronizable*).

Homonyms. Spelling checkers cannot detect the erroneous use of homonyms ("The generals decided to take a *peace* of their neighbor's territory," "She insisted once again that there was too much lint in my *naval*," "There's no *they're their*.").

Compounds. Spelling checkers cannot detect the erroneous use of compounds ("No matter what you do, it may *back fire*" or "He's on his way *down town*.")

Truncations. Spelling checkers cannot find improperly truncated words (" 'A restriction it may be,' he said, 'but this *restrict* is one you'll have to live with.' ")

These limitations add up to one major conclusion: using even the best spelling checker is no substitute for a final, hand proofreading for spelling mistakes.

STYLE ANALYSIS SOFTWARE

Try this paragraph:

> Objective consideration of contemporary phenomena compels the conclusion that success or failure in competitive activities exhibits no tendency to be commensurate with innate capacity, but that a considerable element of the unpredictable must inevitably be taken into account.

Still awake? You'd never know it, but the idea under all the verbiage is from the Bible, and it's from one of the most stirring and beautiful and important collections of sentences ever written. Here's the original (King James version):

> I returned, and saw under the sun, that the race is not to the swift, nor the battle to the strong, neither yet bread to the wise, nor yet riches to men of understanding, nor yet favor to men of skill; but time and chance happeneth to them all.

The first version ("Objective consideration . . .") was penned by George Orwell, the author of *1984*. Orwell wanted to point out what happens to language when bureaucrats get hold of it.

The bureaucrat's language, to be sure, isn't necessarily bad language — it just doesn't communicate. Actually, that's precisely the reason people use bureaucratic language. Bureaucrats write the way they do because, in a bureaucracy, it pays to avoid taking responsibility for projects that may fail. The passive voice (e.g., "The launch decision was made after all relevant data were examined") hides the responsible parties; it's much safer than saying "I approved the launch." Bureaucratic language, in other words, is written in a style that conceals meaning and responsibility. And as the passage from Ecclesiastes shows, the very same message can be written in a different style, one that communicates.

The two examples help to illustrate what the word *style* means. It refers to the form of the presentation — the way verbs are used, the choice of words, the way sentences are structured — rather than its content or meaning. The bureaucratic style can be summed up as follows: bureaucrats, when they write, tend to overuse:

Abstract Nouns (*phenomena, success, failure, activities, capacity*) instead of definite, concrete, and specific ones (*sun, race, swift, battle, bread*);

Nominalizations (*consideration, conclusion*), which add to the passage's abstraction;

Vague Modifiers (*considerable element of unpredictability*) instead of unequivocal, forthright statements (*time and chance happeneth to them all*); and

Passive Voice (*be taken into account*) instead of active verbs (*I returned, and saw . . .*).

To be sure, using these flawed forms isn't always wrong. Sometimes, for instance, you cannot avoid an abstract noun such as *justice*. The danger lies, rather, in overuse. Writing experts agree that, if you really want to communicate, it's best to avoid the bureaucratic style.

Such a consensus is enough to prick up the ears of any good programmer. A major limitation of computers, remember, is that they can process only that information we can explicitly represent. This limitation makes them next to useless for meaning-sensitive tasks, since we're not sure — not yet, anyway — how to represent meaning. But meaning aside, if the writing experts agree that usages *a, b, c,* and *d* are bad, then programmers can put together a program that detects and marks them. And that's just what they did. The results: a host of personal computer **style analysis programs** — programs that detect writing style problems and suggest revision strategies. We now have programs that check for the kind of word choice problems Orwell lampooned and such others as overuse of the passive voice and poor readability: *word choice checkers, passive voice detectors,* and *readability checkers.*

The Granddaddy of Style Analysis Programs: Writer's Workbench. Style analysis programs originated in the research labs of the giants AT&T (Writer's Workbench) and IBM (Epistle). AT&T's Writer's Workbench got widely distributed during the 1970s and early 1980s because, owing to the government's prohibition (since lifted) on AT&T's entry into the computer market, it couldn't sell the software it developed (such as the UNIX operating system). AT&T therefore gave UNIX (often with Writer's Workbench) to many colleges and universities, and a generation of programmers and computer freaks grew up with it. Writer's Workbench, therefore, has inspired legions of programmers, who have developed personal computer versions of it.

Writer's Workbench isn't readily available for personal computers at this writing owing to its huge size (it requires a megabyte of main memory) and its dependence on the UNIX operating system, which is only slowly becoming available for personal computers. Far more than a word choice checker, Writer's Workbench actually contains thirty programs for electronic editing (see the box "Writer's Workbench Writing Aids" for an overview of their functions). The program also analyzes the style of a textual passage, presenting a screen display summarizing its conclusions (for instance, "This text contains a much higher percentage of passive verbs [44%] than is common in good documents of this type [22%]," or "You have appropriately limited your nominalizations").

Writer's Workbench Writing Aids

Programs for Proofreading check for (1) spelling errors, (2) doubled words ("the the"), (3) punctuation errors (such as commas and periods incorrectly positioned outside quotation marks or unbalanced quotation marks or brackets), (4) capitalization errors (such as first letter of sentence not capitalized), (5) diction errors (such as wordy, archaic, or vague words or phrases), (6) split infinitives, and (7) sexist usages (*chairman, man and wife*).

Programs for Analysis of Style compute or identify: (1) percentage of verbs in the passive voice; (2) percentage of sentence types (simple, complex, compound, and compound-complex); (3) percentage of short sentences (fewer than seventeen words) and long sentences (more than thirty-two words); (4) readability grade level (using the Kincaid and other formulas); (5) level of nominalization usage (e.g., *distribution* instead of *distribute*); (6) level of abstract noun usage (e.g., *truth, beauty, justice*), and (7) level of use of long words.

A Program for Improving Organization prints to the screen the first and last sentence of each paragraph (providing a view of the text's organization).

Introducing Word Choice Checkers. A major component of Writer's Workbench is its **word choice checker,** which detects word choice problems such as the use of wordy or archaic phrases. Word choice checkers work in much the same way spelling checkers do, but with a twist. A spelling checker works with a big dictionary of correct words, and as it reads a text file, it marks only those words that it can't square with its dictionary. The word choice checker works in the opposite way. It works with a dictionary of questionable words or phrases, and as it reads a text file, it marks only the words that it *can* find in its dictionary.

All this may seem overly technical, but it raises an important point. Writer's Workbench and other style analysis programs do not contain *all* problematic words and phrases in their dictionaries. Running the program, therefore, may expose some errors, but you shouldn't conclude that the rest of the text is okay. So long as you keep this point in mind, using these programs can be helpful. But a writer who equates running these programs with text revision is headed for trouble.

Microcomputer Word Choice Checkers. Several microcomputer programs are available which perform some (but not all) of Writer's Workbench's functions. These programs include Punctuation & Style (Oasis Systems) and Grammatik (Digital Marketing), two widely used and readily available programs sold directly to computer users. At best, Grammatik and Punctuation & Style are only subsets of Writer's Workbench; they include most of the bigger package's proofreading functions but, sadly, none of the style analysis features. They have word and phrase dictionaries derived from such sources as Strunk and White's *The Elements of Style*. These dictionaries contain the questionable phrase followed by a suggested revision (Figure 6–13).

Punctuation & Style's word and phrase dictionary contains the following kinds of entries:

Awkward Phrases (as a consequence of, includes the necessity of)

Clichés (any and all, intents and purposes)

Erroneous Phrases (cannot help but, irregardless, must of, reoccurrence)

Folksy Phrases (all the farther, more or less, sort of)

Muddy Phrases (a number of, fairly, relatively, seems to)

```
ALONG THE LINE OF+LIKE
ALONG THE LINES OF+LIKE
ALONG THE SAME LINE+LIKE
ALONG THIS LINE+SIMILARLY
ALRIGHT+ALL RIGHT
ALTERNATIVE CHOICE+CHOICE
ALTERNATIVE CHOICES+CHOICES
AN ADDITIONAL+ANOTHER
```

FIGURE 6–13 Part of Punctuation & Style's Word and Phrase Dictionary

Pompous Phrases (a preference for, accentuated, exhibit a tendency, on the order of, take cognizance of)

Redundant Phrases (absolutely complete, collaborate together, generally as a rule)

Wordy Phrases (call your attention to, due to the fact that, in a number of cases, the question as to whether)

How Word Choice Checkers Work. The program reads the document file and, if it finds matches for the words or phrases in its dictionary, presents the matches on the video display, together with a suggestion for revision (Figure 6–14). If you wish, you may mark the word or phrase for editing later with your word processing program. Occasionally, the program wrongly criticizes a correct usage. For example, it's set up to catch the error *media is,* so it will flag "Each investigative journalist in the radio and television *media is* aware of the risks involved." Punctuation & Style's manual warns that only you can decide whether its suggestions are germane. For some, however, the problems of word choice checkers run deeper (see the box, "The Hazards of Electronic Writing").

Using a word choice checker should never substitute for a careful and thoughtful revision of the text. Remember that the major problems in writing

FIGURE 6–14 Punctuation & Style's Screen Display During Text Critiquing

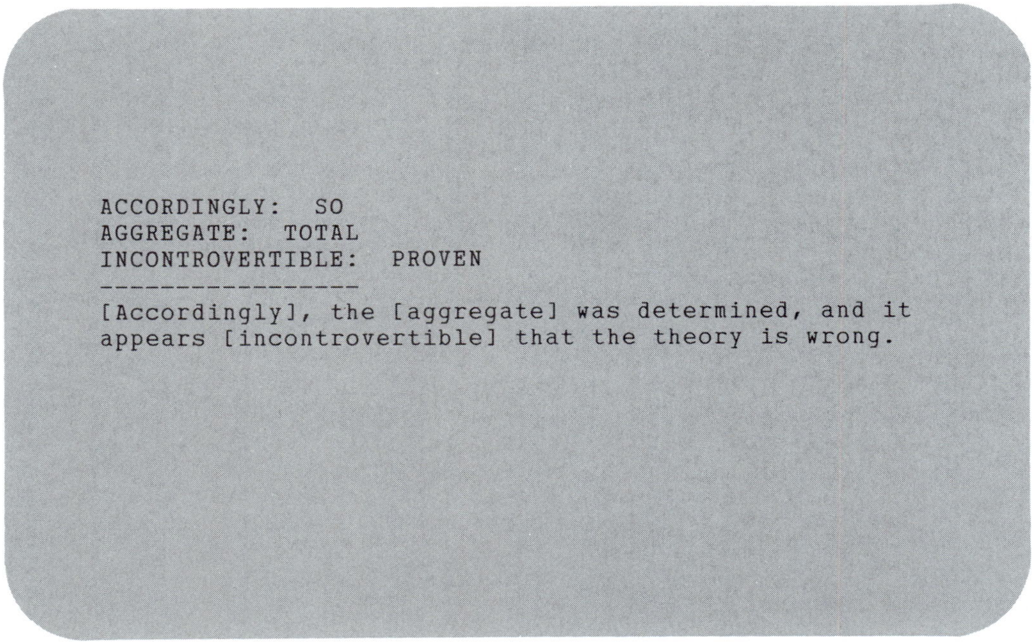

The Hazards of Electronic Writing

Aspen Software's Grammatik is a "style" program that will tell you that using the phrase "on account of" is bad style. Grammatik suggests that you change the phrase to "because." This is a necessary change, yet it becomes superficial if you the writer don't know *why* the change is needed. To use a style program with any dexterity you must know why such a phrase is wordy; how you can identify other, less obvious phrases that the computer might not detect; and why using such phrases in the first place harms your writing. Computerized editing programs have great potential for pounding some arbitrary rules into inexperienced writers, without explaining why the rules were established in the first place.

What's potentially even worse, these programs can numb your writing judgment by fussing over "problems" that don't even exist. Let's say you wrote this paragraph:

> Finally, in case you were curious, the detectives' investigation will demonstrate that Tom is actually the guilty party. He committed the crime while the victim, Fred, slept. Fred shouldn't have decided to employ Tom at the factory, and you can be awfully sure of that.

Zip it through Punctuation & Style (a style checker similar to Grammatik, from Oasis Systems), follow the suggestions to the letter, and you come up with this paragraph:

> Lastly, if you were curious, the detectives' study will show that Tom is really the guilty party. He committed the crime when the victim, Fred, slept. Fred shouldn't have decided to use Tom at the factory, and you can be very sure of which.

The problem is fivefold here. You have the blatant error: "sure of that" to "sure of which." You have the unfocusing of meaning: "investigation" to "study" makes the meaning more general and less precise in the reader's mind. You have a dismantling of "informal" writing, which is perfectly acceptable and often even preferred: "in case" to "if," which sounds stiff. You have a puzzling paradox: Punctuation & Style suggests that you replace "awfully" with "very," yet will point out that "very" is a vague word you should avoid. And finally (or lastly, if you prefer), you have the subtle shift in meaning: "while the victim slept" implies a continuing action, as in the word *during*. On the other hand, "when the victim slept" implies a more distinct cutoff time closer in meaning to "when the victim fell asleep" than to the intended meaning. Changing "employ" to "use" involves a similar shift in meaning.

No style program can tell you the most serious problem with the brief paragraph. It stinks. How about this instead:

> Fred had made two mistakes. First, he had hired Tom to work with him at the factory. Second, he had fallen asleep too early on the night Tom visited him, hate in his mind, knife in his pocket. And that's what the detectives' investigation will prove in court today.

That's not going to win me a Pulitzer Prize for nonfiction, but it's not going to put anyone to sleep, either.

Remember that word "supplement." These programs are just that. And when you come down to it, they don't supplement the word-processing program. They supplement the writer. *You.*

Excerpted with permission from "The Hazards of Electronic Writing," by William Brohaugh, published in the April 1984 issue of *Popular Computing* Magazine, are likely to stem from the big matters of approach, organization, logic, and coherence. Minor revisions in wording aren't likely to cure those problems. If you use a checker, keep it in perspective. Its best use is to keep you from committing such gaffes as writing with inappropriate, erroneous phrases that will make you look silly to your readers. Keep the larger issues of revision in mind and don't let the program do all the revising for you.

Passive Voice Detectors. In his *Revising Prose*, Richard Lanham recommends a revision approach called the Paramedic Method. This approach encourages cutting out useless prepositional phrases, which grow hydra-like when a writer uses the passive voice ("A cold was caught by Joan on Wednesday" vs. "Joan caught a cold Wednesday"). Here's the technique:

1. Mark the prepositions.
2. Mark instances of the verb *to be.*
3. Ask "Who is kicking whom?"
4. Put this "kicking" action in a simple (not compound) active verb.

Punctuation & Style's **passive voice detector** automatically marks sentences. Here's a marked sentence:

> Shown [*in*] the preliminary analysis [*of*] the findings [*of*] the study [*were*] major disagreements [*between*] the hypotheses expressed [*in*] the proposal and the survey data.

Note that this sentence uses twenty-six words and five prepositions. And here's its revision:

> The preliminary study revealed major discrepancies *between* the proposal's hypotheses and the survey findings.

This sentence uses only one preposition and ten fewer words to say exactly the same thing. Note that there's nothing informal about it; this sentence would pass muster in even the stuffiest academic journal.

Be forewarned, however, that using Punctuation & Style's passive voice detector can be a tedious business. It isn't looking, really, for the passive voice. It's looking — mindlessly — for *to be* verbs.[2] And some *to be* verbs have legitimate uses in nonpassive sentences. A case in point is the progressive tense ("The horses are trotting"). The program will show you *all* the sentences in which *to be* occurs, even if you're using the verb in a nonpassive construction.

Measuring Readability. A Florida telephone service admonishes its subscribers:

> Any person who shall willfully refuse to immediately relinquish a party line when informed that such line is needed for an emergency call, and in fact such line is needed for any emergency call, to a fire department or police department or for medical aid or ambulance service, or any person who shall secure the

> use of a party line by falsely stating that such line is needed for any emergency call, shall be guilty of a misdemeanor and be punished by law. Emergency as used in this section means a situation in which property or human life is in jeopardy and the prompt summoning of aid is essential.

Clear as a bell, right? Now here's a translation:

1. You must instantly hang up when a party line member asks to make an emergency phone call. To refuse is illegal.
2. You must not pretend there is an emergency to get use of the party line. This is illegal.

   An emergency exists when human life or property is in danger. Instant help is needed. You must call the fire department, the police, a doctor, or an ambulance.[3]

According to a **readability measurement,** or a quantitative analysis of how readable these two passages are, you'd need at least one year of college to grasp the first one. A seventh grader, in contrast, would have little difficulty with the second one. It's more *readable.*

With that assertion few would argue, but accepting the theoretical premises of readability measurement is another matter. **Readability,** the degree to which the content of a document can be easily comprehended, clearly stems from many qualities of a text, such as logical coherence. But readability measurement tries to reduce all the complexity to a pat formula, such as the Flesch Reading Ease Formula: 205.835 — (sentence length × 1.015) — (number of syllables per 100 words × .846). Readability formulas exemplify what philosophers call reductionism, or a tendency to explain complex things in overly simple terms. And readability *is* complex. It arises not only from the form, but also from the content, of a document. Yet readability formulas ignore content and measure only form (specifically, the average length of sentences and the choice of simple, familiar words, as evidenced by the number of syllables per 100 words). To some critics of readability formulas, that's like measuring the beauty of a sculpture by measuring its breadth and width.

Despite this reductionism, it's clear that readability measurement measures *something.* The Flesch formula, for instance, produces a readability index on a scale of 0 (unreadable) to 100 (very easy), with academic and scholarly writing falling in the 30 to 50 (difficult) range. One can sit down with a collection of texts, some more readable than others, and get surprisingly consistent results. A passage from Veblen's wordy *The Theory of the Leisure Class*, for instance, scores 48, while one from William James's more readable *Psychology* scores 60. A passage from Emerson's eminently readable *The American Scholar* scores 66.

Just what to do with readability measurement has been a hot issue ever since its invention. Its proponents, such as Flesch, have pointed to the evidence that it really does give a rough-and-ready index of readability, while others have jeered and pointed instead to the host of readability factors it ignores. Until recently, the tedium of doing readability measurement by hand kept a lid on its use; most writers ignored it, save for school textbook writers (who were as likely to abuse it as to use it fruitfully). But now you can do readability measurement on a computer. It's a cinch to write a simple program, called a **readability checker,** that measures sentence length and the number of syllables in a manuscript, performs the necessary calculations, and cranks out a score.

Should you give readibility measurement a try? Used with care and caution, a readability measurement can provide a useful and even illuminating way of looking critically at your writing. But watch out for a potential trap. After you use a *readability checker,* you'll discover that you can lower the score by shortening sentences and reducing the number of polysyllabic words. Yet doing so may not really make the text more readable. Above all, readability is really a matter of coherence and intelligibility. A collection of short, choppy sentences that express nothing but nonsense will get a high readability score, but they're not really readable. Coherence, rather than a good readability score, should always stand supreme among a writer's revision criteria.

If you get a high readability score, go through your text and shorten sentences where it's appropriate to do so, especially if you have many sentences longer than 22 words. And if you can use a simple, familiar word instead of a complex, polysyllabic one, use it. Many reading experts believe, for example, that an average sentence length of 17 to 20 words is optimal, as is an average word length of about 5 characters or 1.5 syllables. Remember, however, that sometimes a sentence will have to be longer to express a complex thought. Sometimes, too, longer words are the only ones that will do.

THE COMPUTER'S LIMITATIONS AS A CRITICAL EDITOR

Spelling checkers and memory-resident thesauruses work much better than style analysis software, as you've doubtless concluded, and this fact has no small implication for comprehending the limits of computer technology. Computer technology can match one word with another, and it can do the job at incredible speeds. (Think how long it would take you to check the spelling of words in a 125-page business report by hand if you did it the way a computer does: first, you'd have to determine all the unique words in the manuscript, sort them in alphabetical order, and find out which ones don't match the words listed in a 125,000 word dictionary!) But this technology cannot yet grasp the meaning of words, save in very limited — and rather contrived — experimental situations. A computer that could understand the meaning of everyday language would possess artificial intelligence, and computers (especially personal computers, with their limited memories and slow processing speeds) do not possess artificial intelligence. Not yet, anyway.

What all this means, in practice, is that a personal computer can be trusted so long as it's doing jobs that require simple processing operations such as searching, comparing, matching, counting, or doing arithmetic. That's why the spelling checker and memory-resident thesaurus work so well; all they do is search and match. Whenever a personal computer program is doing something that has to do with meaning, however, some kind of trick is at work: the program pretends to be looking at matters involving meaning, but all it's really doing is the same old simple operations — sorting, searching, comparing, matching, and so on. The word choice checker, for example, claims to be examining the quality of word choice in a document, but all it's really doing is trying to match words and phrases in the document with several hundred questionable words and phrases in its dictionary. A poorly chosen word in the document will escape criticism if the programmer forgot to include it in the dictionary. A similar, and even less convincing, trick is at work in readability checkers. Be skeptical of the results.

It's worth dwelling on this caution because so many people tend to take computer output as if it were handed down to Moses from the heights. Savvy writers of government proposals have known for years that federal and state grants are more easily won when their proposals, however fuzzy and devoid of merit, are stapled to authoritative-looking computer analyses. As I have tried to demonstrate in this chapter, however, you can't really trust anything that comes out of a computer until you know for yourself how the results were obtained.

SUMMARY

Accessory programs for writing and editing can help you write better and more productively, but they must be used with caution. Such programs for writing include outlining and thesaurus programs. Outlining programs overcome a major liability of word processing software, the one-third page limitation on the amount of text that you can view. By creating an outline and collapsing subheadings, a writer can see the overall structure of the document he or she is writing. Memory-resident outlining programs and word processing programs that include outlining functions are now available. These programs help you keep track of your document's structure as it evolves.

Thesaurus programs are *memory resident,* that is, they are stored in the computer's internal memory along with your word processing program. When you want to look up a word in the thesaurus, you press a key. The word processing program's operation is suspended, and the thesaurus shows you synonyms for a word. Using such a program can help improve your sensitivity to the meaning of words.

In the future, optical disk technology is sure to expand the resources available to you as you write. Optical-disk-based encyclopedias and dictionaries (with meanings of words listed) are already feasible and will probably be available by the time you read this book.

Accessory programs for editing include the indispensable spelling checker and software for style analysis. Spelling checkers vary widely in quality. You should use one that has a large dictionary (50,000 words or more), displays your spelling mistakes in context, and inserts the correct spelling in your text file (so that you don't have to do it yourself). Because spelling checkers cannot detect certain mistakes, however, there's no substitute for a final, hand proofreading of your document.

Style analysis programs are based on the idea that the characteristics of bad writing can be objectively identified and detected. These programs include word choice checkers, passive voice detectors, and readability checkers. All are inspired by Writer's Workbench, a mainframe style analysis program.

Word choice checkers work much the same way that spelling checkers do, but with a twist. They compare the words and phrases you've used to a built-in dictionary, and report as questionable the words that *match* the dictionary's contents (instead of displaying the ones that don't match). Microcomputer word choice programs are available, but they are limited in their capabilities. Some writing experts criticize them. These critics have shown that word choice checkers cannot substitute for genuine revision. At best, checkers can point out a few word choice problems. You're on your own for doing the revising that really improves writing quality, such as making sure your writing is well organized and coherent.

Passive voice detectors identify sentences using *to be* verbs, which are often overused in bad or bureaucratic writing. Although passive voice detectors will sometimes flag sentences in the progressive and other tenses, you can use these programs with profit as a guide to revision. Remember, however, that the passive voice isn't always incorrect; it's the overuse of it that presents a problem.

Readability checkers operate on the theory that overly long sentences and polysyllabic words interfere with readability. To measure readability, therefore, these programs measure sentence length and word length. Then they compute a readability score, which is supposed to correspond to the grade level of the text. If the grade level is 10, you need a tenth-grade education to read the text. This idea is close to nonsense because other factors, such as logic and coherence, affect readability. Nevertheless, you can use a readability checker to make sure your sentences and words are not overly long. You'll do well to shorten sentences and words when you see clear ways to do so. But avoid revision efforts that emphasize obtaining a lower readability score. Always strive for coherence, clarity, and intelligibility.

Spelling checkers and thesaurus programs work well because they require of the computer only simple processing operations. Programs that purport to critique meaning must use a programming trick, one that reduces meaning to the features of writing that a personal computer can detect (such as average sentence length). The results may not be valuable and should be viewed with skepticism.

KEY TERMS

memory-resident program
memory-resident thesaurus
outlining program
passive voice detector
readability
readability checker
readability measurement
spelling checker
style analysis software
word choice checker

REVIEW QUESTIONS AND EXERCISES

1. Think of the last time you wrote an essay for a composition class. Did you make an outline or carry out some other kind of prewriting activity? How would an outlining program fit into your approach to prewriting activities? Would an outlining program help you do a better job of planning? Why or why not?
2. What is the drawback of first-generation outlining programs such as ThinkTank? What are the advantages of memory-resident outlining programs? Of word processing programs that incorporate outlining functions?
3. Have you ever used a thesaurus when writing? Would you use one more often if the computer would look up the synonyms for you automatically and almost instantaneously? What other applications do you foresee for memory-resident software technology?
4. Describe how a spelling checker works. Does it really "detect and correct misspellings," as advertisers claim? How could the spelling checker's function be expressed more accurately? What does this more accurate definition tell you about the spelling checker's limitations? (Hint: see the definition of *spelling checker* in the Glossary.) What is the advantage of a large dictionary in a spelling checker?
5. What kinds of spelling mistakes are spelling checkers likely to miss?
6. What is style in writing? What features of writing style are style analysis programs designed to detect? What kind of writing style do style analysis programs encourage?
7. How do word choice checkers work, and what is their chief limitation? What errors are word choice checkers likely to make in critiquing a document?
8. What can happen to writing style if a word choice checker is used as the sole guide to revision? (Hint: see the box, "The Hazards of Electronic Writing.")

9. What is readability? What do readability checkers really measure? What is the potential danger of using a readability checker as the sole guide to revision?
10. How long would it take you to check the spelling of words in a 125-page business report if you did it the way a computer does? (Hint: there are 500 words on a page. Time yourself on just one paragraph of text and extrapolate to get the result.)
11. Why do you think people tend to accept computer output uncritically? Knowing what you know right now, what would you have to know before you could accept computer output as a reliable factor in making an important business decision?

FOR FURTHER READING

WORD PROCESSING ACCESSORY SOFTWARE

Abercrombie, John R. *Computer Programs for Literary Analysis* (Philadelphia: University of Pennsylvania Press, 1984).

Cherry, Lorinda L., Mary L. Fox, Lawrence T. Rase, Patricia C. Gingrich, Stacy A. Keenan, and Nina H. MacDonald. "Computer Aids for Text Analysis [Writer's Workbench]," *Bell Laboratories Record* (May/June 1983).

Dalton, Richard. "Specialized Writing Tools: Developers Are Now Providing Refined Programs to Suit Particular Needs," *Popular Computing* (November 1985).

Foster, Edward. "Outliners: A New Way of Thinking," *Personal Computing* (May 1985).

Friedberg, Jack. *Proofreading in the Word Processing Age* (New York: Irvington, 1985).

Hershey, William. "Idea Processors," *Byte* (June 1985).

Hockey, Susan. *A Guide to Computer Applications in the Humanities* (Baltimore: Johns Hopkins University Press, 1980).

Kamin, Jonathan. *Mastering ThinkTank on the IBM PC* (Berkeley: Sybex Computer Books, 1984).

Kiefer, Kathleen E., and Charles R. Smith. "Improving Students' Revising and Editing: The Writer's Workbench System," *The Computer in Composition Instruction,* William Wresch, ed. (Urbana, Ill.: National Council of Teachers of English, 1984).

O'Malley, Christopher. "Going Beyond Word Processing: Spelling Checkers, Thesauruses, Outliners, and Style Analyzers Pick Up Where Word Processing Software Leaves Off to Help You Sidestep Embarrassing Mistakes," *Personal Computing* (December 1985).

Pearlman, Dara. "A Footnote to Word Processing," *PC: The Independent Guide to IBM Personal Computers* (August 20, 1985).

Pepper, John. "Banish Typos with Spelling Checkers," *PC: The Independent Guide to IBM Personal Computers* (December 24, 1985).

Rosenthal, Steve. "Writing Utilities: PC Wordworking Tools Carve Their Niche among Perfectionists," *PC Week* (April 8, 1986).

READABILITY

Flesch, Rudolf. *How to Test Readability* (New York: Harper & Bros., 1951).

Frase, Lawrence T. "Ethics of Imperfect Measures," *IEEE Transactions on Professional Communication* (March 1981).

Klare, George R. *The Measurement of Readability* (Ames, Iowa: Iowa State University Press, 1963).

WRITING STYLE GUIDEBOOKS

Lanham, Richard. *Revising Prose* (New York: Charles Scribner's Sons, 1979).

Lesikar, Raymond. *Basic Business Communication* (Homewood, Ill.: Richard D. Irwin, 1985).

Strunk, William Jr., and E. B. White. *The Elements of Style,* 3rd ed. (New York: Macmillan, 1979).

Zinsser, William. *On Writing Well: An Informal Guide to Writing Nonfiction,* 2nd ed. (New York: Harper and Row, 1980).

COMPUTERS AND THE PROBLEM OF MEANING

Dreyfuss, Hubert L. *What Computers Can't Do* (New York: Harper and Row, 1972).

Tennant, Harry. *Natural Language Processing* (New York: Petrocelli Books), 1981.

Winograd, Terry. "Computer Software for Working with Language," *Scientific American* (September 1984).

———. *Language as a Cognitive Process* (Reading, Mass.: Addison-Wesley, 1983).

———. *Understanding Natural Language* (New York: Academic Press, 1972).

PART THREE

"Ours is an age of information. Paperwork piles up and numbers fly by so fast we hardly have a chance to organize data, never mind make sense of it. Indeed, data management can be a full-time job. Fortunately, it's a job for which your personal computer at work or home is perfectly suited."

Michael J. Miller and George F. Goley IV *Personal Computing*

Data Base Management: *Strategies for Managing Information*

Linda Martinez is an artist: she's a highly respected photographer. She's also a businesswoman. She sells slides of her work to corporations, newspapers, magazines, and book publishers. When a company's public relations staff needs a slide of an oil well for an annual report, for example, they call Linda to see if she has one. Linda can sell them a picture of an oil well for much less than it would cost the staff to go out and photograph one themselves.

The only problem: She has well over 5,000 slides in her collection. Before Linda got her personal computer, keeping track of what was in her slide inventory became such a time-consuming job that her business was paralyzed. Now, however, she's keeping track of her slides with a data base management program. When she receives a request for a slide portraying the Golden Gate Bridge, she lets the computer search her records. She loads her data base management program, types in "Golden Gate Bridge," and in seconds the computer lists all her slides that contain that subject.

Personal computer data base management programs can put information at your fingertips, too, and Part 3 of this book shows you how. Chapter 7, "Using File Management Software: Tools for Managing Information," introduces file management programs, the simplest and easiest of all data management programs to use. Chapter 8, "The Relational Connection: Introducing Data Base Management Systems," takes you to the next level of sophistication with today's most powerful data base management software.

7 *Using File Management Software:* *Tools for Managing Information*

"[The computer facilitates] all systematic marshallings of bare facts. It does not tire, lose its eyesight, or make more mistakes at the end of the day than at the beginning."
Jacques Barzun and Henry F. Graff *The Modern Researcher*

Every data base management program is designed to do the same thing: to put massive amounts of information at your fingertips. The simplest of these programs, file management programs, let you work with one file of information at a time. More sophisticated ones, called data base management systems (DBMS), let you work with two or more files at once. This chapter begins our exploration of data base management with file management programs.

You can use this chapter to help you learn a file management program. Begin by finding the sheets entitled *Quick Reference Guide: File Management Basics*, which are positioned at the end of this book. Tear them out, and staple them or put them in a folder. Keep these sheets and your file management program's manual handy as you read the chapter. Use your supplementary textbook, if your instructor has assigned one. When this chapter describes a basic file management function, such as deleting a data record, find out from your

manual how to accomplish this function with your program. Then make a note in the *Quick Reference Guide*. When you've finished filling out the *Quick Reference Guide*, keep it next to your computer. You'll find it immensely helpful in day-to-day data base management situations.

MANAGING A DATA BASE WITH FILE MANAGEMENT SOFTWARE: AN OVERVIEW

"Managing a data base" sounds fancy, but chances are you've done it before — by hand. A **data base** is nothing more mysterious than a collection of information pertinent to a particular subject. This collection provides a base or foundation for retrieving information, drawing conclusions, and making decisions. A **data base management program,** therefore, is a program for managing (that is, storing, organizing, and retrieving) the information in the data base. There are two kinds of data base management programs, file management programs (covered in this chapter) and the more sophisticated **data base management systems** (**DBMS**), which are covered in Chapter 8.

DATA BASE MANAGEMENT BY HAND

To illustrate the basic concepts underlying data base management, consider what you do when you research a college paper. If you follow the plan suggested by your high school English teacher, you'll use three-by-five-inch index cards to keep track of the sources you've used. You begin by *creating the form.* Then you *add data.* As you work, you'll take steps to *maintain the data base.* Finally, you'll use your card file to *retrieve information* you need (Figure 7–1).

Creating the Form. File cards help you store and retrieve information. Their usefulness, however, depends on whether you remember to write down *all* the necessary information on each card. Consider a bibliography data base. If you leave out the publisher's name, the citation will be next to useless when it comes to preparing the final draft of a college paper. You'll have to go to the library and look it up again to find the missing information. Using a **form** helps you remember to write down all the needed information. A form is a template that helps you collect and store information. It uses headings (such as AUTHOR'S NAME or DATE OF PUBLICATION), which prompt you to fill in the necessary information.

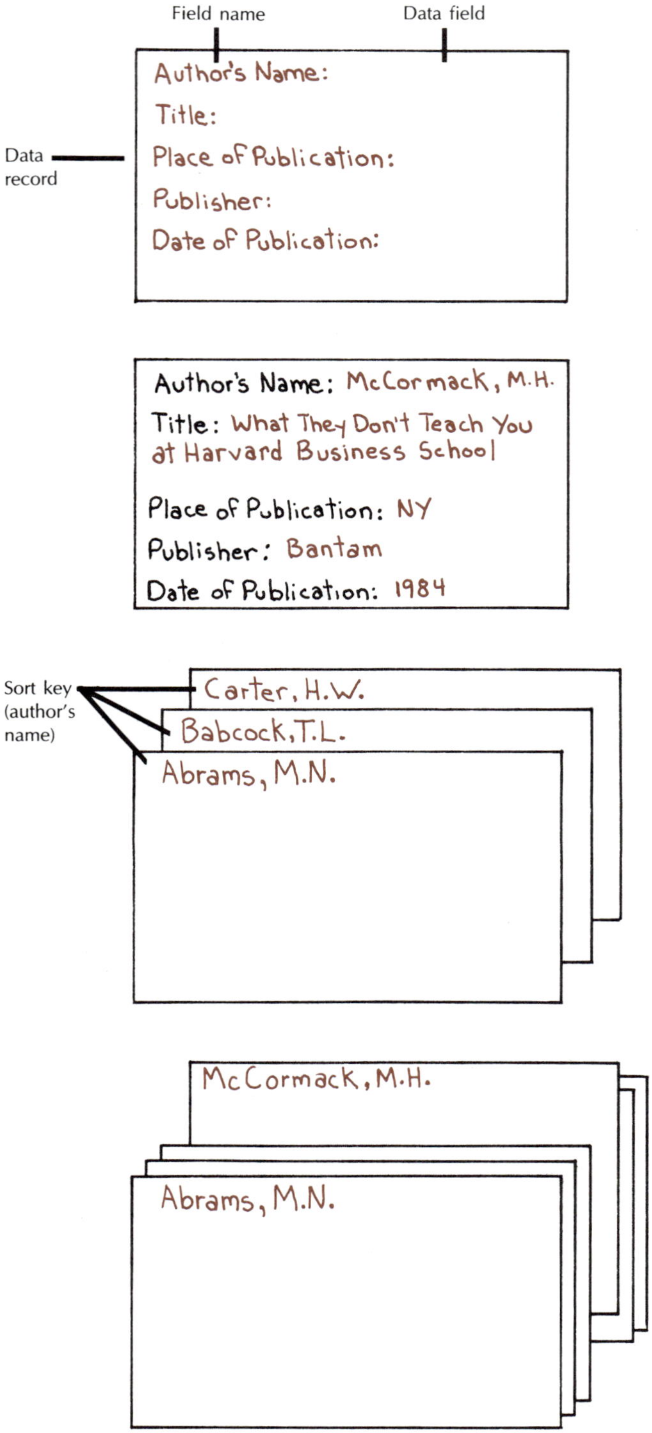

Creating the form
A form is a template that helps you collect and store information.

Adding the data
Field names prompt you to fill in the necessary information so that each data record is complete.

Maintaining the card file
Maintenance steps include editing the data, updating the data, and sorting in alphabetical order. One data field (author's name) serves as the sort key.

Retrieving information
Once the cards are sorted, you can retrieve the data you want.

FIGURE 7–1 File Management by Hand

You've seen plenty of forms already. You fill them out when you apply for a job, pay your taxes, and visit a doctor for the first time. What you already know about forms will help you grasp computerized data management, as long as you learn a few new terms:

Data Field. A **data field** is the space for a particular kind of information in a computerized form. In the field *author's name,* for example, you write down the author of a book.

Field Name. A **field name** is a data field's heading. *Author's name* is a field name.

Data Record (or just record). A **data record** is a filled-out form, containing a unit of related data expressed in named data fields.

We'll start using these terms even though we're still talking about a noncomputerized data base.

Adding Data. Now that you've designed your form, you add data. The field names tell you what kind of information to enter, and the data fields give you enough space to write down the information you need.

Maintaining the Card File. To make sure your card file is useful, you take steps to keep it in good order. These steps include:

Editing the Data. Occasionally, you'll find that you no longer need some records. When using a bibliography card file, for example, you may find that you don't need some of the books you've listed. So you remove their cards.

Updating the Data. Sometimes the information you're tracking changes, and you must reflect those changes in your data base. To maintain a data base of employees, for example, you'll need to update the records to reflect promotions or salary increases.

Sorting the Data. To keep your cards organized, you sort them in alphabetical or numerical order, using one of the fields as a **sort key.** A sort key is a data field that has been chosen as the basis for sorting (i.e., alphabetizing) data records. In an employee's data base, for example, the key might be the employee's name or social security number.

Retrieving Information. When you have finished adding data to your card file, you use it to retrieve information.

Finding Data. Suppose you're using a bibliography card file. You need the place of publication of a book by James N. Smith, so you look at the cards with authors' names starting with *S.*

Printing the Data. When you have finished your paper, you type up the bibliography and put it at the end.

You do all these basic tasks by hand when you're using a precomputer data base. A file management program does the same tasks. It gives you computerized tools for creating a form, adding information to the form, maintaining the data records, and retrieving information when needed.

ADVANTAGES OF COMPUTERIZED FILE MANAGEMENT

A **file management program,** a data base management program that handles only one data file at a time, serves the same function as a card file, but with one major difference: increased productivity. The program turns your computer into a tool for tackling file management tasks with speed and ease. Here's a brief overview of its advantages:

Tools for Creating Forms. File management programs give you tools for creating a form that will appear on the screen every time you want to add new data. Among these tools are many word processing functions, including commands for inserting and deleting text. (Note: Not all file management programs display forms on the screen. The ones that do not are so difficult to use that they should be avoided.)

Ease of Data Entry. The built-in word processing functions make data entry somewhat faster than hand methods. For most applications, however, there's still no alternative to typing in all the data. That's the slowest and least productive step in computerized records management.

Ease and Speed of Maintenance. One major advantage of computerized file management lies in the areas of data base maintenance and information retrieval. You can delete an unwanted record at a keystroke. In seconds, a computer can alphabetize 1,000 records. Because records can be found so quickly and easily, it's easy to update them if the information they contain changes. The built-in word processing functions speed updating tasks.

Ease and Speed of Information Retrieval. File management programs provide powerful tools for extracting information from the data base. Consider a bibliographic data base. Using a file management program, you can find the record of a book by John R. Smith in seconds. Print commands can print out the contents of the entire data base (or just part of it), producing useful **reports** or printed summaries of all or part of the information in the data base. These reports can be sorted in many different ways. For example, you can produce a report that lists the books by author, by call number, by date of publication, or by subject. The computer does all the sorting and printing tasks automatically.

A file management program, in sum, is like a robot programmed to handle information management tasks. When you say, "I want to know who published

Case Study: Data Base Management Aids Research Management Office

Every year, thousands of foundations and government agencies give away millions of dollars in research grants and fellowships supporting scholarly and scientific work in virtually every field of human endeavor.

"There's money out there, all right," says Francie Williams, manager of a major university's research management office. "The problem is that many university researchers are unaware of funding opportunities. A major function of our office is to obtain announcements of research grant opportunities and to get those announcements to the right people."

Before the computer, the job of matching these announcements to faculty interests was a hit-or-miss operation — and it was tedious and time-consuming, too. "We receive as many as two or three dozen such announcements every week," Francie says. To do the job by hand, someone had to sit down and figure out which faculty members should receive the announcements. For every faculty person, there was an index card listing his or her research interests. In practice, however, the cards were rarely consulted. "It would have taken too long," Francie explains. "We just did the best we could with a very imperfect system." As a result, many grant or fellowship announcements were never brought to the attention of the people who could have benefited from them.

Francie's office decided to buy an IBM AT equipped with Notebook II, an easy-to-use, menu-driven file management program. It was the right move. "We created a data base of faculty research interests." Every faculty member interested in research is represented by a data record in the data base. "For each data record, we listed as many as two or three dozen key words about research interests. Now, when we receive an announcement about funding opportunities in, say, cytology, we just sit down and search the data base for all the data records that contain 'cytology.'" After the search, the program prints out the mailing labels for the announcements.

"We're doing a much better job now of matching the announcements with the research faculty," Francie says. "And it's amazing how easy it is to use Notebook II. One of my assistants had only done a little word processing, but she learned how to use Notebook II in an afternoon."

the 1986 book by John R. Davidson," the robot runs to the file cabinet, pulls out the record, and says, "Acme Publishing Company." It does this job, moreover, in a second or two. And it doesn't get tired, lose its eyesight, or make mistakes.

EXPLORING A FILE MANAGEMENT PROGRAM

To manage information with a file management program, you'll need to master its basic functions. The following pages introduce the functions for creating forms, entering data, finding records, modifying records, sorting records, selecting records, and printing records (Figure 7–2).

CREATING A FORM

To use file management software effectively, careful planning is necessary. With many programs, you cannot alter the form after you create it. If you find a problem with the form's design, you may have to scrap the data base and enter all the data over again. (Some programs let you modify the form or add new data fields, but it's still best to get the form right before you start entering data.)

Work out your form on paper before using the computer. After you create your form, enter just a few records — say, a dozen — and try working with your data base. This trial run may expose design flaws that you'll want to correct. You may have to enter the dozen records again after modifying your design, but that's easier than entering several hundred (or several thousand).

The Create Mode. All data base management programs include a **create mode,** or a special section of the program that helps you create an appropriate form for data storage and retrieval. Some programs automatically start this mode the first time you use them. Others require you to give a special command.

Field Names. The program will ask you to list the field names you wish to use. Most programs place limits on the length of field names (12 characters is a common limit). Use field names that clearly indicate what kind of data should be entered in the data field. The field names should prompt the user to enter information; they cannot do so if they are unclear or overly abbreviated.

Field Lengths. Most file management programs require you to define a **field length,** the length (in characters) of every data field. You will need to consider the longest possible entry you'll make in a field. For telephone numbers, you'll need 13 spaces if you want to include the area code in parentheses:

```
(999)355-1234
```

Most file management programs permit no more than one or two lines of text to be entered in a single data field. A few programs, called **text-oriented file management programs,** are designed to store and retrieve large amounts of text. These programs can hold 32,000 characters or more in a single data field.

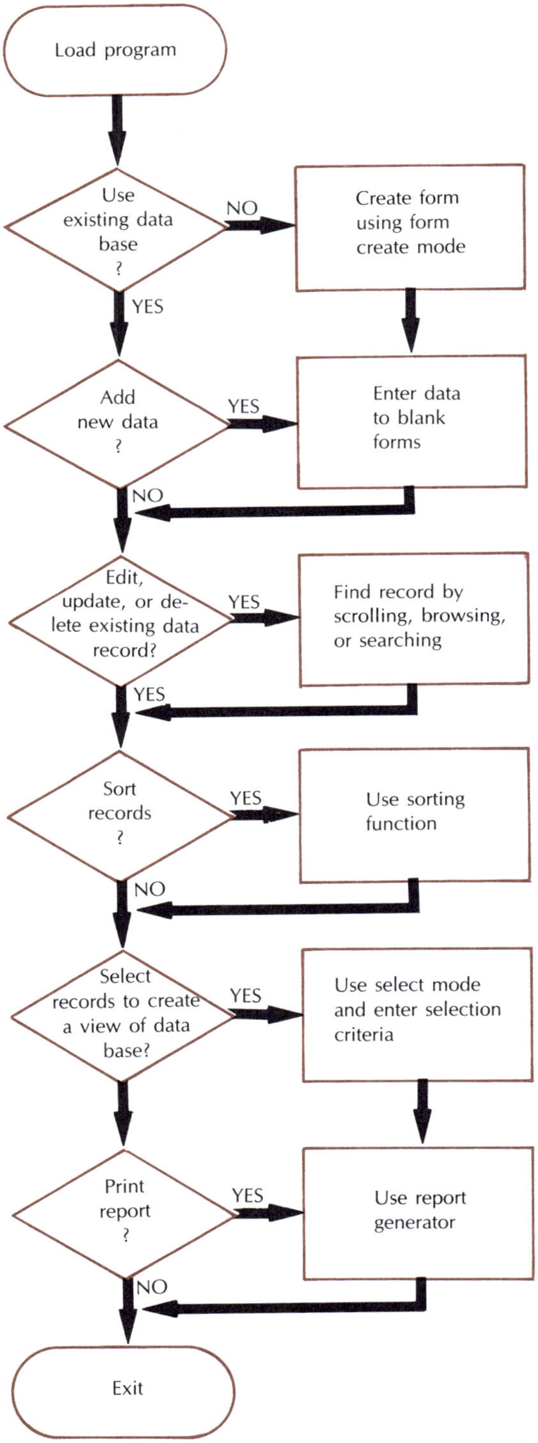

FIGURE 7–2 A Typical Session with a File Management Program

Data Types. Some file management programs also require you to decide in advance what type of data you will enter in a data field. *Data types* include:

Alphabetical Data. These are any data expressed using upper- and lowercase letters. For the field NAME, for example, an alphabetic entry would be *Smith, Harvey*.

Numerical Data. Any data expressed using numbers (*1134.98*).

Numerical Data with Automatic Calculation. Some programs permit you to set up a data field so that the numeric data entered in it will be totaled and averaged automatically. Consider a data base of employees. One of the fields is ANNUAL SALARY. Every time the data base is printed, the program adds up all the salary figures and prints a total and average. Not all programs include this desirable feature, which is useful for many business and scientific applications.

Alphanumeric Data. Data expressed using a combination of alphabetical and numerical data (*Agent 007*) is **alphanumeric** data.

Automatically Supplied Data. Some programs will automatically put today's date and time in a specially defined field. Many will automatically assign a number to the data record.

Figure 7–3 illustrates field names, field lengths, and data types.

ENTERING DATA

Once you have defined a form, you're ready to enter data. After you give a command to display a blank form, the program will position the cursor at the first character of the first field.

Entering Data. File management programs come equipped with limited versions of the word processing software discussed in Part 2. All file management programs give you tools for moving the cursor up, down, left, and right; for moving the cursor to the next field (or the previous one); and for light editing (deleting one character at a time). Some provide more extensive editing commands, which let you delete a whole word or all the text in a data field. Some let you choose between insert and overtype modes.

The Need for Correct Spelling and Consistency. Spelling mistakes can have serious consequences with file management software. Suppose, for instance, you misspell an author's name (*Smuth* instead of *Smith*). Later, you search for the record with the author's name *Smith*. From the computer's point of view, *Smuth* and *Smith* are two completely different names. So it skips *Smuth* and, if no other *Smith* record exists, tells you there's nothing in the data base with that name.

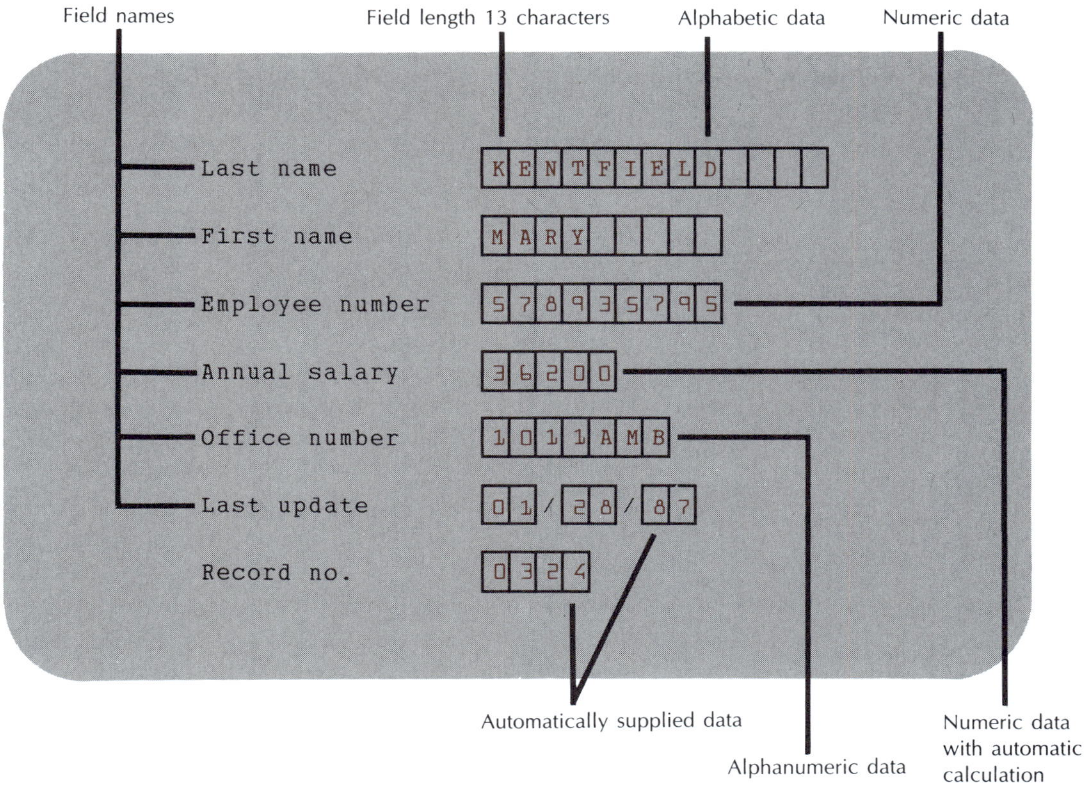

FIGURE 7–3 Form Create Modes Choosing Field Names, Field Lengths, and Data Types

For exactly the same reason, be consistent in the way you enter terms or phrases that will occur in two or more records. Do not enter *University of Chicago Press* in one record and *Univ. of Chicago Press* in another.

Accepting the Data Input. When you have finished filling out the form, a final command tells the computer to accept the data as finished input, and the record is added to the data base. Before you give this command, however, check your work carefully. When the computer has finished adding the record to the data base, you will probably be asked whether you want to add another record. If you wish, you may leave the data entry mode at this point.

Data Encryption. Sometimes the contents of a data base are confidential. An employee data base, for instance, may contain salary rates and performance evaluations. Some programs offer **data encryption** features that hide this data from prying eyes. If you have encrypted your data, no one can see it without typing a secret password when starting the program. Otherwise, the program will produce scrambled information that is impossible to read.

FINDING RECORDS

Most file management programs give you three techniques for finding a particular data record: scrolling, browsing, and searching.

Scrolling. The data records you enter are stored in a linear sequence, one after the other. You can scroll through the data base as you would a word processing document. Scrolling up takes you to the previous record, while scrolling down takes you to the next record. Until you deliberately change the order of data records by sorting the data base (see below), the "beginning" is the first record you entered and the "end" is the latest one.

Browsing. Because scrolling is a slow way to go through a data base, some programs include a **browse mode.** Typically, this mode shows just the first few characters of a dozen or more records at a time (Figure 7–4).

Searching. In a large data base, the quickest way to find a record is to let the computer do it for you. A file management program's **search command** closely resembles the search command of word processing programs discussed in Chapter 5. To use the search function, you type in the search phrase you want to find, just as you would with a word processing program. You must tell the file management program, however, which field you want it to search on. For instance, a search for the author *Smith* must take place in the AUTHOR field. The program will search the AUTHOR field in every data record. It searches the data base in sequence, record by record.

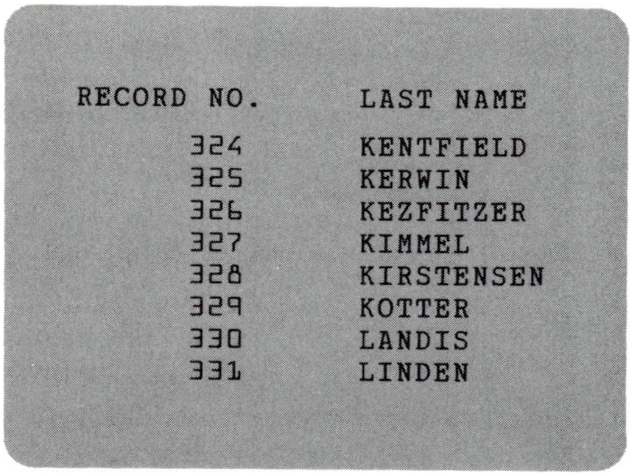

FIGURE 7–4 Browse Mode

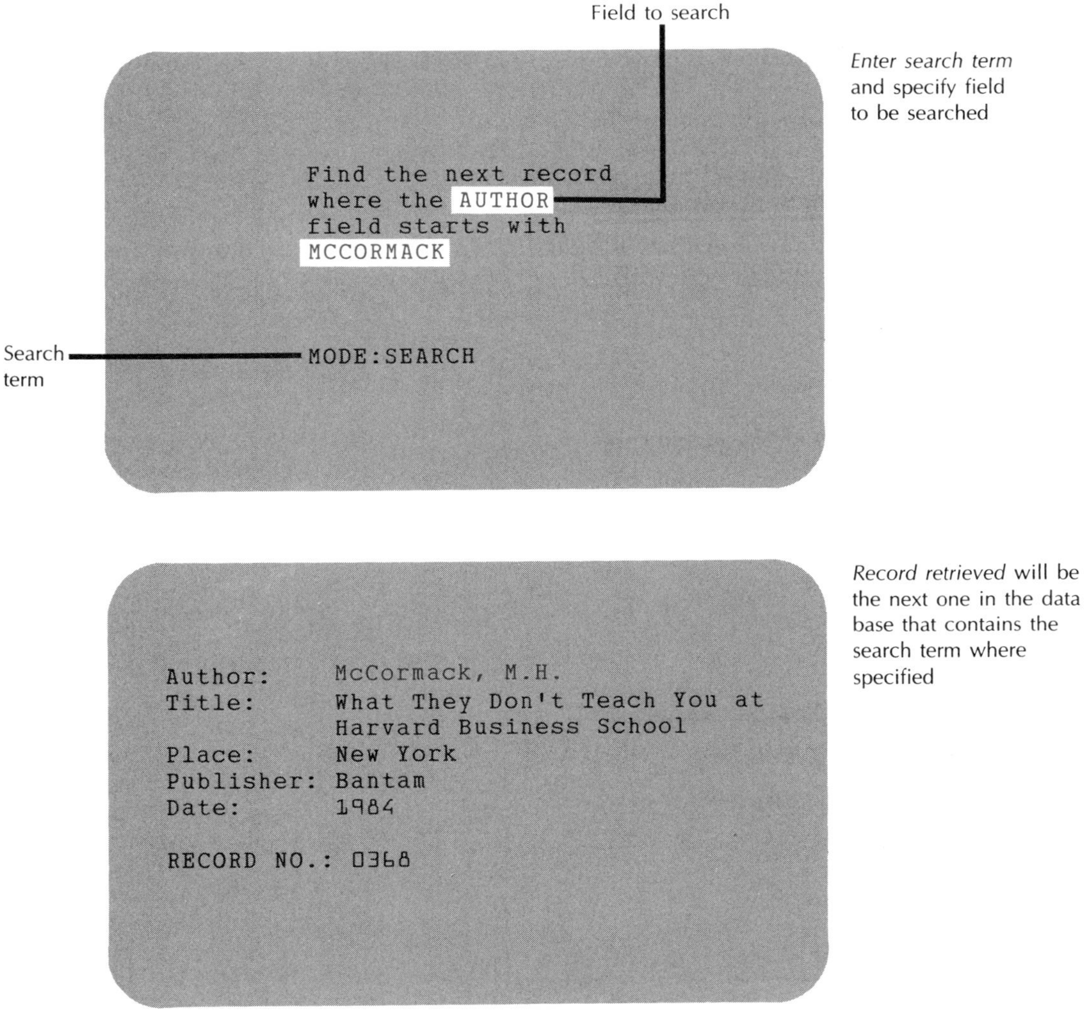

FIGURE 7–5 Search Function

When it finds a **hit,** a record containing data that match the search string, it takes you directly to the record (Figure 7–5).

Using Search Templates. Some programs handle searches in a different way. When you want to find a record with these programs, you are shown a blank form called a **search template.** This template is identical to the form you see when you add new records to the data base, but here it functions as a tool for searching. To use it, you type in the information you want to find. If you're searching for a book by *Williamson*, you type *Williamson* in the AUTHOR field. The program then searches for a record that matches the information you've specified (Figure 7–6).

Advanced Search Functions. Some programs give you more flexible search tools:

Wildcard Characters. Just as a deuce in poker stands for any card, a **wildcard character** stands for any letter or number. Suppose the wildcard character is an asterisk (*). A search for

SYSTEM*

FIGURE 7–6 Searching with a Template

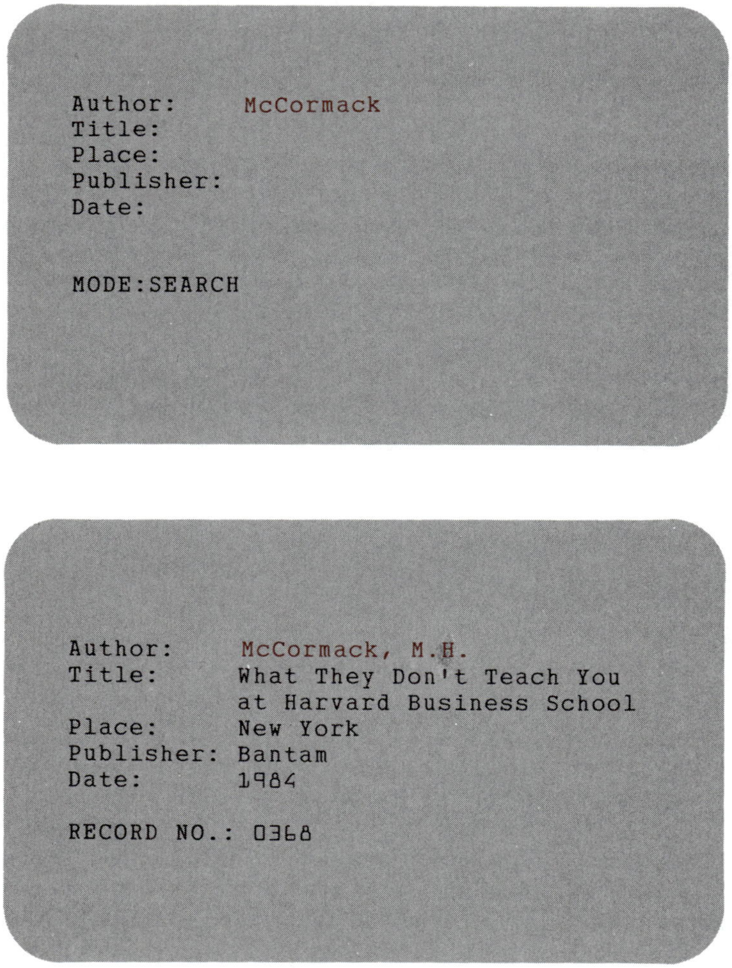

Enter search term by typing it into a blank template

will retrieve any records that contain *system* or *systems*. Using wildcard characters broadens the search and may increase the number of records retrieved.

Truncation. Another advanced search option is to create a search string using a truncated or shortened version of a word, often with a special **truncation** character (such as a question mark). The program then finds all the records that contain words that start with the search phrase, even if these words end with additional characters. Like wildcards, truncation broadens a search. The search phrase SYST?, for example, will retrieve records containing *system, systematic, systematization, systemic, systems, systole,* etc. Sometimes it's not necessary to enter a special truncation character; you simply tell the computer to find records in which a field begins with a search phrase. If you instruct the program to find all the records in which the field NAME begins with *S*, for example, you'll be shown *Sagan, Smith, Stevenson*, etc.

Continuing a Search. Sometimes a search produces more than one hit. Suppose, for instance, you are searching a mailing list data base for records that contain 22901 in the field ZIP CODE. Three records meet that criterion. Most programs take you to the *first* record in the data base that contains 22901. Continuing the search will take you to the *next* record that contains 22901, and so on until you have seen all of them.

MODIFYING RECORDS

A common reason for finding records is to update or delete a particular record.

Updating Records. When the information you are tracking changes, you will want to reflect these changes in your data records. Suppose you are maintaining a data base of employees, and one of them has just changed her address. Some programs do not require you to enter a special mode to change a data record; you simply scroll to the record or use the find function to locate it. Then you use the editing commands to make the changes you want. Other programs require you to enter a special mode before you can make changes to a record.

Deleting Records. Sometimes you will want to remove records from the data base. In the example just mentioned, for instance, you'd want to remove a data record about an employee who has accepted another position. To be useful, the data base should contain only the current employees.

SORTING RECORDS

With most file management programs, the records are initially displayed in the order you entered them. Unless you deliberately entered them in alphabetical or numerical order, they'll be disorganized. This disorganization doesn't matter when you're finding records using search techniques. The program, after all, can find the record you want even if the records aren't in alphabetical or numerical order. Yet you'll still want to sort your records. Almost all programs require you to sort them so they'll be in order when they're printed. To sort your data base, you'll use a special command that takes you to the sort function. Before you do your sort, you'll need to make some decisions.

Which Field to Use as a Sort Key? A big disadvantage of precomputer data bases is that it's so tedious to sort them. Suppose you have 200 bibliography cards, sorted by author. You might want to sort them some other way — for instance, by subject. Yet doing so is so tedious that you probably won't. In contrast, file management programs do the sorting for you at high rates of speed. You can use almost any field as a sort key. You can sort a bibliography, for example, by DATE OF PUBLICATION, PUBLISHER, or SUBJECT just as easily as you can sort it by AUTHOR.

Types of Sorts. You may sort your data base in **ascending sort** (A, B, C or 1, 2, 3) or **descending sort** (C, B, A or 3, 2, 1). Of the two, ascending sorts are most common. In a bibliography data base, for example, you'd normally sort the records by AUTHOR, beginning with *A*. Yet you may wish to look at your data base from another angle. Suppose you want to look only at the most recently published books. To do so, you could sort the data base by DATE OF PUBLICATION, using descending order. The most recently published books will appear first.

Multiple Key Sorts. Some file management programs let you do **multiple key sorts,** or sorts that use more than one sort key. To understand why this is useful, consider the bibliography data base once again. Suppose one of the authors you have listed, Minnie Able, has written five books, so you have five Minnie Able records. You have sorted your data base by AUTHOR. Henry Aardvark's book comes before Minnie Able's books, and Alice Cantrell's book follows them (Figure 7–7). The problem lies in the five records for Minnie Able's books. Although they're grouped together, they're not organized in any way. They're printed the way you entered them in the data base.

A multiple key sort gives you a way of solving sorting problems that aren't taken care of by the first sort key (or **primary sort key,** the one chosen to organize all the records in the data base). Suppose you identify a **secondary sort key,** one that comes into action when there are two or more records with the same data in the field chosen for the primary sort key. For a bibliographic data base, this secondary sort key could be DATE OF PUBLICATION (in ascending order). It would be activated *only* when one author wrote two or

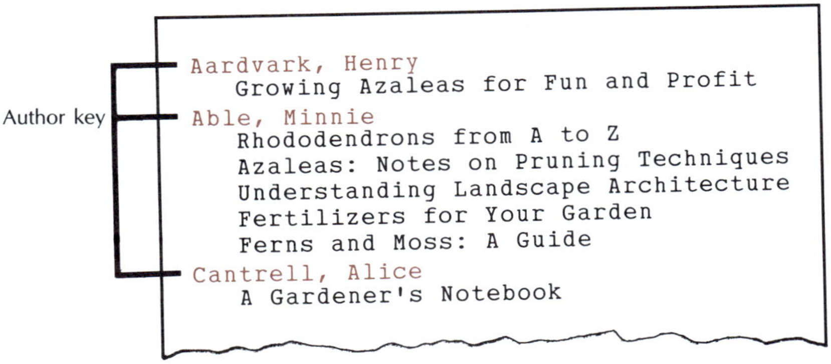

FIGURE 7–7 Report Sorted on One Key Only

more books. It would list Minnie Able's books in chronological order, beginning with the one she published first (Figure 7–8).

What happens if Minnie Able published two books in 1985? Here we have a problem that isn't resolved by the secondary sort key. Some programs let you define a **tertiary sort key** to cope with such cases. A tertiary sort key comes into action when there are two or more records with the same data in the field chosen for the secondary sort key. It resolves problems left unsolved by secondary sort keys. TITLE could be used as a tertiary sort key. Ms. Able's two 1985 books will then be listed in alphabetical order by title. Not all file management programs include multiple key sorting features. As you can see, however, these features are very useful.

FIGURE 7–8 Report Sorted on Two Keys

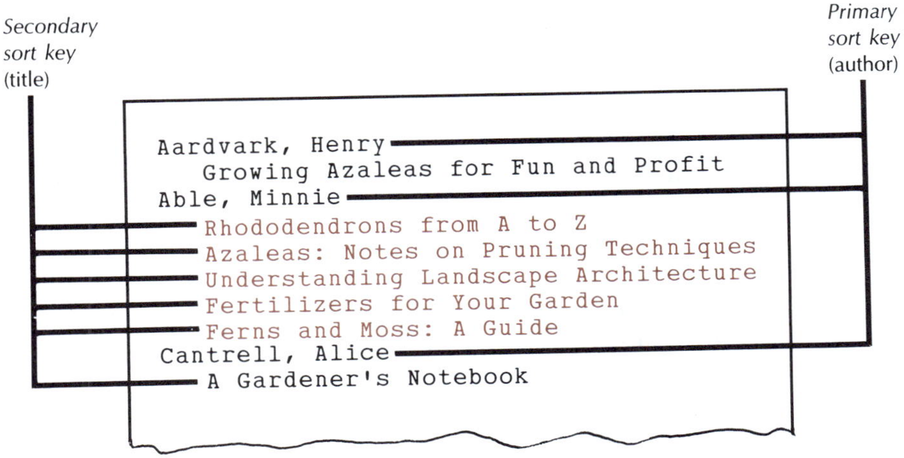

SELECTING RECORDS

To **select** records means to choose which records you want to print. Sometimes, of course, you will want to print your whole data base. More often, however, you will want to see just part of it in a brief, concise list. Suppose, for instance, that you're a music programmer for a radio station. You've a slot to fill with a piece that's less than 25 minutes long. In other words, you want to select for printing all the records in which the field PLAYING TIME is LESS THAN 25. You can then choose from the list a musical composition that fits within the time available.

Learning selection procedures gives you a powerful tool for information management. A major problem we all face today is the overabundance of information; there's more of it than we can conceptualize all at once. Good information management skills include ways to cut down the sheer bulk of information so that you see *only* the information you need. That's precisely what the selection function does. Although it takes some effort to learn how to use it, the effort is well repaid. In return, you get complete control over the information in your data base, which you can retrieve in thousands of different ways. It is one of the most valuable computer skills you can learn.

Entering the Select Mode. To select data records in this way, you'll use a command that takes you into the program's **select mode.** Sometimes this mode is part of the program's printing functions; sometimes it's separate. If it is part of the print mode, you will have to enter that mode before you can select records (see "Printing Records," below).

Entering a Selection Criterion. After you enter the select mode, you'll enter a **selection criterion.** This is a set of specifications you give the program about which records to retrieve. Then the computer goes through the records, ignoring the ones that do not meet the criterion.

To enter a selection criterion, you will make three choices:

Choose the Field to Select On. Here you tell the program which field you want to use as a key for selection purposes. Choose one of the data fields in your data base.

Choose the Search Text or Value. Here you identify a search phrase or numerical value that will provide the basis for the selection of records. To select from the classical music data base, you could enter *Mozart* (search text) or *1900* (numerical value).

Choose an Operator. In data base management, an *operator* is a word, phrase, or symbol that helps you specify search criteria with precision. Operators include **numerical operators** (such as GREATER THAN and LESS THAN), **logical operators** (such as AND, OR, and NOT), and others (such as BEGINS

WITH and CONTAINS). The use of these operators is best understood through examples; you will find several in the following section.

How to Conceptualize Selection Criteria. A useful way to think of selection criteria is to express them as a sentence, using this form:

```
Select all the records where [FIELD] [OPERATOR] [TEXT OR
VALUE].
```

Plug in the specifics of "field," "operator," and "text or value" as needed. Here are some examples:

1. `Select all the records where [DATE OF COMPOSITION] [EQUALS] [1900].` The computer will retrieve *only* those records that contain *1900* in the field DATE OF COMPOSITION.
2. `Select all the records where [COMPOSER] [BEGINS WITH] [MOZART].` The computer will retrieve *only* those records in which *Mozart* begins the field COMPOSER.
3. `Select all the records where [TYPE OF COMPOSITION] [CONTAINS] [STRING QUARTET].` The computer will retrieve *only* the records in which the words *string quartet* occur somewhere in the field TYPE OF COMPOSITION.
4. `Select all the records where [DATE OF COMPOSITION] [IS LESS THAN OR EQUAL TO] [1856].` The computer will retrieve *only* the records in which the field DATE OF COMPOSITION contains a number less than or equal to *1865*.

Using Additional Selection Criteria. Using just one selection criterion, you can cut down the unusable information in your data base substantially. Yet sometimes just one selection criterion isn't enough. Consider this example. Suppose you want to see only those data records that list string quartets before 1865. You start with the criterion, "Select all the records where [DATE OF COMPOSITION] [IS LESS THAN OR EQUAL TO] [1865]." But you're working with a large data base. More than 2,000 data records meet this criterion. It would be tedious to search through all of them to find just the ones that contain *string quartet* in the field TYPE OF COMPOSITION. Expressing your needs in the sentence form just introduced, here's what you want to do. You want to select data records using *two* selection criteria:

1. `Select all the records where [DATE OF COMPOSITION] [IS LESS THAN OR EQUAL TO] [1865]`

   `AND`

2. `Select all the records where [TYPE OF COMPOSITION] [EQUALS] [STRING QUARTET].`

In other words, you want to find *only* those data records which meet *both* criteria. The date of composition must be 1865 or earlier, and the type of composition must be string quartet.

Many programs let you add even more criteria. Here's one that uses three:

1. `Select all the records where [DATE OF COMPOSITION] [IS LESS THAN OR EQUAL TO] [1865]`

   AND

2. `Select all the records where [TYPE OF COMPOSITION] [EQUALS] [STRING QUARTET]`

   AND

3. `Select all the records where [CONDITION OF LP RECORDING] [EQUALS] [EXCELLENT].`

The data records you retrieve have to meet all *three* criteria before you'll accept them. It's not enough that the record contains *1865* or earlier in the DATE OF COMPOSITION field or *string quartet* in the TYPE OF COMPOSITION field. It must also contain *excellent* in the CONDITION OF LP RECORDING data field.

Logical Operators. In the above examples, you noticed that the three selection criteria are connected using the word AND. As it's used here, AND is an operator in the same way that LESS THAN or EQUAL TO are operators — they help you write precise search criteria. Logical operators, however, are used to link two or more search criteria (as in the example above), giving you tools for even greater precision in telling the computer just which records to include and which to exclude. Logical operators are sometimes called **boolean** operators, after an English mathematician and logician who invented an algebra based on logical rather than numerical relationships.

Most programs let you use two logical operators, AND and OR.

AND. When two selection criteria are linked with **AND** logic, records must satisfy *both* criteria to be retrieved (Figure 7–9). Consider this expression: "Select all the records where TYPE OF COMPOSITION equals STRING QUARTET *AND* COMPOSER equals HAYDN." This search retrieves *only* those records about Haydn string quartets. The AND operator, in short, is exclusive; it narrows the selection criteria and reduces the number of data records retrieved.

OR. The second way to connect selection criteria is to use **OR** logic. Using OR logic results in a less restrictive search and increases the number of records retrieved. Consider this expression: "Select all the records where TYPE OF COMPOSITION equals STRING QUARTET *OR* COMPOSER equals HAYDN." This expression will retrieve records about any composer's string quartets (not just Haydn's). It will also retrieve any compositions by Haydn — not just his string quartets (Figure 7–10).

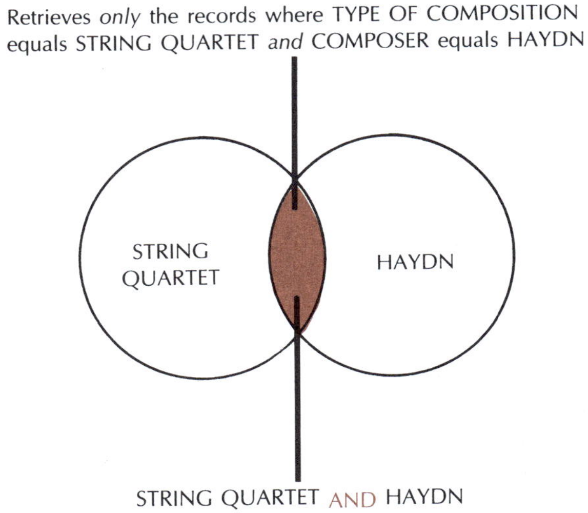

FIGURE 7–9 AND Operator Retrieves a Highly Focused Set

Some programs include a third operator, called NOT or BUT NOT.

NOT. The third way to connect selection criteria is to use the **NOT** operator, which is exclusive and reduces the number of records retrieved. Here's an example: "Select all the records where TYPE OF COMPOSITION equals STRING QUARTET, *BUT NOT* the records where COMPOSER equals HAYDN." This expression will retrieve all the string quartet data records, *except* the ones where Haydn is listed in the COMPOSER field (Figure 7–11).

FIGURE 7–10 OR Operator Is Inclusive

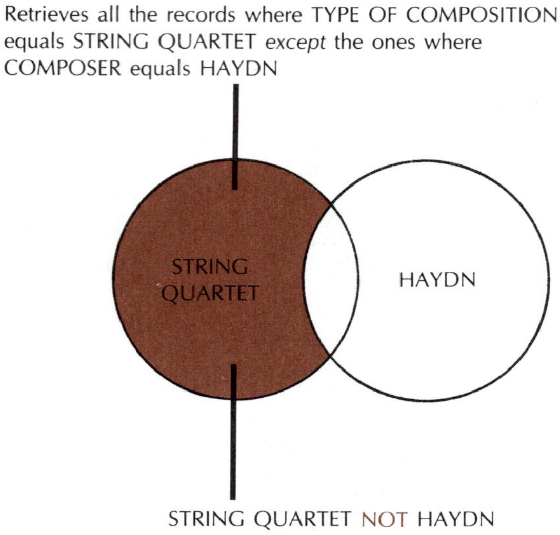

FIGURE 7–11 NOT Operator Excludes Unwanted Records

As you can see, selection criteria and logical operators provide a powerful way of thinking about information. You should practice using these information-management tools until they become second nature to you.

Creating a View. Once you have finished entering your selection criteria, the program begins searching for all the records that meet them. It then shows you (on the screen or at the printer) a list that contains only the records you selected. The set of selected records is called a **view.** The idea behind the term *view* is that you're looking at the data base from a certain angle. If you've selected the records where TYPE OF COMPOSITION equals STRING QUARTET, for example, you're looking at a string quartet view.

PRINTING RECORDS

Printing a data base creates a report of its contents. You may print the whole data base, if you wish, or a view of it that you have created using selection criteria. In either case, you will need to create a report format before you can print.

Creating the Report Format. To create the report format, you'll have to make some decisions.

Deciding Which Fields to Print. You may, if you wish, print all the fields in your data records. Yet reports with extraneous information are hard to read. It's best to include only those fields that are really required. In the classical music record data base just mentioned, for instance, suppose you're interested in listing the playing times of compositions. It would make sense to include PLAYING TIME, COMPOSER, and RECORD NUMBER. However, the information in other fields, such as TYPE OF COMPOSITION, CONDUCTOR, SOLOIST, etc., is not needed.

Formatting the Report. Most file management programs produce **columnar reports,** in which the data are listed in columns running down the page (Figure 7–12). Usually, this format is the **default format,** or the one the program will use unless you deliberately alter it. You may choose to turn on page numbering. If you wish, you can add running heads.

POTENTIAL PITFALLS OF FILE MANAGEMENT SOFTWARE

File management programs can be a lifesaver for people who must manage large amounts of information. Yet using these programs can be risky.

The Data Entry Problem. File management programs speed data manipulation and retrieval, but there's not much you can do about data entry: in most cases, you'll have to type the information you want to store into the computer (or pay someone else to do it). If you're thinking about computerizing a card file or some other precomputer data base, you will need to think about costs and benefits. The cost of conversion (aside from the cost of the computer and software) will be the expense and time required to type the data into the computer. If you do not really need the information management tools that these programs give you, the cost of data entry may not be worth it.

Limitations of Particular Programs. File management programs vary in their capabilities. Some let you enter as many as 1,000 characters in each data field; others restrict you to only 24. Some let you define a dozen sort keys, some let you define only one. Before going to all the trouble and expense

Playing Time	Composer	Record No.
5:32	Haydn	0126
6:15	Mozart	1019
7:35	Beethoven	0015
8:59	Mozart	1036
9:02	Verdi	2294

FIGURE 7–12
Columnar Report

TABLE 7–1 File Management Program Features

	Maximum size of data field	Maximum number of fields in record	Maximum number of records in Database	Can new fields be added after adding data?	Can fields be rearranged after adding data?
Notebook II	30,000	50	limited only by disk capacity	yes	yes
PC-File 4.0	65†	42	32,767	yes	no
*Symphony 1.0**	80	256‡	8192‡	yes	no

*Symphony is an integrated program that includes other software functions. Listed here are its file management functions only.
†One "super field" may be defined with up to 1,665 characters.
‡May be less depending on availability of internal memory.

of typing data into one of these programs, make sure it has the features you need. Many personal computer users have entered hundreds or even thousands of records before discovering that the program they're using cannot do what they want it to do. For a list of the capabilities of popular file management programs, see Table 7–1, "File Management Program Features."

Program Inflexibility. Using a file management program is risky for yet another reason: the inflexibility of the form once you've started entering records. Imagine this scenario: after entering 3,000 records, you discover that you should have devoted more thought and planning to the design of your form. A few programs let you add data fields at any time, but very few let you redesign the whole data form.

The Backup Problem. Backing up data regularly is particularly important when using file management software. Computers fail; programs crash. A business can be all but devastated by losing a list of sales contacts. The only safe course is to back up the whole data base every time any change, no matter how small, is made to it.

Personal computer literacy gives you the knowledge you need to avoid these problems, and most of it has already been presented in this book. Before you can be sure a file management program will meet your needs, however, you'll need to learn what a data base management system (DBMS) can do. A DBMS is far more powerful than file management software. In Chapter 8 we introduce data base management systems and show when they are preferable to file management programs.

Automatic numeric field calculation	Browse mode	Wildcard search?	Trunca-tion?	Sort keys	Logical operators
no	no	no	yes	1	AND, OR
yes	yes	yes	yes	10	AND, OR
yes	yes	yes	yes	3	AND, OR

SUMMARY

A data base is nothing more mysterious than a collection of information pertinent to a particular subject. A data base management program is a program for managing (that is, storing, organizing, and retrieving) the information in the data base. This chapter discusses the simplest data base management programs, called file management programs. A file management program can handle one file of data at a time.

Basic file management functions include creating a form (with data fields and field names); filling out records by adding data to forms; maintaining the file by editing; updating, and sorting records; retrieving data; and printing data. You perform these functions yourself when you maintain a manual data base using index cards. When your personal computer helps you perform these functions, you can get big gains in performance and productivity.

The first step in creating a data base is to design the form. You will need to think about what kind of data you want to store and how much space each field will need. Choose field names that clearly indicate the data field's contents. After you create the form, you may enter data. Be careful about spelling and be consistent in your usage of terms or phrases that will occur in more than one record. Check your work before you give the command that adds the record to the data base.

You can find records by scrolling, browsing, or searching. Some programs let you use wildcard characters or truncation. One reason to find records is to update or delete them.

So that your data will be printed in a well-organized way, you will sort your data base frequently. You may choose any field in the data record to use as a sort key, and you may sort in ascending or descending order. Some programs let you define secondary and tertiary sort keys, which resolve sorting problems left unresolved by the primary sort key.

You may print all the records in your data base. You may also select just the ones that meet criteria you specify. You specify which records you want by using a selection criterion. Many programs let you combine selection criteria using logical operators. Printing a data base produces a report of its contents. To print, you will have to decide which fields you want printed and, with some programs, how to arrange them on the page.

File management programs, like word processing programs, are valuable tools, but using them does pose some risks. Entering data is a tedious and time-consuming process. Before spending time or money entering hundreds or thousands of records into a data file, make sure the program you are using really meets your needs. Be sure, too, that the form you've designed will continue to work satisfactorily; not all programs let you change the form after you have added data. Back up your data base every time you make a change in it.

KEY TERMS

alphanumeric
AND
ascending sort
browse mode
columnar report
create mode
data base
data base management program
data base management system (DBMS)
data encryption
data field
data record
default format
descending sort
field length
field name
file management program
form
hit
logical (boolean) operator
multiple key sort
NOT
numerical operator
OR
primary sort key
report
search command
search template
secondary sort key
select
select mode
selection criterion
sort
sort key
tertiary sort key
text-oriented file management program
truncation
view
wildcard character

REVIEW QUESTIONS AND EXERCISES

1. Design a form on paper for a data base of practical value to you (suggestions: books and articles of use to you in your areas of academic interest or a collection of some kind [compact disks, rocks, or souvenirs]). Work out a format for the field names and data fields. For each field, specify the field length and the data type.
2. Think about what you want your data base to do. What kind of information are you likely to want to retrieve from it? In what situations would you be likely to do so? Does your form (the one you created on paper in exercise 1) include all the information you need? More than the information you need? Revise your form so that it is more useful to you.
3. What are the advantages of computerized file management over hand methods?
4. Why is correct spelling and the use of consistent nomenclature so important when you're using file management programs?
5. What is the purpose of a data base search? How is it different from selection? from sorting?
6. Make up a form for a data base on popular LP records or compact disks. For sorting purposes, identify the primary, secondary, and tertiary sort keys and explain why you have chosen them.
7. For the LP or compact disk data base, write selection criteria that use all the numerical operators. Then write a second set of selection criteria that use logical operators.
8. What are the shortcomings and potential drawbacks of file management software?

FOR FURTHER READING

Becker, Laurence. "Notebook II: A Data Base Manager for Text," *Computers and the Humanities* (January-March 1985).

Casella, Phil. "Tracking Electronic Paper," *InfoWorld* (January 21, 1985).

Chiang, Katherine S., et al. "Creating Bibliographies for Business Use: Literature-Retrieval Programs Can Help You Organize Unwieldy Collections of Brochures, Legal Documents, and Corporate Reports," *PC: The Independent Guide to IBM-Standard Personal Computing* (November 12, 1985).

Dickenson, John. "Lexical Electronic Filing: A Lexical, or Word-Oriented, Database Manager Organizes Document Files by Keywords — A Godsend When Searching Material from Public Databases or Maintaining Large-Scale Electronic Files," *PC: The Independent Guide to IBM-Standard Personal Computing* (August 20, 1985).

Hunter, Beverly. "Problem Solving with Data Bases," *Computing Teacher* (March 1986).

Krasnoff, Barbara. "Project Database II: Flat-File Databases," *PC Magazine* (August 1986).

Markoff, John, and Ezra Shapiro. "Public-Domain Gems [incl. PC-FILE III]," *Byte* (March 1985).

Mendrinos, Roxanne B. "Use of Data Bases in the Classroom," *Computers in the Schools* (Winter 1985/86).
Miller, Michael J. "Database Frontiers," *Popular Computing* (August 1985).
———, Michael J., and George F. Goley IV. "Making Sense of Database Software," *Popular Computing* (June 1984).
Phillips, Brian. "Nutshell: A Software Review of a File Manager," *Online* (March 1986).
Powledge, Fred. "FYI 3000 and Zyindex," *Popular Computing* (March 1985).
Ruff, Laura B., and Mary K. Weitzer. *Understanding and Using pfs:FILE/REPORT* (St. Paul, Minn.: West, 1986).
Trost, Stanley R. *Doing Business with PFS* (Berkeley: Sybex Computer Books, 1984).
Urschel, William. "Data Base/Filer Software," *Personal Computing* (April 1985).

8 *The Relational Connection:* *Introducing Data Base Management Systems*

"The concepts behind DBMS personal computer software are taken directly from the mainframe domain. In many ways, they represent quintessential 'computerness.' But that's part of the excitement of having these programs available on a micro. There is probably no other type of software that so firmly places mainframe-like power in your hands."

Alfred Glossbrenner *How to Buy Software*

The 1957 invention of the high-capacity hard disk brought computers into a new era. For the first time, immense amounts of data could be stored in one place and accessed almost immediately. And soon afterward, the data base management system (DBMS) was born. Data base management systems were originally designed to meet the data-crunching needs of large organizations. Mainframe DBMS programs can deal with several data bases at once, linking the data tracked by marketing, accounting, and production departments into a single information system. Updates made by one department are immediately reflected in the data bases kept by others. With the more sophisticated mainframe DBMS packages, hundreds of users can share a truly massive reservoir of data.

Now available for personal computers, data base management programs bring an immense amount of computing power to individuals. Whether you'll really

need that power, however, is something only you can judge. After all, DBMS programs were originally created for sharing data, but most personal computers are single-user machines. For many personal computer users, a file management program will suffice.

Even in a single-user environment, however, a DBMS can do things a file management program can't. For this reason, DBMS power is becoming increasingly attractive in the personal computer world, where more than 2 million data base management programs are now in use. Most programs are now sold to first-time buyers. Yet according to a senior analyst at Future Computing, a famous industry forecasting service, by 1990 two out of every five data base management programs sold will replace file management programs that no longer meet users' needs. Adds a southern California software distributor: "People grow out of a product like PFS:FILE pretty quickly."[1] And growing out of a data base product can be a painful and expensive experience. The message seems clear: you'll be doing yourself a big favor to find out what a DBMS can do — and whether you need its power.

You can use this chapter to help you learn the basics of a data base management system (DBMS). Begin by finding the sheets entitled *Quick Reference Guide: Data Base Management System Basics*, which are positioned at the end of this book. Tear them out, and staple them or put them in a folder. Keep these sheets handy as you read this chapter. When in this chapter we describe DBMS functions and procedures, such as creating a new data base or using the display command, consult your program's manual, handouts your instructor has given you, or the supplementary text you are using. Find out how to carry out the function or procedure with your DBMS package, and make a note of the command on the *Quick Reference Guide*. When you've finished filling out the *Quick Reference Guide*, keep it with you whenever you use the computer. You'll find it helpful in day-to-day operating sessions.

MANAGING DATA WITH A DBMS: AN INTRODUCTION

To distinguish a DBMS from a file management program, it's usually stressed that a DBMS is more powerful. One author stresses, for instance, that a DBMS can handle two or more files at once and it greatly eases the task of updating information contained in the data base. This claim is quite valid, yet it doesn't really convey the staggering improvement in performance that you get with a DBMS. A DBMS truly puts information at your fingertips. To understand just what this performance improvement means, let's look once more at the limitations of file management programs.

WHY USERS GROW OUT OF FILE MANAGEMENT PROGRAMS

File management programs provide major performance improvements over manual information-handling techniques. But once you've gotten over the initial flush of enthusiasm, file management procedures start to seem clumsy and slow. Since these points are best conveyed by example, we'll use an example that runs through this entire chapter.

The Update Problem. Let's suppose you're running a high-class shop for stereo freaks, and part of your stock includes a select line of audiophile-quality compact disks. You stock only those disks that a major national magazine ranks 9 or 10 in sound and performance quality. To track your stock and the magazine ratings, you buy a file management program, design a form, and enter the data. Figure 8–1 shows the file management program's data record for Buzzy Punk's "Same to You."

It's useful, obviously, to have the wholesale price and distributor's address and phone right there on the data record. When your stock gets low (as it is here), you've all the information you need right on the screen. But after six months of business, you know otherwise. Most compact disks are still pressed overseas, and the fluctuating price of the dollar has put audio compact disk prices on a roller coaster. Fast Delivery, Inc., has changed its wholesale price three times. And on top of that, they've just changed their phone number. As a result, you're spending more time in front of your computer than you can afford to spend. Here's why.

If you only had one data record for the disks that Fast Delivery markets, there would be no problem — you'd just update the one record. But you've over 900 data records in your data base, and about 40 percent of them list disks that you get from Fast Delivery (you get the others from other suppliers, whose prices have also changed — but by varying amounts). And so a horrible limitation of your file management program appears. You'll have to scroll through the data base, record by record, changing every entry by hand. It takes so much work, in fact, that you might decide just to chuck the whole idea of computerized record management.

How a DBMS Tackles the Update Problem. Here's how a DBMS solves the update dilemma. You sit down at the computer and phrase two quick commands in a

```
LABEL                   |Sterling
CATALOG NUMBER          |ZX-149
ARTIST                  |Buzzy Punk
TITLE                   |"Same to You"
SOUND QUALITY           |9.5
PERFORMANCE QUALITY     |10
DISTRIBUTOR             |Fast Delivery, Inc.
ADDRESS                 |11219 Forest Park Drive
CITY                    |Woodville
STATE                   |VA
ZIP                     |22900
PHONE                   |999-123-9876
WHOLESALE PRICE         |$7.90
STOCK                   |1
```

FIGURE 8–1 File Management Program Data Record

query language. A query language is a command language that lets you create a data base, ask questions about the data, update or modify the data as necessary, and perform other data-processing operations. Here's the first command (Figure 8–2). It's phrased in a simplified version of SQL (pronounced "sequel"), an IBM-developed query language that is widely used for DBMS applications. As you can see, the command is easy to understand. It's telling the computer: "Update the data base called POPDISK. When you find a record in which the DISTRIBUTOR field contains the text 'Fast Delivery,' change the WHOLESALE PRICE to $7.50." The operation takes just seconds.

Here's the second command (Figure 8–3). It, too, takes just seconds to do its job. In about five minutes, you've taken care of the other price changes too. (Actually, there's even a better, safer, and faster way to do these two jobs, but we'll need to introduce the idea of working with two or more data bases at once before you'll understand why.)

The Report Problem. A customer comes in with a question you hear, in various forms, every day: "Of the several available versions of Vivaldi's *Four Seasons*, which has the best sound?" And so you sit down with your personal computer and your file management program and select a view that contains all the *Four*

```
UPDATE POPDISKS

SET WHOLESALE PRICE = $7.90

WHERE DISTRIBUTOR = "Fast Delivery"
```

FIGURE 8–2 Update Command in SQL

Seasons data records. The program displays six records. To find the answer, you have to scroll through each of them, one by one. The whole procedure takes about five minutes. That's not bad, but try this DBMS approach (Figure 8–4). You ask to have the data records ordered according to quality of sound, and the reply appears in seconds (Figure 8–5).

Two facts about DBMS packages should be apparent after this example. First the good news:

Power. A data base management program puts information-crunching power at your fingertips. These programs do more than just store and retrieve

```
UPDATE POPDISKS

SET PHONE NUMBER = 999-123-9876

WHERE DISTRIBUTOR = "Fast Delivery"
```

FIGURE 8–3 Another Update Command

```
SELECT LABEL, CATALOG NUMBER, SOUND, DISTRIBUTOR
FROM CLASSICS
WHERE TITLE = "FOUR SEASONS"
AND SOUND > 7
ORDER BY SOUND
```

FIGURE 8–4 Data Base Query in SQL

FIGURE 8–5 Screen Display After Query

LABEL	CATALOG NUMBER	SOUND	DISTRIBUTOR
Golden	HQ-9973	10	Amalgamated
Hifalutin	889-43-1	10	International
Venus	CD-3550	9.5	Amalgamated
Coconut	77-555-2	9	Fast Service
Ziba	Z-30-971	8	International
Cabo	CD-275	8	International

Case Study: Putting PC Power Where It's Needed (Even If It's Halfway Around the World)

A trio of [IBM] PCs help Don Buschek and Goodyear Tire & Rubber squeeze extra dividends from the company's 36,000-acre rubber plantation on the tropical island of Sumatra, Indonesia.

Rubber from rubber trees is not just a quaint throwback to the Dutch and British colonial days of pith helmets, ceiling fans, and gin and tonics. About 30 percent of the rubber used in the United States is natural rubber.

In Sumatra since 1917, Goodyear has accumulated voluminous records of the yields from Dolok Merangir (Doe-lock Merangue-gay), an estate covered with neatly manicured lawns, exotic shrubs, and graceful palms, in addition to the company's 4 million rubber trees. Goodyear's goal is straightforward: Find a way to make sense of all the information and exploit it for higher yields.

Buschek, the plantation's finance director, oversees a project to develop a dBASE III database that will eventually store all known information about the trees and their yields, sort and report the information for in-house use, and send regular updates to Goodyear's corporate headquarters in Akron, Ohio. "Our goal is to use the database to isolate the factors that are most significant in establishing high yields or high resistance to disease," says Buschek.

Rubber tree records are arranged on a block-by-block basis, with each block measuring 500 × 5000 meters, consisting of 25 hectares (a hectare is 2.471 acres). Each acre is planted with 500 tall and spindly *Havea brasiliensa* trees, which look nothing like the broad-leafed rubber trees that grace many American living rooms. The data available for each block includes the number of trees planted; the number of healthy, producing trees (usually about three of five); the incidence of leaf blight, root disease, or other diseases; the yield of rubber latex per block; the frequency of tapping (usually every third day); the type and amount of fertilizer applied; the stimulant applied to the tapper's cut; the age of the tree; tree breed; soil acidity; and geographic conditions.

Once the data base is perfected, the plantations production manager, Jock Young, might be able to see, for instance, that one kind of tree does especially well when planted on hilly areas. He would have clearer evidence about the point where yields begin to fall off as a block of trees reaches old age (about 25 years) and would more accurately know when to order "slaughter tapping," an aggressive tapping process that maximizes the falling yield while hastening the tree's decline.

From William K. Howard, "PCs on the Rubber Plantation," *PC Magazine* (July 9, 1985), pp. 158–160.

information; they give you the electronic equivalent of a garage full of power tools for shaping information to your needs. That's why DBMS packages are useful for single-user applications, even though these packages were originally designed for use by many people at once.

And now the bad news:

Difficulty. Most data base management systems are substantially more difficult to use than file management programs. Almost all file management programs are menu driven. To use them, you need not memorize many commands; you simply choose them from a menu shown on the screen. In contrast, most DBMS packages are command driven. You must learn how to express the commands using a query language.

Don't let the second point scare you away from a DBMS. After all, if you're using an IBM, Apple, or CP/M computer, you've already learned how to use commands you type in at the keyboard. As you know, you need to learn only a few DOS commands for day-to-day work. Much the same applies to DBMS packages; you need to understand only a few basic commands to use them.

A NOTE ON DATA BASE DESIGN

In the mainframe world, three different DBMS designs compete for the marketplace, each with its adherents (and detractors). In the personal computer world, however, the battle has been all but won by the relational design. Most personal computer DBMS packages are relational DBMSs, so there's little need to understand the other design strategies. The term *relational* will be defined at the end of the chapter, after you've seen some more examples.

EXPLORING A RELATIONAL DBMS

Six basic functions figure in everyday work with a relational DBMS: creating the data base, adding records, retrieving information, updating information, deleting information, and calculating information. The terms used for these commands vary from program to program, but the underlying function is the same.

CREATING A DATA BASE

The **create command** constructs a new data base. Here's an example of a create command:

```
CREATE CLASSICS
```

This command creates a new data base called CLASSICS.

Command Functions and Names in Relational DBMS Packages

Relational data base packages use different commands to accomplish a core of basic functions that all or most of them can accomplish. Here's a comparison of SQL and dBASE II commands.

Function	**Query language**	
	SQL	*dBASE II*
Creating a Data Base	CREATE	CREATE
Adding New Records	INSERT	APPEND
Retrieving Information	SELECT	DISPLAY
Modifying Information	UPDATE	REPLACE
Deleting Information	DELETE	DELETE

The program responds with a screen that lets you define the data record form (including field names, data type, field length in characters, and the number of decimal places to be used in numeric fields [Figure 8–6]). These terms were introduced in Chapter 7; they have the same meaning in the DBMS context as they do in the file management context.

FIGURE 8–6 Creating the Data Base

```
   FIELD NAME    TYPE         WIDTH   DEC
1  LABEL         Char/Text      6
2  CATNO         Char/Text      8
3  COMPOSR       Char/Text     10
4  TITLE         Char/Text     20
5  SOUND         Numeric        3      1
6  PRICE         Numeric        4      2
7  DISTRIB       Char/Text      3
```

For the first field (LABEL) in Figure 8–6, you've told the program, "Create a field called LABEL [short for "record label"]". It will contain characters, and should be six spaces in length. The second field, CATNO (short for "catalog number"), is also a character field, because many catalog numbers combine letters, punctuation marks, and numbers (such as A-119). The numeric option can be chosen only if all the characters in the field will be numbers. The next two fields, COMPOSR (short for "composer") and TITLE, are also character fields. The SOUND field is numeric with one decimal place, and is long enough to hold the highest number (10.0). The PRICE field is also numeric, and has room for four characters. Only three are needed right now, but the wholesale price may go up.

As you can see, creating a data base with a relational package requires you to plan carefully, just as you must do with a file management program such as the ones discussed in Chapter 7. You must consider how much space you need for data entry. A major difference between file management programs and relational DBMS packages, however, is that a relational DBMS stores and displays data records in a columnar format (see Figure 8–5). For this reason the data fields are kept as short as possible — you want to see the whole record, if possible, on the 80-character-wide video display. Accordingly, short codes (such as INT) are used instead of spelling out lengthy text entries (such as International CD, Inc.).

ADDING RECORDS

Commands for adding records to the data base, such as the **append command** (dBASE) or the insert command (SQL), add records to an existing data base. After using the append or insert command, what appears to be a file management program's form (see Chapter 7) is displayed (Figure 8–7). You type in the information just as if you were using a file management program.

RETRIEVING INFORMATION

Data base management systems provide powerful tools for displaying information in the data base. To illustrate what a relational package can do, we'll look at only one of them here: the dBASE **display command,** the command that selects data for display on the screen. Using the CLASSICS data base, here's a dBASE DISPLAY FOR expression:

```
DISPLAY FOR label = "Cabo"
```

And here's the result (Figure 8–8). The query we've just used retrieved the whole record, showing all the fields (label, catalog number, composer, title,

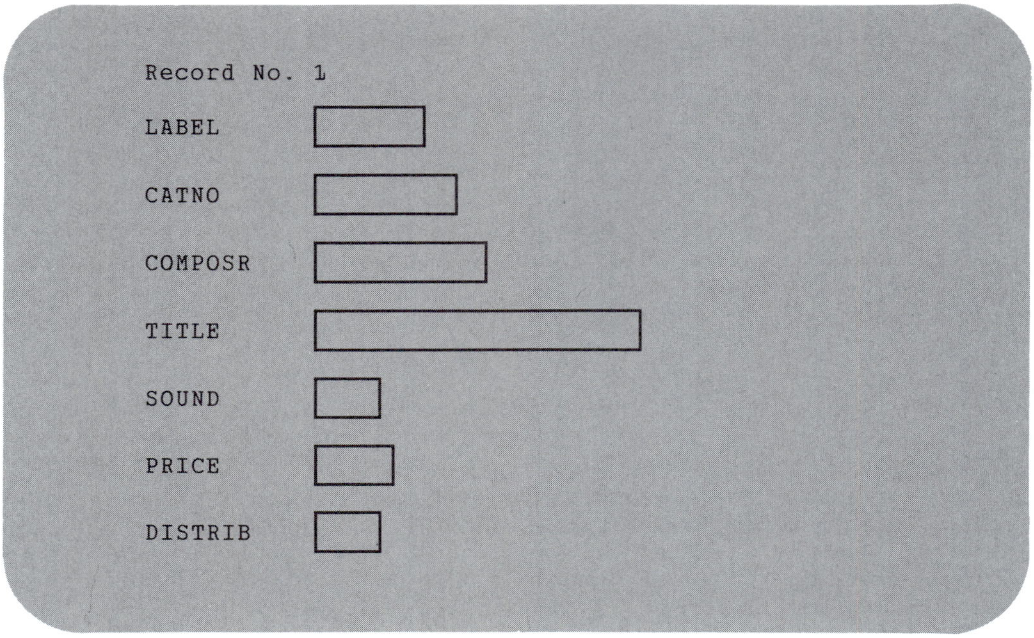

FIGURE 8–7 Blank Data Record in Append Mode

FIGURE 8–8 Result of Retrieval with DISPLAY FOR

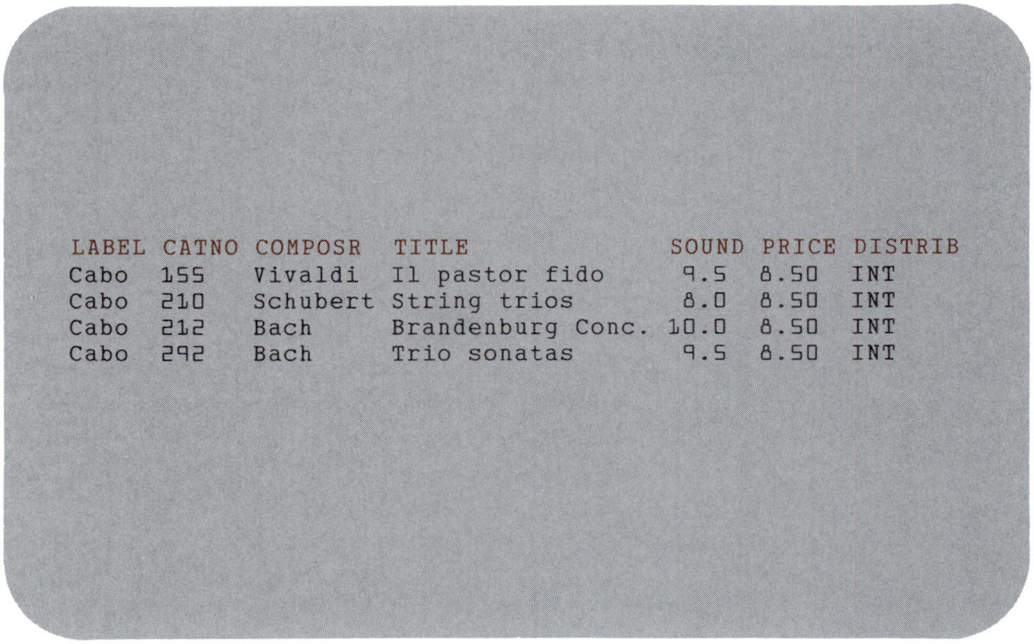

LABEL	CATNO	COMPOSR	TITLE	SOUND	PRICE	DISTRIB
Cabo	155	Vivaldi	Il pastor fido	9.5	8.50	INT
Cabo	210	Schubert	String trios	8.0	8.50	INT
Cabo	212	Bach	Brandenburg Conc.	10.0	8.50	INT
Cabo	292	Bach	Trio sonatas	9.5	8.50	INT

COMPOSR	TITLE	SOUND
Vivaldi	Il pastor fido	9.5
Schubert	String trios	8.0
Bach	Brandenburg Conc.	10.0
Bach	Trio sonatas	9.5

FIGURE 8–9 Reducing Information by Eliminating Fields

sound quality, wholesale price, and distributor). We can limit the fields shown by modifying the command.

```
DISPLAY composr,title,sound FOR label = "Cabo"
```

And here's the result of this information buzzsaw (Figure 8–9).

Logical operators (see Chapter 7) provide even more powerful tools. Suppose a customer comes in and says, "I'm looking for a string quartet by Mozart that's a 10 in sound quality." First, the query:

```
DISPLAY FOR composr = "Mozart" .AND. sound = "10"
```

This query produces the results shown in Figure 8–10.

FIGURE 8–10 Retrieval Using Logical Operators

LABEL	CATNO	COMPOSR	TITLE	SOUND	PRICE	DISTRIB
Cabo	396	Mozart	Quartet Nos. 10,13	10.0	8.35	INT
Venus	15541	Mozart	Quart/Divertimenti	10.0	7.10	SOC
Ziba	A-119	Mozart	Quartet Nos. 11,14	10.0	8.50	INT

UPDATING INFORMATION

The **replace command** (called **update** in SQL) lets you update information quickly, even if the updates must be made to many records or the whole data base. Let's suppose you've just received an apologetic note from International Associates, Inc., a compact disk supplier, pointing out a 75-cent wholesale price increase for all the CDs in their catalog. Here's the query.

```
REPLACE price WITH price + .75 WHERE distrib = "INT"
```

This is precisely the same updating operation, remember, that would have required you to scroll through your entire data base, making change after change by hand, were you using a file management program.

DELETING INFORMATION

An order for a compact disk (Venus 3550–15) comes back from International Associates, Inc., with the unhappy news that it has been deleted from the catalog. Here's the dBASE II **delete command** you'll use:

```
DELETE FOR label = "Venus" .AND. catno = "3550-15"
```

AGGREGATE FUNCTIONS

Relational data base management programs provide equally supple tools for managing the numbers in a data base. These functions, called **aggregate functions,** scan the entire data base to compute an answer. Among these functions are SUM (sum the numbers in a field), COUNT (count the number of records), AVG (average), MIN (minimum amount listed in a field), and MAX (maximum value in a field).

Here's an example of how useful these functions can be. Suppose you're wondering whether your distributors are giving you a good deal. To find out the average price you're paying, you use the AVG query:

```
AVG price
```

And the program responds,

```
7.28
```

Now you're wondering what average price you're paying per disk from one of the distributors, International (abbreviated INT):

```
AVG price FOR distrib = "INT"
```

And the program returns the answer:

```
8.11
```

Hmm. It might be a good idea to check out another supplier for these disks!

OTHER RELATIONAL DBMS FEATURES

Other relational DBMS features include a procedural language, backup with restore, the ability to restructure data bases, and a report generator.

Procedural Language. A major advantage of relational DBMS packages is the **procedural language** that comes with them. This procedural language is a genuine programming language with many uses. You can use it, for instance, to automate day-to-day data base maintenance procedures (such as the procedure described above to determine which disks to order). You can also use it to set up a menu-driven, custom installation of a DBMS. Part 5 of this book, "Application Horizons," returns to DBMS procedural languages.

Backup with Restore. Imagine this scenario. You're working with your data base, thinking to yourself, "I'm totally in control. This is wonderful. Look how well I'm doing entering this command." And then — "Oh no! I just wiped out all the data records about disks provided by CD Distributors!" Most relational data base management packages are designed to give you a graceful way out of such errors. They use a **backup with restore** feature that comes into play whenever you use the delete command. You don't really delete the records you think you're deleting; the program saves them for you, just in case you change your mind. You can bring the deleted records back into the database with a RESTORE command.

Restructuring Capabilities. When we set up our compact disk data base, we defined the PRICE field with space for three numbers. We never imagined, did we, that the wholesale price of compact disks would require four digits? But freak accidents have blown up both United States compact disk plants, and the dismal decline of the dollar has sent the price of all imports rocketing upward.

With some file management programs, you'd be out of luck at this point. But most relational DBMS packages include features that let you create new data bases with altered field specifications. You give a few simple commands that instruct the program, in effect, to make a new data base with a PRICE field that contains four characters instead of three.

Report Generator. As you've seen throughout this chapter, the immediate screen display of data operations is one of the factors that distinguishes a DBMS from a file management program. Even so, printed reports remain useful, especially because DBMS packages can print reports with subtotals for each column and totals for the entire report. Think of the report generator as a way to produce on paper what a DBMS is showing you on the screen.

The functions we've discussed so far lie at the heart of dBASE II. Every one of them is a power tool for working with information. Yet we've not touched on the most powerful feature of dBASE II and other relational data base managers: their ability to work with multiple data bases.

USING TWO OR MORE DATA BASES

A major advantage of relational data base management programs is their ability to use two or more data bases at the same time. This saves time by making it unnecessary to enter the same data twice. To illustrate, let's return to our example.

WHY MULTIPLE DATA BASES ARE USEFUL

One apparent advantage of using a file management program is that you've plenty of room on the form to show the distributor's address and phone number. That way, after you've looked up a compact disk, you see the information you need for ordering it, right on the display screen. This approach seems convenient at first, but it turns out that it isn't. Suppose you have listed 211 disks distributed by Fast Delivery, Inc. And now suppose they go out of business. You'll have to get all those disks from some other supplier. What's even worse, you'll have to go into your data base and type in the new distributor's name, address, and telephone number 211 times! You'll almost certainly make data entry errors, which can cripple your program's accuracy in retrieving data.

It's much better to come up with a way to list that information just *once.* To put it another way, it's a good idea to eliminate **data redundancy,** or the storage of the same data item in two or more places. And with multiple data bases, you can do just that. The key is the **join command.** This command lets you put together the information in two or more separate data bases. Using this command, for instance, you could combine the information in the CLASSICS data base (a catalog of classical compact disks) with another, much shorter one called SUPPLIERS, in which the distributors' addresses are listed just once for each. The result will be an accurate report that lists, for every disk, the suppliers' addresses. The process is completely automatic and takes very little time.

DISTRIB	COMPANY	ADDRESS	CITY	ST	ZIP	PHONE
CDD	CD Distributors	921 Elm St.	Richmond	VA	22504	804-999-9999
INT	International CD	1221 6th St.	New York	NY	10011	212-111-1001
SOC	Sonic Corp.	950 Loud Av.	Ft.Worth	TX	71633	512-000-2000

FIGURE 8–11 SUPPLIERS Data Base

USING THE JOIN COMMAND

Here's a brief illustration. In addition to your data base called CLASSICS, you create another one called SUPPLIERS to list the addresses and telephone numbers of compact disk wholesale distributors (Figure 8–11). There's a key point to notice here. The field DISTRIB (short for "distributor code") is the same one that appears in the CLASSICS data base (see, for instance, Figure 8–10). The DISTRIB field creates a link between the two data bases. And now let's see what you can do with it.

Suppose you've added the field STOCK to your CLASSICS data base to indicate the number of disks you have in stock (see the last column in Figure 8–12). As a supplier of audiophile-quality compact disks to your exclusive clientele, you want to make sure you stock all the disks that rate a 9 or 10 in sound quality. So you decide to print a list of your 9s and 10s, complete with an up-to-date list of how many disks you have on hand and, for the sake of convenience, the distributor's phone number. To do so, you'll need to combine data from the CLASSICS and SUPPLIERS data bases using the JOIN command.

FIGURE 8–12 CLASSIC Data Base with STOCK Field Added

LABEL	CATNO	COMPOSR	TITLE	SOUND	PRICE	DISTRIB	STOCK
Cabo	396	Mozart	Quartet Nos. 10,13	10.0	8.35	INT	2
Dill	D-129	Bach	Trio sonatas	8.5	7.50	CDD	0
Venus	15541	Mozart	Quart/Divertimenti	10.0	7.10	SOC	4
Ziba	Z-150	Bach	Goldberg Vars.	8.0	8.50	INT	3
Ziba	A-119	Mozart	Quartet Nos. 11,14	10.0	8.50	INT	1

LABEL	CATNO	SOUND	PRICE	DISTRIB	STOCK	COMPANY	PHONE
Cabo	396	10.0	8.35	SOC	2	International	212-111-1001
Dill	D-129	8.5	7.50	CDD	0	CD Distributors	804-999-9999
Venus	15541	10.0	7.10	SOC	4	Sonic Corp.	512-000-2000
Ziba	Z-150	8.0	8.50	INT	3	International	212-111-1001
Ziba	A-119	10.0	8.50	INT	1	International	212-111-1001

FIGURE 8–13 ORDER Data Base

Because the JOIN command needed to accomplish this task is complex, it's omitted here. It says, in effect, "Join the two data bases currently in use [that is, CLASSICS and SUPPLIERS] to a new data base called ORDER. Use DISTRIB as the key field. In the new data base, list the information by label, catalog number, sound, price, distributor code, company name, and phone" (Figure 8–13).

Since you don't want to order disks that have a sound quality of less than 8, and you don't want to order if you already have 2 or more disks in stock, you use a DISPLAY FOR command.

```
DISPLAY FOR sound > 7.5 .AND. stock < 2
```

("Display all the records where sound is greater than 7.5 and stock is less than 2.") Here's the result, in Figure 8–14. So pick up the phone and call!

THE ADVANTAGES OF ELIMINATING DATA REDUNDANCY

The Chapter 7 discussion of file management programs stressed correct spelling and consistency — and with good reason. When you have the same data item

FIGURE 8–14 ORDER Data Base After DISPLAY FOR

LABEL	CATNO	SOUND	PRICE	DISTRIB	STOCK	COMPANY	PHONE
Dill	D-129	8.5	7.50	CDD	0	CD Distributors	804-999-9999
Ziba	A-119	10.0	8.50	INT	1	International	212-111-1001

entered in two different records, it must be entered in *exactly* the same way. If it isn't, search procedures and reports will not function correctly.

With a relational data base program, you can do away with the worst of this data redundancy problem. The address and the phone number of International CD, a compact disk distributor, are listed in just *one* place. When you use REPLACE to change the address and phone number, you're changing just one record. There's no question of problems in data retrieval caused by varying spellings of the information. (You must still be careful, however, in how you spell the data entered in the DISTRIB field. Yet these data are three-letter codes. Mistakes will be easy to detect on data entry.)

THE RELATIONAL MODEL

Now that we've gone through these examples, it's time to define the term **relational DBMS.** The task isn't easy, since computer scientists are currently involved in a wrangle over the term's meaning. From the user's viewpoint, however, it's safe to say that a relational DBMS has two critical features, both of which involve relationship among data: (1) it stores data in tables, and (2) it has the ability to link two or more data bases through a common data field.

A table, if you think about it, expresses a relationship between the columnar headings and the data stored beneath them. And all the data in a single data record (listed by a DBMS as a horizontal line across the screen) is related; it's unified by the fact that it's all stored as one record. A relational DBMS makes use of these table relationships to give you all that data-crunching power. As you've seen throughout this chapter, tables are very important in relational DBMSs: indeed, the result of any information retrieval operation with a relational DBMS is — you guessed it — another table.

The linking of two or more data bases through a common field, such as the field DISTRIB in the example this chapter has used, illustrates the second sense of the term relational. The common field establishes a relationship between the two data bases, and this relationship can be used to reduce data redundancy. Reducing (or preferably, eliminating) data redundancy greatly increases the data base's accuracy, usefulness, and reliability.

DBMS HORIZONS

What we've discussed thus far may seem like the last word in personal computer sophistication, but there's more. Let's look at attempts to make relational data base packages easier to use.

NATURAL LANGUAGE INTERFACES

As you've seen throughout this chapter, you must use a query language such as SQL to use a relational data base package. Although some query language expressions are straightforward, others are complicated and cumbersome. The truth is that query languages keep many users away from relational packages.

That's what motivates the efforts now going on to develop **natural language interfaces** to DBMS packages. A natural language interface is a computer control program that allows a person to interact with the computer using human (rather than computer) language. In other words, instead of using the JOIN statement described above (and several others omitted for simplicity), one could simply type in, "Give me the telephone numbers of distributors for all disks with a sound quality over 8 and a stock less than 2."

You might think that we're talking about the computers of the next century, but programs exist right now that have this capability. Natural language interfaces are one outgrowth of research into artificial intelligence (AI). A company called Artificial Intelligence Corporation has created a natural language interface program called INTELLECT, which runs on IBM mainframes and has been installed in more than 150 Fortune 1000 companies.[2] Other companies market natural language interfaces for personal computer DBMS packages.

Natural language interfaces sound like a great idea on first hearing, but some computer scientists don't think so. For one thing, the "natural language" statement just mentioned ("Give me the telephone numbers . . .") actually shows a pretty good understanding of what's in the data base and how to retrieve it. Formulating a statement in such precise terms as these is much different from saying, "Hey, what disks should I order?" Critics of the natural language interface question, therefore, whether such queries really are being phrased in natural language. To make these queries work, you have to use very precise terms. Moreover, you have to know just what you're doing. And if you know that much, why not save typing time by using the query language instead?[3] The way to make these programs easier to use, these experts say, isn't to sidestep the complexity of using the program. The right way is to make it easier for users to get the expertise they need.

IMPROVING THE USER INTERFACE

New programs help users develop querying expertise by using improved user interfaces. A user interface is the part of the program that handles the interaction between computer and user.

An excellent example of this trend is dBASE III Plus, a successor to dBASE III. Instead of asking the user to learn how to use a query language, dBASE III Plus uses a series of pull-down menus that help users construct complex commands. As you construct a command, its syntax is clearly displayed. Even novice users can learn to use dBASE III Plus quickly. To be sure, the user still must understand how the data base is laid out and what the commands do. But the program does everything it can to remove the burden on the user's memory.

MULTIPLE-USER DBMS PACKAGES

Now that local area networks are available for personal computers, several DBMS makers have announced multiple-user versions of popular relational data base packages. Local area networks (LAN) are high-speed communication linkages among several personal computers and a central disk storage unit (see Chapter 12). Multiple-user DBMS programs can support the creation of one large, master data base that can be used by several people with their own personal computer workstations.

SUMMARY

Data base management systems (DBMS) were originally devised for huge information-crunching jobs in big organizations, but they're now available for personal computers. For many data base applications, DBMS power may come in handy.

Data base management systems go beyond storage and retrieval operations to give you almost instantaneous access to the information in your data base. With one command, for example, you can update information that appears throughout the data base. Select operations are far more flexible than they are with file management programs, and the results appear in tabular form right on the screen. However, DBMS packages are harder to learn and use than file management programs. You must learn how to use a query language — a language for giving commands and asking questions about the data.

Six basic functions figure in everyday work with a relational DBMS, the type of DBMS discussed in this chapter: creating the data base, adding records, retrieving information, updating information, deleting information, and calculating information using aggregate functions.

When you create a data base and add data to it, the program shows you what looks like a file management program's form. The data records are actually stored as tables, however, with field names for column headings and the data expressed as horizontal rows.

The most powerful feature of relational DBMS packages is their ability to work with two or more data bases at the same time. This feature helps to eliminate data redundancy, or the entry of the same data in two or more places.

A relational data base represents information using tables. You can think of the word *relation* as being synonymous with *table.* The emphasis on tables runs through every aspect of a relational DBMS. The result of any retrieval operation, for instance, is another table. Relational data bases also establish relationships between two or more data bases by linking them through a common field.

Attempts to make relational DBMS packages easier to use have employed natural language interfaces and improved user interfaces. Some programs now support use by several people at the same time.

KEY TERMS

aggregate functions
append command
backup with restore
create command
data redundancy
delete command
display command
join command
natural language interface
procedural language
query language
relational DBMS
replace (update) command

REVIEW QUESTIONS AND EXERCISES

1. Why do users tend to grow out of file management programs such as pfs:FILE? What advantages does a DBMS have over a file management program?
2. Why is it important to keep field lengths to a minimum when using a DBMS such as dBASE III?
3. Describe the functions of the five basic DBMS commands (called, in dBASE III, create, append, display, replace, and delete).
4. Why do a DBMS's aggregate functions, which file management programs usually lack, make it far more attractive than file management programs for business purposes?
5. Why is it useful to work with more than one data base at a time? (Hint: What are the advantages of eliminating data redundancy?)
6. Why are some computer scientists less than enthusiastic about natural language interfaces for DBMS packages?
7. Draw on your personal experience and think of an application that would make use of the JOIN command.
8. What are the two chief characteristics of a relational DBMS?

FOR FURTHER READING

Clifford, Michael J. *The dBASE Book of Business Applications* (Englewood Cliffs, N.J.: Prentice-Hall, 1985).

Date, C. J. *An Introduction to Database Systems,* 2 vols. (Reading, MA: Addison-Wesley, 1981, 1983).

Date, C. J. *Database: A Primer* (Reading, MA: Addison-Wesley, 1983).

Hill, I. D. "Wouldn't It Be Nice if We Could Write Computer Programs in Ordinary English — Or Would It?" *British Computer Society Bulletin* (June 1972).

Krassnoff, Barbara, and John Dickenson. "Project Database II," *PC: The Independent Guide to IBM-Standard Personal Computing* (June 24, 1985).

Kruglinski, David. *Data Base Management Systems: A Guide to Microcomputer Software* (New York: Osborne/McGraw-Hill, 1983).

Lesk, Michael. "Computer Software for Information Management," *Scientific American* (September 1984).

Martin, James. *An End-User's Guide to Data Base* (Englewood Cliffs, N.J.: Prentice-Hall, 1981).

Ross, Steven C. *Understanding and Using dBASE III* (St. Paul: West, 1986).

Simpson, Alan. *Advanced Techniques in dBASE III* (Berkeley: Sybex, 1985).

———. *Understanding dBASE II* (Berkeley: Sybex Computer Books, 1984).

———. *Understanding dBASE III* (Berkeley: Sybex Computer Books, 1986).

PART FOUR

"In the old days, a spreadsheet was manufactured out of actual paper and ink. It was white-collar sweatshop work."

Robert Mamis Inc. *Magazine*

Electronic Spreadsheets: *Strategies for Number-Crunching*

In the summer of 1957, the scientist J. C. R. Licklider decided to study just how he spent his time while working. Licklider found, to his dismay, that "about 85 percent of my 'thinking' time was spent getting into a position to think, to make a decision, to learn something I needed to know." Licklider spent this time doing tasks that waste a scientist's intelligence, such as adding up huge columns of numbers or plotting charts.

Here's an example of the Licklider dilemma. One of his projects was a study of noise ratios in communication. The subject had already been studied by several researchers, but they had used slightly different measures of the noise ratio. All the data they used had to be recalculated so that they would be comparable. "When they were in comparable form," Licklider complains, "it took only a few seconds to determine what I needed to know."[1] But the drudgery required to get there made the whole project almost intolerably difficult.

Since Licklider voiced his complaint, computers have come to the rescue. That's no news, of course, to veteran and expert number crunchers, who use mainframe statistical packages and supercomputers to work at the very forefront of mathematics. Yet most of the work people do with numbers isn't at the forefront of anything. It involves the kind of simple calculations Licklider found himself doing by hand — simple but monstrously repetitive arithmetic calculations that produce subtotals, totals, averages, and the like. It's exactly this kind of calculating that spreadsheet software is designed to do.

The term *spreadsheet* (sometimes called *worksheet*) derives from precomputer accounting practices. Accountants have long worked with spreadsheets — large pieces of paper lined with vertical columns and horizontal rows. Electronic spreadsheets simulate an accountant's spreadsheet. You can enter headings and numbers just as you would on paper. But there's a big, wonderful difference between paper and electronic spreadsheets. You place simple formulas into the electronic spreadsheet that automatically perform arithmetic and other operations on the numbers you've entered. At the bottom of a long column of figures, for example, you can place a simple command that says, "Add up this column of numbers," and at once the answer appears.

Just by itself, this number-crunching capability would have ensured the electronic spreadsheet's success. But that's only the beginning. What's truly exciting about spreadsheets is what happens after you've put in the numbers and formulas. At this point, you can change one of the numbers, and the results of the change are immediately reflected in the totals or averages or whatever other calculations you've asked the program to do. For this reason, you can ask what-if questions, such as "What if my salary were raised by $250 per month? How much more could I save?"

Some experts believe that spreadsheets, more than any other kind of software, set off the personal computer stampede. Today, about seven out of every ten personal computers in business are equipped with this highly useful software, and spreadsheet programs consistently top the software bestseller charts. You'll want to learn as much as you can about this wonderful new tool for managing numbers. And that's true, moreover, whether you pursue a career in business or out of it. Spreadsheets have found happy homes on the desks of historians, schoolteachers, anthropologists, freelance writers, and many others.

Part 4 of *Personal Computer Applications* takes you to the heart of this highly useful software. Chapter 9, "Electronic Spreadsheets: Tools for Manipulating Numbers," explores the basic functions of any spreadsheet program. Chapter 10, "Advanced Spreadsheet Skills: Making the Most of the Visible Calculator," explores advanced spreadsheet functions and techniques such as multiple windows and templates.

9 *Electronic Spreadsheets: Tools for Manipulating Numbers*

"What I find new and wonderful about computerized spreadsheets is that you can have a vast array of meaningful numbers, and all the numbers know about each other. *Change any one of them, and they all adjust immediately."*

Stewart Brand

All spreadsheet programs do the same thing: they help people work with numbers the way they would on paper, and then automate the formerly tedious job of doing the calculations. Perhaps more than any other software we've examined in this book, all spreadsheet programs share a core of functions and command procedures. This core of functions and commands originated with VisiCalc, the first spreadsheet program. Although VisiCalc is no longer sold, its legacy lives on in dozens of programs that resemble it closely. This chapter provides an overview of these functions and commands.

You can use this chapter to help you learn any spreadsheet program. Begin by tearing out the sheets entitled *Quick Reference Guide: Electronic Spreadsheet Basics*, which are positioned at the end of this book. Keep these sheets, your spreadsheet program's manual, and your supplementary textbook (if any) handy as you read the chapter. When in this chapter we describe a basic

spreadsheet function, such as loading an existing spreadsheet or widening a column, find out from your manual how to accomplish this function with your program. Then make a note in the *Quick Reference Guide*. When you've finished filling out the *Quick Reference Guide*, keep it next to your computer. You'll find it helpful in day-to-day number-crunching situations.

A typical session with an electronic spreadsheet program boils down to these steps: loading the program, using a blank spreadsheet (or loading an existing one), changing the spreadsheet's appearance, entering labels, entering constants, using formulas, copying formulas, editing the spreadsheet, saving the spreadsheet to disk, and printing (Figure 9–1).

LOADING THE PROGRAM

To begin a spreadsheet session with most personal computers, you turn on the computer, insert the disk containing the disk operating system (DOS), and wait until you receive the system prompt. Then you insert the disk containing your spreadsheet program. With command-line operating systems, loading the program into the computer's internal memory is simple. You type the program's name (or an abbreviation of it) and press the RETURN key. To load Lotus 1-2-3, for example, you type LOTUS and press RETURN. A moment later, you choose 1-2-3 from a menu of options.

USING A BLANK SPREADSHEET

After the spreadsheet program is successfully loaded, you're shown a blank spreadsheet, which consists of vertical **columns** and horizontal **rows,** each with an identifying number (rows) or letter (columns). Starting from the left side of the spreadsheet, the first 26 columns are labeled A through Z. After Z, columns are labeled AA, AB, AC, AD, and so on. Each intersection of a row and column forms a rectangular box called a **cell.** The intersection of column C and row 3, for example, forms cell C3.

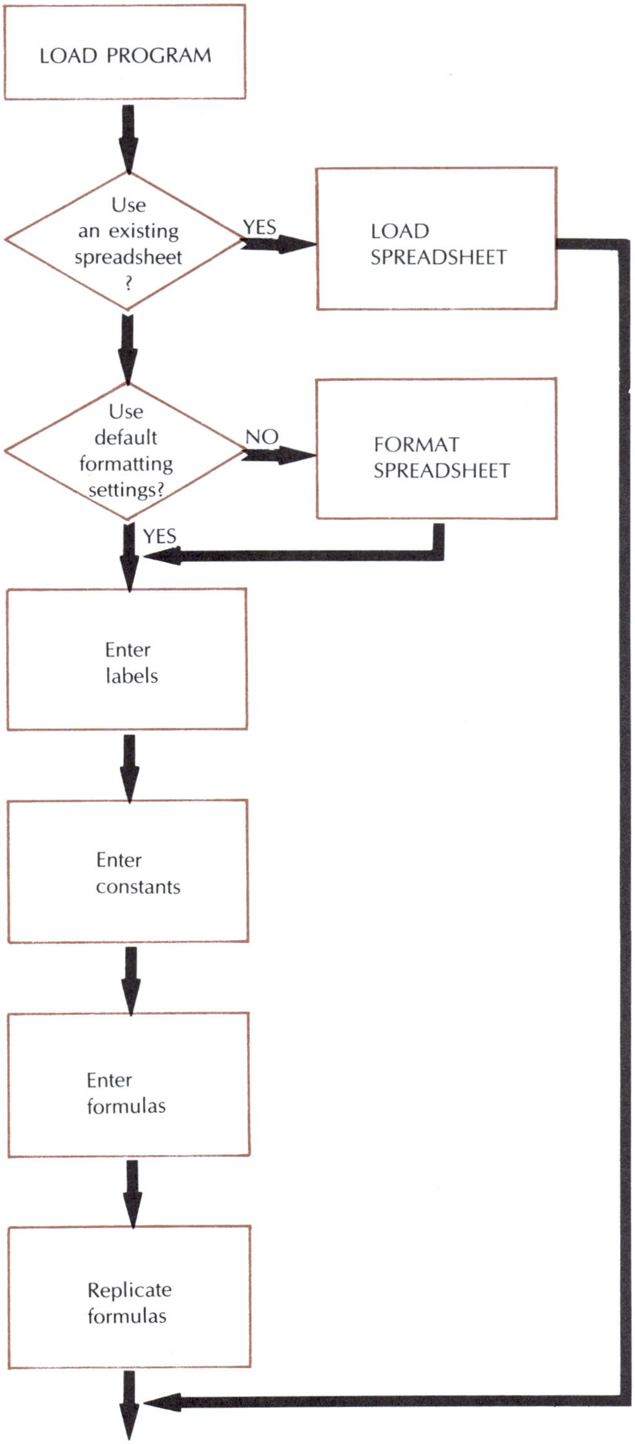

FIGURE 9–1 A Typical Session with a Spreadsheet Program

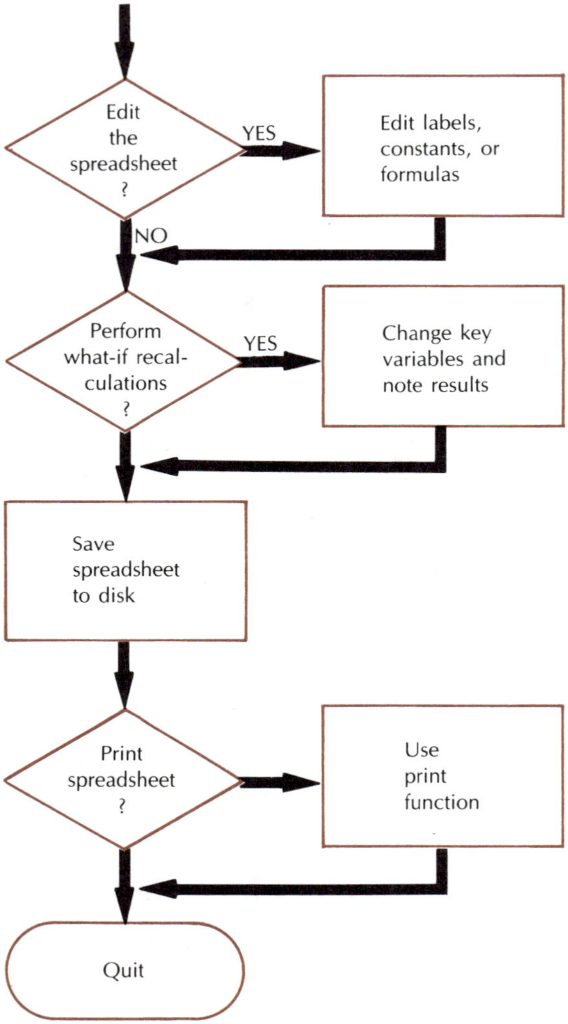

FIGURE 9–1 A Typical Session with a Spreadsheet Program (*continued*)

In addition to the matrix of rows and columns, you'll see the following on the display screens of most spreadsheet programs (Figure 9–2):

Active Cell. The cell in which the cursor is currently located is the **active cell,** the cell in which characters will appear if you start typing. You can control the active cell's location by using the keyboard's cursor control keys.

Cell Coordinates Indicator. The **cell coordinates indicator** shows you the active cell's coordinates (such as A1).

Entry Line. The procedure for number and text entry differs from that for

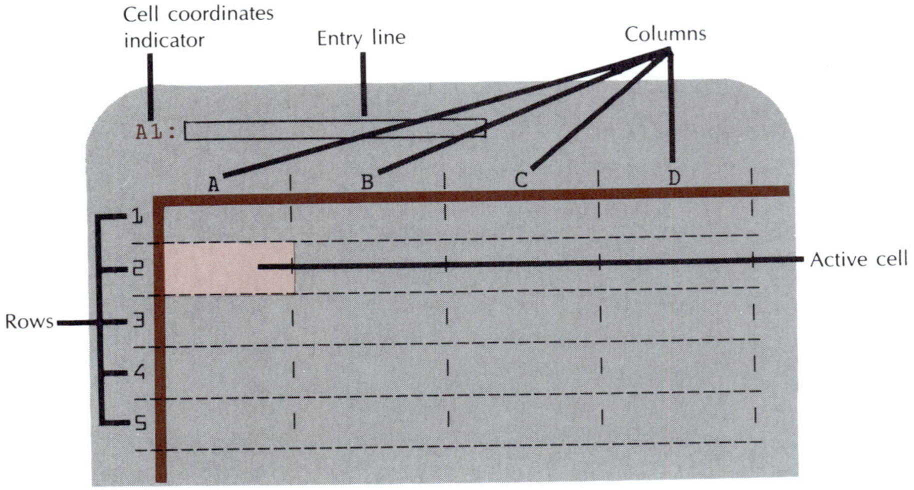

FIGURE 9–2 Blank Spreadsheet

word processing and file management programs, where you type directly in a document or form. When you enter a label, value, or formula in a spreadsheet program, what you type doesn't appear immediately in the active cell. It appears instead on the **entry line,** a line outside the **spreadsheet window** (the window in which the spreadsheet appears). After you finish typing the entry, you press the RETURN key. The entry disappears from the entry line and reappears in the active cell. Now there are only two ways to alter it: (1) by typing something else on the entry line and pressing RETURN, which erases the cell's old contents and inserts the new; or (2) by using the edit command. The edit command puts a cell's contents on the entry line, where you may make a change.

THE COMMAND MENU

Most spreadsheet programs use a pop-up command menu very much like the word processing command menus discussed in Chapter 4.

Entry Mode vs. Command Mode. Spreadsheet programs operate in two modes, an **entry mode** and a **command mode.** When you load a spreadsheet program, it's in the entry mode. In the entry mode, the characters you type at the keyboard appear on the entry line. You may enter them into the spreadsheet by pressing RETURN. To enter the command mode with most programs, you press the slash (/) key. In the command mode, the characters you type set commands in motion. The use of the slash key, incidentally, is part of the legacy left by the first spreadsheet program, VisiCalc. Almost all commercially successful spreadsheet programs emulate VisiCalc's features to some extent, although they may offer more features.

Command Menus. The command menu that appears may list the commands using single letters or key words (Table 9–1).

One-Letter Command Menus. One-letter command menus list the commands' first letter in alphabetical order (Figure 9–3). To select the command, you type the letter. Choosing F, for example, sets the FORMAT command in motion. One-letter command menus take up little room on the screen, but they force the user to memorize the command names.

Key Word Command Menus. These list command names without abbreviation. You don't have to memorize the command names, but the menu takes up more room. In Lotus 1-2-3, for example, two menu lines are required; the first line lists the commands, and the second lists submenus for the selected line. The second line's contents change when you select a different command

TABLE 9–1 Spreadsheet Commands

Command name	Function
Blank	Erase the contents of the active cell (also called ERASE).
Clear	Erase the entire worksheet from memory and start over with a blank spreadsheet.
Column width	Set column width for the column in which the active cell is positioned.
Copy	Copy a formula to a range of cells (also called REPLICATE).
Delete column	Delete column in which the active cell is positioned.
Delete row	Delete row in which the active cell is positioned.
Global column width	Sets formats for entire spreadsheet (hence "global") for width of columns. The default is 9 characters.
Global format	Sets formats for entire spreadsheet (hence "global") for display of values and labels.
Insert column	Insert new column to the left of the active cell.
Insert row	Insert new row above the active cell.
Load file	Erase the spreadsheet currently in memory and load an existing spreadsheet (also called RETRIEVE).
Move	Move a range of cells to another location on the spreadsheet.
Print	Start printing.
Save	Save the current spreadsheet to disk.
Sort	Arrange labels or values in a range in ascending or descending order (also called ARRANGE).

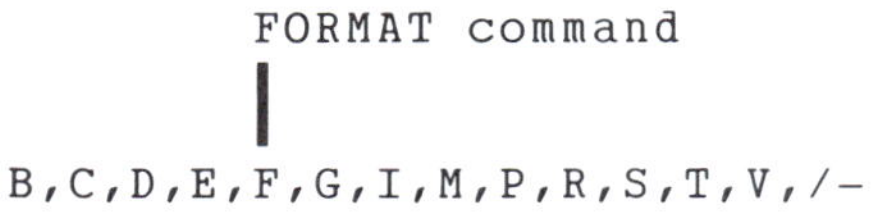

FIGURE 9–3 One-Letter Command Menu (VisiCalc)

(Figure 9–4). Understanding the roadmap of command menus and submenus is a key to mastering spreadsheet programs (Figure 9–5).

Notice that you can see only a small portion of the worksheet on the screen. When you start the program, the window reveals only the top left corner of the worksheet (Figure 9–6). You're seeing only the upper-left corner of a vast piece of electronic "paper" — and vast is an understatement. Even inexpensive spreadsheet programs give you a worksheet that's approximately 25 square feet in size (64 columns by 256 rows), about the floor size of a large closet. The Godzilla of spreadsheets, Lotus Symphony, gives you more than 850 square feet of spreadsheet — about the size of a large, two-car garage! But don't worry

FIGURE 9–4 Keyword Command Menu and Submenu

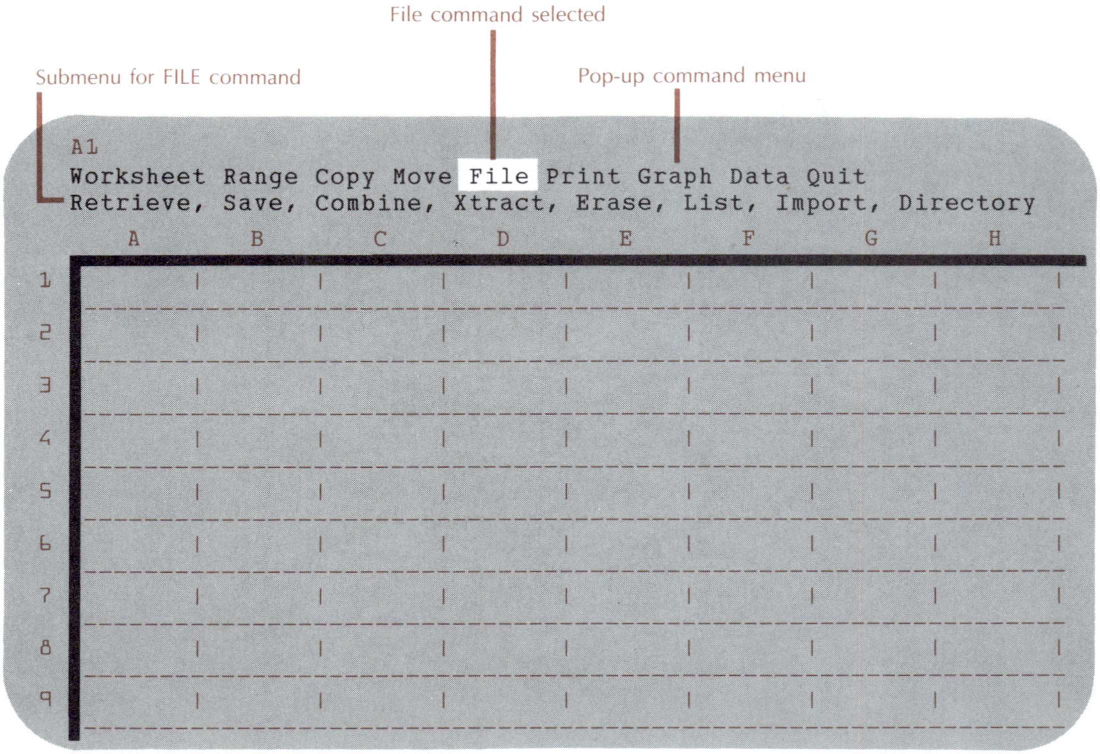

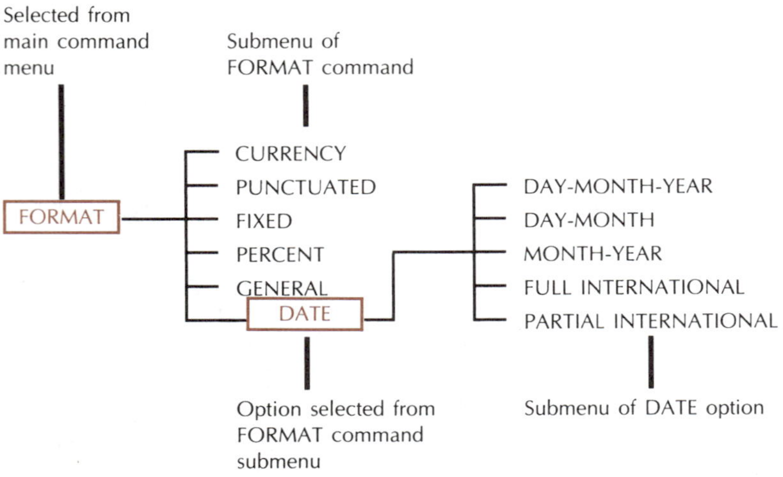

FIGURE 9–5 "Roadmap" to Lotus Symphony FORMAT Command

FIGURE 9–6 The Spreadsheet Window

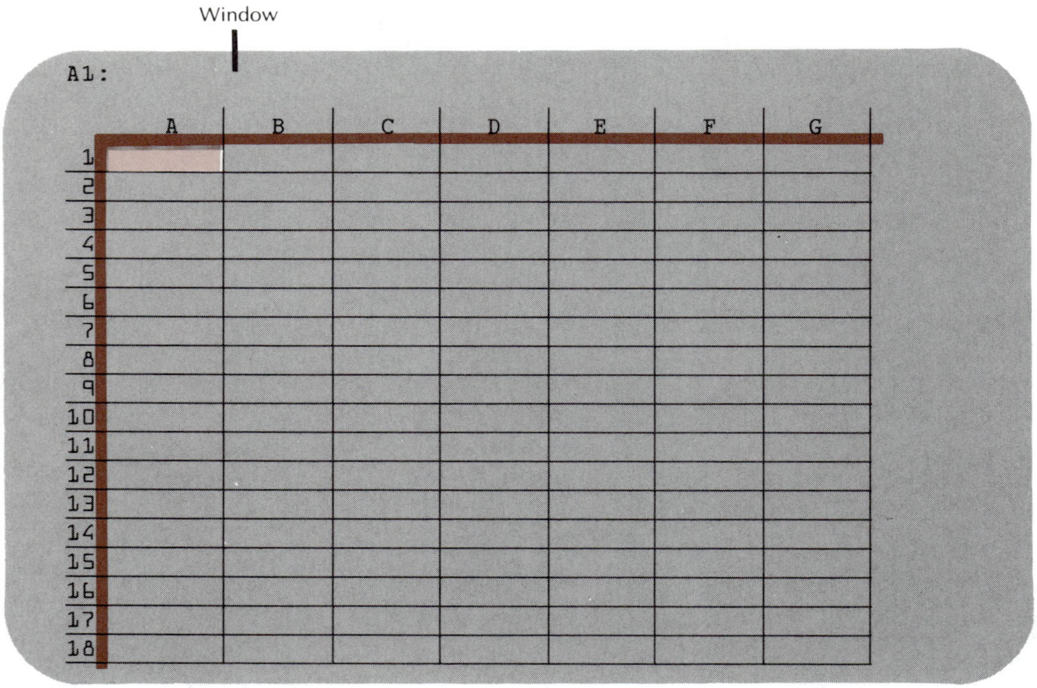

about getting lost in a wilderness of rows and columns. Almost all the spreadsheets you'll create will use no more than a fraction of the space available. It's better to create several small spreadsheets than one huge one, because big spreadsheets are hard to understand — most of it isn't visible — and invite errors.

Even though you'll probably never use the whole spreadsheet workspace, many of the spreadsheets you do create will take up more than one windowful. You will need to learn some scrolling commands to position the window "over" the spreadsheet as you wish. All programs let you scroll the program one column or one row at a time using the cursor control keys. Some programs let you scroll windowful by windowful, too. A useful command that some programs offer is a GO TO command, which lets you jump immediately to a cell you specify.

Invention of the Visible Calculator

Has anyone ever said to you, "Forget it — you don't know what you're talking about, and besides, it will never sell"? Well, read on. Here's what happened to someone who didn't listen to this discouraging advice.

In 1978, Dan Bricklin was a Harvard MBA candidate. Like other MBA students, he stayed up late every night doing — and redoing — tedious calculations needed for homework assignments. These assignments required endless analyses of projections, budgets, and other financial data. One night, after a particularly long session with a sharp pencil and a calculator, Bricklin started dreaming about a visible calculator — a program that would let you work with numbers in the same way as you do on paper, but it would do the calculations automatically. If the program ran on personal computers, this capability could be put on the desks of the people who needed it most.

Bricklin took his idea to a Harvard finance professor, who ridiculed him. The professor pointed out that dozens of financial analysis programs already existed; how could he hope to compete with them? And besides, the professor added, personal computer software would never sell. People wouldn't use personal computers when more powerful mainframe computers were available. But the professor mentioned an ex-student of his, Dan Fylstra, who was interested in marketing personal computer software.

Fylstra and Bricklin got together, and Fylstra liked the idea. Fylstra hired a programmer, Bob Frankston, who worked day and night in an attic to create the program. By spring 1979, it was ready. They called it VisiCalc, short for "visible calculator." The product's reception was cool at first, but the program quickly soared to the top of the software bestseller charts. In the first year, Fylstra and Bricklin shipped 500 copies per month of VisiCalc. By 1981, it was shipping 12,000 copies a month.

Paraphrased from Paul Freiberger and Michael Swaine, *Fire in the Valley: The Making of the Personal Computer* (Berkeley: Osborne/McGraw-Hill, 1984), pp. 229–230.

CHANGING THE SPREADSHEET'S APPEARANCE

Every spreadsheet uses default formats to determine the width of columns and the appearance of letters and numbers on the screen. These formats are used unless you specifically change them by giving formatting commands. You will probably want to change some of these settings; the default formats will prove unsatisfactory for most applications.

THE DEFAULT FORMATS

Default formats control the appearance of columns, numbers (**values**), and headings (**labels**).

Default Column Width. Most programs display the new, blank spreadsheet with equally spaced columns (generally, they are 9 or 10 spaces wide). You may want to widen some or all of the columns, because a width of 9 or 10 spaces may be insufficient for lengthy headings or numbers with many digits. There's a good reason, however, to keep columns as narrow as possible: with an average width of 9 spaces, you can see as many as seven or eight columns on the screen. Remember, too, that many programs have **soft cell boundaries,** which means that headings can go over the right cell boundary into the next cell right (so long as it's empty) (Figure 9–7). Numbers, however, must fit inside the column. If there's a number that's too lengthy to fit, the program will display an error signal in the cell (usually, a series of punctuation characters such as ########) (Figure 9–7).

Values. The numbers that appear in a spreadsheet can come from two sources: you can type them in yourself (in which case they are called **constants**),

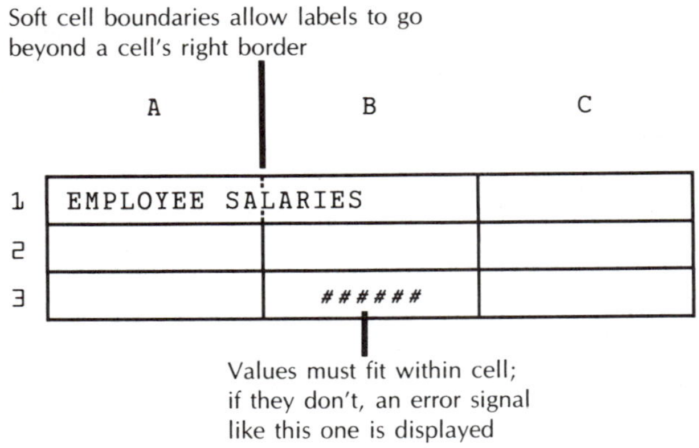

FIGURE 9–7
Soft Cell Boundaries and Error Signals

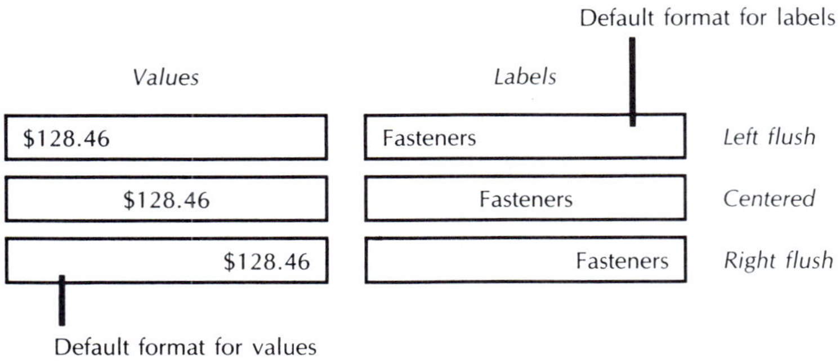

FIGURE 9–8
Positioning Values and Labels in the Cell

or formulas can produce them. (We'll explore this distinction later.) The default display format for values is right flush with most programs (Figure 9–8). Furthermore, numbers are often displayed with all significant decimal places.

Labels. The headings you type in the spreadsheet are usually formatted left flush (Figure 9–8).

Because one or more of these default settings will prove unsatisfactory, you will probably do some formatting at the beginning of your spreadsheet session. You must first decide, however, whether you want these changes to apply to the entire spreadsheet (**global formatting**) or just part of it (**range formatting**).

GLOBAL FORMATTING

Global formatting commands apply to the entire spreadsheet. Using these commands, you can control these formats:

Position of Values and Labels. You may elect to position values and labels left flush, centered, or right flush (Figure 9–8).

Numeric Display Formats (Figure 9–9). Most users change the global format for the display of values at the beginning of a spreadsheet session. For business spreadsheets, the currency format is ideal.

Column Width. If you are using a spreadsheet for scientific applications, in which the display of all significant decimal places is desirable, you may wish to widen all the columns in the spreadsheet. It's usually better, however, to format values so that only two or fewer decimal places appear rather than widening the spreadsheet; in that way, you'll see more of it on the screen at any one time. If one column needs widening (perhaps a column of names), use the range formatting commands.

1.2987	*General format* All significant numbers (but not trailing zeros) displayed up to 15 decimal places
3.95E+1	*Scientific format* For display of very large or very small numbers
1.30	*Fixed format* Allows user to specify how many decimal places will be displayed; numbers are rounded if necessary
$2,998.54	*Currency format* Dollar signs, commas, and two decimal places (with rounding) automatically inserted
9.5%	*Percent format* Converts decimal (.095) to percent and displays with percent sign

FIGURE 9–9 Numeric Display Formats

RANGE FORMATTING

Any of the formatting options just discussed can apply to a **range,** an area of the spreadsheet that you define for formatting and other purposes. Some programs give you two ways to define a range:

Defining a Range by Typing a Range Expression. All spreadsheet programs let you define a range by typing a **range expression,** which defines the range by establishing its upper-left and lower-right corners. The range expression is typed with a special symbol that defines it as a range expression (such as two dots, as in the expression A1..E1). Using this technique, you can define a variety of ranges, including an entire column or row (Figure 9–10).

Defining a Range by Pointing. Newer programs let you define a range by giving you a **pointer.** A pointer is a cell highlighted in reverse video on the screen. To define the range, you begin by "anchoring" the pointer in a beginning cell. Using the cursor control keys (or, with some programs, a mouse), you can expand the highlighted area until it encompasses all the cells in the range.

ENTERING LABELS

Normally, you'll begin creating your spreadsheet by entering labels. A label uses words or dates to explain the material in the spreadsheet. Figure 9–11 shows the labels for a simple spreadsheet that, when completed, will provide a

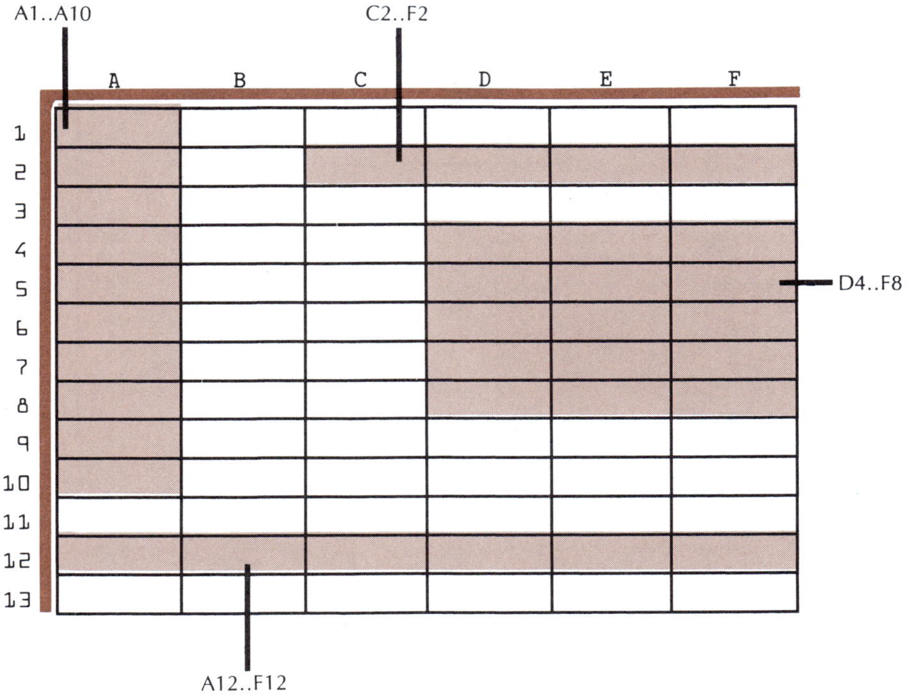

FIGURE 9–10 Ranges and Range Expressions

way of estimating net pay (salary after deducting taxes) over a three-month period. Notice that column A has been widened to make room for the long labels, such as "GROSS PAY AMOUNT." You can size each column as you please using range formatting commands.

Most programs are designed to interpret anything that starts with upper- and lower-case letters as a label entry. If you type an entry that uses nothing but numbers, it's interpreted as a value entry — and formatted accordingly. And so if you want to use a number as a label, it will be formatted right flush while all other headings are formatted right flush. If you want to use a number as a heading, you'll have to take special steps, such as starting the entry with a quotation mark ("1984). The quotation mark tells the program to interpret the entry as a label (not as a value).

To make sure your spreadsheet makes sense to you after you've created it, use labels that explain the data. Overly cryptic titles might confuse you later on if you forget what they stand for. "West Coast Sales," for instance, tells the story better than "WCS."

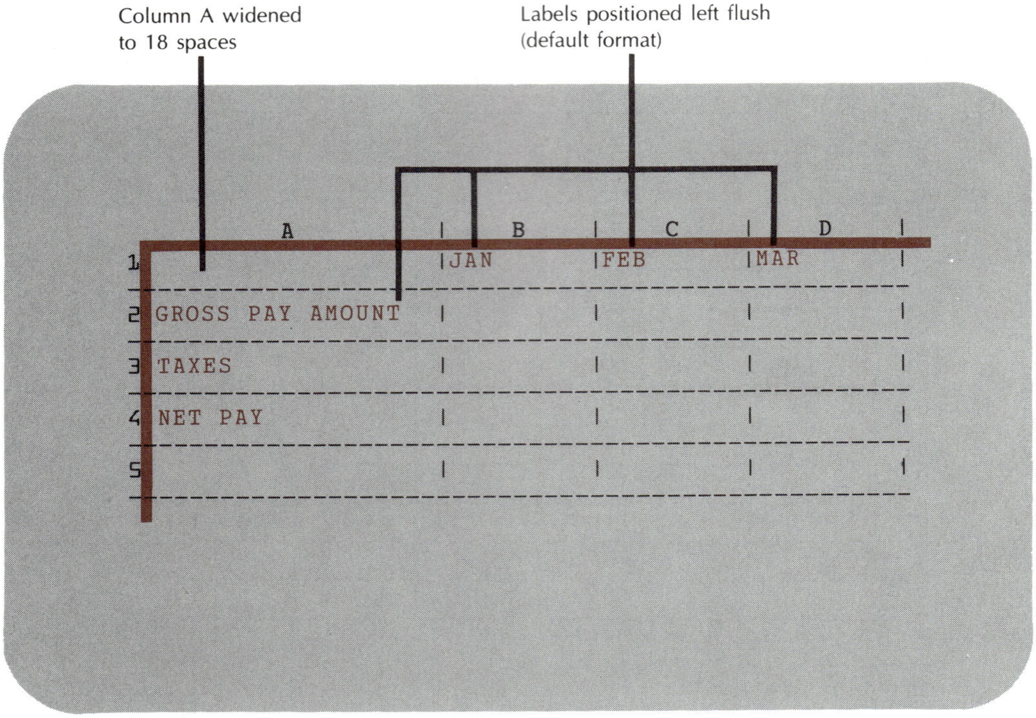

FIGURE 9–11 Labels for a Simple Spreadsheet

ENTERING CONSTANTS

The values that appear in cells can come from two sources: numbers you type in (called constants) and numbers that result from a formula placed in the cell. The term constant is an apt one for the first type of value; whenever you type a number into a cell directly, it stays put until you deliberately alter it by typing another number. You need do nothing special to enter a value; when you're in the entry mode, anything that begins with a number and consists solely of numbers will be interpreted as a value. (If you want to enter figures in dollars and cents, do not type commas or dollar signs. If you do, the program will probably interpret what you've entered as a label, not a constant.) Use the global currency format instead, and the program will put them in for you automatically.)

Figure 9–12 shows the constants entered into cells in a spreadsheet. These constants reflect the amounts the spreadsheet designer expects to receive for gross pay (pay before withholding taxes are subtracted) over a three-month period.

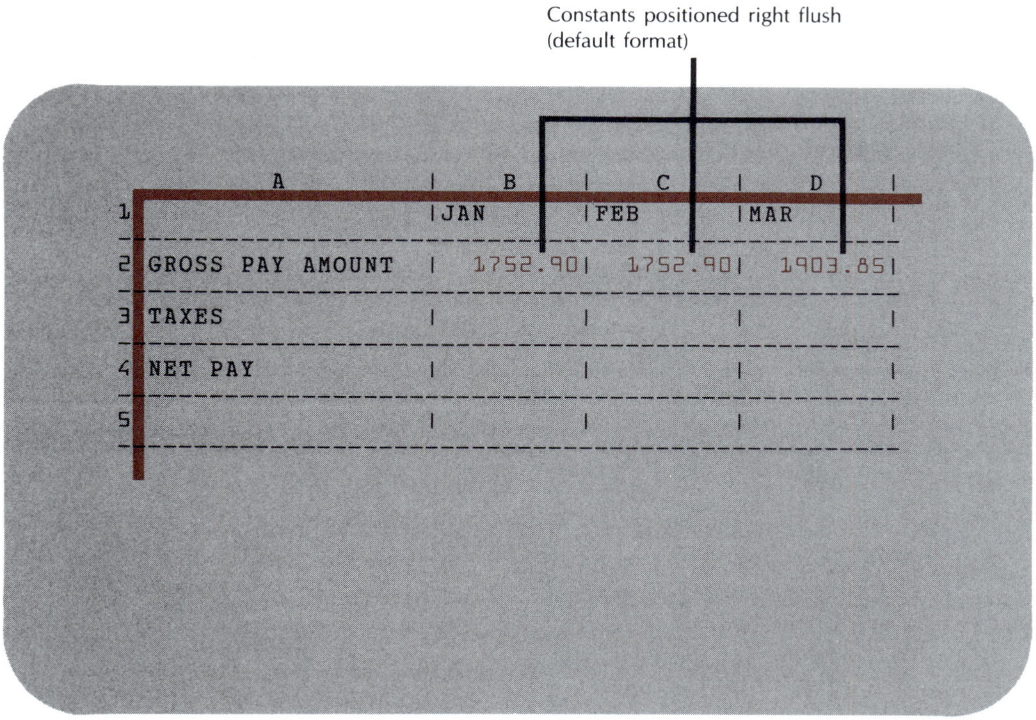

FIGURE 9–12 Entering Constants

USING FORMULAS

To get a spreadsheet program to do calculations on the values you have entered, you write a **formula** in a cell. A spreadsheet formula is a mathematical rule or principle (such as NET PAY = GROSS PAY − TAXES) that is expressed in a way the spreadsheet program can interpret. The formula is "attached" to the cell, but you don't see it there; instead, you see the value that the formula returns. You can see the hidden formula, however, if you make the formula's cell the active cell. The formula will be displayed on the entry line, where you can edit it if you wish.

ENTERING FORMULAS

A formula may contain these elements:

Formula Marking Character. The formula must begin with a formula marking character, such as a plus sign. The character tells the program that what follows is neither a constant nor a heading.

Constants. When you use a constant in a formula, the constant does not change unless you deliberately alter it.

Cell References. A **cell reference** tells the program to go to the cell you've named, find the value in that cell, and use it in the formula. Suppose, for instance, you place the value 5 in Cell A1. Then you write the formula A1 + 2 in Cell A5. The program will go to Cell A1, find the value 5, and use this value in solving the formula. The value retrieved by a cell reference can be a value you type in yourself. However, it can also be a value that results from a formula in the referenced cell. Suppose I write the formula 2 + 3 in Cell A1. The program solves the formula and displays 5 in Cell A1. Then I go to Cell A5 and write the formula A1 + 2. The program will go to Cell A1 and retrieve the value 5.

Built-in Functions. All spreadsheet programs offer several — sometimes as many as dozens of — **built-in functions,** which include many ready-made formulas. To use built-in functions, you must first type a marking character — usually the "at" sign, @ — that tells the program you're typing a formula. Following the marking character, you type the function's keyword (an abbreviation such as AVG for average or STDEV for standard deviation). In most cases, the keyword is followed by an **argument,** which is enclosed in parentheses. The argument tells the program on what cells or data to perform the built-in function. An argument can include a range expression, a cell reference, or a constant.

Operators. **Operators** are symbols that indicate an arithmetic operation (such as addition or multiplication) or a logical operation (such as making a decision using IF/THEN logic).

Figure 9–13 shows the formula that will be entered into Cell B3. It says, in effect, "Take the value in Cell B2 and multiply it by .24, showing the result in Cell B3." Figure 9–14 shows the result. Figure 9–15 shows the entry of another formula, this one using a subtraction operator. Figure 9–16 shows the result of this formula.

OPERATORS

The operators available for use in most spreadsheet programs fall into two categories, **arithmetic operators** and **logical operators.**

Arithmetic Operators. As you write formulas, you will frequently use arithmetic operators. Operators tell the program what kind of arithmetic operation to perform. Table 9–2 (page 269) lists the operators available with the spreadsheet program PC-CALC.

Spreadsheet programs evaluate arithmetic operators in a specific order.

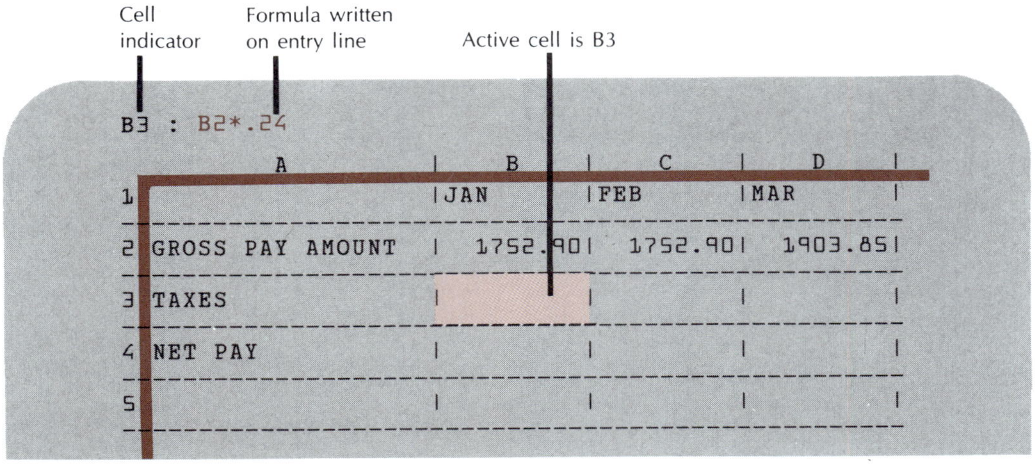

FIGURE 9–13 Entering a Formula

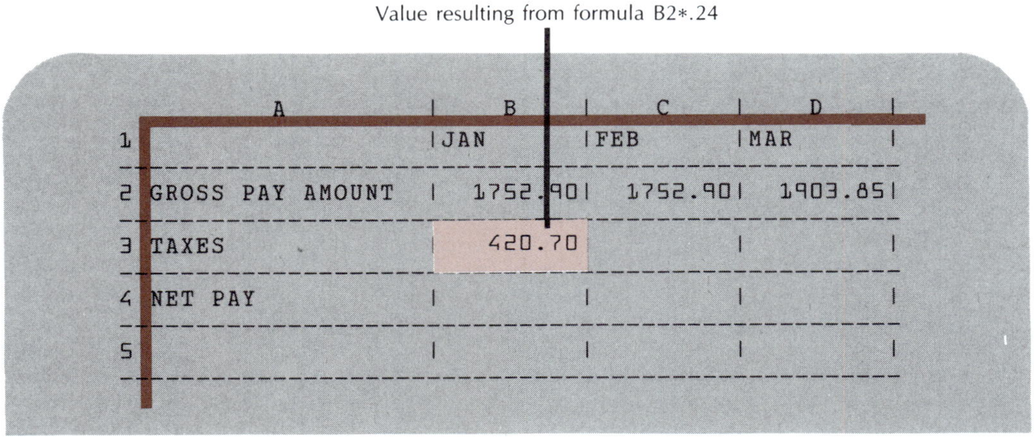

FIGURE 9–14 Result of Formula Inserted in Cell B3

Some programs evaluate formulas left to right. More commonly, expressions are evaluated as they would be in algebra or computer programming; multiplication and division come before addition and subtraction.

The evaluation process may involve as many as five or six steps. PC-CALC, for instance, evaluates exponents first, and only afterwards looks at multiplication, division, and percentage operators; later, remainders, addition, and subtraction are considered (Table 9–3).

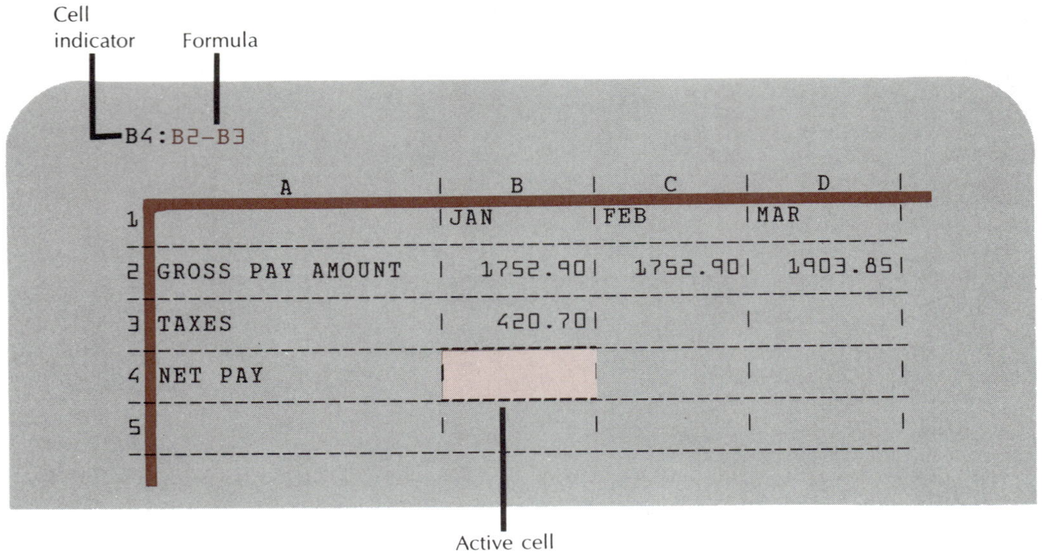

FIGURE 9–15 Entering Another Formula

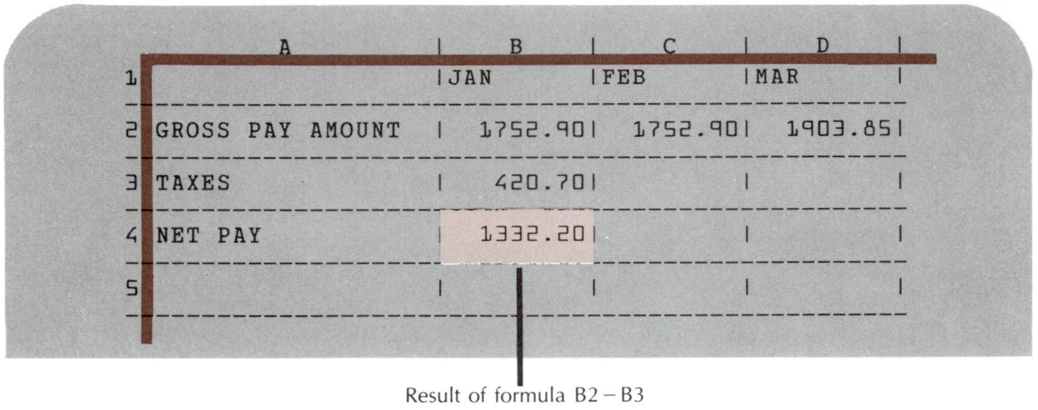

FIGURE 9–16 Result of Formula Inserted in Cell B4

To grasp the importance of the order in which operators are evaluated, consider this formula.

```
8*2^2
```

As evaluated by PC-CALC, this formula returns 32 (8 * 4), *not* 256 (16 ^ 2). Obviously, you will need to learn the order of evaluation for the program you're

TABLE 9–2 Spreadsheet Operators: PC-Calc

Operator	Purpose	Example
+	Addition	A1 + A2
−	Subtraction	A1 − 10
*	Multiplication	A1 * 250
/	Division	A1 / 3.75
^	Exponentiation	A1 ^ 2
%	Percent	A1 % A2
\	Modulo (remainder)	A1 \ 10

using. In addition to reading the program's manual carefully, try experimenting with the program. Type in the examples used here and see what happens.

You can override the normal order of evaluation using parentheses. When used with parentheses in this way,

```
(8*2)^2
```

the expression returns 256.

You may nest parentheses. Consider this expression:

```
((8*2)^2) - 10
```

This expression tells the program to multiply 8 times 2 to find 16. Then it squares 16 to find 256; finally, it subtracts 10.

Most programs allow many levels of nesting. Consider this expression:

```
(((8*2)^2) - 10)^2
```

Notice that you must use an equal number of left and right parentheses. If you do not, the program will show an error message. The formula will not be entered into the active cell.

As you can see, nested formulas are hard to read. When formulas are hard to read, it's more difficult to check your spreadsheet for accuracy. For this

TABLE 9–3 Order of Evaluation: PC-Calc

1. Exponentiation (^)
2. Multiplication (*), Division (/), Percentage (%)
3. Modulo (\)
4. Addition (+) and subtraction (−)

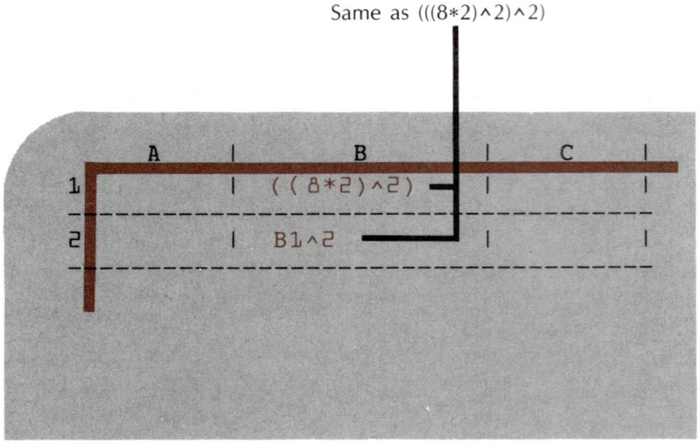

FIGURE 9–17 Formula Split Up and Placed in Two Cells

reason, keep your formulas short and simple. Break up long formulas over two cells if possible. Figure 9–17 shows the same formula placed in two cells.

Logical Operators. Less frequently used than arithmetic operators, logical operators are operators used to perform logical operations, such as comparing two statements to see whether one of them is true or false or evaluating a statement. These operators (Table 9–4 lists the ones Lotus 1-2-3 includes) are frequently used with conditional expressions using the IF-THEN built-in function, which will be discussed below. This function allows you to write formulas that translate, into English, like this one: "If the value in A1 is greater than zero, AND if the

TABLE 9–4 Logical Operators: Lotus 1-2-3

Operator	Purpose	Example
=	equal to	A1=A2
<	less than	A1>A2
<=	less than or equal to	A1<=A2
>	greater than	A1>A2
>=	greater than or equal to	A1>=A2
<>	not equal to	A1<>A2
#NOT#	exclusion	A1#NOT#A2
#AND#	both of	A1#AND#A2
#OR#	either of	A1#OR#A2

value in A2 equals 10, then place the value 1 in A3." You are familiar with the AND operator from reading the chapters on data base management, and so you know that both conditions (A1 > 0 and A2 = 10) must be true before 1 will be placed in A3.

COPYING FORMULAS

Most spreadsheets use at least some formulas over and over again. In Figures 9–13 through 9–16, for example, the formula that appears in Cell B3 (B2*.24) can be used repeatedly in Row 3 (TAXES). When finished, this spreadsheet will compute the figures for the whole year, January through December, and so the formula will be needed twelve times. It would be tedious, obviously, to type the formula so many times; it would be much easier to let the computer do it for you automatically.

You can do precisely that with a spreadsheet program's copy command (often called replicate command). This command is unlike a word processing program's copy command in that it does not make an exact copy of the formula. To understand why, consider again the formula in Cell B3 (B2*.24). If you copy this formula to cell D3 without changes, it will give you the wrong answer. The reason? It's looking to Cell B2, not Cell D2, for the monthly paycheck amount. The copy command solves this problem by making the necessary adjustments automatically. In other words, when you copy the formula in Cell B3 to the range C3 through M3, the cell references in the formula are changed so that they always refer to the cell right above the formula. And so the formula in Cell D3 reads D2*.24, the formula in Cell E3 reads E2*.24, and so on.

All this may sound magical and mysterious until you know what's going on. The program doesn't really store the formula the way it's shown on the screen. On the contrary, when you write a formula such as B2*.24 in Cell B3, it's stored in Cell B3 in this way: "Take the value *in the next cell up in the same column* and multiply it by .24." And this is what you copy. When you copy this formula to C3, the copied formula looks in the next cell up, same column, for the value — and that cell just happens to be C2, the correct one.

Figure 9–18 shows the first step in copying a formula. The formula (B2*.24) is copied from Cell B3. Figure 9–19 shows the second step. The formula is copied to a range of cells (here, C3 through D3). Figure 9–20 shows the results; the correct values appear in Cells C3 and D3. Notice that, in Cell D3, your taxes have gone up! Replicating the formula in Cell B4 to Cells C4 through D4 produces the results shown in Figure 9–21.

As you can see, replication is an extremely valuable and convenient feature. Just imagine how much work it would save if this spreadsheet listed taxes and net pay for twelve months instead of three.

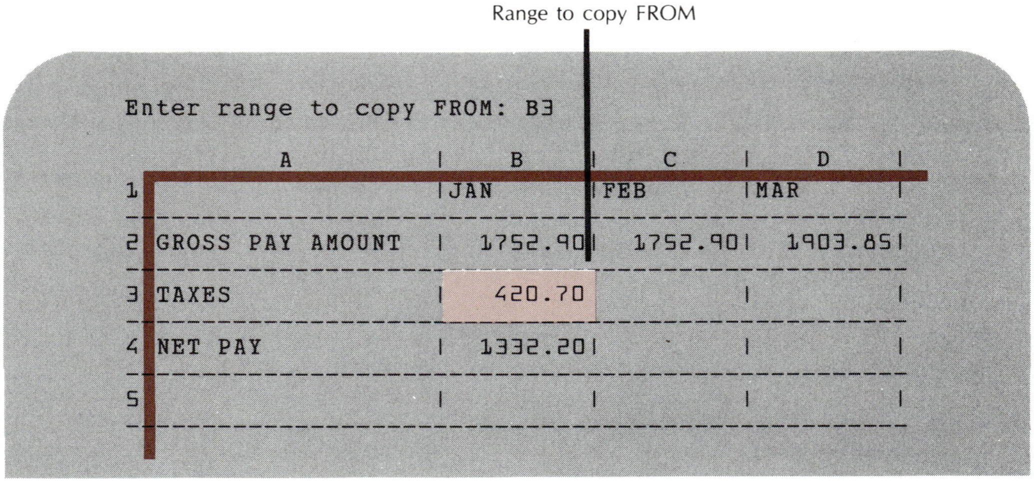

FIGURE 9–18 First Step in Replication

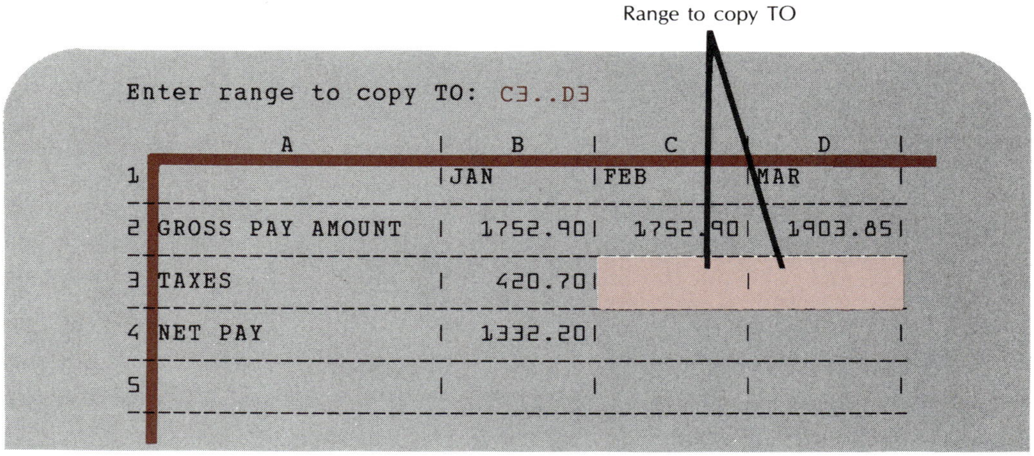

FIGURE 9–19 Second Step in Replication

ABSOLUTE AND RELATIVE CELL REFERENCES

Successful work with spreadsheets requires you to distinguish between absolute and relative cell references when writing formulas.

Relative Cell References. In the brief example at the beginning of this chapter, you saw that copied formulas change so that they work in adjacent columns

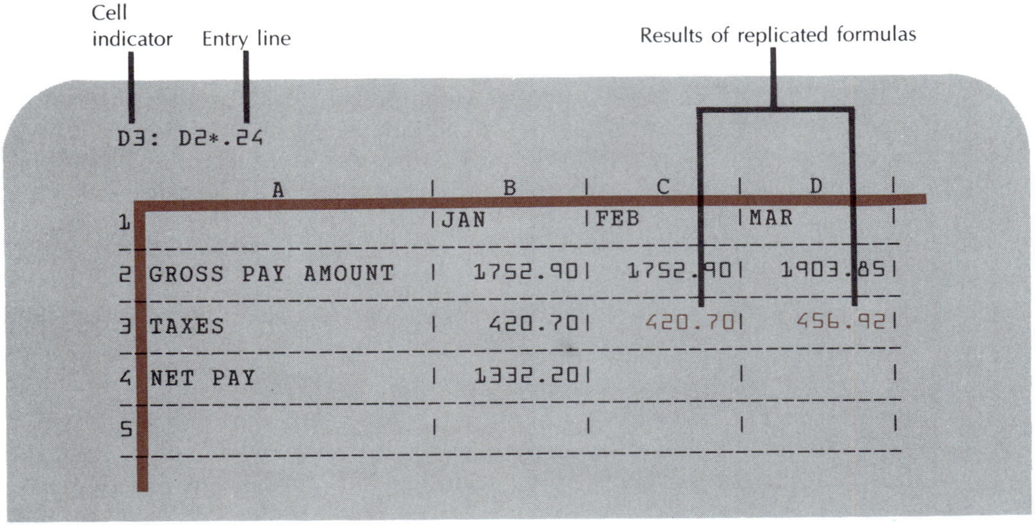

FIGURE 9–20 Result of Replication

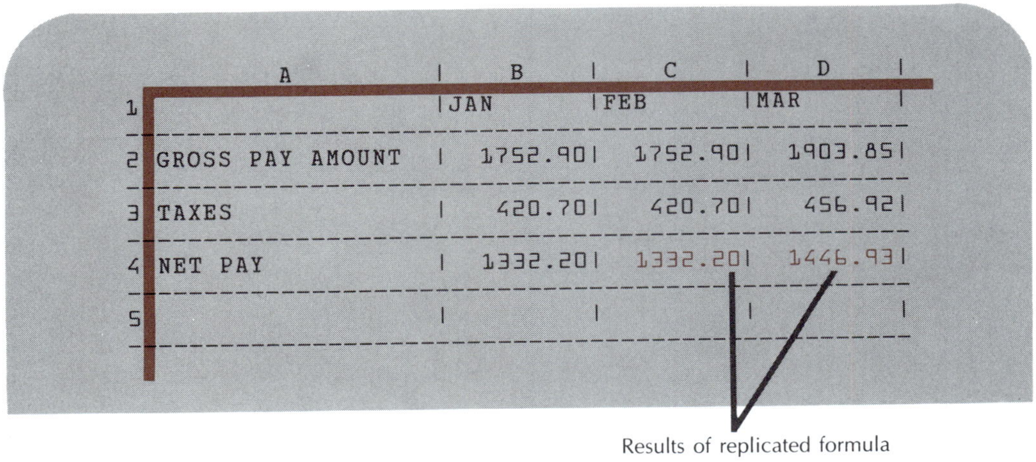

FIGURE 9–21 Result of Second Replication

or rows. That is because the cell references contained in the formulas are **relative cell references;** that is, cell references that state the referenced cell's position relative to others in the spreadsheet (for instance, "one row up in the same column"). Relative cell references are the default in most programs; you need do nothing special to enter relative cell references in your formulas. All cell references will be adjusted automatically when copied.

Absolute Cell References. An **absolute cell reference** "pins down" a cell reference in a formula so that it *doesn't* change when you replicate it. An absolute cell reference usually begins with a marking character, such as a dollar sign, which tells the program to interpret what follows as an absolute rather than a relative cell reference. When copied, absolute cell references do not change. If you copy the absolute cell reference B2, for example, it reads the same way (and points to the same cell) no matter where it is copied.

As you'll see, absolute cell references are useful for constructing **keys,** or cells that contain key variables that can be inserted in formulas throughout the spreadsheet.

KEYS

Almost always, it's better to use cell references instead of constants when you're writing formulas. The point of creating a spreadsheet is to link cells so that the whole spreadsheet recalculates when you change a variable. A cell that uses nothing but constants, however, isn't linked to any other cell.

Some constants are necessary, of course, in every spreadsheet. In a spreadsheet that computes net pay, for example, you will need to use a constant for the tax rate. Even so, it's better to put such constants in their own cells, called keys, rather than use them in formulas throughout the spreadsheet. Here's an example that shows why.

In Figure 9–22, the formulas in Cells B4, C4, and D4 use the constant .24. The constant works just fine. But what if the tax rate goes down to .21? You'll have to go through the spreadsheet and edit each formula, one by one. For a large spreadsheet, the job can be very tedious. And tedium causes errors.

FIGURE 9–22 Spreadsheet with Formulas Using Constant

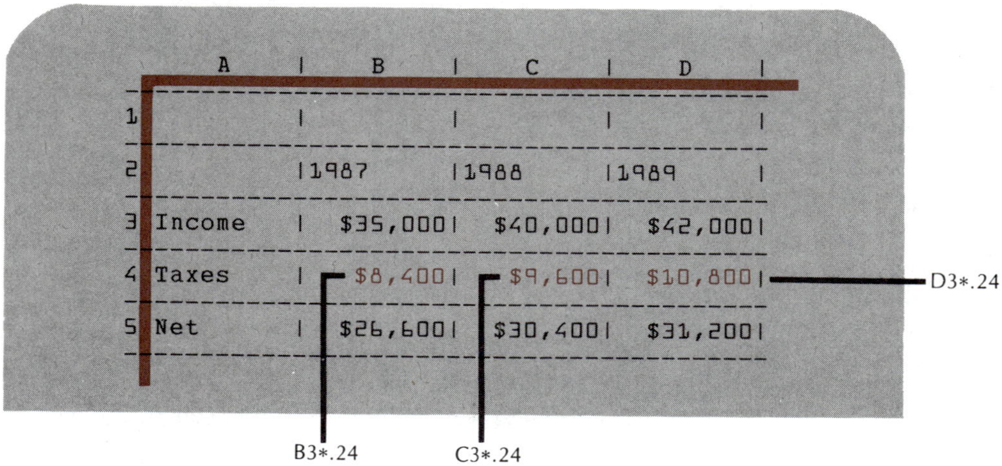

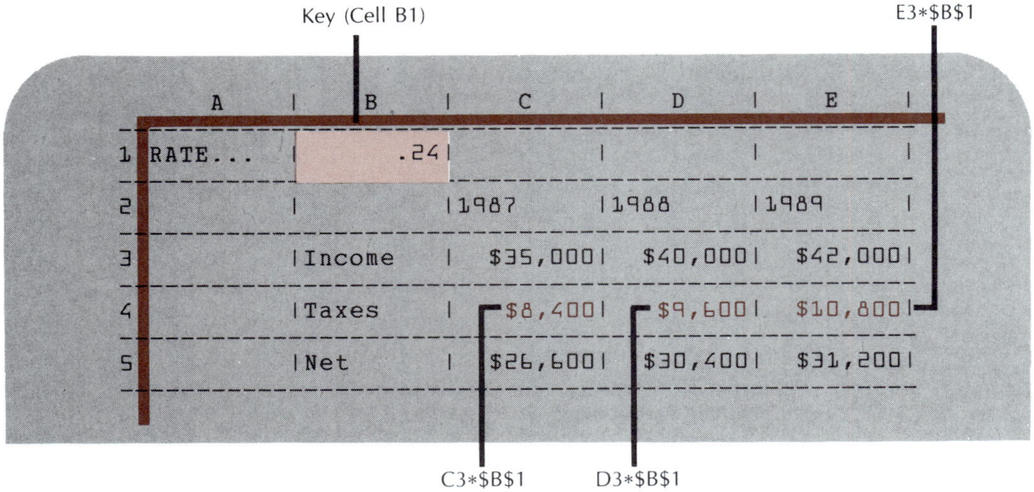

FIGURE 9–23 Spreadsheet Using Key for Constant

Instead of using constants in a formula, it's much better to enter the constants in a key. In Figure 9–23, for instance, the key cell B1 contains the constant .24. The formulas in Cells B4, C4, and D4 do not use the constant. Instead, they refer to the key cell, B1. Notice that these references are absolute cell references.

If the tax rate changes, you simply type the new value into the key cell and the results ripple through the spreadsheet. Because you type the key value only once, there's no chance of errors in repeated entries of the same value. And because the key is entered as a value, you see it on the screen (constants in formulas, remember, are hidden from view). You can see any mistakes you make right away.

BUILT-IN FUNCTIONS

All spreadsheet programs include a variety of built-in functions, which consist of a marking character, a keyword, and — usually — an argument. Here's a formula written using a built-in command:

```
@SUM(C1..C45)
```

In English, it reads "Add up the cells C1 through C45 and put the answer here." As you can see, using built-in functions can save time. If the program lacked the @SUM function, you'd have to type C1 + C2 + C3 + C4 + C5 . . . (etc.). Becoming familiar with your program's built-in functions, therefore, is part of the pathway to spreadsheet mastery (Table 9–5).

TABLE 9–5 Built-in Functions (Lotus 1-2-3)

Function	Explanation
	Mathematics functions
@ABS(x)	Shows absolute form of a value *x* (converts to positive if *x* is negative).
@INT(x)	Shows integer of the value *x* (no decimal places). Numbers are stored, however, with an accuracy of up to 11 decimal places.
@MOD(x,y)	Finds the remainder of *x* divided by *y*.
@ROUND(x)	Rounds the value *x* to a specified number of decimal places.
@SQRT(x)	Finds the square root of the value *x*.
	Statistical functions
@AVG(range)	Computes the mean value of a range of numbers and shows the result in the cell (also called AVERAGE).
@COUNT(range)	Counts the number of non-empty cells in a range and shows the number in the cell.
@MAX(range)	Finds the maximum value in a range of numbers and shows the result in the cell.
@MIN(range)	Finds the minimum value in a range of numbers and shows the result in the cell.
@STD(range)	Finds the standard deviation of a range of numbers.
@SUM(range)	Sums a range of numbers and shows the result in the cell.
@VAR(range)	Finds the variance of a range of numbers.
	Engineering and applied science functions
@ACOS(x)	Finds the angle in radians when the cosine is *x*.
@ASIN(x)	Finds the angle in radians when the sine is *x*.
@ATAN(x)	Finds the angle in radians when the tangent is *x*.
@COS(x)	Finds the cosine of *x* in radians.
@EXP(x)	Raises the constant *e* to the exponent *x*.
@LN(x)	Finds the $\log_e$ of *x*.
@LOG(x)	Finds the $\log_{10}$ of *x*.
@PI	Returns the value of *pi*.
@RAND	Returns a random number between 0 and 1.
@SIN(x)	Finds the sine of *x* in radians.
@TAN(x)	Finds the tangent of *x* in radians.
	Date functions
@DATE(yr,mo,day)	Assigns a serial number to each day of a calendar beginning January 1, 1900.
@TODAY	Finds today's date from the operating system and returns its serial number.
	Financial functions
@FV(pmt,int,term)	Finds the future value of an annuity with payments of *pmt* at an interest rate of *int* and a term of *term*.

TABLE 9–5 (continued)

Function	Explanation
@IRR	Internal rate of return.
@NPV(x, range)	Finds the net present value of a series of cash flows listed in the range, assuming they are discounted by the value *x*.
@PMT(prn,int,term)	Finds the periodic payment on a loan with the principal of *prn* at an interest rate of *int* and a term of *term*.
@PV(pmt,int,term)	Finds the present value of an annuity with payments of *pmt* at an interest rate of *int* and a term of *term*.
	Logical functions
@FALSE	Returns a zero (false).
@TRUE	Returns a 1 (true).
@NA	Shows "NA," short for "not available," in the cell.
@ERR	Shows "ERR," short for "error," in the cell (or any cell that references this cell).
@IF(cond,x,y)	If the condition is true or larger than zero, then *x* is displayed in the cell. Otherwise, *y* is displayed in the cell.

Note: Not all Lotus 1-2-3 built-in functions are listed here.

RANGE NAMING

An exceptionally useful feature of the newer spreadsheet programs (such as Lotus 1-2-3) is **range naming.** With this feature, you can assign a name to a range. The range B2..B5 in Figure 9–24, for example, could be named SALES. Later, you can use the name instead of the range in formulas. The formula

```
SUM(SALES)
```

means exactly the same thing to the computer as

```
SUM(B2..B5)
```

As you can see, range naming helps you work with a spreadsheet program in a way that makes more sense to the eye.

CONTROLLING RECALCULATION

A major advantage of spreadsheet programs is that every time you change a value, the program recalculates the total. **Recalculation** is fun to watch and gives you a real sense of computing power. When recalculation occurs, you see

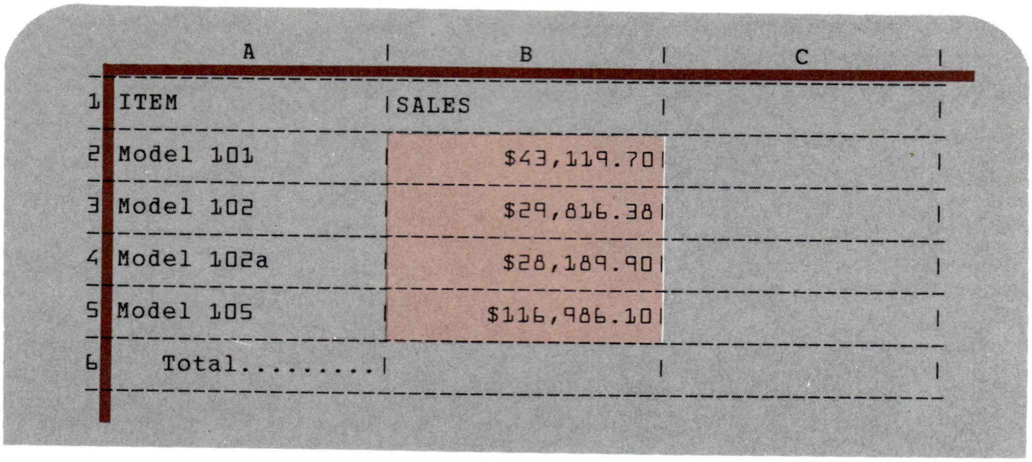

FIGURE 9–24 Spreadsheet with Range of Values

the cursor ripple down the spreadsheet, and values change right before your eyes. These programs are truly "visible calculators." To use a spreadsheet effectively, however, you will need to understand how recalculation occurs.

Spreadsheet programs recalculate all cells in a single pass, beginning at the upper left-hand corner of the spreadsheet and ending in the lower right. Just how this recalculating occurs, however, depends on which recalculation mode the program is set to use. Most spreadsheet programs can recalculate spreadsheets row by row or column by column.

Row-wise Recalculation. A **row-wise recalculation** program begins by calculating across Row 1, left to right. When it is finished, it moves back to the beginning of Row 2 and works across. It continues until all the rows are calculated.

Column-wise Recalculation. A **column-wise recalculation** program begins by calculating down Column A. When it is finished, it goes to the top of Column B and works down. It continues until all the columns are calculated.

One of these recalculation modes is the default. In other words, your program will automatically use one of these recalculation modes unless you tell it to use the other one. VisiCalc, for instance, recalculates the spreadsheet column by column in its default mode. But PC-Calc recalculates row by row. If you don't know which mode the program is using, mistakes may occur.

The Forward Reference Problem. All this information about automatic recalculation modes may seem technical, but understanding it can help you avoid the serious errors that can occur when you use **forward references** in formulas. A forward reference is a cell reference that refers "forward" to a cell that comes later in the single-pass recalculation. In a spreadsheet set up for row-wise recalculation, a forward reference refers to a cell one or more rows below. In one set up for column-wise recalculation, however, a forward reference refers to a cell one or more columns to the right.

Here's an example to demonstrate the danger of forward references (Figure 9–25). The formulas in Cells B3 and C3 contain forward references. But they won't cause a problem in the row-wise recalculation mode. Row 2 is calculated left to right. The program solves the formula in Cell D2. Then calculation moves down to Row 3.

In the column-wise recalculation mode, however, the formulas in Cells B3 and C3 will cause an error. They now contain a forward reference (D2). Working column by column, recalculation first takes place in Column A, then Column B, then Column C, and so on. And when the program gets down to Cell B3, it will look for a value in Cell D2. But that value may not have been computed yet; nothing in Column D has been recalculated. In other words, the figure that the formula in Cell B3 retrieves using the cell reference D2 may be wrong.

Changing from one recalculation mode to the other can solve some forward reference problems, but it's better to avoid using *any* reference to cells positioned right or down in the spreadsheet.

The Natural Recalculation Mode. Advanced programs such as Lotus Symphony avoid forward reference problems by using the **natural recalculation mode.** In the natural recalculation mode, recalculation does not occur by row or column. Rather, it follows the cell references in formulas. If the references take the program from Cell B1 to H20 and then back to C25, that's the way the recalculation occurs.

The Circular Reference Problem. Perhaps the biggest "no-no" in spreadsheet design is the use of circular references (although some esoteric applications use them deliberately). A **circular reference** takes recalculation on a circular path:

```
A1 (D5 * 10)
B1 (A1 * 10)
D5 (B1 / 2)
```

Most programs will display an error message if you try to use a circular reference.

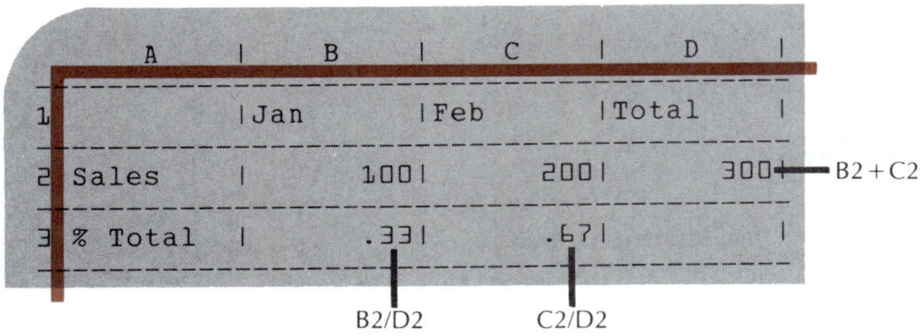

FIGURE 9–25 Spreadsheet with Forward Reference

Automatic vs. Manual Recalculation. With most programs, recalculation occurs automatically every time you make a change in a cell (**automatic recalculation**).

When a spreadsheet gets large, however, automatic recalculation can slow data entry. Suppose you're entering a long series of sales figures. Every time you make an entry on the entry line and press RETURN, the program recalculates the entire spreadsheet. In a large spreadsheet this recalculation can take as much as 15 seconds to a minute.

To speed data entry with large spreadsheets, you can select a **manual recalculation** mode. Choosing this option shuts down automatic recalculation. To get the program to recalculate the spreadsheet, you must use a special command. Most programs follow VisiCalc in using the exclamation point key (!) as the recalculation command.

Manual recalculation has one major shortcoming. If you forget to give the recalculation command before printing, you might print out erroneous results. Whenever you're using the manual recalculation mode, make sure you shift back to automatic recalculation before you print. That way there's no chance of this error's occurring.

EDITING THE SPREADSHEET

As you create your spreadsheet, you may find that you need to revise your work. A formula, for instance, may not work properly. You may have used the wrong cell reference or misspelled a built-in function's keyword. To edit the cell's contents with most programs, you need only scroll to the cell containing the error and use the edit command. The edit command moves the cell's contents to the entry line (Figure 9–26), and a cursor appears. Now available to you is a miniature version of a word processing program. You may use the destructive backspace to rub out characters to the left of the cursor, and you may use the left or right cursor control keys to go over characters without erasing them. After you make the needed changes, pressing the RETURN key inserts them in the active cell. The whole spreadsheet is then recalculated automatically, and you can see whether the edited formula is working correctly.

You may also insert new rows and columns, or delete old ones if they prove unnecessary. The program automatically readjusts all cell references so that column or row deletions or insertions do not destroy formula references (Figure 9–27, page 282).

SAVING TO DISK

The spreadsheet you create exists only in your computer's internal memory, which is volatile. You must deliberately save it to disk if you want your work saved. Professional spreadsheet users save their work every 15 minutes to protect themselves from power failures or command errors.

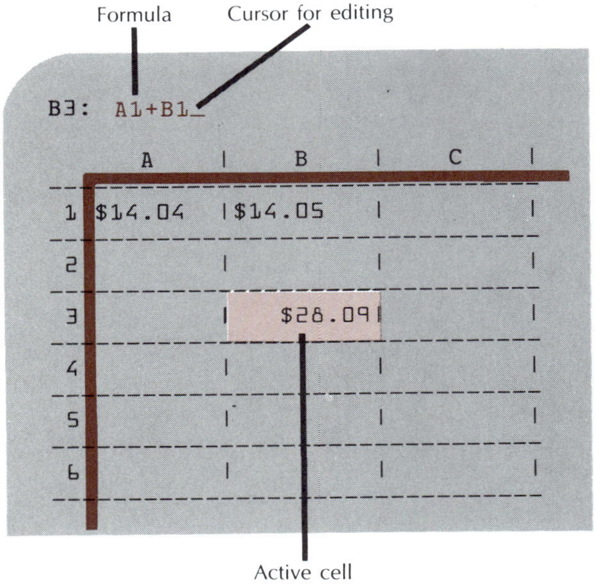

FIGURE 9–26 Edit Mode

PRINTING

A spreadsheet program's print command does not work the way a word processing program's does. You must first tell the spreadsheet program what part of the spreadsheet you want printed. To tell the program what to print, you'll use a range expression like the ones used in formulas (such as A1..D15). The range expression defines the upper-left and lower-right corners of a rectangle, within which every cell will be printed (Figure 9–28, page 283).

Because spreadsheets are often larger than a piece of $8\frac{1}{2}$ by 11 inch paper, it can prove impossible to print a spreadsheet on just one page. In such cases the program will automatically break up the spreadsheet so that each segment fits on one page. Page 1, for example, might contain the cells A1 through J28, while page 2 contains K1 through T28, and so on. This printing technique is far from satisfactory; you have to paste or tape the pages together to see on paper what you're seeing on the screen. There are, however, two ways around this problem:

Compressed-Mode Printing. Most dot-matrix printers offer compressed-mode printing, in which characters are squeezed together so that 132 of them will fit on one line.

Print Accessory Programs. These programs, such as Sideways are available that reorient the printout vertically (instead of horizontally). Printing continuously on tractor-fed paper, these programs can print a spreadsheet dozens of columns wide.

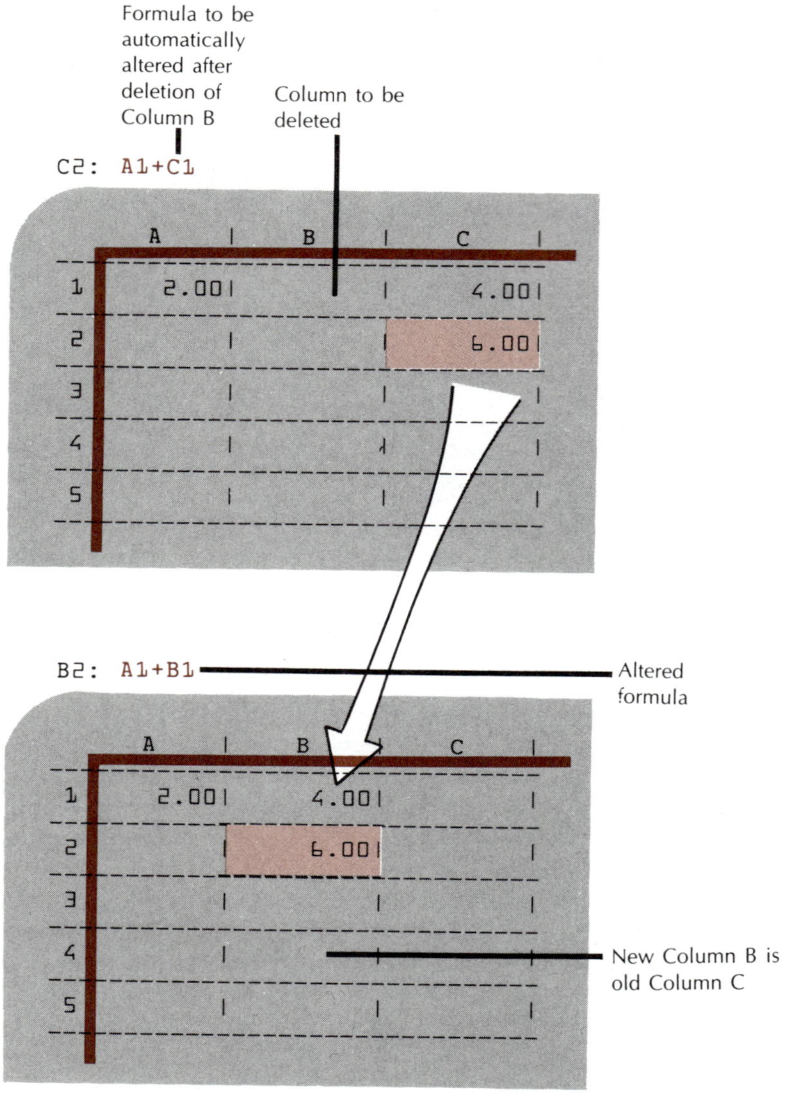

FIGURE 9–27 Automatic Readjustment of Formulas After Column Deletion

QUITTING

A spreadsheet program's quit command returns you to the operating system. Before using it, however, be sure you have saved your work. Unlike most word processing and data base management programs, spreadsheet programs rarely include "fail-safe" error messages that prevent you from quitting without saving your work. The reason for this apparent disregard for the user is that, when using a spreadsheet program, it's frequently advisable to quit without saving.

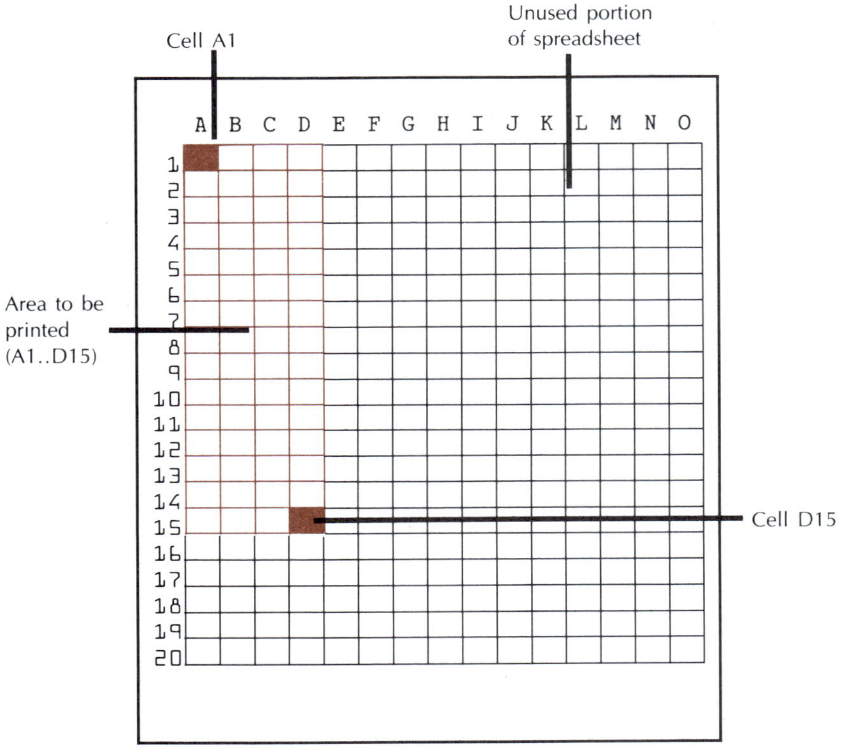

FIGURE 9–28 Range to Be Printed

Suppose you've created a spreadsheet that calculates your take-home salary for a year. You've saved it to disk. Now you're interested in exploring some what-if questions, such as "What will my take-home pay look like if I receive $2,220.00 per month?" Then you plug in the figures; however, it's not advisable to save this altered spreadsheet. You were just playing around with the figures, and you want to keep the original version unaltered.

THE LIMITATIONS OF SPREADSHEET SOFTWARE

Spreadsheets are powerful and exciting tools for solving the Licklider dilemma (the task of performing relatively simple calculations on many numbers). Yet using them can be risky, even if you manage to avoid the pitfalls we've discussed (such as forward and circular references).

The Hidden Formula. Formulas are placed "beneath" cells, and you can see them only by making a cell active and looking at the cell contents indicator. Very few programs give you a way to see all the formulas at once. Hidden formulas discourage the proofreading and checking that accurate work requires.

The Data Entry Problem. Another problem caused by the hidden formula may occur when you try what-if operations. To the user, all the values in the spreadsheet look like constants; that is, numbers you typed in. But some of these values may be the results of hidden formulas. If you put a new value in a cell containing a formula, it overwrites the cell and destroys the formula. The interlinkages among cells are destroyed and the spreadsheet will almost certainly contain errors.

The Limited View of the Spreadsheet. The spreadsheet window shows you only a few columns and rows. You don't have to scroll very far before your headings disappear from view. Without the headings to guide you, you might type data in the wrong place.

These and other spreadsheet problems can be avoided by checking your work, using good spreadsheet design principles, and using advanced spreadsheet functions. These subjects are covered in Chapter 10.

SUMMARY

A spreadsheet program gives you a blank worksheet, which contains a matrix of dozens of columns and hundreds of rows. Each intersection of row and column is a cell. You can enter labels, values, and formulas in cells. Replication functions let you copy formulas across a row or down a column, with automatic adjustment of the formulas. The result is a powerful tool for calculating that is also easy to use. Because formulas interlink the spreadsheet's cells, plugging in new variables causes changes to ripple through the whole spreadsheet. You see the results of these changes immediately. For this reason, spreadsheet programs are truly "visible calculators."

Spreadsheet programs have two modes, an entry mode and a command mode. In the entry mode, you enter labels, values, and formulas by typing them on the entry line. Pressing RETURN puts the entry into the active cell. In the command mode, typing letters sets commands in motion. To become an expert user of a spreadsheet program, you will need to develop a "map" of its command menus and submenus.

When writing formulas, bear in mind the order by which arithmetic operators are evaluated. Use parentheses to control the order evaluation if necessary. Use cell references rather than constants when writing formulas. Put constants in key cells.

When replicating formulas, distinguish between relative and absolute cell references. Use absolute cell references to refer to constants in keys.

Use ranges liberally. Name them if your program permits.

Be sure you understand how your program recalculates the spreadsheet. Does it recalculate using row-wise or step-wise recalculation? Design your spreadsheet with the recalculation mode in mind. To play it safe, avoid any cell reference that is potentially a forward reference. Do not use circular references. Use manual recalculation to speed data entry with large spreadsheets, but don't forget to recalculate the spreadsheet before saving it or printing it.

Spreadsheets are easy to use, but they do have two major pitfalls for inexperienced users. You can't see more than one formula at a time, and so it's hard to check your work. Moreover, you might ruin your spreadsheet by trying to type a new value into a cell that contains a formula. Finally, your headings may scroll out of view when you are entering data, raising the chance that you will make errors in data entry. You can avoid these errors by checking your work, using good design principles, and using advanced spreadsheet functions. These subjects are covered in Chapter 10.

KEY TERMS

absolute cell reference
active cell
argument
arithmetic operator
automatic recalculation
built-in function
cell
cell coordinates indicator
cell reference
circular reference
column
column-wise recalculation
command mode
constant
entry line
entry mode
formula
forward reference
global format
key
label
logical operator
manual recalculation
natural recalculation mode
operator
pointer
range
range expression
range format
range naming
recalculation
relative cell reference
row
row-wise recalculation
soft cell boundaries
spreadsheet window
value

REVIEW QUESTIONS AND EXERCISES

1. What is a spreadsheet? What was using one like before the personal computer came along? What's the advantage to using an electronic spreadsheet?
2. Identify the elements visible on the screen of the spreadsheet program you're using. Identify the active cell, cell coordinates indicator, entry line, spreadsheet window, and command menu.
3. What is the difference between global and range formatting commands?
4. What elements can go into a spreadsheet formula?
5. Why is it possible to copy formulas across or down a spreadsheet and have them function properly?
6. Under what circumstances is it advisable to use an absolute cell reference rather than a relative cell reference?
7. Why is it advisable to use keys for constants rather than embedding them in formulas?
8. Why is range naming such a desirable feature?
9. What is a forward reference and how is it avoided?
10. What is a circular reference and how is it avoided?
11. How are forward reference problems affected by the way the spreadsheet recalculates (i.e., row-wise or column-wise)?
12. What are the limitations of spreadsheet software?
13. It is often said that electronic spreadsheets are useful for business purposes. What other applications are they suitable for? (Hint: Think of work you're doing in other classes.)

FOR FURTHER READING

Foster, Edward. "Building Simple Spreadsheets," *Personal Computing* (January 1985).

Henderson, Thomas B., Douglas Cobb, and Gena B. Cobb. *Spreadsheet Software: From VisiCalc to 1-2-3* (Indianapolis: Que, 1983).

Hergert, Douglas. *Mastering VisiCalc* (Berkeley: Sybex, 1983).

Ingalsbee, Lon. *Lotus 1-2-3 for the IBM PC* (Columbus, Ohio: Merrill, 1986).

LeBlond, Geoffrey T., and Douglas F. Cobb. *Using 1-2-3* (Indianapolis: Que, 1983).

McLaughlin, Hugh. *1-2-3 for Business* (Indianapolis: Que, 1983).

Ross, Steven C. *Understanding and Using Lotus 1-2-3* (St. Paul, Minn.: West, 1986).

Trost, Stanley R. *Doing Business with SuperCalc* (Berkeley: Sybex, 1984).

Trost, Stanley R., and Charles Pomernacki. *VisiCalc for Science and Engineering* (Berkeley: Sybex, 1983).

Weitzer, Mary K., and Laura B. Ruff. *Understanding and Using MultiMate* (St. Paul, Minn.: West, 1986).

Witkens, Ruth. *Managing Your Business with Multiplan* (Seattle: Microsoft Press, 1984).

10 *Advanced Spreadsheet Skills:* *Making the Most of the Visible Calculator*

"The first day I got VisiCalc I started preparing financial projections with it. I couldn't believe its capabilities; there is hardly any limit to what you can do with a spreadsheet."
Allen Sneider *Laventhol & Horwath Co.*

The visible calculator's abilities have led to their widespread use far beyond the accountant's workstation. According to a survey carried out by the research firm Software Access, about 61 percent of spreadsheet users put their software to work on applications other than budgeting or financial analysis. They use the programs for scheduling production, tracking personnel, planning projects, and many other applications. Software Access's Mary Ellen Dick concludes: "Spreadsheets really are an all-purpose tool."[1]

No matter what you use a spreadsheet for, however, you'll do better work if you know how to get the most out of your spreadsheet program. This chapter helps you achieve this goal by introducing the principles of good spreadsheet design, the basics of modeling and forecasting, and advanced features of spreadsheet software.

PRINCIPLES OF GOOD SPREADSHEET DESIGN

Don Jewel, a spreadsheet expert employed by a major Canadian accounting firm, had a funny feeling about an important spreadsheet. *Important* is an understatement. The next day, Jewel planned to present the spreadsheet as evidence in a $100,000 lawsuit. "Intuitively, I suddenly felt that two of the pages didn't look right." And when he added up the figures using a hand calculator, he found a mistake: a tiny error in a hidden formula. Jewel was lucky to find the error before going to court. Had the error gone unnoticed, Jewel says, "it would have cast a shadow over all the financial evidence we presented."[2]

Spreadsheet errors occur more commonly than most users realize — and after reading the last chapter, you know why. Because you can't see the formulas, which are hidden "behind" a spreadsheet's cells, it's all too easy to ignore formula mistakes. But here's the good news. Experienced spreadsheet users have developed strategies to ensure accuracy. The best way to protect yourself against errors is to follow the principles of good spreadsheet design. These principles include the use of documentation, keys, appropriate cell formats, calculation areas, formulas split up over several cells, cell protection, routine checking procedures, templates, and relatively small spreadsheets. We'll discuss each in turn.

DOCUMENTING YOUR WORK

To document a spreadsheet is to indicate, at the minimum, who created it, when it was created, what it does, and how to use it. Even if you're the only person who uses a spreadsheet you create, documentation makes good sense. After all, you might forget over time how you set it up, thus making it difficult or impossible to use. If the spreadsheet will be used by more than one person, documentation is even more necessary. A user unfamiliar with the formulas might, for instance, inadvertently enter a value into a cell containing a formula. That mistake may ruin the spreadsheet and, what is worse, lead to spurious results that could go undetected.

Here's an example of a documented spreadsheet. Jane Smith is a real estate agent with Happy Homes, Inc. Like real estate agents everywhere, Jane helps her clients determine how much they can afford to pay for a home. Normally, she looks up monthly mortgage payments in a book of payment tables. Yet — happily for home buyers — interest rates have fallen below 10 percent for the first time in years. The tables she has do not show monthly payments for loans below 10 percent. Instead of ordering a new book of loan tables at $20, Jane decides to create a spreadsheet that will calculate monthly payments right on the screen. She plans to let the other agents in her office use it too, so she sets it up with clear instructions on its use (Figure 10–1).

```
                    A                  B              C
 1 MONTHLY PAYMENT OF HOME LOAN
 2 Developed by:  Jane Smith
 3 Date: January 27, 1987
 4 ==========================================================
 5 DIRECTIONS:  This spreadsheet computes the monthly payment
 6 of a home loan from data you supply.  Enter the required
 7 figures in the data entry area.
```

FIGURE 10–1 Documented Spreadsheet

USING KEYS

The second principle of good spreadsheet design is to create a separate and distinct **data entry area** (Figure 10–2), which contains the spreadsheet's keys. It should include headings that clearly indicate just where the user should enter the data (and what kind of data should be entered). As you learned in the previous chapter, good spreadsheet design requires the use of keys. Using keys

FIGURE 10–2 Data Entry Area with Keys

```
                    A                  B              C
 1 MONTHLY PAYMENT OF HOME LOAN
 2 Developed by:  Jane Smith
 3 Date:  January 27, 1987
 4 ==========================================================
 5 DIRECTIONS:  This spreadsheet computes the monthly payment
 6 of a home loan from data you supply.  Enter the required
 7 figures in the data entry area.
 8
 9 ==========================================================
10 DATA ENTRY AREA
11 ==========================================================
12 Purchase price      =  $75,000.00
13 Down payment (%)    =          5%   [Type in as a decimal]
14 Interest rate (%)   =        9.5%   [Type in as a decimal]
15 Loan term (months)  =        360
```

instead of cell references makes what-if analysis possible. It also reduces the chance of forward reference errors.

USING CALCULATION AREAS

Good spreadsheet design principles require a distinct **calculation area** containing the hidden formulas that produce the values shown in cells. By setting the calculation area apart, the spreadsheet designer lessens the chance that someone will ruin the spreadsheet by accidentally erasing a formula. The calculation area should be clearly demarcated, and its heading should warn the user: "Do not enter data here" (see Figure 10–3).

Position the calculation area below the data entry area if your program uses row-wise recalculation; if it uses column-wise recalculation, position the calculation

FIGURE 10–3 Spreadsheet Design Elements

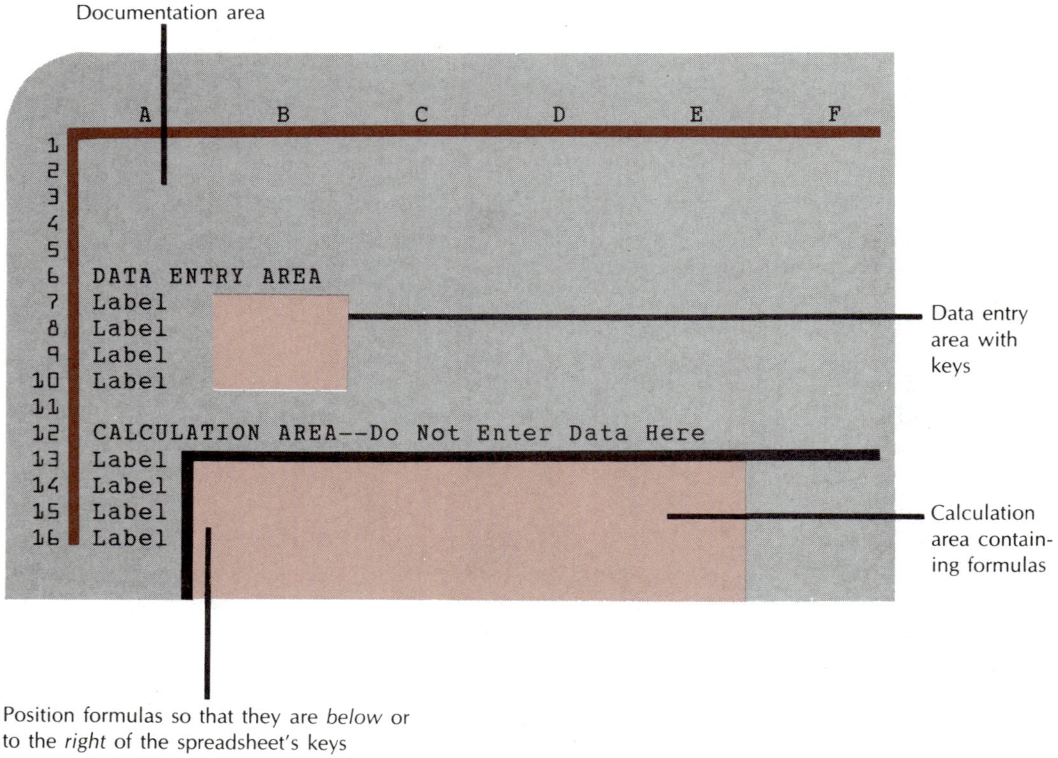

area to the right of the data entry area. This design will help to eliminate forward reference areas by ensuring that all references to keys point up or left.

USING APPROPRIATE CELL FORMATS

As you learned in the previous chapter, you can format cells so that they display numbers or characters in a variety of ways. You can format numbers, for instance, so that they are displayed as currency ($75,000.00) or as integers (360). You can format characters so that they appear in the left, middle, or right of the cell. Choose formats that clarify your spreadsheet's meaning and purpose. Here's how Jane formats her data entry cells (B12 through B15):

- B12 Currency format (displays the entered value with a dollar sign and two decimal places)
- B13 Percentage format (displays the entered decimal value as a percentage)
- B14 Percentage format (displays the entered value as a percentage)
- B15 Integer format (displays the entered value as an integer with no decimal places)

Figure 10–4 shows the formatted data entry area. Note how the formatted entries help to clarify the spreadsheet's function.

SPLITTING UP COMPLEX FORMULAS

The formula[3] used to calculate monthly mortgage payments is complex, and one look at it will tell you why real estate agents look up monthly payments in tables rather than computing them by hand. Here's the formula, expressed using spreadsheet operators:

```
PMT = I*A/(1-((1/(1+I))^360))
```

FIGURE 10–4 Formatted Values

```
 9 ==========================================================
10 DATA ENTRY AREA
11 ==========================================================
12 Purchase price       =   $75,000.00
13 Down payment (%)     =           5%    [Type in as a decimal]
14 Interest rate (%)    =         9.5%    [Type in as a decimal]
15 Loan term (months)   =        360
```

where

```
A  =  amount financed
I  =  interest rate per loan period (annual rate/12
      if the loan period is one month)
N  =  number of periods
```

This formula requires so many nested expressions that it all but invites errors. To find the monthly payment for an 8.75 percent loan of $78,850, for example, you'd have to enter this unwieldy formula in a cell:

```
.00729166*78850/(1-((1/(1+.00729166))^360))
```

To simplify this formula, let's express one of the nested expressions as a variable, V:

```
PMT = I*A/(1-(V^N))
```

where

```
A  =  amount financed
I  =  interest rate per loan period
N  =  number of periods
V  =  1/(1+I)
```

That's better, isn't it? Expressing 1/(1 + I) as V cleans up the formula and makes it much easier to detect typing errors. Jane's design for the calculation area (Figure 10–5) carries this idea further. The design solves the equation one step at a time.

1. Cell B20 finds the down payment by multiplying the purchase price (cell B12) by the down payment percentage (cell B13) using the formula

   ```
   B12*B13
   ```

2. Cell B21 computes the amount financed by subtracting the down payment (cell B20) from the purchase price (cell B12) using the formula

   ```
   B12-B20
   ```

3. Cell B22 computes I, the interest rate for each loan period (one month), by dividing the annual interest rate (B14) by 12.

   ```
   B14/12
   ```

4. Cell B23 finds I*A (interest rate per loan period * amount financed) using the formula

   ```
   B21*B22
   ```

5. Cell B24 finds the intermediate variable V using the formula

   ```
   1/(1+B22)
   ```

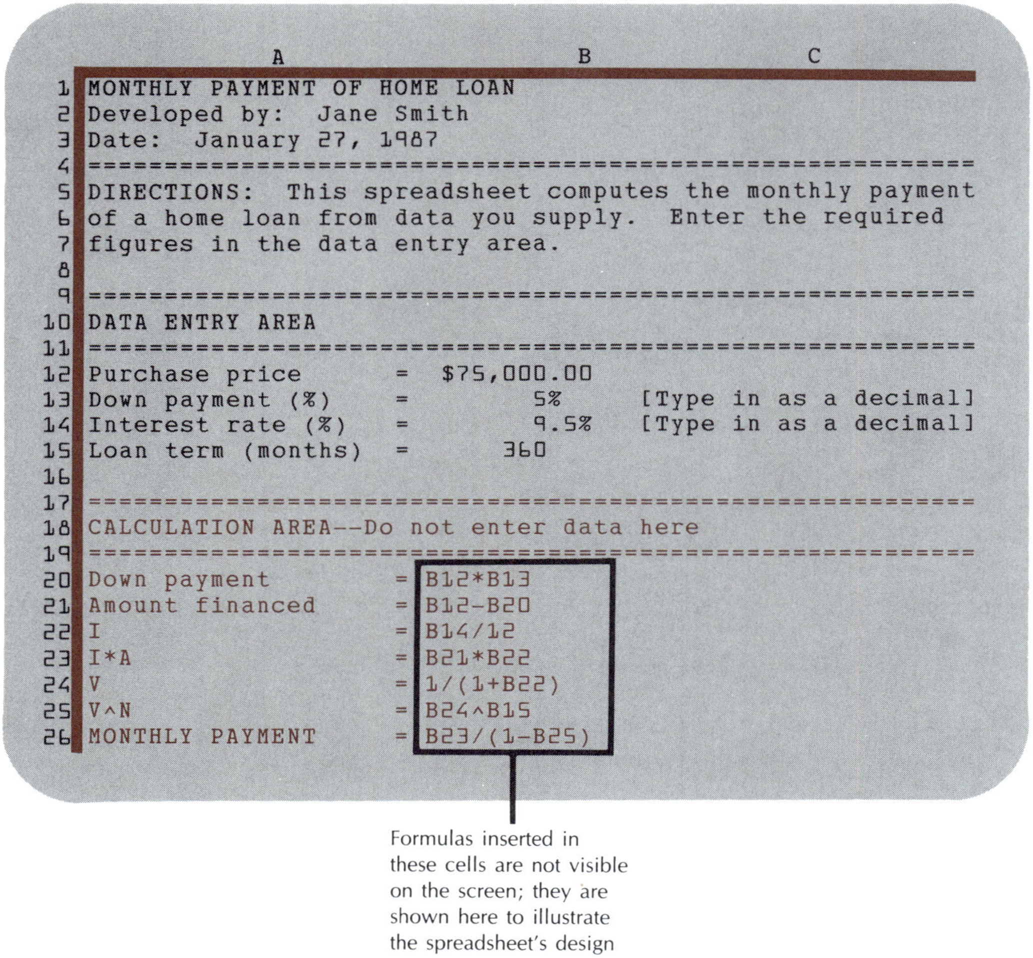

FIGURE 10–5 Design for Calculation Area Showing Formulas

6. Cell B25 solves the expression V^N using the formula

   B24^B15

7. Finally, cell B26 computes the monthly payment. It divides I∗A (that is, the value shown in cell B23) by the expression 1 − V^N. Since cell B25 has solved for V^N, we can use the simple formula

   B23/(1-B25)

All these formulas can readily be checked for errors.

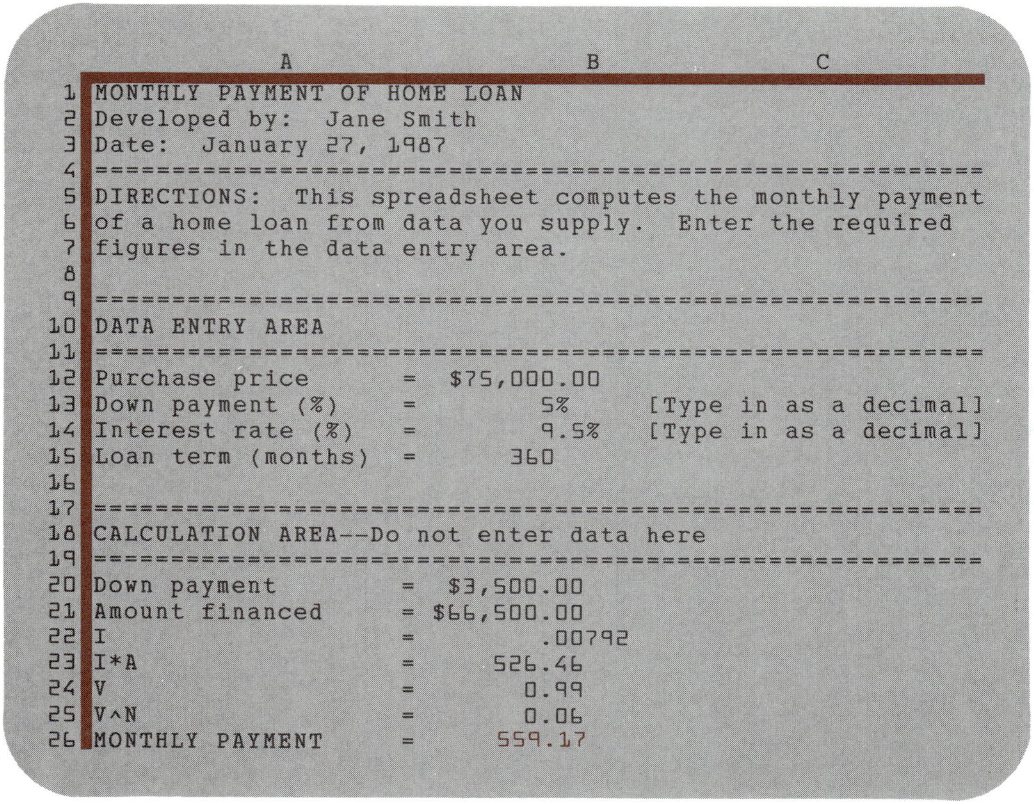

FIGURE 10–6 Completed Spreadsheet in Action

Figure 10–6 shows how the completed spreadsheet finds the monthly payment on a $75,000 house, assuming a 9.5 percent loan, a 5 percent down payment, and a 30 year loan period.

USING CELL PROTECTION

Labeling the calculation area "Do not enter data here" helps to discourage work-destroying entries in cells containing formulas. But it doesn't *prevent* an unusually determined miscreant from ruining your spreadsheet. Suppose, for instance, someone typed $5,000 in cell B20. That would erase the formula in the cell — that is, B12 (purchase price) * B13 (down payment percentage). From that point on, the spreadsheet would also assume a $5,000 down payment, no matter what you type in cell B12 or cell B13. And the result, almost certainly, would be an error. Even worse, the program will not warn you that an erroneous calculation has been made!

To forestall this catastrophe, spreadsheet programs let you protect the formulas in a range of cells. This **cell protection** feature should *always* be used in calculation areas. When cells are protected, no changes of any kind can be made to them. If someone tries to put data in these cells, the program will display an error message such as "This cell is protected."

CHECKING YOUR WORK

A spreadsheet such as the one Jane has created is a tool of real value. It can be used over and over again. But that value will be wasted if the spreadsheet contains an error. There's no substitute for a careful hand checking of a spreadsheet. To be sure, many errors will be obvious because they produce noticeably peculiar results. In Jane's spreadsheet, for instance, using a multiplication instead of a division operator will produce a ridiculous monthly payment such as $22,540. Other errors aren't so obvious. You can't really be sure your spreadsheet is accurate until you've solved all the formulas by hand or by using a pocket calculator. Note, however, that spreadsheet programs calculate all values to an accuracy of up to fifteen decimal places, even if only two decimal places are shown on the screen. If you get a small discrepancy between your calculator and spreadsheet, it may be attributable to rounding errors.

CREATING A TEMPLATE

Any successful spreadsheet — one that's documented, carefully designed, and checked — represents a considerable investment of your time. It's worth saving so that you can use it over and over again. Consider, for instance, Jane's monthly payment spreadsheet. She could save it with the key values shown in Figure 10–4. If she does, however, she will have to erase these values deliberately (and plug in new ones) the next time she wants to analyze a different situation.

It's far more convenient to save a version of this spreadsheet that has no entries in the cells for key values (Figure 10–7). A ready-to-go spreadsheet like this one is called a **template.** Notice in Figure 10–7 that an error message occurs in cell B26; it occurs whenever a division by zero is attempted. It will disappear when you plug in the necessary values in cells B12 through B15.

USING SMALL SPREADSHEETS

Experienced spreadsheet users find that, in most cases, it's better to create a series of relatively small spreadsheets rather than one huge one. A large spreadsheet

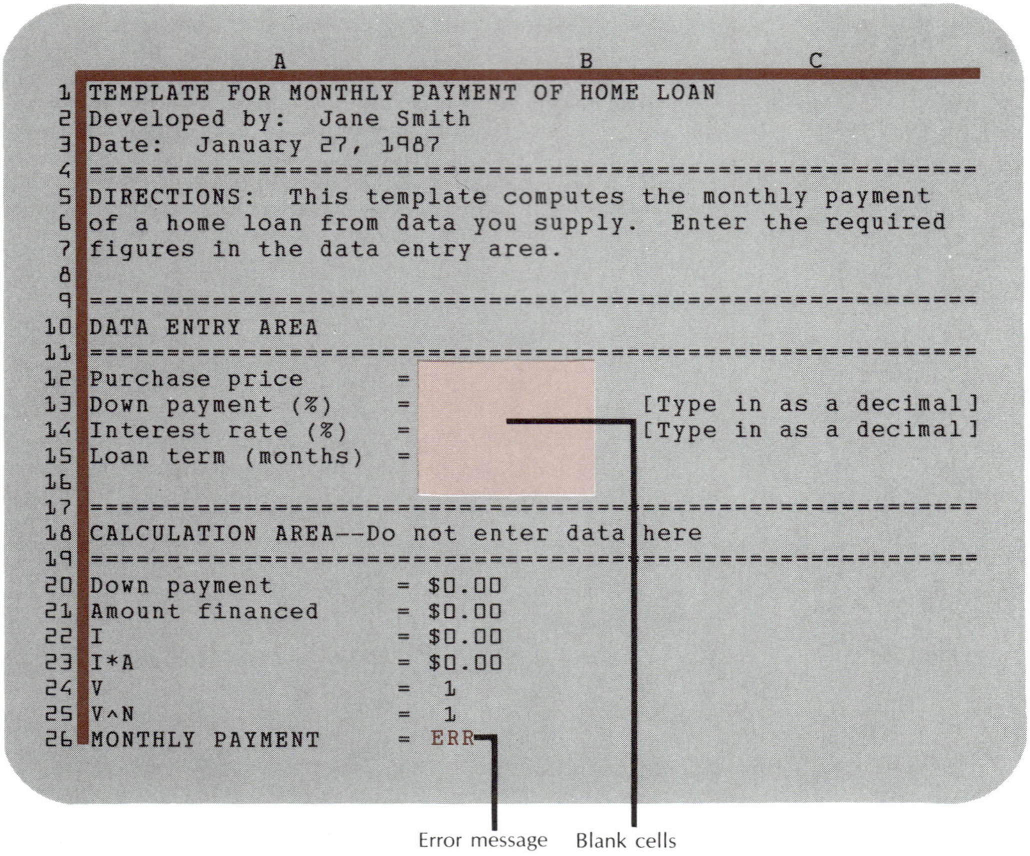

FIGURE 10–7 Blank Template for Monthly Loan Payment (Error message will disappear when data are keyed in)

responds very slowly when recalculation occurs, and the limited view of the spreadsheet permitted by the spreadsheet window makes it hard to see the spreadsheet's structure. These two shortcomings of large spreadsheets conspire to make work with the spreadsheet as tedious as it is prone to error.

A series of smaller spreadsheets solves these problems, but creates new ones. The advantage of having a single, large spreadsheet is that a truly massive amount of information can be interlinked. If you split the spreadsheet up into smaller files, you may lose this capability. There are two ways, however, in which you can avoid this loss: first, by moving data through a series of spreadsheets using the program's features for copying data from one spreadsheet to another, and second, by using file linkage features in some of the more sophisticated spreadsheet programs.

Moving Data Through a Series of Spreadsheets. Suppose Bethany Roberts is a secondary school teacher, and she has worked out a very large spreadsheet for keeping track of students' scores. The spreadsheet — and it's a monster — begins with a list of students' names and the scores they've achieved on thirty quizzes and tests. Each column of scores, moreover, is subjected to a standardized score analysis, in which the raw scores — the number of points each student obtained on the quiz or test — is converted (by a lengthy and complicated process) into standardized scores with a normal distribution. Finally, the standardized scores are multiplied by weighting factors (e.g., the final exam is worth 30 percent of the grade) to determine the course grade. It's a terrific spreadsheet, but it's so large that it takes three to five minutes to recalculate!

Bethany decides to break up the spreadsheet into three parts. Here's her plan:

1. The first spreadsheet, the raw scores spreadsheet, is used as a giant data area. There are no formulas anywhere in the spreadsheet; all it contains is a list of students' names and the scores for each of the thirty quizzes or tests.
2. The second spreadsheet, the grade analysis spreadsheet, contains no data. It is a template that is used to compute the standard scores for one set of quiz or exam scores at a time.
3. The last spreadsheet, the grade averaging spreadsheet, records the standardized scores for each test. Weights attached to the scores for each quiz or test produce the final course grade.

Here's how Bethany uses her three spreadsheets. When her students have taken their first quiz at the beginning of the term, she records the raw scores in Spreadsheet 1, the raw scores spreadsheet. She names the range of new quiz scores Quiz 1, saves the spreadsheet to disk, and clears the screen. Then she loads the grade analysis worksheet and, using a file combining command that retrieves a range of cells from another spreadsheet, copies the Quiz 1 scores into it. Moments after the Quiz 1 scores appear, the standardized scores ripple down the right side of the grade analysis spreadsheet. She names these scores Quiz1std ("Quiz 1 standardized scores"), saves the spreadsheet, and clears the screen again. Now she loads the grade averaging worksheet and, using again the command that retrieves a range of cells from another spreadsheet, copies the Quiz 1 standardized scores into it. Finally, she saves the grade averaging worksheet to disk. She repeats this procedure for each new set of quiz or test scores.

File Linkage Features. A few spreadsheet programs give you the ability to write references to a cell or range of cells in spreadsheets other than the one you're using, so long as the spreadsheet is on the same disk. With this feature, a spreadsheet user can create a series of linked spreadsheets, each of which is manageable in size. Getting all the links to function properly is tricky, however, and extensive documentation becomes more important than ever: if the user forgets to place all the necessary files on the disk at the same time, for instance, the program will not be able to find the cells or ranges it's looking for.

Case Study: Avoiding Bottom-Line Disaster

"There have been times when I used a spreadsheet, set it aside for a month or so, then looked at it again — and found an error," says Jonathan Yarmis, personal computer analyst for General Instrument Corporation of Clifton, N.J. "I consider myself above average in my computer skills — which made me wonder: If I make these kinds of mistakes, what were other people doing?"

The answer, Yarmis found, is that they were making plenty of errors, too. For example, he ran across one spreadsheet user — "fairly high up in the company," according to Yarmis — who ignored a circular reference error message showing on the computer screen, a dangerous practice. "He told me the program was giving him the right answers anyway," Yarmis says. "But how does he know they're right?"

Accounting firms, attuned as they are to financial controls, have developed some of the earliest formal spreadsheet policies and procedures. Arthur Young, for example, treats spreadsheets like computer programs: each requires a manual.

Corporations are starting to follow the accountants' lead in instituting spreadsheet controls. Last fall, General Instrument introduced its "personal computer documentation/programming standards," which apply to all personal computer applications that could affect "initiation of payments or recording of assets," Yarmis says. Under this policy, all spreadsheets must be accompanied by a written narrative explaining how the model works. "So many users aren't even aware of what proper business conduct in this area is," Yarmis says. "This is an attempt to make people aware that the effects of what they do could be serious."

He also encourages people to include a printout of the spreadsheet model made with a program called Spreadsheet Auditor. This $99 package by Consumer Software of Vancouver, British Columbia, prints the equations from a spreadsheet in a form that the programs themselves don't: in a table in the same relative position they occupy in the spreadsheet.

"There was some initial resistance on the part of some people," Yarmis says. "They said writing documentation would take away their initial productivity gains." Yarmis challenged them by betting that if he examined five of their spreadsheets, he could find mistakes in at least two of them. Several people took up Yarmis on the challenge — and lost.

From Doran Howitt, "Avoiding Bottom-Line Disaster," *InfoWorld* (February 11, 1985).

MODELING AND FORECASTING

Spreadsheets provide a highly visible and intuitively sensible way to work with complex formulas (such as the formula for calculating periodic payments with compounded interest). Two additional spreadsheet applications lie in **modeling** and **forecasting.** Both are widely used by business managers.

MODELING

You've already seen how spreadsheets can answer what-if questions, such as "What will the monthly payment be if the down payment is 20 percent instead of 5 percent?" This same capability can be used to model a real-world situation.

Modeling Defined. To model something is to create an artificial version of it, one that has at least some characteristics in common with the real thing. To put it another way, the model simulates some aspects of a prototype's behavior. Next, you vary the model, trying it out in different situations. As you do, you come to understand the real thing better. Consider, for instance, an aeronautical engineer's model airplane. It models the aircraft's aerodynamic properties in a wind tunnel. By changing the model's shape, the engineer can determine the best design. Notice that modeling is far cheaper, quicker, and safer than experimenting with a real airplane!

Modeling and Decision Making. A spreadsheet model uses mathematics instead of a physical substance, but it has exactly the same advantages: it can help you make decisions at far less cost than experimenting with the real world. A business manager, for example, can construct a spreadsheet model of the business's financial transactions. By changing key variables, the manager can test alternative scenarios; for instance, what would happen to company profits if costs were reduced 5 percent? Or if sales increased 10 percent?

The results can be seen immediately, without any of the cost, expense, and stress of making actual changes in day-to-day business practices. It's no wonder so many business executives and managers are using spreadsheets to help them make decisions.

Here's an example of spreadsheet-based decision making in action. A prospective home buyer, Edward Thomas, comes into Happy Homes, Inc., and sits down with Jane Smith to discuss his situation. Edward has saved $10,000, and he is thinking about spending some of it on a down payment. He would like, however, to keep the down payment to a minimum. He would also like to keep his payments down to roughly $475 per month. He has identified a house in which he's interested; it costs $65,000.

Exploring Edward's situation with her spreadsheet, Jane begins by assuming the currently available interest rate, 9.5 percent. At this interest rate, Edward would need a down payment of almost $10,000 to keep his monthly payments below $475. Now Jane experiments with lowering the interest rate, and the effects are dramatic. If Edward can obtain a loan at 8.5 percent interest, he can pay only 5 percent down — $3,250 — and look forward to monthly payments of $474.80. Jane's company and other industry analysts believe the trend is toward lower interest rates, and so Jane advises her client to wait before making an offer on the house.

Limitations of Spreadsheet Modeling. A spreadsheet model, like any other model, is useful only if it accurately reflects reality. It's only as good as its underlying assumptions. If the assumptions you make while creating the model are wrong, the spreadsheet will not help you to make better decisions. Many companies encourage middle managers and professionals to create their own spreadsheets. After all, these people know their slice of the business better than anyone else and are most likely to spot erroneous assumptions in a spreadsheet and correct them. Moreover, they're most likely to include all the relevant information.

Even so, it's impossible for even the best-informed person to include every aspect of a real-world situation in a model, just as it's impossible for an aeronautical engineer to build a model airplane that's a perfect miniature of the real thing. Remember that a model is just that — a model, or a depiction of a *few aspects* of a much more complex reality. What actually happens may be caused by some factor your model didn't take into account.

FORECASTING

Spreadsheets provide useful tools for forecasting, or predicting future values by extrapolating from present trends. Forecasting is a necessary activity in any business: every manager must prepare for the future. If sales continue to go up 25 percent each year for the next five years in a row, for instance, a manager will have to predict how many additional workers to hire.

Here's an example to show how useful spreadsheets can be for forecasting purposes. Jim Scofield is an executive of Amalgamated Veeblefitzer Corporation (AVC). AVC has been improving its position in the veeblefitzer market; steady increases have given it a 38.5 percent share of the total market. If present trends continue, AVC's market share will rise to a solid 50 percent in the next five years. Jim's job is to predict what AVC's sales will be for each of the next five years, assuming constant progress toward that goal. The firm's managers need the sales figures so that they will know how many veeblefitzer parts to order.

Predicting sales is complicated because the total market for veeblefitzers is increasing at a 4.6 percent annual rate. So when AVC achieves its 50 percent

Case Study: Economists Use Spreadsheets to Forecast Economic Problems in the Third World

The economies of developing nations are fragile things. A sudden downturn in the international price levels of a country's products can destroy an economic development effort. When oil prices plummeted in 1982, for instance, Mexico's economy followed suit — and Mexico joined a growing list of countries that cannot meet principal payments on massive international debts.

Since more than $800 billion is owed to Western banks by Third World countries, keeping track of the economic performance of these countries is more than a curious past-time. Predicting debt repayment failures and developing strategies to cope with them has become a regular practice at the Institute of International Finance (IIF), a Washington, D.C.-based consortium of nearly 200 member banks. A team of 15 economists track the economic performance of 41 developing countries using personal computers and Lotus 1-2-3, the best-selling spreadsheet program.

Greg Fager, senior economist at IIF, says that Lotus is ideal for this application. A vast range of economic data for each debtor nation — approximately 150 factors crucial to a country's economic performance — must be entered, updated, and analyzed. And once all the data have been entered, "what-if" analysis — changing key variables to see what impact they have on the totals — becomes possible. "There are some very obvious ways of assessing countries' performance and economic policies," Fager says. IIF economists can manipulate key variables, and as they do, they ask, " 'How does this affect our constituency, the commercial banks?' "*

IIF economists generate regular reports for member banks, including Continental Illinois, which has loaned to dozens of developing nations. Whenever Continental loan officers need to make a decision, the IIF data are ready and waiting — including projections for future performance, which help the bank minimize the risk of making loans in inherently risky situations.

*Quoted in Paul Karon, "Getting a Handle on Third-World Debt," *PC Week* (October 14, 1986), p. 40.

market share five years down the road, it will get a bigger slice of a *bigger* pie. Figure 10–8 shows Jim's design for a spreadsheet that does the necessary forecasting.

Here's how Jim's spreadsheet works. Cells D15 through D18 take the initial data:

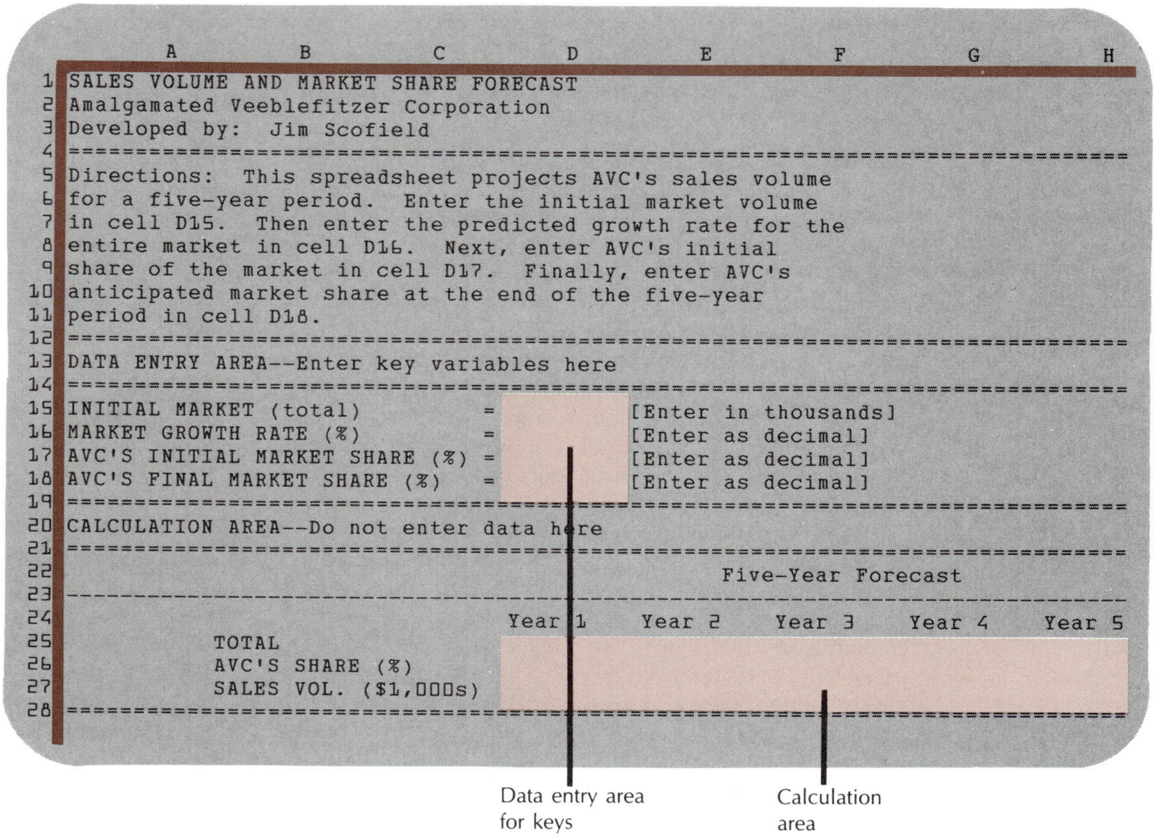

FIGURE 10–8 Spreadsheet for Business Forecasting

- D15 Total value (in $1,000s) of the veeblefitzer market
- D16 The rate at which the total veeblefitzer market is growing per year (expressed as a percentage)
- D17 AVC's present share of the veeblefitzer market (expressed as a percentage)
- D18 AVC's share of the market five years from now, assuming the present growth plan works (expressed as a percentage).

Notice that the spreadsheet design includes messages instructing the user to enter the D16, D17, and D18 values as decimals. These decimals, when entered, will be displayed as percentages because these cells use the percent display format. If .385 is entered in cell D17, for example, it will be displayed as 38.5 percent.

The calculation area stores the formulas and shows the projections. To calculate the growth in total sales volume (row 25), Jim starts by placing a cell reference (D15) in cell D25. This reference takes the value in cell D15 (the total veeblefitzer market for Year 1) and places it in cell D25, the total for Year 1 of the forecast. Now Jim uses a formula[4] to project the total market for Years 2 through 5 (to appear in cells E25 through H25). Here's the formula:

$$\text{Volume}_2 = \text{Volume}_1 + (\text{Growth Rate} * \text{Volume}_1)$$

where

$$\text{Volume}_2 = \text{Year 1 volume}$$
$$\text{Volume}_2 = \text{Year 2 volume}$$

In spreadsheet notation, here's the formula for cell E25:

```
D25+(D25*($D$16))
```

It states in English: Take the quantity in cell D25 and multiply it by the percentage in cell D16. (The dollar signs [D16] indicate an absolute cell reference.) Then add the product to the quantity in cell D25.

Reducing this equation algebraically, we get the simpler:

```
D25*(1+$D$16)
```

Replicating this formula across row 25 gives the projected total market volumes for all five years.

Now Jim uses a formula to calculate AVC's market share for each of the five years. He begins formatting the range D26 through H26 so that decimals will be displayed as percentages. Next, he places the cell reference D17 in cell D26, which then shows the value in cell D17. Now he uses the formula

```
(Final Share - Initial Share)/4 + last year's share
```

In spreadsheet notation, here's the formula Jim places in cell E26:

```
($D$18-$D$17)/4+D26
```

Replicated across row 26, this formula shows AVC's increasing market share.

Now Jim enters the formula to calculate AVC's annual slice of this growing pie. He begins by entering in cell D27 the formula

```
D25*D26
```

In this formula, the total market (cell D25) is multiplied by AVC's market share (D26) to give the AVC sales volume for that year. Replicating this formula across row 27 shows the projected sales for the entire five-year period. Figure 10–9 shows the results, assuming the figures shown in cells D15 through D18.

Now that his spreadsheet is completed, Jim can use it to blend what-if modeling and forecasting. Here's what happens if Jim assumes an annual market growth rate of 8.5 percent instead of the more modest 4.6 percent (Figure 10–10).

Any forecast is only as good as the assumptions that underlie it. Jim may have good reasons for assuming that the overall veeblefitzer market will continue to grow (and AVC's market share along with it), but if these trends don't continue the projection will be worthless. Experienced forecasters develop several alternative forecasts, with assumptions ranging from optimistic to pessimistic. Spreadsheets ease this job by making it easy to change key variables. In Jim's spreadsheet, for instance, one could easily draw up a prediction that assumed slower growth for the overall market and equally slow growth for AVC's share of it.

FIGURE 10–9 Sales Volume and Market Share Forecast

```
          A        B        C        D        E        F        G        H
 1 SALES VOLUME AND MARKET SHARE FORECAST
 2 Amalgamated Veeblefitzer Corporation
 3 Developed by:  Jim Scofield
 4 ========================================================================
 5 Directions:  This spreadsheet projects AVC's sales volume
 6 for a five-year period.  Enter the initial market volume
 7 in cell D15.  Then enter the predicted growth rate for the
 8 entire market in cell D16.  Next, enter AVC's initial
 9 share of the market in cell D17.  Finally, enter AVC's
10 anticipated market share at the end of the five-year
11 period in cell D18.
12 ========================================================================
13 DATA ENTRY AREA--Enter key variables here
14 ========================================================================
15 INITIAL MARKET (total)       =     205   [Enter in thousands]
16 MARKET GROWTH RATE (%)       =    4.6%   [Enter as decimal]
17 AVC'S INITIAL MARKET SHARE (%) = 38.5%   [Enter as decimal]
18 AVC'S FINAL MARKET SHARE (%)   = 50.0%   [Enter as decimal]
19 ========================================================================
20 CALCULATION AREA--Do not enter data here
21 ========================================================================
22                                            Five-Year Forecast
23 ------------------------------------------------------------------------
24                              Year 1    Year 2    Year 3    Year 4    Year 5
25          TOTAL              $205.00   $214.43   $224.30   $234.61   $245.40
26          AVC'S SHARE (%)     38.50%    41.38%    44.25%    47.13%    50.00%
27          SALES VOL. ($1,000s) $78.93  $88.72    $99.25   $110.56   $122.70
28 ========================================================================
```

MARKET GROWTH RATE = 8.5% [Enter as decimal]

Five-Year Forecast

	Year 1	Year 2	Year 3	Year 4	Year 5
TOTAL	$205.00	$222.43	$241.33	$261.84	$284.10
AVC'S SHARE (%)	38.50%	41.38%	44.25%	47.13%	50.00%
SALES VOL. ($1,000s)	$78.93	$92.03	$106.79	$123.40	$142.05

FIGURE 10–10 Sales Volume Forecast with a Higher Annual Market Growth Rate

USING ADVANCED SPREADSHEET FEATURES

Like computer hardware, spreadsheet programs have been through several generations of development. First-generation programs, such as the early versions of VisiCalc, had most of the spreadsheet features already discussed. Second-generation programs, such as Lotus 1–2–3 and SuperCalc[3], include advanced features that have made spreadsheeting even more attractive, productive, and useful. These features include *advanced built-in functions, titles, macros,* and *look up tables.*

ADVANCED BUILT-IN FUNCTIONS

Most spreadsheet programs are at work in the business environment, so it's not surprising that many include built-in functions for business purposes. Using these functions can simplify spreadsheets and help you avoid errors.

Lotus Symphony is an integrated program that includes a business-oriented spreadsheet module. Among its several built-in functions for business computing is @PMT, a function that computes the payment of a loan for a specified period. This function requires you to enter arguments, or additional values that Symphony needs to compute the payment. The arguments are entered as follows, with each element in the argument separated by a comma:

```
@PMT(principal, interest, periods)
```

For Jane's spreadsheet (the one that computes the monthly payment of a home loan), this function can replace several rows in the calculation area. Here's the @PMT function, with cell references used instead of values (B21 = principal, B14/12 = monthly interest rate, and 360 = number of payments).

```
@PMT(B21,B14/12,360)
```

Figure 10–11 shows the simplified spreadsheet using the @PMT function.

USING TITLES

In a large spreadsheet, headings and titles may scroll out of view as you enter data. In Figure 10–12, for example — a spreadsheet for recording test scores — the students' names will no longer be visible once you start entering the Quiz 6 scores. That could lead to data entry errors.

Many spreadsheet programs solve this problem by letting you define rows or columns as **titles.** Titles do not scroll; they stay put. In Figure 10–13, for example, rows 1 through 8 and column A are titles. As you enter data, therefore, the spreadsheet's documentation (rows 1 through 8) and the students' names (column A) always remain in view.

FIGURE 10–11 Advanced Business Math Function

```
            A                        B                  C
 1 MONTHLY PAYMENT OF HOME LOAN
 2 Developed by:  Jane Smith
 3 Date:  January 27, 1987
 4 ===========================================================
 5 DIRECTIONS:  This spreadsheet computes the monthly payment
 6 of a home loan from data you supply.  Enter the required
 7 figures in the data entry area.
 8
 9 ===========================================================
10 DATA ENTRY AREA
11 ===========================================================
12 Purchase price        =  $75,000.00
13 Down payment (%)      =          5%   [Type in as a decimal]
14 Interest rate (%)     =        9.5%   [Type in as a decimal]
15 Loan term (months)    =         360
16
17 ===========================================================
18 CALCULATION AREA--Do not enter data here
19 ===========================================================
20 Down payment          = B12*B13
21 Amount financed       = B12-B20
22 MONTHLY PAYMENT       = @PMT(B21,B14/12,360)
```

```
                A                 B    C    D    E    F    G    H
 1 GRADES FOR MR. WILLIAM'S 5th GRADE CLASS
 2 Developed by:  Marie Smith, Teacher's Aide
 3 Date:  March 8, 1987
 4 =========================================================
 5 DIRECTIONS:  Enter student grades in the data entry area.
 6 =========================================================
 7                       DATA ENTRY AREA
 8 =========================================================
 9 Students'           Quiz  Quiz  Quiz  Test  Quiz  Quiz
10 Names                  1     2     3     1     4     5
11 =========================================================
12 Clarisse              18    20    21    23    28    33
13 Edward                10     9    12    12    11    18
14 James                 22    25    27    21    30    19
15 Kelly                 20    21    22    29    22    28
16 Mary A.               10     8    11    29    27    21
17 Mary N.               10     9    12    12    11    18
18 Nancy                 22    25    27    21    30    19
19 Robert                10     8    11    29    27    21
20 Steven                22    25    27    21    30    19
21 Vita                  18    20    21    23    28    33
22 =========================================================
```

FIGURE 10–12 Grade Record Spreadsheet

MACROS

When you work on a day-to-day basis with a template you've created, you'll find yourself entering the same long series of keystrokes over and over again. To save a spreadsheet with Lotus Symphony, for example, you must enter the following keystrokes:

F9 To bring up the SERVICES command menu

F To choose the FILE option

S To choose the SAVE option

Y Tells Symphony to overwrite the previous version of the same file

Second-generation spreadsheet programs give you a way to store a series of keystrokes like this one and enter them by pressing just one key. This feature, called keyboard macros (or, more simply, macros), helps you work more rapidly and efficiently.

The macro itself is nothing more mysterious than a range within the spreadsheet (preferably tucked away out of view) that contains a list of the keystrokes. Once you've listed the keystrokes, you use a special LEARN command. This

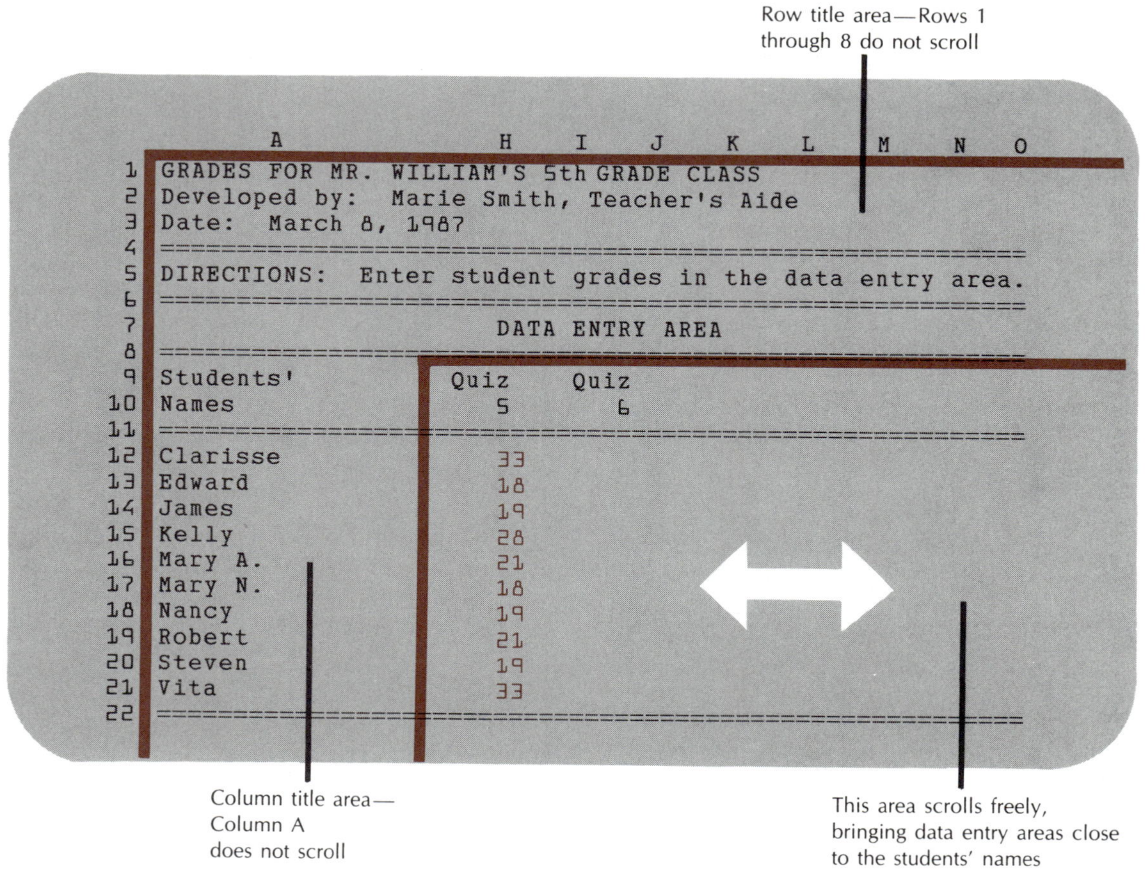

FIGURE 10–13 Grade Record Spreadsheet with Titles

command reads the keystrokes and names them using a letter or number you select. The keystrokes needed to save a spreadsheet, for example, could be named with the letter S (short for "save"). Once the program has learned the macro, you can set it in motion at any time simply by holding down the keyboard's CONTROL or ALT keys and depressing the key corresponding to the macro's name (for instance, ALT-S would set the "save the spreadsheet" macro in motion with Lotus Symphony).

Second-generation programs such as Lotus 1–2–3 offer extensive macro capabilities. Macros can be used to set up a customized installation of the program. You can write complex macros that will, for instance, present the user with a menu and prompt for specific kinds of data entry. So complex are these capabilities that they are correctly regarded as a programming language in themselves. We will return to this point in the chapter on programming.

LOOKUP TABLES

A feature of newer, more sophisticated spreadsheet programs is the lookup table, a table of values that the program can use to transform one kind of information into another. For example, with a lookup table in a teacher's grading worksheet, numerical scores can be converted automatically to letter grades.

Here's how the lookup table works. The table itself is positioned at the bottom of the spreadsheet (see cells A8 through B12 in Figure 10–14). It lists the numerical scores and their letter equivalents (0 to 49 is an F, 50 to 64 is a D, 65 to 79 is a C, etc.). The lookup function, a built-in function, sets the lookup table in motion. Here's the lookup function that's placed in cell C1:

```
@LOOKUP(B1,$A$8..$A$12,1)
```

and it says, in English, take the value in cell B1. Now look in the first column of the lookup table, which is located in the range A8 through A12. If a value greater than the lookup value is found, stop searching and move back to the lower value. Then go one column right and put whatever is in that cell in cell C1. Alternatively, if a value equal to the search value is found, stop searching, go one column right, and report the contents of that cell to C1.

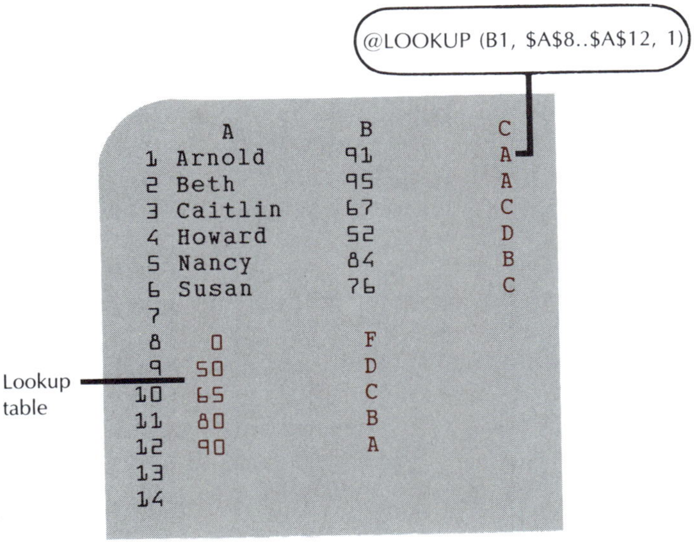

FIGURE 10–14 Lookup Table

Copied down column C from C2 to C6, the lookup function automatically reports letter scores for each of the students' grades. Notice that the cell references to the lookup table are absolute references (marked with dollar signs). They are needed because relative cell references would change during the copying process.

SUMMARY

Spreadsheets are like power tools: they can help you get through the work more quickly, but they also raise the likelihood of major errors. Because spreadsheets "hide" formulas, errors are all too common. It's easy to enter a value in a cell already containing a formula, destroying the formula and with it the spreadsheet's pattern of cell interlinkages. You can avoid most of these errors, however, by adhering to principles of good spreadsheet design.

Document your work. Even if you're the only person to use the spreadsheet, documentation will help you remember how your own creation works. If others will use it, the documentation may help them avoid major mistakes. At the minimum, the documentation should state who created the spreadsheet, what it does, and how to use it.

Create a separate and distinct data entry area, which is designed for the entry of key variables. It should include headings that clearly indicate just where the user should enter the data (and what kind of data should be entered). The key variables should be placed as near as possible to the upper left corner of the spreadsheet. This location will aid what-if calculations. It will also help to avoid forward reference errors.

Format your spreadsheet in a way that clarifies its meaning and purpose. Use currency, integer, percentage, and other formats whenever their use is appropriate.

Use a separate and clearly demarcated calculation area, an area that contains the hidden cell formulas. By setting this area apart, the designer lessens the chance that someone will ruin the spreadsheet by accidentally erasing a formula. The heading of the calculation area should warn the user: "Do not enter data here."

Split up complex formulas. By breaking down a formula so that it is spread over several adjacent cells, you reduce the formula's complexity and make errors easier to spot and fix.

Use cell protection in the calculation area. This feature prevents users from altering the contents of the protected cells.

Check your work manually. Use a pocket calculator and make sure your results are the same as the ones shown on the screen.

When you have finished developing a successful, checked spreadsheet, save it with blank data entry values. This blank version of the spreadsheet, called a *template,* can be used whenever you need it.

Keep your spreadsheets small. Link a series of spreadsheets together rather than creating one huge spreadsheet.

You can use a spreadsheet to build a model of a real-world situation. By changing key variables, you can test alternative scenarios. This kind of analysis can help you make better decisions. Remember, however, that any model reflects only a part of reality. What actually happens may be caused by some factor your model didn't take into account.

Spreadsheets are also useful for forecasting, or projecting future values by extrapolating from present trends. Remember, however, that any forecast is only as good as the assumptions that underlie it.

Advanced features of spreadsheet software can help you work more accurately and productively. These features include advanced built-in functions, titles, and macros. Advanced built-in functions simplify the entry of several complicated financial formulas. Titles aid the entry of data in large spreadsheets, in which the headings may scroll out of view. Macros automate the entry of a series of keystrokes. Lookup tables can translate one kind of information (such as numerical scores) into another (such as letter grades).

KEY TERMS

calculation area
cell protection
data entry area
forecasting
modeling
template
titles

REVIEW QUESTIONS AND EXERCISES

1. Why is it so hard to see the errors in spreadsheet formulas?
2. If you're the only person who uses a spreadsheet, is it really worth the effort it takes to document it properly? What's involved in good documentation?
3. Why should you put keys in a separate data entry area? Why should this data entry area be positioned above or to the left of the calculation area?
4. How do numeric display formats help to clarify a spreadsheet's meaning and function?
5. Why is it advisable to split up lengthy formulas?
6. Which part of the spreadsheet should be protected with cell protection, and why?

7. Under what circumstances would you be well advised to check all the formulas in your spreadsheet with a hand calculator?
8. What is the advantage of saving a template to disk?
9. Why is it advisable to keep spreadsheets as small as possible?
10. What is the inherent limitation of modeling? Of forecasting? If you were asked to prepare a model or forecast for your boss, what would you say to him or her about the reliability of its conclusions?
11. Why is desirable to have a spreadsheet with advanced functions such as @PMT?
12. Under what circumstances would you be likely to use titles?

FOR FURTHER READING

Anderson, Dick, and Douglas Cobb. *1–2–3 Tips, Tricks, and Traps* (Indianapolis: Que, 1984).

Fawcette, James. "Using Spreadsheets to Model Your Business," *Personal Computing* (December 1984).

Fersko-Weiss, Henry. "Avoiding Spreadsheet Disaster," *Personal Computing* (March 1985).

Howitt, Doran. "Avoiding Bottom-Line Disaster," *InfoWorld* (February 11, 1985).

Rubin, Charles. "How to Track an Investment," *Personal Computing* (February 1985).

———. "Moving up with Spreadsheet Math," *Personal Computing* (January 1985).

Taylor, Jared. "Keeping Your Spreadsheet Honest," *PC: The Independent Guide to IBM-Standard Personal Computing* (May 13, 1986).

———. "Spreadsheet Clinic," *PC: The Independent Guide to IBM-Standard Personal Computing* (column appears in each issue).

PART FIVE

"The Analytical Engine is therefore a machine of the most general nature. Whatever formula it is required to develop, the law of its development must be communicated to it by two sets of cards. Thus the Analytical Engine will possess a library of its own."

Charles Babbage (1864)

Application Horizons

The three fundamental software tools for information work (word processing, data base management, and spreadsheets) are only part of a wider world of personal computer applications. As Babbage foresaw, the more programs you add to your personal software library, the more flexible your computer will become.

Part 5 of *Personal Computer Applications* surveys the most popular applications beyond the three fundamental programs. (We won't limit ourselves exclusively to software, however, since some of these applications require the addition of special hardware to a personal computer system.) Covered are graphics (Chapter 11), telecommunications (Chapter 12), integrated software that combines up to five software functions in one package (Chapter 13), special-purpose software for specific applications (Chapter 14), and application programming (Chapter 15).

11 *Personal Computer Graphics:* *Making Your Point with Pictures*

"Wherever pictures relate to man's work, computer graphics will have an impact."
Stanley Klein *Computer Industry Analyst*[1]

The old proverb "One picture is worth a thousand words" has been amply confirmed by experimental science: tests show that people understand graphic images more quickly than they grasp the meaning of words. What's more, the mind retains a graphic image longer, and with more accuracy, than it does its verbal equivalent.

You can put these well-established facts to work for you as you seek to understand information and communicate your understanding to others. Growing recognition of this communication potential has helped to make graphics one of the fastest-growing areas in the personal computer world. According to one estimate, the installed base of personal computer graphics packages will approach 10 million by 1989. The personal computer is well on its way to becoming the preferred graphics workstation for business, science,

scholarship, and industry. This chapter introduces you to the ways in which people are using personal computer graphics right now — and the ways in which we may use graphics in the future.

As you know, word processing software makes writing easier by dramatically decreasing the work involved in revising the text. Because a document's text is stored in the computer's memory, you need not retype the whole document every time you want to make a change; you can keep working on it until it's just right. The result is a big increase in writing productivity — and, if the technology is used properly, in writing quality too.

Software for personal computer graphics offers exactly the same advantage for anyone who creates graphs, charts, illustrations, or other pictorial images. Like high-quality written work, high-quality pictures require multiple revisions. Before the computer redoing a drawing usually meant starting from scratch and doing the whole tedious job over again. With the computer, however, the image is stored in memory. It can be altered, redone, expanded, contracted, inverted, recolored, and otherwise transformed until it's just right. The result is high productivity and — potentially — high quality. The potential for high quality can be realized only if you know how to observe the standards of good taste and accuracy in graphic communication. Surveying those standards is beyond the scope of this book, but you can learn them quickly by consulting a good graphics handbook.

Personal computer graphics applications require special hardware. Fortunately, most personal computers now come equipped for graphics applications. So that you can better understand what hardware is required (and how to evaluate its quality), this chapter begins with graphics hardware before surveying graphics software and applications.

HARDWARE FOR GRAPHICS

Computer graphics, broadly speaking, refers to any computer-generated information that isn't expressed with text or numbers. This definition encompasses everything from a child's computer-generated picture of a house to an ultra-sophisticated, multi-million-dollar flight simulator. Even so, most personal computer graphic images are based on the same underlying principle: pictorial images are created out of hundreds or thousands of tiny pixels (picture elements) on the screen. If you've ever been to a football game where a cheering section puts on a card show, you'll grasp this basic principle right away. To put on a card show, each member of the cheering section is assigned a seat and receives a big colored card. When the people in the cheering section hold up their picture elements (cards), the result — seen at a distance — is a picture of something, such as an American flag.

Card shows are fun, but as you can see right away they have one major drawback: poor resolution. The term resolution refers to a graphic device's ability to resolve, or make visible, the details in an image. To provide high resolution and highly detailed images, the picture elements must be both very numerous and very small. With most personal computers, special hardware provides the resolution and flexibility needed to portray detailed images.

VIDEO CIRCUITS FOR GRAPHICS APPLICATIONS

Not all personal computers are designed to depict high-quality, detailed graphic images. Personal computer designers tackle the display of graphics in two ways, and one of them is unsatisfactory for all but the most primitive graphics applications. The first approach is to provide the computer with a fixed set of alphabetic, numeric, and graphics characters, no more than 256 in number. No other shapes or images can be displayed. If the user wishes to show pictorial images on the screen, they must be built up from the characters supplied. A computer designed to operate in this way is said to operate in a **character mode.** The second approach is to give the computer control over every pixel on the display screen, so that each one can be switched on or off as required. With this approach, any two-dimensional shape can be displayed. A computer designed to operate in this way is said to operate in a **graphics mode.**

For graphics applications, the character mode imposes severe limitations: the computer can display only those images that a programmer can build up using the supplied characters. Even so, many personal computers still use the character mode approach, offering a graphics mode only as an option. Considering the popularity of personal computer graphics, you might find it surprising that character modes are used at all. When you know more about how the computer displays images on the video screen, however, you'll understand why the character mode is still attractive to computer makers and programmers.

How a CRT Works. Inside personal computer monitors is a cathode ray tube (abbreviated CRT), which forms images on the screen by bombarding a thin layer of phosphor with a beam of electrons. The beam sweeps across each line of the screen in an operation called a **raster scan.** The beam switches on and off to energize each individual picture element on the screen (Figure 11–1). Because the phosphor does not hold the image for long, the beam must refresh

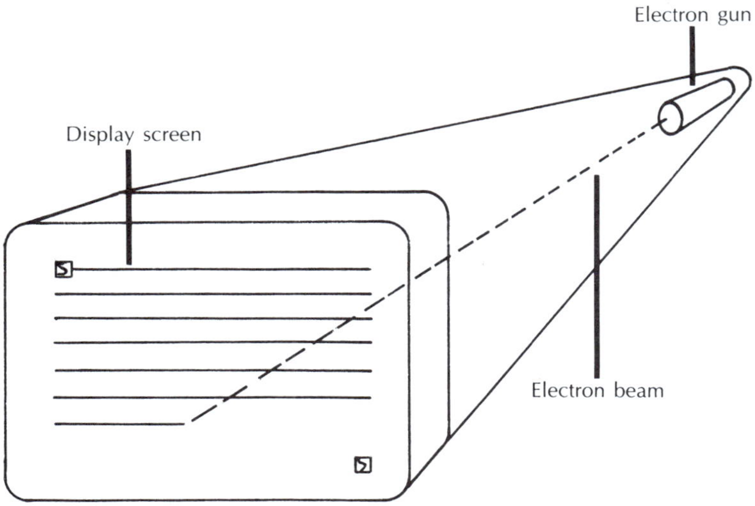

FIGURE 11–1 Raster-Scan CRT

the image about thirty times each second. Refreshing the image so often makes excessive demands on the computer's processing ability. Consider: in a standard personal computer, every line has 640 pixels. There are 200 lines of pixels on the screen. The entire screen is refreshed thirty times per second: the computer must belt out more than 3 million bits of information per second to keep the screen display going!

Were this information-crunching responsibility given to the CPU, the computer would have precious little time to do computation. For this reason, personal computers use video display circuits that have their own memory (called a **frame buffer**). The frame buffer stores the screen image, and the refresh circuits get the image from the frame buffer without putting any burden on the CPU (Figure 11–2). The CPU gets involved only when it's necessary to send new information to the screen. This approach is used by all personal computer video circuits, whether they're designed to operate in the character or the graphics mode. But there's a major difference in complexity (and cost) between character mode and graphics mode circuitry.

Character Mode Video Circuits. In the early days of personal computing, memory chips were still very expensive. To keep the cost of a personal computer down to a reasonable level, therefore, designers skimped on the size of video frame buffers. They accomplished this by designing the computer to use a fixed character set and operate in the character mode. This approach requires only a small frame buffer. The information needed to produce the characters is stored permanently in a read-only memory (ROM) circuit called a **character generator.** Each character is assigned its own unique value, which can be expressed

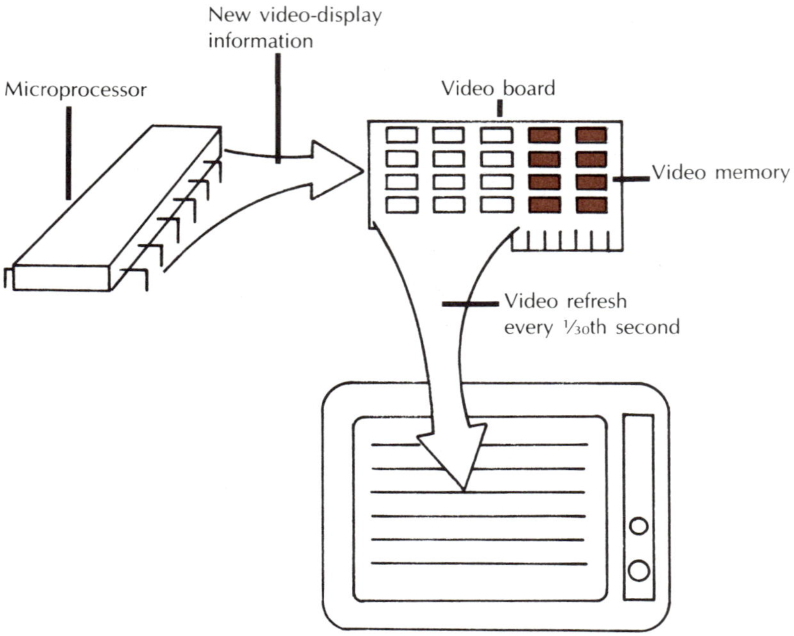

FIGURE 11–2 Frame Buffer

as a single byte (8 bits) of information. As a result, the frame buffer needs to store only about 2,000 bytes of information to keep an 80 column by 25 row screen refreshed (Figure 11–3). Demands on the CPU are light, and so programs that run in the character mode tend to operate speedily.

The character mode, however, imposes major limitations on computer graphics. All images have to be made up from the supplied graphics characters. Moreover, it's very difficult to manipulate the graphics images once they're created.

Graphics Mode Video Circuits. Now that memory chips are inexpensive, there's no cost obstacle to putting large memories on video boards. Some of today's computers offer a graphics mode as an alternative to the character mode; others are equipped to run in the graphics mode at all times. In the graphics mode, every pixel on the screen is represented by a bit of storage in the video memory. The video memory, in other words, uses bits of information to map the screen image (Figure 11–4), and so this technique is often called **bit-mapped graphics.**

From the computer designer's and programmer's point of view, bit-mapped graphics have both advantages and disadvantages. The advantages are significant. A computer operating in a graphics mode can display any two-dimensional

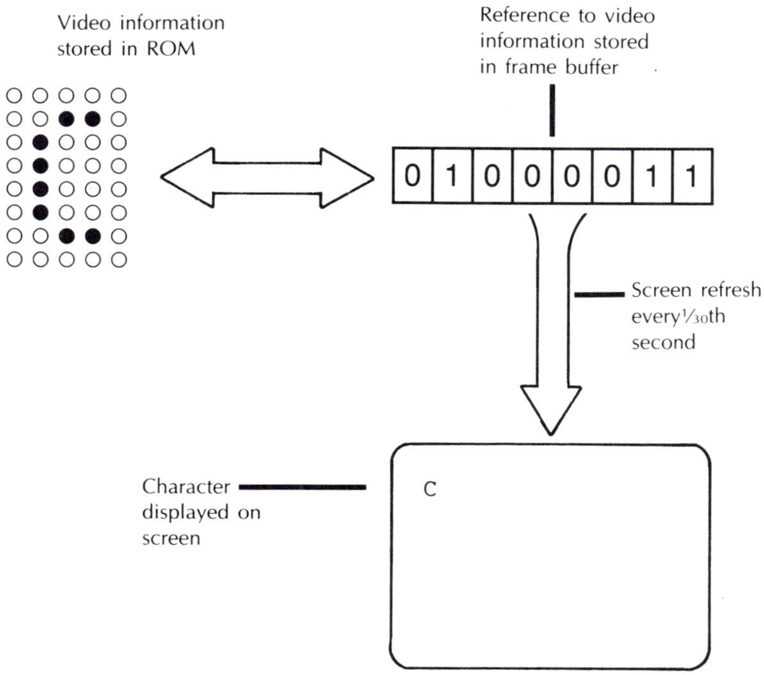

FIGURE 11–3
Character Generation

image. Since the screen display isn't tied to a fixed set of characters, moreover, the computer can display foreign language characters and technical symbols with ease. Finally, graphics capabilities make it possible to design graphics-based user interfaces, making the computer easier for ordinary people to use.

Bit-mapped graphics do, however, have their disadvantages. The graphics mode places a heavy demand on processing circuitry and slows down program execution. To achieve a tolerable degree of screen resolution, the frame buffer must hold and manipulate at least 128,000 bits of video data. Updating the screen image can keep a fast, 32 bit microprocessor so busy that it seems to operate only very sluggishly. For this reason, programmers try to create programs that work in the character mode if they're writing for a computer that lets you choose.

The new generation of microprocessor technology will eventually make this issue irrelevant. Graphics-intensive programs that run sluggishly on the 1981 IBM Personal Computer, for instance, now run tolerably well on the 80286-powered AT. Even newer and more powerful chips are already in production, and more are on the drawing board. Tomorrow's personal computers will take bit-mapped graphics in stride.

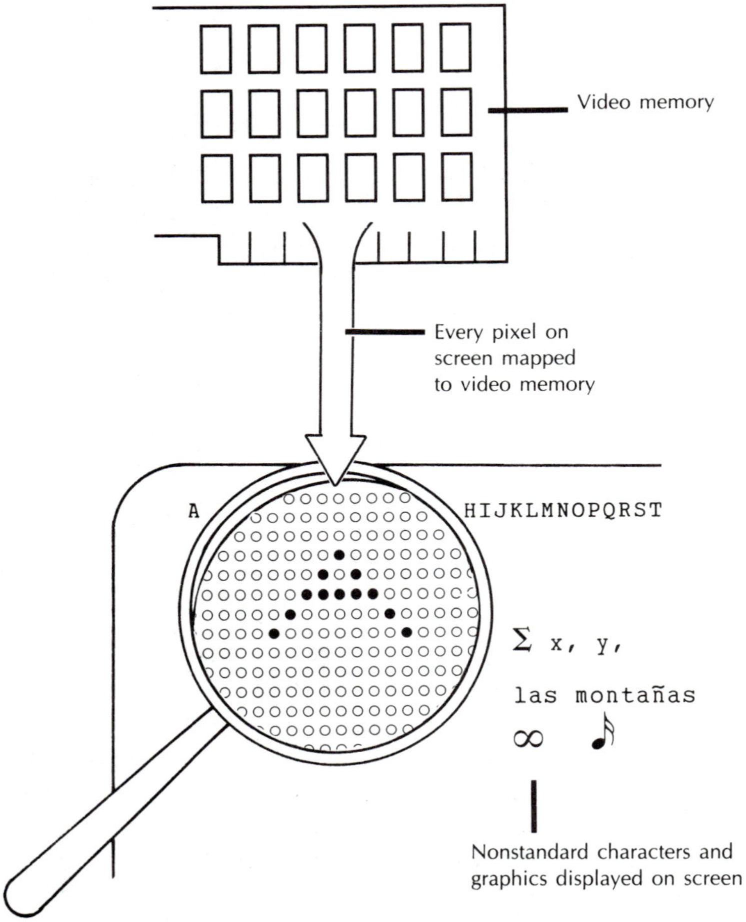

FIGURE 11–4 Bit-Mapped Graphics Screen

RESOLUTION

Just because a computer can operate in a graphics mode, however, doesn't necessarily mean that the images it produces are of acceptable quality. The video screen and CRT must be capable of resolving the image so that the image's details become visible. Most personal computers do not display enough pixels on the screen to resolve highly detailed images. The IBM Personal Computer, for instance, produces a resolution of 640 horizontal pixels and 200 vertical pixels (128,000 total), producing results that are only marginally acceptable for graphic images. Noting the PC's primitive graphics capabilities, Apple gave the PC a run for its money with the Macintosh. The Mac was designed in the beginning for high-resolution graphics (Figure 11–5). It displays 512 horizontal

FIGURE 11–5 High-Quality Graphics

and 342 vertical pixels (175,104). Recently, IBM responded to Apple by offering an enhanced graphics adapter (EGA) and an enhanced graphics monitor for the IBM PC. The EGA circuitry provides a resolution of 640 horizontal and 350 vertical pixels (224,000 total).

The Apple Macintosh and the EGA-equipped IBM PC have advanced personal computer graphics, but there's still progress to be made. Professional workstations are capable of 1,000 horizontal and 1,000 vertical pixels (1 million in all), producing superbly detailed, lifelike images. At present the technology needed to produce this very high resolution is expensive, but the trend — as with almost all computer components — is toward lower prices. The next generation of personal computers may offer 1 million pixels as a standard configuration.

GRAPHICS INPUT AND OUTPUT DEVICES

The computer keyboard and standard printers are acceptable only marginally — if at all — for graphics applications. Special graphics input and output devices have been developed to meet graphics applications needs.

Graphics Input Devices. These include the graphics tablet, the light pen, the mouse, and the digitizer.

Graphics Tablet. A **graphics tablet** allows an artist, designer, or engineer to work naturally — that is, by drawing with a stylus on a flat plane. It automatically transforms the strokes of the stylus into a graphic image that appears on the screen (Figure 11–6). Software designed to work with the tablet straightens out poorly drawn lines and makes hand lettering look as though it were typeset.

Light Pen. A **light pen,** a stylus containing a photocell that detects light, allows you to draw right on the computer screen. It works by detecting precisely when a particular pixel is being illuminated by the raster scan. Since the pixels are illuminated one by one in the raster scan's sweep over the screen, the computer can tell precisely where the pen is located. Software provided with the pen allows the entry of lines of varying thicknesses and the selection of image areas on the screen for further manipulation (such as inversion, moving, or copying).

Mouse. A mouse can be used to enter graphics images into the computer. As the mouse rolls around on the desktop, it translates its movements into a series of numerical coordinates, which refer to pixel locations on the

FIGURE 11–6 Graphics Tablet

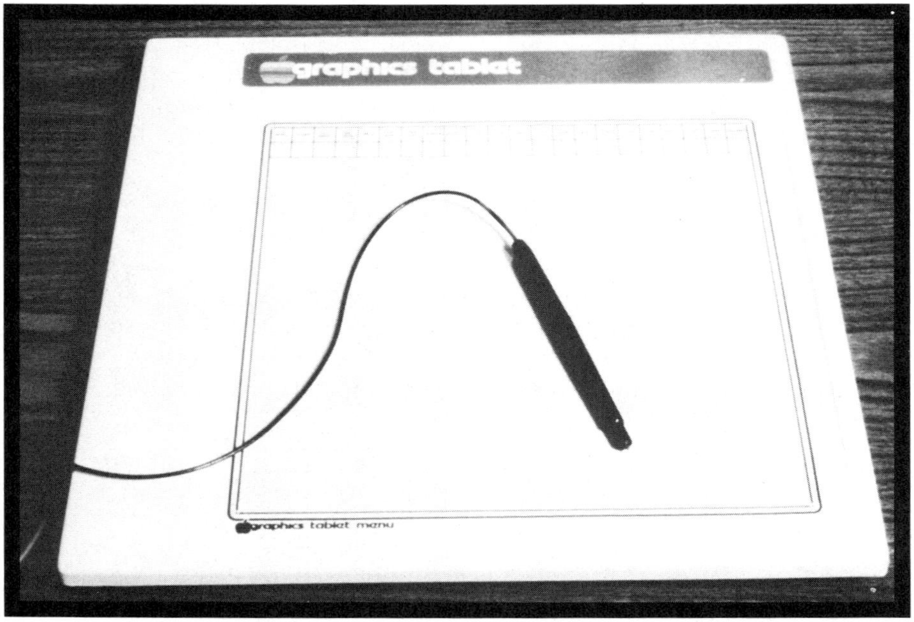

screen. The coordinates 280,19, for instance, refer to the pixel 280 columns to the right and 19 rows down. Like a light pen, the mouse can be used to draw shapes and select images for further manipulation.

Digitizers. The graphics tablet, the light pen, and the mouse allow the direct entry of pictorial information into the computer. A **digitizer,** however, takes a different approach. It scans an *existing* drawing or photograph, and transforms the picture into its digital equivalent (hence *digitizer*) for display on a computer screen.

Graphics Output Devices. These include the dot-matrix printer, the laser printer, the plotter, and the image recorder.

Dot-Matrix Printer. Most dot-matrix printers operate in a graphics mode, which resembles the bit-mapped graphics mode on the computer display screen — and in more ways than one, because resolution is poor. At best, dot-matrix printers can produce a resolution of 240 dots per inch. That may seem like a lot, but graphics produced with this level of resolution will probably have the "jaggies" — ragged edges that bespeak a graphic's computer origins (Figure 11–7). Some software, however, overcomes this hardware

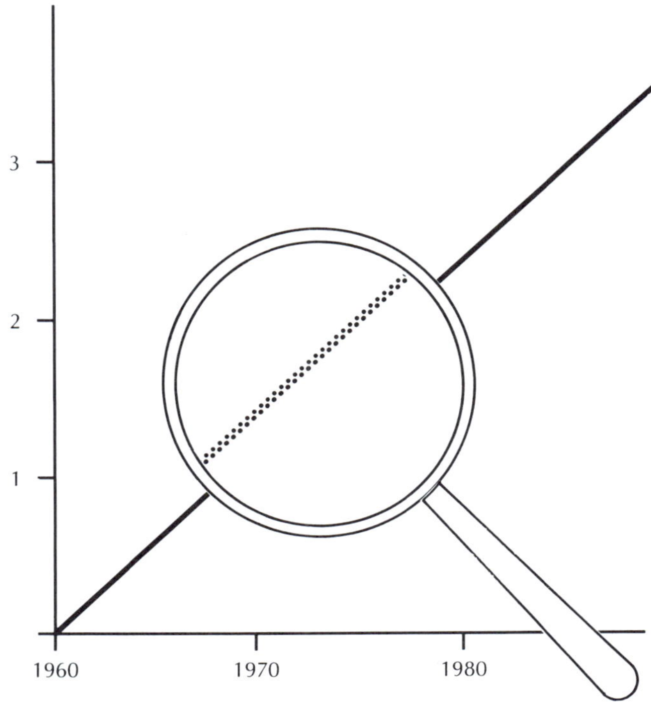

FIGURE 11–7 The "Jaggies"—Dot-Matrix Graphics Printout

limitation through craftsmanship; examples include Fancy Font from SoftCraft, Inc., and Lotus Symphony. The key lies in the ability of most dot-matrix printers to scroll the paper 1/216th line at a time. At each head pass, the page is scrolled a tiny fraction of an inch. Repeated head passes, each slightly out of register with the preceding one, build up a high-quality, high-resolution image (Figure 11–8). This **multiple head pass** approach has, however, a major drawback: it's very slow. Text, for example, may print at only two or three characters per second. A lengthy document or complex chart may take hours.

Laser Printer. Laser printers produce results superior to those of dot-matrix printers operating in the multiple head pass mode, and do so at speeds of up to eight pages per minute. Laser printer output compares favorably, in fact, to that of professional typesetting machines. Offsetting their advantages, however, is their high price.

Plotter. A reasonably cost-effective solution to the graphics output problem is the plotter; many cost less than $500. A plotter is accurately described as an electronic artist's hand. Most personal computer plotters are flatbed or roller-bed plotters. In a flatbed plotter, the paper is anchored on a flat surface. A pen, contained in a holder, is mounted on a movable arm, which can range back and forth across the bed. Pulleys move the pen laterally along the arm. A roller-bed plotter works in much the same way, except that the pen arm stays put and the paper is scrolled back and forth under it. Plotters produce high-quality images with outstanding resolution, and they work rapidly; the pen moves at speeds of up to 30 inches per second. Plotters can produce transparencies for overhead projectors by working directly on clear sheets of plastic.

Image Recorder. For presentation purposes, 35mm color slides are hard to beat. They're colorful, bright, and sharp. One way to produce slides is to use a 35mm camera to photograph a display monitor, but the results are usually unsatisfactory. As you'll discover when you develop the film, the image is more than slightly convex; the sides bow out. When you're looking directly at a display monitor, the eye tunes out the distortion. But the camera, always faithful to reality, captures it with precision. A better choice

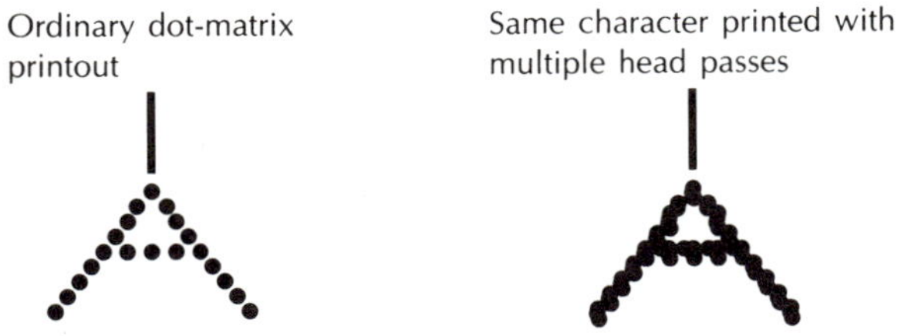

FIGURE 11–8 Multiple Head Pass Printing

is an output peripheral called an **image recorder.** Image recorders produce 35mm slides of screen images without the convex distortion. They also enhance color and image quality.

GRAPHICS SOFTWARE AND APPLICATIONS

If you had to worry about just which pixels were to be illuminated to make up a computer image, chances are you'd produce very few computer graphics! Fortunately, graphics application packages are available. These application packages have the same function as the application programs we've already discussed: they insulate you from the second-by-second minutiae of low-level hardware operations so you can concentrate on your work. Personal computer packages for graphics include analytic graphics programs, presentation graphics programs, paint programs, and software for computer-aided design (CAD).

ANALYTIC GRAPHICS PACKAGES

Analytic graphics packages are designed to transform numerical data into charts and graphs. These packages seek to give you a way of viewing your data — and through doing so, they allow you to reach a new, better level of understanding about the numbers you're working with. To create a chart with an analytic graphics program, you'll begin with a **data series.** This is a list of numbers containing the information you want expressed in graphic form. Next, you'll choose the type of chart you want made. The program then constructs the chart for you, and displays a preliminary version of it on the screen.

The Data Series. Such a series consists of two columns, titled **categories** and **values** (Figure 11–9). It is nothing more than a list of headings (categories)

Categories	Values
Year	*Sales* (millions)
1980	4.3
1981	4.7
1982	5.2
1983	5.4
1984	5.7
1985	5.7
1986	5.9
1987	6.1

FIGURE 11–9 Data Series

and values (numbers) that correspond to them. When the graphics program creates the chart, it automatically assigns the categories and values to their own axes (singular: axis), or the horizontal and vertical arms of the chart (Figure 11–10). In a column chart, the horizontal axis is called the **X axis** or **category axis,** and the vertical axis is called the **Y axis** or **values axis.** To put it another way, the X axis names or categorizes the data being measured, and the Y axis provides the numerical scale by which the categories are measured.

Data Importation. Many analytic graphics programs are designed to read data directly from files created by spreadsheet or data base management programs. To import data from a spreadsheet, you must specify the range (in columns and rows) in which the data are stored. To import data from a data base management program, you must specify the fields from which you want the data drawn.

A major advantage of integrated software (see Chapter 13) is that spreadsheet, data base management, and graphics functions are combined in a single program. Without leaving the program, you can switch back and forth between, for instance, a spreadsheet and a graph. The benefits go beyond convenience. With an integrated program, you can extend what-if analysis into the realm of graphics.

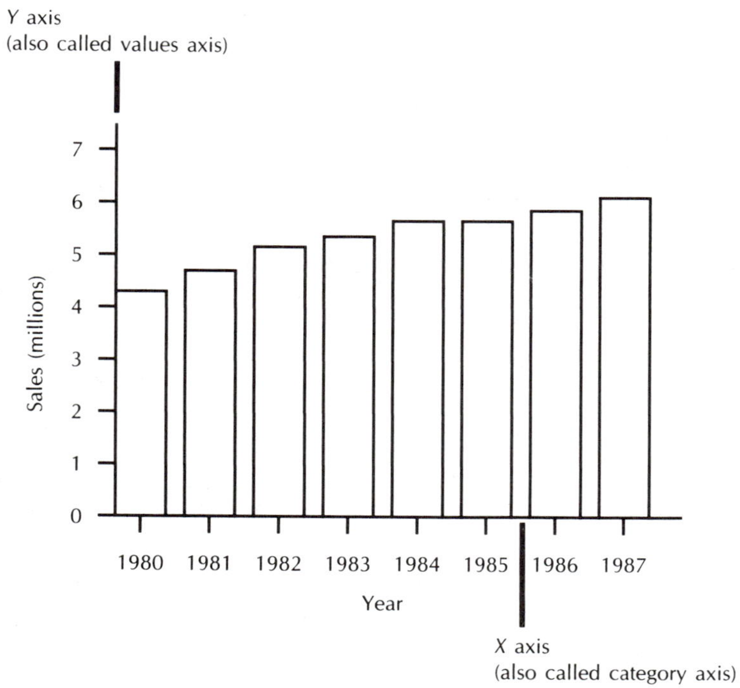

FIGURE 11–10
Column Chart

Graphics: A Two-Edged Sword

Business graphics can put you at the cutting edge of information management, even if you are unable to draw a straight line or don't know an easel from a pixel. For only a few hundred dollars, graphics software packages will transform your PC into an art department that can generate colorful charts and graphs, custom drawings, professionally rendered images, and even screen-based slide shows.

Graphics software can help you cut through to the heart of a message, making an impact that no amount of verbiage or data can match. People remember what they see but forget or filter out much of what they hear and read. Graphics can also let you condense mounds of data into manageable patterns and useful information. According to some experts, the quantity of technical knowledge is now doubling every 5½ years. And soon the rate will jump to perhaps 40 percent each year, meaning that data will double every 20 months. To succeed in the face of this ever-growing volume of information, one corporate vice president now uses business graphics to summarize monthly reports, saving himself the tedium of studying 150 pages of data each month.

Business graphics can even help the bottom line. In a recent survey, over 40 percent of computer graphics users reported an increase in revenues attributable to the use of business graphics.

Because images carry great impact, business graphics can weaken your credibility if you're not careful. The colors you choose for your graphics can have a tremendously positive impact or just as easily have a negative effect — something I learned the hard way. As part of the opening sequence of slides during a presentation, I showed a multicolored map of Canada with the northern part of the U.S. visible. At the end of the presentation, a member of the audience dressed in full military uniform came up to me, indignant that the United States had been shown in red during the opening.

Another possible mistake is graphic distortion of your data, which could lead to poor decisions with disastrous consequences. One or two simple changes in a graph can make the same data convey very different messages. For example, squeezing the *x* axis of a graph on floppy disk sales gives the impression of sharp growth after a big dip while stretching it conveys slow growth. Distorted graphics can mask the facts, leaving you worse off than you were with piles of printouts.

If you want to succeed with business graphics, you should learn as much as you can about the software capabilities and bolster your "visual IQ."

From Kathryn Alesandrini, "Graphics: A Two-Edged Sword," *PC Magazine* (June 11, 1985), pp. 239–249.

After you change key variables, you can switch to the graphics mode to view the change's impact. For any application involving frequent use of analytic graphics, integrated programs are highly desirable.

Choosing the Chart Type. Graphics programs provide several choices for expressing the data series in visual form. Options often provided with analytic graphics software are illustrated in Figure 11–11.

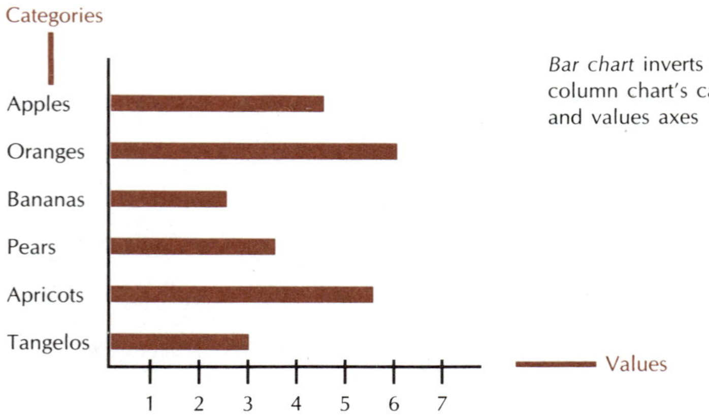

Bar chart inverts the column chart's categories and values axes

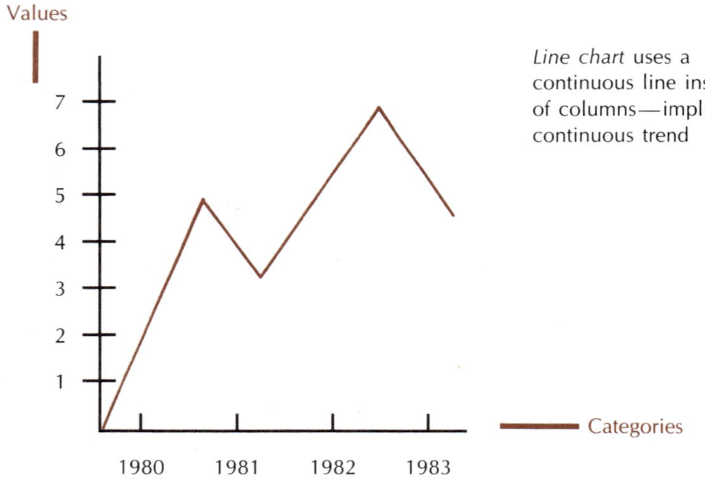

Line chart uses a continuous line instead of columns—implies a continuous trend

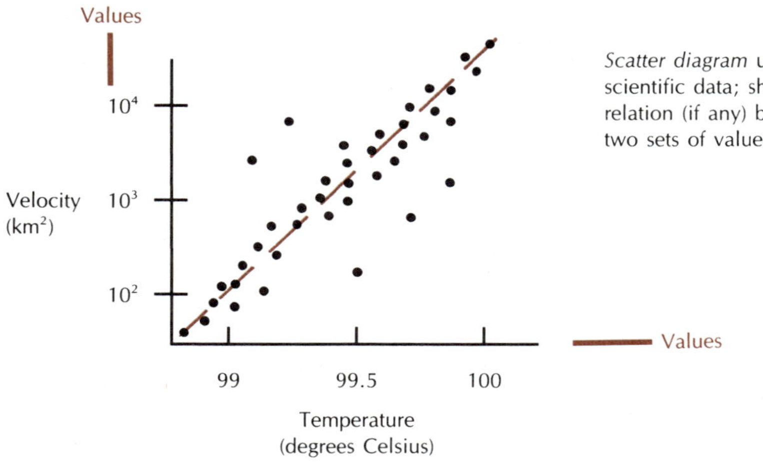

Scatter diagram used for scientific data; shows relation (if any) between two sets of values

FIGURE 11–11
Analytical Graphic Options

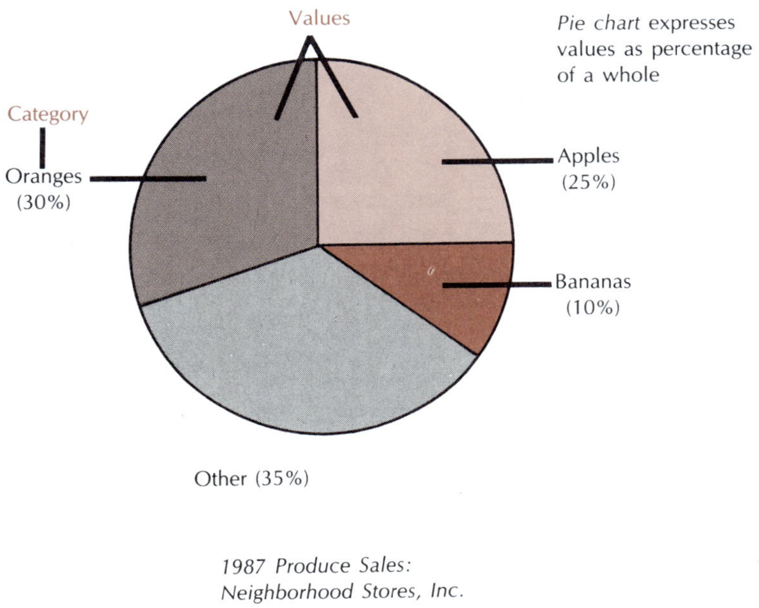

FIGURE 11–11
Analytical Graphic Options (*continued*)

PRESENTATION GRAPHICS: PRESENTING THE DATA

Presentation graphics packages often include analytic graphics capabilities; they can take a series of numbers and transform them into a chart or graph. But they also have the features necessary to prepare graphics for public presentations. These features include:

Clip-Art. **Clip-Art** or **image libraries** are collections of pictures that can enliven an otherwise dull chart (Figure 11–12).

Exploded Pie Charts. An **exploded pie chart** has a slice removed for emphasis (Figure 11–13).

Color Enhancement. If used carefully, color can enhance a graph's meaning. For instance, everyone is familiar with the traffic-light symbolism of red, yellow, and green. These colors can be used to suggest danger, caution, and safety.

Titles and Legends. Analytic graphics programs usually include only the minimum features necessary to add titles (headings) and **legends** (keys to a graph's meaning). For presentations, it's often necessary to reduce the amount of extraneous textual information and highlight a particular pattern. The best presentation graphics packages provide tools for adding clarifying titles (Figure 11–14).

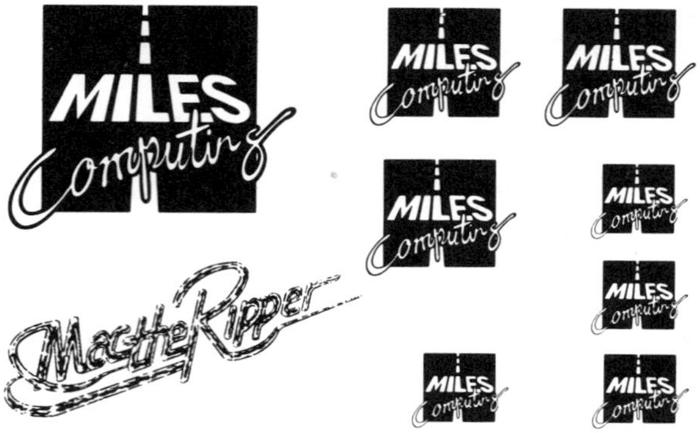

(MTK01) Mac the Knife, Vol. 1 (A Clip-Art Treasury)

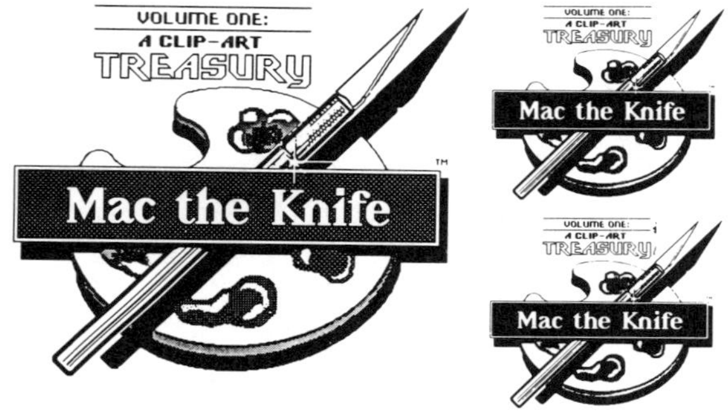

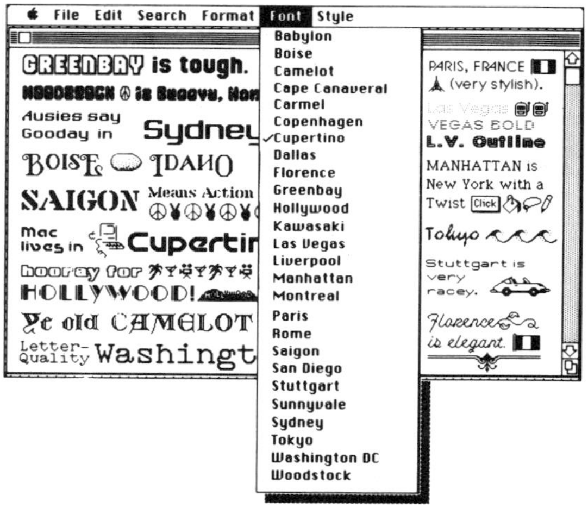

(MTK02) Mac the Knife, Vol. 2 (World Class Fonts)

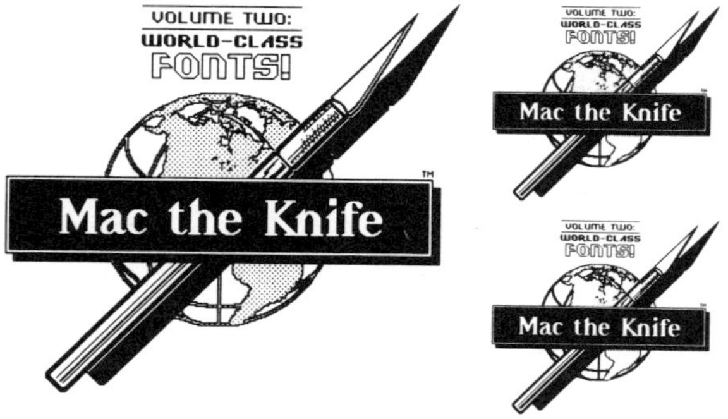

FIGURE 11–12 "Mac the Knife"— Clip-Art by Miles Computing

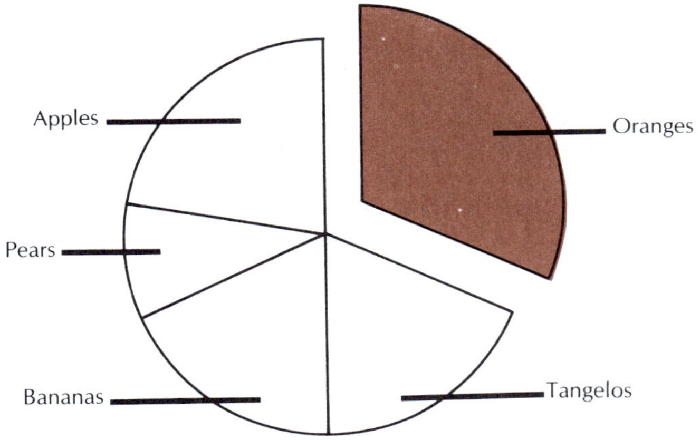

FIGURE 11–13
Exploded Pie Chart

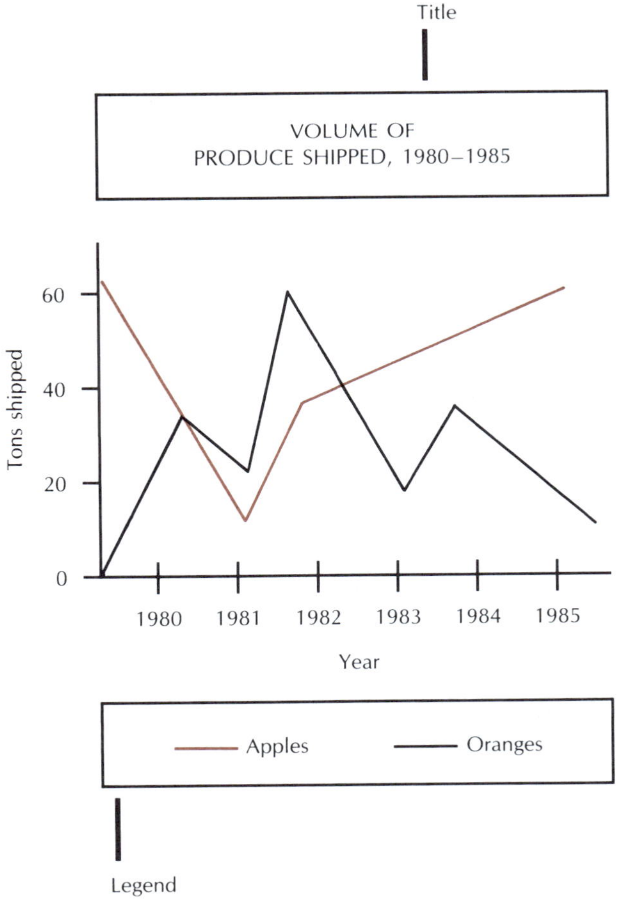

FIGURE 11–14 Chart with Titles and Legend

PAINT PROGRAMS

Paint programs provide a set of graphics tools for creating illustrations. Using an input device such as a mouse, an illustrator can use a paint program to create pictures of virtually anything, not just business charts and graphs. Paint programs give the user a space to work in and a menu of options. From the menu, the user can select a variety of tools that enter circles, squares, rectangles, ellipses, straight lines, filled-in shapes, text (with multiple fonts and type sizes), and patterns. Additional tools allow the user to manipulate the image. An optional screen grid moves all lines or text so that they're aligned with the grid. A zoom function allows the user to magnify a particular area for work on tiny details. Areas of the image can be selected for deletion, copying, or moving. Additional commands invert, shrink, or expand selected portions of the image.

COMPUTER-AIDED DESIGN (CAD)

Before graphics computers came along, preliminary sketches, design drawings, and production diagrams ate up huge portions of every company's production budget. And when an analysis of a new product showed the inevitable flaws, it was "back to the drawing board" — with the inevitable delays and added costs. It's no wonder **computer-aided design (CAD)** is one of the fastest-growing areas of computer applications. In brief, CAD allows an engineer or designer to create a production-quality drawing on the display screen and to modify it with ease until it's right. Even more sophisticated systems perform structural analyses of the designed parts (**computer-aided engineering** or **CAE**) and can also program machines to create them (**computer-aided manufacturing** or **CAM**).

Until recently, the computer-aided design field was dominated by expensive systems designed to work with mainframe and minicomputers. These systems cost as much as $600,000. Even so, from 1980 to 1984 the CAD market grew from $480 million to $1.8 billion, averaging 40 percent growth annually.[2] Now CAD has come to the personal computer, and a repeat of the mainframe CAD boom is under way. In 1983, manufacturers shipped only 1,900 CAD systems for personal computers. By 1985, the figure had risen to 32,000. By 1988, the figure will have rocketed to 205,000 packages annually.[3]

Personal computer CAD programs are intended for professionals in fields such as architecture, civil engineering, electrical engineering, mechanical engineering, and interior planning. They resemble the paint programs just discussed, but they're more sophisticated and precise in several ways. Indeed, according to one estimate, they offer approximately 70 to 80 percent of a mainframe CAD system's performance for about 10 percent of the cost.

Unlike paint programs, CAD software is designed for precision applications. A CAD program, therefore, can render an image so that it conforms to a precise scale. An airplane, for instance, can be drawn so that every inch on the screen equals precisely 350 inches on the actual aircraft. Another sophisticated feature of CAD software is the ability to render images in three dimensions. The image can be rotated on the screen, so that it may be viewed from any angle.

GRAPHICS HORIZONS

The coming generation of personal computers will combine fast microprocessors with high resolution, bit-mapped graphics displays. And if what's happening in mainframe and minicomputer graphics right now is any indication of what's to come, these new computers may change not only the way we work with knowledge but the way we acquire it as well.

Mainframe and minicomputers have sufficient power to simulate real-world events or processes using on-screen animation. Anyone who has played a computer video game has seen computer animation in action, but the systems we're talking about here are a world apart. They produce highly complex, highly detailed images that simulate equally complex and detailed processes in the real world. And the result is a major new resource for education. Flight simulators, for example, help pilots learn how to fly new, multi-million-dollar jetliners without risk and without consuming any fuel. Other large computer systems are simulating nature's behavior on the display screen, and they're helping scientists achieve a better understanding of complex natural phenomena.

As personal computers become more powerful and more capable of realistic simulation, the benefits for education will be enormous. Schools that cannot now afford expensive laboratory equipment will be able to buy graphics microcomputers programmed to simulate experiments in a chemistry or physics lab. Textbook concepts (such as the life cycle of a biological cell or the formation of a bell curve) will come to life on computer displays. Engineering students will see for themselves how much pressure can be applied to a girder before it deforms and causes a catastrophic structural collapse. Students, in other words, will be able to experience and perform what-if experiments on aspects of reality that they might otherwise only read about.

The prospects for personal computer graphics are exciting indeed, a point best made by the founder of computer graphics himself, Ivan E. Sunderland:

> I think of a computer display as a window on Alice's Wonderland in which a programmer can depict either objects that obey well-known natural laws or purely imaginary objects that follow laws he has written into his program. Through computer displays I have landed an airplane on the deck of a moving carrier . . . flown in a rocket at nearly the speed of light, and watched a computer reveal its innermost secrets.[4]

Computer graphics techniques, in sum, are extending not only our ability to improve how we communicate, but also our ability to learn about the world around us.

SUMMARY

Personal computer graphics hardware and software offer the same productivity and quality improvement advantages that word processing does. Just as a word processing program allows you to revise a document easily until it's just right, so too does a graphics package let you redo pictorial images until they're ready for printing.

Graphic images on computer screens are made up of thousands of tiny dots or pixels. To render objects realistically, the dots must be small and numerous enough to show details. The term *resolution* refers to a graphic device's ability to resolve, or make visible, the details in an image.

Personal computers tackle the display and manipulation of graphic images in two ways. The first approach is to provide the computer with a fixed set of alphabetic, numeric, and graphics characters. No other shapes or images can be displayed. If the user wishes to show pictorial images on the screen, they must be built up from the supplied characters. A computer designed to operate this way is said to operate in a *character mode.* The character mode prohibits the display of images that require elements other than those included in the character set, but it makes light demands on processing circuitry and speeds processing.

The second approach is to give the computer control over every picture element (pixel) on the display screen, so that each one can be switched on or off as required. In this mode, every pixel on the screen is represented by a bit stored in the video memory. The video memory, in other words, uses bits of information to map the screen image; so this approach is often called *bit-mapped graphics.* With this approach, any two-dimensional shape can be displayed. A computer designed to operate this way is said to operate in a *graphics mode.* Its advantages are significant. A computer operating in a graphics mode can display any two-dimensional image. Since the screen display isn't tied to a fixed set of characters, moreover, the computer can display foreign language characters and technical symbols with ease. Finally, graphics capabilities make it possible to design graphics-based user interfaces, making the computer easier for ordinary people to use. However, the graphics mode taxes microprocessors and slows down program execution.

Today's personal computers operate in the bit-mapped graphics mode, but improvements are needed in resolution. The new generation of superfast microprocessor chips will help speed program execution in the graphics mode. Tomorrow's personal computers may display one million pixels at a time.

Special graphics input devices — especially the graphics tablet, light pen, mouse, and digitizer — speed the entry of images into the computer. Graphics output devices — including the dot-matrix printer, laser printer, plotter, and image recorder — are all capable of producing high-quality output.

Like all application software, graphics software insulates you, the user, from the minutiae of low-level hardware operations so you can concentrate on your work. Personal computer packages for graphics include analytic graphics programs, presentation graphics programs, paint programs, and software for computer-aided design (CAD).

Analytic graphics packages are designed to transform numerical data into their graphic equivalents. To create a chart with an analytic graphics program, you'll begin with a *data series* — a list of numbers containing the information you want expressed in graphic form. Next, you'll choose the type of chart you want made. The program then constructs the chart for you, and displays a preliminary version of it on the screen. Data may be imported from a spreadsheet or data base management program, although integrated programs are preferable where data importation is frequent.

Presentation graphics packages often include analytic graphics capabilities; they can take a series of numbers and transform them into a chart or graph. But they also include the features necessary to prepare graphics for public presentations. These features include clip-art or image libraries, exploded pie charts, color enhancement, titles, and legends.

Paint programs provide a set of graphics tools for creating illustrations. Using an input device such as a mouse, an illustrator can use a paint program to create pictures of virtually anything.

Unlike paint programs, CAD software is designed for precision applications. A CAD program, therefore, can render an image so that it conforms to a precise scale. Another sophisticated feature of CAD software is the ability to render images in three dimensions.

KEY TERMS

analytic graphics package
bit-mapped graphics
categories
character generator
character mode
clip-art
computer-aided design (CAD)
computer-aided engineering (CAE)
computer-aided manufacturing (CAM)
computer graphics
data series
digitizer
exploded pie chart
frame buffer
graphics mode
graphics tablet
image library
image recorder
legend
light pen
multiple head pass
paint program
raster scan
values
X (category) axis
Y (values) axis

REVIEW QUESTIONS AND EXERCISES

1. In what way does personal computer graphics software offer advantages similar to those of word processing?
2. What is the technique used to display most personal computer graphic images? What is its major drawback?
3. Why is it that not all computers can display high-quality, detailed graphic images?
4. Why do graphics circuits have their own bank of memory chips?
5. Why are character mode video circuits generally less costly than graphics mode video circuits?
6. What advantage does the Macintosh have over the IBM PC when it comes to the display of graphic images?
7. What is the difference between an analytic graphics package and a presentation graphics package?
8. Name the functions of the x axis and y axis in a column chart.
9. What is the value of an integrated program that combines spreadsheet and graphics functions?
10. Why does Kathryn Alesandrini call presentation graphics a "two-edged sword"?
11. What is the advantage of creating engineering drawings on a computer?
12. What role might computer graphics play in future classrooms?

FOR FURTHER READING

Alesandrini, Kathryn. "Graphics That Dress for Success," *PC: The Independent Guide to IBM-Standard Personal Computing* (January 8, 1985).

Alperson, Jay. "Graphics: Before and After," *PC World* (June 1985).

Bauman, Verne. *Power Painting: Computer Graphics on the Macintosh* (New York: Bantam, 1985).

Bishop, Jack. "Charting Your Course on the PC," *PC: The Independent Guide to IBM-Standard Personal Computing* (January 8, 1985).

Cannon, T. M., and B. R. Hunt. "Image Processing by Computer," *Scientific American* (October 1981).

Dam, Andries van. "Computer Software for Graphics," *Scientific American* (September 1984).

Dunn, S. Thomas. "Into the Electronic Age: A Lasers-in-Graphics Preview," *American Printer* (July 1985).

Glau, Gregory R. *Business Graphics for the Macintosh* (Homewood, Ill.: Dow Jones-Irwin, 1985).

Hounsfield, Godfrey N. "Computed Medical Imaging," *Science* (October 3, 1980).

Hyman, Michael I. *Advanced IBM PC Graphics: The State of the Art* (New York: Brady, 1985).

Krummel, Larry. "Merging Text and Graphics: The Good, the Bad," *American Printer* (October 1983).

Lambert, Steve. *Presentation Graphics on the Apple Macintosh: How to Use Microsoft Chart to Create Dazzling Graphics for Professional and Corporate Applications* (Seattle: Microsoft Press, 1984).
Mar, Jerry. *MacGraphics for Business* (New York: Scott, Foresman, 1986).
Maran, Richard. *The Graphic Macintosh Book* (New York: CBS Educational and Professional Publishing, 1985).
Pfaffenberger, Bryan. *Business Communication in the Personal Computer Age* (Homewood, Ill.: Richard D. Irwin, 1987).
Raskin, Robin, and Tom Christopher. "PC Systems for Pie Chart Picassos," *PC: The Independent Guide to IBM-Standard Personal Computing* (January 8, 1985).
Stallings, Stephanie. "Design Tools for the PC," *PC: The Independent Guide to IBM-Standard Personal Computing* (October 1, 1985).
Whitted, Turner. "Some Recent Advances in Computer Graphics," *Science* (February 12, 1982).
Wilcox, David L. "The Boom in Business Graphics," *PC World* (May 1985).
Young, Jeffrey S. *Inside MacPaint: Sailing Through the Sea of Fatbits on a Single-Pixel Raft* (Seattle: Microsoft Press, 1985).

12 *Personal Computer Communications:* *Strategies for Computer Networking*

"Modern communications are rapidly shrinking our world to distanceless dihensions so far as the communications environment is concerned. . . . We are moving into electronic space. . . . We are on the cusp of something big."

Frederick Williams *The Communications Revolution*

A California doctor has reason to believe that the Information Age has begun: computer-based communications helped him save a life. Late one night, a patient of his developed a rare, but serious, postoperative complication, and standard intensive care procedures weren't working. The doctor sat down at his microcomputer, placed a computer call through the telephone system, and contacted a service that sells access to a huge data base of medical journal articles. In seconds, the doctor found a recently published article reporting a successful therapy for the complication. He phoned the hospital and instructed the intensive care unit to try the new therapy — and it worked.[1]

The California doctor's experience shows why so many experts believe, like Frederick Williams, that we're on the verge of something big. By providing a major new resource for communication, computers are putting people every-

where in all-but-instantaneous contact with the information and knowledge they need. This contact, even over vast distances, will become indispensable as the information explosion runs its course. As the Carnegie Corporation recently found in a major study of education for the Information Age, tomorrow's workers will need more than the knowledge they acquire in course work. That knowledge will quickly become obsolete. Like the California doctor, they'll also have to know "how to figure out what they need to know, where to get it, and how to make meaning out of it."[2] Computer use will become even more widespread as tomorrow's knowledge workers use computer-based communication as a fundamental tool for knowledge acquisition.

As a personal computer user, you've already put your hands on almost everything you need to take a trip in electronic space. This chapter tells you what you need to know to complete the journey.

Data communications is the catchall term for any transfer of information from one point to another, whether the transmission medium is a carrier pigeon or a Telstar satellite. Computer data communications fall into two categories: telecommunications, or connections via the telephone system, and **direct-wire communications** that link computers using high-speed direct cables.

TELECOMMUNICATIONS: AN INTRODUCTION

The telephone system provides a communications resource of incredible dimensions. At any time, anyone in the United States can pick up a telephone and, within seconds, connect with any of 175 million other telephones in the United States and millions more abroad. The number of potential interconnections has been estimated at six quadrillion (6×10^{15}). This mind-boggling flexibility is made possible by a capital investment of about $170 billion, which includes over 1 billion miles of transmission paths.[3]

If the phones at both ends of the line are replaced by properly equipped computers, a major new resource for data communications becomes available. Possessing a personal computer equipped for telecommunications could well be your ticket to the Information Age.

HARDWARE FOR TELECOMMUNICATIONS

The telephone system is reliable and extensive, but it was designed for the human voice, not computer data. Special equipment — an *asynchronous communications board,* an *RS–232C Serial Port,* and a *modem* — is needed to enable computers to communicate over the telephone lines.

The Asynchronous Communications Board. Communications within the computer's confines occur at high speeds because there's a wire for each of the eight bits in a byte. An entire byte can, therefore, be communicated simultaneously, with each bit traveling in synchrony along the parallel circuits (hence the term **parallel transmission**). And that's exactly why you can't hook your computer up to the telephone system without some extra equipment. Phone lines don't have eight wires. They can't send and receive eight bits simultaneously. In fact, they can only send and receive one bit at a time in a series (Figure 12–1). The **asynchronous communications board,** a special circuit board within your computer, converts the parallel data stream within your computer to the bit-after-bit **serial transmission** that the telephone system can handle.

At the board's heart is a tiny chip called the **Universal Asynchronous Receiver/Transmitter (UART).** Its main job, as its name indicates, is to *receive* serial transmissions and convert them so that the computer's parallel circuits can handle them, and to *transmit* serial data that's been converted from its parallel counterparts.

The term **asynchronous** in the UART's name gives you a good clue to another of its functions. In a parallel data transmission circuit, all eight bits in a byte arrive simultaneously, so there's no need for any special signal that tells the receiving device "That's a byte." What's more, the arrival and departure of data are synchronized by the heartbeat of the computer's clock, which pulses one million or more times per second. When data are transmitted serially, one bit after another, there's a problem: how does the receiving device know where one byte stops and the next begins? Worse, serial transmission occurs at much slower (and uneven) speeds. It's inherently asynchronous. The UART copes with this problem by inserting special bits in the transmission, called start and stop bits, which tell the receiving computer "Here's where a byte starts" and "Here's where a byte stops" (Figure 12–2).

The RS–232C Serial Port. **The RS–232C serial port,** a data channel into and out of the computer, is a standardized input/output connector designed to facilitate connections between a wide variety of computers, printers, and modems. The RS–232C standard is controlled by the Electronic Industries Association (EIA), and it grew out of collaboration in the late 1960s between EIA, Bell Laboratories, and manufacturers of telecommunications equipment. It's one of the few things about personal computers that's reasonably standardized.

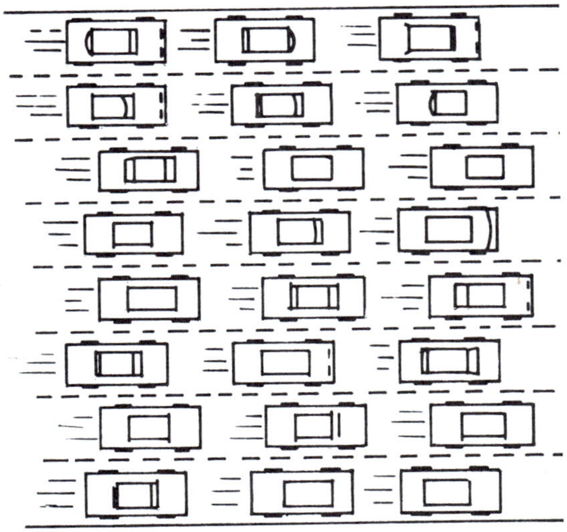

Parallel wiring within the computer allows large volumes of data to travel simultaneously at high speed, just as traffic does on an eight-lane freeway.

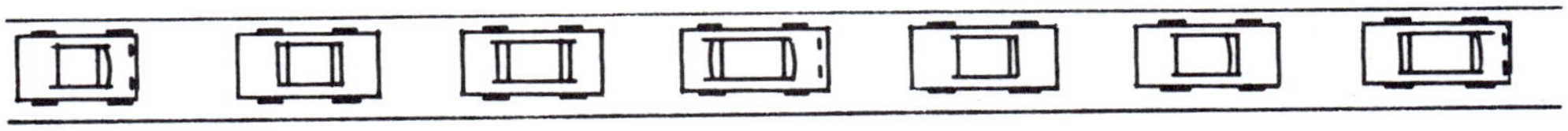

Serial wiring of ordinary telephone lines forces bits of data to travel in a series, one after the other; result is reduced volume of data transmitted and slow speed, just as traffic is held up on a one-lane road.

FIGURE 12–1 Parallel vs. Serial Wiring

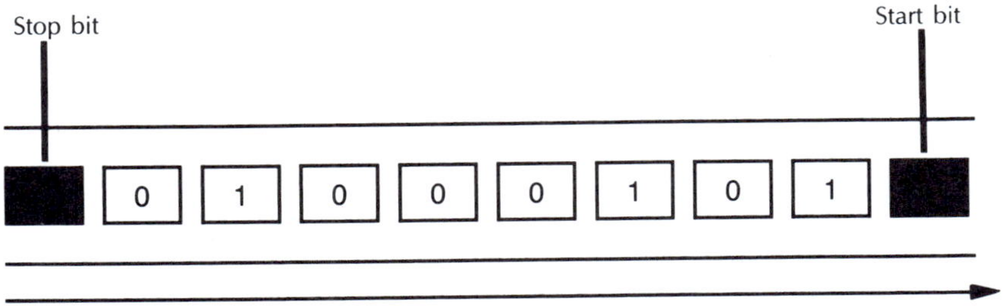

FIGURE 12–2 Start and Stop Bits

The Modem. Just because the data format has been converted from a parallel transmission to an asynchronous serial one doesn't mean the telephone lines are ready for it. The signals coming out of the RS–232C port are still *digital* signals: they're all-or-nothing pulses that have little in common with the kind of information that normally flows over telephone wires. Indeed, the telephone system isn't very good at transmitting unmodified digital information accurately. Here's why. It is designed for the human voice, which produces a remarkably complex configuration of sound frequencies that oscillate between 300 and 4,000 cycles per second. The system is designed to encode, transmit, and decode electrical versions of the human voice, with its particular frequency range and complex patterning. To transmit digital information accurately, then, you need an additional device that transforms the digital signals coming out of the computer into a form that the phone system was designed to handle.

That's exactly what a **modem** (*mo*dulator-*dem*odulator) is for. The modem takes the digital signals coming out of the computer and converts them (or *modulates* them) into the electrical equivalent of warbles that oscillate between 1,050 and 2,250 cycles per second, smack dab in the center of the human vocal range (Figure 12–3). Like the asynchronous communications board, the modem is also a device not only for transmitting but also for receiving. When it receives properly modulated signals coming over a telephone line, it *demodulates* them and transforms them back into their digital equivalent.

FIGURE 12–3 Hardware for Communication via the Telephone System

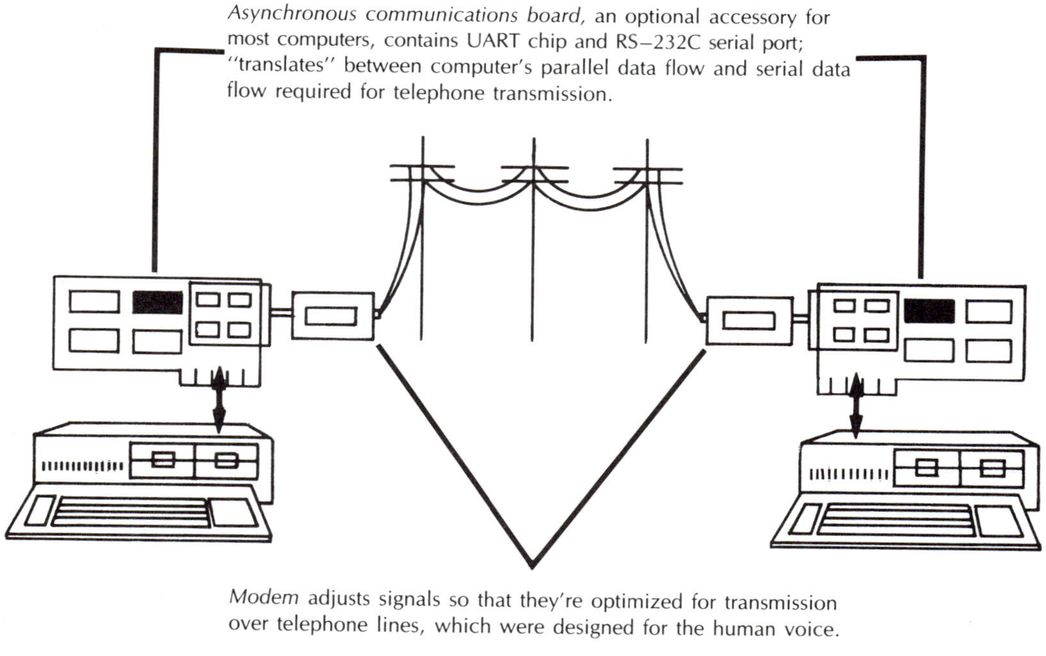

Not all modems, however, can transmit and receive simultaneously. A **half-duplex** modem, like a citizen's band radio, can only do one thing at a time. Such modems are quite satisfactory for simple, remote terminals, to which data flow in only one direction. **Full-duplex** modems, which are needed for two-way data communication, can receive and transmit data at the same time. Personal computer users will select full-duplex modems.

Modems vary, too, in the speed with which they can transmit and receive data. Modem transmission speeds are measured in **bauds,** a measurement that's a survival from the age of the telegraph. The term refers to the number of signals (or in digital terms, bits) transmitted each second.

A *300 baud modem* transmits information at speeds up to about 350 to 400 words per minute, which is quite slow. It could take a 300 baud modem an hour to transmit (or receive) a document of appreciable length. Offsetting the slow speed, however, is the low price and the fact that, at roughly 30 characters per second, you can read the incoming data on the screen.

A *1,200 baud modem* transmits information at speeds up to about 2,000 words per minute. A 1,200 baud modem is highly desirable when you're working with long-distance telecommunications or online data base services, but the initial cost is higher.

A *2,400 baud modem* transmits information at speeds of up to about 4,000 words per minute. These 2,400 baud modems, although expensive, will become widely used among professional and business users; savings on telephone and online service charges quickly repays the additional expense.

The earliest personal computer modems were **acoustic couplers,** or modems designed to receive a telephone handset on molded rubber cups (Figure 12–4). The acoustic coupler converts the digital data stream to analog sounds, which the headset picks up and transmits. Prone to error, acoustic couplers are still valuable for portable computers, since it's not always possible to find a phone jack. Most of today's modems, however, are **direct-connect modems** that plug directly into a modular telephone jack.

The same microprocessor intelligence that made personal computers possible is improving computer peripherals. Modems are no exception. Today's popular modems are **intelligent** or **smart modems;** a built-in microprocessor chip controls the modem's functions. Intelligent modems can be set up, for example, to answer incoming calls automatically or dial distant computers at regular intervals.

VALUE-ADDED NETWORKS

Long-distance data communications often travel the bulk of their journey over special, high-speed communication channels specially designed for computer data. These channels are maintained by companies called **value-added networks.**

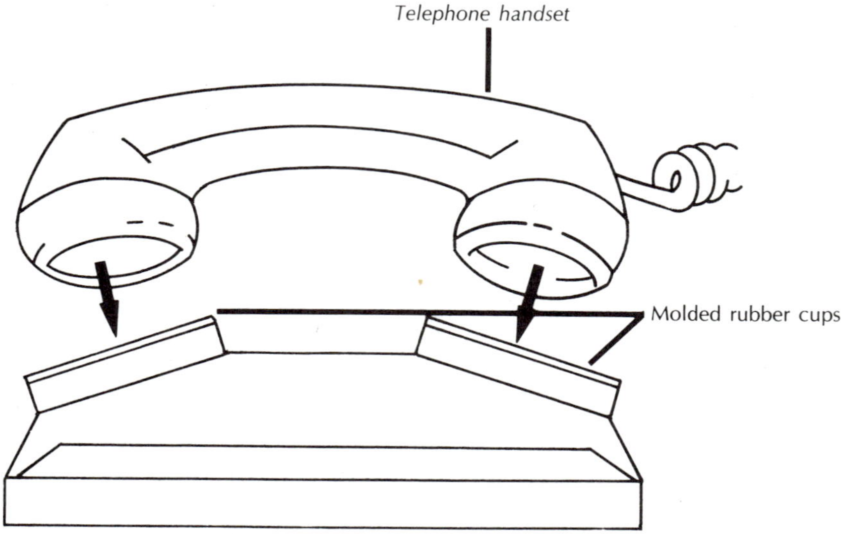

FIGURE 12–4 Acoustic Coupler Modem

These networks, such as Telenet and TYMNET, "add value" (compared to ordinary telephone services) because they use high-speed transmission techniques and provide advanced error correction. In most large and middle-sized cities, a personal computer user can gain access to a value-added network by dialing a local telephone number.

Value-added networks are often called **packet-switching networks** after the way they send and receive data. Data are broken up into units (**packets**) of 128 characters, which are then transmitted across the network at very high speeds. Along the way, a traveling packet may follow one of several alternative routes; the service will switch to the one that's working best at the moment of transmission. Aside from ordinary telephone cables and high-speed, private cables, this route may include the following communication channels (Figure 12–5):

Microwave Relay. Microwaves are high-frequency waves that travel in straight lines through the atmosphere. They must be captured and relayed every 30 to 35 miles because they cannot bend with the curvature of the earth.

Satellite Relay. Communication satellites, positioned in stationary orbits thousands of miles above the earth, can be used to relay microwaves across continents and oceans (Figure 12–6).

Fiber Optics. Fiber optics technology uses hair-thin filaments of light-conducting material to carry huge amounts of digital data.

As the user of a value-added service, you needn't worry about the details of just how your message reaches its destination. To contact or **log on** to a

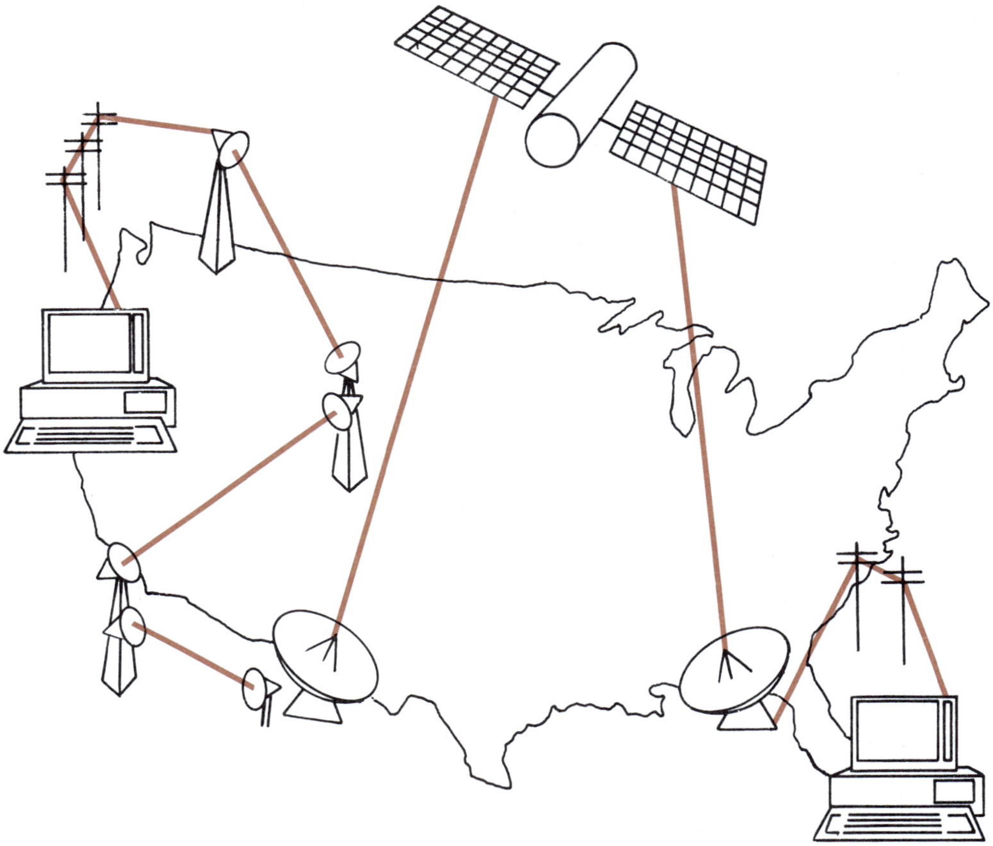

FIGURE 12–5 Alternative Routings of Data via Packet-Switching Network

distant information service, for example, you use your computer to dial the network's local number. The network's computer answers the phone and asks you where you'd like to call. After naming the information service you want and pressing the RETURN key, the network establishes the connection in an instant, and you're ready to go.

SOFTWARE FOR COMMUNICATIONS

Communications software organizes a personal computer system (including the asynchronous communications board, the RS–232C port, and the modem) for data communications. Telecommunications applications require that you use a communications program.

FIGURE 12–6
Communications Satellite

Types of Communications Software. Two kinds of communications programs are available for personal computers:

Dumb terminal emulation programs transform your computer into a device that, electrically speaking, is indistinguishable from the telecommunications-based remote workstations (or terminals) you've probably seen working with mainframe computer systems. When the program is loaded, your computer becomes a standard, "vanilla" terminal, so that anything typed at the keyboard will be displayed on the screen and sent out through the computer's serial port. The messages received from the distant computer will be shown on the display screen. These are basic terminal functions. Dumb programs, however, ignore your computer's processing power and storage capabilities. You cannot capture the incoming data to disk or print it.

Smart communications programs take advantage of your computer's processing, storage, and printing capabilities. They permit you to capture on disk (or, to use a synonym, **download**) the information that's coming in via the serial port. You may also prepare letters or other documents prior to an online session, and send them (that is, **upload** them). Other features include **automatic log on** (automatic execution of all steps necessary to achieve a connection with a distant computer), remote control (automatic answering of incoming calls with control placed in the hands of the calling

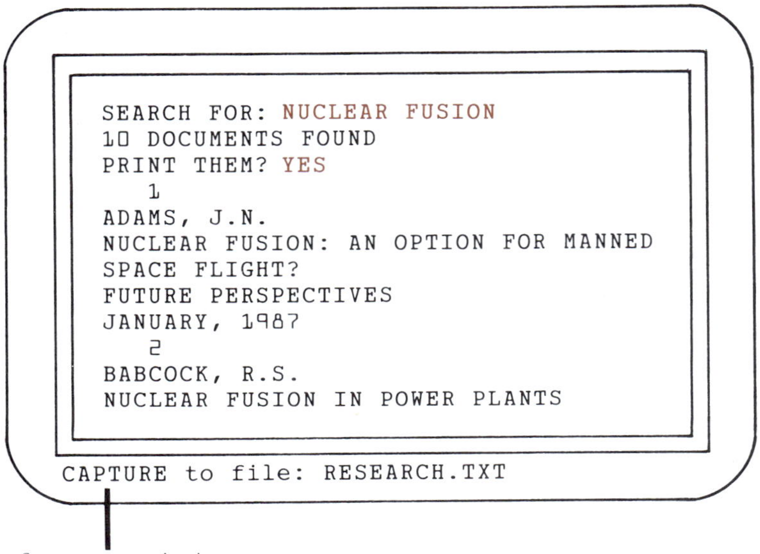

Smart communication program can capture retrieved data to disk.

FIGURE 12–7 Smart Communications Program

computer), and switching between data and voice communication (Figure 12–7).

Error Correction. As you know only too well from your telephone experience, phone lines are often noisy. Other conversations, static, and other disturbances can corrupt the data stream, causing errors. Fortunately, **communications protocols,** or standards for data communication interchange, include procedures for automatically correcting a high proportion of these noise-induced errors. The most commonly used communications protocol is the XMODEM protocol, which was created — and placed in the public domain — by a personal computer hobbyist named Ward Christiansen. All personal computer communications programs are based on the XMODEM protocol. That means, therefore, that any two such computers running virtually any communications program can exchange files and programs with each other via telecommunications links.

TELECOMMUNICATIONS APPLICATIONS

Telecommunications applications for personal computers include *electronic mail, bulletin boards, computer conferencing, telecommuting,* and *online bibliographic data base research.*

ELECTRONIC MAIL

Electronic mail refers broadly to the transmission, storage, and reception of letters, memos, and other documents via computer media. Electronic mail is a one-way, one-to-one form of communication; a message travels in one direction from a sender to a receiver (Figure 12–8).

In its simplest form, electronic mail involves only two computers, linked via direct connections in a local area network or via the telephone system (**point-to-point electronic mail**). The major disadvantage of point-to-point electronic mail is that the timing of the transmission has to be carefully coordinated. An auto-answer modem, to be sure, simplifies the process, but the receiver still has to know roughly when the transmission is coming so that the computer and modem will be ready.

A commercial variant is **point-storage-point electronic mail,** in which a commercial vendor provides massive storage facilities. Subscribers equipped with their own computers or computer terminals send messages to the vendor, who stores them until the recipient calls into the system. On contacting the vendor, a participant first sees a list of messages addressed to him or her, and may choose to read or delete them. The participant sends mail to others by typing the message and then specifying to whom it should be sent.

Point-storage-point electronic mail solves the problem of timing the reception (Figure 12–9). Instead of uploading the material directly to the receiver, you send it to an electronic mail service that stores it in its computer's auxiliary memory. The receiver's computer then contacts the electronic mail service (at the receiver's convenience) and, when the receiver logs on, the service displays a message: "Mail waiting." A few keystrokes send the document on its way through the telephone lines, and the transmission is completed.

FIGURE 12–8 Electronic Mail Provides a One-way Information Transfer

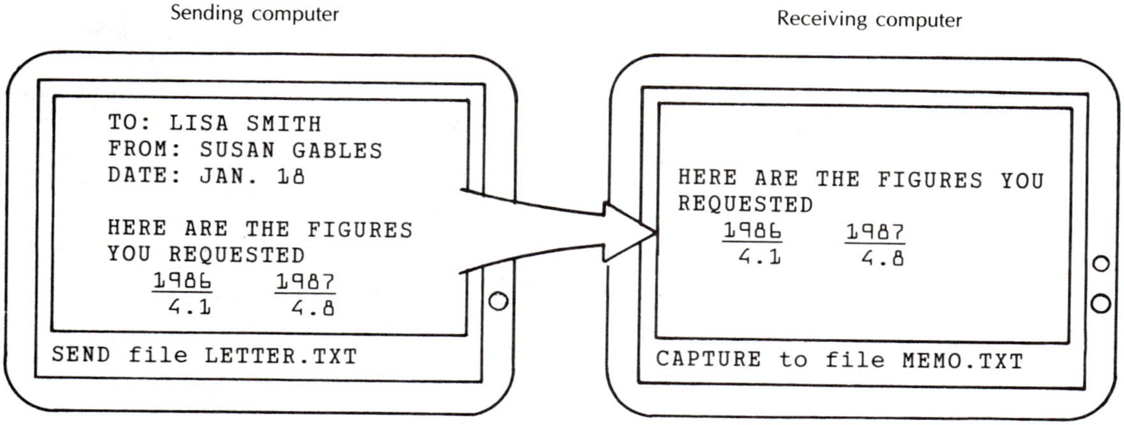

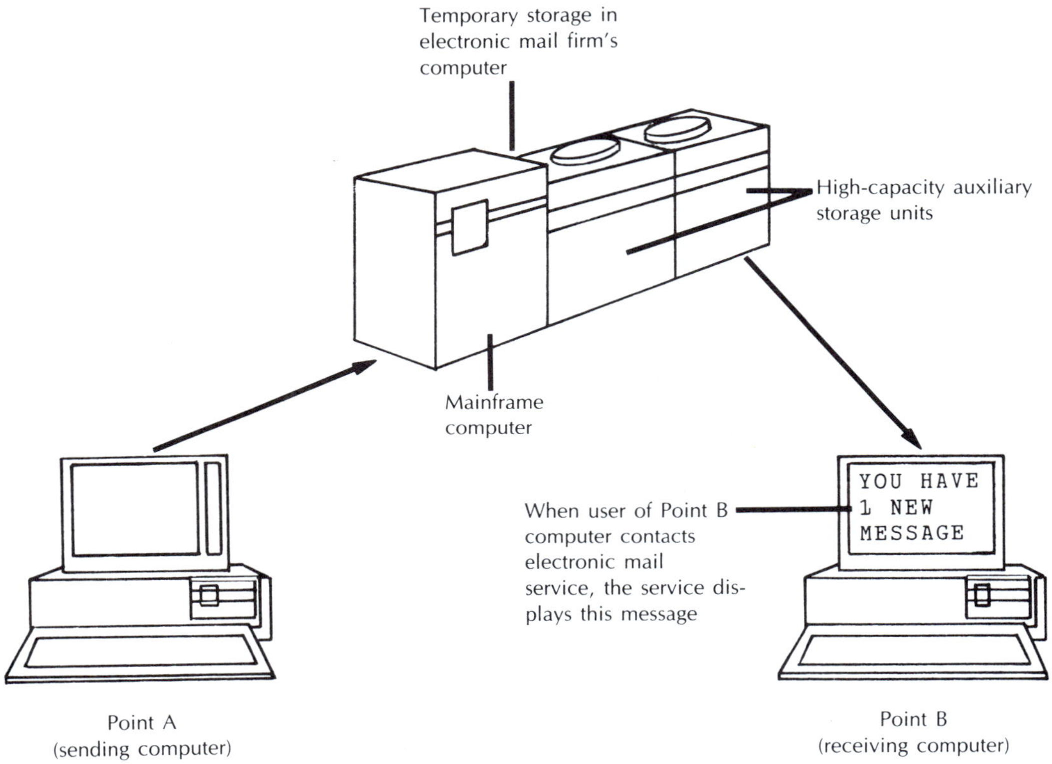

FIGURE 12–9 Point-Storage-Point Electronic Mail

The use of electronic mail services is becoming increasingly widespread in business, and for the following reasons:

Transferring Information in One Direction. In contrast to a telephone conversation, electronic mail allows only a one-way transfer of information. That rules out electronic mail for many applications, including informal chatting, contract negotiation, or sales communications. But many business communications — especially those between management and staff — are essentially one-way transfers of information ("Raise the price of Model 101 by 15 percent, effective July 1").

Avoiding Telephone Tag. For one-way transfers of information, electronic mail is far superior to the telephone: chances are much better that you'll get your message through. According to one estimate, about 70 percent of all business telephone calls fail to connect with their target. The result is telephone tag. The person you called calls back but you're out; you return the call but he's out, and so on.

Rapid Transmission. Suppose you've just written a twenty-page report in your New York office, and the Los Angeles branch must have it tomorrow morning. What's the fastest way? An express mail service? Wrong! It's electronic mail.

These advantages have led to widespread acceptance of this new medium. In 1984, commercial electronic mail firms such as Western Union, General Electric, and MCI Mail sent more than 100 million electronic mail messages through their computers. Because the cost of electronic mail services is dropping rapidly, industry analysts expect continued growth in the volume of electronic mail. With your personal computer skills, you'll be well positioned to take advantage of this new communication channel.

Electronic mail services are provided by several firms, including **information utilities** such as The Source, CompuServe, and Delphi (Table 12–1). Information utilities are companies that sell public access to huge mainframe computer systems whose auxiliary memories are loaded with information of public interest. They provide personal computer users with a wide variety of services, including up-to-the-minute stock quotes, special interest group (SIG) conferences, current news, home banking, and computer shopping (Figure 12–10).

TABLE 12–1 Electronic Mail Services

CompuServe	Electronic mail services offered in addition to investment information and material of interest to personal computer hobbyists (5000 Arlington Centre Boulevard, P.O. Box 20212, Columbus, OH 43220).
Delphi	Electronic mail services offered in addition to investment information and material of interest to personal computer hobbyists (General Videotex Corporation, 3 Blackstone Street, Cambridge, MA 02139).
EasyLink	Major vendor of electronic mail services; also provides access to FYI News Service (Western Union Telegraph Co., One Lake Street, Upper Saddle River, NJ 07458).
ECHO	This new entrant in the electronic mail sweepstakes offers lower rates (4739 Alla Road, Marina Del Rey, CA 90291).
MCI Mail	Major vendor of electronic mail services; also provides access to Dow-Jones News/Retrieval Service (Box 1001, 1900 M St., N.W., Washington, D.C. 20036).
The Source	Electronic mail services offered in addition to investment information and material of interest to personal computer hobbyists (Source Telecomputing Corporation, 1616 Anderson Rd., McLean, VA 22102).

```
                 <<MAIN MENU>>

    Conference                  News
    Entertainment               Shop-by-Computer
    Financial Services          Sports
    Movie Reviews               Weather

Choose one: <<C, E, F, M, N, SHOP, SPORTS, W>>? F
```

FIGURE 12–10
Information Service Main Menu

BULLETIN BOARDS

Electronic mail, whether point-to-point or point-storage-point, involves just two people: the sender and receiver. A computer **bulletin board,** in contrast, provides electronic tools that one person can use to send a message to many people (Figure 12–11). Bulletin boards are variants of electronic mail systems that allow

FIGURE 12–11
Bulletin Board Message

```
     TO: ALL
   FROM: JANICE JENNINGS
SUBJECT: DATA BASE MANAGEMENT CLASSES

THE CORPORATE INFORMATION CENTER, LOCATED IN
ROOM 172 OF THE PARKER COMPLEX, ANNOUNCES
A NEW SERIES OF OUR POPULAR COURSES ON
MICROCOMPUTER DATA BASE MANAGEMENT. STOP
BY FOR REGISTRATION SOON.
```

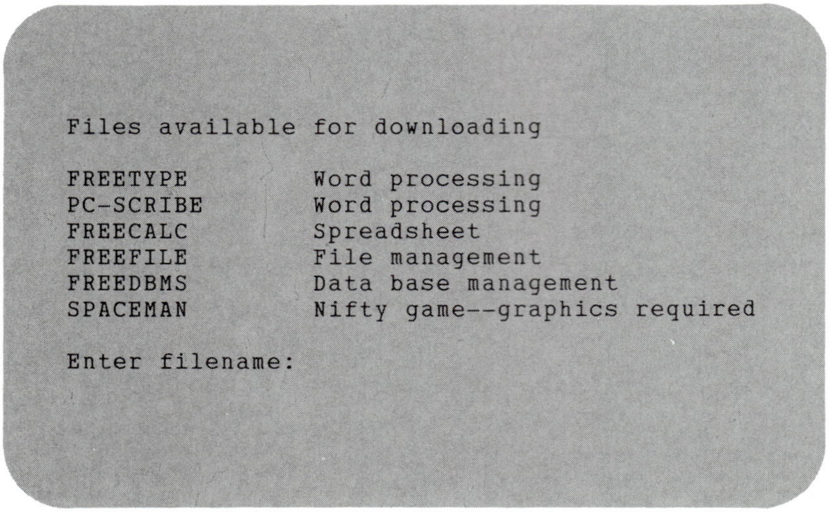

FIGURE 12–12 Public-Domain Software Menu on Bulletin Board System (BBS)

for public mailboxes, that is, electronic mailboxes that are publicly accessible and may be read by any participant.

Personal computer-based **bulletin board systems (BBS)** can be set up by anyone who has a personal computer, a spare telephone line, an auto-answer modem, and the necessary software. Usually started by hobbyists, bulletin board systems address the concerns of computer hobbyists, amateur programmers, and people who share special interests. In addition to electronic mail and bulletin boards, they offer downloading of **public domain software** — software that programmers have deliberately refrained from copyrighting (Figure 12–12).

COMPUTER CONFERENCING

Computer conferencing goes the computer bulletin board one step better: it provides a way for many people to communicate with one another simultaneously. Conferences are an important part of professional and managerial activity. Every day, about 20 million business conferences are held — but a high proportion of them don't really require that all the participants sit down in the same room (Figure 12–13). According to one estimate, as many as 60 percent of them could be handled by a teleconference, a special telephone call that links several people.

Ordinary meetings and teleconferences will continue to meet most business needs, but computer technology has provided a new alternative: the **computer conference** (Figure 12–14). A computer conference uses, as a communications

FIGURE 12–13 Appletalk Personal Network

```
DAVIS

The committee on new projects
recommends we open the
Fernville branch. What do
you think?

==============================================
MCINTIRE                 | ROBBINS
                         |
OK, the sales            | I think we need
forecast looks           | more data on
good.                    | local economic
                         | conditions.
                         |
```

FIGURE 12–14 Computer Conference

medium, computers linked by data communications. Conference coordination is usually handled by an electronic mail or information utility, whose computers have the necessary storage and processing capacities. In a computer conference, several people participate at once (although not everyone has to be sitting in front of a terminal at the same time). The most recent messages by participants are instantly available on all the display screens in the conference.

The chief advantage of a computer conference over a teleconference is that lengthy textual materials can be read and discussed by all participants. In addition, the host computer (the central computer on which the conference is taking place) compiles a complete written record of the conference. When the goal of the conference is to produce or modify a written document (such as a technical report or a court brief), computer conferencing is an excellent choice.

Information utilities such as The Source, CompuServe, and Delphi make private computer conferences available to their subscribers. The person who sets up the conference establishes a list of invited participants; no other persons can gain access to the conference or see the document it creates.

TELECOMMUTING

The availability of electronic mail, information utilities, and computer conferencing — coupled with the widespread use of personal computers — has made it possible for increasing numbers of people to avoid the daily trip to the office. Instead of reporting for work each morning, an employee can spend at least part of the work week at home. Work assignments, memos, and completed documents can flow back and forth via the computer instead of the office mail system.

Telecommuting, as this new work pattern is called, is slowly gaining in popularity. According to a 1986 estimate, some 2 to 3 million salaried employees work at least a full day or more per week at home. Some experts believe the figure will rise to 10 million by 1990. If telecommuting becomes widespread, it could produce major savings for the economy; a 12.5 percent reduction in automobile commuting would be enough to free the United States from dependence on foreign oil.

Telecommuting, to be sure, isn't for everyone. It's best suited to self-motivated professionals whose work (unlike that of salespeople and managers) does not depend on face-to-face contact. Moreover, some people find it hard to avoid the distractions of the home — children, stereos, refrigerators, neighbors, television. And the office has its advantages. Contact with people who share your goals is stimulating. Even the staunchest advocates of telecommuting believe that occasional trips to the office are needed.

ONLINE BIBLIOGRAPHIC DATA BASE RESEARCH

Suppose you've just been handed a work assignment by your boss, who's interested in getting some perspective on the decline in the synthetic fuels industry. You're instructed to go to the nearest college library and make a list of every article on that subject that's appeared within the past 5 years in five major newspapers: the *New York Times*, the *Washington Post*, the *Christian Science Monitor*, the *Los Angeles Times*, and the *Wall Street Journal*. Big job, isn't it? Guess again. All the information you need is accessible via telecommunications, and you can do the job in 15 or 20 minutes. You can make use of an **online data base vendor,** a firm that sells telecommunications access to computer-readable data bases (Table 12–2). Many of these data bases correspond to the bibliographic indexes shelved in major research libraries. One of them, NATIONAL NEWSPAPER INDEX, is precisely suited to your needs. After contacting the service and choosing the NATIONAL NEWSPAPER INDEX data base, you type in your search term ("synthetic AND fuel"). In seconds, your personal computer printer starts listing the references — dozens of them.

If this information gold mine sounds amazing to you, you're on the right track. Much of the world's knowledge — technical, scientific, commercial, and scholarly — is indexed in more than 2,800 of these data bases. Getting access to this knowledge, moreover, is surprisingly inexpensive, especially in comparison to the costs involved in traditional library research. Data base searching via telecommunications can save hours, days, and even weeks of library research time.

Online data base vendors have been in business for more than a decade. Until the personal computer came along, however, the only people who made use of this information resource were trained searchers and professional librarians. Now that personal computers have been diffused throughout society, millions of people have the equipment they need to access these services and retrieve knowledge for themselves. Online data base vendors, hoping to cultivate this market, have lowered their prices and made their user interfaces more friendly. Many people will continue to seek the assistance of trained searchers, but increasing numbers of personal computer users will attempt searches themselves.

Data Bases. The data bases available online are computer-readable collections of information in a single subject area, which may be highly focused (for example, bilingual education) or multidisciplinary (biomedicine and nursing). They fall neatly into two categories:

Reference Data Bases. **Reference data bases** refer the reader to the original source document. To do so effectively, individual data records contain complete **citations** (full bibliographic data, including author, title, name of journal, date of publication, etc.) and, usually, **abstracts** (summaries of the referenced

TABLE 12–2 Online Data Base Vendors

BRS	Major vendor of reference and source data bases with emphasis on academic information; requires user training and online charges are high (BRS Information Technologies, Inc., 1200 Route 7, Latham, NY 12110).
BRS/After Dark	Budget-priced nighttime/weekend version of BRS with a wide selection of BRS data bases, emphasizing academic information; user-friendly, menu-driven interface suitable for untrained users (BRS Information Technologies, 1200 Route 7, Latham, NY 12110).
BRS/Brkthru	Version of BRS that uses user-friendly, menu-driven software; like BRS, online charges are high, but are reduced nights and weekends (BRS Information Technologies, 1200 Route 7, Latham NY 12110).
Chase Econometrics	Major vendor of numerical source data in business and economics (486 Totten Pond Road, Waltham, MA 02154).
DIALOG Information Services	Largest vendor of reference data bases; more than 100 million items accessible. Expensive and requires training (3460 Hillview Avenue, Palo Alto, CA 94304).
Dow-Jones News/Retrieval Service	Major vendor of business information to personal computer users; inexpensive access to source data bases specializing in investment data (Dow Jones & Co., Inc., P.O. Box 300, Princeton, NJ 08540).
Knowledge Index	Budget, nighttime/weekend version of DIALOG; offers only a small subset of DIALOG data bases. Search software, which does not use menus, is a simplified version of DIALOG's (DIALOG Information Services, 3460 Hillview Avenue, Palo Alto, CA 94304).
I. P. Sharp Associates	Major vendor of source data bases; specializes in economic and financial statistics (Box 418, Exchange Tower, 2 First Canadian Place, Toronto, Canada MFX 1E3).
Lexis/Nexis	Source data bases specializing in the legal literature (Mead Data Central, 9393 Springboro Pike, Dayton, OH 45401).
NewsNet	Vendor of full-text, online versions of more than 100 industry newsletters (945 Haverford Road, Bryn Mawr, PA 19010).
ORBIT/SDS Information Service	Vendor of reference data bases with an emphasis on academic subjects; expensive and requires user training (SDC Information Service, 2500 Colorado Avenue, Santa Monica, CA 90406).

work's aims and chief conclusions) (Figure 12–15). Reference data bases are frequently computer-readable versions of print-based reference works, such as *Chemical Abstracts*, which can be found in the reference sections of college and university libraries.

Source Data Bases. **Source data bases** do not refer you elsewhere; they contain the complete data or full original text you're looking for. Source data bases include **numeric data bases** containing such data as commercial or investment statistics (Figure 12–16), and **full-text data bases** containing the full text of, say, an encyclopedia or a journal (Figure 12–17).

From the user's viewpoint, reference data bases seem like supersophisticated versions of the file management software discussed in Chapter 7. Bibliographic information is contained in data records (see Figure 12–15), which contain data fields. Search procedures make use of search terms and logical operators (Figure 12–18). If you are already familiar with a file management program, you will probably find it easy to master online searching too.

Data Base Producers vs. Data Base Vendors. Access to these data bases isn't often sold by **data base producers,** the people who create the data bases and add information to them. On the contrary, data base producers commonly lease this information to online data base vendors. Data base vendors sell access to dozens, even hundreds, of computer-readable data bases, making all of them

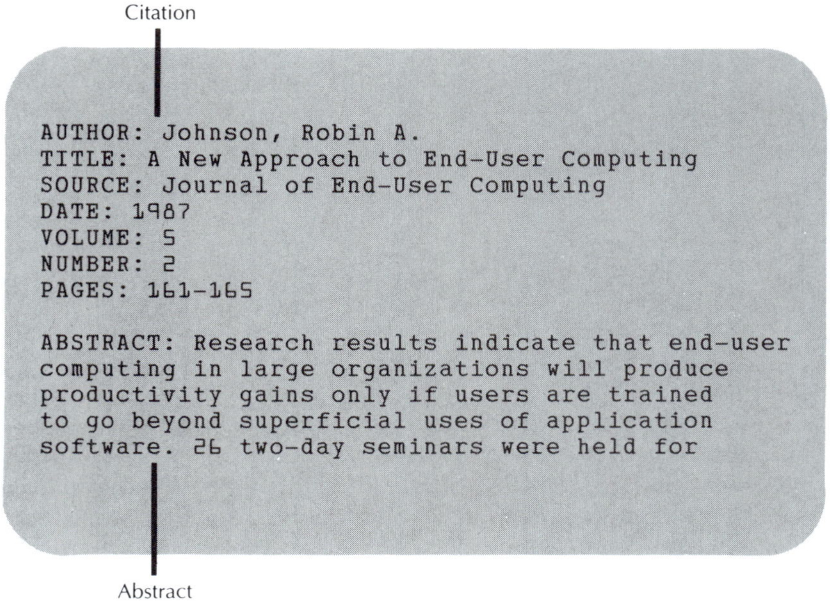

FIGURE 12–15 Online Data Base Data Record: Citation and Abstract

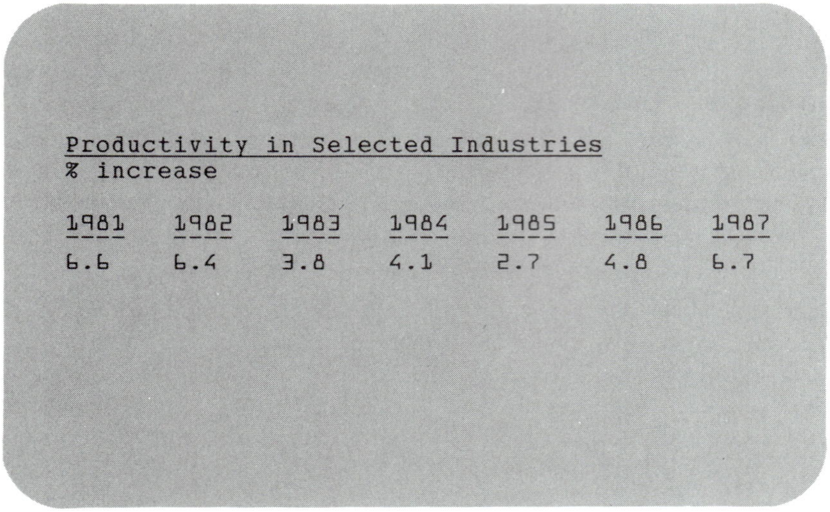

Productivity in Selected Industries
% increase

1981	1982	1983	1984	1985	1986	1987
6.6	6.4	3.8	4.1	2.7	4.8	6.7

FIGURE 12–16 Numeric Data Base

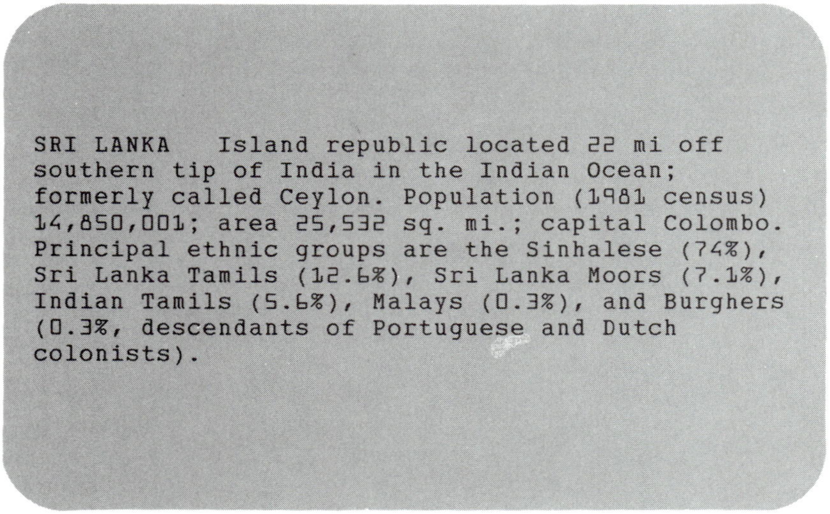

SRI LANKA Island republic located 22 mi off southern tip of India in the Indian Ocean; formerly called Ceylon. Population (1981 census) 14,850,001; area 25,532 sq. mi.; capital Colombo. Principal ethnic groups are the Sinhalese (74%), Sri Lanka Tamils (12.6%), Sri Lanka Moors (7.1%), Indian Tamils (5.6%), Malays (0.3%), and Burghers (0.3%, descendants of Portuguese and Dutch colonists).

FIGURE 12–17 Full-Text Data Base

available in what appears to the user as a single, huge system. These firms, such as Lockheed's DIALOG Information Service, maintain huge, ultrasophisticated host computers capable of storing up to 100 million or more data records. When you log on to DIALOG, any one of these 100 million records is available to you within seconds or minutes, even if you're sitting at a personal computer thousands of miles away.

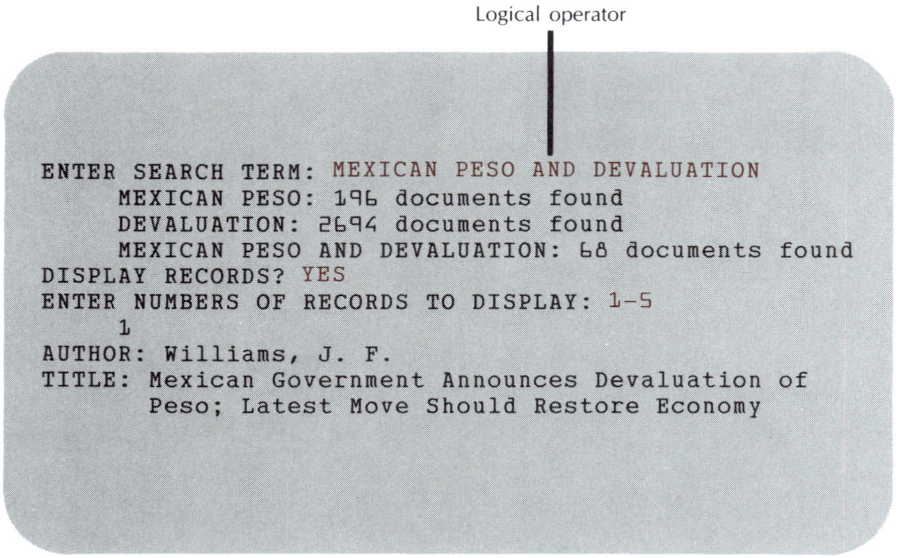

FIGURE 12–18 Search Procedure Using Logical Operator AND

Knowledge Index and BRS/After Dark. Online data base research is inexpensive in comparison to library research costs, but until the early 1980s online searching was still prohibitively expensive for most personal computer users. Search costs on systems such as DIALOG's average about a dollar per minute. The bulk of usage on these systems, however, occurs during normal business hours; the big computers lie all but unused at night and on weekends. Two of the major online data base vendors, DIALOG and BRS Information Technologies, realized that they had nothing to lose by opening budget-priced nighttime/weekend services for personal computers. And so Knowledge Index (DIALOG) and BRS/After Dark were born. Both offer a subset of the daytime service's data bases at about one-third the price (for a list of BRS/After Dark data bases, see Table 12–3). Further, their user interfaces are simplified (Knowledge Index) or menu-driven (BRS/After Dark) (Figure 12–19, page 363), so that untrained searchers can make productive use of them.

DIRECT-WIRE COMMUNICATIONS

Linking computers by direct cabling would seem to offer many advantages over telecommunications. Telecommunications, after all, take place at a snail's pace compared to the data transfer speeds that can be achieved with cables (often in excess of a megabyte of data per second). And for this reason, much effort

TABLE 12–3 BRS/After Dark Data Bases

ABI/INFORM (business)
ABLEDATA (resources for the disabled)
ABSTRACTS OF WORKING PAPERS IN ECONOMICS
ABSTRAX 400 (popular periodicals)
ACADEMIC AMERICAN ENCYCLOPEDIA (full text)
AGRICOLA (agriculture)
AMERICAN CHEMICAL SOCIETY JOURNALS ONLINE (full text of chemistry journals)
ASSOCIATION PUBLICATIONS IN PRINT
BILINGUAL EDUCATION BIBLIOGRAPHIC ABSTRACTS
BIOSIS PREVIEWS (biology)
BOOKS IN PRINT
CA/SEARCH (chemistry)
CATALYST: RESOURCES FOR WOMEN
DISC (microcomputers)
DISSERTATION ABSTRACTS
EDUCATIONAL RESOURCES INFORMATION CENTER
EDUCATIONAL TESTING SERVICE TEST COLLECTION
EXCEPTIONAL CHILD EDUCATION RESOURCES
FAMILY RESOURCES
HBR/ONLINE (full text of *Harvard Business Review*)
HEALTH PLANNING AND ADMINISTRATION
ICRS MEDICAL SCIENCES DATA BASE (full text of medical journals)
INSPEC (physics and computer science)
INSTITUTE OF ELECTRICAL ENGINEERS DATA BASE
INTERNAL REVENUE SERVICE PUBLICATIONS (full text)
INTERNATIONAL PHARMACEUTICAL ABSTRACTS
KIRK-OTHMER ENCYCLOPEDIA OF CHEMICAL TECHNOLOGY (full text)
LANGUAGE AND LANGUAGE BEHAVIOR ABSTRACTS
MANAGEMENT CONTENTS (business)
MATHFILE (mathematics)
MEDLARS (clinical medicine)
MENTAL MEASUREMENTS YEARBOOK
NATIONAL COLLEGE DATABANK
NATIONAL INFORMATION SOURCES ON THE HANDICAPPED
NATIONAL REHABILITATION INFORMATION CENTER
NATIONAL TECHNICAL INFORMATION SERVICE

(continued)

TABLE 12–3 (continued)

ONLINE MICRO-SOFTWARE DIRECTORY
ONTARIO EDUCATION RESOURCES INFORMATION SYSTEM
PATDATA (patents)
PRE-MED (current publications in clinical medicine)
PRE-PSYC (current publications in clinical psychology)
PSYCINFO (online version of *Psychological Abstracts*)
PUBLIC AFFAIRS INFORMATION SERVICE
RELIGION INDEX
RESOURCE ORGANIZATIONS AND MEETINGS FOR EDUCATORS
RESOURCES IN COMPUTER EDUCATION
RESOURCES IN VOCATIONAL EDUCATION
ROBOTICS INFORMATION
SCHOOL PRACTICES INFORMATION FILE
SOCIOLOGICAL ABSTRACTS
SOCSCISEARCH (*Social Science Citation Index*)
TEXAS EDUCATION COMPUTER COOPERATIVE
VOCATIONAL EDUCATION CURRICULAR MATERIALS

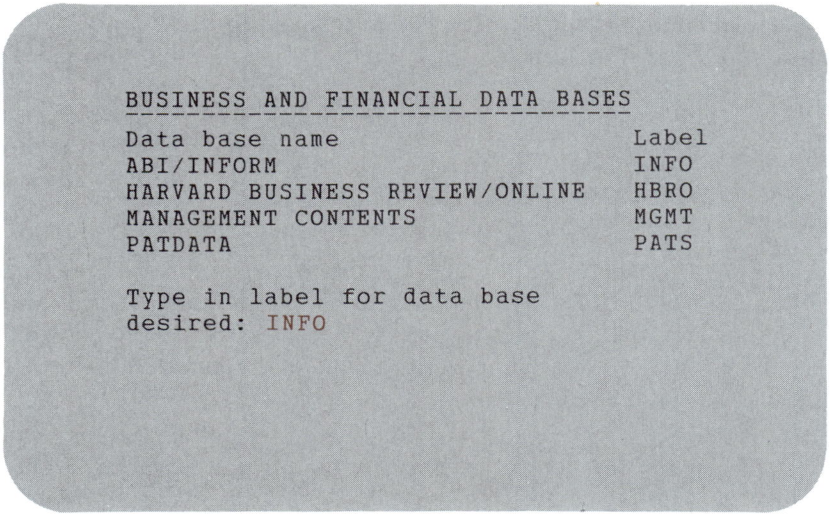

FIGURE 12–19 Menu-Driven User Interface (BRS/After Dark)

has been expended to create local area networks (systems that link a group of contiguous personal computers together) and micro-to-mainframe connections, which link an organization's many personal computers with its central mainframe computer. Progress in the development of direct-wire connections, however, has been slowed by lack of standardization and by technical problems.

LOCAL AREA NETWORKS

Local area networks (LANs) are networks of personal computers directly connected by high-speed cable links. They require special hardware apart from the cable connectors. Each computer in the network needs a special communications circuit board that gives it access to the special, high-speed communication system the network provides. The term *local area* is right on target: most LANs permit cable lengths of no more than several hundred feet or, at the extreme, half a mile. Within that range, networks of as many as several hundred personal computers have been achieved. Most, however, are small, linking five to twenty computers (Figure 12–20).

LANs vs. Timesharing Systems. LANs should be distinguished from the timesharing systems available with most mini- and mainframe computers. Timesharing systems permit many users — several hundred or more — to gain access to a big computer using a remote terminal. The terminal itself has no processing capabilities; it's just a way of communicating with the big computer, which may be positioned some distance away. Even though many people might be using the big computer at the same time, each user has the illusion of private access to the system and complete control over it. As more users access the computer, however, its performance degrades. LANs, in contrast, are linkages among full-fledged computers. Each station in the network has its own processing capabilities.

Rationales for LAN Installations. If every computer in a local area network has its own processing capabilities, what, then, is the point of the network? Three major rationales underlie the installation of most local area networks at this writing:

Sharing Expensive Peripherals. Many personal computer accessories, such as laser printers and high-capacity hard disks, are extremely expensive, and it's impossible to equip each computer in the network with all the desired accessories. When that's the case, a network permits several personal computer users to share a printer or disk drive.

Creating Local Electronic Mail Linkages. A local version of electronic mail becomes available for the network's participants. If the participants are members of a work group, a group of people who routinely cooperate with

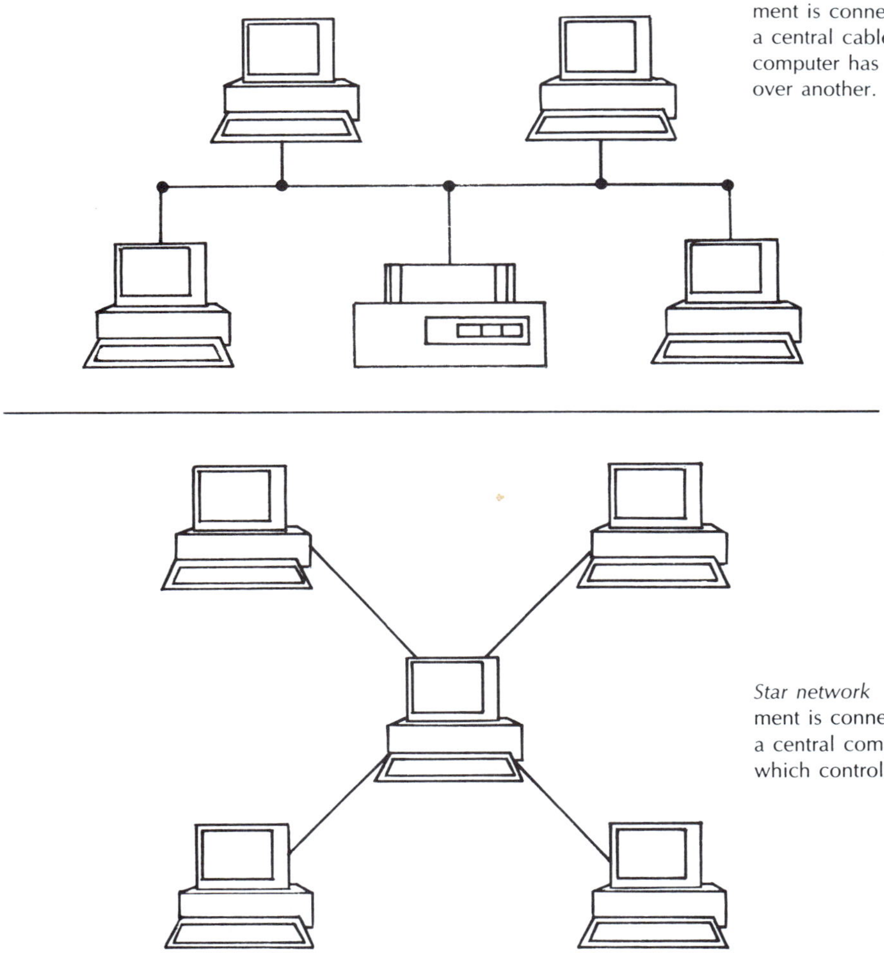

FIGURE 12–20 Two Alternatives in Local Area Network Design

each other, installing a local area network can speed and streamline the communication process among them considerably.

Creating Personal Computer-Based Transaction Processing Systems. Much of what business people do from day to day is to process transactions, such as sales or returns. In an office full of transaction workers, each equipped with a LAN-linked personal computer, much paperwork can be avoided. These workers can post the results of transactions to a shared data base directly, without having to retype the information for the company's records.

Sharing Software. Another common rationale for installing LANs is the prospect of sharing expensive programs. Most personal computer programs, however, are not designed for use by more than one person at a time.

Because many organizations find these advantages attractive, local area networks are increasing in popularity. In 1983, for instance, there were only 15,000 LAN installations; by 1985, the number had quadrupled.[4] Growth would probably occur even more quickly were a single LAN system to emerge as the standard. At this writing, the market was divided among dozens of competing, mutually incompatible systems. Many observers believe that IBM's recently introduced local area network will become the standard, as so many IBM products have in the past (including the IBM Personal Computer).

MICRO-TO-MAINFRAME CONNECTIONS

According to a recent study by the consulting firm Future Computing, by 1989 more than 28 million personal computers will be at work in business settings. And 76 percent of Fortune 2000 companies want to connect their personal computer with company mainframe computers.[5] Why all the excitement about the micro-to-mainframe connection? In many companies, you'll find personal computers working in offices where mainframe terminals are also present. That's a waste of space, of course, but it's a waste in other ways, too. An industry observer recalls seeing one employee reading sales figures off the mainframe terminal while another typed the figures, one by one, into a personal computer spreadsheet! Linking the personal computer directly with the mainframe would solve that problem, and many others as well.

Unfortunately, as many companies are finding out, achieving the micro-to-mainframe link isn't easy. Special equipment is required, usually in the form of an optional circuit board, cabling, and devices that translate between microcomputer and mainframe data formats. And once the electronic connection is established, another problem emerges: personal computer and mainframe programs may not be able to exchange data. Solving these problems may require a new generation of personal computer and mainframe software. There's every indication, however, that these problems will soon be solved. Micro-to-mainframe connections will become widespread. And when they do, the personal computer will have fulfilled its potential of providing individuals with a window on the entire world of computing.

SUMMARY

Data communications is the catchall term for any transfer of information from one point to another. Computer data communications fall into two categories: *telecommunications,* or connections via the telephone system, and *direct-wire connections* that link computers using high-speed direct cables.

Computer-based telecommunications make use of the telephone system, which is incredibly extensive and flexible. However, the system was designed for the human voice, not computer data. Special equipment is needed to enable computers to communicate over the telephone lines. This equipment (asynchronous communications board, RS–232C serial port, and a modem) translates between the computer's internal data flow (which occurs in parallel using digital signals) and the requirements of telephone lines (which transmit analog signals in series).

Most long-distance data communications are handled by value-added networks (often called packet-switching networks). These networks, such as Telenet and TYMNET, "add value" (as compared to ordinary telephone services) because they use high-speed transmission techniques and provide advanced error correction. In most large and middle-sized cities, a personal computer user can gain access to a value-added network by dialing a local telephone number.

Communications software organizes a personal computer system for data communications. Two kinds of communication programs are available for personal computers: dumb terminal emulation programs and smart communications programs. Dumb terminal emulation programs transform your computer into a device that, electrically speaking, is indistinguishable from the telecommunications-based remote workstations. Anything typed at the keyboard will be displayed on the screen and sent out through the computer's serial port. The messages received from the distant computer will be shown on the display screen. Dumb programs, however, ignore your computer's processing power and storage capabilities. Smart communications programs take advantage of your computer's processing, storage, and printing capabilities. They permit you to capture on disk or print the information that's coming in via the serial port.

Communications protocols provide standards for data communication interchange. Communications programs that use them can automatically correct a high proportion of noise-induced errors. The most commonly used communications protocol is the XMODEM protocol, on which all personal computer communications programs are based.

Telecommunications applications for personal computers include electronic mail, bulletin boards, computer conferencing, telecommuting, and online bibliographic data base research.

Electronic mail refers broadly to the transmission, storage, and reception of letters, memos, and other documents via computer media. Electronic mail is a one-way, one-to-one form of communication. In its simplest form, it involves only two computers, linked via direct connections in a local area network or via the telephone system (point-to-point electronic mail). A commercial variant is *point-storage-point* electronic mail, in which a commercial vendor provides massive storage facilities. Electronic mail speeds one-way transfers of information and avoids telephone tag.

A bulletin board provides a way for one person to send a message to many people. Bulletin boards are variants of electronic mail systems that allow for public mailboxes, that is, electronic mailboxes that are publicly accessible and may be read by any participant.

Computer conferencing provides a way for many people to communicate with one another simultaneously. In a computer conference, several people participate at once (although not everyone has to be sitting in front of a terminal at the same time). The most recent messages by participants are instantly available on all the display screens in the conference. Lengthy textual materials can be read and discussed by all participants. In addition, the host computer compiles a complete written record of the conference.

Telecommuting, or working at home and using telecommunications to communicate with the office, is slowly gaining in popularity. It could produce major savings for the economy, but it isn't for everyone. It's best suited to self-motivated professionals whose work (unlike hat of salespeople and managers) does not depend on face-to-face contact.

Online data base services sell telecommunications access to computer-readable data bases. The data bases available online are computer-readable collections of information in a single subject area, which may be highly focused (for example, bilingual education) or multidisciplinary (biomedicine and nursing). They fall into two categories. Reference data bases refer the reader to the original source document. Such data bases are frequently computer-readable versions of print-based reference works, such as *Chemical Abstracts*, which can be found in the reference sections of college and university libraries. Source data bases do not refer you elsewhere; they contain the complete data or full original text you're looking for. Such data bases include *numeric data bases* containing such data as commercial or investment statistics, and *full-text data bases* containing the full text of, for example, an encyclopedia or a journal.

From the user's viewpoint, reference data bases seem like supersophisticated versions of the file management software discussed in Chapter 7. Bibliographic information is contained in data records, which contain data fields. Search procedures make use of search terms and logical operators. If you are already familiar with a file management program, you will probably find it easy to master online searching too.

Direct-wire linkages among computers can, unlike telecommunications systems, achieve high data transfer speeds. Efforts have been made, therefore, to create local area networks and micro-to-mainframe links using direct cabling. Progress in this area has been slow owing to technical problems and lack of standards.

Local area networks (LANs) are networks of personal computers directly connected by high-speed cable links. Most LANs are small, linking five to twenty computers. LANs, in contrast to timesharing systems, are linkages among full-fledged computers. Each station in the network has its own processing capabilities. The stations are linked to share expensive peripherals, create local electronic mail linkages, create transaction processing systems, and share software.

Creating links between a company's personal computers and its mainframe makes good sense; that way, company personnel can gain access to mainframe data, which they can then analyze on their personal computers. The personal computers, in turn, can take the place of mainframe terminals for remote mainframe operations. But special equipment and software are required. Only now is that equipment and software becoming available.

KEY TERMS

abstract
acoustic coupler
asynchronous
asynchronous communications board
automatic log on
baud
bulletin board
bulletin board systems (BBS)
citation
communications protocol
communications software
computer conference
data base producer
direct-connect modem
direct-wire communications
downloading
dumb terminal emulation program
electronic mail
full-duplex modem
full-text data base
half-duplex modem
information utility
local area network (LAN)
log on
modem
numeric data base
online data base vendor
packet
packet-switching network
parallel transmission
point-storage-point electronic mail
point-to-point electronic mail
port
public domain software
reference data base
RS-232C serial port
serial transmission
smart communications program
smart (intelligent) modem
source data base
telecommuting
Universal Asynchronous Receiver/Transmitter (UART)
uploading
value-added network

REVIEW QUESTIONS AND EXERCISES

1. In what way does the telephone system provide an incredibly large resource for computer networking?
2. Name three hardware components necessary for computer-based communication via the telephone system. Why are these components necessary for telecommunication?

3. What are the features of smart communications programs? Why would these features be desirable for telecommunications?
4. Distinguish between point-to-point and point-storage-point electronic mail.
5. What are the advantages of electronic mail over other communications media?
6. Distinguish between bulletin boards and computer conferencing.
7. Do you think telecommuting will become widespread? Why or why not?
8. What is the difference between a reference and a source data base? What is the difference between a data base producer and a data base vendor?
9. Which BRS/After Dark data bases look as if they would interest you, given your academic major and career plans?
10. What is the difference between telecommunications and direct-wire communications?
11. Distinguish local area networks from timesharing systems. Which would be most appropriate, in your view, for a business manager? A professional writer? A computer scientist?
12. Why do so many corporate users of personal computers want to connect their machines to central mainframe computers?

FOR FURTHER READING

HARDWARE AND SOFTWARE FOR COMMUNICATIONS

Cambell, Joe. *The RS-232 Solution* (Berkeley: Sybex Computer Books, 1984).

Froehlick, Robert A. *The Free Software Catalog and Directory* (New York: Crown Publishers, 1984).

Glossbrenner, Alfred. *How to Get Free Software* (New York: St. Martin's, 1984).

———. *The Complete Handbook of Personal Computer Communications: Everything You Need to Know to Go Online With the World,* Rev. ed. (New York: St. Martin's, 1986).

Jordan, Larry. "What Makes Modems Run?" *PC World* (May 1985).

Kruglinksi, David. *The Osborne/McGraw-Hill Guide to IBM PC Communications* (Berkeley: Osborne/McGraw-Hill, 1984).

Lamb, John. "How Computers Can Talk to Each Other," *New Scientist* (September 9, 1982).

Lu, Cary. "[Macintosh] Communications Primer," *MacWorld* (July/August 1984).

Melin, Michael, and Michael Mikus. *Connections: The Micro-Communications Handbook* (Berkeley: The Book Company, 1984).

Niles, Jack. *Micros and Modems: Telecommunicating with Personal Computers* (Reston, Va.: Reston, 1983).

Stanton, Tom. "Shareware: Nominal Fees Can Yield Big Value," *PC: The Independent Guide to IBM-Standard Personal Computing* (May 13, 1986).

COMPUTER CONFERENCING, TELECOMMUTING, ELECTRONIC MAIL, AND BULLETIN BOARDS

Beeston, Tom, and Tom Tucker. *Hooking in: The Underground Computer Bulletin Board and Guide* (Westlake Village, Calif.: Computerfood Press, 1984).

Crawford, A. "Corporate Electronic Mail: A Communication-Intensive Application of Information Technology," *MIS Quarterly* (Fall 1982).
Epstein, Nadine. "Et Voilà! Le Minitel," *New York Times Magazine* (March 9, 1986).
Fersko-Weiss, Henry. "Electronic Mail: The Emerging Connection," *Personal Computing* (January 1985).
Gabel, David. "Making a Habit of Electronic Mail," *Personal Computing* (August 1984).
Hiltz, Starr Roxanne, and Murray Turoff. *The Network Nation: Human Communication via Computer* (Reading, Mass.: Addison-Wesley, 1984).
Jaffe, Louis. "Convenient Conferences," *Popular Computing* (March 1985).
Johansen, Robert, and Christine Bullen. "What to Expect from Computer Conferencing," *Harvard Business Review* (March-April 1984).
Kiesler, Sara, Jane Siegel, and Timothy McGuire. "Social Psychological Aspects of Computer-Mediated Communication," *American Psychologist* (October 1984).
Mandela, Audrey. "Electronic Express," *Popular Computing* (March 1985).
Mayo, John S. "Evolution of the Intelligent Network," *Science* (February 12, 1982).
Newell, Allen, and Robert F. Sproull. "Computer Networks: Prospects for Scientists," *Science* (February 12, 1982).
Poppel, Harvey L. "Who Needs the Office of the Future?" *Harvard Business Review* (November-December 1982).
Rice, Ronald E., ed. *The New Media: Communication, Research, and Technology* (Beverly Hills, Calif.: Sage, 1986).
Slatta, Richard. "The Problems and Challenges of the Computer-Commuter," *Link-Up* (June 1984).
Wicklein, John. *Electronic Nightmare: The New Communications and Freedom* (New York: Viking, 1981).

ONLINE BIBLIOGRAPHIC DATA BASE RESEARCH

Cook, Peter R. "Electronic Encyclopedias," *Byte* (July 1984).
Cuadra Associates. *Directory of Online Databases* (Santa Monica, Calif.: Cuadra Associates, Inc., 1983).
Fenichel, Carol H., and T. H. Hogan. *Online Searching: A Primer* (Marlton, N.J.: Learned Information, 1981).
Hewes, Jeremy Joan. "Combing the Electronic Archives," *MacWorld* (May 1985).
Hoover, Ryan. *Executive's Guide to Online Information Services* (White Plains, N.Y.: Knowledge Industry Publications, 1984).
Lambert, Steve. *Online: A Guide to America's Leading Information Services* (Bellevue, Wash.: Microsoft Press, 1984).
Levy, Steve. "Cutting On-Line Costs," *Popular Computing* (October 1983).
Li, Tze-chung. *An Introduction to Online Searching* (Westport, Conn.: Greenwood Press, 1985).
Newlin, Barbara. *Answers Online: Your Guide to Informational Databases* (Berkeley: Osborne/McGraw-Hill, 1985).
Williams, Martha E. "Electronic Databases," *Science* (February 12, 1982).
———. *Computer-Readable Data Bases: A Directory and Data Sourcebook* (White Plains, N.Y.: Knowledge Industry Publications, 1982).

LANS AND MICRO-MAINFRAME LINKS

Brooner, E. G. *The Local Area Network Book* (Indianapolis: Howard W. Sams, 1984).

Daney, Charles. "A Micro-to-Mainframe Primer," *PC: The Independent Guide to IBM-Standard Personal Computing* (January 22, 1985).

Davis, George R., ed. *The Local Network Handbook* (New York: McGraw-Hill, 1982).

Derfler, Frank J. "Micro to Mainframe: Making the Right Connection," *PC: The Independent Guide to IBM-Standard Personal Computing* (May 13, 1986).

Hiltz, Starr Roxanne. *Online Communities: A Case Study of the Office of the Future* (New York: Ablex, 1983).

Kelleher, Joanne. "Microcomputer Networking: Learn from Successful Users," *ComputerWorld* (March 24, 1986).

McKean, Kevin. "The Computerization of the Telephone," *Personal Computing* (July 1984).

Mello, Adrian. "The Mac Lines Up With Mainframes," *MacWorld* (July/August 1984).

Saal, Harry. "Local Area Networks: An Update on Microcomputers in the Office," *Byte* (May 1983).

Zuboff, S. "The New Worlds of Computer-Mediated Work," *Harvard Business Review* (September-October 1985).

13 *Integrated Software:* *Putting It All Together*

"Why should (or shouldn't) you scrap your Acme Whizbang Word Dicer and your Peerless Number Spreader programs in favor of an all-in-one package?"

Alfred Poor PC Magazine

A Saint Louis–based barbecue sauce maker expressed his computer frustrations in these terms: "If I were typing a letter to a broker . . . and I wanted to check his sales figures over the last three months, I had to shut down WordStar, switch over to VisiCalc, run out his report, shut down VisiCalc, bring WordStar back up, and then try to copy the stuff in. That's a lot of trouble. . . . I had three computers. . . . One was for word processing, one for data base management, and one for VisiCalc."[1]

Why not put all five basic software functions — word processing, data base management, spreadsheets, graphics, and communications — into a single, big program? That's precisely the idea behind integrated software, the subject of this chapter.

When personal computer memories broke the 64K RAM barrier with the introduction of the IBM Personal Computer, integrated software became possible. The personal computer, a computer designed originally for running just one program at a time, had become powerful enough to run a very large program that incorporated all or most of the five basic software functions (word processing, data base management, spreadsheets, graphics, and communications). Software developers were quick to offer integrated products for the IBM Personal Computer. By 1984, Lotus Development Corporation's Symphony and Ashton Tate's Framework vied with more than a dozen competitors for what everyone assumed would be a growing market share.

These days, however, the integrated software market is much quieter. Framework, Symphony, and a few other integrated programs are still around, but experts agree that these programs have failed to pry most users away from their favorite, **standalone application packages.** (A standalone program offers just one software function, such as word processing or data base management.)

The reasons users have been slow to accept integrated programs aren't hard to discern. Integrated programs seem very promising at first glance, but the reality all too often falls short of the promise: rarely do the software functions of integrated programs compare favorably with their standalone counterparts. And what's more, other ways of achieving the integration of software functions, including desktop organizers and windowing environments, have encouraged people to stick with the standalone application programs they like best.

INTEGRATED SOFTWARE: THE PROMISE

An ideal **integrated program** would make it easy to switch among the basic software functions while you're working, ease the transfer of data from one program to the next, and provide a consistent user interface for all five functions.

CONTEXT SWITCHING

One major advantage of integrated software is the ability to move quickly among the five software functions. All five — word processing, data base management, spreadsheets, graphics, and communications — are usually available within one integrated program. Each of these functions is called a **context;** to move from one context to the next is called **context switching.** Integrated programs make it easy to switch context. You may move, for example, from the data base management context to the spreadsheet context without exiting the program or changing disks.

Consider these three situations:

Searching the Data Base While Using the Spreadsheet. You're working up a spreadsheet to calculate annual sales commissions, and you've forgotten to make a note of Al Smith's sales for the year. You need to look up his sales in the data base.

Using the Spreadsheet While Word Processing. You're writing a report that discusses some figures. You realize you need to analyze the figures with a spreadsheet before going on.

Using Communications While Word Processing. You're writing a report on new management techniques, but you've forgotten the author of a business management journal article you want to discuss. You need to interrupt your writing and use your communications program to log on to a bibliographic data base.

Without integrated software, each of these situations would force you to save your work, exit the program, load another one, retrieve the data you need, exit the second program, and reload the original one. If you frequently work with more than one software context, integrated software can reduce the time you spend switching from one context to the next (Figure 13–1).

DATA TRANSFER

Integrated programs do more than merely ease the process of switching. They also provide easy pathways for the transfer of data among software contexts.

Separate, standalone application packages do not usually facilitate data transfer unless they have been designed to work together. Most programs use their own, nonstandard data file formats, which have been chosen to optimize the single software context they serve. A data file format is a technique for storing data in a disk file. A word processing program, for example, will use a data file format that speeds the formatting of text. A spreadsheet program, in contrast, will use one that speeds the calculation of formulas. Chances are that the two programs cannot exchange information with each other easily.

In an integrated program, however, data file formats are designed from the beginning to allow easy transfer from one context to another. Here are some ways you might find this capability useful:

Data Base to Spreadsheet. You want to transfer sales data from the data base to the spreadsheet, where you'll analyze it.

Telecommunications to Spreadsheet. You want to download investment data from an information service and analyze it with your spreadsheet.

Spreadsheet to Graphics. You want to express two columns of numbers in a spreadsheet as a bar graph.

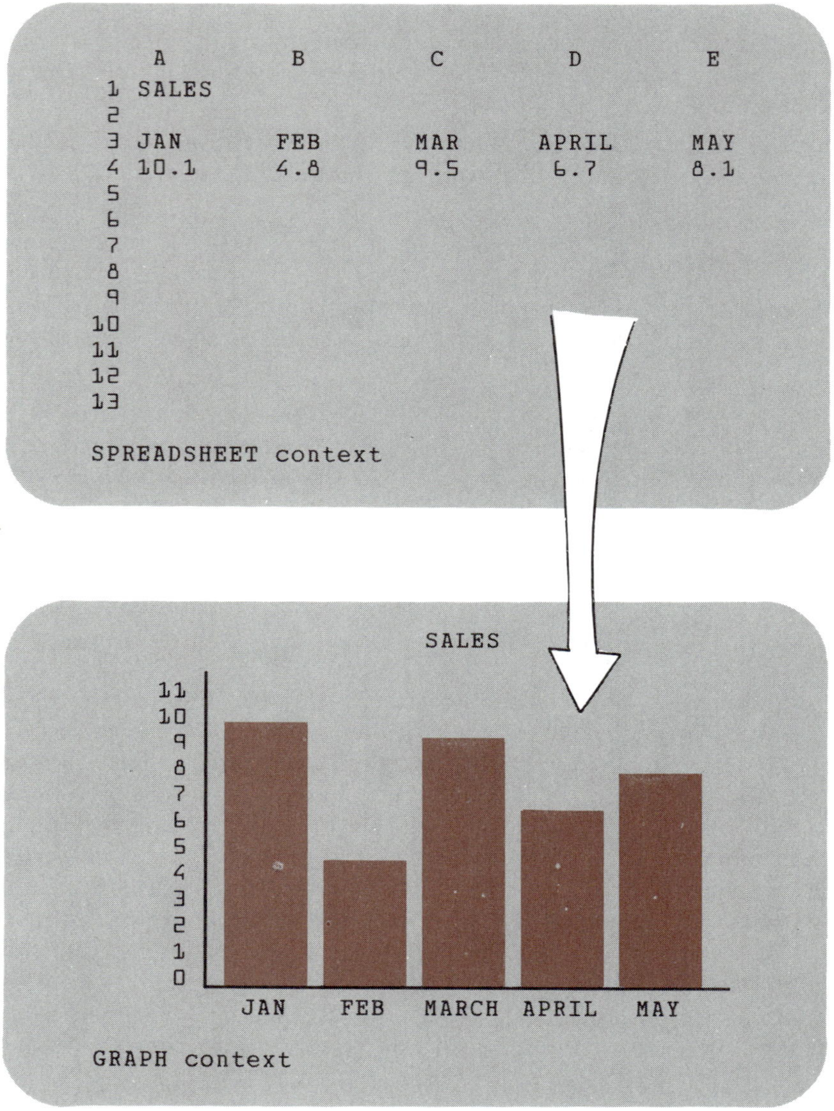

FIGURE 13–1 Context Switching: Spreadsheet to Graphics

Spreadsheet to Word Processing. You want to include a spreadsheet as a table in a word processing document you're writing.

Graphics to Word Processing. You want to include a graph you've created in a word processing document you're writing.

Word Processing to Telecommunications. You want to upload, or send via telecommunications links, a document you've written to an electronic mail service.

Some integrated programs not only ease the data transfer process, they also let you work on the same data with more than one software context. This capability is especially fruitful for what-if analyses using graphics. With a spreadsheet displayed in one window and a graph of the data displayed in a second window, exploratory changes in the data are immediately reflected in the graph (Figure 13–2).

FIGURE 13–2 What-If Analysis with Graphics

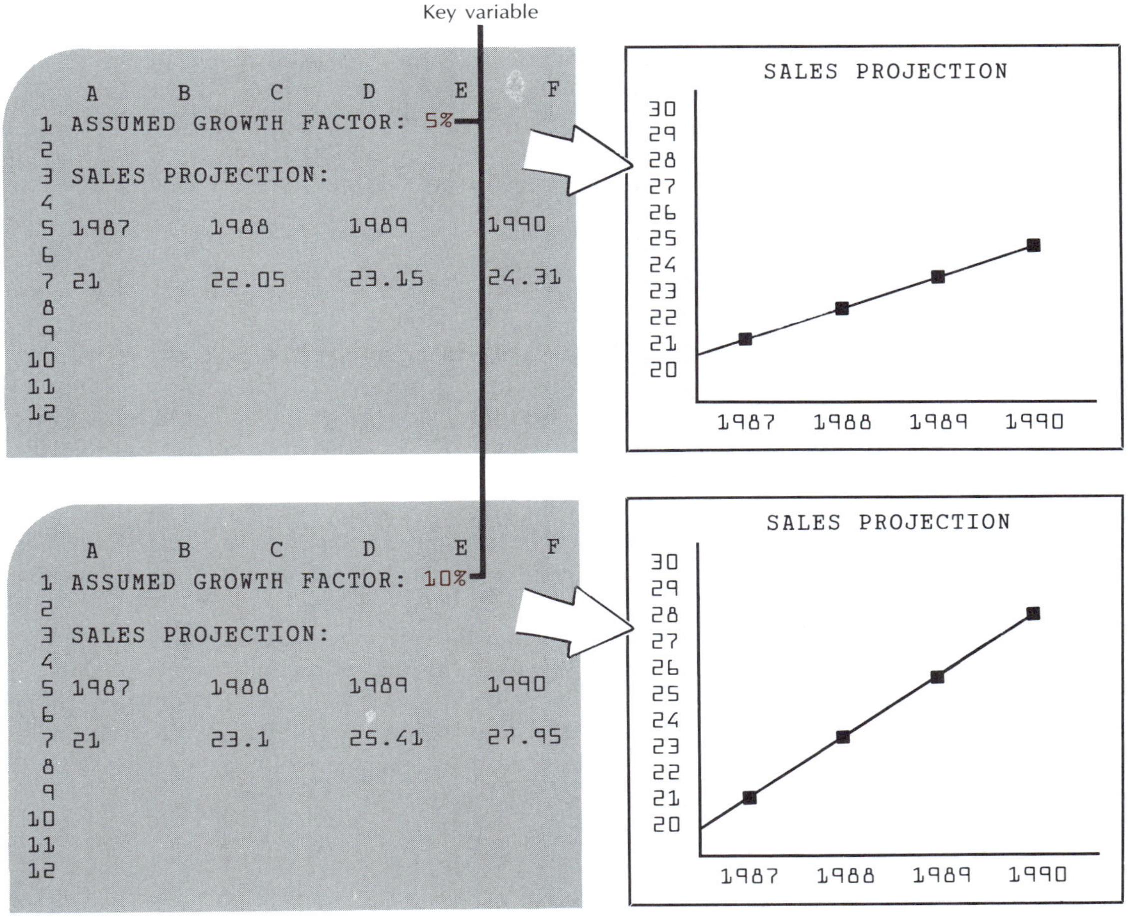

CONSISTENCY OF USER INTERFACE

A third potential advantage of integrated software is that a consistent user interface can be used for all five contexts. To grasp why this would be an advantage, consider what's involved in learning five standalone application programs. For each program, you have to learn a lengthy set of commands and operating procedures. One program's commands and procedures probably do not apply to the next. It's even possible that one command (such as the keyboard command CONTROL-Y) will accomplish completely different tasks in two programs. If you frequently work with two or more progams, the confusion and stress involved in this and other inconsistencies can lower your productivity.

INTEGRATED SOFTWARE: THE REALITY

The integrated software ideal sounds very good. Unfortunately, however, the integrated programs available for today's personal computers fail to live up to the ideal. Some, to be sure, do a better job than others. But many users find that integrated programs present the user with too much complexity, skimp on one or more of the software contexts, or tax the computer beyond reasonable levels.

COMPLEXITY

Integrated programs ease the learner's task by providing a consistent user interface for all five contexts. Yet these programs still present a formidable challenge to someone trying to learn how to use them. Any program that contains all five software functions is bound to be complex. As a measure of this complexity, consider the size of integrated program software manuals. Lotus Symphony's manual weighs in at a hefty 8.5 lbs (Figure 13–3); Framework's weighs 7.75 lbs., and Enable's is only slightly less bulky at 6.5 lbs. Put together, the documentation for these three programs weighs as much as a Compaq portable computer!

Beginners in personal computing may find an integrated program's complexity (and the ocean of documentation supplied with the program) to be overwhelming. To be sure, anyone who wants to achieve mastery of the personal computer will eventually learn all five types of application programs. But the bulky documentation and wilderness of procedures tends to discourage new users.

INADEQUATE SOFTWARE FUNCTIONS

The ideal integrated program would include all five software functions, and all five of them would match the best standalone application packages in quality,

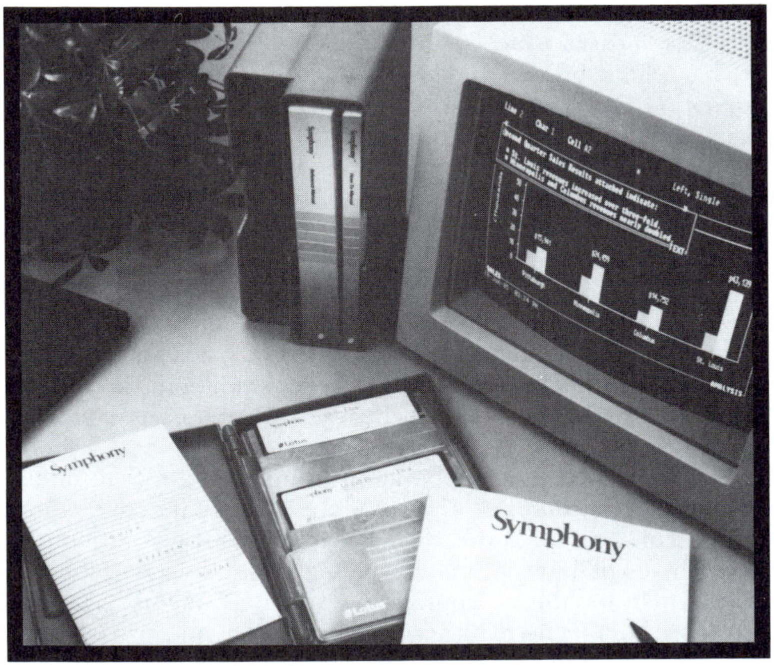

FIGURE 13–3 Lotus's Symphony and Its Manual

flexibility, and power. Unfortunately, today's personal computers do not have enough memory to achieve this ideal. And so programmers tend to create integrated programs in which some of the contexts are excellent but others are inadequate.

The spreadsheet context in integrated software often surpasses the best standalone spreadsheet programs in size, flexibility, and power. Lotus Symphony's spreadsheet, for example, presents the user with 256 rows and 8,192 columns, and includes more than ninety built-in functions. Not all this space, to be sure, can be used, because the entire spreadsheet must fit within the available RAM memory. And since Symphony is such a big program, it leaves little room for the spreadsheet. This isn't a serious limitation, however, since it's almost always better to create a series of simple, well-designed spreadsheets rather than one big, complicated one.

Also of generally excellent quality is the graphics context in integrated software programs. And the communications context usually works at least as well as standalone communications programs.

Less attractive, in general, are the data base management and word processing contexts of integrated software. In most integrated programs, the data base management context is better described as a spreadsheet modified to perform a limited set of file management tasks. And in any case, it's likely to be of limited use. Many integrated programs require that the whole data base reside in active memory (RAM), most of which is already taken up by the big program itself. So there's a sharp limit on the number of data records you can create. That's a serious limitation for serious data base management applications.

The same limitations apply to the word processing context. In most programs, this context provides only a fraction of the feature found in standalone programs. Moreover, document length may be sharply limited by lack of memory. These document length limitations may be acceptable for memos or letters, but they're not acceptable for professional writing applications.

Expanded Memory. Since integrated program performance is sharply constrained by the memory limitations built into today's personal computers, it is not surprising that makers of integrated software have led the way in demanding more memory in new personal computer models. One result of this campaign is an expanded memory system for the IBM Personal Computer.

Developed by Lotus Development Corporation (the makers of Symphony) in association with Intel and Microsoft Corporation, the expanded memory board — an add-on circuit board for the IBM PC — allows the 8088 chip to address up to 8 megabytes of internal memory. The board uses a technique called **bank switching.** Within the computer's conventional memory, a 64K bank of RAM chips is set aside. The bank serves as a window on the additional memory, which is switched in and out of the window in 64K-sized chunks (Figure 13–4). The user needn't worry about the details, however. So far as you know when you are using expanded memory, your computer has a huge amount of RAM.

When document and data base length limitations disappear thanks to expanded memory, integrated programs become more useful. However, the data base and word processing contexts of integrated programs may still lack the features some users need. So it's still not likely that most personal computer users will give up their standalone packages for an integrated program.

AN ALTERNATIVE TO INTEGRATED SOFTWARE: WINDOWING ENVIRONMENTS

Many users still prefer to use standalone application programs rather than integrated software. Two recent advances in software technology, desktop organizers and windowing environments, encourage the continued use of standalone programs.

DESKTOP ORGANIZERS

Increasing numbers of personal computer users are putting **desktop organizers** to work (Figure 13–5). These are *memory resident programs* that, like the thesaurus

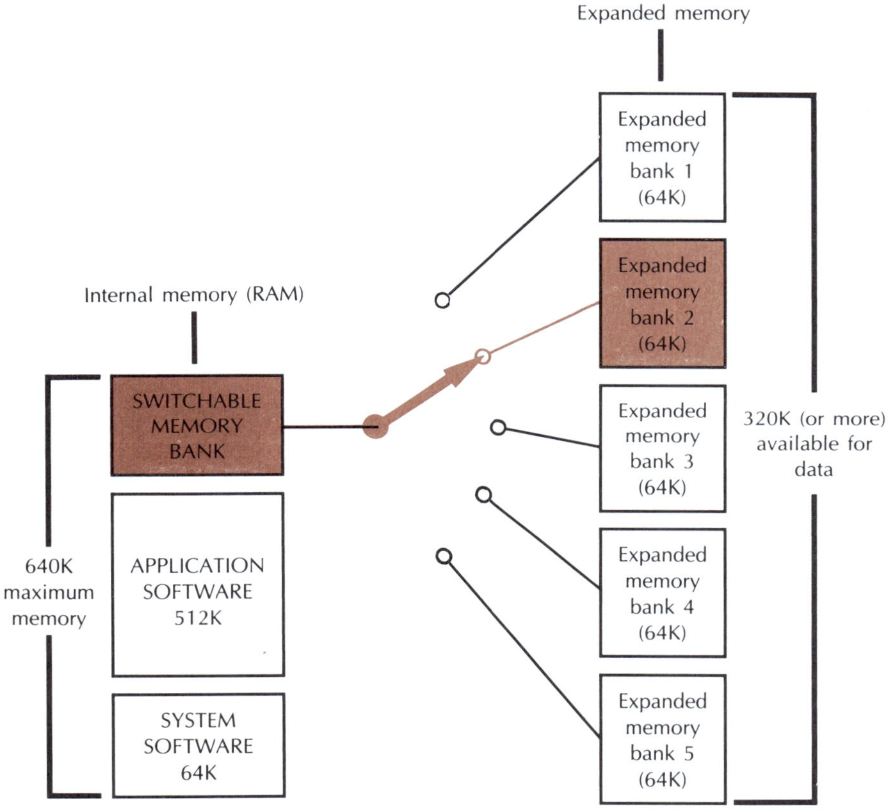

FIGURE 13–4 Bank Switching

program discussed in Chapter 6, reside in your computer's internal memory while you're using another application program. At the press of a key, however, they interrupt the application program and pop into view. The desktop organizer's features include a clipboard for data transfer between standalone applications. Using the clipboard, you can easily transfer data from a spreadsheet, for instance, into a word processing document.

In addition, several helpful utilities are available at a keystroke (Figure 13–6):

Notepad. This is a mini-word-processor for making notes to yourself.

Address/Phone Number Data Base. This is a computer version of the desktop Rolodex.

Calculator. Non-computer-using friends and spouses of personal computer freaks are often amused when, in the midst of a computing session, a computer user gropes for a desktop calculator. Desktop organizers solve

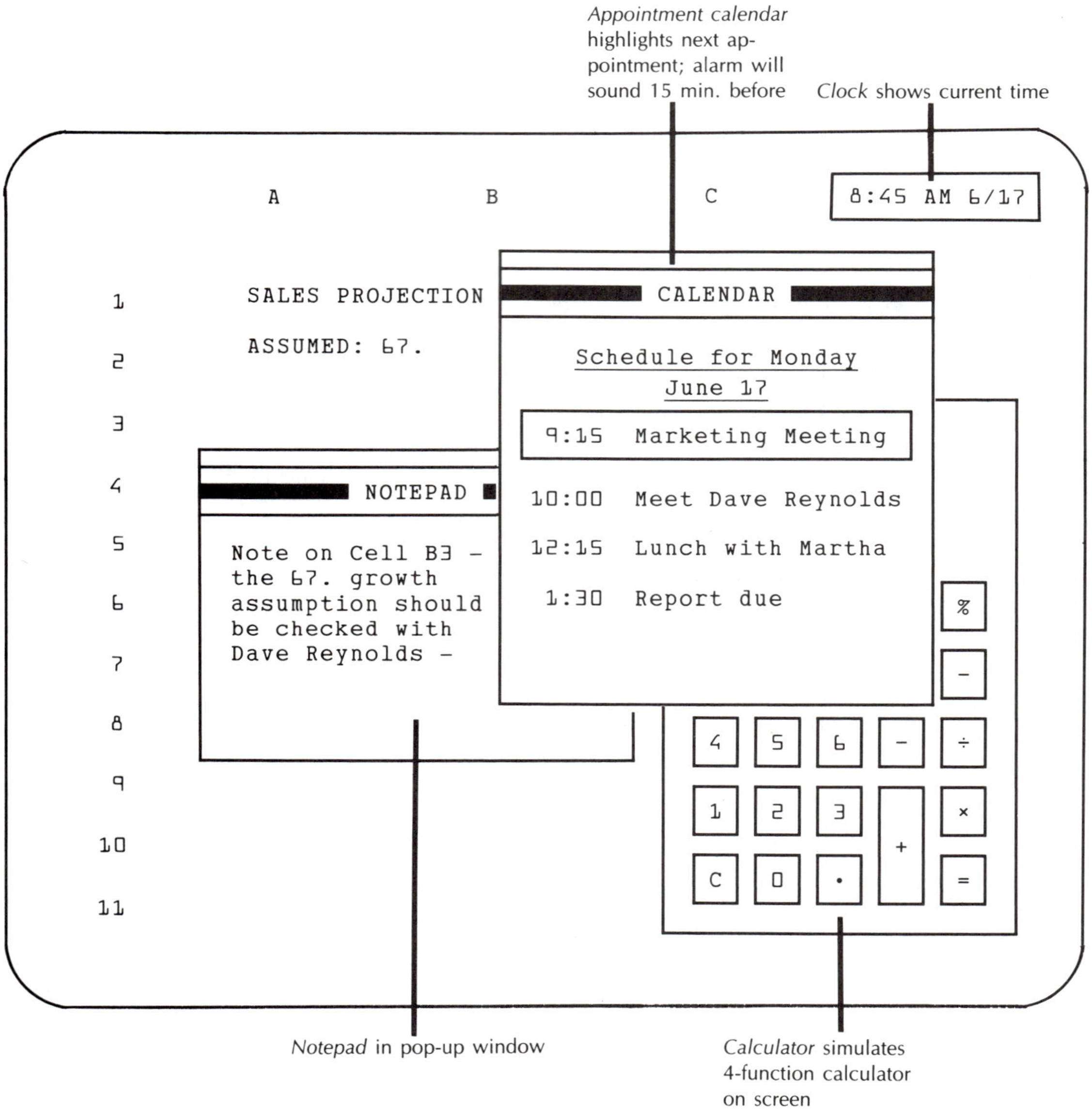

FIGURE 13–5 Desktop Organizer with Pop-Up Windows

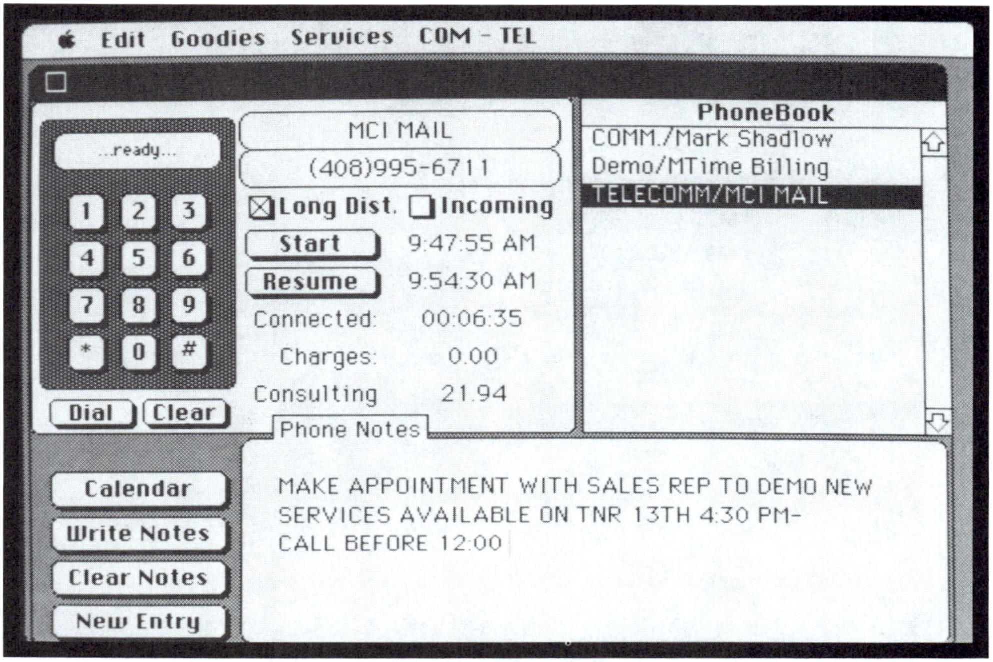

FIGURE 13–6 Borland International's Sidekick Desktop Organizer

this problem by simulating a calculator on the screen. In addition to the four arithmetic functions, the calculator includes hexadecimal and binary conversions (useful for programmers).

Calendar/Daily Organizer/Appointment Schedule. This computer version of an appointment book warns you of impending deadlines or meetings.

Desktop organizers cannot perform context switching, so moving from one standalone application program to another is still a tedious, slow process.

WINDOWING ENVIRONMENTS

Windowing environments such as Microsoft Windows and the Macintosh Finder are extensions of a computer's operating system. Indeed, they take it over, substituting a visual command interface for the more difficult, command-line technique (see Chapter 3). They include the utilities (such as a notepad, calculator, and appointment book) that make desktop organizers so valuable (Figure 13–7). Further, they manage standalone application programs, allowing you to load

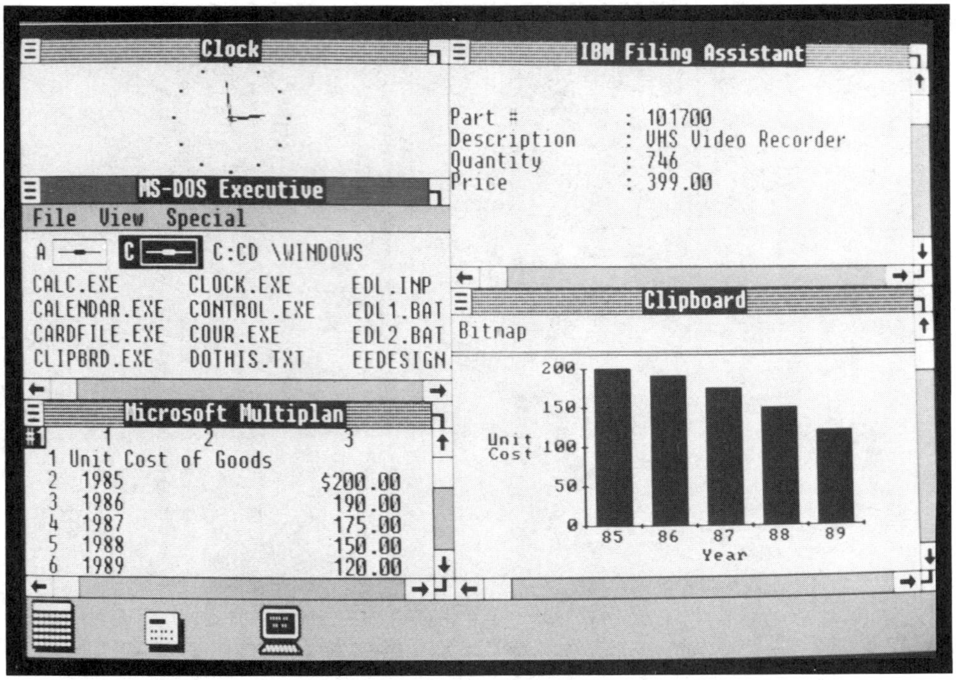

FIGURE 13–7 Microsoft Windows

two or more of them into windows (Figure 13–8). The result is that you get the two chief advantages of integrated software (data transfer between applications and context switching), and you can continue to use the standalone programs of your choice.

With most windowing environments, only one application program is actually running at any one moment; the other may be visible on the screen, but it is "frozen" or inactive. But you can rapidly switch from one program to the next, giving you the equivalent of context switching in an integrated program. While you're writing a document with word processing software, for instance, you can switch to a data base management program and look up some figures you need. Some windowing environments can actually run two programs simultaneously (multitasking), but multitasking tends to overtax the processing capabilities of personal computer CPUs.

Like desktop organizers, windowing environments also provide the easy-to-use data transfer device called the **clipboard** for transferring data from one standalone program to another. A clipboard is a temporary storage place. To use the clipboard to copy information from a spreadsheet into a word processing

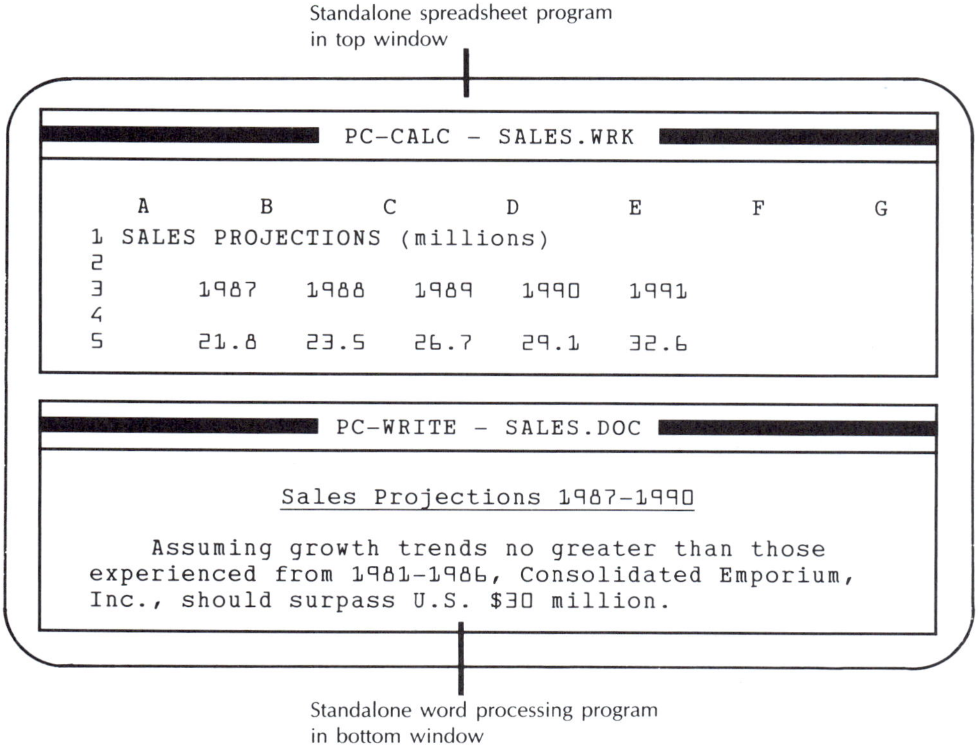

FIGURE 13–8 Windowing Environment: Two Applications Running Simultaneously

document, for example, you begin by using the command that copies the information from the spreadsheet to the clipboard. Then you switch to the word processing program and position the cursor where you want the spreadsheet information to appear. Finally, you use the command that copies the information from the clipboard into the document (Figure 13–9).

HORIZONS OF SOFTWARE INTEGRATION

Integrated software, in sum, has so far failed to conquer the world of personal computing. The reasons for this failure lie in the limitations of today's personal computing technology rather than in any inherent shortcoming of the integrated software ideal itself. Unquestionably, this ideal points the way to the future of personal computing.

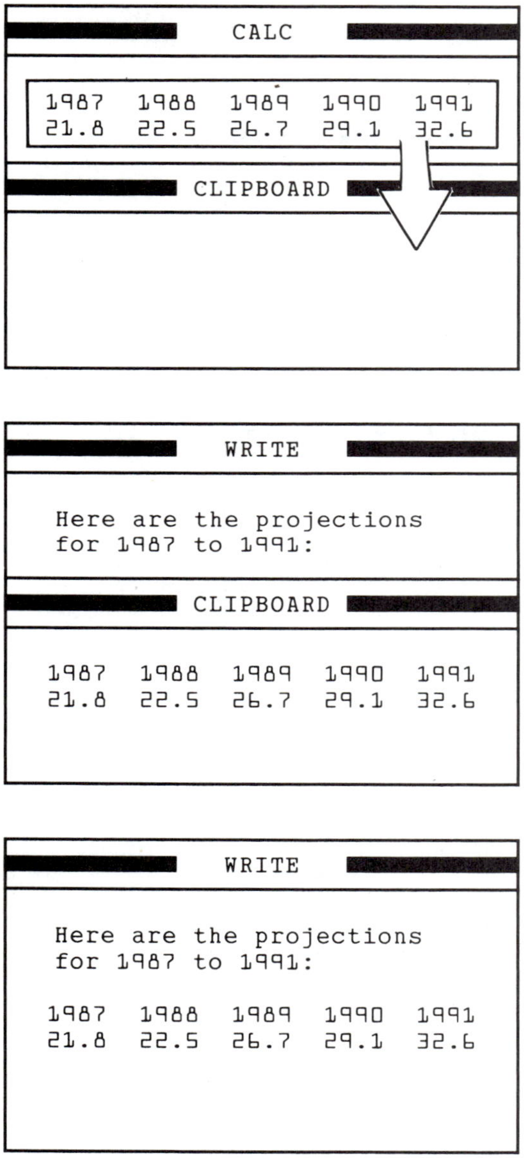

Step 1 Highlight the text to be copied and use the command that places a copy of it temporarily in the clipboard.

Step 2 Open a second standalone application program.

Step 3 Use the command that inserts stored material from the clipboard.

FIGURE 13–9 Windowing Environment: Using the Clipboard

The future may already be visible in professional workstations. Professional workstations are ultrasophisticated microcomputers, most of which use 32 bit microprocessor chips, huge amounts of internal memory (1 to 4 megabytes or more), and high-resolution display screens (with at least a million pixels). Because many professional workstations execute over a million instructions per second, use over a million bytes of memory, and display a million or more pixels, they're sometimes called 3M machines.

Most professional workstations are expensive, single-purpose machines used for graphics-intensive applications such as computer-aided design (Figure 13–10). Yet no one doubts that, in the near future, 3M computers will sell for approximately the cost of today's top-of-the-line personal computers (about $3,000 to $4,000). When they do, the era of software integration will begin in earnest. They've the power to run several programs at once and also to give the user a highly detailed, bit-mapped display screen.

The promise of things to come is already evident in the Xerox 6085 (Figure 13–11), a professional workstation designed for information workers (rather than designers or architects). The computer comes with an integrated software package called ViewPoint. ViewPoint blends a visual operating system with word

FIGURE 13–10
Complex Graphics on a Desktop Plotter

FIGURE 13–11
Professional Workstation — the Xerox 6085

processing, data base management, spreadsheets, graphics, and communications contexts. Unlike today's integrated packages for personal computers, each of these software contexts is fully equal — if not vastly superior — to the best standalone packages. And if you still prefer a standalone package, ViewPoint is capable of running any program written for the IBM Personal Computer.

SUMMARY

Integrated programs incorporate all or most of the five basic software functions (word processing, data base management, spreadsheets, graphics, and communications) in a single large program. An ideal integrated program would make it easy to switch among the five basic software functions while you're working, ease the transfer of data from one program to the next, and provide a consistent user interface for all five software functions.

Within an integrated program, each of the five software functions is called a *context*. To move from one context to the next is called *context switching*. If you frequently work with more than one software context, integrated software can reduce the time you spend switching.

A second advantage of integrated programs is that they provide easy pathways for the transfer of data among software contexts. Data file formats are designed from the beginning to allow such easy transfer. Some integrated programs not only ease the data transfer process, but also let you work on the same data with more than one software context.

A third potential advantage of integrated software is that a consistent user interface can be used for all five contexts.

Integrated programs have been available since 1984, but most personal computer users still prefer standalone application programs. A standalone program offers just one software function, such as word processing or data base management. Many users find that integrated programs present the user with too much complexity, skimp on one or more of the software contexts, or tax the computer beyond reasonable levels. Integrated software spreadsheet and graphics functions, to be sure, may surpass standalone packages. But limited features and limited data base or document length make the data base management and word processing contexts compare unfavorably with standalone packages. Expanded memory techniques can cure the data base and document length problems, but standalone programs offer more features.

Two alternatives to software integration, desktop organizers and windowing environments, encourage the continued use of standalone programs. Desktop organizers are memory-resident programs that include a clipboard for data transfer between standalone applications. Windowing environments give you data transfer and context switching, the two chief benefits of integrated software, yet they let you continue to use the standalone programs of your choice. However, windowing environments, which use bit-mapped graphics, tax the present generation of personal computer hardware to its limits. They tend to run very sluggishly.

The integrated software ideal is a good one. It has failed to take over the personal computer world, however, because the present crop of personal computers is technically limited. Professional workstations show us tomorrow's personal computers. These 3M computers, which are capable of executing a million instructions per second, displaying a million pixels, and storing over a million characters in internal memory, have the power needed for true software integration.

KEY TERMS

bank switching
clipboard
context
context switching
desktop organizer
integrated program
standalone application package
windowing environment

REVIEW QUESTIONS AND EXERCISES

1. Why would a user of several standalone application programs believe an integrated package to be desirable?
2. What technological advance made integrated software possible?
3. What are the three potential advantages of integrated software?
4. Do integrated programs deliver on their potential? In what areas do integrated programs tend to succeed more than others?
5. What are the alternatives to integrated software?
6. Describe three functions of a desktop organizer.
7. Differentiate windowing environments from integrated programs.
8. Why is it likely that software integration, despite its present shortcomings, represents the future of personal computing?

FOR FURTHER READING

Aarons, Richard. "The Organizing Principle: Desktop Organizer Programs," *PC: The Independent Guide to IBM-Standard Personal Computing* (February 11, 1986).

Baker, Richard H. *Framework Applications* (Blue Ridge Summit, Pa.: Tab Books, 1985).

Baras, Edward W. *Symphony Master: The Expert's Guide* (Berkeley: Osborne/McGraw-Hill, 1985).

Bernard, Josef. "Windows: At Panes to Integrate Software," *Computers & Electronics* (March 1984).

Bonner, Paul. "Forks in the Road to Integration," *Personal Computing* (January 1985).

Burns, Diane, S. Venit, and Vincent Puglia. "Desktop Organizers: Top-Notch Efficiency Tools," *PC: The Independent Guide to IBM-Standard Personal Computing* (May 27, 1986).

Dinerstein, Nelson T. *The Dynamics of Framework* (Homewood, Ill.: Dow Jones-Irwin, 1985).

Hogan, Thom. "Beyond the Finder: Resources and the Macintosh," *A+* (November 1984).

Jenkins, Avery. "Desktop Organizer Software: Uncluttering a Manager's Space and Time," *PC Week* (February 26, 1985).

Jennings, Mark S. "Evaluating the Macintosh Finder: The Macintosh's Operating System Is Friendly, But at What Price?" *Byte* (December 1984).

King, Brian L. *Framework: The Decision-Maker's Guide to Business Applications* (New York: Random House, 1985).

Lighthouse Publishing Staff. *The Complete Book of Symphony Macros* (Berkeley: Osborne/McGraw-Hill, 1985).

Lotus Development Corporation, *The Lotus Guide to Learning Symphony* (Reading, Mass.: Addison-Wesley, 1985).

Petzold, Charles, Jeff Duntemann, Paul Chisholm, and M. David Stone. "Operating in a New Environment," *PC: The Independent Guide to IBM-Standard Personal Computing* (February 25, 1986).

Poor, Alfred. "Integration with Integrity: Framework, Symphony, and Enable," *PC: The Independent Guide to IBM-Standard Personal Computing* (June 10, 1986).

Sullivan, Kristina B. "Memory Residency a Standard Feature of Newer Desktop-Organizer Packages," *PC Week* (August 27, 1985).

14 *Special-Purpose Software:* *Tailored to Get a Specific Job Done*

"Efficiency consultants agree: You can't just move faster or work harder and expect your productivity to move up the scale. You need the right tools."
Charles Petzold *PC Magazine*

Once you've mastered the five basic software functions, you'll have most of the tools you need for full participation in the Information Age — most, but not all. Personal computer users often discover that, in some cases, special-purpose programs meet their needs better than the general-purpose software we've been discussing. In this chapter, you'll find a survey of special-purpose software for business, education, and science.

Special-purpose application programs are tailored to get a specific job done, such as tracking investments or billing patients. Although many of these jobs could be approached with one of the five general-purpose programs, sometimes a special-purpose program offers clear advantages. Consider, for instance, a small-business accounting application. A data base management program can be used to set up a complete accounting system or a small business. But accounting systems are complex — far more complex than any of the data base management examples we've discussed so far. It's a big job to create an accounting system from scratch using general-purpose software, and the result may be a system that only its creator finds easy to use.

Several small-business accounting packages sell for less than $500, and some of them are reasonably user friendly. The programs come equipped with pre-defined forms for employee records, inventory, and business transactions. The better ones use procedures that conform to the highest standards of accounting practice. Special-purpose programs lack the flexibility of general-purpose software, but sometimes sacrificing flexibility makes good sense. Special-purpose programs are especially attractive when they offer application-specific features that would be difficult or impossible to emulate with general-purpose programs.

With the exception of special-purpose programs for business, the software discussed in this chapter may be hard to find in computer stores. Many are **vertical market programs,** which are aimed at a highly specific clientele. To find advertisements for these products, you may have to look in specialized publications, such as journals for engineers, attorneys, or scientists.

BUSINESS

Special-purpose programs for business include software for accounting, encrypting data, planning investments, and managing projects.

ACCOUNTING

An effective accounting system keeps track of a company's financial position, both for internal reasons (effective management and planning) and external ones (accurate reporting to stockholders and revenue agencies). It records all the company's financial transactions, classifies them into company accounts, and summarizes these accounts in financial reports. Accounting requires the constant manipulation of facts and figures and, as such, it's well suited to computerization. Most medium- to large-scale companies use computers for accounting — in fact, many large companies could not do business at all if they had to go back to manual methods. According to one estimate, a large corporation could not operate longer than four days if all computer accounting capabilities were lost.

Many small businesses, however, still plod along with pen-and-pencil techniques — but their numbers are decreasing. Accounting packages of good to excellent quality are now available for personal computers, and hundreds of thousands of small businesses put them to work every day. The typical personal computing accounting package assumes that the user has some accounting background. Some, however, require of the user only a brief overview of basic accounting principles.

Personal computer accounting packages include five modules (Figure 14–1):

General Ledger. The **general ledger program** is the heart of any accounting system; it's the scoreboard for all business transactions. Reports from the general ledger, such as balance sheets and income statements, tell a manager where a business stands at any moment in time.

Accounts Receivable. The **accounts receivable program** keeps track of individuals and firms that owe you money. All transactions involving sales of goods or services are entered into accounts receivable. Reports indicate which accounts are overdue.

FIGURE 14–1 Five Modules of Accounting Packages

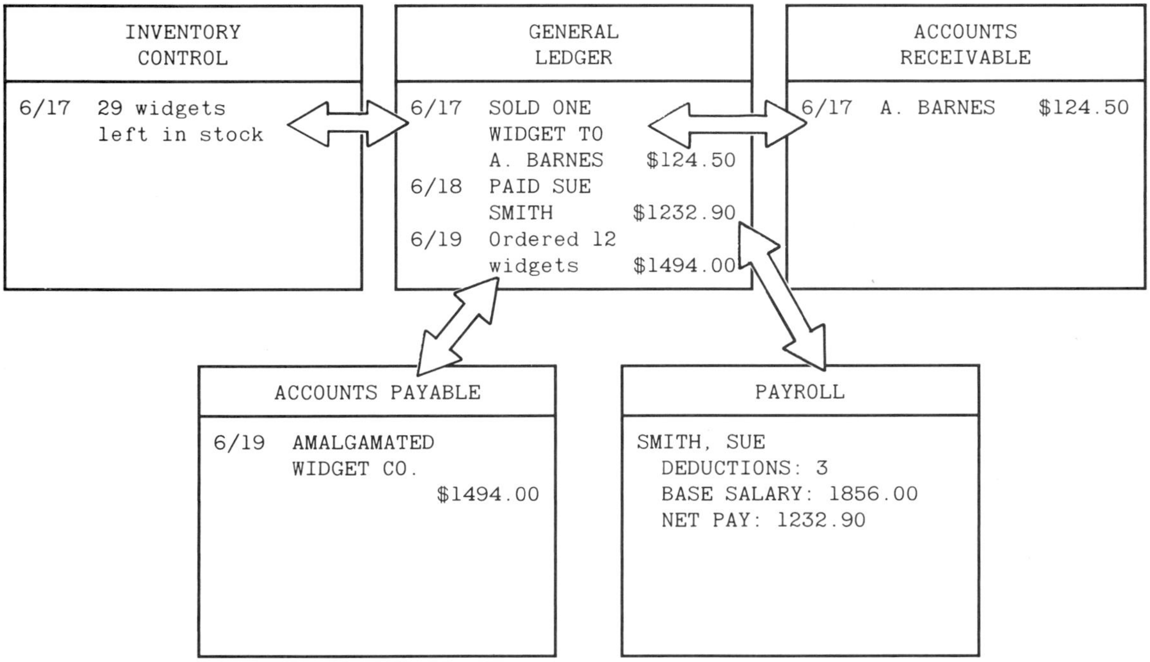

Accounts Payable. The **accounts payable program** is the mirror image of the accounts receivable program; it keeps track of those to whom *you* owe money.

Inventory Control. The **inventory control program** keeps track of the goods you have in stock. It alerts you when inventory levels fall too low.

Payroll. The **payroll program** keeps records on employees, calculates paychecks after subtracting taxes, and prints the checks.

Highly desirable in accounting packages is **account automation,** in which an entry made in one account, such as accounts payable, is automatically reflected in all other relevant accounts. Consider, for instance, what happens when a sales transaction is entered in accounts receivable. If the customer has paid cash, the income should be posted in the general ledger. And since inventory has been reduced by the sale, the inventory control program should show the reduction. Personal computer accounting packages that offer account automation are called **integrated accounting packages.**

A new development in the integrated accounting software field is the **multiuser accounting package** (Figure 14–2). Designed to operate on local area networks (see Chapter 12), the package can acccommodate a half dozen or more users, each with a personal computer as a workstation. Account automation is standard. When a sale is made, for instance, a clerk can enter the sales invoice into accounts receivable. At the same time, another worker in the purchasing department is told that the inventory has dropped. With these packages, a business that employs just a few people can install a computer system that rivals the ones big corporations use.

Not every small business needs a computer-based accounting system. A fundamental principle of accounting as a management tool is that innovations should be cost-effective; that is, the benefits should exceed the costs. An inflexible, unfriendly accounting system may cost thousands to install, force the business to grind to a halt while everyone learns it, and require major changes in day-to-day transaction procedures just so they'll fit the program's demands. It might be better to keep using dear old dependable Mr. Smith, who knows your business — even though he keeps all your receipts in a collection of shoeboxes.

ENCRYPTING DATA

Managers of data processing departments of major corporations have developed an obsession with the security of their computer systems — and with good reason. A company's computer contains information that's both sensitive and valuable. For example, in 1974 more than 3 million customer names were downloaded from a data base created by the company that markets the *Encyclopaedia Britannica.* The list was sold for $1 million. Worse, that information can be

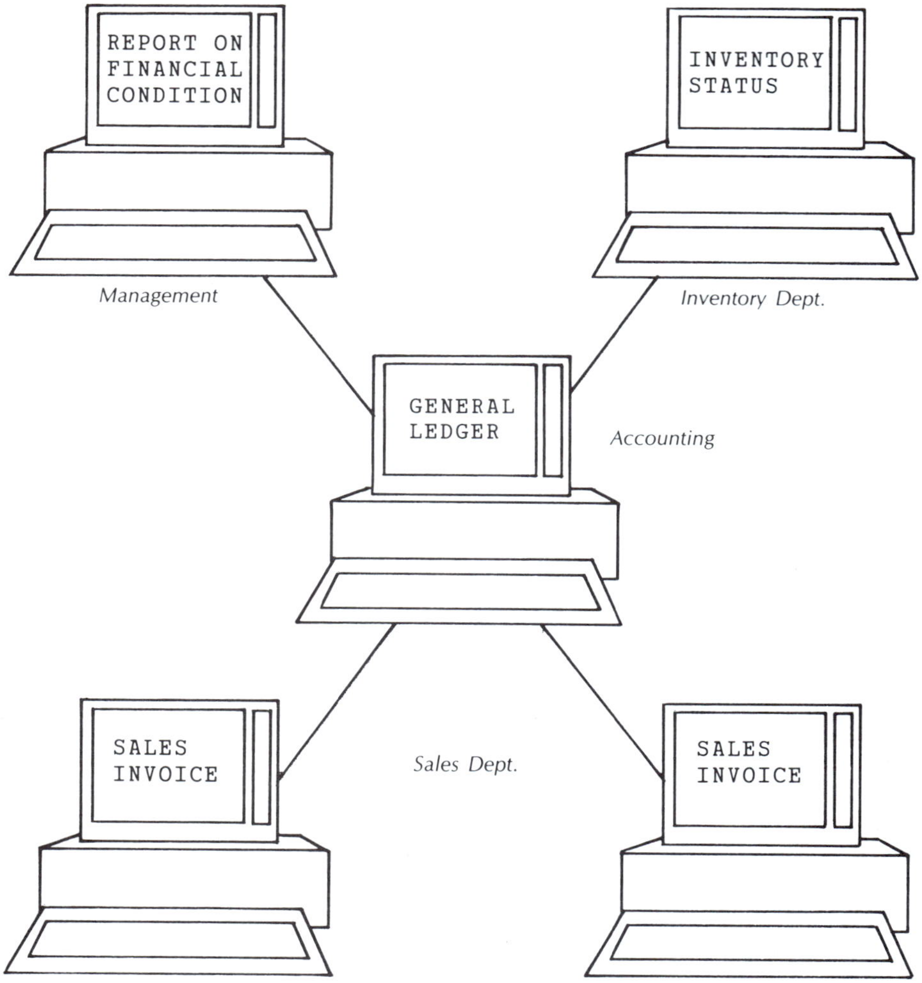

FIGURE 14–2 Multiuser Accounting Package and Local Area Network

manipulated for criminal purposes. In 1972, a Penn Central computer was instructed to deliver 217 railway cars, worth $60,000 each, to a lonely siding in the country. Once they were delivered and were being repainted with fake markings, the computer was instructed to forget all about the whole transaction.

To protect companies against computer crimes, data security personnel have devised many schemes, including the translation or encryption of data into a code that cannot easily be read or deciphered. These and other techniques have helped protect a company's mainframe or minicomputers from much (but not all) computer crime. Now that personal computers have come along, however, new opportunities for computer crime exist. Left alone in a deserted office, a PC is defenseless against the computer criminal who wishes to vandalize, alter, or steal valuable company data. For this reason, many companies now require that personal computer users emulate mainframe security techniques. In particular, sensitive data — data that others shouldn't see or that computer criminals might want to steal — should be encrypted.

To be completely secure, data encryption must go beyond the encryption or data hiding features found in some spreadsheet or data base management programs. These are too easy to circumvent. Data encryption software does a much better job. Such a program codes the data in a form that can be broken, if at all, only by the world's most sophisticated decryption devices.

INVESTMENT PLANNING

In 1985, 47 million people — about one out of every five people in the United States — participated in one way or another in buying and selling stocks. Out of these millions, only a fraction were able to afford the expertise of sophisticated market analysts, who use quantitative tools to identify good buys. But the personal computer's out to change all that. Right now, you can go down to your local software store and buy a good part of that expertise right off the shelf.

Three kinds of special-purpose business software — technical analysis program, fundamental analysis program, and investment portfolio managers — bring sophisticated investment analysis tools to the desk of anyone with a personal computer:

Technical Analysis Programs. **Technical analysis programs** create charts that analyze a stock's historical trends. Their goal is to predict short-term price changes so that you can pick a stock for a quick profit. Technical analysis programs do the tedious calculating and charting for you.

Fundamental Analysis Programs. **Fundamental analysis programs** go beyond the surface of a stock's price movements and volume; it examines the actual value of a company as judged by its assets and profits. Its goal is to find companies whose stock is undervalued in comparison with its potential. Fundamental analysis programs can go through thousands of publicly available company records and pick out the companies that meet predefined criteria.

Portfolio Managers. **Portfolio managers** keep track of your stocks and other investments, producing periodic reports that let you know how you're doing.

Why not use a spreadsheet program for these applications? You can, but you'll spend some time — days, at least — setting up the templates. Special-purpose programs come ready-made for these applications, some of them with tools that spreadsheets don't offer. N^2 Computing's Metastock, for example, is a technical analysis package that will automatically download stock data from seven online information services. A fundamental analysis program, Standard & Poor's Stockpack-II, comes with data disks containing detailed information on 1,500 companies; you can subscribe to an update program that sends you an information-packed disk each month.

Investment software spreads investment expertise throughout society, and that sounds like a great idea. But as Wall Street analysts have recently discovered, there may be a major, unanticipated side effect: wild swings in a stock's prices. Consider: everyone's using investment software, and the programs all say "Sell!" about a certain stock. So the bottom drops out of its price. At the same time, the programs all say "Buy!" about another one, and its price skyrockets. This pattern, to be sure, is part of the market and always will be, since investors try to make rational decisions about investments. Yet if everyone has computer assistance, price swings could grow out of proportion. According to some Wall Street observers, this pattern may already be visible. Major brokerage houses engage in program trading, the use of computers to guide huge corporate and institutional investments. Program trading, many believe, is responsible for the big price swings that have characterized stock market performance in recent years. If more people use investment software, this pattern is virtually certain to become more pronounced.

PROJECT MANAGEMENT

Managing a big project, like building a submarine or the New York World Trade Center, isn't easy. Thousands of separate jobs have to be coordinated so that they're done in the correct sequence and finished at the right time. To help managers cope with big projects, management scientists have invented project management techniques called CPM (critical path method) and PERT (program evaluation and review technique).

CPM and PERT both approach project management in the same way. (There are some differences between them, but we can leave them aside here.) First, a manager identifies *all* the individual activities that must be completed to get the job done. Second, the correct *sequence* of activities is determined; which ones have to be completed before the rest can be started? Third, the time required to complete the tasks is estimated. Finally, the *longest sequence* of activities is identified and graphed on a chart. The time it takes to complete these activities is the critical path (Figure 14–3). If any of these activities is delayed, the whole project will be delayed. So once the critical path has been identified, a manager can track critical path activities carefully to make sure they're on schedule.

PERT and CPM have proven their worth in large-scale projects. To use them, managers must sit down and identify all of a project's tasks, an exercise

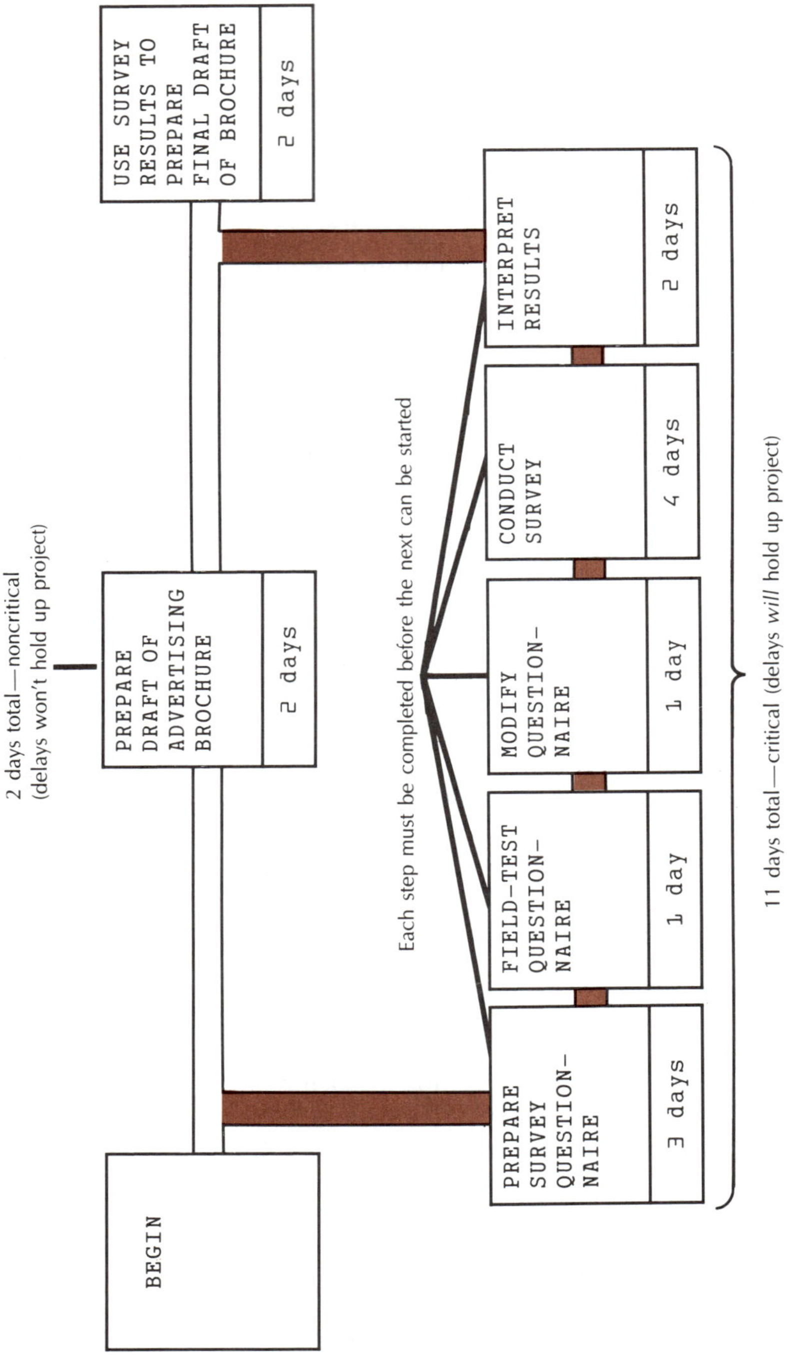

FIGURE 14–3 Critical Path Method of Project Management

that is beneficial in itself. These techniques help managers identify problems before they get out of hand; if a critical path activity is getting behind, more resources can be committed to it. Using PERT and CPM, the Navy completed its Polaris missile program 3 years ahead of schedule, and DuPont saved $1 million on a $10 million construction project.

Are CPM and PERT useful for small-scale projects? Before computers came along, they weren't. The expense of solving the formulas and preparing the diagram was so great that only large-scale projects could benefit. Now **project management programs** (such as Software Publishing Company's Harvard Total Project Manager) are available for personal computers, and they do all the calculating and charting for you. You can bring the benefits of PERT and CPM to small-scale projects, such as carrying out a one-person laboratory study or organizing an office for a direct mail campaign.

EDUCATION

Special-purpose software for education falls into two categories: software for computer-assisted instruction (CAI) and software for computer-managed instruction (CMI).

COMPUTER-ASSISTED INSTRUCTION (CAI)

Computer-assisted instruction (CAI) refers broadly to the use of the computer for instructional purposes. In a typical CAI session, the student engages in a dialogue with the microcomputer. The computer presents the student with a question or problem. The student responds. Then the computer analyzes the student's answer and provides immediate feedback.

All CAI programs share these basic attributes, but they can be placed in three broad categories:

Drill-and-Practice. Drill-and-practice programs reinforce material the student has already learned (Figure 14–4). These programs are well suited to areas in which memorization must play a role (for instance, mathematics, foreign languages, or spelling).

Tutorials. Tutorials introduce new material, guiding the student through it step by step (Figure 14–5). The student can proceed at his or her own pace; the program does not move on to the next level until the present one has been mastered. A wide variety of tutorial software is offered by Wicat Systems Co., a subsidiary of Control Data Corporation. Designed to run on a minicomputer system or a microcomputer local area network, this software — called PLATO — has produced impressive results. In one troubled,

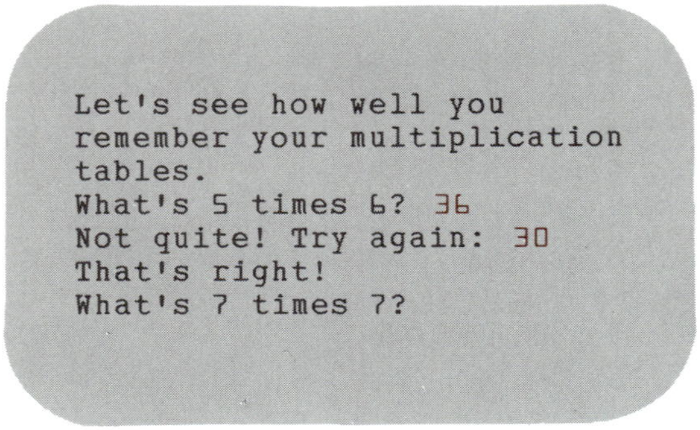

FIGURE 14–4 CAI: Drill-and-Practice Software

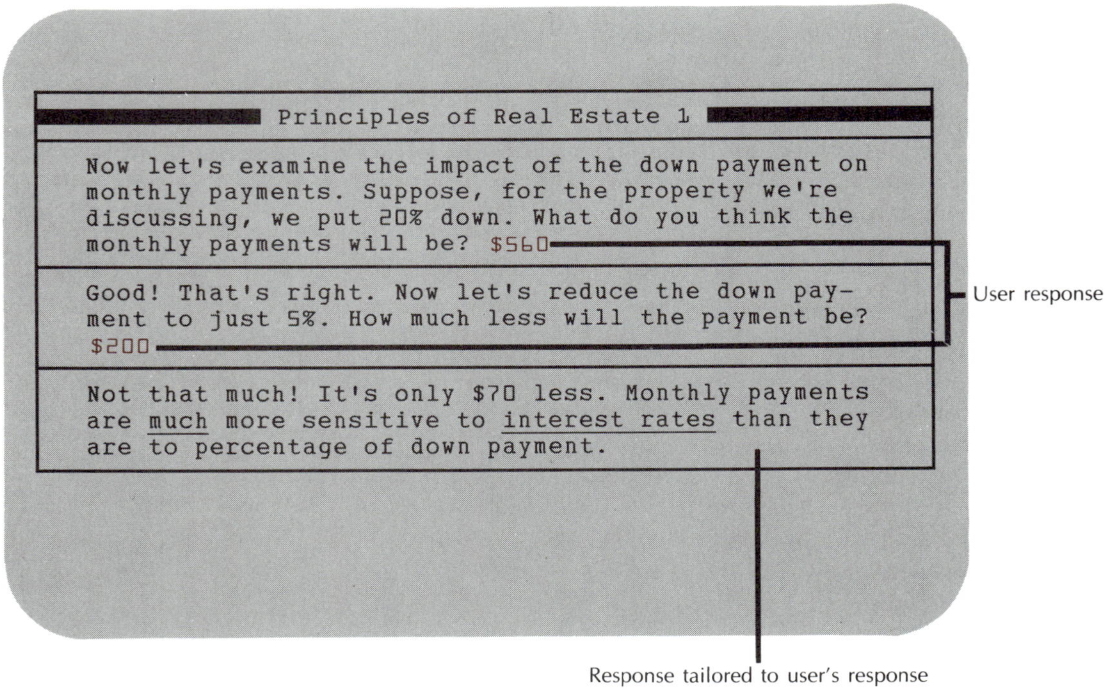

FIGURE 14–5 CAI: Tutorial Software

inner-city high school, for instance, a PLATO math course raised students' SAT scores by 120 points.

Simulation. Simulation programs teach facts and concepts by simulating real-world experiences on the display screen (Figure 14–6). The program SCRAM, for instance, simulates a nuclear power plant meltdown. Students must react to the unfolding situation and make decisions to prevent catastrophe. MOON

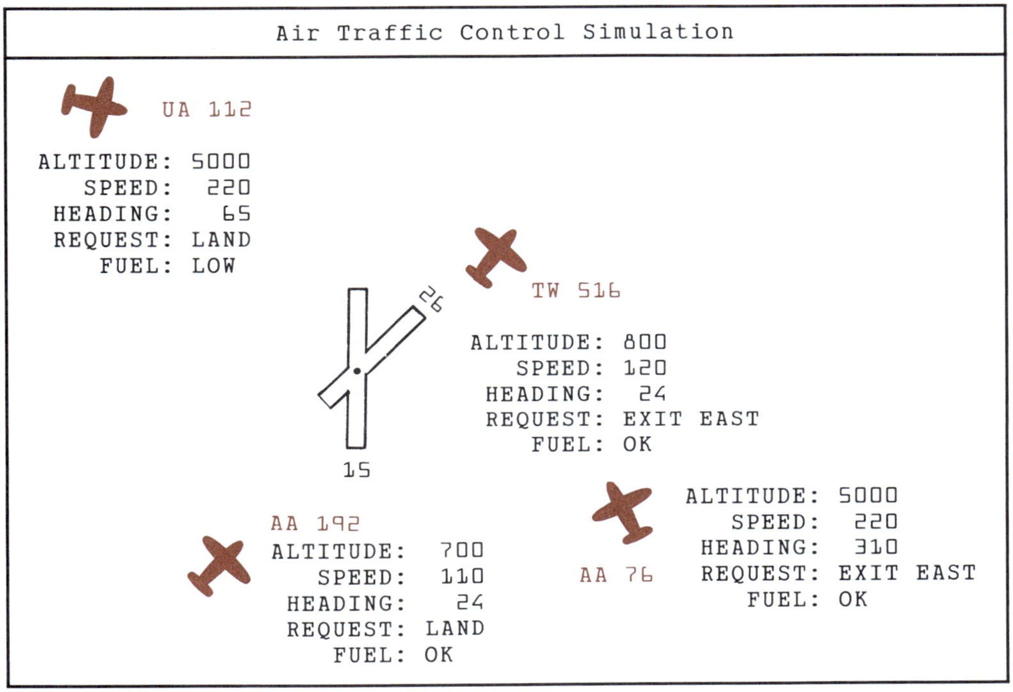

FIGURE 14–6 CAI: Simulation Software

LANDER simulates an Apollo lunar-landing module. The craft is descending at 3,600 m.p.h. at an altitude of 120 miles; fuel is sharply limited. To avoid a crash, students must learn how to calculate the allocation of fuel for the descent.

Computer-assisted instruction has advantages over traditional instruction methods. The computer provides individualized attention to students who might otherwise be ignored. Moreover, the instruction is pitched to the student's abilities; students learn at their own pace, so both the slower and more gifted students gain. Finally, the computer is infinitely patient. It never gets tired or shows bias.

Despite CAI's advantages, many schools and teachers have been slow to put computers in classrooms. One reason for this slow pace is a shortage of quality CAI software. Creating good CAI software is a huge job; it can take hundreds of hours of programming to produce just one hour of quality software-based instruction. Many teachers, moreover, lack computer skills, and some resist CAI out of fear that the computer is intended to replace them. Still others feel that the benefits of CAI have not been demonstrated sufficiently to warrant changes in the school curriculum.

Even so, CAI is likely to become more popular in the years to come. Parents are pushing for CAI, fearing that lack of computer skills will decrease their children's chances in the job market. Moreover, the pool of high-quality CAI software is growing steadily. Finally, a new generation of young teachers, trained in computer-assisted instructional methods and familiar with computers, is coming into the schools. In time, CAI will take its place along with other instructional resources (such as films and field trips) as a standard, familiar part of the educational experience.

COMPUTER-MANAGED INSTRUCTION (CMI)

Unlike most other professionals, teachers must spend as much as half of their workday on menial paperwork, such as filling out forms and grading student papers. Many experts believe the paperwork load to be a major enemy of instructional quality; it takes teachers away from students. Teachers have a new ally in the war against paperwork: the personal computer. Personal computers are useful for *managing* instruction — that is, doing the background paperwork that instruction requires — as well as for providing it. Software for **computer-managed instruction (CMI)** includes programs for computing grades, generating quizzes or exams out of data bases of test questions, scoring tests automatically, and tracking attendance.

SCIENCE

Special-purpose software for science includes software for managing bibliographic citations, working with statistical data, writing in technical fields, and managing huge amounts of text.

BIBLIOGRAPHIC MANAGEMENT

Every working scientist keeps track of the literature, and it's a big job. According to one recent estimate, between 6,000 and 7,000 scientific articles are written every day. In the face of an information crunch of this magnitude, scientists must develop new ways to track the literature in their fields.

Bibliographic data managers offer a new approach to scientific information management. These programs closely resemble the file management program discussed in Chapter 7, but with one major difference: they're preconfigured for bibliographic data base management. They come with predesigned data record forms for such materials as books, journal articles, conference papers, technical publications, and unpublished manuscripts. Data may be keyed in directly, or captured automatically from online data bases. At any time, a bibliography can be printed, and it will conform to established scientific and publishing standards.

In tandem with online data base services, bibliographic data managers can dramatically reduce the time scientists spend looking for new publications in their field. A zoologist specializing in whales, for example, can log on to an online data base vendor, and select the data base BIOSIS PREVIEWS. She then frames a search question that tells the computer, in effect, "Show me all the whale publications that have been added to the data base since I last logged on." In minutes, she downloads the new citations on disk. Next, the bibliographic data manager reads the disk file, and places each citation in its own data record. Finally, she prints out an alphabetized bibliography of the new sources. She has accomplished in about twenty minutes what might have taken a full day to do in the library. And the library search wouldn't have been as up-to-date. There's often a lag of a year or more before journal articles are indexed in print-based reference works. In contrast, the same articles may appear in an online data base within two or three weeks.

STATISTICAL PACKAGES

Statistics is the science of collecting, analyzing, and interpreting quantitative data, and it's just one of many academic disciplines that computers have aided. Before the computer, statistical studies were extremely tedious and, for this reason, were avoided or simplified. In sociology, for instance, doing a statistical study in the 1940s meant hiring a small army of research assistants, each equipped with an electromechanical calculator. In the 1960s, however, **statistical packages** — programs for doing a variety of statistical procedures on the computer — were developed.

Mainframe statistical packages quickly changed the face of most subjects that deal with quantitative data, such as sociology, economics, psychology, epidemiology, and others. For the first time, a large-scale statistical studies became economically feasible. Scientists could go beyond the simple statistical procedures and use more complex ones, which require huge amounts of computation.

Mainframe statistical packages have one serious limitation, however. To pay off the huge cost of a mainframe computer, most universities charge everyone who uses it. The fact that you're paying for every minute you spend with the computer discourages **exploratory data analysis,** the exploration of data with alternative statistical procedures. Exploratory data analysis can prove illuminating; it can even lead to major new interpretations of the data.

A variety of statistical packages are now available for personal computers. Comparable in flexibility and power to most mainframe packages, personal computer statistical programs offer one major advantage: there's no penalty attached to exploratory data analysis. To be sure, these packages don't run as fast on a personal computer as they do on a mainframe or minicomputer. A procedure that runs in 35 seconds on a minicomputer may take 3 or 4 minutes on a personal computer. In reality, however, this time difference is negligible compared to the convenience of having powerful statistical tools right on your desktop.

TECHNICAL WORD PROCESSING SOFTWARE

Engineers and scientists have special word processing needs; they must include special symbols and mathematical equations in their work. Technical word processing programs use bit-mapped graphics techniques to display and print equations, nonstandard characters, and chemical diagrams.

UTILITIES

Utilities are programs that help you use your personal computer more effectively. The transient programs provided with a personal computer's operating system include all the basic utilities you need for day-to-day work, but many users find additional utilities attractive. Among the top sellers are programs for creating a RAM disk, enhancing the keyboard, printing while performing other tasks, and recovering deleted files.

CREATING A RAM DISK

A **RAM disk utility** pulls off a neat trick: it fools a computer's operating system into thinking that part of the internal memory is a disk drive. To understand why this trick is so neat, you'll need to understand why many personal computer programs operate sluggishly.

Computer operations occur far more quickly when they occur solely in internal memory (RAM) without any disk access. You would think, therefore, that programmers would create programs that avoid disk access. With today's personal computers, internal memory sizes of 512K, 640K, or 1 megabyte are common. That's plenty of room for, say, a word processing program and 100 pages of text. But many users have not expanded their computers' internal memories beyond the 128K or 256K that the factory installs. So programmers, who want to sell as many copies of their programs as they can, must create programs that will run even in machines with small memories.

To create a big, complicated program that will run in a 128K or 256K computer, programmers use techniques that store portions of the program and data on the program disk. When these stored portions are needed, program execution stops and they're retrieved from the disk. This operation, called swapping, slows down program execution considerably. Annoyingly, it can freeze the keyboard for 20 seconds, 1 minute, or more. Even more annoyingly, the programs won't function any differently even if you install extra RAM. They just ignore it.

Now you can see why the RAM disk is such a neat trick. Once you've used a RAM disk utility to define part of the computer's internal memory as if it were a disk, you can copy a program and data to the "disk drive." But you haven't really copied anything to an actual disk; you've put it in RAM, where all operations occur at speeds ten to twenty times those involving disks and disk drives. The result is a major improvement in program performance. This improvement carries with it a big danger, though. As you'll recall from Chapter 3, RAM is volatile — that is, any information present in RAM is lost when the power is switched off. So if you "save" a word processing document to a RAM "disk," it isn't really saved at all. If you switch off the power, all your work will be lost. The way to avoid this disaster is to save your work frequently to real disks.

ENHANCING THE KEYBOARD

Let's say you like your favorite word processing or spreadsheet program, except for one thing: to accomplish a routine operation, such as saving a document to disk, you have to enter a long string of keyboard commands. And since you save to disk often, entering all those commands gets boring — and what's worse, it's lowering your productivity. All that time you spend punching keys could have been spent on more productive activities.

Key enhancement programs are designed to solve this problem; they store keyboard commands and let you enter a long string of them with a single keystroke. These programs are memory-resident; that is, they are active in memory while you're working with another program. When you're ready to use the key enhancement program, it pops onto the screen with a keystroke. Next, you enter the keyboard commands you want to store, and save them. Finally, you assign a single keyboard command (such as COMMAND-M) that enters all the keyboard commands at once — that is, as a *macro*.

PRINTING WHILE PERFORMING OTHER TASKS

Printing a lengthy document can tie up your computer, especially when it's used with a slow letter-quality printer. The problem here isn't the computer — it's the printer. The computer can send data to the printer much faster than the printer can accept it, so the computer has to wait until the printer's ready for it. In the meantime, almost all of the computer's processing power is going to waste.

Print spoolers (also called background printing programs) allow personal computer users to print and work with an application program at the same time. The print spooler operates even while the user is working with another program. Whenever there's a lull in the processing action, the print spooler automatically sends another batch of data to the printer.

RECOVERING DELETED FILES

Sooner or later it will happen to you. Accidentally, you'll erase a file containing hours, days, or even weeks of work — a file for which you've made no backup. People respond to this situation in different ways: tears, Donald Duck–style tantrums, or violent acts toward the computer are common. If you're ever in this situation, stop the string of invective: there's hope. Even though you've used the disk-operating utility to erase the file, it's probably still on the disk. Here's why: when you erase something on a disk, the read/write head doesn't actually remove all the information in the file. On the contrary, all it does is erase the file's entry in the disk directory. So long as you haven't written anything else to the disk, your data are probably still intact. A **file recovery program** can restore them.

SPECIAL-PURPOSE PROGRAM HORIZONS

In the early days of personal computing, very little application software was available. To use the computer, you were all but forced to learn some programming skills (usually in BASIC). Now that special- and general-purpose application software is widely available, programming skills have become unnecessary — and, some would say, pointless. After all, why should you spend a year learning how to write your own spreadsheet program when you can buy one for as little as $19.95 — or get one free, if you're willing to use a public domain spreadsheet program such as FREECALC? For this reason many educators believe that programming skills are of little relevance to a course on personal computers that focuses on application software.

Yet many people who use application software have found it worthwhile to learn at least some programming skills. *PC Magazine* found in 1985 that 60 percent of its readers programmed their computers, even though only 4 percent of them were professional programmers. Most of these people probably programmed their computers because they found it intellectually stimulating and fun. Yet there are other reasons to learn programming skills, and these reasons are completely consistent with a focus on application software. Chapter 15 explains these reasons and shows you how to get started with personal computer programming.

SUMMARY

Special-purpose application programs are tailored to get specific jobs done. Although many of these jobs could be approached with the five general-purpose programs, sometimes a special-purpose program offers clear advantages. In contrast to spreadsheet or data base management programs, special-purpose programs do not require extensive modification before they can be used for specific applications. Moreover, the better programs offer application-specific features that would be difficult or impossible to emulate with general-purpose programs.

Special-purpose programs for business include software for accounting, creating publication-quality documents, encrypting data, planning investments, and managing projects.

Accounting packages for personal computers include five modules: the general ledger, accounts receivable, accounts payable, inventory control, and payroll. Integrated accounting packages feature account automation, in which an entry made in one account, such as accounts payable, is automatically reflected in all other relevant accounts. A new development in the integrated accounting software field is the multiuser accounting package, which is designed for use in a local area network.

Unattended personal computers pose a security risk for many companies. Confidential or sensitive information stored on disk can be read, altered, or vandalized. To prevent security violations, some companies require employees to use data encryption software on sensitive data. These programs code data in unbreakable, unreadable codes.

Software for investment purposes gives any personal computer owner some of the expertise used by big brokerage houses. Investment programs include technical analysis packages (analysis of a stock's historical trends), fundamental analysis packages (analysis of a company's real value and prospects), and portfolio managers (analysis of an individual's package of investments).

Software for project management brings to personal computer users the expertise of a manager trained in CPM (critical path method) and PERT (performance evaluation and review technique). CPM and PERT are quantitative project management strategies initially developed for big projections. Personal computer project management software makes these approaches cost-effective for small ones too.

Special-purpose software for education falls into two categories: software for computer-assisted instruction (CAI) and software for computer-managed instruction (CMI). Computer-assisted instruction (CAI) refers broadly to the use of the computer for instructional purposes. CAI software engages the student in a dialogue; it presents questions, accepts and analyzes the student's responses, and provides immediate feedback. Instruction is pitched to the student's level and learning speed. CAI programs fall into three categories: (1) drill-and-practice programs, which reinforce knowlege the student has already acquired; (2) tutorial programs, which teach new material; (3) simulation programs, which teach facts and concepts by simulating real-world experiences. Software for computer-managed instruction can lighten teachers' paperwork loads and enable them to spend more time with students. CMI programs can help teachers compute grades, generate quizzes or exams out of data bases of test questions, score tests automatically, and track attendance.

Special-purpose software for science includes software for managing bibliographic citations, working with statistical data, writing in technical fields, and managing huge amounts of text. Bibliographic data managers capture bibliographic citations and abstracts from online data base services, downloading them automatically into a personal computer data base. Statistical packages bring to personal computers the power of mainframe packages. Because there is no charge for CPU time when one is using a personal computer, these statistical packages may improve the quality of scientific work by encouraging exploratory data analysis. Technical word processing programs use bit-mapped graphics techniques to display and print equations, nonstandard characters, and chemical diagrams.

Utilities are programs that help you use your personal computer more effectively. Popular utilities include RAM disk programs for defining part of RAM as a disk drive; keyboard enhancers that let you create elaborate keyboard macros and use them with application programs; print spoolers that let you work while you're printing; and file recovery programs that restore disk files you've accidentally deleted.

KEY TERMS

account automation
accounts payable program
accounts receivable program
bibliographic data manager
computer-assisted instruction (CAI)
computer-managed instruction (CMI)
exploratory data analysis
file recovery program
fundamental analysis program
general ledger program
integrated accounting package
inventory control program
multiuser accounting package
payroll program
portfolio manager
print spooler
project management program
RAM disk utility
special-purpose application program
statistical package
technical analysis program
vertical market program

REVIEW QUESTIONS AND EXERCISES

1. Why is it sometimes preferable to purchase a special-purpose application program rather than modifying a general-purpose program?
2. What are the advantages of account automation, integrated accounting software, and multiuser accounting packages for a small- or medium-sized business?
3. Imagine yourself working as the manager of a department in a corporation. What kinds of data would you be well advised to encrypt? Why?
4. What kinds of tasks can investment software perform? Why is it preferable to use these special-purpose programs rather than a spreadsheet?
5. Do project management techniques such as CPM or PERT make sense for the kinds of projects an individual or small business might take on? Why?
6. What are the three kinds of computer-assisted instructional software? Have you ever been exposed to any in school? If so, what were your reactions to it? Was it helpful? How could the programmer have done a better job?
7. Most professionals — lawyers, doctors, dentists, engineers, and so on — have support staff (secretaries, assistants, and custodians). Teachers don't, and, according to a recent national study, this fact is a chief reason teachers believe themselves to be undercompensated in comparison to other professionals. Will computers help to change this situation?
8. What is one advantage of doing a statistical analysis on a microcomputer instead of on a large, central mainframe computer?
9. Of the utilities discussed in the latter part of this chapter, which one or ones would you consider essential to professional or business use of a computer? Which ones are not essential but would be convenient to have?

FOR FURTHER READING

ACCOUNTING, PROJECT MANAGEMENT, AND INVESTMENT SOFTWARE

Badgett, Tom. "Getting a Handle on Your Business," *Personal Computing* (April 1986).

Hixson, Amanda C. *A Buyer's Guide to Microcomputer Business Software: Accounting and Spreadsheets* (Reading, Mass.: Addison-Wesley, 1984).

Meyers, Thomas A. "Rating Investment Software," *PC: The Independent Guide to IBM-Standard Personal Computing* (April 15, 1986).

Tanner, C. Kenneth, and C. Thomas Holmes. *Microcomputer Applications in Educational Planning and Decision Making* (New York: Teacher's College Press, 1985).

The, Lee. "All-in-one Accounting," *Personal Computing* (March 1985).

———. "Low-cost Accounting with Extras," *Personal Computing* (November 1985).

White, Thomas W., and G. William Dauphinais. "4-in-1 Accounting: The Basics from Real World," *PC: The Independent Guide to IBM-Standard Personal Computing* (October 1, 1985).

DATA SECURITY

Bonner, Paul. "Secret Disk a Lock-in Winner in Encryption," *PC Week* (February 18, 1986).

The, Lee. "Controlling Access to Your Data," *Personal Computing* (September 1985).

White, Lee. "Data Security: You Can't Work Without It," *ComputerWorld* (March 20, 1985).

KEYBOARD ENHANCEMENT SOFTWARE

Bonner, Paul. "Keyboard Enhancers: The Artful Means of Saving Strokes," *PC Week* (June 18, 1985).

Liskin, Miriam. "Conserving Your Keystrokes: Techniques for Building Better Macros," *Personal Computing* (April 1986).

Obregon, David. "Power Plays at Your Keyboard," *PC: The Independent Guide to IBM-Standard Personal Computing* (October 29, 1985).

COMPUTER-ASSISTED INSTRUCTION WITH MICROCOMPUTERS

Bitter, Gary, G., and Ruth A. Camuse. *Using a Microcomputer in the Classroom* (Reston, Va.: Reston, 1984).

Bonner, Paul. "Computers in Education: Promise and Reality," *Personal Computing* (September 1984).

Boruta, Marcia, and Hugh Mehan. "Computers in the Classroom: Stratifier or Equalizer?" *Science for the People* (March/April 1985).

Davidson, Melvin. "Computer-Assisted Instruction on a Microcomputer," *Byte* (November 1978).

Gleason, Gerald T. "Microcomputers in Education: The State of the Art," *Educational Technology* (March 1981).

Michaels, Sarah, Courtney Cazden, and Bertram Bruce. "Whose Computer Is It, Anyway?" *Science for the People* (March/April 1985).

Sorensen, Peter R. "Simulating Reality with Computer Graphics," *Byte* (March 1984).

STATISTICAL SOFTWARE FOR MICROCOMPUTERS

Carpenter, James, Dennis Deloria, and David Morganstein. "Statistical Software for Microcomputers: A Comparative Analysis of 24 Packages," *Byte* (April 1984).

Collins, T. W. "Social and Science Research and the Microcomputer," *Sociological Methods and Research* (May 1981).

Fridlund, Alan J. "Taking the Numbers Bull by the Horns," *InfoWorld* (February 11, 1985).

Stahr, Lisa B. "Working with Statistical Analysis," *Personal Computing* (October 1984).

Vanderbok, William G. "SPSS Arrives on the PC," *PC: The Independent Guide to IBM-Standard Personal Computing* (March 5, 1985).

15 *Application Programming:* *From Problem to Solution*

"Programming is not like neurosurgery, nuclear physics, or flying the space shuttle. Programming is like writing, woodworking, or photography. Anybody can do it."
Chris Crawford *Popular Computing*[1]

Now that so much application software is available, anyone can use a computer fruitfully without possessing advanced programming skills. Even so, there's no shortage of arguments in support of learning some programming fundamentals. Some say a little experience with programming helps you think more logically. Others point out that, on occasion, a problem crops up that no commercially available application program can solve. In such a case, you'll have to write your own program — or hire someone else to do it for you. Even if you hire someone else, they say, knowing something about programming can help you evaluate the hired programmer's work.

Perhaps the most compelling argument for readers of this book, however, is to point out that some elementary programming skills can help you get more — much more — out of your application software. Many spreadsheet, data

base, and integrated programs contain their own programming languages. A few simple programs written in these languages will suffice to automate many tasks that might otherwise have taken hours to perform. The skills you'll need aren't difficult to acquire, and when you have them, you'll be on your way to becoming a *power user:* a personal computer user who harnesses every available tool in the service of application productivity.

SPEAKING COMPUTERESE: AN INTRODUCTION

A program is a series of instructions to the computer that tell it what to do. It embodies an algorithm, or a step-by-step approach to solving a problem. **Programming,** then, is the process of transforming an algorithm into a program — a series of instructions the computer can understand.

The key word here is "understand." Computers do not speak English, nor are they likely to anytime soon. One reason is that English (like all natural human languages) is wonderfully rich in ambiguity; a high proportion of words in the dictionary have more than one meaning. *Plant,* for instance, is both a noun and a verb — and that's not the end of the ambiguity. As a noun, it can mean either "vegetable" or "factory." Humans have no problem with this kind of ambiguity, but computers can't tolerate it at all. Every program statement made to a computer must be completely unambiguous.

That's why we need *programming languages.* **Programming languages** are formalized systems of computer-readable notation that allow algorithms and data to be expressed in an unambiguous, precise manner. And for this reason, they're not like English or any other naturally occurring language (even though they often use English words as commands).

Programming languages do share one characteristic with human languages, however. There's no single, universal programming language that everyone uses, and most programming languages are mutually unintelligible. Hundreds of programming languages already exist, and new ones are constantly being created. So far as programming languages are concerned, we're living after the fall of the Tower of Babel. Fortunately, you don't need to be an accomplished field linguist or intrepid explorer to find your way among this confusion of competing tongues. All existing programming languages sort neatly into four categories: *machine languages, assembly languages, high-level languages,* and *very high level languages.* We'll discuss the first three now; very high level languages we will discuss at the end of this chapter in the section titled "Programming Horizons."

MACHINE LANGUAGE

Machine language uses binary numbers to tell the computer what to do. Actually, machine language is the only language that a computer can understand. All other kinds of computer languages must be translated into machine language before the computer can understand them.

Machine language instructions are highly specific. They tell the computer, for instance, to move a single byte of data at a time to a particular location within the microprocessor. To illustrate, suppose you're asking your roommate to go get a soft drink from the refrigerator, and you're using the human equivalent of machine language. You'd have to tell him, "Contract your stomach muscles so that you lean forward in the chair. As you lean forward, grasp the arms of the chair with your hands. Push upward to lift your body from the chair. Use your thigh muscles to straighten your legs and lift you to a standing position," and so on.

Hardly anyone programs in machine language these days, and for obvious reasons. It takes many machine language instructions to accomplish a simple function, such as adding two numbers together. What is more, programming in machine language is extremely tedious — and prone to error, as well, because people do not find binary numbers easy to read or work with. No alternative to machine language existed, however, in the early days of computing.

Machine languages are called **low-level languages** because they involve the programmer deeply in the actual, internal movement of data within the CPU. Programming in a low-level language is like driving a car using only the lowest gear: a great deal of work is going on in the engine, but you don't get very far very fast (Figure 15–1).

FIGURE 15–1 Machine Language Program to Add Two Numbers

Memory address	*Instruction*	
00000000	00111110	Load the next byte of data into a temporary storage area
00000001	00000101	Data: the number 5
00000010	11000110	Add next byte to storage area
00000011	00001001	Data: the number 9
00000100	00110010	Store amount accumulated in temporary storage area
00000101	00000111	Least significant half of address
00000110	00000000	Most significant half of address
00000111	00001110	Sum

ASSEMBLY LANGUAGE

Assembly language programming was developed in the late 1940s and early 1950s to speed programming tasks and reduce errors. In place of binary numbers, the programmer uses two- or three-letter instructions (such as ADD or MVI), which are abbreviations for the functions the instruction performs. The instruction ADD, for instance, stands for a series of machine language instructions that add two numbers together. To make assembly language instructions easier to use, they're *mnemonic* (ni-MON-ik) — that is, they remind the programmer what they stand for (Figure 15–2). Extending the analogy above, a human language counterpart of assembly language would use the mnemonic DECHAIR (raise body from chair) in place of all the instructions needed to get the friend out of his chair.

Assembly language brought about major productivity and accuracy improvements in computer programming; however, a program written in assembly language cannot be used directly by the computer. Because the computer can understand only machine language, a program had to be devised to translate the assembly language code into its machine language counterpart. This program, called an **assembler,** does this job automatically. It begins with the **source code,** or the code that the programmer has written. Then it translates the source code into **object code,** or instructions given solely in the machine language that the computer understands.

Despite its superiority to machine language, assembly language is still a low-level language. The programmer must know the hardware intimately to program well in assembly language. He or she must think in terms of what the machine is to do rather than in terms of the problem at hand. And even though one assembly language instruction may take the place of a half dozen or more machine language instructions, it still takes many assembly language instructions to produce a full-scale, functioning program. One has the sensation, as Charles Petzold puts it, of "trying to construct a suspension bridge out of toothpicks."[2]

Another limitation of assembly language is its lack of **portability,** or usability on other brands of computers. Assembly language statements pertain to a particular CPU's instruction set, the list of operations that it has been designed to perform. Instruction sets vary among competing computer brands. So an assembly language program written for one computer is very unlikely to run on another; in other words, it's not portable.

Instruction	
MV1 NUMB 1	Load the first number to be added into the temporary storage area
AD1 NUMB 2	Add the second number to be added to the temporary storage area
STA SUM	Store the sum in a memory location called SUM

FIGURE 15–2 Assembly Language Version of Program in Figure 15–1

To be sure, programs written in assembly language have merit: like machine language programs, they're designed around the computer's architecture. So they execute very rapidly and take full advantage of the hardware's capabilities. For this reason, many people still program in assembly language when they want programs to run quickly. Yet computer scientists saw a clear need for a more portable programming language, one that would let programmers think in terms of the problem at hand rather than requiring them to focus on the details of CPU processing. Their efforts led to high-level programming languages.

HIGH-LEVEL LANGUAGES

High-level languages, first developed in the mid- to late-1950s, insulate the programmer from the details of what's going on inside the CPU. Instead of many specific instructions, high-level languages allow the programmer to express algorithms using a set of English-sounding words and mathematical symbols. For example, the addition of the two numbers A and B can be expressed in a natural way:

```
X = A + B
```

The same expression in assembly language would involve several statements, all having to do with precisely what is to go on inside the CPU.

High-level languages are closer to natural languages than to assembly language. Even so, programs written in high-level languages still have to take into account the general contours of what the computer is to do. In this brief BASIC program, for example, you can see the general outline of standard computer procedure (input and storage, followed by processing and output). The line numbers indicate the precise sequence in which the instructions are to be carried out.

```
10 INPUT A
20 INPUT B
30 X = A + B
40 PRINT X
50 END
```

The first statement, INPUT A, means "accept a number from the keyboard. Call it A, and store it in the memory." The second statement does exactly the same thing for the variable B. The third statement, on line 30, means "Add A and B, call the sum X, and store the sum in the memory." The statement on line 40 means "Display the value called X on the screen." The last statement ends the program's execution.

As you can see, one statement in a high-level language such as BASIC may correspond to many assembly language instructions. For this reason, programs written in high-level languages are shorter — and much easier to use and understand — than their assembly language or machine language counterparts.

If you were using a high-level language to tell your roommate to go get a soft drink, you could say, "Please get up, go to the kitchen, open the fridge, and get out a soft drink. Close the fridge, come back here, and give the soft drink to me." Notice that you still have to spell out the procedure, but you can use general terms and ignore the specifics (for instance, the specifics about how one opens a refrigerator door).

Like assembly language programs, programs written in a high-level language must be translated into machine language code before the computer can understand them. The programs that make such translations are called *compilers* and *intepreters.*

Compilers. A **compiler** operates in a batch-processing mode — that is, it goes through the entire text of the source code, automatically translates it into machine language object code, and quits. It generates a product: a **compiled program** (that is, one that will run on the computer by itself, without any further assistance from the compiler). Think of the compiler as being like a professional, multilingual translator, who translates an English short story by writing out a new, separate version of it in Spanish. Once the translation is finished, you can use it without the translator hanging around.

Interpreters. An **interpreter** does not produce a compiled program. On the contrary, it remains in the memory and executes the source code directly, without leaving behind any permanent record of the translation it has done. The user types in a program, and the interpreter executes it immediately. If there are any programming errors, they can be fixed and the program can be run again right away. Think of the interpreter as being like a professional human interpreter who goes with you along the streets of Madrid. You tell the interpreter to ask the waiter to bring you a glass of water; the interpreter says *"Tráigale a él un vaso de agua, por favor"* ("Please bring him a glass of water"). No record is made of the interpretation; the interpreter does her job right on the spot, and that's that.

Interpreters have many advantages, especially for learning purposes. With the interpreter present in the memory, you sit at the keyboard and try out program instructions. Just after you finish writing the source code, the interpreter executes it — and if there are any problems (*bugs,* or flaws in the program design), they'll show up right away. You can then display the program again and edit it. Today's interpreters will automatically detect problems in the way you've written the program and point them out to you. Furthermore, you can expand the program right on the screen, adding new functions to see how they work. Interpreters are, in short, highly interactive.

Interpreters do have two major disadvantages. The first is slow speed. A compiled program runs as much as ten to twenty times faster than the same program run through an interpreter. The second disadvantage is inefficient use of memory. To run a program through an interpreter, the interpreter must be present in the computer's memory along with the source code. Because of these disadvantages, most commercial software is sold in compiled form.

High-level languages are designed to be portable, that is, to operate on a wide variety of computers. Ideally, the language itself is standardized in a single, unvarying form. Compilers and interpreters take care of translating the program for a particular hardware environment. If a high-level language truly lives up to this ideal, a source code program written for one computer could be compiled or interpreted for another one, and it would run just fine. Unfortunately, few high-level languages live up to this ideal in practice.

High-level programming languages got their start in 1954, when John Backus and coworkers at IBM created FORTRAN (*For*mula *Tran*slator). FORTRAN, which is intended for scientific calculations, epitomizes the high-level language ideal; it closely follows the principles of mathematical and algebraic notation, so the programmer can express the program in terms natural to the problem. FORTRAN was initially greeted with much skepticism; few believed that a compiled program could work as efficiently and well as a hand-done assembly language program. The skepticism quickly turned to enthusiasm when it was proved that a machine-translated compiled program could equal an assembly language program in quality.

At about the same time, Grace Hopper and her coworkers at Remington Rand began work on what was to become COBOL, and in the late 1950s an international committee produced ALGOL (Algorithmic Language). In many respects, FORTRAN, COBOL, and ALGOL can be accurately regarded as the progenitors of almost all modern programming languages, which try — with only mixed success — to improve on the past (Table 15–1). Indeed, FORTRAN and COBOL are still widely used.

The rapid proliferation of programming languages has concerned computer scientists. After all, one of the reasons mathematics is such a powerful tool is that there is only one worldwide system of notation. For this reason, efforts have been made periodically to create a universal programming language, one that would meet everyone's needs and become the standard. PL/I, ALGOL, APL, Pascal, Ada, and others have been offered as nominees. Although all these programs have become popular, none suffices for every programmer or application, and these efforts have failed. Programmers will continue to choose the language they believe best suited to the task at hand — as did Charles V, who remarked "I speak Spanish to God, Italian to women, French to men, and German to my horse."

The tendency of programming languages to become identified with a particular task is well illustrated by the remarkable survival of the two oldest ones, FORTRAN and COBOL. FORTRAN is still the language of choice for many scientists and engineers, and COBOL — outmoded as it is — is still a standard

(*text continues on p. 422*)

TABLE 15–1 A Capsule History of Programming Languages

Date	Language	
1945	*Plankalkul*	Arguably the first programming language, Plankalkul was a system of programming notation created by the German computer inventor Konrad Zuse. Zuse never implemented the language, but many of his ideas found their way into modern programming languages.
1954	*FORTRAN*	Initially, FORTRAN was developed for performing calculations in the sciences, mathematics, and engineering. The language is outmoded in many respects; lengthy FORTRAN programs tend to have many GOTO statements that transfer control to another part of the program. These statements make the program difficult to understand and maintain. But FORTRAN's ability to express mathematical problems keeps its popularity high. FORTRAN programs are almost always compiled. It is virtually alone among programming languages for its high degree of standardization; its programs are, in consequence, highly portable from one computer environment to the next.
1958	*ALGOL*	A language that never caught on in the United States, ALGOL is the creation of an international committee. Widely used in Europe until recently, ALGOL blends the mathematical prowess of FORTRAN with the logical elegance of Zuse's Plankalkul. ALGOL is still used, but its chief importance today is its contribution to modern programming languages that emphasize logical structure, such as Pascal.
1959	*LISP*	Developed in 1959 by John McCarthy at the Massachusetts Institute of Technology, LISP (List Processor) was developed for nonnumerical applications, such as simulations of human problem solving. It is well suited to performing repetitive operations on textual data. In recent years, LISP has become one of the languages of choice for artificial intelligence research.
1960	*COBOL*	Developed specifically for business applications, COBOL (Common Business-Oriented Language) excels in handling large volumes of business data, such as financial or inventory records. Although COBOL uses GOTO statements and does not suit modern standards of program design, it is remarkably user-friendly. COBOL programs use English words (EXAMINE INVENTORY TALLYING MUFFLERS) and, for this reason, are especially easy to use. These features have made COBOL the most widely used programming language of all. COBOL programs are compiled. Although efforts are made to standardize COBOL periodically, several competing versions exist. For this reason, COBOL programs may not be portable.
1964	*BASIC*	Invented by John Kemeny and Thomas Kurtz, two Dartmouth College professors, BASIC (Beginner's All-Purpose Symbolic Instruction Code) was developed as a teaching language. BASIC shows a strong FORTRAN influence, and has many of FORTRAN's shortcomings, such as poor facilities for lending logical structure to programs. BASIC has other shortcomings, too; the program does not handle large volumes of data well, for instance, and it is the least standardized of all programming languages. A BASIC program written for one microcomputer will almost certainly need rewriting before it will run on another. Despite its shortcomings, BASIC is very popular; about 90 percent of a microcomputer magazine's readers, for example, use the language. BASIC programs are usually interpreted, although BASIC compilers are available.

Date	Language	
1964	*PL/I*	PL/I (Programming Language I) represents an attempt to create a universal programming language — a language that would include features that appeal to everyone. So PL/I includes features of both FORTRAN and COBOL. An IBM-developed language, PL/I is identified with the mainframe programming environment. It is considered by many to be unwieldy and difficult to learn. PL/I programs are compiled.
1968	*APL*	Although APL (A Programming Language) has been nominated for universal use like PL/I, it has found a niche among programmers who use it for advanced computation in statistics. Also produced by IBM, APL requires special equipment and is not widely used.
1970	*Pascal*	Pascal is named after the eighteenth-century mathematician Blaise Pascal, who invented an early calculating machine. Created by the Swiss computer scientist Niklaus Wirth, Pascal shows ALGOL influence in its strong emphasis — indeed, insistence — on the prominence of logical structure in program design. Pascal was originally designed as a teaching language. Attempts to elaborate it have created several competing versions, so Pascal programs may not be portable. Nevertheless, Pascal is growing in popularity, particularly among microcomputer users; about 30 percent of one microcomputer magazine's readers program in Pascal. Pascal programs are compiled.
1973	*PILOT*	Designed for applications in computer-assisted instruction (CAI), PILOT (Programmed Inquiry, Learning, and Teaching) was developed by John A. Starkweather at the University of California, San Francisco. PILOT programs involve the user in a dialogue as the user types responses to questions the computer poses. Although useful for CAI, PILOT is not a good choice for other programming applications.
1974	*C*	Developed by Dennis Ritchie at Bell Laboratories, C is a high-level language that nevertheless gives programmers a high degree of control over the computer. For this reason, compiled C programs execute very rapidly. It is also highly portable. These two features combine to make C the language of choice for many professional software houses, such as Microsoft. The language is cryptic and difficult to learn, however. It does not enforce good programming practices, so an untrained user may produce poor-quality work with it.
1980	*Ada*	Named after Ada Augusta, the Countess of Lovelace and a coworker of the nineteenth-century inventor Charles Babbage, Ada is sponsored by the U.S. Department of Defense for use by all government contractors and defense-related agencies. Like PL/I, Ada stems from an attempt to create a language that will do everything. Some criticize it as unwieldy and inefficient; others believe it to be a major breakthrough. Ada incorporates the emphasis on logical structure found in ALGOL and Pascal. Yet it goes far beyond Pascal in its flexibility.
1980	*PROLOG*	Initially developed by a French team headed by Alain Colmerauer, PROLOG (Programming in Logic) was polished by a group of computer scientists at the University of Edinburgh. PROLOG is unlike any other programming language. Its statements are designed to perform inferences from a knowledge base, and can answer questions such as "If all good parents buy their children encyclopedias, is it true that all encyclopedias are bought by good parents?" PROLOG is widely used by artificial intelligence programmers.

Writing a Program in BASIC

Brenda Smith is a fifth-grade teacher at Willow Run Elementary School, and — after years of good service — her desk calculator has quit for good. Since she has a personal computer on the same desk, she decides to write some BASIC programs instead of buying a new calculator. One program she will write finds the average score her students make on spelling quizzes.

Brenda recalls how she added up the quiz scores on her calculator. She began by clearing the calculator. Then she punched in the scores, one by one. As she did, the number shown in the plasma display would grow as the scores accumulated. When she came to the end of the scores, she would count the number of scores. (Although there are twenty-one students in Brenda's class, the number of scores goes up or down depending on absences or students visiting from other teachers' classes.) Finally, she would divide the accumulated score, the one shown on the display, by the number of scores, and write down the result (the average).

Brenda wants her program to do exactly what she used to do with her calculator. After doing a good deal of advance planning, she starts her computer, loads BASIC, and types the following:

```
10  REM ****************************************************
20  REM *      Program to compute average test scores      *
30  REM ****************************************************
40
```

Note that each line in a BASIC program has a number. The computer follows these numbers when it executes the program. Instead of numbering the lines 1, 2, 3 . . . , however, Brenda — following the usual practice — has numbered them by 10. This way, if she decides to add a line between two existing ones, there will be plenty of room without renumbering every line in the program.

The word REM is a *statement* that tells the computer to do something. The REM (for remark) statement doesn't accomplish much — it just tells the computer to ignore the rest of the line, which contains Brenda's reminder to herself about what this program does.

While planning her program, Brenda realizes that, when she averages scores with a calculator, she starts out with two different counts. The first count, which she decides to call the *accumulator,* accumulates the scores (by addition) and shows them on the plasma screen. The second count, which she decides to call the *counter,* keeps track of how many scores have been added up. Both start out at 0.

Lines 50 and 60 clear the "calculator" for the start of a score-averaging session. The LET statement allows Brenda to assign an *initial* value to a numeric variable. A numeric variable is a quantity with a name (here A and C, for accumulator and counter). These initial values will change as the program operates. Every program statement has its own syntax, or rules governing the exact order and form in which the statement is expressed. In the LET statement, for instance, the variable must come before the quantity assigned to it.

At the right of both lines is a comment, or a note added to explain how the program works. Each comment begins with an apostrophe, which tells BASIC to ignore what follows.

```
10   REM  **********************************************
20   REM  *  Program to compute average test scores    *
30   REM  **********************************************
40
50   LET A = 0      'Set accumulator to 0
60   LET C = 0      'Set counter to 0
```

When Brenda adds up test scores using her calculator, she performs the same action several times. She takes the score, adds it to the accumulator, and adds 1 to the counter. Then she takes the next score, adds it to the accumulator, adds 1 again to the counter, and so on. In other words, she's performing a *loop* — an action that she performs over and over again until there is no more data. So she decides to use a loop structure in her program.

The loop begins with line 70 and the INPUT statement. The INPUT statement allows the program's user to type in data from the keyboard. It displays a question mark on the screen, and waits for the user to press a key. When the computer has received the input, it assigns the variable name X to it. (We'll skip over line 80 for now; you'll see why it's necessary in a moment.) Line 90 uses the LET statement again to modify the A (accumulator) variable, which — at this point — is still 0. It sets a new value for the variable A. Line 100 moves up the counter by 1.

Line 110 uses a new statement, GOTO. The GOTO statement branches the program back to the line number specified (here, line 70). And when the computer gets back to line 70, it asks for another score by displaying a number on the screen — and the whole process repeats itself. Now line 90 adds the second score to the first score, and line 100 changes the count to 2.

```
70    INPUT X                      'Begin loop
80    IF X = -99 THEN GOTO 120     'Test for end of data
90    LET A = A+X                  'Add data to accumulator
100   LET C = C+1                  'Add one to counter
110   GOTO 70.                     'End loop
```

You've probably already seen why line 80 is necessary. If it weren't for line 80, there would be no way to get out of this loop. The computer would just keep asking for more scores. Line 80 gives you a way out. It checks for the entry of a sentinel value, an impossible data item (here, −99) that is used to tell the program that all the scores have been entered. (*box continues on next page*)

Writing a Program in BASIC (continued)

When Brenda types in −99, the program jumps to line 120. Line 120 names a new variable, M (for mean or average), and assigns to it the value derived from dividing A (the accumulator's final value) by C (the counter's final value).

```
120 LET M = A/C     'Mean = Accum./Counter
```

The program isn't quite finished yet. Line 120 determines the average score, but it doesn't display the average on the screen. Line 130, with its PRINT statement, is needed.

```
130  PRINT "AVERAGE = ";M     'Print the mean
```

The PRINT statement provides an excellent example of how persnickety even easy programming languages can be about syntax. The statement won't work unless all the punctuation is done just right. The material to be shown on the screen is enclosed in quotes, and the semicolon tells the computer to insert the value stored for the variable named M.

So here's the finished program:

```
10   REM ***********************************************
20   REM *  Program to compute average test scores     *
30   REM ***********************************************
40
50   LET A = 0                      'Set accumulator to 0
60   LET C = 0                      'Set counter to 0
70   INPUT X                        'Begin loop
80   IF X = -99 THEN GOTO 120       'Test for end of data
90   LET A = A+X                    'Add data to accumulator
```

for business programming. Indeed, about 80 percent of currently operating computer programs are written in COBOL.[3] To some, FORTRAN and COBOL are "living fossils"; others, however, "would point out that even a very old species might still be filling a particular ecological niche."[4]

The failure to establish a single, universal programming language may not have the grave consequences some imagine. In fact, it may be best to *avoid* ambitious programming languages, the ones that try to do everything. According to some computer scientists, these programs may be overly complex and prone to errors.[5] In recent years, computer scientists have become less concerned about which programs are being used; instead, they've become more concerned with *how* programs are being written. Traditional programming techniques are giving way to a new approach called *structured programming.*

```
100  LET C = C+1                    'Add one to counter
110  GOTO 70                        'End loop
120  LET M = A/C                    'Mean = Accum./Counter
130  PRINT "AVERAGE = ";M           'Print the mean
140  END
```

And here's what it looks like when it runs on the screen, as it is interpreted by BASIC:

```
Ok
RUN
?10
?15
?11
?18
?9
?19
?11
?15
?12
?19
?13
?15
?8
?18
?14
AVERAGE = 13
Ok
```

STRUCTURED PROGRAMMING

Jeff Duntemann, a technical editor of *PC Tech* magazine, recalls — none too avidly — his first experience with programming. Using APL at a mainframe terminal, Duntemann created a 300-line text editor. Several months later, his company switched computers, and the program wouldn't run on the new system. He suspected that a little rewriting would get the program running again — and then he looked at the source code.

> I realized with welling horror that I hadn't the slightest idea how my program worked. The code was literally Greek to me. No matter how hard I tried, I could not dope out the algorithm by looking at the code. I ended up abandoning the old formatter and writing a new one from scratch.[6]

Duntemann's experience illustrates why so many programming experts are disenchanted with **traditional programming** techniques, preferring newer, structured techniques instead. To understand why, let's take a closer look at the distinction between traditional and structured programming.

TRADITIONAL PROGRAMMING

Until semiconductor memory chips dramatically lowered the price of internal memory, programmers knew they'd be working with very limited amounts of memory. Moreover, early computers were slow. And so programmers tried to write efficient programs, that is, programs that would use very little memory and operate quickly. A mystique grew up around the programming wizards who, with great cleverness and often highly idiosyncratic techniques, wrote the most compact codes. There was a built-in payoff, too, to using idiosyncratic techniques. If you were the only person in the whole company who knew how the payroll program worked, the boss could hardly afford to fire you!

Traditional programming, however, presents two major problems. The first problem is that the source code will probably be unintelligible to other people. To make the program execute rapidly and use little memory, programmers removed spaces between program statements, placed several statements on one line, eliminated statements that only served to clarify the program's function, and removed comments that explained what an instruction did. The result, called "good code," might look like this:

```
250  IFE=10ORE=15THEN30ELSE80;GOTO290
```

The problem with this kind of code, however, is that it's unintelligible to others — and, as Duntemann's experience shows, it might even be unintelligible to the person who wrote the program! If the program has to be altered by someone else, it may be necessary to throw the whole thing out and start over.

The second problem created by traditional programming techniques is poor program structure. Encouraged by programs such as APL, COBOL, FORTRAN, or BASIC, which do not force programmers to use clearly defined program structures, traditional programmers sometimes string lines of code together without forethought. Often they use the GOTO statement, which transfers program control to another section of the program. When the GOTO statement is overused, which it frequently is, the result is spaghetti code: a program that has no clear logical structure and presents itself as a welter of interconnections. Spaghetti code programs will run, but attempts to alter them later may prove catastrophic. Changes may reverberate through the program structure, leading to unpredictable consequences.

The shortcomings of traditional programming were amply illustrated in the early 1960s, when IBM undertook the development of an operating system for

Case Study: The Risks of Faulty Programming

The countdown was coming to an end. Lying on their backs in the cockpit of the space shuttle *Columbia,* astronauts John Young and Robert Crippen could see pelicans flying along the beach at Cape Canaveral. Straight ahead the stars had given way to the deep blue of early morning. Within less than an hour they would be the first people to fly the space shuttle into orbit, the first Americans in space in more than five years.

Then, 20 minutes before launch time, warning lights at Mission Control began to flash. Something was wrong with the computer system. The countdown was halted; the computer analysts went to work. They had three hours before the flight would have to be scrubbed.

It became apparent that nothing was physically wrong with the computers. All the circuits were working. The communication lines were intact. The problem seemed to lie instead in the programs, in the software, that told the computers what to do.

Technicians immediately realized they faced a serious problem. The software on board the space shuttle consists of nearly 500,000 elaborately woven instructions. Finding a programming error, a bug, in that web would be like trying to find a single misspelled word in an encyclopedia. Soon the news began to circulate. The maiden flight of the space shuttle would have to be delayed.

"It was precisely the type of error that one would expect," says the Dutch computer scientist Edsger W. Dijkstra (pronounced DIKEStra). He inhales on his cigarette, then continues. "You see, most of NASA's software is full of bugs."

His eyebrows arch with pleasure, a sure sign that a story follows. "I saw the first moon shot in 1969, when Armstrong, Aldrin, and Collins went to the moon, and shortly thereafter I met Joel Aron of IBM's Federal Systems Division, who I knew had been responsible for a large part of the software. So when I saw Joel at the swimming pool of our hotel in Rome, I said, 'Joel, how did you do it?' 'Do what?' he said. I said, 'Get that software to work okay.' 'Okay?' he said. 'It was full of bugs. In one of the trajectory computations, we had the moon's gravity repulsive rather than attractive, and this was discovered by accident five days before count zero.' "

Dijkstra draws back in his chair, the picture of astonished outrage. "When I had regained my composure, I said, 'Those three guys, they have been lucky.' 'Oh yes,' Joel said."

For more than twenty years, Dijkstra has been fighting against the kind of programming that inevitably leads to bugs in computer software. To him, the way organizations like NASA program computers is foolhardy at best, perilous at worst. He believes there is another way, a better way. It involves structuring how a person thinks about programming so that programs themselves acquire a firm mathematical basis. The discipline his work has spawned, called structured programming, has been one of the most important advances in computer software of the past two decades.

From Steve Olson, *Science '84* (January/February 1984)

its new System/360 computers. The project fell seriously behind, so the project managers — using standard management techniques — put more programmers to work on it. But the new people did not clearly understand what their predecessors were doing, and the project was delayed even more.

IBM eventually delivered the System/360 operating system, but the experience taught the computer industry a hard lesson. The cost of creating software was rising just as rapidly as the cost of hardware was declining. In some large-scale computing systems, 10^7 lines of code must work together to manipulate 10^{12} bits of information — more than the total number of circuits in a huge mainframe computer. Programming for these large-scale systems clearly ranks among the most complex tasks humans have ever undertaken. As problems with programming increased, computer scientists began to wonder whether problems with software would put an end to the computer industry's rapid progress.

THE STRUCTURED APPROACH

The term **structured programming** is used in two ways. Originally, the term meant following Edsger Dijkstra's suggestion that spaghetti code should be avoided. In large corporate programming departments, however, the term now refers to a project management technique that is designed to improve programming efficiency and lower development costs. To add to the confusion, the project management approach called structured programming also includes an emphasis on structured programming the way Dijkstra defined it.

For our purposes, we can blend these two meanings and say that structured programming is founded on three fundamental principles:

1. The program should be carefully planned before any coding begins.
2. The program should use logical control structures to accomplish its aim. Spaghetti code should be avoided.
3. Documentation and program readability are more important than program efficiency.

Planning. A common mistake made by traditional programmers (and programming beginners) is to start writing codes without doing much planning in advance. If problems arise when the program is tested, or so the traditional thinking goes, they can be solved through **debugging,** or the process of finding and fixing bugs in a faulty program. Epitomizing this process is the computer *hacker,* a programming enthusiast who boasts of the ability to get any program, no matter how faulty, to work.

Research on improving the productivity of programmers, however, has demonstrated that program quality is best achieved through careful planning rather than through debugging. Detecting a problem is far easier and cheaper in the design stage than it is in the debugging stage.[7] To avoid errors, increasing numbers of programming experts recommend a type of planning known as **top-down programming.** In top-down programming, the programmer begins with a clear formulation of just what the program will accomplish. This includes an exact specification of the data to be used and the output to be produced. The program is then designed using *modules.*

A **module** is a set of logically related program statements that accomplish a specific task in a program, and a **modular program** is made up of a series of modules (Figure 15–3). **Modularity** (said of a program that uses modules extensively) has its origins in ALGOL, in which program modules always used BEGIN and END statements. Modularity is also a prominent feature of ALGOL's descendant, Pascal. Modularity makes programs easier to read, understand, and check. It also makes it possible to divide work among a team of programmers, a technique that has produced huge programs in the space of six months or a year.

Modular programs follow strict rules:

All modules and program statements have *single* entry and exit points. This practice makes the program's organization much clearer if anyone besides the programmer needs to understand it.

Each module should be of modest size (no nore than forty or fifty statements at the most). This restriction makes the program easier to read.

A module's function should be logically independent of other modules' functions. Moreover, each module should perform just one, clearly identifiable

FIGURE 15–3 Modular Program (in True BASIC)

Defines variables

```
LET answer = 3
```

Establishes contact with user

```
PRINT "Guess my number (between 1 and 5)!"
INPUT guess
```

Makes decisions based on user input

```
SELECT CASE guess
    CASE 2
      PRINT "Close! Answer=";answer
    CASE 4
      PRINT "Close! Answer=";answer
    CASE guess=answer
      PRINT "Right!"
    CASE ELSE
      PRINT "Answer=";answer
END SELECT
```

```
END
```

function in the overall program. That way, if some change needs to be made to the module in the future, only one part of the program will be affected. Ideally, a new, altered module can be inserted without affecting any other part of the program.

The modules and program statements should occur in an order that is logical considering the program's function. Each module should pass on program control to the next in an orderly, sequential fashion.

Many traditional programmers do not like programming under these restrictions. Yet evidence is mounting that these rules reduce programming costs, diminish programming errors, and dramatically lower the cost of program maintenance.

Control Structures. A well-structured program accomplishes everything it does using the three basic **control structures — sequence, selection,** and **loop** (Figure 15–4). These control structures govern the sequence in which program instructions are executed. In a structured program, they control all aspects of program execution, and GOTO statements are avoided. This rule strikes many traditional programmers as overly strict and confining, for it's often easier to use GOTO statements than it is to think up a control structure that will do the job. Yet it has been proven mathematically that any problem a computer can solve can be solved using the three control structures. (This is the "firm mathematical basis" for structured programming that Dijkstra mentioned in the case study, above.) In other words, *there is always a way to express an algorithm using these three control structures.* If there isn't, the program can't be solved by a computer. This proof is as significant in the history of computer science as was Turing's 1937 demonstration that a digital computer could solve virtually any problem in mathematics or logic (see Chapter 2).

On grounds of program readability, control structures are preferable to GOTO statements. Programs with numerous GOTO statements are exceptionally difficult to read and understand, whereas those which use control structures instead are far more readable.

Documentation and Readability. A computer program is a medium of communication — not merely between the programmer and the computer, but also between *people.* A successful program, for instance, must be maintained; it is sure to receive upgrades and changes as conditions change. (Tax laws, for example, change every year, and so do accounting programs.) Since program maintenance may be done by others, a program should be readable by someone besides the person who created it. There's no discounting the importance of program maintenance; in large-scale installations, maintenance can cost ten to twenty times as much as creating the program in the first place.

Top-down structured programming techniques help make programs more readable. To help clarify the function of program modules, moreover, each

SEQUENCE CONTROL STRUCTURE

Executes a series of program statements in the order they are listed	Input population Multiply population by 1.03 Print population

SELECTION CONTROL STRUCTURES

IF/THEN Executes a single statement if a condition is true	net pay is more than $1 print check
IF/THEN/END IF Executes several statements if a condition is true	net pay is more than $1 deduct net pay amount from payroll acct. print check
IF/THEN/ELSE Executes one or more statements if a condition is true; otherwise, executes an alternative statement or series of statements	net pay is more than $1 print check print "Help yourself to 2 cups of coffee"
SELECT CASE Allows branching on more than one condition	year year = 1985 print "Good year for Beaujolais" year = 1984 print "Good year for white wines" year = 1983 print "Good year for German wines" print "Sorry no data"

LOOP STRUCTURES

FOR/NEXT Executes one or more statements a predetermined number of times	year = 1987 to year = 2087 Multiply population by 1.03 Increase year by 1 year
DO/WHILE Executes one or more statements until a condition is satisfied	there are more employee records figure net pay print paychecks

FIGURE 15–4 Control Structures

"Street BASIC" and True BASIC

The BASIC supplied with most of today's microcomputers has an increasingly bad reputation among programming teachers — and, according to BASIC's inventors, John Kemeny and Thomas Kurtz, it's well deserved. This may sound surprising coming from the language's own inventors, but they are dead serious. According to Kemeny and Kurtz, the people who created BASIC interpreters for early microcomputers had to make compromises because these machines had such small memories. Unfortunately, they say, some of these compromises became "features" of the language, and were retained even after the reason for the compromises had disappeared. The result was what they call "street BASIC."

The problem with microcomputer BASICs, Kemeny and Kurtz add, isn't merely that they contain compromises — although that's bad enough. Even worse, microcomputer BASICs lack the new features that Kemeny and Kurtz have added to the language in recent years. These features reflect the growing acceptance of structured programming. Microcomputer BASICs contain an insufficient number of logical control structures, so people trying to program in the language are virtually forced to use GOTO statements.

A look at the program written by the schoolteacher Brenda (see pp. 420–422) shows that the program — which is well written and documented by BASIC standards — violates two major rules of top-down structured programming. First, it isn't modular. To be sure, lines 70 through 110 could be considered a module, but it's not clearly separated from the rest of the program. Second, the "module" has two exit points. If the X value does not equal −99, the exit point is line 110. If the X value does equal −99, the exit point is line 80.

Brenda's program isn't particularly hard to follow as it is, yet the beginnings of spaghetti code are already in evidence. In a really big program, one with several hundred lines of code, the result may be an unreadable mess.

should be well documented, both with textual materials (manuals and records) and ample comments in the program itself. This emphasis on program readability, to be sure, works to the disadvantage of program efficiency. Unfortunately, well-documented, readable programs do not run as fast as the tightly written, undocumented code produced by adept traditional programmers.

Sometimes efficiency is so important that it isn't worth sacrificing for the sake of readability. An interactive data base system used for posting day-to-day business transactions, for instance, shouldn't keep people waiting for five minutes while it searches for data records. The structured programming approach favors readability over efficiency. Whether that bias is appropriate in any one situation is up to the judgment of a professional programmer.

To bring BASIC up to date, Kemeny and Kurtz have published a new version of the language — True BASIC. Here's Brenda's program in True BASIC:

```
LET A = 0
LET C = 0

DO
     INPUT X
     IF X <> -99 THEN
          LET A = A+X
          LET C = C+1
     ELSE
          LET M = A/C
          PRINT "AVERAGE = ";M
          STOP
     END IF
LOOP
END
```

After setting the accumulator and counter to 0, this program uses a single, highly readable module. Translated into English, it says: "Begin a loop. Accept X from the keyboard. If X doesn't equal −99, then let A = A+X and let C = C+1. Now do the loop over again. Otherwise (ELSE), let M = A/C and print "Average = ," placing the value stored for variable M after the equals sign. Now stop looping and end." Note how the indentations accentuate the program's structure and help to communicate what it does.

Structured Programming in Action. Mounting evidence suggests that the bias implicit in structured programming — a bias in favor of readability and against efficiency — makes excellent sense in most situations. The first large-scale test of structured programming was carried out in a huge project for *The New York Times* in the early 1970s. The task was to automate the retrieval of citations from the newspaper's voluminous records. The program came to 83,000 lines of code, and took twenty-two calendar months to write — but it was finished ahead of schedule and cost *less* than originally anticipated. Only twenty-one errors were found during testing, a remarkable achievement for a program that large.

PROGRAMMING APPLICATION SOFTWARE

It isn't difficult to write short, simple programs in a language such as BASIC, True BASIC, or Pascal. On the other hand, becoming an accomplished application software programmer requires more than merely learning the meaning of program statements and mastering program syntax. It also requires the master of a huge number of algorithms for tackling day-to-day programming challenges, such as positioning the cursor on a bit-mapped graphics screen or sorting a list the fastest way. Mastering these algorithms, and learning how to express them in a programming language, requires a major investment of time.

Most people, in short, will never become accomplished programmers of full-scale application software — nor should they. It's absurd to spend 350 hours of your time to learn how to develop a word processing program when you can buy one for $10. For this reason, many people now say that only those who wish to become professional programmers should bother learning a programming language. What this argument ignores, however, is the very real relevance of a little programming expertise to the use of application software. For example, consider this simple program, which is written in a language designed to work with a popular data base management program. The progam is simplified and altered a little so that you can understand it, but is close to the real thing:

```
LET CHOICE = 0

DO WHILE CHOICE < 4

     ERASE SCREEN
     DISPLAY "MAIL MENU
              1.  Add new names
              2.  Sort data
              3.  Print mailing labels"
     INPUT "Enter your choice (1 to 3) " TO CHOICE

     IF CHOICE = 1
          DISPLAY BLANK DATA RECORD
     END IF

     IF CHOICE = 2
          SORT DATA RECORDS ON LAST NAME
     END IF

     IF CHOICE = 3
          DO LABELS
     END IF
END DO
```

You probably saw right away that this is a well-structured program; we're looking at a program module that displays a screen menu for a data base management system. In English, the program says: "Set the variable choice to 0. While the choice is less than 4, erase all the junk on the display screen. Now display the menu ("Mail menu . . . ."), with its three choices. If the user picks No. 1, display a blank data record on the screen. If the user picks No. 2, sort the data records by the last name. If the user picks No. 3, print mailing labels from the data base."

This program is really very simple; it's the kind of program Brenda wrote to average her class's test scores. And that program, as you saw, was rather simple and trivial. And yet, sitting on top of a huge data base, the program just presented becomes another sort of beast entirely — it produces some very impressive results. Indeed, it transforms a very user-*un*friendly data base management program into a user-friendly one, so that even an untrained person can add data to it, sort records, or print mailing labels. To understand why, we'll need to focus on the concept of *leverage* — because that's exactly what we're talking about here.

The word *leverage* refers to the substantial advantage in power one can gain by using a lever. All by yourself, for example, you probably can't lift that big boulder way out in the field. If you set up a fulcrum for support, however, and get a good, strong length of steel rod to use as a lever, you'll find yourself able to do an absolutely amazing job of lifting all by yourself. You really aren't applying any more force to the rod than you did when you tried to lift the boulder without assistance. But when you apply the modest force you can exert to the *lever,* spectacular things happen.

Using the programming languages provided with many spreadsheet, data base management, and integrated programs gives you exactly the same kind of leverage. Simple programming skills, the kind that Brenda has, won't get you very far in programming if you try to write your own software from scratch. But when you use those skills to write programs using the languages provided by applications software, something amazing happens: you have leverage. The same skills that could produce only simple programs with a language such as BASIC all of a sudden become capable of doing some very impressive things.

PROGRAMMING HORIZONS

Computer scientists have been looking in earnest for other ways to get the kind of programming leverage just discussed. We'll cover two of them here: *automatic programming* and *very high level languages.*

AUTOMATIC PROGRAMMING

Program generators present the user with a series of questions, such as "What is the name of the input variable?" The user responds in everyday language and, when the dialogue is finished, the program generator constructs a program in some high-level language. The result is **automatic programming,** or programming that does not require any programming expertise at all from the person using the computer. Thus far, automatic programming has shown some promise, but it has succeeded only with relatively simple applications.

VERY HIGH LEVEL LANGUAGES

The high-level languages discussed so far allow programmers to think in terms of the problem at hand, but they are still *procedural:* the program tells the computer how to get a result, and goes through the instructions step by step.

Very high level languages (also called **nonprocedural** or descriptive languages) free the programmer from concern with procedure. To put it another way, the programmer can state "what result is wanted without specifying how to get it."[8] All this may sound mysterious and abstract, but in fact you've already used a very high level language: the electronic spreadsheet. In a spreadsheet, you use expressions very much like the ones you would use in a BASIC program (such as X = A+B). However, you needn't worry about the procedure the computer should follow to solve the problem. Your only concern is to set up the spreadsheet model in a way that conforms to how you would naturally think about it. Very high level languages produce leverage in a big way. Simple spreadsheet models, which may take only an hour or two to create, would take many hours — perhaps days or even weeks — to program in a high-level language such as BASIC or Pascal.

So why bother to learn how to program at all? Simple — if you can learn a few elementary structured programming techniques and use them to enhance the application software you're using, you can get double leverage. You're getting the leverage of a very high level language when you use a spreadsheet or a data base management program's query language. And when you apply your programming skills to automate what a spreadsheet or data base management program is doing, you've put leverage on leverage. You've become a power user.

SUMMARY

A program is a series of instructions to the computer that tell it what to do. It embodies an algorithm, or a step-by-step approach to solving a problem. Programming, then, is the process of transforming an algorithm into a program — a series of instructions the computer can understand. Programming languages are formalized systems of notation that allow algorithms to be expressed in an unambiguous, precise manner. Hundreds of programming languages already exist, and new ones are constantly being created.

All existing programming languages sort neatly into four categories: machine languages, assembly languages, high-level languages, and very high level languages.

Machine language uses binary numbers to tell the computer what to do; it is the only language that a computer can understand. All other kinds of computer languages must be translated into machine language before the computer can understand them. It takes many machine language intructions to accomplish a simple function. Machine languages are called low-level languages because they involve the programmer deeply in the actual, internal movement of data within the CPU.

Assembly language programming was developed in the late 1940s and early 1950s to speed programming tasks and reduce errors. In place of binary numbers, the programmer uses two- or three-letter instructions, which are abbreviations for the functions the instruction performs. A program written in assembly language cannot be used directly by the computer. Assemblers transform the source code into the machine language object code the computer can understand. Assembly language programming is an improvement over machine language programming, but the programmer must still write programs that focus on what the CPU is doing. Moreover, assembly language programming goes very slowly.

High-level languages, first developed in the mid- to late-1950s, insulate the programmer from the details of what's going on inside the CPU. Instead of many specific instructions, high-level languages allow the programmer to express algorithms using a set of English-sounding words and mathematical symbols. Even so, programs written in high-level languages still have to take into account the general contours of what the computer is to do. Programs written in a high-level language must be translated into machine language code before the computer can understand them. The programs that do this translation are called compilers and interpreters.

A compiler operates in a batch processing mode — that is, it goes through the entire text of the source code, automatically translates it into machine language object code, and quits. It generates a product: a compiled program. An interpreter does not produce a compiled program. On the contrary, it remains in the memory and executes the source code directly, without leaving behind any permanent record of the translation it has done. The user types in a program, and the interpreter executes it immediately. If there are any programming errors, they can be fixed and the program can be run again at once. Interpreters are, in short, highly interactive. However, they are slow and inefficient.

High-level languages are designed to be portable, that is, to operate on a wide variety of computers. Unfortunately, few high-level languages live up to this ideal in practice.

The first high-level languages were FORTRAN, COBOL, and ALGOL. FORTRAN (a language for scientific calculations) and COBOL (a language for business data processing) are still in widespread use. ALGOL (a language that emphasizes logical control structures) has influenced many newer languages, such as Pascal and Ada, which are growing in popularity. Attempts to create a single universal programming language have failed. Many people still prefer to use FORTRAN and COBOL, even though they are outmoded. And the evidence suggests that a single universal programming language would be far too complex to be useful in practice.

Traditional programming techniques emphasized the creation of efficient programs, which use very little memory and operate quickly. However, traditional programs are often unintelligible to others who must figure out how they work in order to maintain them. The overuse of GOTO statements, moreover, led to spaghetti code — code that has so many overlapping branching statements that no one save the programmer can figure out what the program does just by looking at it. Spaghetti code cannot easily be maintained. Changes made on one line may reverberate unpredictably throughout the entire program.

Structured programming is founded on three fundamental principles: (1) the program should be carefully planned before any coding begins; (2) the program should use logical control structures to accomplish its aim, and should avoid spaghetti code; and (3) documentation and program readability are more important than program efficiency.

Program quality is best achieved through careful planning rather than through debugging. To avoid errors, increasing numbers of programming experts recommend a type of planning known as top-down programming, in which the programmer begins with a clear formulation of just what the program will accomplish. Included in this formulation is an exact specification of the data to be used and the output to be produced. The program is then designed using modules. A module is a set of logically related program statements (Figure 15–1), and a modular program is made up of a series of modules. Modular programs follow strict rules: (1) all modules and program statements have *single* entry and exit points; (2) each module should be of modest size (no more than forty or fifty statements at the most); (3) a module's function should be logically independent of other modules' functions; and (4) the modules and program statements should occur in an order that is logical considering the program's function, each module passing on program control to the next in an orderly, sequential fashion.

A well-structured program accomplishes everything it does using the three basic control structures — sequence, selection, and loop. GOTO statements are avoided. It has been proven mathematically that any problem a computer can solve can be solved using the three control structures. On grounds of program readability, control structures are preferable to GOTO statements. Programs with numerous GOTO statements are exceptionally difficult to read and understand, whereas those which use control structures instead are far more readable.

A computer program is a medium of communication — not merely between the programmer and the computer, but also between *people.* Readability is vital for program maintenance. Top-down structured programming techniques help make programs more readable. Readability, however, works to the disadvantage of program efficiency.

Most people will never become accomplished programmers of full-scale applications software — nor should they. Yet learning some elementary programming skills can help you become a power user of spreadsheet, data base management, and integrated software.

Very high level languages (also called nonprocedural or descriptive languages) free the programmer from concern with procedure. The programmer can specify the result wanted without specifying the procedures for getting it. You have already used a very high level language if you have used a spreadsheet or a data base query language.

KEY TERMS

assembler
assembly language
automatic programming
compiled program
compiler
control structure
debugging
interpreter
loop
low-level language
machine language
modular program
modularity
module
nonprocedural language
object code
portability
program generator
programming
programming languages
selection
sequence
source code
structured programming
top-down programming
traditional programming
very high level language

REVIEW QUESTIONS AND EXERCISES

1. Someone asks you, "You're taking a computer course. So what's programming?" Answer in twenty-five words or fewer.
2. What is one major difference between human and programming languages? Hint: list all the possible meanings of several common words such as *tree* or *fish*.
3. What is the major disadvantage of machine language?
4. Why do people still program in assembly language sometimes?
5. What's the difference between a low-level and a high-level language? Is a high-level language procedural or nonprocedural?

6. Program your roommate to go get you a pizza, first in machine language and then in an assembly language. List the instructions you would use.
7. What's the difference between a compiler and an interpreter? Between source code and object code?
8. What became of efforts to create a single massive programming language that would benefit everyone equally?
9. What's the difference between structured and traditional programming techniques?
10. What are the three basic principles of structured programming?
11. In what sense is source code a vehicle for communication between people as well as between people and computers?
12. Think of some common, everyday activities, such as doing laundry at the laundromat, and draw a flowchart expressing one of these activities using only the three basic control structures.
13. What's wrong with "street BASIC," according to BASIC's creators?
14. Critique this statement: "95% of personal computer users will use application software, and for this reason they should completely forget about programming. They don't need to know anything about programming to use the computer at maximum efficiency."
15. Explain this statement: "A personal computer spreadsheet is a very high-level programming language."

FOR FURTHER READING

PROGRAMMING SKILLS AND LANGUAGES

Aarons, Richard. "BASIC [for the IBM Personal Computer]," *PC: The Independent Guide to IBM-Standard Personal Computing* (October 29, 1985).

Brooks, Fredrick P. *The Mythical Man-Month* (Reading, Mass.: Addison-Wesley, 1975).

Crawford, Chris. "Why You Should Learn to Program," *Popular Computing* (September 1983).

Dickenson, John. "Programming Makes Sense for Business," *PC: The Independent Guide to IBM-Standard Personal Computing* (October 29, 1985).

Dijkstra, Edsger. *A Discipline of Programming* (Englewood Cliffs, N.J.: Prentice-Hall, 1976).

Duntemann, Jeff. "Pascal [for the IBM Personal Computer]," *PC: The Independent Guide to IBM-Standard Personal Computing* (October 29, 1985).

Field, Tim, and Jim Heid. "Step by Step with Mac Pascal," *MacWorld* (April 1985).

Helms, Harry L. *Computer Language Reference Guide* (Indianapolis: Howard W. Sams, 1980).

Kemeny, John G., and Thomas E. Kurtz. *Back to BASIC* (Reading, Mass.: Addison-Wesley, 1985).

Knuth, Donald. *The Art of Computer Programming* (Reading, Mass.: Addison-Wesley, 1973).

Martin, James. *Application Development Without Programmers* (Englewood Cliffs, N.J.: Prentice-Hall, 1982).

Sandberg-Diment, Eric. "Does Everyone Need to Learn Programming?" *The New York Times* (January 17, 1984).

Tesler, Lawrence G. "Programming Languages," *Scientific American* (September 1984).

Wirth, Nicklaus. "Data Structures and Algorithms," *Scientific American* (September 1984).

———. *Algorithms + Data Structures = Programs* (Englewood Cliffs, N.J.: Prentice-Hall, 1976).

Yourdon, Edward, and Larry Constantine. *Structured Design* (New York: Yourdon Press, 1978).

PROGRAMMING APPLICATION SOFTWARE

Ewing, David P. *One-Two-Three Macro Library* (Indianapolis: Que, 1985).

Lotus Development Corporation. *The Lotus Guide to Symphony Macros* (Reading, Mass.: Addison-Wesley, 1986).

McMahon, Marilyn. *Report Writing in dBASE II* (Englewood Cliffs, N.J.: Prentice-Hall, 1986).

Prague, Cary N. *Programming with dBASE II* (Blue Ridge Summit, Pa.: Tab Books, 1985).

Ridington, Richard W. *The Hidden Power of Lotus 1-2-3: Using Macros* (New York: Brady Books, 1985).

———. *More Hidden Power of Lotus 1-2-3: Advanced Macro Applications* (Englewood Cliffs, N.J.: Prentice-Hall, 1986).

Simpson, Alan. *Simpson's 1-2-3 Macro Library* (Berkeley: Sybex Computer Books, 1986).

PART SIX

"Any medium powerful enough to extend man's reach is powerful enough to topple his world."

Alan Kay

The Impact of Computing

Computer applications skills give you the tools you need to cope with the information society — a society in which what counts is knowing how to acquire, manipulate, and communicate information. You will find these skills to be of value to you in many ways. Yet no survey of personal computing applications would be complete without considering the risks as well as the benefits. And that's the purpose of Chapter 16.

16 *The Benefits and Risks of Personal Computing*

"Every technological change has an equal capacity for the enhancement or degradation of the quality of life, depending on how it is used."

Barry Jones *Sleepers, Wake! Technology and the Future of Work*

Large- and middle-sized computers are benefiting us in many ways: they're guiding jet aircraft safely from takeoff to touchdown, raising the quality of health care, improving the distribution of goods and services, opening major new channels of communication, and widening our knowledge of the universe. Yet the same technology poses risks as well. Huge data banks maintained by both government and private agencies, for example, may work to erode our individual liberties.

Precisely the same point can be made about the personal computer: it brings with it risks as well as benefits. We'll look at the good news first.

BENEFITS

The personal computer's benefits are most striking in helping small business compete more effectively, improving public access to knowledge, helping the handicapped, providing new channels for communication, and opening new opportunities for employment.

NEW TOOLS FOR SMALL BUSINESS

Computers help people in business make better decisions, work more efficiently, broaden the scope of their enterprises, and position themselves advantageously vis-à-vis their competition. Companies that use computer technology creatively have been able to price their products lower, provide new customer services, and produce higher-quality goods. Here's just one of thousands of possible examples. A medical information system at El Camino Hospital in California is helping the hospital to offer inpatient services at rates as much as 40 percent lower than other area hospitals. Even with these price reductions, the system is producing savings at an estimated $20 to $21 per patient per day, above and beyond the cost of installing and maintaining the system.

The personal computer has given small businesses the same cost-cutting, profit-raising advantages formerly enjoyed only by large firms. And if small businesses can cut costs and improve profits, the United States economic outlook may brighten considerably. Just consider this fact: small businesses, according to one study, were responsible for the creation of about 80 percent of new jobs in the United States between 1969 and 1976. In the future, small businesses will probably continue to produce new jobs at a faster rate than large companies.

The personal computer could not have arrived at a better time, for entrepreneurship is on the upswing. More people than ever before are becoming entrepreneurs by organizing and managing new business ventures. "Entrepreneurship will be the major impetus of the decade immediately ahead of us," says the founder of People Airlines, Donald C. Burr.[1] Burr is undoubtedly right; entrepreneurship is exploding. In 1950, Americans were creating only 93,000 new businesses per year. By the end of 1983, the figure had skyrocketed to 600,000.[2]

IMPROVED PUBLIC ACCESS TO KNOWLEDGE

The United States economy may gain in another way by the growing use of personal computers: improved access to knowledge is virtually certain to encourage new, profitable business ventures. In today's information economy, information and know-how are just as important as capital — perhaps *more* important. During the heyday of heavy industry, knowing how to build an automobile factory would not give you much of an advantage, unless you were able to come up with the millions needed to build it. Today, however, many highly profitable companies are started on shoestring capital. Steve Jobs scraped up part of the capital needed to start Apple Computer (a Fortune 1000 company these days) by selling his old Volkswagen bus. Apple's strategic resource? Knowledge of personal computers and their prospects in the economy.

The management guru Peter Drucker stresses that "Knowledge has already become the key to productivity, competitive strength, and economic achievement. Knowledge has already become the primary industry, the industry that supplies the economy with the essential and central resources of production."[3] And so the more knowledge is available, the more entrepreneurs will use it to create new enterprises. And the personal computer, as you've seen throughout this book, is opening a major new chapter in the history of access to information and knowledge. Already a $4 billion per year business, the online information industry will experience steady growth as personal computer owners begin taking advantage of online knowledge.

The personal computer's role in widening public access to knowledge may do more than stimulate the economy. It may also save lives. "The failure in medicine," says Dr. Mark Toups, a general practitioner, "are failures of information"[4] — and the personal computer seems to be the ideal remedy. Doctors in rural areas, for instance, may not be prescribing the latest and best therapies for their patients. Eighty to 85 percent of cancer patients are seen by community physicians. The most serious problem for these doctors, according to Vincent T. DeVita, the director of the National Cancer Institute, is keeping up with the amazing pace of new discoveries in cancer treatment. A potential solution: Physician Data Query (PDQ), an online data base service that specializes in up-to-date cancer treatment information. Physicians can use personal computers to search PDQ, which often lists important new findings months before they are published in medical journals.[5]

HELPING THE HANDICAPPED

The personal computer is playing an impressive role in improving the welfare of handicapped people. Until recently, the loss of some natural function, such as speech, hearing, or sight, was almost sure to lead to diminished quality of life and reduced employment prospects. Personal computers, however, are helping to change this picture.

Because personal computer technology is both cheap and transportable, computer-based helping devices can be positioned where handicapped people need them. Here are a few examples of one of the personal computer's most positive roles in today's society.

Handicapped people whose mobility is impaired can work at home by telecommuting, an innovation that is opening up a new world of meaningful careers for the handicapped.

Hearing-impaired people can now communicate with others through computer-based communications media, such as electronic mail. After receiving work instructions via the computer, a hearing-impaired person can perform the work at the computer console and, when finished, upload the results. A major new source of careers has opened for the hearing-impaired in various fields, such as accounting, data processing, and computer programming.

Personal computers equipped with voice synthesis systems are opening new worlds of literature to the blind. One system can read text from virtually any printed book. Formerly, blind people were restricted to books that had already been transcribed into Braille or recorded on tape.

NEW CHANNELS FOR COMMUNICATION

One reason for the United States' remarkable record of economic development is the freedom and ease of communication its citizens have enjoyed. The telegraph and telephone brought about virtually instantaneous message and voice communications; document delivery, in contrast, has lagged. By 1970, it still took one to three days to deliver documents from coast to coast. Now that personal computers are becoming widespread, the prospects for electronic mail — and instant document delivery — are becoming brighter.

Via electronic mail, a five-page report can be communicated from coast to coast in a matter of minutes. To be sure, there's nothing new about this rapid delivery speed; offices equipped with facsimile ("fax") machines have been doing it for years. Facsimile machines form an electronic image of a page of text or graphics, send the image over the telephone lines, and reproduce it on the other end. However, facsimile works only when you've facsimile machines at both ends of the transmission. Although many large companies have them, growth rates are not strong enough to suggest that facsimile-based electronic mail will displace the postal service.

If 50 million personal computers are in use by 1995, as one study suggests, the picture may be very different. Personal computers may do for electronic mail what facsimile probably won't — that is, give millions of people the transmission and reception devices they'll need to get involved. And the prospects for this kind of electronic mail look good; corporate use is expected to grow substantially in the coming years. If the new communications media do for the economy what the telephone and telegraph have already done, the results suggest increased prosperity.

NEW EMPLOYMENT OPPORTUNITIES

Your involvement with the personal computer may lead to enhanced job opportunities. Over the next decade, some of the fastest-growing job areas will be in computer-related fields. According to the Bureau of Labor Statistics, between 1982 and 1995 the number of jobs will grow by 96.8 percent for computer service technicians, 85.3 percent for computer systems analysts, and 65 percent for electrical engineers. The *total number* of new jobs in computer fields, to be sure, is not large; only about 6 percent of new jobs will require advanced scientific or electrical engineering expertise.[6]

Your personal computer skills are far more likely to help you obtain and succeed in a job not directly connected with the design, manufacture, or programming of computers. Rapid growth is expected for many jobs for which computer application skills are highly useful. These jobs include:[7]

> *Business Services.* Approximately 3 million new jobs will open by 1995 for accountants, business consultants, legal assistants, personnel officers, public relations workers, security officers, and people skilled in computer applications.
>
> *Professional Services.* The economy will require about 850,000 new attorneys, engineers, accountants, and architects.
>
> *Health Professions.* About 3 million more new positions will open in health-related fields, with exceptionally high growth rates expected for positions in physical therapy, medical insurance records processing, occupational therapy, and medical and dental instrumentation.

In all these fields and more, your personal computer applications skills may improve your chances of getting the job you want — and of keeping it.

RISKS

Personal computer technology — and microelectronics technology in general — poses risks as well as bringing benefits. These risks may be greatest for blue-collar workers and service workers, as well as for small-business owners who ignore the rules for secure computer operation.

DISPLACED BLUE-COLLAR WORKERS

The most serious risk posed by microprocessor-based computer technology may lie in the displacement of blue-collar workers (factory employees or nonagricultural manual laborers). Displacement refers to the elimination of jobs through technology-based automation; for this reason, it is often called **technological unemployment.** Displacement, therefore, is a problem apart from unemployment caused by the inability to find a job for which one is skilled. Displaced workers possess outmoded skills *for which no more jobs exist.* The blue-collar worker's biggest enemy, many believe, is the microprocessor-based industrial robot — a machine that will work without getting tired, without calling in sick, and without demanding higher wages. Some predictions suggest that displacement caused by industrial robots will be severe. According to an estimate by the Congressional Budget Office, by 1990 approximately 15 percent of today's blue-collar manufacturing jobs will have been eliminated by the use of industrial robots.

These job losses could be offset by new jobs in high-technology industries, such as robotics and computers. Yet it appears unlikely that the number of high-tech jobs created by 1993 will offset job displacement. According to one estimate, by 1990 robots will displace an additional 50,000 workers in the automobile industry; yet robotics-related jobs will employ only 3,000 to 5,000 workers. High-tech industries, in general, employ far fewer people than other industries. In 1978, for example, IBM — one of the world's largest high-tech corporations — employed 325,000 people. In the same year, in strong contrast, General Motors employed nearly one million people. If industrial production continues to decline, in short, high-technology companies will not make up the shortfall by providing enough new jobs.

If job displacement is severe, it could contribute to the growth of a permanently unemployed, rebellious underclass — a development that could have ominous implications for social peace in the future. Bergen County, New Jersey, illustrates the plight of displaced workers and the danger it poses. Highly dependent on the automobile, aluminum, and aerospace industries, Bergen County was a model of industrial prosperity until the 1970s. Several major companies closed their Bergen County plants, which they considered old and inefficient. The final blow was the closing of a Ford plant in 1980. The result was the growth of a chronically unemployed and severely impoverished underclass of former factory workers, predominantly black and Hispanic. At the same time, this scenic area has become a fashionable location for weekend and summer homes for wealthy New Yorkers. Displaced workers stand on streetcorners watching a parade of Mercedes-Benz automobiles go by. Many sociologists fear the widening social gap between the very poor and the very rich; similar gaps have produced intractable social unrest in many countries.

Efforts have been made to retrain a few of these workers for other jobs, but the existence of a permanently unemployed underclass in this country is a problem unlikely to disappear overnight. In Bergen County, a highly successful retraining program landed computer-related jobs for two-thirds of the twenty-six students enrolled.[8] Such programs, however, seem to reach very few displaced workers, despite the expenditure of more than $80 billion under the Manpower Development and Training Act and its successor, the Comprehensive Employment and Training Act. According to one estimate, less than 1 percent of the $80 billion has actually benefited the displaced workers who were supposed to be aided by the bills.[9] Maryland, for instance, has 35,000 displaced workers, but only 700 of them receive retraining per year.[10]

There is no denying that the United States has growing numbers of displaced workers and that their problems are real and severe. It is by no means certain, however, that computer technology is solely responsible for the displacement. Most job displacement is actually being caused by increased foreign competition rather than automation. Heavy industries in the United States cannot hope to compete with plants in Japan, Taiwan, Singapore, and South Korea, where equipment is newer and workers receive as little as $1 per hour. Out-of-date plants in places like Bergen County, New Jersey, might still be in operation were it not for stiff foreign competition. Job losses caused by computers, in sum, are minor compared to the grave cost of America's inability to compete in world markets.

Computers and robots, moreover, are displacing far fewer workers than originally feared. Many studies show that few, if any, employees lose their jobs when companies install computers, despite the claims of computer vendors that manpower can be reduced significantly when computers are installed. The mayor of San Francisco, Dianne Feinstein, recently complained that despite spending $60 million on office automation systems for the city she was unable to dismiss a single employee. There are, of course, examples to the contrary. Yet projections of job displacement generally overestimate — often by a wide margin — the displacement that actually occurs.

One reason for the failure of robotics to displace workers so far is that the technology has not made rapid progress. Robots have turned out to be far less attractive in the factory than they are on paper. "In a lot of applications where we start out looking at robots," says Larry J. Kerr, a vice president of manufacturing at Firestone Tire and Rubber Co., "we wind up finding another way to do the job at half the cost and a quarter of the complexity." Only 15,000 industrial robots are now in use, and in 1995 it now is expected that robots will have displaced fewer than 5 percent of all factory workers.[11]

Just how severe the job displacement problem will be in the future no one can say. But this much is already clear: the displacement of blue-collar workers is part of a larger historical trend that is changing the very nature of United States society. We are leaving behind a world-dominant role as a producer of goods and taking on a new role, an equally dominant one, as a producer of services and knowledge. In any social transformation of this magnitude, someone's going to get hurt.

LOW QUALITY OF EMPLOYMENT IN SERVICE OCCUPATIONS

Over the next decade, the United States economy will create an estimated 31 million jobs, and about three-quarters of them will become available in service-producing industries such as retail stores, transportation, food service, entertainment, business services, professional services, and dozens more. About 75 percent of these service-related jobs will require computer skills. This statistic provides the major rationale for the computer literacy boom in public schools. According to many educational experts, today's students will need computer skills to compete effectively in tomorrow's work force.

Yet, some say, most of the new service jobs won't require computer skills at all. Certainly, workers will be using computer-based machines — but these machines will require skills that take only a week or two to learn. Indeed, it's not just computer skills that will be obsolete in the future, some say. People will be able to perform these jobs with even *fewer* skills than workers have now. A fast-food cashier, for instance, needs no mathematical ability to ring up a sale; he or she merely pushes one button with a picture of a hamburger on it and another one with a picture of a small soft drink.

Devices such as computerized cash registers make work easier, but some sociologists believe their impact on society could be negative. People feel better about their jobs when they can use their skills. Studies of workers show that psychological well-being, employee self-respect, and overall job satisfaction correlate closely with the use of employee skills on the job. As the computer "de-skills" millions of jobs, growing numbers of workers will find themselves in positions that lack intrinsic satisfactions. Potential social consequences of a highly dissatisfied work force include higher rates of alcoholism, child abuse or neglect, and workplace vandalism, among others.

The computer's potential for "de-skilling" service occupations is another — and much less appealing — side of the quest for user-friendliness. By making computers easier to use, computer manufacturers are also making it possible for people to work without using skills. For instance, a secretary whose word processor has a built-in spelling checker need not use spelling skills on the job.

Labor unions have been particularly concerned about another facet of the growing role of computers in service occupations. Millions of American workers spend most or all of their working day sitting in front of video display terminals (VDTs). Are VDTs a health hazard? VDTs emit very small amounts of radiation, but carefully conducted tests by the National Occupational Safety and Health Administration show that this radiation cannot be distinguished from background radiation levels.[12] Many VDT workers, however, have been disturbed by reports of higher miscarriage rates among pregnant users of VDTs. Many VDT workers complain of eyestrain and muscle aches after spending long hours at the terminal. The most likely cause of eye and muscle complaints, however, lies not in VDT radiation but rather in unreasonable demands for worker productivity.

COMPUTERS AND WOMEN

Occupations in the United States are still segregated by sex to a remarkable degree. Women are concentrated in a sharply limited range of occupations, and they are very likely to receive less pay than males who do substantially the same tasks. Some sociologists fear that the computer may have a sharply negative impact on "feminized" occupations, the ones in which more than half the workers are women. In the late 1970s more than one-third of working women were employed in clerical occupations, which are strongly feminized — that is, disproportionately staffed with women. More than 90 percent of secretaries, typists, receptionists, bank tellers, and telephone operators are women. Yet it is precisely these occupations that, some say, are most likely to experience severe displacement as the use of office automation grows.

A major rationale for the installation of office automation systems, in fact, is the elimination of jobs. An office automation project undertaken by Los Angeles County sought to save $10 million annually by eliminating more than 900 clerical positions. One West Coast bank is said to have saved half a million dollars by setting up word processing pools; the number of secretaries was cut in half.[13] If the personal computer accelerates the pace of office automation, as most experts expect it will, the impact on women workers could be severe.

Up to the present, however, widespread job displacement among clerical workers has not materialized. Many managers, for instance, are not willing to give up their secretaries, believing that having a secretary is a sign of high status and power in an organization.[14] What is more, as the pace of the information explosion accelerates, it is likely that more clerical staff will be needed even if office automation systems are installed. During the past decade, and contrary to expectations, growth in clerical occupations has been rapid.

Personal computer technology may not play the negative role some have predicted in displacing women from their jobs. But what concerns many educators is that the world of personal computing is discouraging women from seeking careers in computer-related areas. By any standard, the world of personal computing — as defined by the social environment of computer stores, hacker clubs, and computer science organizations — is a decidedly masculine one. Personal computer hardware and software companies know this perfectly well, and pitch their advertising accordingly. In computer magazine advertising, a recent study revealed, only 27.7 percent of the individuals shown are girls or women. What is more, males were portrayed as the active users or experts while women were shown passively watching. If women were shown using the computer, it was in roles that suggested secretarial duties.[15]

Why is the personal computer world so decidedly masculine among adults? It isn't among young children. Observations of preschool children show that relatively few sex differences can be observed in patterns of computer use.[16] Children in the lower grades of elementary school, too, show few sex-related differences in how they perceive or use the computer (Figure 16–1). By the seventh or ninth grade, however, girls show marked declines in computer interest,[17] and the lower interest levels continue into the college years. Male college students have significantly more exposure to computing, and female students discuss computers less frequently.[18] Male freshmen and sophomores were more likely

FIGURE 16–1 Personal Computers as Learning Aids

than females to have taken computer courses, played computer games, used computer application software, and written computer programs.[19]

Many theories have been advanced to explain these patterns, but the most likely explanation is simply that women are actively discouraged from getting involved in computers. In school, girls and boys quickly learn that it is more appropriate for boys to express interest in electronics and machines. Computer clubs and magazine advertisements drive home the message that computing is essentially a male activity. And if these messages are not discouraging enough, consider this one: the median pay of women professionals in the computer science field is only 78 percent of what men receive for the same work.[20] The real earnings differences often amount to as much as $5,000 to $7,000 a year.

Given the persistence of these very real barriers, it is hardly surprising that only 30 percent of computer programmers, 4 percent of electrical engineers, and 1 percent of technical managers are women.[21] However, people who are involved with computer education and manufacturing are working to change this picture. Increased efforts are being made to recruit and retain female students in computer science programs. In the end, changing this picture will require courage — the courage of women who are willing to resist social pressure and enter male-dominated occupations, and the courage of men who are willing to welcome a very different world in the workplace.

NEW RISKS FOR BUSINESSES

The computer may give businesses greater efficiency and competitive advantages, but it also brings a host of new risks. Among them:

Computer-Assisted Disaster. Not every computer system helps the businesses that buy it. A San Francisco law firm went bankrupt in the late 1970s, thanks in part to its reliance on computers for customer billings. The firm's accounting software never worked properly; hundreds of thousands of dollars were lost because customers were never billed.[22] Other computer-assisted disasters occur when vital or sensitive data are lost owing to accidental erasure or interruptions in electrical power. To safeguard against accidental data loss, business users must learn to exercise great care to back up all work. Losses due to power line interruption can be minimized by regular backups; if data are saved every 10 minutes, for instance, no more than 10 minutes' work will be lost. For highly important applications, backup power supplies can be installed.

Crackers. Thousands of small, informal groups of teenage computer whiz kids exist in this country. A favorite pastime of some of these kids — called **crackers** — is to break into private computer systems through telecommunications links. Once they have entered the system, they may destroy data or plant software versions of practical jokes. Many businesses are beefing up security systems to guard against computer trespassers.

Computer Crime. A serious problem for all businesses is computer crime — the use of the computer for thievery, embezzlement, and fraud. By any crook's yardstick, computer crimes are lucrative: they net, on average, $430,000 per heist (in comparison to an average take of $10,000 in bank holdups).[23] Many computer crimes go undetected, and even the criminal who is caught may not be prosecuted, because of fear that the public would lose confidence in the business's security system.[24] Juries, moreover, are sympathetic to white-collar criminals, and rarely impose jail sentences; only 17 percent of those convicted of embezzling bank funds go to jail, compared with 91 percent of convicted bank robbers.[25]

Unauthorized Software Duplication. A major problem for the software industry has been the unauthorized, illegal copying of software. According to one estimate, about half the application programs now in use are unauthorized duplicates — and some believe this estimate to be low. A business employee who uses unauthorized copies of software is punishable by law, but the existence of unauthorized copies on a business's premises also renders it liable to lawsuits. In several highly publicized cases, Lotus Development Corporation filed multi-million-dollar lawsuits against companies using unauthorized copies of Lotus products.

These risks can be greatly reduced by the cautious use of computers in business settings.

THE FUTURE

Only time will tell us whether the benefits the personal computer offers will outweigh the risks it poses for life in the Information Age.

Consider this example from the world of military computing. The computer was originally devised as a device to make weapons of war more accurate, and by any measure it has succeeded admirably. Intercontinental ballistic missiles now possess what is called "absolute accuracy." With the aid of computerized guidance mechanisms, these missiles can land within a few hundred yards of their target. With a huge nuclear warhead on board, that's more than enough accuracy to wipe out the intended target. This high degree of accuracy has been made possible by computer technology. Will it benefit us by reducing the risk of nuclear war, as the proponents of mutually assured destruction (MAD) suggest? Or does it increase the risk of war, by deluding leaders into thinking they might be able to wipe out the enemy in a sneak attack?

However much we may fear the risks of computing, no alternative exists to widespread public use of computer technology today. Massive increases in population, in societal complexity, and in information require of us that we adopt computer-based knowledge processing systems. To give up computers would mean resigning ourselves to many unsatisfactory outcomes. Consider just this one: most banks and corporations could function no more than three or four days without computerized information systems. We are no more free to dispense with computing than early Mesopotamians were to dispense with writing.

The analogy to writing is apt in other ways as well. Writing has been an instrument both of liberation and destruction; the memoirs of Mohandas Gandhi sit alongside Hitler's *Mein Kampf* on library shelves, and both were produced with the same technology. This point has been made about technology many times, and by many people, but it deserves to be made one more time here: No technology is intrinsically good or evil, beneficial or risky, favorable or unfavorable — at least, not so much that a good technology cannot be put to evil uses by evil people. What determines the outcome of history is not, therefore, the victory of a "good" technology over a "bad" one. On the contrary, the outcome of history has to do with the moral integrity, courage, and vision of the people who use a technology.

SUMMARY

Computers help people in business make better decisions, work more efficiently, broaden the scope of their enterprises, and position themselves advantageously vis-à-vis their competition. The personal computer has given small businesses the same cost-cutting, profit-raising advantages formerly enjoyed only by large firms. And if small businesses can cut costs and improve profits, the United States economic outlook may brighten considerably. Small businesses are responsible for most new jobs.

In today's information economy, information and know-how are just as important as capital — perhaps *more* important. So the increasing use of personal computers to gather information and knowledge will help even small businesses compete more effectively. Health care will benefit, too, by getting up-to-date information to physicians, even if they are isolated in rural communities.

The personal computer is playing an impressive role in improving the welfare of handicapped people. Because personal computer technology is both cheap and transportable, computer-based helping devices can be positioned where handicapped people need them.

The personal computer may revolutionize communications by giving millions of people new devices for immediate transmission and reception of text. If the new communications media do for the economy what the telephone and telegraph have already done, the result would be increased prosperity.

Your involvement with the personal computer may lead to enhanced job opportunities, perhaps in the computer field itself. You are far more likely, however, to use your computer applications skills in a field not directly connected with computers, such as professional, business, and health services occupations. Rapid job growth is expected in these fields.

The most serious risk posed by microprocessor-based computer technology may lie in the displacement of blue-collar workers. Displacement refers to the *elimination* of jobs through technology-based automation. Most of these jobs will not be replaced by new jobs in high-tech industries, which employ fewer people than heavy manufacturing industries do. Experts disagree on just how severe job displacement will be; in any case, much more displacement is being caused by foreign competition from Singapore, Taiwan, South Korea, and Japan. Robotics, moreover, has made slow progress. Job displacement may become more severe in the future as the United States moves to a service-based economy.

Most new jobs will be in service-related occupations, and of these three-quarters will require computer skills. So today's children are learning the computer skills (such as BASIC programming) that many believe will be necessary in tomorrow's work force. Yet, others say, most of these service jobs will require few computer skills. Computers will be used, but they'll be so user-friendly that their operators will not need computer skills. Nor, perhaps, will they need other skills, such as the ability to read or do arithmetic. The computer, in short, may "de-skill" service jobs, with ominous implications for job satisfaction and the quality of work.

Women are actively discouraged from computing by the masculine nature of the computer's social world and by pronounced patterns of salary discrimination in computer-related occupations. The computer science industry and computer scientists are working hard to change this pattern. In the end, however, changing it will require women with the courage to move into male-dominated areas and men with the courage to accept changing patterns.

Personal computers bring many benefits to businesses, but if they are not used carefully they can bring risks too. Poorly designed systems and lost data can bankrupt companies. Crackers can break into telecommunications-based systems and ruin data. The computer provides new opportunities for crime. Unauthorized software duplication can get a company into big trouble with software publishers. These risks can be minimized by the cautious use of computers in business.

KEY TERMS

cracker
technological unemployment

REVIEW QUESTIONS AND EXERCISES

1. Why is the personal computer an especially important resource for entrepreneurs?
2. Why is it often said that improved public access to information and knowledge will lead to economic growth and better professional performance?
3. What are some of the ways in which computers have helped handicapped people?
4. What is the advantage of rapid communication?
5. What areas are likely to experience rapid growth in job availability over the next decade? How can personal computer skills help you in these areas?
6. What is the difference between temporary or cyclic unemployment and technological unemployment? Which is more serious as a social problem? Does the evidence thus far indicate that massive technological unemployment is likely to occur?
7. What are some of the possible social and economic consequences of the widespread de-skilling of service jobs?
8. Do video display terminals constitute a health hazard?
9. In what ways are women particularly at risk in the computer age?
10. How can using computers harm a business?

FOR FURTHER READING

Bolter, J. David. *Turing's Man: Western Culture in the Computer Age* (Chapel Hill, N.C.: University of North Carolina Press, 1984).

Bylinsky, Gene. "The Race to the Automatic Factory," *Fortune* (February 1983).

Crompton, Rosemary, and Gareth Jones. *White-Collar Proletariat: Deskilling and Gender in Clerical Work* (New York: Macmillan, 1984).

Ehrbar, A. F. "Grasping the New Employment," *Fortune* (May 16, 1983).

Fishman, Katarine D. *The Computer Establishment* (New York: Harper and Row, 1981).

Friedrichs, Gunter, and Adam Schaff. *Microelectronics and Society: For Better or Worse* (Elmsford, N.Y.: Pergamon, 1982).

Ginzberg, Eli, and George J. Vojta. "The Service Sector of the U.S. Economy," *Scientific American* (March 1981).

Gottleib, C. C., and A. Borodin. *Social Issues in Computing* (New York: Academic Press, 1973).

Huws, Ursula. *Your Job in the Eighties: A Woman's Guide to the New Technology* (London: Pluto Press, 1982).

Jones, Barry. *Sleepers, Wake! Technology and the Future of Work* (Brighton, U.K.: Wheatsheaf, 1982).

Kaplinksy, Raphael. *Automation: The Technology and the Society* (Harlow, Eng.: Longman, 1984).

Kidder, Tracy. *The Soul of a New Machine* (Boston: Little, Brown, 1981).

Laver, Murray. *Computers and Social Change* (Cambridge, Eng.: Cambridge University Press, 1980).

Mankin, Don, Tora K. Bikson, and Barbara Gutek. "The Office of the Future: Prison or Paradise?" *Futurist* (June 1982).

McGahey, Richard. "High Tech, Low Hopes," *The New York Times* (May 15, 1983).

Mosco, Vincent. *Pushbutton Fantasies: Critical Perspectives on Videotex and Information Technology* (Norwood, N.J.: Ablex, 1982).

Norman, Colin. "The New Industrial Revolution," *Futurist* (February 1981).

Nulty, Peter. "How Personal Computers Change Managers' Jobs," *Fortune* (September 3, 1984).

Shaiken, Harley. "Computers as Strikebreakers," *Technology Review* (April 1982).

Slack, Jennifer Daryl, and Fred Fejes. *The Ideology of the Information Age* (Norwood, N.J.: Ablex, 1981).

Stanley, Amy Dru. "High Tech Will Hurt Women," *The New York Times* (September 19, 1983).

Twiss, Brian C., ed. *The Managerial Implications of Microelectronics* (London: Macmillan, 1981).

Woodward, Kathleen, ed. *The Myths of Information: Technology and Postindustrial Culture* (Bloomington, Ind.: Indiana University Press, 1980).

Appendix A
Guidelines for Selecting Personal Computer Hardware and Software

Buying personal computer hardware and software is like entering a maze or hall of mirrors: it's more than a little difficult to find your way. Dozens of computers and thousands of programs compete for your attention in the marketplace. Moreover, it's difficult to find reliable advice. Sales personnel in computer stores are, quite naturally, interested in selling you the products they carry (and not the ones you can get through mail order or the store's competitors). Even worse, you will find that people who have adopted a brand of computer or program behave like converts to an intolerant religion: converts to the IBM credo sneer at the Macintosh, and vice versa.

Even professionals in the field of equipment procurement (the science of justifying purchases of equipment) offer precious little help. These professionals advise careful study of costs and benefits before buying a computer. Yet corporate experience demonstrates that the cost of performing such studies may well exceed the cost of the computers. A vice president in charge of personal computer acquisitions at a major West Coast bank remarked that, in his former job, the company spent $40,000 in administrative costs to justify purchasing $15,000 worth of computer equipment.[1] As personal computers get even less expensive, the rationale for preparing these costly justifications becomes even less convincing. The attitude spreading among many corporate purchasers of personal computer equipment is simply to see the computer as a way of investing in an individual — especially, an individual who is likely to benefit from it.

In contemplating the purchase of hardware or software for yourself, then, the question you really need to ask is: "Am I the kind of person who is likely to benefit from a personal computer?" Or: "Should I invest in myself?" And the answer is simple enough. Almost all readers of this book are aiming for careers or professions in areas that will touch (or even emphasize) the acquisition, manipulation, and communication of information. And that means the right personal computer can benefit you enormously.

HARDWARE

Which computer is, for you, the right one? To answer this question, you will need to consider carefully the work you plan to do with it over the next five years, which is the probable life span of the system. Try formulating answers to these questions:

1. As you know, computer software must be prepared for a particular configuration of microprocessor, operating system, and disk drive. Software publishers are quite naturally reluctant to issue programs for a computer that has been sold to only a few thousand people. Therefore the most popular computers are also the ones for which the greatest variety of software is available. That variety may — or may not — be important to you; let's find out. Do you plan to make one and only one application of your computer — for example, word processing? If so, have you identified exactly the program you want? It's rather unlikely that you would have answered yes to both of these questions, but if you did, a computer's popularity needn't sway you. You can simply select the computer that runs the software you want. For everyone else, you'll be well advised to look at the popular computers for which a large and varied pool of software is available. If you're looking at an off-brand computer that is claimed to be "100% compatible" with one of these popular computers, make sure that these claims can be verified.
2. Consider the type of writing you plan to do. Is there any possibility that you will need to display and print foreign-language, technical, or scientific characters (characters that do not appear in the standard ASCII character set)? If you answer yes to this question, you will be well advised to select a computer that (1) includes the characters you want in its built-in character set; or (2) uses a bit-mapped graphics display and is capable of printing exactly what appears on the screen. If your answer is no, you needn't consider a computer's character-display capabilities.
3. Let's talk graphics. Do you envision yourself using programs that require bit-mapped graphics displays, such as analytical or presentation-graphics software? If so, you will want to select a computer that offers video circuitry for bit-mapped graphics, reasonably high screen resolution, the ability to use an RGB monitor, and a printer capable of reproducing these images. If you plan to focus on such applications, make sure plotters and laser printers will work with the computer.

4. Now consider your internal memory needs. Do you anticipate working with extremely large spreadsheets, integrated software, windowing environments, memory-resident software, desktop organizers, or multitasking? If your answer is yes, you will need a computer that is capable of working with at least 512K — and preferably more — of internal memory.
5. Think of your auxiliary memory needs. Is speedy system response important to you? Do you plan to work with more than two or three programs routinely? Do you plan to create lengthy document or data files? If you answer yes to any of these questions, consider a system that includes a hard disk.
6. Let's look at the system's expandability — and in particular the cost of accessories you may wish to add. Is the computer you're looking at based on open or closed-architectural principles (that is, can the user easily add circuit boards and make system modifications)? Are accessories for this system, such as hard disks and memory-expansion boards, reasonably priced? Watch out for this one. Closed-architecture systems place barriers to system expansion, and so adding extra peripherals (such as a hard disk) or extra memory can cost significantly more than you would pay for a system with open architecture. Disk drives for the Macintosh 128 — a closed system — once cost $500, and memory-expansion kits cost $995, when a disk drive for an IBM Personal Computer (an open system) could be obtained for $85 and a memory-expansion board for $250.
7. Sooner or later, you'll burst into the world of electronic space. Does the computer you're looking at have a built-in asynchronous communications board and an RS-232C serial port? There's a trend nowadays to make the buyer pay extra for these all-but-essential items. If you're looking at two machines which are comparable in all other ways, but one of which throws in these goodies free, take it.
8. What's the warranty? It's common for computer manufacturers to provide only three-month limited warranties, which are insufficient. You may, however, have to accept this risk if you can't find a competing (and otherwise comparable) product with a six-month or full-year warranty.
9. What do you have to do to get it fixed? Don't buy a computer if you have to mail it to Cucamonga or Timbuktu to get repairs done. You'll quickly become professionally dependent on the machine, and its prolonged absence would be intolerable.
10. Now that you've come this far, hold it: look at software. Work through the software questions and make sure the machine you've picked out will run precisely the software you need.

SOFTWARE

1. Let's start with word processing. Do you have any compelling reason to select a program that formats the text offscreen? Few such reasons exist, unless you're a professional programmer preparing and printing program

manuals, an application for which many offscreen formatters were expressly designed. Otherwise, you'll be best off with an onscreen formatter. Beware: Many programs that advertise themselves as "what you see is what you get" word processors actually use embedded commands here and there.

2. What do you plan to do with your word-processing package? If you plan to use it only for an occasional letter, memo, or short report, you needn't worry about fancy features. If, however, you plan to write lengthy manuscripts that will include footnotes, running heads, varied paragraph formats, or superscripted numbers, you'd better make sure the program you're looking at has the features you need.
3. Now think about all those wonderful word-processing accessories we discussed in Chapter 6. Will the word-processing program you've picked out work with a memory-resident thesaurus? Is a good-quality spelling checker available for it (good = dictionary of at least 80,000 words)? Most people don't think about these questions until they've made a major commitment to a program — and by then it may be too costly to switch. Think, too, about outlining software. If you write frequently — and especially if the quality of the writing you do will in any way affect your career progress — consider a word-processing program that integrates outlining and word-processing functions.
4. On to data base management programs. Which do you need, a file management program or a data base management system (DBMS)? What counts here is the importance, to you, of avoiding redundant data. Think about the data base management applications you're planning and sketch a design for a data record. Are there some data fields that will have the same information, over and over, on many records? Will retrieval of this information be harmed if you do not enter this information in exactly the same way every time it is entered? If you answer yes to both these questions, you may be better off with a relational DBMS rather than a file management program.
5. Now let's consider electronic spreadsheets. Do you want to transform numerical data into their analytical graphics counterpart? Pick up a spreadsheet program that includes graphics capabilities.
6. Another vexing little matter: Do you want to exchange data between your spreadsheet program and data-base manager? Better make sure they can read each other's data files (unlikely). If this function is extremely important to you, consider an integrated program.
7. These questions will help you identify some programs that you may be interested in. For each of them, ask:

   Will it be difficult to learn? Avoid programs that hit you with dozens of keyboard commands. A few are tolerable, but you'll be well advised to prefer programs that have user-friendly ways, such as using command menus. Pay particular attention to the way in which keyboard functions are allocated. Is the program's use of familiar keys such as RETURN,

BACKSPACE, or PGDN likely to conflict with habits you've acquired with other software?

How good is the documentation? Does it include a tutorial that helps you learn the program quickly? Is there an index? Can you get help over the telephone from the company if the documentation doesn't answer your question? Does it have a reference guide to all commands? Program documentation is improving, but there are still some notable exceptions.

Do you have friends, classmates, or business associates who are now using the program and can help you get started? This is a genuine plus — enough, in some circumstances, to overrule other considerations.

Do you really have to pay several hundred dollars for each program? Take a good, hard look at software—particularly programs such as PC-Write, PC-Calc, and PC-File (if you're using an IBM Personal Computer or compatible). They're available on a shareware basis: you pay the registration fee (approximately $50 for each program) only if you like the software and decide to use it.

Appendix B
Resources for Personal Computing

MAGAZINES AND NEWSPAPERS

Business Software (P.O. Box 2795, San Diego, CA 92128). Excellent coverage of new developments in software for business managers and professionals.

Byte (70 Main Street, Peterborough, NH 03458). Emphasizes technical aspects of microcomputer hardware and software.

ComputerWorld (375 Cochitutate Road, Box 880, Framingham, MA 01701). Trade newspaper covering entire computer industry, including personal computers. Special in-depth supplements (*ComputerWorld Focus*) highlight new developments.

Computing Teacher: Journal of the International Council for Computers in Education (University of Oregon, 1787 Agate Street, Eugene, OR 97403-1923). Excellent coverage of computer-assisted instruction from the teacher's point of view.

InfoWorld (1060 Marsh Road, Suite C-200, Menlo Park, CA 94025). Trade newspaper covering the personal computer industry. Widely respected for its objective and critical review policies.

MacWorld (PC World Communications, Inc., 555 De Haro Street, San Francisco, CA 94107). Excellent coverage of Macintosh hardware and software with a flair for creative graphics.

Online: The Magazine of Online Information Systems (Online, Inc., 11 Tannery Lane, Weston, CT 06883).

PC World (PC World Communications, Inc., 555 De Haro Street, San Francisco, CA 94107).

PC: The Independent Guide to IBM-Standard Personal Computing (PC Communications Corporation, One Park Avenue, New York, NY 10016). Good coverage of IBM-standard hardware and software.

Publish! The Magazine of Desktop and Personal Computer Publishing (PC World Communications, Inc., 555 De Haro Street, San Francisco, CA 94107). Magazine focusing on desktop publishing in both the Macintosh and IBM Personal Computer environments.

Research in Word Processing Newsletter (Liberal Arts, South Dakota School of Mines and Technology, Rapid City, SD 57701). Newsletter specializing in desktop publishing, professional-level word processing, and computer-assisted writing instruction. Features lively software reviews and articles.

PUBLIC DOMAIN SOFTWARE AND SHAREWARE

Public-domain software has not been copyrighted and may be freely copied and distributed by the user. Shareware programs are usually copyrighted, but the company or person who markets it grants users the right to duplicate the program (but not the documentation) for others: if you receive one of these programs and like it, you are expected to pay a modest registration fee. Excellent sources for public-domain software and shareware products are personal-computer users' groups and public bulletin-board systems. To determine whether there are users' groups and bulletin boards in your area, contact a local computer store.

ButtonWare (P.O. Box 5786, Bellevue, WA 98006). Offers several excellent shareware programs, including PC-File III (a very good file-management program), PC-Calc (an excellent spreadsheet, superior to VisiCalc), PC-Style (a style-analysis program), and others.

Headlands Press, Inc. (P.O. Box 862, Tiburon, CA 94920). Offers PC-TALK, a highly respected shareware communications program.

PC-SIG (1030 E. Duane Avenue, Suite D, Sunnyvale, CA 94086). Mail-order source for disks containing public-domain software.

Public Domain Software Library (1533 Avohill Drive, Vista, CA 92083). Mail-order source for disks containing public-domain software.

Quicksoft (219 First N., #224C, Seattle, WA 98109). Offers an outstanding shareware word-processing program called PC-WRITE; compares favorably to commercial products priced in the $300 to $400 range.

INFORMATION UTILITIES

All three of these information utilities offer low rates nights and weekends; online bulletin boards and conferences focus on personal-computer topics.

CompuServ (5000 Arlington Center Boulevard, Columbus, OH 43200).

Delphi (General Videotext Corporation, 3 Blackstone Street, Cambridge, MA 02139).

The Source (Source Telecomputing Corporation, 1616 Anderson Road, MacLean, VA 22012).

Notes

PROLOGUE

[1]On the origins of writing in Mesopotamia, see Denise Schmandt-Besserat, "The Earliest Precursor of Writing," *Scientific American* (June 1978), pp. 51–60.

CHAPTER 1

[1]Figures cited in Donald H. Sanders, *Computers Today* (New York: McGraw-Hill, 1983), p. 557.

[2]E. Daniel, "Information Resources and Organizational Structure," *Journal of the American Society for Information Science,* 34 (1983), pp. 222–228.

[3]Lewis Branscomb, "Electronics and Computers: An Overview," *Science,* 215 (February 12, 1982), p. 759.

[4]Christopher K. Heaney, "Micros: After the Hype Wears Off," *ABA Banking Journal,* 77 (February 1985), pp. 39–40.

[5]Judy A. Gordon, "Computers Are the Future: And the Future Is Here Today," *Credit and Financial Management,* 87 (January/February 1985), pp. 36–39.

[6]"Typewriters Said No Match for WP," *ComputerWorld* (June 28, 1982), p. 106.

[7]Peter G. W. Keen and Lynda A. Woodman, "What to Do with All Those Micros," *Harvard Business Review* (September–October 1984), p. 146.

[8]Lee White, "You Can Get There from Here: Office Automation Survey Shows How," *ComputerWorld* (February 6, 1985), pp. 23–26.

CHAPTER 2

[1]Paraphrasing Hoo-Ming D. Toong and Amar Gupta, "Personal Computers," *Scientific American* (December 1982), p. 87.

[2]Christopher Evans, *The Micro Millennium* (New York: Washington Square Press, 1979), pp. 2–3.

[3]Paraphrasing Peter Laurie, *The Joy of Computers* (Boston: Little, Brown, 1983), p. 16.

[4]The figures are from Robert E. Lynch and John R. Rice, *Computers: Their Impact and Use* (New York: Holt, Rinehart and Winston, 1977), pp. 46–48.

[5]*Wall Street Journal* (September 16, 1985), p. 1C.

CHAPTER 3

[1]Paraphrasing John Wilson, "Superchips: The New Frontier," *Business Week* (June 10, 1985), p. 83.

[2]Virginia Bubek, "Automating the Office," *Wall Street Journal* (September 16, 1985), p. 7C.

CHAPTER 4

[1]J. D. Gould, "Composing Letters with Computer-Based Text Editors," *Human Factors*, 23 (October 1981), pp. 593–606.

[2]Richard M. Collier, "The Word Processor and Revision Strategies," *College Composition and Communication*, 34 (May 1983), pp. 149–155.

CHAPTER 6

[1]Preface to the first edition of *Roget's Thesaurus* (1852), reprinted in *Roget's International Thesaurus* (New York: Thomas Y. Crowell Co., 1962), p. xii.

[2]Detected are *is, are, was, were, shall be, will be, have been, has been, had been, shall have been,* and *will have been.*

[3]The example is from Glenda M. McClure, "Computerized Writeability Analysis," *Conference Record: The Many Facets of Computer Communications,* IEEE Professional Communication Society, Atlanta, Georgia (October 19–21, 1983), pp. 31–33.

CHAPTER 8

[1]Alfred Poor, "The Latest on Databases," *PC Magazine* (July 9, 1985), p. 139.

[2]Jane Eisenberg and Jeffrey Hill, "Using Natural Language Systems on Personal Computers," *Byte* (January, 1984), p. 230.

[3]C. J. Date, *Database: A Primer* (Reading, Mass.: Addison-Wesley, 1983), p. 39.

PART FOUR

[1]The Licklider quotations are from his "Man-Computer Symbiosis," originally published in *ETC: A Review of General Semantics,* 24 (1967), and reprinted in Zenon Pylyshyn, ed., *Perspectives on the Computer Revolution* (Englewood Cliffs, N.J.: 1970), p. 309.

CHAPTER 10

[1]Edward Foster, "Building Simple Spreadsheets," *Personal Computing* (January 1985), pp. 61–62.

[2]Henry Fersko-Weiss, "Avoiding Spreadsheet Disaster," *Personal Computing* (March 1985), p. 112.

[3]Stanley R. Trost, *Doing Business with SuperCalc* (Berkeley, Calif.: Sybex Computer Books, 1983), p. 181.

[4]Ibid., p. 118.

CHAPTER 11

[1]Quoted in James C. Condon, "Charts on Computer Graphics Are Trending Upwards," *New York Times* (March 27, 1983), 7:20.

[2]Bud Anderson, "CAD/CAM: Big Markets for Factory Systems," *High Technology* (January/February, 1982), p. 99.

[3]Glenn Hart, "CAD Overview," *PC Magazine* (March 11, 1986), pp. 107–8.

[4]Cited in Andries van Dam, "Computer Software for Graphics," *Scientific American* (September, 1984), p. 146.

CHAPTER 12

[1]Paraphrased from James Radlow, *Computers and the Information Society* (New York: McGraw-Hill, 1986), p. 2.

[2]Carnegie Forum Task Force on Teaching as a Profession, "A Nation Prepared: Teachers for the 21st Century," *Chronicle of Higher Education* (May 21, 1986), p. 45.

[3]John S. Mayo, "Evolution of the Intelligent Network," *Science* (February 12, 1982).

[4]Joanne Kelleher, "Microcomputer Networking: Learn from Succesful Users," *ComputerWorld* (March 24, 1986), p. 59.

[5]Cited in Frank J. Derfler, Jr., "Micro to Mainframe: Making the Right Connection," *PC Magazine* (May 13, 1986), p. 116.

CHAPTER 13

[1]Quoted in Paul Bonner, "When You'd Rather Switch than Swap," *Personal Computing* (August, 1983), p. 73.

CHAPTER 15

[1]"Why You Should Learn to Program," *Popular Computing* (September 1983), p. 154.

[2]"Assembler," *PC Magazine* (October 29, 1985), p. 133.

[3]John Dickenson, "Programming Makes Sense for Business," *PC Magazine* (October 29, 1985), p. 114.

[4]Alan Kay, "Computer Software," *Scientific American* (September 1984), p. 54.

[5]Glenn Bacon, "Software," *Science* (February 12, 1982), p. 776.

[6]"Pascal," *PC Magazine* (October 29, 1985), p. 141.

[7]Bacon, "Software," p. 777.

[8]Lawrence G. Tesler, "Programming Languages," *Scientific American* (September 1984), pp. 77–78.

CHAPTER 16

[1]Quoted in Leslie Wang, "A Pioneer Spirit Sweeps Business," *New York Times* (March 25, 1984), 3:1.

[2]Figure cited in John Naisbitt, *Megatrends: Ten New Directions Transforming Our Lives* (New York: Warner Books, 1984), p. 145.

[3]Quoted in a speech by N. B. Hannay, Vice President, Research and Patents, Bell Laboratories (March 5, 1980).

[4]Quoted in Thomas Maremaa, "Computerizing the Medical Profession," *Popular Computing* (October 1984), p. 92.

[5]Barbara J. Culliton, "Information as a 'Cure' for Cancer," *Science* (February 15, 1985), p. 732.

[6]Andrew Pollack, "Job Outlook for the 80s Is Generally Optimistic," *New York Times* (March 25, 1984), pp. 12, 14.

[7]Leslie Wayne, "America's Astounding Job Machine," *New York Times* (June 17, 1984), 3:25.

[8]David L. Westin and Alan F. Westin, "Giving Unemployment the Boot," *Popular Computing* (January 1984), pp. 135–39.

[9]Eli Ginzberg, "The Mechanization of Work," *Scientific American* (September 1982), p. 68.

[10]Joseph Menosky, "Computer Worship," *Science '84* (May 1984), p. 42.

[11]Gregory Stricharchuk and Ralph E. Winter, "Second Thoughts: Experience with Robots Shows They Can Be More Costly and Complicated Than Expected," *Wall Street Journal* (September 16, 1985), p. 14C.

[12]National Institute of Occupational Safety and Health, *Potential Health Hazards of Video Display Terminals* (Cincinnati: NIOSH, 1981).

[13]Z. Zerman, *The Impacts of Computer/Communications on Employment in Canada* (Montreal: Institute for Research on Public Policy, 1979).

[14]Diane Werneke, *Microelectronics and Office Jobs: The Impact of the Chip on Women's Employment* (Geneva, Switzerland: International Labor Organization, 1983).

[15]Mary C. Ware, "Sex-Role Messages vis-à-vis Computer Use: A Look at the Pictures," paper delivered at the 1983 meeting of the New York State Sociological Association.

[16]Karl S. Rosengren et al., "An Observational Study of Preschool Children's Computing Activity," paper presented at the conference "Perspectives on the Young Child and the Computer" (Austin, TX, Sept. 28, 1985).

[17]Karen Swoope and Carole S. Johnson, "Students' Perceptions of Interest in Using Computers: Boys, Girls, or Both," paper presented at the Annual Meeting of the American Educational Research Association (Chicago, IL, March 31–April 4, 1985).

[18]Joan McCord, "Computers, Sex, and Society: The Microcomputing Program at Drexel University," Working Paper Series, Microcomputing Program, Office of the Vice President for Academic Affairs, Drexel University, 1984.

[19]Joan McCord, "At the Brink: Baseline Data. The Microcomputing Program at Drexel University," Working Paper Series, Microcomputing Program, Office of the Vice President for Academic Affairs, Drexel University, 1986.

[20]"Women Seen Suffering 'Subtle' Discrimination," *ComputerWorld* (June 18, 1979), p. 16.

[21]Russ Adams and Jan Zimmerman, "Women in Computing," *Interface Age* (December 1983), pp. 78–88.

[22]Peter Dworkin, "Hard Times for a Law Firm That Went Big on Advertising," *San Francisco Chronicle* (August 6, 1982), pp. 6–7.

[23]Thomas Whiteside, *Computer Capers: Tales of Electronic Thievery, Embezzlement, and Fraud* (New York: T. Y. Crowell, 1978), p. 9.

[24]Thomas Whiteside, "Annals of Crime: Dead Souls in the Computer," *New Yorker* (August 29, 1977), pp. 34–64.

[25]*Business Week* (June 3, 1977).

APPENDIX A

[1]Susan Bryant, "Are Corporate PCs Earning Their Keep?" *PC World* (August 1986), p. 178.

Glossary

abacus An ancient calculating device in which movable beads function as digits to represent quantities and facilitate calculations (Chapter 2). *See also* digit, digital computer.

absolute cell reference A spreadsheet cell reference that does not change when copied to other cells (Chapter 9). *See also* cell, cell reference.

abstract A brief and informative summary of an article or book that states its objectives, its methodology (if any), its principal conclusions, and its implications (Chapter 12). *See also* citation, reference data base.

access time The time it takes for an auxiliary storage device to locate the desired program or data and begin feeding information into the internal memory (Chapter 3). *See also* auxiliary storage device, data transfer rate, internal memory.

account automation The integration of accounting software such that an update in one program module (such as accounts receivable) is automatically posted to all affected modules (such as general ledger and inventory control) (Chapter 14). *See also* accounts receivable program, general ledger program, inventory control program.

accounts payable program A special-purpose application program that keeps track of those to whom a business owes money (Chapter 14). *See also* special-purpose program.

accounts receivable program A special-purpose application program that keeps track of individuals and firms that owe a business money (Chapter 14). *See also* special-purpose application package.

acoustic coupler An early modem designed to couple directly with telephone handsets (Chapter 12). *See also* direct-connect modem, modem.

active cell The cell in which the cursor is positioned in a spreadsheet program. When a cell is active, the user may enter constants, formulas, or labels on the entry line (Chapter 9). *See also* constants, entry line, formula, label.

aggregate functions In a data base management system (DBMS), a set of commands that quickly and automatically perform calculations on a selected data field in a set of data records. The functions include SUM, COUNT, AVERAGE, MINIMUM, and MAXIMUM (Chapter 8). *See also* data field, data record.

algorithm A strategy for solving a problem using

step-by-step procedures. A computer program embodies an algorithm in computer-readable form (Chapter 2). *See also* program.

alphanumeric An expression of data that uses both alphabetical and numeric data (such as *Agent 007*) (Chapter 7).

alternate key (ALT) A command key used to enter commands by typing them at the keyboard of the IBM Personal Computer. It is necessary to hold down the alternate key while pressing the second key in the command (such as ALT-U) (Chapter 3). *See also* command key.

analog computer A computer that performs measurements using a comparison or analogy. A thermometer, for instance, measures by using an analogy between the expansion of mercury and increase in air temperature. Analog computers are useful for performing measurements, but they are less useful than digital computers for counting (Chapter 2). *See also* digital computer.

analytic graphics package A graphics program that transforms a data series into a chart or graph; its purpose is to provide you with further insight into the data you're working with (rather than to present this data to others) (Chapter 11). *See also* data series, presentation graphics packages.

AND A logical operator that narrows a selection by including only those records that meet all selection criteria ("Retrieve all the records that contain TAIWAN *and* BALANCE OF TRADE") (Chapter 7). *See also* logical operator, NOT, OR.

append command A query language command in a data base management system (DBMS) that allows the user to add new data to blank data records (Chapter 8). *See also* query language.

application software Ready-to-run programs created to do specific tasks such as word processing, working with electronic spreadsheets, or managing a data base (Chapter 1).

argument Information that tells a spreadsheet program which cells a built-in function should affect (Chapters 3, 9). *See also* built-in function, parameter.

arithmetic-logic unit (ALU) The part of the central processing unit (CPU) that actually performs the processing operations, which are of two kinds: arithmetic operations (adding, subtracting, multiplying, and dividing) and logical operations (such as comparing two numbers to see which one is bigger) (Chapter 2). *See also* central processing unit (CPU).

arithmetic operator An operator, used in writing spreadsheet formulas, that indicates addition (+), subtraction (−), multiplication (*), and division (/) (Chapter 9). *See also* operator.

arrow keys *See* cursor control keys.

artificial intelligence (AI) The intelligence possessed by an artifact or machine capable of mimicking human processes of reasoning and judgment (Chapter 2). *See also* knowledge.

ascending sort In a sort, the organization of a data base so that records are sorted alphabetically from A to Z or numerically from the lowest to the highest number (Chapter 7). *See also* data base, descending sort.

ASCII Acronym for the American Standard Code for Information Interchange, an input coding system widely used with personal computers and for data communications (Chapter 3). *See also* ASCII file, coding system.

ASCII file A file that contains nothing but the 126 characters that conform to the ASCII code. *See also* ASCII.

assembler A program that transforms assembly language source code into object code (Chapter 15).

assembly language A low-level programming language in which machine instructions are expressed in a mnemonic code (a code that reminds the programmer what the instructions stand for); the completed program is compiled by an assembler (Chapter 15). *See also* assembler, object code, source code.

asynchronous Not occurring at the same time and not governed by regulating pulses (Chapter 12). *See also* asynchronous communications board, universal asynchronous receiver/transmitter (UART).

asynchronous communications board A circuit board within the computer that converts the internal parallel data stream to the serial transmission that the telephone system can handle (Chapter 12). *See also* asynchronous, universal asynchronous receiver/transmitter (UART)

automatic hyphenation In a word processing program, a feature that goes through the document, word for word, and inserts hyphens whenever doing so would create more even character counts on each line (Chapter 5).

automatic logon A feature of smart terminal emulation programs that automatically executes all the steps necessary to achieve a connection with a distant computer (Chapter 12). *See also* smart terminal emulation program.

automatic programming An advanced programming technique in which the user, who need not possess programming technique, creates a computer program using a program generator (Chapter 15). *See also* program generator.

automatic recalculation The default recalculation mode in most spreadsheet programs; recalculates the spreadsheet automatically after any insertion (Chapter 9). *See also* manual recalculation, recalculation.

automatic reformatting A feature of newer word processing programs that automatically readjusts the right margin after new text is inserted within a line of existing text (Chapter 4). *See also* reformatting command.

auxiliary storage A peripheral device designed for the long-term storage of massive amounts of programs and/or data. In contrast to the internal memory, which keeps programs and data accessible for processing, the auxiliary storage is like a filing cabinet in which programs and data can be stored when they are not being used (Chapter 2). Common auxiliary storage devices for personal computers are disk drives and hard disks; their performance is measured by access time and data transfer rate (Chapter 3). *See also* access time, data transfer rate, disk drive, floppy disk, hard disk, internal memory, mass storage, peripheral.

backspace key On most personal computer keyboards, a destructive key that rubs out characters to the left of the cursor (Chapter 3). *See also* cursor, delete key, destructive.

backup with restore A feature that safeguards data in a data base management system; preserves and restores deleted data in case the deletion turns out to be an accident or is otherwise undesirable (Chapter 8).

bank switching A memory expansion technique in which a single bank of internal memory serves as a window on additional memory, which is switched in and out of the window as necessary (Chapter 13).

batch processing A data processing technique in which all four stages of the processing operation — input, storage, processing, and output — occur in a rigid, unalterable sequence. Batch processing was once the only processing technique possible with computers, but today's computers also offer interactive processing (Chapter 2). *See also* interactive processing.

baud A unit of measurement that denotes the number of bits per second transmitted via a data communications medium (Chapter 12). *See also* data communications.

begin block command In a word processing program, a command that demarcates the beginning of a block of text (Chapter 4). *See also* block, block move, copy block command, delete block command, end block command, move block command.

bibliographic data manager A special-purpose file management program designed for the storage and rapid retrieval of data records containing bibliographic data (Chapter 14).

binary digit A digit, either 0 or 1, used to represent a single unit of data in a binary number system (Chapter 2). *See also* binary numbers, bit.

binary number A number system that uses a radix or base of 2 and employs just two digits, 0 and 1. *See also* binary digit, bit.

biochip An experimental integrated circuit fabrication technique in which genetically engineered organic molecules are "grown" to create extremely small electronic components (Chapter 2). *See also* integrated circuit.

bistable device An electronic circuit that can be switched between just two states, on and off. Modern electronic digital computers are made up of these simple switching devices in huge quantities (Chapter 2). *See also* electronic digital computer.

bit Contraction of *bi*nary digi*t* (Chapter 2). *See* binary digit.

bit-mapped graphics A graphics display technique in which every pixel on the screen is represented or mapped by a bit of storage in the frame buffer or video memory (Chapter 11). *See also* frame buffer, graphics mode, pixel.

block A unit of text that you have demarcated for editing purposes, such as moving it elsewhere (Chapter 4). *See also* begin block command, block move, copy block command, delete block command, end block command.

block move An editing procedure by which a text block is positioned elsewhere in the text, and the gap left by its departure is automatically closed up (Chapter 4). *See also* block, begin block command, end block command.

boilerplate Standard passages of text that are used to respond to writing situations that come up repeatedly, such as answering routine inquiry letters or printing standard legal documents (Chapter 5). *See also* glossary.
boolean operator *See* logical operator.
booting the system *See* cold boot, warm boot.
browse mode In a data base management program, a mode that permits the user to scan several data records at a time (Chapter 7). *See also* data record.
built-in function A formula that may be inserted into a spreadsheet cell by typing a keyword and, usually, an argument (Chapter 9). *See also* argument, cell, keyword.
bulletin board A computerized tool that one person can use to send a message to many people; bulletin board systems provide public mailboxes that are publicly accessible and may be read by any participant (Chapter 12). *See also* computer conferencing, electronic mail.
bulletin board system (BBS) A public access, online bulletin board, usually started by a personal computer hobbyist (Chapter 12). *See also* bulletin board.
byte A basic unit of information as it is stored and processed in personal computers. A byte contains 8 bits (that is, eight binary digits). Because it takes one byte to represent a single character in internal memory, the terms byte and character are synonymous in the personal computing world (Chapter 3). *See also* character, internal memory.

calculation area an element in good spreadsheet design; an area of the spreadsheet that is set aside for cells containing formulas that the user should not disturb. To avoid forward reference errors, the calculation area should be situated beneath or to the right of the data entry area (Chapter 10). *See also* data entry area, forward reference.
case-sensitive search In a word processing or data base management program, a search that takes the case of letters (i.e., uppercase or lowercase) into consideration when looking for matches. In a case-sensitive search for the search string *Strong*, the search command will retrieve *Strong* but not *strong* (Chapter 5). *See also* search command, search string.
categories In a data series, the column that contains the headings that will be placed on the *X* axis or category axis (Chapter 11). *See also* data series, values, *Y* axis.
cathode-ray tube (CRT) A visual display output device commonly used with personal computers that contains a cathode-ray tube similar to those used in televisions (Chapter 2). *See also* monochrome monitor, pixels, resolution, RGB monitor.
CD-ROM A read-only optical storage medium that uses compact disks (Chapter 3). *See also* compact disk, optical disk, read-only storage medium.
cell A rectangular space within a spreadsheet within which the user may enter a constant, a formula, or a label. The cell is named by the row and column intersection at which it appears (e.g., A1 stands for the cell positioned in Column A and Row 1) (Chapter 9). *See also* active cell, cell coordinates indicator, column, constant, formula, label, row.
cell coordinates indicator An indicator found on the display screen of most spreadsheet programs; shows the location (expressed as a coordinate in rows and columns) of the active cell (Chapter 9). *See also* active cell.
cell protection A feature of spreadsheet programs that prevents users from replacing the formulas found in a range of cells (Chapter 10). *See also* formula, range.
cell reference A reference to a spreadsheet cell that is used in a formula (Chapter 9). *See also* absolute cell reference, cell, formula, relative cell reference.
central processing unit (CPU) The part of a computer's hardware devoted to interpreting the program's instructions and directing the computer to carry them out. The CPU consists of three parts, the control unit, the arithmetic-logic unit (ALU), and the internal memory (Chapter 2). *See also* arithmetic-logic unit, control unit, internal memory.
character A letter, number, or punctuation mark, represented within the computer by an 8-bit (or 1 byte) binary number (Chapter 3). *See also* bit, byte.
character format A document format that pertains to the appearance of individual characters, such as boldface type, italics, underlining, superscripts, and subscripts. Some newer programs also let you control fonts and type sizes (Chapter 4). *See* font, format, type size.
character generator A read-only memory that stores the information needed to display the

characters used in a character-mode video display circuit (Chapter 11). *See also* character mode, read-only memory (ROM).

character mode A video display mode in which the computer can only display a fixed set of alphabetic, numeric, and graphics characters, generally no more than 256 in number (Chapter 11). *See also* graphics mode.

circular reference A cell reference error that takes recalculation on a circular path (Chapter 9). *See also* cell reference, recalculation.

citation A bibliographic account of an article or book in a reference data base that contains all the information needed to retrieve the referenced work (such as the author's name, the work's title, name of journal or press, place of publication, page numbers, date of publication, etc.) (Chapter 12). *See also* abstract, reference data base.

clip art *See* image libraries.

clipboard A buffer or temporary storage area used for data exchange among programs in a windowing environment (Chapter 13). *See also* windowing environment.

closed architecture A computer design approach that frustrates user attempts to expand the computer with third-party peripherals (and sometimes third-party software as well) (Chapter 2). *See also* open architecture.

COBOL Acronym for *C*ommon *B*usiness-*O*riented *L*anguage. COBOL, one of the first high-level programming languages, is designed specifically for business programming applications (Chapter 2).

coding Representing data with a physical object, a mark, or the presence or absence of current in an electronic circuit (Chapter 2). *See also* input.

coding system A set of standards for the inputting of data into a computer, such as that established by the American Standard Code for Information Interchange (ASCII) (Chapter 3). *See also* ASCII, input.

cold boot Slang for the automatic operating system processes that prepare the computer for operation after the power is switched on (Chapter 3). *See also* operating system, warm boot.

column 1. A vertical series of cells in a spreadsheet (Chapter 9). 2. A vertical line of characters on a display screen or printout. *See also* cell, row, pixel.

columnar report A data base report that lists data in columns running down the page; the default format for most data base management programs (Chapter 7). *See also* default format.

column-wise recalculation A mode of spreadsheet recalculation in which calculation proceeds down column 1, then down column 2, and so on (Chapter 9). *See also* natural recalculation, recalculation, row-wise recalculation.

command An instruction to the computer that tells it to do something (Chapter 3). *See also* command processor.

command key A key, such as the escape key or control key, used to enter commands by typing them at the keyboard (Chapter 3). *See also* alternate key (ALT), control key (CTRL), escape key (ESC).

command-line operating system An operating system that requires you to control the computer by typing commands at the keyboard (Chapter 3). *See also* extension, keyword, object-oriented operating system, operating system, parameter, primary file name.

command menu A menu of command options displayed on the screen (Chapter 4). *See also* menu, pointer, pop-up command menu, pull-down command menu.

command mode A spreadsheet program mode in which characters typed at the keyboard may be interpreted as commands. In most spreadsheet programs, the command mode is entered by pressing the slash key (/) (Chapter 9). *See also* entry mode.

command processor The part of an operating system that provides the user interface, accepts and executes user commands, and presents error and other messages on the screen (Chapter 3). *See also* command, operating system, user interface.

communications protocols Standards for data communication interchange, including procedures for correcting a high proportion of communication errors automatically (Chapter 12).

communications software Software that organizes a personal computer system (including an asynchronous communications board, an RS-232C serial port, and a modem) for data communications (Chapter 12). *See also* asynchronous communications board, dumb terminal emulation program, modem, RS-232C serial port, smart communications programs.

compact disk (CD) An optical disk widely used in

high-fidelity audio systems and increasingly popular as a read-only storage medium for personal computers (Chapter 3). *See also* CD-ROM, optical disk, read-only storage medium.

compiled program A program that has been translated by a compiler into computer-readable object code, which will execute on a given brand of computer (Chapter 15). *See also* interpreter.

compiler A program that compiles a list of instructions written in a high-level language (source code) into the machine language the computer can understand (object code) (Chapters 2, 15). *See also* machine language, object code, program, source code.

compressed mode printing A dot-matrix printing mode in which characters are squeezed together so that 132 will fit on one standard line; useful for printing spreadsheets (Chapter 9).

computer *See* analog computer, digital computer.

computer-aided design (CAD) A computer graphics program that provides an engineer or designer with graphics tools for the creation of high-quality engineering or architectural drawings (Chapter 11).

computer-aided engineering (CAE) The automatic, simulated testing and analysis of parts drawn with computer-aided design (CAD) packages (Chapter 11). *See also* computer-aided design (CAD).

computer-aided manufacturing (CAM) The automatic programming of machines to create parts drawn with computer-aided design packages (Chapter 11). *See also* computer-aided design (CAD).

computer-assisted instruction (CAI) The use of computers for instructional purposes, including drill and practice sessions, tutorials, and simulation (Chapter 14).

computer conference A conference that uses, as a medium, computers linked by data communications; conference coordination is usually handled by electronic mail or information utilities, whose computers have the necessary storage and processing capabilities. In a computer conference, many people can communicate with many others, creating a document that is a group effort (Chapter 12). *See also* electronic mail, information utility.

computer graphics Any computer-generated information that is not expressed with text or numbers (Chapter 11). *See also* information.

computer-managed instruction (CMI) The use of computers for managing administrative and clerical tasks related to teaching, such as preparing tests, computing grades, and tracking attendance (Chapter 14).

confirmation message In interactive processing, a message that asks the user to confirm a command that may have work-destroying consequences (Chapter 2). *See also* interactive processing.

confirmation option In a search-and-replace command, an option that displays a confirmation message before each substitution is made (Chapter 5). *See also* confirmation message, search-and-replace option.

constant A value typed into a cell in a spreadsheet program; does not change unless the user deliberately alters it by typing over the cell's contents (Chapter 9). *See also* cell, value.

context A basic software function, such as word processing or data base management, within an integrated program (Chapter 13).

context switching Moving from one software function to another in an integrated program (Chapter 13). *See also* integrated program.

continuous paper *See* tractor feed paper.

control key (CTRL) A command key used to enter commands by typing them at the keyboard. With most computers, it is necessary to hold down the control key while pressing the second key in the command (such as CONTROL-Y) (Chapter 3). *See also* command key.

control structures A logical structure for the design of program modules that governs the sequence in which program instructions are executed (Chapter 15). *See also* looping, sequence, selection.

control unit The part of a computer's central processing unit (CPU) that supervises the computer's operation by executing a program's instructions, one after another (Chapter 2). *See also* central processing unit, program.

copy block command In a word processing program, a command that copies a block of text to a selected location (Chapter 4). *See also* block, begin block command, end block command.

copy command A resident operating system command that copies a file from one disk to another (Chapter 3). *See also* operating system, resident command.

cracker A computer hobbyist, usually juvenile, who takes delight in gaining unauthorized (and often illegal) entry into corporate and government computer systems (Chapter 16).

create command A query language command in a data base management system (DBMS) that allows the user to create a new data base (Chapter 8). *See also* query language.

create mode A mode of a file base management program that assists the user in the creation of an appropriate form for data storage and retrieval (Chapter 7). *See also* form.

currency format A numeric display format that displays spreadsheet values with dollar signs, commas, and two decimal places (Chapter 9). *See also* numeric display format.

cursor A blinking spot or line on the video display screen that shows where characters will appear when typed at the keyboard. The cursor's position is controlled with the cursor control keys (Chapter 3). *See also* cursor control keys.

cursor control keys On the keyboard, the keys that position the cursor on the display screen. Also called arrow keys, the cursor control keys are usually four in number and are indicated by left, right, down, and up arrows printed on them (Chapter 3). *See also* cursor.

cut sheet Paper that has been separated into distinct pages before printing (Chapter 4). *See also* cut sheet feeder.

cut sheet feeder A printer accessory that feeds standard-sized pages of paper into a printer automatically (Chapter 4). *See also* cut sheet paper.

daisywheel printer *See* letter-quality printer.

data Raw, unorganized facts about the world, such as a cardboard box full of unsorted customer receipts (Chapter 1). *See also* information.

data base A collection of information pertinent to a particular subject; serves as a base or foundation for retrieving information, drawing conclusions, or making decisions (Chapter 7).

data base management program An application program that provides computerized tools for managing (that is, storing, organizing, and retrieving) the information normally stored in file cabinets, such as mailing lists, customer account data, or patient records. Data base management programs speed tasks related to the creation, storing, retrieving, and summarizing of information (Chapters 1 and 7). There are two kinds of data base management programs, file management programs and data base management systems (DBMS) (Chapters 7 and 8). *See also* application software, data base, data base management system (DBMS), file management program.

data base management system (DBMS) A data base management program that can work with more than one data file at a time. A DBMS usually includes a programming language, called a procedural language, that lets a sophisticated user modify the program for use in a specific business setting (Chapter 7). *See also* file management program, procedural language.

data base producer *See* online data base producer.

data base vendor *See* online data base vendor.

data communications The transfer of information from one point to another via telecommunications or direct-wire communications (Chapters 2, 12).

data disk A floppy disk containing data, that is, work created with a word processing, data base management, spreadsheet, or some other program (Chapter 3). *See also* program disk.

data encryption The translation of confidential information into a code that cannot be read or easily deciphered; the information is shown in English only when the user types a password (Chapters 7, 14).

data entry area An element of good spreadsheet design in which an area is set aside at the top or left of the spreadsheet for the entry of spreadsheet keys; the calculation area is situated to the right or down (Chapter 10). *See also* calculation area.

data field In a data base management program (Chapter 7) or the mail merging function of a word processing program (Chapter 5), a named data-storage area that is designed to store a particular kind of information (such as a first name, a last name, or a street address). *See also* data base management program, data record, field name, mail merging.

data file 1. A file containing data, that is, work created with a word processing, spreadsheet, data base management, or some other program (Chapters 3, 5). 2. In a mail, the file that contains names and addresses used for mail merging. *See also* file, mail merging, program file.

data file format The format used by a program to store data in disk files (Chapter 13).

data record In a data base management program or a mail merging data file, a unit of related data expressed in named data fields (such as one person's name, address, city, state, zip code, and telephone number) (Chapters 5, 7). *See also* data base management program, data field, mail merging.

data redundancy The storage of one data item in two or more places in a data base (Chapter 8).

data series A two-column list of numbers to be expressed in graphic form; the first column contains the categories (headings) and the second contains the values (numbers) (Chapter 11). *See also* analytic graphics, categories, presentation graphics, value.

data transfer rate The number of bits per second transferred to internal memory after information stored in an auxiliary storage device has been located (Chapter 3). *See also* access time, auxiliary storage device, internal memory.

data type The type of data (alphabetic, numeric, or alphanumeric) to be entered in a data field; the selection is made during use of the create mode of a data base management program (Chapter 7). *See also* data field.

debugging The process of detecting program faults or bugs and correcting them (Chapter 15).

default drive The disk drive or hard disk to which the computer is currently logged on; unless you instruct it otherwise (or change the default drive using the switch drives command) files will be stored and retrieved from this drive. The default drive is usually indicated by a letter (such as A or B) in the system prompt (Chapter 3). *See also* disk drive, hard disk, switch drives command, system prompt.

default formats In a word processing, data base management, or spreadsheet program, the format settings that will be used unless you specifically and deliberately countermand them (Chapters 4, 7, 9). *See* format.

default formatting settings *See* default formats.

default option In a command menu, the option that will be chosen unless you deliberately move the pointer to a different option (Chapter 4). *See also* command menu, pointer.

delete block command In a word processing program, a command that deletes a block of text and closes up the resulting gap automatically (Chapter 4). *See* begin block command, block, end block command.

delete buffer A temporary storage place for deleted text, which may be recovered and replaced in the document if the deletion is reconsidered. However, the delete buffer stores only one deletion at a time; when the buffer's contents are replaced by a new deletion, the old contents cannot be recovered (Chapter 4). *See also* undo command.

delete command In a data base management system (DBMS), a query language command that provides powerful tools for deleting out-of-date or unwanted information from the data base (Chapter 8). *See also* query language.

delete key On the keyboards of most personal computers, a key that deletes the character on which the cursor is positioned (Chapter 3). *See also* cursor.

delimiter In a command-line operating system, a space or punctuation mark that separates components of the command, such as the keyword and parameter (Chapter 3). *See also* keyword, operating system, parameter.

descending sort In a sort, the organization of a data base so that records are sorted alphabetically from Z to A or numerically from the highest to the lowest number (Chapter 7). *See also* data base, ascending sort.

desktop organizer A memory-resident program that includes features such as an address/phone book, a notepad, an onscreen calculator, and an appointment schedule (Chapter 13). *See also* memory-resident program.

desktop publishing The in-house production of publication-quality documents (such as price lists, newsletters, or brochures) using tools that fit readily on a desktop (i.e., a personal computer, a laser printer, a word processing program, a graphics program, and a page layout program) (Chapter 5). *See also* laser printer, page layout program.

destructive Property of a key or command such that it erases or destroys data entered into the computer (Chapter 3). *See also* backspace key, nondestructive.

device independence A feature of modern computers such that the operating system masks the electronic and other differences among auxiliary storage or other devices. So far as the user is concerned, for example, a floppy disk drive and a hard disk are merely places for the storage and retrieval of files; the user can use exactly the same commands to work with both, even though they are, in reality, very different devices (Chapter 3). *See also* auxiliary storage, disk drive, file, floppy disk, operating system.

digit A discrete object, such as a finger or a charged electronic circuit, that aids counting by representing a quantity in a way that is clearly separate and differentiated from other quantities (Chapter 2). *See also* digital computer, electronic digital computer.

digital computer A computer that performs computations by manipulating quantities represented by digits. An abacus is an ancient digital computer (Chapter 2). *See also* abacus, analog computer, digit, electronic digital computer.

digitizer A graphics input device that scans a picture, such as a photograph, and transforms it into its digital equivalent for display on a bit-mapped graphics monitor (Chapter 11). *See also* bit-mapped graphics.

direct access *See* random access.

direct-connect modem A modem designed to plug directly into a modular telephone jack (Chapter 12). *See also* acoustic coupler, modem.

directory command In a personal computer operating system, a resident command that displays the disk directory (Chapter 3). *See also* disk directory.

direct wire communications Computer communication via high-speed cable rather than the telephone system (Chapter 12). *See also* telecommunications.

disk copy program In a personal computer operating system, a transient system utility that copies the entire contents of one disk on another (Chapter 3). *See also* operating system, system utility, transient utility.

disk directory A screen display listing the files present on a floppy or hard disk (Chapter 3). *See also* file, floppy disk, hard disk.

disk drive An auxiliary storage device designed to read information from (and write information to) floppy disks (Chapter 3). *See also* auxiliary storage, floppy disk, read, write.

disk format program In a personal computer operating system, a transient system utility that formats a blank disk for use (Chapter 3). *See also* format, operating system, system utility, transient utility.

disk operating system (DOS) *See* operating system.

display command A query language command in a data base management system (DBMS) that selects data for display on the screen (Chapter 8). *See also* query language, select.

distributed computing The distribution of computing resources throughout an organization using minicomputers or microcomputers linked to a central mainframe or minicomputer (Chapter 2). *See also* mainframe computer, microcomputer, minicomputer.

document A unit of written work (such as an essay, a play, a business report, or a poem) created with a word processing program (Chapter 4). *See also* word processing program.

document display screen In a word processing program, a display screen that provides the user with a document window, a status line, a cursor, a ruler, and other features (Chapter 4). *See also* cursor, document window, ruler, status line, window.

document format In a word processing program, a format that pertains to an entire document (such as the default margin settings, position of page numbers, and running heads) (Chapter 4). *See also* format.

document window In a word processing program, the portion of the document display screen in which text can be entered and revised (Chapter 4). *See also* document display screen, window.

dot-matrix printer A computer printer that forms an image by extruding a pattern or matrix of tiny wires which strikes a ribbon, forming a character made up of tiny dots (Chapter 3).

download To capture on disk text files or software that have been received through data communications media (Chapter 12). *See also* data communications, upload.

dumb terminal emulation program A program that transforms a personal computer into a remote terminal lacking its own processing capabilities (Chapter 12). *See also* smart communications program.

electronic digital computer A digital computer that represents data using electronic bistable devices, such as vacuum tubes or transistors (Chapter 2). *See also* bistable device, digital computer.

electronic mail The transmission, storage, and reception of letters, memos, and other documents via computer media; a one-way information transfer from a sender to a receiver (Chapter 12). *See also* point-storage-point electronic mail, point-to-point electronic mail.

embedded command A formatting command inserted within the text to be formatted; does not affect the appearance of the text on the screen. Usually, the command consists of a special command symbol, such as an asterisk, followed by the command name (e.g., CENTER or JUSTIFY). Delimitors, generally parentheses or brackets, are often used to indicate the text to be affected by the command. The command is read by a formatting program, which follows its instructions to prepare the print output file (Chapter 4). *See also* formatting, formatting program, onscreen formatter, print output file.

end block command In a word processing program, a command that demarcates the end of a block of text (Chapter 4). *See also* begin block command, block, block move, copy block command, delete block command, move block command.

endnotes Footnotes that are positioned at the end of the document rather than the bottom of the page (Chapter 5).

entry line An area outside the spreadsheet window in which constants, formulas, and labels may be entered in the active cell (Chapter 9). *See also* active cell, constants, formulas, labels, spreadsheet window.

entry mode A spreadsheet program mode in which characters typed at the keyboard will appear on the entry line (Chapter 9). *See also* entry line.

erase command A resident operating system command that erases a file on a disk (Chapter 3). *See also* operating system, resident command.

error message In interactive processing, a message displayed on the screen informing the user that the computer was not able to carry out an operation or that something has gone wrong with the equipment (Chapter 2). *See also* interactive processing.

escape key (ESC) A command key on the computer's keyboard that is used (in combination with other keys) to enter commands (such as ESCAPE-X, a command requiring you to press the escape key and then the X key). With most computers, it is not necessary to hold down the escape key while you enter the second key in the keyboard command (Chapter 3). *See also* command key.

execute To carry out a program's instructions (Chapter 2). *See also* program.

exploded pie chart A pie chart from which a slice has been removed for emphasis (Chapter 11).

exploratory data analysis A technique for the analysis of statistical data in which a variety of alternative analytical strategies are employed (Chapter 14).

extended memory *See* auxiliary storage.

extension In a command-line operating system, the second and optional part of the file name; consists of up to 3 letters, numbers, or punctuation symbols (except that many symbols are illegal in extensions). Often used to indicate the type of information contained in the file (e.g., DOC = word processing document) (Chapter 3). *See also* command-line operating system, primary file name.

field length The length in characters of a data field; defined while using the create mode of a data base management program. The field length should be long enough to accommodate the longest possible data entry in the field (Chapter 7). *See also* data field.

field name A word or phrase (such as AUTHOR'S NAME or CUSTOMER IDENTIFICATION NUMBER) that serves as the heading or title of a data field. The field name tells the user what kind of information to enter in the field (Chapter 7). *See also* data field.

fifth generation computer The next generation of computers, which may possess artificial intelligence (AI) (Chapter 2). *See also* artificial intelligence (AI).

file A named unit of data or program instructions stored on an auxiliary storage device, such as a disk drive (Chapter 3). *See also* auxiliary storage, data file, disk drive, extension, primary file name, program file.

file management program A data base management program designed to work with only one data file at a time (Chapter 7). *See also* data base management program.

file manager The part of an operating system that automatically stores and retrieves information on auxiliary storage devices such as disk drives (Chapter 3). *See also* operating system.

file merge command A word processing program command that inserts or merges one file with another. Generally, the file is inserted at the cursor's location (Chapter 5). *See also* file.

file name The name of a file, which is used for storage and retrieval operations (Chapter 3). *See also* extension, file, file specification, primary file name.

file recovery program A utility program that can recover an accidentally deleted file, so long as the user has not saved any other files to disk since the accidental erasure (Chapter 14).

file specification In a command-line operating system, a file name prefix that tells the computer where the file is located (Chapter 3). *See also* command-line operating system, file name.

first generation computer Any of the first electronic digital computers (ca. 1951–1959), which used vacuum tubes. First generation computers failed every few minutes, were slow and costly to operate, and had small internal memories. Programs were written in machine language, and data were input on punched cards (Chapter 2).

fixed disk *See* hard disk.

fixed format A numeric display format that shows spreadsheet values with a user-specified number of decimal places (Chapter 9). *See also* numeric display format.

flexible disk *See* floppy disk.

floppy disk A thin, flexible disk of plastic coated with a magnetically sensitive material and wrapped in a cardboard envelope. Floppy disks and disk drives are the most common auxiliary storage medium for personal computers (Chapter 3). *See also* disk drive.

footnote reference mark The mark (usually a superscripted number) that calls the reader's attention to a footnote or endnote (Chapter 5). *See also* endnotes.

font A set of letters, numbers, and punctuation symbols that are all designed to conform to a distinctive type style, such as Times Roman or Helvetica (Chapter 4). *See also* character format, type size.

forecasting An analytical technique that seeks to predict future values by extrapolating from present trends (Chapter 10).

forced page break command In a word processing program, a command that overrides automatic pagination and inserts a page break precisely where you wish it (Chapter 4). *See also* page break.

form A template, containing a series of headings and data fields, that assists in the collection and storage of information when using a file management program (Chapter 7). *See also* heading, data field, file management program.

format 1. (noun) A design for the appearance of printed text on the page so that it conforms to aesthetic and professional standards. 2. (verb) To modify text so that it conforms to aesthetic and professional standards when printed. 3. (verb) To prepare a blank disk for use with the computer by imposing a pattern of magnetic tracks and sectors on it (Chapter 4).

formatting 1. The process of imposing a magnetic pattern of tracks and sectors on a new, unused floppy disk or hard disk so that the disk drives can use it to store and retrieve information (Chapters 3, 4). *See also* floppy disk, hard disk. 2. The process of modifying computer-based text so that it conforms, when printed, to established aesthetic and professional standards. *See also* offscreen formatting, onscreen formatting.

formatting program 1. A system utility program that imposes a pattern of magnetic tracks and sectors on a floppy or hard disk. 2. A word processing program that accompanies an offscreen formatter, reads embedded commands, and follows their instructions to create a print output file (Chapter 4). *See also* embedded command, floppy disk, hard disk, offscreen formatting, onscreen formatting, print output file, system utility.

form letter A standard letter mailed to many people (often with some measure of personalization) (Chapter 5). *See also* mail merging.

formula A mathematical rule or principle that is expressed in a form a spreadsheet program can interpret. A formula begins with a formula marking character, and can contain constants, cell references, built-in functions, and operators (Chapter 9).

forward reference A cell reference error in a spreadsheet formula; references a cell situated to the right of the formula in column-wise recalculation or below the formula in row-wise recalculation (Chapter 9). *See also* cell reference, column-wise recalculation, recalculation, row-wise recalculation.

fourth generation computer A computer created since 1971 that uses large-scale and very large-scale integrated circuits (Chapter 2).

frame buffer The memory in a video display circuit that holds the image used to refresh the screen during raster-scan operations (Chapter 11). *See also* raster scan.

full-duplex modem A modem that can transmit and receive simultaneously; required for use with personal computers (Chapter 12). *See also* half-duplex modem, modem.

full-text data base A source data base that contains the full text of journal articles, encyclopedias, legal documents, and other materials (Chapter 12). *See also* reference data base, source data base.

function keys Special keys (usually labelled F1, F2, F3, etc.) that programs can use for program control purposes (Chapter 3).

functional organization The way a modern electronic digital computer is organized so that it processes data automatically. All electronic digital computers contain two kinds of components, the central processing unit (CPU) and peripherals (Chapter 2). *See also* central processing unit (CPU), peripherals.

fundamental analysis program An investment analysis program that goes through publicly available data on companies and selects those whose stock is undervalued in comparison with its potential (Chapter 14).

general format A numeric display format that displays spreadsheet values with all significant numbers past the decimal point (up to 15 decimal places with some programs) (Chapter 9). *See also* numeric display format.

general ledger program The central program in an accounting package; provides a scorecard for all business transactions and allows a manager to see where a business stands (Chapter 14).

general-purpose computer A computer designed so that, with the aid of application software, it can serve a wide variety of purposes (Chapter 2). *See also* special-purpose computer.

gigabyte Approximately 1 billion bytes or characters (more precisely, 1,024 megabytes) (Chapter 3). *See also* byte, character, megabyte.

global format A format that applies to every cell in a spreadsheet (Chapter 9). *See also* range format.

glossary A memory-based text-storage facility provided by some word processing programs; used for the storage and retrieval of frequently used passages of text called boilerplate (Chapter 5). *See also* boilerplate.

graphics *See* computer graphics.

graphics mode A video display mode in which the computer can switch any pixel on or off independently of the others (Chapter 11). *See also* bit-mapped graphics, character mode.

graphics tablet A graphics input device that transforms images traced on its surface into images displayed on the monitor (Chapter 11).

hacker Slang for an amateur programmer who takes delight in finding and repairing bugs in programs (Chapter 15). *See also* cracker.

half-duplex modem A modem that cannot send and receive information simultaneously; acceptable for use with remote terminals but not with personal computers (Chapter 12). *See also* full-duplex modem, modem.

hanging indentation A paragraph format in which the first line of the paragraph is flush to the left margin but subsequent lines (called turnover lines) are indented (Chapter 4). *See also* paragraph format, turnover line.

hard disk An auxiliary storage device that uses a hard or rigid platter. Coated with a magnetically sensitive substance, the platter spins in a dust-proof environment at speeds of up to 3,000 r.p.m. The dust-proof environment is necessary because the read/write head "floats" just above the disk's surface, so close that a human hair or dust particle on the disk's surface would collide with the head. Thanks to the disk's high speed and the head's proximity to the platter, access times and data transfer are greatly increased (Chapter 3).

hardware The physical parts of the computer, the ones you can see and touch (Chapter 1). *See also* software.

heading *See* field name.

high-level programming language A programming language (such as COBOL or FORTRAN) in which the programmer uses instructions that resemble familiar English words, the Arabic numbers we use every day, and ordinary mathematic expressions (rather than cryptic instructions written in binary code). After writing the program in a high-level language, the program is translated or compiled into the machine language the computer understands (Chapter 2). *See also* compiler, machine language.

hit A data record containing data that match a search string entered during a search of a data base (Chapter 7). *See also* data base, search string.

idea processing program *See* outlining program.

image library A collection of images and pictures that can be inserted into charts, graphs, or free-form illustrations (Chapter 11).

image recorder A graphics output device that captures a high-quality graphics image on 35mm slide film (Chapter 11).

incompatibility Inability to run software or use peripherals designed for another computer. The Apple IIe, for instance, is incompatible with the IBM Personal Computer (Chapter 3).

information Data that has been organized and made useful for some purpose, such as a cardboard box full of customer receipts sorted by customer's last name (Chapter 1). *See also* data.

information society An emerging social order in the Western industrialized nations in which, according to sociologists, most people will be concerned with the production of information and knowledge rather than the production of goods (Chapter 2). *See also* information, knowledge.

information utility A company that sells public access to huge mainframe computer systems, which are stocked with information of public interest (including up-to-the-minute stock quotes, current news, special interest group [SIG] conferences) and services such as electronic mail, home banking, and computer shopping (Chapter 12).

input The process of representing data for computer processing purposes (Chapter 2). *See also* coding, output.

input device A peripheral that takes in data in a form humans understand (such as letters, numbers, or pictures) and translates it into a form the computer can understand (such as binary numbers) (Chapter 2). *See also* peripheral.

input/output manager The part of an operating system that automatically manages the flow of information to and from input and output devices (Chapter 3). *See also* operating system.

insertion point *See* cursor.

insert mode In a word processing program (or others that incorporate text entry and revision features), a text-entry mode in which characters typed at the keyboard push existing text right and down (Chapter 4). *See also* overtype mode.

instruction set A list of the tasks that a microprocessor is designed to carry out. Each instruction has its own, unique code, expressed in binary numbers. Programs contain lists of instructions that use this code. The microprocessor follows these instructions to carry out, or execute, the program (Chapter 3). *See also* binary numbers, execute, microprocessor, program.

integrated accounting package An accounting package that includes accounts payable, accounts receivable, general ledger, payroll, and sometimes inventory control modules, all of which are linked by account automation (Chapter 14). *See also* account automation, accounts payable program, accounts receivable program, general ledger program, inventory control program.

integrated circuit A complex electronic component that is printed on a small, wafer-like chip of silicon. The result, which can be mass-produced at low cost, is a tiny electronic component that replaces a much larger and more expensive circuit board containing many hand-soldered elements (Chapter 2).

integrated program A program that includes all five basic software functions (word processing, spreadsheet, graphics, communications, and data base management), allows rapid and easy context switching, facilitates the exchange of data among programs, and provides a consistent user interface for all software functions (Chapter 13). *See also* standalone application program.

interactive processing A computer operating technique in which the user can actively control the computer's operations, correcting (for example) problems in the middle of processing operations if something goes wrong. The computer engages in a dialogue with the user, presenting error messages, prompts, menus, and confirmation messages (Chapter 2). *See also* confirmation message, error message, menu, prompt.

internal memory The part of the computer's central processing unit (CPU) that stores data and programs so that they are directly accessible for processing purposes (Chapter 2). In a personal computer, the internal memory consists of the read-only memory (ROM) and the random-access memory (RAM) (Chapter 3). *See also* auxiliary storage, central processing unit (CPU), program, random access memory (RAM), read-only memory (ROM).

interpreter A program that translates source code instructions into executable machine language and executes each program statement; does not produce a compiled program (Chapter 15). *See also* compiled program, compiler.

inventory control program A special-purpose program that keeps track of a business's stock of goods and alerts a manager when inventory levels fall too low (Chapter 14).

join command In a data base management system (DBMS), a command that lets the user join two or more data bases by linking them through a common data field (Chapter 8). *See also* data field.

justification *See* right margin justification.

key A spreadsheet cell that contains an important constant, which will be referenced by formulas in calculation areas (Chapter 9). *See also* calculation area, cell.

keyboard command A command entered by holding down one of the keyboard's command keys (such as the control or alternate keys) and pressing one or two other keys (Chapter 4). *See also* alternate key (ALT), command key, control key (CTRL), escape key (ESC).

key enhancement program An accessory program that adds macro capabilities to programs that lack them (Chapters 5, 14). *See also* macro.

keyword 1. In a command-line operating system, the first part of a keyboard command; a verb such as PRINT, TYPE, or DELETE, the keyword tells the computer what to do. It is usually followed by a parameter (Chapter 3). 2. A command name in a command menu (Chapter 9). 3. The name of a built-in function in a spreadsheet program. *See* built-in function, command-line operating system, command menu, parameter.

kilobyte (K) Approximately 1,000 bytes or characters (more precisely, 2^{10} = 1,024 bytes) (Chapter 3). *See also* byte, character.

knowledge Information that has been subjected to reasoning and judgment (Chapter 2). *See also* data, information.

label A heading or title in a spreadsheet cell (Chapter 9). *See also* cell.

large-scale integration (LSI) A technique, developed in the late 1960s, for the fabrication of integrated circuits containing between 100 and 100,000 discrete electronic components on a single chip (Chapter 2). *See also* integrated circuit.

laser printer A computer printer that uses a high-speed laser to etch an image of the text on a rotating drum; the image is fused to the paper using a heat process. The result is a high-quality printout that untrained eyes cannot distinguish from the work of a professional printer (Chapter 3).

left flush alignment A paragraph format in which text is aligned flush to the left margin; the right margin is ragged (Chapter 4). *See also* paragraph format.

legend A key to the meaning of shapes, patterns, or colors in a chart or graph (Chapter 11).

letter-quality printer A computer printer that forms an image by striking an embossed, fully-formed image of a character against a ribbon. Letter-quality printers emulate the typescript produced by fine office typewriters (Chapter 3).

light pen A stylus containing a photocell that detects light and allows the user to draw directly on the screen of a computer monitor; it works by detecting precisely when a particular pixel is being illuminated by the raster scan so the pen's position can be determined on the screen (Chapter 11). *See also* pixel, raster scan.

line break The place where a new line must be started to keep the text from going over the right margin (Chapter 4). *See also* line break.

loading a program Transferring a program from auxiliary storage to the internal memory for use (Chapter 4). *See also* auxiliary storage, internal memory.

load program command A resident operating system command that loads a program from disk (Chapter 3). *See also* operating system, resident command.

local area network (LAN) A network of personal

computers directly connected by high-speed cable links (Chapter 12). *See also* timesharing.

logical operator An operator used to specify relationships of inclusion or exclusion among two or more criteria (Chapters 7, 9). *See also* AND, NOT, OR, selection criteria.

log on 1. To switch to a disk drive so that it becomes the default drive (Chapter 3). 2. To contact a computer bulletin board, electronic mail service, or online data base vendor (Chapter 12). *See also* bulletin board, electronic mail, default drive, disk drive, online data base vendor, switch drives command.

looping A program control structure made possible by the storage of the program in internal memory that causes the computer to keep doing an operation over and over until a specified condition is fulfilled (Chapter 2). *See also* control structure, internal memory, stored program concept.

low-level language A programming language that involves the programmer in the internal movement of data within the central processing unit (CPU) (Chapter 15). *See also* central processing unit (CPU), high-level language, programming language.

machine language A programming language that expresses program instructions in terms of machine codes that can be directly executed by a specific kind of computer (Chapters 2, 15). *See also* assembly language, high-level language.

macro A stored list of program commands which, when retrieved by a keyboard command, are executed automatically in the sequence in which they are written. A variety of commands can be included in the macro, including commands for positioning the cursor, scrolling, formatting, and storing a document on disk. Macros can be used to automate complex document, data base, or spreadsheet processing tasks (Chapter 5).

magnetic core memory An internal memory storage device widely used in second and third generation computers; information is stored by imparting a magnetic charge to a tiny length of wire (Chapter 2). *See also* internal memory, second generation computers, semiconductor memory, third generation computers.

magnetic disk *See* floppy disk, hard disk.

mail merging In a word processing program, a feature that automates the production of personalized form letters from a data file of names and addresses (Chapter 5). *See also* data field, data file, data record, form letter, main document.

main document The document containing the form letter text used in mail merging (Chapter 5). *See also* mail merging.

mainframe computer A large computer designed to meet the computing needs of an entire organization (Chapter 2). *See also* microcomputer, minicomputer, personal computer.

manual recalculation A mode of recalculation in a spreadsheet program in which recalculation does not proceed until the user specifically requests it; useful for large spreadsheets in which data entry is hampered by delays caused by automatic recalculation (Chapter 9). *See also* automatic recalculation, recalculation.

mass storage An auxiliary storage system capable of storing virtually all of the information an organization uses on a day-to-day basis (Chapter 2). *See also* auxiliary storage.

matrix letter *See* main document.

megabyte (M) Approximately 1 million bytes or characters (more precisely, 2^{20} = 1,048,576 bytes) (Chapter 3). *See also* byte, character.

megaflop A unit of measurement of computer speed; one megaflop is equal to one million computational operations per second (Chapter 2).

memory *See* auxiliary storage, internal memory.

memory address A number referring to a unique location in a computer's internal memory. Personal computer memory addresses are made up of 16-, 20-, or 24-digit binary numbers. The maximum size of the internal memory is determined by the number of digits in the memory address. A computer that has a 20-bit memory address, for instance, can use a maximum of 2^{20} unique memory locations. In personal computers, each memory location holds a maximum of eight binary numbers (one byte or one character) (Chapter 3). *See also* byte, character, internal memory.

memory chips *See* semiconductor memory.

memory-resident program An accessory program (such as an appointment calendar, a spelling checker, a thesaurus, or an outlining program) designed to work in tandem with application software such as word processing programs. The memory-resident program occupies memory space that the program does not use. At a keystroke, the application program's operation is suspended and the memory-resident program "pops" onto the screen. When work with the memory-resident program is finished, the user is returned immediately to the application program, with the cursor positioned precisely where it was when the program's operation was suspended (Chapter 6). *See also* memory-resident thesaurus, outlining program.

memory-resident thesaurus A word processing accessory program that functions in a memory-resident mode. After typing a word with a word processing program, the user can see — at a keystroke — a list of synonyms in a window that opens on the screen. If one of the synonyms works better than the word originally typed, it can be selected and, with another keystroke, automatically inserted in the document (Chapter 6). *See also* memory-resident program, window.

menu A list of options that is displayed on the computer screen; by choosing one of them, the user can control the computer without having to remember complicated keyboard commands (Chapter 3). *See also* submenu.

microcomputer A general-purpose computing system constructed around a microprocessor chip (Chapter 2). *See also* microprocessor; *compare* personal computer.

microprocessor An outgrowth of large and very large-scale integration technologies, a microprocessor is a computer's central processing unit (minus the internal memory) fabricated on a tiny chip of silicon. Because microprocessors can be produced in massive quantities at low unit costs, they have made possible the distribution of computing resources throughout society (Chapter 2). *See also* central processing unit (CPU).

microspacing The insertion of spaces as small as one-twentieth of an inch to even out the gaps between words in right-justified text (Chapter 5). *See also* proportional spacing, right-margin justification.

minicomputer A multiple-user, timesharing computer — essentially a junior version of a mainframe computer — designed to meet the needs of a medium-sized or small organization, or of a department within a large organization (Chapter 2). *See also* mainframe computer.

modeling A simulation process in which an artificial version of a prototype (a model) is constructed; the artificial version has some features in common with the prototype or mimics its behavior in some ways. The prototype's properties can be investigated, therefore, by studying the model (Chapter 10). *See also* simulation.

modem A device that modifies (modulates) the digital data stream coming from the computer so that the telephone system can transmit the data; it also demodulates (hence *mo-dem*) data coming in via the telephone lines so that the computer can use it (Chapter 12). *See also* acoustic coupler, direct-connect modem, full duplex modem, half-duplex modem, smart modem.

modularity The degree to which a programming language enables modular programming techniques (Chapter 15). *See also* module.

modular program A program written using modules (Chapter 15). *See also* module.

module A logically related set of program statements that accomplish a specific task in a program; each module has single entry and exit points, is of modest size, is logically independent of other program modules, and passes on program control to the next module in a logical, sequential fashion (Chapter 15).

monitor *See* cathode-ray tube (CRT) monitor.

monochrome monitor A cathode-ray tube (CRT) monitor that produces an amber or green image against a deep black background, or a black image against a white background (Chapter 3). *See also* cathode-ray tube (CRT) monitor.

monospace type A type font in which every character is the same width, producing a result that resembles typescript (Chapter 5). *See also* font, proportional spacing.

mouse A hand-held computer control device designed to roll about on the desktop next to a computer's keyboard. As it rolls, its movements are reflected in the movement of a small arrow, or pointer, on the screen. A standard input device on some computers (such as the Macintosh) and an option on others (such as the IBM Personal Computer), mice are widely used to select items from lists, point to commands on the screen, and edit text (Chapter 3). *See also* input device, menu.

move block command In a word processing program, a command that accomplishes a block move, in which a block of text is moved from one location to another and the gap left by the block's departure is closed up automatically (Chapter 4). *See also* begin block command, block move, delete block command, end block command.

multiple head pass A printing technique used with dot-matrix printers in which the print head makes multiple passes over the page, each of which is slightly out of register with the preceding one; the result is a high-quality graphics image (Chapter 11). *See also* dot-matrix printer.

multiple key sort A sort in which the records are first sorted using a primary sort key, and then subsequently sorted by a secondary sort key and perhaps additional sort keys. In a multiple key sort, several records that share a single primary sort key will be internally sorted on the secondary sort key. If the primary sort key is AUTHOR and the secondary sort key is DATE OF PUBLICATION, for instance, all data records will first be sorted by AUTHOR and, if there are several records by the same author, these records will be sorted by DATE OF PUBLICATION (Chapter 7). *See also* primary sort key, secondary sort key, sort key, tertiary sort key.

multiple-user system A timesharing computer designed to meet the computing needs of a work team, a department within an organization, or an entire organization (Chapter 2). *See also* single-user system, timesharing.

multiple windows A feature of application programs capable of opening two or more windows on a document or documents (Chapter 5). *See also* document window, window.

multitasking operating system An operating system that can run several programs simultaneously, such as UNIX (Chapter 3). *See also* operating system.

multiuser accounting package An accounting package designed to operate on a local area network (Chapter 14). *See also* local area network (LAN).

natural language interface A user interface that, ideally, would allow the user to communicate with the computer using conversational English and without worrying about precise command syntax (Chapter 8). *See also* user interface.

natural recalculation mode A mode of spreadsheet recalculation in which calculation follows the cell references in formulas rather than proceeding row by row or column by column; avoids forward reference errors (Chapter 9). *See also* forward reference, recalculation.

near-letter-quality A text printing mode of some dot-matrix printers that is claimed to come close to the quality of letter-quality printers (Chapter 3). *See also* dot-matrix printer, letter-quality printer.

nondestructive A command that, when used, does not obliterate or erase data already entered into the computer (Chapter 3). *See also* destructive.

nonprocedural language A very high-level programming language in which the programmer is freed from concern with the procedures the computer must follow to execute the program (Chapter 15). *See also* very high level programming language.

nonproprietary operating system An operating system produced by an independent, third-party software house that is designed to run on several manufacturers' computers, so long as they conform to a de facto standard (Chapter 3). *See also* operating system.

nonvolatile A memory that does not lose its contents when the current is switched off (Chapter 3). *See also* volatile.

NOT A logical operator that narrows a search by excluding unwanted records that meet the first criterion but also meet a second criterion ("Retrieve all the records that contain TAIWAN but *not* the ones that also contain BALANCE OF TRADE") (Chapter 7). *See also* AND, logical operator, OR.

number lock key (NUM LCK) A key that "toggles" or switches the numeric keypad back and forth between its numerical entry and cursor control functions (Chapter 3). *See also* cursor control keys, numeric keypad.

numerical operator A word, phrase, or symbol (such as EQUALS, GREATER THAN, or <) that establishes a relationship of magnitude between two variables (as in the expression, "x is greater than y"). Numerical operators are frequently used in data base searching to establish selection criteria (Chapter 7) and in spreadsheet programs to create formulas (Chapter 9). *See also* formula, logical operator, selection criteria.

numeric data base An electronic, online data base that permits the rapid storage and retrieval of statistics, such as economic indicators (Chapter 12).

numeric display format A format that applies to all the numbers in a range or throughout the entire spreadsheet (Chapter 9). *See also* currency format, fixed format, general format, percent format, scientific format.

numeric keypad A set of keys that uses a standard format for the high-speed, one-handed entry of numbers (Chapter 3). *See also* number lock key (NUM LCK).

object code A computer program that has been translated into the machine language, which the computer can directly execute (Chapter 15). *See also* machine language, source code.

object-oriented operating system An operating system that represents computer programs, files, and operations as objects on the screen, which can be manipulated with a mouse (Chapter 3). *See also* mouse, operating system.

office A place where people carry out six fundamental activities with information: creating information, storing and retrieving information, analyzing information, summarizing information, communicating information, and using information to make decisions (Chapter 1).

office automation The application of computer technology to office work (Chapter 1). *See also* office.

offscreen formatting In a word processing program, an approach to text formatting in which formatted text does not appear on the screen the way it will print on paper. Formatting is accomplished through the use of embedded commands, which are placed in text along with delimiters (usually parentheses or brackets) that mark the text to be affected. The commands are read by a formatting program, which constructs a print output file. Finally, the print output file is sent to the printer (Chapter 4). *See also* embedded command, formatting, formatting program, onscreen formatter, print output file.

online data base producer A company that creates and leases computer-readable data bases to online data base vendors (Chapter 12). *See also* online data base vendor.

online data base vendor A company that sells telecommunications access to computer-readable data bases (Chapter 12). *See also* online data base producer.

onscreen formatting In a word processing program, an approach to formatting in which the text appears on the screen the way it will appear when printed. Formatting commands directly affect the appearance of the displayed text; embedded commands are avoided. For this reason, no separate formatting procedure is necessary before printing (Chapter 4). *See also* embedded commands, formatting, offscreen formatting.

open architecture A microcomputer design technique that invites third-party suppliers to provide additional circuit boards, software, and peripherals. Plug-in slots and connectors are provided so the user can easily attach these accessories to the computer (Chapter 2). *See also* closed architecture.

operating system The system software that manages computer functions from moment to moment, including the flow of information within the computer, the flow of information to and from output and input devices, the storing and retrieving of data on auxiliary storage units, handling user commands and presenting error and other messages on the screen, and providing utility programs for day-to-day system maintenance (Chapter 2). *See also* auxiliary storage, command-line operating system, command processor, file manager, input device, input/output manager, multitasking operating system, nonproprietary operating system, object-oriented operating system, output device, proprietary operating system, supervisor, system disk, system software.

operator A symbol that indicates an arithmetic or logical operation (Chapter 9). *See also* arithmetic operator, logical operator.

optical disk A read-only storage medium that stores information in the form of tiny pockmarks on a reflective plastic surface. The pockmarks are detected optically by a laser beam (Chapter 3). *See also* CD-ROM, compact disk (CD), read-only storage medium.

OR A logical operator that broadens a search by including all the records that meet two or more criteria ("Retrieve all the records that contain TAIWAN or BALANCE OF TRADE") (Chapter 7). *See also* AND, logical operator, NOT.

outlining program A word processing accessory program that facilitates the creation, revision, storage, and printing of outlines. Subordinate headings in the outline can be collapsed or hidden so that the outline's overall structure can be seen; at a keystroke, the hidden headings can be expanded or revealed. Some outlining programs are memory-resident, and a few word processing programs include outlining functions (Chapter 6). *See also* memory-resident program.

output A stage in the processing of data in which the now-processed data are displayed on a display screen or printed on a printer (Chapter 2).

output devices A peripheral designed to show the results of computer processing operations in a form that people can understand, such as a cathode-ray tube (CRT) display screen or a printer (Chapter 2). *See* cathode-ray tube (CRT), peripheral.

overtype mode In a word processing program (or others that incorporate text entry and revision features), a text-entry mode in which characters typed at the keyboard will erase the characters shown on the screen (rather than push them aside) (Chapter 4). *See also* insert mode.

packet A unit of data (such as 128 characters) that is transmitted at high speed via a packet-switching network (Chapter 12). *See also* packet-switching networks.

packet-switching networks *See* value-added networks.

page break The place where a new page must be started to keep the text from going over the bottom margin (Chapter 4). *See also* line break.

page layout program A desktop publishing program that goes beyond a word processor's formatting capabilities and provides tools for blending text and graphics in page design (Chapter 5). *See also* desktop publishing.

paint program A program that provides graphics tools for creating illustrations (Chapter 11).

paragraph format A format that affects the way a paragraph of text appears on the page, such as left flush alignment (Chapter 4). *See also* format, hanging indentation, left flush alignment, right flush alignment, right margin justification.

parallel processing A computer design technique in which several linked central processing units (CPU) each work simultaneously on a part of a complex problem (Chapter 2).

parallel transmission The synchronous transmission of bits representing a character simultaneously over several parallel wires (Chapter 12). *See also* serial transmission, synchronous.

parameter In a command-line operating system, the part of a command typed at the keyboard that tells the computer on what file, disk, or other object the computer should perform an action; provides an object for the keyword's verb (Chapter 3). *See also* command-line operating system, keyword.

passive voice detector A program that detects many (but not all) instances of the passive voice in a document created with a word processing program (Chapter 6).

payroll program A special-purpose application program that keeps employee records, calculates paychecks after subtracting withholding taxes and other deductions, and prints the checks (Chapter 14).

PC-compatible A personal computer capable of running software and using peripherals designed for the IBM Personal Computer (Chapter 2). *See also* personal computer.

percent format A numeric display format that shows spreadsheet values as percentages. The user types in a decimal (such as .0875), and the screen shows the percentage (8.75%) (Chapter 9). *See also* numeric display format.

peripheral All components of the computer that are outside, or peripheral to, the central processing unit (CPU), such as auxiliary storage devices (disk drives), input devices (keyboards), and output devices (display screens and printers) (Chapter 2). *See also* auxiliary storage, central processing unit (CPU), input device, output device.

personal computer An easy-to-use, inexpensive, and small microcomputer, which is designed for use by ordinary people with little previous background in computers or computer programming. Personal computers are designed to meet the computing needs of individuals, not organizations (Chapters 1, 2). *See also* mainframe computer, microcomputer, minicomputer.

pixel Acronym for *pi*cture *el*ement, or a tiny dot on the screen of a cathode-ray tube (CRT) monitor that can be switched on or off independently of the others (Chapter 3). *See also* cathode-ray tube (CRT) monitor.

pointer In a command menu or spreadsheet, an area highlighted by reverse video or a special color; shows the currently selected command option or defines a spreadsheet range. The pointer may be moved using the cursor control keys (Chapters 4, 9). *See also* command menu, range, reverse video.

point-storage-point electronic mail The one-way transmission of a message from one computer to another with an intermediate storage stage in the auxiliary memory of a host computer system; the document is stored until the recipient calls into the system (Chapter 12). *See also* point-to-point electronic mail.

point-to-point electronic mail The one-way transmission of a message from one computer to another through direct linkages via the telephone system or a local area network (Chapter 12). *See also* point-storage-point electronic mail.

pop-up command menu An approach to the provision of command options to the user in application programs. A command menu is displayed (normally at all times) on the screen. When the user selects one of the command options by moving the pointer and pressing the return key, a submenu appears (pops up) that contains additional command options (Chapter 4). *See also* command menu, menu, pointer.

port A channel leading into and out of the computer (Chapter 12). *See also* RS-232C serial port.

portability The extent to which a computer program or programming language can be used on other brands of computers (Chapter 15).

portfolio manager A program that keeps track of an investor's stocks and produces periodic reports (Chapter 14).

primary file name In a command-line operating system, the first and mandatory part of the file name; consists of up to 8 letters, numbers, or punctuation symbols (except that many symbols are illegal in file names). Primary file names are used to identify the material stored in the file (Chapter 3). *See also* extension, file.

primary sort key In a multiple-key sort, the data field that is chosen to organize all the records in a data base. In a bibliographic data base, for example, a good primary sort key would be AUTHOR (Chapter 7). *See also* secondary sort key, sort key, tertiary sort key.

print merging *See* mail merging.

print output file A file of formatted text prepared by a formatting program (Chapter 4). *See also* embedded commands, formatting, formatting program, offscreen formatting.

print spooler A utility program that allows a personal computer user to print a file and work with an application program at the same time (Chapter 14).

procedural language A programming language provided with many data base management systems (DBMS); used to automate day-to-day data base maintenance procedures and to set up menu-driven, custom installations of the DBMS (Chapter 8).

processing Performing operations on data such as addition, multiplication, or comparison to see what of two quantities is the larger. Processing takes place according to the directions of a program (Chapter 2). *See also* program.

professional workstation A special-purpose, single-user computer designed to meet the needs of professionals in disciplines such as electrical engineering, aerospace technology, and laboratory science (Chapter 2). *See also* special purpose computer, single-user system.

program A list of step-by-step instructions that the computer follows to accomplish a task. A program embodies an algorithm (Chapter 2). *See also* algorithm.

program disk A floppy disk containing a single application program and the accessory programs it needs to function properly (Chapter 3). *See also* data disk.

program file A file containing a program (that is, compiled object code), which is ready to execute (Chapter 3). *See also* compiler, data file, file, object code.

program generator A program that creates a computer-readable program by guiding the user (who need not possess programming expertise) through a series of questions, such as

"What is the name of the input variable?" (Chapter 15). *See also* automatic programming.

programming The task of translating an algorithm into a program, a series of instructions the computer can understand (Chapter 15).

programming languages Formalized systems of computer-readable notation that allow algorithms and data to be expressed in an unambiguous, precise manner (Chapter 15).

project management program A special-purpose application program that automates the calculations involved in project management techniques such as the critical path method (CPM) and the program evaluation and review technique (PERT) (Chapter 14). *See also* special-purpose application package.

prompt In interactive processing, a message or symbol displayed on the screen informing the user that the computer is ready to receive instructions (Chapter 2). *See also* interactive processing.

proportional spacing The assignment to each letter in a font of a space proportional to its size, so that an *m* gets more space than an *l* (Chapter 5). *See also* microspace justification, monospace font.

proprietary operating system An operating system produced by the same company that manufactures the computer it runs on and that will not operate on any other manufacturer's computer (Chapter 3). *See also* operating system.

public domain software Software (often of excellent quality) that programmers have refrained from copyrighting and is freely copiable without risk of legal prosecution (Chapter 12).

pull-down command menu An approach to the provision of command options to the user in application programs. A command menu is displayed (normally at all times) along the screen's top margin. When the user selects one of the command options (generally by pointing to it with a mouse and clicking the mouse's button), a submenu is "pulled down" vertically under the command's name. The submenu contains additional command options (Chapter 4). *See also* command menu, menu, mouse, pointer.

query language A command language in a data base management system (DBMS) that lets you create a data base, ask questions about the data, update or modify the data as necessary, and to perform other data-processing operations (Chapter 8).

radix The base of a number system. Our system, the decimal system, uses base 10, except that our timekeeping system uses base 60 (Chapter 2). *See also* binary numbers.

RAM *See* random-access memory (RAM).

RAM disk utility A utility program that transforms unused portions of internal memory so that it can be treated as if it were a super-fast disk drive (Chapter 14).

random access An access technique in which all information in memory can be accessed directly without having to go through a sequence of items (Chapter 3). *See also* sequential access.

random-access memory (RAM) One of two types of internal memory in personal computers, RAM refers to the portion of the memory used for storing programs and data so that they are accessible for processing. The microprocessor can access these programs and data directly through random access techniques (Chapter 3). *See also* internal memory, random access.

range An area of a spreadsheet, defined by a range expression, that is defined by the user (Chapter 9). *See also* range expression.

range expression An expression that defines a range by delimiting the upper left and lower right corners of a rectangle (e.g., A1..T28) (Chapter 9). *See also* range.

range format A format that applies only to a range of cells in a spreadsheet (Chapter 9). *See also* range.

range naming A convenient way to refer to ranges in some spreadsheet programs; allows a range of cells to be given a name (such as SALES) and referenced by that name in formulas (Chapter 9). *See also* formula, range.

raster scan The projection technique of repeated, line-by-line sweeps by which a cathode-ray tube displays images on the video screen (Chapter 11). *See also* cathode-ray tube (CRT).

read To retrieve information from memory. Reading is a nondestructive operation; retrieving information from memory does not erase or alter the stored information, which may be read again (Chapter 3). *See also* write.

readability The extent to which a document's content can be easily comprehended (Chapter 6). *See also* readability checker.

readability checker A program that attempts to assess a document's readability by performing quantitative analyses of its style or form, such as the choice of familiar words and the use of short sentences (Chapter 6). *See also* readability.

readability measurement A quantitative measure of readability, performed by hand or by a readability checker (Chapter 6). *See also* readability, readability checker.

read-only memory (ROM) One of two parts of a personal computer's internal memory, the one from which the computer can read information (but not write it). ROM is used to channel essential operating programs into the computer when power is switched on (Chapter 3). *See also* internal memory, random-access memory (RAM), read, write.

read-only storage medium An auxiliary storage medium from which the computer can read (but not write) information, such as an optical disk (Chapter 3). *See also* auxiliary storage, CD-ROM, optical disk, read, write.

read/write head An electromagnetic device, similar to the record/play head of a tape recorder, that is designed to read information from and write information to a floppy or hard disk. The read/write head moves back and forth across the disk's surface, providing the computer with random access to the information the disk contains (Chapter 3). *See also* floppy disk, disk drive, hard disk, random access.

read/write memory A memory designed so that the computer can both read information from it and write information to it (Chapter 3).

recalculation The automatic refiguring of all formulas in a spreadsheet that occurs after any constant, formula, or label is inserted (Chapter 9). *See also* automatic recalculation, circular reference, column-wise recalculation, constant, formula, forward reference, label, natural recalculation, row-wise recalculation.

record *See* data record.

reference data base A data base that refers the user to the full text of a book or article; contains citations and, frequently, abstracts of the referenced work (Chapter 12). *See* abstract, citation, source data base.

reformatting command In an inexpensive or outmoded word processing program, a command that readjusts the right margin after new text is inserted within an existing line of text. Use of the reformatting command is not necessary with newer programs, which usually offer automatic reformatting (Chapter 4). *See also* automatic reformatting.

relational DBMS A data base management program that represents information in tables and has the ability to link two or more data bases together through a common data field (Chapter 8). *See also* data base management system (DBMS), data field.

relative cell reference A cell reference that states the referenced cell's position relative to the one in which the formula is placed; the reference therefore changes when the formula is copied (Chapter 9). *See also* absolute cell reference, cell reference.

replace command A query language command in a data base management system (DBMS) that lets the user update information in data records quickly and automatically, even if the updates have to be made in many or all data records in the data base (Chapter 8).

replication Copying of a formula to an adjacent cell or range of cells (Chapter 9).

report A printed summary of all or part of the information contained in a data base (Chapter 7). *See also* data base.

reset command A resident operating system command that initiates a warm boot or system reset (Chapter 3). *See also* operating system, warm boot.

resident utilities System utilities that are built into the operating system so that they are always available when the system prompt is present (Chapter 3). *See also* operating system, system prompt, system utilities, transient utilities.

resolution A cathode-ray tube (CRT) monitor's ability to display information clearly and crisply, as measured by the number of horizontal and vertical lines that can be shown on the screen (Chapter 3). *See also* cathode-ray tube (CRT) monitor.

return key A key that, when used with the operating system, sends a typed command to the computer's central processing unit (CPU) (Chapter 3). When used with a word processing program, it creates a new paragraph (Chapter 4). Because most programs that include text entry features use automatic word wrapping, the return key is only very rarely used to prevent words from going over the right margin when entering text (Chapter 4). *See also* central processing unit (CPU), operating system, paragraph, word processing program, word wrapping.

reverse video A display technique used for highlighting something on the screen of a monochrome monitor; in a monitor that normally displays green characters against a black background, highlighted characters will appear black against a green background (Chapter 4). *See also* monochrome monitor.

RGB monitor A color cathode-ray tube (CRT) monitor that employs separate cathodes or electron guns for the three primary colors (red, green, and blue) (Chapter 3). *See also* cathode-ray tube (CRT) monitor.

right flush alignment A paragraph format in which text is aligned flush to the right margin; the left margin is ragged (Chapter 4). *See also* paragraph format.

right margin justification A paragraph format in which text along the right margin is aligned so that it appears as if it had been professionally printed (Chapter 4). *See also* paragraph format.

robot A machine that possesses humanlike skills or dexterity (Chapter 2).

row A horizontal series of cells in a spreadsheet (Chapter 9).

row-wise recalculation A mode of spreadsheet recalculation in which recalculation proceeds across row 1, then row 2, and so on (Chapter 9). *See also* column-wise recalculation, natural recalculation, recalculation.

RS-232C serial port A standardized input/output connector designed to facilitate connections between a wide variety of computers, modems, and printers (Chapter 12). *See also* port.

ruler In a word processing program, a calibrated line along the top or bottom margin of the document window; shows current margin settings and tab stops (Chapter 4). *See also* document window.

running head A short version of a document's or chapter's title, or some other identifying title, that "runs" through a document (i.e., appears on every page within the top margin, bottom margin, or both) (Chapter 4).

scientific format A numeric display format that displays very large or very small numbers in scientific notation (Chapter 9). *See also* numeric display format.

scroll To move "up" (toward the beginning) or "down" (toward the end) of a word processing document or spreadsheet (Chapter 4).

search-and-replace command A command that automatically substitutes one word or phrase for another throughout a manuscript. Normally, the command should be used with the confirmation option, which asks you to okay each substitution (Chapter 5). *See also* confirmation option, search command.

search command In a word processing program, a command that accepts one or more words (a search string), searches a document, and scrolls to the text that matches the search string (Chapter 5). In a data base management program, a command that accepts a search string, searches a data base, and finds the next record that contains the string (Chapter 7). *See also* case-sensitive search, data base, search string, whole-word search.

search function *See* search command.

search string In a word processing or data base management program, a series of characters and spaces (which may form one or more words) that is entered in a search command (Chapters 5, 7). *See also* search command.

search template A blank form that functions as a tool for searching a data base (Chapter 7). *See also* form.

secondary sort key A sort key that comes into operation when there are two or more records with the same data in the field chosen for the primary sort key (Chapter 7). *See also* primary sort key, sort key, tertiary sort key.

second generation computers Electronic digital computers, based on transistors rather than vacuum tubes, that were created during the years 1959 and 1964. Second generation computers were substantially faster and less costly to operate than their first generation predecessors, and improvements in auxiliary storage, internal memory, and programming techniques (specifically, the development of high-level languages) made them much more useful (Chapter 2).

select To choose the data records in a data base that the user would like to print (Chapters 4, 7). *See also* data records, select mode.

selection A program control structure, made possible by the storage of programs in internal memory, that permits the computer to choose alternative pathways in the execution of a program (Chapters 2, 15). *See also* control structure, internal memory, stored program concept.

selection criteria A set of specifications that is used to tell the computer which data records to retrieve in its select mode (Chapter 7). *See also* data record, select mode.

select mode A data base management program mode that helps the user choose records for printing purposes (Chapter 7). *See also* select.

semiconductor memory An internal memory that uses integrated circuit memory chips (instead of magnetic cores or earlier memory technologies) (Chapter 2). *See also* integrated circuit, internal memory, magnetic core memory.

sequence A simple program control structure in which program statements are excecuted in sequential order (Chapter 15). *See also* control structure.

sequential access A storage technique in which information can be located only by going through a sequence of items, one by one (Chapter 3). *See also* random access.

serial port *See* RS-232C serial port.

serial transmission The asynchronous transmission of one bit at a time over a single line; start and stop bits must be added to demarcate each character (Chapter 12). *See also* asynchronous, synchronous.

simulation A technique for analyzing information in which a model of something in the real world — a prototype — is made, and the prototype's properties are investigated by manipulating the model.

single-user system A computer designed for one person's use, rather than for use by several people or an entire organization (Chapter 2). *See also* multiple-user system, professional workstation.

smart communications program *See* smart terminal emulation program.

smart modem A modem equipped with its own microprocessor circuitry and capable of performing automatic operations, such as answering incoming calls (Chapter 12). *See also* modem.

smart terminal emulation program A communications program that takes full advantage of the personal computer's processing capabilities, offering features such as file and software downloading, automatic log on, remote control, and switching between data bases (Chapter 12).

soft cell boundaries A feature of some spreadsheet programs that allows the user to type labels too long to fit in one cell. So long as there is nothing in the cell or cells to the right, the label can go "through" the cell boundary (Chapter 9). *See also* cell, label.

software The programs that run on a computer, giving it the instructions it needs in order to do something useful. *See also* system software, application software.

sort To place items in alphabetic or numerical order (Chapter 7).

sort key A data field that has been chosen as the basis for sorting operations, such as alphabetizing, performed on a data base. An employee's data base, for instance, might be sorted using the employee's name or social security number as the sort key (Chapter 7). *See also* data base, data field, primary sort key, secondary sort key, tertiary sort key.

source code A computer program expressed in the code the programmer uses and readable by trained programmers; must be translated into machine language before the computer can read it (Chapter 15). *See also* assembler, compiler, object code.

source data base A computer-readable data base that does not refer the searcher elsewhere (as do reference data bases) but rather contain the full text or complete data that is the object of the search (Chapter 12). *See also* full text data base, numeric data base, reference data base.

special-purpose application program A program that is designed to do a specific job, such as tracking investments or billing patients, rather than serving as a general-purpose tool for manipulating information (Chapter 14).

special-purpose computer A computer that has been designed or "dedicated" to a single application, such as computer-aided engineering or word processing. *See also* general-purpose computer.

spelling checker A program that detects spelling mistakes and typographical errors in files created with word processing software. To be more precise, the spelling checker tries to find matches between the words in its dictionary and the words in the document; if no match is found, the program reports the questionable word (which may not be misspelled) (Chapter 6).

spreadsheet program An application program that simulates an accountant's worksheet, except that it provides ways to link numbers written on the worksheet with hidden mathematical formulas (Chapter 1). *See also* application software.

spreadsheet window The window on the display screen in which a portion of the spreadsheet is displayed (Chapter 9). *See also* window.

standalone application package An application program that performs only one function, such as word processing or communications (Chapter 13). *See also* integrated program.

statistical package A bundle of programs that automatically perform a variety of statistical analyses on the computer (Chapter 14).

status line In a word processing program, a line that conveys information on the status of the program, such as the file name of the current document and coordinates that describe the cursor's location on the screen (Chapter 4). *See also* cursor, file name.

storage A step in the processing of data in which represented data are stored so that they can be processed conveniently (Chapter 2). *See also* internal memory, memory.

stored program concept A design concept that underlies the functional organization of all modern electronic digital computers: the program is stored in the internal memory alongside the data the computer will process. Because the entire program is present in the internal memory, the computer can jump around in the program as necessary (instead of executing the program in a rigid, unalterable sequence). Stored programs make advanced computer functions such as selection and looping possible (Chapter 2). *See also* functional organization, internal memory, looping, program, selection.

streaming tape drives A backup storage medium frequently used to provide secure backup storage for information contained on hard disks (Chapter 3). *See also* hard disk.

structured programming 1. The avoidance of traditional programming techniques in which program readability was sacrificed for efficiency and rapid execution. 2. The avoidance of go to statements and the use of modular programming techniques. 3. A project management approach that emphasizes program readability (Chapter 15). *See also* traditional programming.

style analysis software Software designed to critique the style in which a document is written (that is, the form of expression rather than its meaning or content). Style analysis programs designed for personal computers include word choice checkers, passive voice detectors, and readability checkers. They tend to enforce a writing style that is appropriate for business letters, instruction manuals, children's books, and other documents in which clarity, short sentences, and familiar words contribute to communicative success. They are less useful for critiquing scholarly work or fictional narrative (Chapter 6). *See also* word choice checker, passive voice detector, readability, readability checker.

style sheet In a word processing program, a feature that allows the simultaneous entry of a variety of formats (including margins, lines per page, header or footer position, page number position, and other characteristics) so that they affect all the text in a document (Chapter 5). *See also* format, macro.

submenu A list of command options that appears on the screen after selecting an item in a menu (Chapter 4). *See also* menu.

supercomputer An ultra-sophisticated research computer capable of performing more than 100 million arithmetic operations per second (Chapter 2).

supervisor The part of an operating system that automatically supervises the flow of information within the computer (Chapter 3). *See also* operating system.

switch drive command In a personal computer operating system, a resident command that changes the default drive to the one specified by an argument in the command (Chapter 3). *See also* argument, default drive.

synchronous Occurring at the same time; regularized by a clock so that events occur at exactly the same time (Chapter 12). *See also* asynchronous.

system disk A floppy disk containing the computer's operating system and utility programs (Chapter 3). *See also* operating system, utility software.

system prompt A prompt informing you that the operating system has been successfully loaded into the computer's memory and that it is ready to load an application program or perform other functions (Chapter 3). *See also* operating system, prompt.

system software Collectively, the programs that help the computer's components to work together and provide programmers the tools they need to create new programs (Chapter 1). *See also* disk operating system (DOS).

system utilities Programs of two kinds (resident and transient) that help the user maintain the computer system on a daily basis (Chapter 3). *See also* resident utilities, transient utilities.

technical analysis program An investment analysis program that analyzes a stock's historical trends (Chapter 14).

technological unemployment Displacement of workers through technology-based automation (Chapter 16).

telecommuting A new work pattern in which employees work at home occasionally and communicate with the office via electronic mail, computer conferencing, and other computer-based communications media (Chapter 12). *See also* computer conferencing, electronic mail.

template A corrected and tested version of a spreadsheet that has been saved to disk with no data in its keys (Chapter 10). *See also* keys.

terminal A keyboard and video display that are connected to a central mainframe or minicomputer (Chapter 2).

tertiary sort key A sort key that comes into action when there are two or more records with the same data in the field chosen for the secondary sort key (Chapter 7). *See also* primary sort key, secondary sort key, sort key.

text-oriented file management program A file management program designed for the storage and retrieval of large amounts of text (as many as 32,000 characters can be placed in a single data field) (Chapter 7). *See also* data field, file management program.

third generation computers Computers created during the years 1964–1971 using small- and medium-scale integrated circuits. More reliable and faster than their second generation predecessors, third generation computers offered large internal memories, massive auxiliary memories, timesharing, and ready-to-run application software packages (Chapter 2).

timesharing A computer operation technique in which many people may use a computer simultaneously, even though each of them has the impression of possessing exclusive control over the computer and its peripherals (Chapter 2).

titles In a spreadsheet, a set of rows or columns that do not scroll as the rest of the spreadsheet does; useful for entering row and column headings (Chapter 10). *See also* column, row.

top-down programming A programming technique in which the programmer begins with a clear statement of what the program is supposed to accomplish, including an exact specification of the data to be used and the output to be produced. The program is then designed using modules (Chapter 15). *See also* module.

tractor feed paper Paper that is designed to be used in a printer designed for tractor feeding; supplied with 1/4-inch perforated strips along each side so that the printer's ratchet can drive it through the printer. Also called continuous paper because the paper is supplied in a long, continuous strip; the user must separate the pages by tearing along their perforations after printing (Chapter 4). *See also* cut sheet paper.

traditional programming A programming style that places central emphasis on program efficiency rather than program readability (Chapter 15). *See also* structured programming.

transient utilities System utilities that cannot be used unless they are deliberately loaded into internal memory like any other program (Chapter 3). *See also* internal memory, resident utilities, system utilities.

transistor An electronic device that duplicates the functions performed by vacuum tubes (amplification and switching) but does so at a tiny fraction of the vacuum tube's cost, power requirements, and failure rate (Chapter 2).

truncation The shortening of a word in a search string so that, in a search, a data base management program will retrieve all records containing the first few letters of the word, even if the rest of the letters in the word vary. A search for SYST, for example, will retrieve records containing system, systematic, systematization, etc. (Chapter 7).

turnover line The second and subsequent lines of a paragraph, which may be aligned flush to the left margin (as in a normal paragraph) or indented (as in a footnote or a hanging indentation) (Chapter 4). *See also* hanging indentation, paragraph format.

type size The height of characters in a font, measured in printer's points (Chapter 4). *See also* character format, font.

undo command A command that restores the document to the state it was in prior to the last editing command (Chapter 4). *See also* delete buffer.

unerase program A program that restores a file that has been erased from a disk, so long as no writing operations have occurred since its erasure (Chapter 3). *See also* file, write.

Universal Asynchronous Receiver/Transmitter (UART). A chip on an asynchronous communications board that translates between the computer's internal data stream, which is synchronous and parallel, and external data communications, which are asynchronous and serial (Chapter 12). *See also* asynchronous, data communications, parallel, serial, synchronous.

update command *See* replace command.

upload To send previously prepared files (text files or software) to bulletin boards or electronic mail services via data communications media (Chapter 12). *See also* bulletin board, electronic mail, download.

user interface The part of a program that handles the interaction between the user and the computer in a system designed for interactive processing (Chapter 2). *See also* interactive processing.

value 1. A number that appears in a spreadsheet cell. A value may have its origin as a constant typed in by the user or it may result from a formula (Chapter 9). 2. A number in the data series prepared for an analytic graphics package; corresponds to a certain category (Chapter 11). *See also* analytic graphics package, categories, constant, data series, formula.

value-added networks A data communications network that transmits data over high-speed communication channels, often involving microwave, satellite, and other sophisticated communications technologies (Chapter 12). *See also* data communications.

vertical market programs Special-purpose application programs targeted to a highly specific clientele (Chapter 14).

very high level programming language A programming language that frees the programmer from concern about the procedure the computer must follow to carry out the program's instructions. Instead, the programmer can focus on the nature of the problem to be solved, working solely in the problem's terms (rather than those imposed by the computer) (Chapters 2, 15). *See also* high-level programming language, program.

very large scale integration (VLSI) A technique for the fabrication of integrated circuits containing more than 100,000 discrete components (Chapter 2). *See also* integrated circuit, large-scale integration.

view A set of selected data records from a data base that meet selection criteria (Chapter 7). *See also* data base, data records, selection criteria.

voice recognition A computer input technique in which a computer, equipped with a microphone and special voice-recognition circuitry, responds to the human voice. Voice recognition equipment may be used both for commanding the computer and data input (Chapter 2). *See also* input.

volatile Susceptible to loss of stored information when electrical current fails (Chapter 3). *See also* nonvolatile.

warm boot Slang term for a system reset operation carried out during an operating session; resets the computer to its state at the beginning of an operating session and clears the memory of all save the essential operating system software (Chapter 3). *See also* operating system, cold boot.

what-if modeling An information analysis technique in which key variables are changed to see the change's effect on a computed outcome ("What would our profits look like if we were able to obtain the parts for $2.50 per thousand instead of $2.75?") (Chapter 1). *See also* simulation.

white-collar workers A sector of the work force encompassing those who work in professional, technical, managerial, sales, and clerical jobs (Chapter 1).

whole-word search In a word processing or data base management program, a search that seeks to match the search string (a single word) *only* when it is surrounded by spaces (and not when it is preceded or followed by other characters). A whole-word search for *very*, for example, will retrieve *very* but not *every* or *bravery* (Chapter 5). *See also* search command, search string.

wild card A character (such as an asterisk) that, when entered, stands for any letter or number (Chapters 3, 7).

Winchester drive *See* hard disk.

window Used to describe the work display area of an application program and suggest the idea that the screen is floating just over the surface of the work, such as a document or spreadsheet, revealing only part of it as if it were a window or picture frame (Chapter 5). *See also* document window, multiple windows.

windowing environment An extension of a computer's operating system that allows standalone application programs to run in windows provided by the windowing environment; several such applications can be present on the screen at one time (although only one of them is active). Windowing environments combine the advantages of integrated software (ease of data exchange and context switching) with those of standalone application packages (Chapter 13). *See also* context switching, integrated program, window.

word choice checker A program that detects the use of certain overused or doubtful words or phrases in a document created with a word processing program (Chapter 6).

word processing program An application program that turns a computer into a tool for creating, revising, and printing written work (Chapter 1). *See also* application software.

word wrapping An automatic feature of word processing software that prevents words from going over the right margin; automatically "wraps" them to the beginning of the next line down. The user, therefore, does not have to worry about pressing the return key at the end of the line (Chapter 4). *See also* return key.

write To store information in memory. Writing is a destructive operation; when information is written to an auxiliary storage device or to the internal memory, it overwrites information previously stored there (Chapter 3). *See also* auxiliary storage, internal memory, read.

WYSIWYG Acronym for "what you see is what you get," describing the onscreen formatting approach to text formatting in a word processing program (Chapter 4). *See* onscreen formatting.

***X* axis** The axis in a chart or graph that contains the categories (headings) (Chapter 11). *See also* categories, *Y* axis.

***Y* axis** The axis in a chart or graph that contains the values (Chapter 11). *See also* value, *X* axis.

Index

Abacus, 22, 24–25
Absolute cell reference, 272–274
Abstract, 357
Access time, 79, 82
Account automation, 394
Accounting software, 392–394
Accounts payable program, 394
Accounts receivable program, 393
Acoustic coupler, 345
Active cell, 254
Ada, Countess of Lovelace, 36
Aggregate functions (DBMS), 237–238
ALGOL, 417, 427
Algorithm, 29
Allen, Paul, 54
Alphabetical data type, 206
Alphanumeric data type, 206
Altair, 54
Alternate key (ALT), 85
Analog computer, 26
Analytic graphics packages, 327
Append command (DBMS), 234
Apple I, 55
Apple II, 55
Apple Macintosh, 56–57, 99, 104, 322–323, 383
Application software, 13, 50, 60, 105
Argument, 97, 266
Arithmetic functions in word processing programs, 160
Arithmetic-logic unit, 30
Arithmetic operations, 30
Arithmetic operators, 266–270
Artificial intelligence, 60
Ascending sort, 212
ASCII, 84–85
Assembler, 414
Assembly language, 414
Asynchronous, 342
Asynchronous communications board, 342
AT. *See* IBM Personal Computer AT
Automatically supplied data, 206
Automatic equation numbering, 160
Automatic hyphenation, 155
Automatic log on, 348
Automatic pagination, 135
Automatic recalculation, 280
Automatic reformatting, 123
Auxiliary storage, 31, 78–84

Babbage, Charles, 34–36
Background printing, 406
Backspace key, 88
Backup with restore (DBMS), 238
Bank switching, 380

BASIC, 54–55, 415, 420–422
Batch processing, 41
Baud, 345
BBS. *See* Bulletin board system
Begin block command, 125
Bibliographic data managers, 402–403
Binary digit, 28
Binary numbers, 28
Biochips, 61
Bit-mapped graphics, 320–321
Block, 125
Block move, 126
Blue-collar workers, 446–448
Boilerplate, 143–144
Booting the system, 94
Browse mode, 208
BRS/After Dark, 361
BRS Information Technologies, 361
Built-in function, 266, 275–277
Bulletin board, 353
Bulletin board system (BBS), 354
Byte, 74

CAD. *See* Computer-aided design
CAE. *See* Computer-aided engineering
CAI. *See* Computer-assisted instruction
CAM. *See* Computer-aided manufacturing
Calculation area, 290–291
Case-sensitive search, 154
Cassette tapes, 79
Categories, 327–328
Category axis (*y*-axis), 328
Cathode ray tube (CRT), 47
CD. *See* Compact disc
CD-ROM, 83
Cell(s), 252
  protection of, 294–295
Cell coordinates indicator, 254
Cell reference, 266
Central processing unit (CPU), 30, 72–78
Character(s), 74
  formats for, 132
Character generator, 319–320
Character mode, 318
Christiansen, Ward, 349
Circular reference, 279
Citation, 357
Clip-art, 331
Clipboard, 384–385
Clones, 55
Closed architecture, 57
CMI. *See* Computer-managed instruction
COBOL, 45, 53, 417, 422
Coding, 23
Coding systems, 84–85
Cold boot, 102
Colossus, 39
Column, 252
Columnar reports, 219
Column chart, 330
Column-wise recalculation, 278
Command, 96, 119–121, 146–147, 255–259
Command keys, 87
Command-line operating system, 97–98
Command menus, 119, 256–259
Command mode, 255
Command processor, 95, 96–100
Communication protocol, 349
Communications software, 347–349
Compact disc (CD), 83
Compiled program, 416
Compiler, 45, 416
Compressed-mode printing, 281
CompuServe, 352
Computer conferencing, 354–356
Computer crime, 452
Computer graphics, 317
Computer-aided design (CAD), 334–335
Computer-aided engineering (CAE), 334
Computer-aided manufacturing (CAM), 334
Computer-assisted disaster, 452
Computer-assisted instruction (CAI), 399–402
Computer-managed instruction (CMI), 402
Confirmation message, 48, 98
Confirmation option, 154
Constants, 260, 264
Context, 374
  switching of, 374
Control key (CTRL), 85
Control structures, 429
Control unit, 30
Copy block command, 125
Copy command, 100
Cost savings of computer use, 443
CP/M-80 operating system, 94, 104
CPM. *See* Critical path method
CPU. *See* Central processing unit
Crackers, 452
Create command (DBMS), 232
Create mode, in file management programs, 204
Critical path method (CPM), 397–399
CRT. *See* Cathode ray tube
Cursor, 85
Cursor control keys, 85, 122

Cut sheet feeder, 135
Cut sheets, 135

Data, 6
  rate of transfer of, 79, 82
  redundancy of, 239–241
  transfer of, among contexts, 374–377
Data base, 189
Data base management program, 14–15, 199
Data base management system (DBMS), 199, 225–244
Data base producer, 359
Data communications, 48
Data disk, 96
Data encryption, 207
Data entry area, 289
Data field, 156, 201
Data file, 96, 156
Data record, 201
Data series, 327
Date functions, in spreadsheet software, 276
DBMS. *See* Data base management system
Debugging, 426
Decision making, 299
Default drive, 96–97
Default formatting settings, 131, 219
Default option, 119
Defining blocks of text, 124–126
Delete block command, 126
Delete buffer, 126
Delete command (DBMS), 237
Delete key, 87
Deleting records, 211
Deleting text from a document, 123–124
Delimiter, 98
Delphi, 352
Descending sort, 212
Deskilling of service occupations, 448–449
Desktop organizer, 380–383
Desktop publishing, 156–160
Destructive, 88
Device independence, 95
DIALOG Information Service, 360–361
Digit, 23
Digital computer, 23
Digital Electronic Corporation MicroVAX, 57
Digitizer, 324
Dijkstra, Edsger W., 425
Direct access, 78
Direct-connect modem, 345
Directory command, 100
Direct-wire communications, 341, 361–366
Disk copy program, 103
Disk directory, 100
Disk drives, 79
Disk format program, 103
Disk operating system (DOS), 95
Display command (DBMS), 234
Distributed computing, 53
Document, 114
Document display screen, 114, 118–119
Document formats, 134–135
Document window, 118
DOS. *See* Disk operating system
Dot-matrix printer, 90, 325–326
Download, 348
Drill-and-practice program, 399
Drucker, Peter, 64, 444
Dumb terminal emulation program, 348
Duntemann, Jeff, 423

Eckert, J. Presper, 39
Editing text, 151–154, 179–190
Educational software, 399–402
EGA. *See* Enhanced graphics adapter
8-bit microprocessor, 73
Electronic digital computer, 23
Electronic mail, 350–352, 445
Embedded commands, 128
Employment, and computers, 446–451
End block command, 125
Endnotes, 149
Engineering functions, 276
Enhanced graphics adapter (EGA), 323
ENIAC, 39
Entry line, 255
Entry mode, 255
Epistle, 183
Equation mode, 160
Erase command, 102
Error message, 48, 98
Escape key (ESC), 85
Expanded memory (Lotus-Intel), 380
Exploded pie chart, 331–333
Exploratory data analysis, 403
Extension, 97

Fernandez, William, 55
Fiber optics, 346
Field
  length of, 204
  name of, 201
Fifth-generation computers, 60

File(s), 95
  management program for, 198–220
  recovery program for, 406
  specification of, 98
File manager, 94, 95–96
File merge command, 144
Financial functions, 276–277, 305–306
First-generation computer, 41, 59
Fixed disk. *See* Hard disk
Floppy disk, 79–82, 84
Fonts, 132
Footnote(s), 149–150
  floating of, to next page, 150
  formatting control for, 150
  numbering of, automatic, 150
  reference mark for, 149
Forced page break command, 117
Forecasting, 300–305
Foreign language characters, 160
Form, 199–200
Form letters, 156
Formatting
  disks for, 96
  program for, 128
  of spreadsheet, 291
  of text, 117, 132–135
Formulas, 265–274, 291–294
  marking character for, 265
FORTRAN, 45, 53, 417, 422
Forward reference, 278–279
Fourth-generation computers, 50, 59
Frame buffer, 319
Full-duplex modem, 345
Full-text data base, 359
Functional organization, 30
Function keys, 87
Fundamental analysis program, 396

Gates, Bill, 54, 104
General ledger program, 393
General-purpose computer, 37
Gigabyte, 76
Global formatting, 261–262
Glossaries, 142
GOTO statements, 423
Grammatik, 183, 186
Graphics, 160
  software for, 327–335
Graphics mode, 318
Graphics tablet, 324

Half-duplex modem, 345
Handicapped, 444–445
Hanging indention, 134
Hard disk, 82
Hardware, 13, 72–94, 317–324, 342–347, 380
Harvard Total Project Manager, 399
High-level programming languages, 45, 415–419
Hit, 208
Hoff, Ted, 53
Hollerith, Herman, 37
Horizontal scrolling, 160
Horizon technologies, 61

IBM Personal Computer, 55–56, 97, 321, 322, 380, 388
IBM Personal Computer AT, 57, 321
IBM System/360, 47
  operating system for, 424–426
Idea processing programs. *See* Outlining programs
Image libraries, 331–332
Image recorder, 326–327
Importing data, 328–329
Incompatible, 76
Index generation, 160
Industrial society, 63
Information, 6
Information society, 62–64
Information utilities, 352
Input, 22
Input devices, 32, 84–89
Input/output manager, 94
Inserting text in a document, 122–123
Insertion point, 122
Insert mode, 123
Integrated accounting package, 394
Integrated circuit, 46
Integrated program, 374–380
Intel 8008 microprocessor, 54
Intel 8080 microprocessor, 73, 94
Intel 8088 microprocessor, 57, 75
Intel 80286 microprocessor, 57, 321
Intelligent modem. *See* Smart modem
Interactive processing, 48
Internal memory, 28, 31, 74, 75, 76–78, 380, 404–405
Interpreter, 416
Inventory control program, 394
Investment planning software, 396–397

Jobs, Stephen, 55, 444
Join command (DBMS), 239–241

Kemeny, John, 430–431
Key(s)
  enhancement programs for, 146
  in spreadsheet, 274–275, 289–290. *See also* Sort key
Keyboard, 85–88
  enhancement software for, 405
Keyboard commands, 119
Keyword, 97
Kildall, Gary, 104
Kilobyte, 76
Knowledge, 60, 444
Knowledge Index, 361
Kurtz, Thomas, 430–431

Labels, 260, 262–263
LAN. *See* Local area network
Lanham, Richard, 187
Large-scale integration (LSI), 50
Laser printer, 92, 326
Left flush alignment, 132
Legend, 331–333
Leibniz, Gottfried, 34
Letter-quality printer, 92
Light pen, 324
Line breaks, 114
Line chart, 330
Linking spreadsheets, 297–298
Load program command, 102
Local area network (LAN), 244, 364–366
Logged on, 96
Logical functions, 277
Logical operations, 30
Logical operators, 214, 216–218, 270–271
Log on, 346–347, 348
Lookup tables, 309
Looping, 41
Lotus 1-2-3, 270, 276–277
Lotus Symphony, 220, 257–258, 279, 305, 307–309, 379
Low-level language, 413
LSI. *See* Large-scale integration

Machine language, 41, 413
Macros, 146, 307–309, 405
Magnetic core memory, 46
Magnetic disks, 48
Main document, 156
Mainframe computer, 46, 57–58, 403
Manual recalculation, 280
Mass storage, 53
Mathematics functions, in spreadsheet software, 276
Matrix letter, 156
Mauchly, John, 39
Medicine, 444
Megabyte, 76
Megaflops, 58
Memory chips, 52
Memory, 28. *See also* Internal memory
Memory address, 74
Memory-resident program, 175
Memory-resident thesaurus, 175
Menus, 48
Microcomputer, 54
Microprocessor, 53
Microsoft Windows, 383
Microsoft Word, 161, 173
Microspacing, 155
Micro-to-mainframe connections, 366
Microwave relays, 346
Minicomputer, 52, 57
Modeling, 299–300
Modem, 344–345
Modularity, 427
Modular programming, 427
Module, 427
Monitor, 89
Monochrome monitor, 89
Monospace type, 156
MOS Technology 6502 microprocessor, 75
Motorola Corporation 68000 microprocessor, 75
Mouse, 88–89, 324
Move block command, 125
MS-DOS operating system, 104
Multiple column printing, 160
Multiple sort keys, 212
Multiple windows, 147–149
Multiple-user DBMS, 244
Multiple-user system, 57
Multitasking operating system, 104
Multiuser accounting package, 394

Natural language interface, 243
Natural recalculation mode, 279
Near-letter-quality, 90
Nondestructive, 85
Nonproprietary operating system, 104
Nonvolatile, 78
Notebook II, 220
Noyce, Robert N., 58
Numerical data type, 206

Numerical operators, in file management programs, 214
Numeric data base, 359
Numeric keypad, 87

Object code, 414
Object-oriented operating system, 99
Office, 6–13
Office automation, 450
Offscreen formatting, 127–128
Online data base vendor, 357
Onscreen formatting, 128–129
Open architecture, 56
Operating systems, 45
Optical disk, 83
Order of evaluation, 268–269
Outlines, 149
Outlining programs, 167–175
Output, 30
Output device, 32, 89–94
Overtype mode, 123

Packet, 346
Packet-switching network, 346
Page breaks, 114
Page layout program, 159
Paint programs, 334
Paragraph formats, 132–134
Parallel processing, 61–62
Parallel transmission, 342
Parameter, 97
Parentheses, 269
Pascal, Blaise, 34
Payroll program, 394
PC-Calc, 266–270
PC-compatible computer, 56
PC-DOS operating system, 97, 104
PC-File, 220
PC-Outline, 175
PC-Write, 161
Peripheral, 31
Personal computer, 55
PERT. *See* Program evaluation and review technique
PFS: File, 220
PFS: Write, 161
Pie chart, 331
Pixel, 89
PLATO, 399–400
Plotter, 326
Pointer, 119, 262
Point-storage-point electronic mail, 350
Point-to-point electronic mail, 350
Pop-up command menu, 119
Portability, 414
Portfolio manager, 396
Primary file name, 97
Primary sort keys, 212
Print accessory programs, 281
Printers, 89–94
Printing text, 135, 154–160
Print merging, 155–156
Print output file, 128
Print spooler, 405–406
Procedural language (DBMS), 238
Processing, 29
  accuracy of, 33
  speed of, 32, 58, 73
Professional workstation, 57, 323, 387
Program, 29
Program disk, 96
Program evaluation and review technique (PERT), 397—399
Program files, 96
Program generators, 433–434
Programming, 412
  traditional, 424–426
Programming languages, 412–419
Program trading, 397
Project management program, 399
Project management software, 397–399
Prompts, 48
Proportional spacing, 156
Proprietary operating system, 104
Public domain software, 354
Pull-down menu, 119
Punctuation & Style, 183

Query language (DBMS), 228

Radix, 28
RAM disk utility, 404–405
Random-access memory (RAM), 78
Range
  formatting of, 261–263
  naming of, 277
Raster scan CRT, 318
Read, 78
Readability, 187–188
  measurement of, 188
Readability checker, 189
Read-only memory (ROM), 78
Read-only storage medium, 83
Read/write head, 79

Read/write memory, 78
Recalculation, 278, 280
Recovering lost work, 406
Reference data base, 357
Reformatting command, 122
Relational data base management system, 242
Relative cell reference, 272–273
Replace command (DBMS), 237
Report, 202
Research notes, 149
Reset command, 102
Resident utilities, 100
Resolution, 89
Reverse video, 119
RGB monitor, 89
Right flush alignment, 133
Right margin justification, 133
Robots, 61, 448
ROM. *See* Read-only memory
Row, 252
Row-wise recalculation, 278
RS-232C serial port, 342
Ruler, 119
Running heads, 134

Satellites, 346
Scatter diagram, 330
Schickard, William, 34
Scrolling, 117, 123, 147
Search-and-replace command, 154
Search command, in file management programs, 208
Search function, 153
Search string, 153
Search template, 208
Secondary sort keys, 212
Second-generation computers, 45, 59
Select, 214
Selecting text, 125
Select mode, in file management programs, 214
Selection, 41
  criteria for, 214–218
Semiconductor memory, 52
Sequence, 427
Sequential access, 79
Sex differences in computer use, 450–451
Signpost paragraph, 147
Simulation software, 400–401
Single-user system, 57
16-bit microprocessor, 73
Smart communication program, 348
Smart modem, 345
Soft cell boundaries, 260
Software, 13
Sort key, 201, 212–213
Source, The, 352
Source code, 414
Source data base, 358
Special-purpose application programs, 392–407
Spelling checker, 179–181
Split-screen editing, 147
Spreadsheet programs, 16
Spreadsheet window, 255
Standalone application package, 374
Statistical functions, in spreadsheet software, 276
Statistical packages, 403–404
Status line, 118
Storage, 28
Stored program concept, 39
Streaming tape drive, 84
Structured programming, 423–424, 426–431
Style analysis programs, 181–191
Style sheet, 146
Submenu, 119
Sunderland, Ivan, 335
Supercomputer, 58
Supervisor, 94
Switch drive command, 100
System disk, 94
System prompts, 96
System software, 13, 94–104
System utilities, 95, 100–103, 404–406

Table of contents generation, 160
Technical analysis program, 396
Technical characters, 160
Technological unemployment, 446
Telecommuting, 356
Telephone tag, 351
Template, 295
Terminal, 47
Tertiary sort keys, 213
Text-oriented file management software, 204
ThinkTank, 168–173
Third-generation computer, 47, 59
32-bit microprocessor, 73
Timesharing, 47, 57, 364
Titles, 306
Titus, Jonathan, 54
Top-down programming, 427
Tractor feed paper, 135
Transaction processing systems, 365
Transient utilities, 102
Transistor, 45

TRS-80, 55
True BASIC, 430–431
Truncation, in file management programs, 211
Turing, Alan, 37
Turnover lines, 134
Tutorial program, 399–400
Type sizes, 132

Unauthorized software duplication, 452
Undo command, 126
Unerase program, 103
UNIVAC, 41
Universal Asynchronous Receiver/Transmitter (UART), 342
UNIX operating system, 104
Updating records, 211
Upload, 348
User interface, 56

Value-added network, 345–346
Values, 260, 327–328
Values axis (*x*-axis), 328
VDT. *See* Video display terminal
Vertical market program, 392
Very high level programming language, 53, 434
Very large scale integration (VLSI), 50, 58, 60, 77
Video display terminal, hazards of, 449
View, 218
Voice-recognition systems, 61
Volatile, 78
von Neumann, John, 39–41

Warm boot, 102
Webster's New World On-Line Thesaurus, 176
What-if analysis with graphics, 377
White-collar workers, 6
Whole-word search, 154
Wildcard character, 210–211
Winchester drive. *See* Hard disk
Window, 47
Windowing, 147
Windowing environment, 383–385
WordPerfect, 161
Word processing programs, 14, 114–161
WordStar, 173
Word wrapping, 121
Work losses, 78
Wozniak, Stephen, 55
Write, 78
Writer's Workbench, 183
WYSIWYG ("What you see is what you get"), 129

x-axis (values axis), 328
Xerox 6085, 387
XMODEM protocol, 349

y-axis (category axis), 328

Zilog Z-80 microprocessor, 73

Quick Reference Guide: Operating System Basics

Directions

Tear out pp. A–1—A–3, which are keyed to Chapter 3. Chapter 3 discusses basic operating system functions, such as formatting disks and setting the default drive. As you read Chapter 3, consult your operating system's manual, your instructor's handouts, or the supplementary textbook you are using to find out how to carry out the function with your program. Make a note of the command you should use in the "Do this" column. When you've finished filling out this *Quick Reference Guide*, keep it with you when you write with your computer. You'll find it an invaluable aid.

STARTING AN OPERATING SESSION

If you want to:	Do this:
Turn on the computer	______________________
Load the operating system	______________________
	______________________

Note: Some computers perform the next two operations automatically.

Set today's date	______________________
Set the current time	______________________
View the disk directory	______________________
Switch from Drive A to Drive B	______________________
Switch from Drive B to Drive A	______________________
Load a program	______________________
Format a disk	______________________

MANAGING DISKS ON A DAY-TO-DAY BASIS

If you want to:	Do this:
Refer to a file in a command when the file is on the default disk	______
Refer to a file in a command when the file is *not* on the default disk	______
Erase an unwanted file on the default disk	______
Erase an unwanted file on a disk other than the default disk	______
Copy a file from Drive A to Drive B	______
Copy a file from Drive B to Drive A	______
Copy an entire disk	______
______	______
______	______
______	______
Load an application program	______
Reset the system	______
End an operating session	______

Quick Reference Guide: Word Processing Basics

Directions

Tear out pp. A–5—A–11, which are keyed to Chapter 4. Chapter 4 discusses basic word processing functions, such as loading a program or loading an existing document. As you read Chapter 4, consult your word processing program's manual to find out how to carry out each function with your program. Make a note of each command you should use in the "Do this" column. When you've finished filling out this *Quick Reference Guide*, keep it with you when you write with your computer. You'll find it an invaluable aid. Note: your program may not be able to do all of the functions listed here. Functions that some programs lack are indicated with an asterisk.

GETTING STARTED

If you want to:	Do this:
Install the program for your computer	______________________________
Start the program	______________________________
Ask for onscreen help*	______________________________
Quit the program	______________________________

FUNCTION KEY GUIDE

(Skip this section if your computer does not have function keys)

F1 ______________________________

F2 ______________________________

F3 ______________________________

F4 ______________________________

F5 ______________________________

F6 ______________________________

F7 ______________________________

F8 ______________________________

F9 ______________________________

F10 ______________________________

MANAGING DOCUMENTS

If you want to:	Do this:
Load an existing document	______________________
Merge two documents*	______________________
Save a document to disk	______________________
	______________________

CURSOR CONTROL AND SCROLLING

If you want to:	Do this:
Move cursor up	______________________
Move cursor down	______________________
Move cursor left	______________________
Move cursor right	______________________
Move cursor to end of line	______________________
Move cursor to beginning of line	______________________
Scroll up one line	______________________
Scroll down one line	______________________
Scroll up one windowful	______________________
Scroll down one windowful	______________________
Scroll to beginning of document	______________________
Scroll to end of document	______________________

SELECTING PROGRAM MODES

If you want to:	Do this:
Select insert mode	______
Select overtype mode	______

TEXT DELETION

If you want to:	Do this:
Delete character to left of cursor	______
Delete character on which the cursor is positioned	______
Delete word left*	______
Delete word right*	______
Delete sentence*	______
Delete line*	______
Delete paragraph*	______

BLOCK COPY AND MOVE

If you want to:	Do this:
Mark beginning of block	____________
Mark end of block	____________
Copy block	____________
Move block	____________
Delete block	____________
Recover deleted text from buffer*	____________
	____________
Write block to different file*	____________
	____________
	____________
Undo last editing command*	____________

DEFAULT FORMATTING SETTINGS

Line spacing	______	line(s)
Left margin	______	from left side of page
Right margin	______	from right side of page
Tabs	______	spaces
Page breaks	[ ] yes	[ ] no
Page numbering	[ ] yes	[ ] no

FORMATTING THE TEXT

If you want to:	Do this:
Boldface characters	______
Italicize characters*	______
Underline characters	______
Superscript characters*	______
Subscript characters*	______
Position paragraph left flush	______
Position paragraph right flush	______
Right justified paragraph	______
Centered paragraph	______
Use a hanging indentation*	______
Indent first line automatically*	______
Double line spacing	______
Set right margin	______
Set left margin	______
Set top margin	______
Set bottom margin	______
Insert header or footer*	______
Turn on automatic pagination	______
Force page break	______

PRINTING THE DOCUMENT

If you want to:	Do this:
Get the printer ready	______
	______
	______
Select continuous printing (no pause for page breaks)	______
	______
	______
Pause for page breaks	______
Start printing	______
Stop printing	______
Print selected pages	______
Print multiple copies	______

Quick Reference Guide: Advanced Word Processing

Directions

Tear out pp. A–13—A–16, which are keyed to Chapter 5. Chapter 5 discusses advanced word processing functions, such as using multiple windows. As you read Chapter 5, consult your word processing program's manual to find out how to carry out each function with your program. Make a note of each command you should use in the "Do this" column. When you've finished filling out this *Quick Reference Guide*, keep it with you when you write with your computer. You'll find it an invaluable aid. Note: no word processing program has all the features listed here; the one you're using probably lacks some (perhaps most) of them.

GLOSSARIES

If you want to:	Do this:
Create and store a glossary entry	______________________
	______________________
Insert the glossary entry in the text you're writing	______________________
Store the glossary entry on disk for future use	______________________
	______________________

BOILERPLATING

If you want to:	Do this:
Insert a separate disk file in the document you're writing	______________________
	______________________

MACROS, PROGRAMMABLE KEYBOARD COMMANDS, AND STYLE SHEETS

If you want to:	Do this:
Create a macro file (a file containing a series of commands)	______ ______
Use a macro file you have created	______
Program a single key to enter two or more commands at the same time	______
Store formatting specifications in a style sheet	______ ______
Attach a style sheet to a document	______

MULTIPLE WINDOWS

If you want to:	Do this:
Split the window horizontally to show two parts of the same file	______ ______
Move from one window to the other	______
Enlarge or reduce the size of a window	______
Close a window	______
Display two or more documents at the same time	______ ______

FOOTNOTES

If you want to:	Do this:
Create a footnote	____________
Format the footnote reference mark	____________
Format the footnote test	____________
Select endnotes instead of footnotes	____________

SEARCH AND SEARCH-AND-REPLACE

If you want to:	Do this:
Enter a search string	____________
Start the search	____________
Cancel the search	____________
Do a case-sensitive search	____________
Do a whole-word search	____________
Search-and-replace	____________
Search-and-replace with confirmation each time	____________

PRINTING TECHNIQUES

If you want to:	Do this:
Print with microspacing	______________________
Start automatic hyphenation	______________________
Print with proportional spacing	______________________
Enter data field in a main document	______________________
Start printing form letters	______________________

Quick Reference Guide: File Management Basics

Directions

Tear out pp. A–17—A–23, which are keyed to Chapter 7. Chapter 7 discusses basic file management functions, such as creating a form or finding a record. As you read Chapter 7, consult your file management program's manual to find out how to do each function with your program. Make a note of each command you should use in the "Do this" column. When you've finished filling out this *Quick Reference Guide*, keep it with you when you write with your computer. You'll find it an invaluable aid. Note: your program may not be able to do all of the functions listed here. Functions that some programs lack are indicated with an asterisk.

GETTING STARTED

If you want to:	Do this:
Install the program for your computer	______________________
Start the program	______________________
Ask for onscreen help*	______________________
Quit the program	______________________

FUNCTION KEY GUIDE

(Skip this section if your computer does not have function keys)

F1 ______________________

F2 ______________________

F3 ______________________

F4 ______________________

F5 ______________________

F6 ______________________

F7 ______________________

F8 ______________________

F9 ______________________

F10 ______________________

CREATING THE DATA BASE

If you want to:	Do this:
Enter the create mode	______________________
Enter new field names	______________________
Enter field lengths*	______________________

What data types are available for your program?

Text or character? [ ] yes [ ] no
Numerical data? [ ] yes [ ] no
Date field? [ ] yes [ ] no
Automatic record number? [ ] yes [ ] no

Enter data type*	______________________
Instruct the program to compute totals and averages for a field*	______________________
Automatically insert today's date in a field*	______________________
Automatically insert current time in a field*	______________________
Automatically insert record number in a field*	______________________
Save form as defined	______________________

ENTERING DATA

If you want to:	Do this:
Display a blank form	______
Move cursor up	______
Move cursor down	______
Move cursor left	______
Move cursor right	______
Move cursor to next field	______
Move cursor to previous field	______
Delete character to left of cursor	______
Delete character to right of cursor	______
Delete all text in field*	______
Switch on insert mode*	______
Switch on overtype mode*	______
Accept data as finished input	______
Add another record	______
Stop adding records	______

FINDING RECORDS

If you want to:	Do this:
Display previous record	______
Display next record	______
Turn on browse mode	______
Search for data record	______
Search for a data record with a wildcard character	______
Search for a data record with truncation	______
Continue the search for additional hits	______

MODIFYING RECORDS

If you want to:	Do this:
Make changes to a record	______
Accept the changes as finished input and add the modified record to the data base	______
Delete a record	______

SORTING RECORDS

If you want to:	Do this:
Sort the data records	____________
Choose ascending sort	____________
Choose descending sort	____________
Name a field to serve as the primary sort key	____________
Name a field to serve as the secondary sort key*	____________
Name a field to serve as the tertiary sort key*	____________

SELECTING RECORDS

If you want to:	Do this:
Enter the select mode	____________
Select all records for printing	____________
Select certain records to be printed	____________
Choose field to select on	____________
Choose an operator	____________
State the selection text or value	____________
Add another criterion with AND logic	____________
Add another criterion with OR logic	____________
Begin the selection	____________

PRINTING THE DATA RECORDS

If you want to:	Do this:
Define a new report format	
Choose which fields to print	
Turn on page numbering	
Add running heads	
Start printing	
Stop printing	

Quick Reference Guide: DBMS Basics

Directions

Tear out pp. A–25—A–32, which are keyed to Chapter 8. Chapter 8 discusses basic data base management systems (DBMS) and their functions, such as creating a form or displaying records. As you read Chapter 8, consult your file management program's manual to find out how to do the function with your program. Make a note of the command you should use in the "Do this" column. When you've finished filling out this *Quick Reference Guide*, keep it with you when you write with your computer. You'll find it an invaluable aid. Note: your program may not be able to do all of the functions listed here. Functions that some programs lack are indicated with an asterisk.

GETTING STARTED

If you want to:	Do this:
Install the program for your computer	______________
	______________
	______________
Start the program	______________
	______________
	______________
Ask for onscreen help*	______________
Quit the program	______________

FUNCTION KEY GUIDE

(Skip this section if your computer does not have function keys)

F1 ______________

F2 ______________

F3 ______________

F4 ______________

F5 ______________

F6 ______________

F7 ______________

F8 ______________

F9 ______________

F10 ______________

CREATING THE DATA BASE

If you want to:	Do this:
Enter the create mode	______________________
Enter new field names	______________________
Enter field lengths	______________________

What data types are available for your program?

Text or character? [ ] yes [ ] no
Numerical data? [ ] yes [ ] no
Logical data (Yes/No)? [ ] yes [ ] no
Date field? [ ] yes [ ] no
Automatic record number? [ ] yes [ ] no

How do you enter:

Text or character?	______________________
Numerical data?	______________________
Logical data (Yes/No)?	______________________
Date field?	______________________
Automatic record number?	______________________
Save form as defined	______________________
Quit the create mode	______________________

ENTERING DATA

If you want to:	Do this:
Select a data base for use	____________
Display a blank form	____________
Move cursor up	____________
Move cursor down	____________
Move cursor left	____________
Move cursor right	____________
Move cursor to next field	____________
Move cursor to previous field	____________
Delete character to left of cursor	____________
Delete character to right of cursor	____________
Delete all text in field*	____________
Switch on insert mode*	____________
Switch on overtype mode*	____________
Accept data as finished input	____________
Add another record	____________
View previous record	____________
Stop adding records	____________

DISPLAYING DATA

If you want to:	Do this:
Display one record	______________
Display several records	______________
Display all records	______________
Display records that meet a criterion you specify	______________
Display only certain fields	______________

MODIFYING RECORDS

If you want to:	Do this:
Find first record in file	______________________
Find last record in file	______________________
Move to a particular record	______________________
Locate only those records that meet a criterion you specify	______________________
Make changes to a record	______________________
Accept the changes as finished input and add the modified record to the data base	______________________
Delete a record	______________________
Delete all records that meet a criterion you specify	______________________
Undelete a record	______________________
Remove deleted records from file	______________________
Change the structure of the data base (alter form)	______________________

OBTAINING SUMMARY STATISTICS

If you want to:	Do this:
Count the number of records in a file	
Count only the records that meet a specified condition	
Add up numeric fields in all records	
Add up numeric fields in only the records meeting a criterion you specify	
Average a numeric field	
Average a numeric field in only the records meeting a criterion you specify	

SORTING RECORDS

If you want to:	Do this:
Name a primary sort key and sort the data records to a new file	
Choose ascending sort	
Choose descending sort	
Name a field to serve as the secondary sort key*	
Name a field to serve as the tertiary sort key*	
Index a data file	

PRINTING THE DATA RECORDS

If you want to:	Do this:
Define a new report format	______________________
Choose which fields to print	______________________
Turn on page numbering	______________________
Add running heads	______________________
Insert totals for numeric fields	______________________
Start printing	______________________
Stop printing	______________________

Quick Reference Guide: Electronic Spreadsheet Basics

Directions

Tear out pp. A–33—A–39, which are keyed to Chapter 9. Chapter 9 discusses basic electronic worksheet functions, such as loading the program or widening a column. As you read Chapter 9, consult your spreadsheet program's manual to find out how to carry out each function with your program. Make a note of each command you should use in the "Do this" column. When you've finished filling out this *Quick Reference Guide*, keep it with you when you write with your computer. You'll find it an invaluable aid. Note: your program may not be able to do all of the functions listed here. Functions that some programs lack are indicated with an asterisk.

GETTING STARTED

If you want to:	Do this:
Install the program for your computer	______________________
______________________	
______________________	
Start the program	______________________
______________________	
______________________	
Ask for onscreen help*	______________________
Quit the program	______________________

FUNCTION KEY GUIDE

(Skip this section if your computer does not have function keys)

F1 ______________________

F2 ______________________

F3 ______________________

F4 ______________________

F5 ______________________

F6 ______________________

F7 ______________________

F8 ______________________

F9 ______________________

F10 ______________________

MANAGING THE SPREADSHEET

If you want to:	Do this:
Enter the command mode	____________
Escape from the command mode (without giving a command)	____________
Load an existing spreadsheet	____________
Erase the entire worksheet from memory and start over with a blank worksheet	____________
Save a spreadsheet to disk	____________

CURSOR CONTROL AND SCROLLING

If you want to:	Do this:
Move spreadsheet window right, one column at a time	____________
Move spreadsheet window right, one window at a time*	____________
Move spreadsheet window left, one column at a time	____________
Move spreadsheet window left, one window at a time*	____________
Move spreadsheet window down, one row at a time	____________
Move spreadsheet window down, one window at a time*	____________
Move spreadsheet window up, one row at a time	____________
Move spreadsheet window up, one window at a time*	____________
Go to a cell you specify	____________

EDITING THE SPREADSHEET

If you want to:	Do this:
Erase the contents of the active cell	____________________
Set width of one column	____________________
Set width of all columns	____________________
Delete a column	____________________
Delete a row	____________________

FORMATTING LABELS AND VALUES

If you want to:	Do this:
Enter a number as a label entry	____________
Format labels flush to the left side of the cell	____________
Format labels flush to the right side of the cell	____________
Format labels centered in the cell	____________
Select number of decimal places for display of values	____________
Display values with dollar signs, two decimal places, and commas	____________
Select floating decimal point display of values	____________
Display values in scientific notation	____________
Display values as percentages	____________
Display values flush to the left side of cell	____________
Display values flush to the right side of cell	____________
Display values in center of cell	____________

ORDER OF EVALUATION OF OPERATORS

	Operator
First operator evaluated	________
Second operator evaluated	________
Third operator evaluated	________
Fourth operator evaluated	________
Fifth operator evaluated	________

WRITING FORMULAS

If you want to:	Do this:
Write an absolute cell reference	________
Write a relative cell reference	________
Define a range of cells by typing on the entry line	________
Define a range of cells using the cursor control keys*	________
Name a range*	________
Replicate a formula to a range of cells	________
Use a built-in function in a formula; command prefix needed?	________
See the formula in a cell	________
Edit a formula you have already entered	________

CONTROLLING RECALCULATION

If you want to:	Do this:
Set recalculation by row	____________________
Set recalculation by column	____________________
Select manual recalculation mode	____________________
Give recalculation command	____________________
Select automatic recalculation	____________________